Routledge Handbook of the History of Global Economic Thought

Routledge Handbook of the History of Global Economic Thought offers the first comprehensive overview of the long-run history of economic thought from a truly international perspective. Although globalization has facilitated the spread of ideas between nations, the history of economics has tended to be studied either thematically (by topic), in terms of different currents of thought, or individually (by economist). Work has been published in the past on the economic thought traditions of specific countries, but this pioneering volume is unique in offering a wide-ranging comparative account of the development of economic ideas and philosophies on the international stage.

The volume brings together leading experts on the development of economic ideas from across the world in order to offer a truly international comparison of the economics within nation-states. Each author presents a long-term perspective on economics in their region, allowing global patterns in the progress of economic ideas over time to be identified.

The specially commissioned chapters cover the vast sweep of the history of economics across five world regions, including Europe (England, Scotland, Ireland, Italy, Greece, Spain, Portugal, Germany, Sweden, Russia and Ukraine), the Americas (the USA, Canada, Mexico and Central America, the Caribbean, Spanish-speaking South America, and Brazil), the Middle East (Turkey, Israel, Arab-Islamic economics, Persia/Iran and North Africa), Africa (West Africa, Southern Africa, Mozambique and Angola), and the Asia-Pacific region (Australia and New Zealand, China, Southeast Asia, the Asian Tigers and India).

This rigorous, ambitious and highly scholarly volume will be of key interest to students, academics, policy professionals and to interested general readers across the globe.

Vincent Barnett has been a Research Fellow for over two decades at numerous universities across the UK. His most recent books are the Routledge Historical Biography *John Maynard Keynes* (2013), and the first monograph in English exploring the work of *E.E. Slutsky as Economist and Mathematician* (2011).

Routledge Handbook of the History of Global Economic Thought

Edited by
Vincent Barnett

Routledge
Taylor & Francis Group

LONDON AND NEW YORK

First published 2015 by Routledge

2 Park Square, Milton Park, Abingdon, Oxfordshire OX14 4RN

52 Vanderbilt Avenue, New York, NY 10017

Routledge is an imprint of the Taylor & Francis Group, an informa business

First issued in paperback 2019

British Library Cataloguing in Publication Data
A catalogue record for this book is available from the British Library

Library of Congress Cataloging in Publication Data
Routledge handbook of the history of global economic thought/ edited by Vincent Barnett.
　　pages cm
　　ISBN 978-0-415-50849-0 (hardback) –
　　ISBN 978-1-315-76108-4 (ebook) 1. Economics–History.
　　2. Economic history. I. Barnett, Vincent, 1967–
　　HB75.R67484 2014
　　330.09–dc23　　　　　　　　　　　　2014005761

ISBN: 978-0-415-50849-0 (hbk)
ISBN: 978-0-367-86692-1 (pbk)

Typeset in Bembo and Stone Sans
by Florence Production Ltd, Stoodleigh, Devon, UK

Contents

Contents

Contributors

François Allisson, Centre Walras-Pareto, Switzerland.

Gareth Austin, The Graduate Institute, Geneva, Switzerland.

Vincent Barnett, Independent Scholar, England.

Luis Perdices de Blas, Complutense University of Madrid, Spain.

José Luís Cardoso, University of Lisbon, Portugal.

Balakrishnan Chandrasekaran, Rajiv Gandhi Institute of Contemporary Studies, India.

William Coleman, Australian National University, Australia.

Alexander Dow, University of Victoria, Canada.

Sheila Dow, University of Sterling, Scotland.

Hamed El-Said, Manchester Metropolitan University, England.

Mark Figueroa, University of the West Indies, Jamaica.

Patrice Franko, Colby University, USA.

S.M. Ghazanfar, University of Idaho, USA.

Erik Grimmer-Solem, Wesleyan University, USA.

Hamid Hosseini, King's College, Wilkes-Barre, USA.

Takashi Kanatsu, Hofstra University, USA.

Nene Ernest Khalema, University of Kwazulu-Natal, South Africa.

J.E. King, La Trobe University, Australia.

Arie Krampf, Academic College Tel Aviv Yaffo, Israel.

Steven Kyle, Cornell University, USA.

Cassey Lee, University of Wollongong, Australia.

Zagros Madjd-Sadjadi, Winston-Salem State University, USA.

Lars Magnusson, Uppsala University, Sweden.

Roger Middleton, University of Bristol, England.

Verónica Montecinos, Penn State University, USA.

Tidings P. Ndhlovu, Manchester Metropolitan University, England.

Robin Neill, University of Prince Edward Island, Canada.

Eyüp Özveren, Middle East Technical University, Turkey.

Pier Luigi Porta, University of Milan-Bicocca, Italy.

Renee Prendergast, Queen's University Belfast, Northern Ireland.

Michalis M. Psalidopoulos, Tufts University, USA.

Gerardo Serra, London School of Economics, England.

Thee Kian Wie, Australian National University, Australia.

Richard Weiner, Indiana-Purdue University, Fort Wayne, USA.

Yuval Yonay, University of Haifa, Israel.

1

Introduction

Vincent Barnett

This volume is devoted to documenting the development of economic thinking across the world and in all historical eras, partitioned on nation-state/geographical lines. If Ptolemy's *Cosmographia* was an early attempt to delineate the world's physical geography, then this *Cosmoconomy* (or *Economographia*) is a much more modest attempt to map the global contour-lines of economic ideas. As this is a very expansive focus, the volume cannot claim to provide an exhaustive account of the topic, or even an entirely comprehensive one: not every nation-state that exists today (or has existed in the past) is covered.

Part of the limitation here was the existing state of knowledge in this field: as the authors of the chapter on Southeast Asia imply, no-one had ever thought of writing a history of economics in the Malay Peninsula before. Hence, although an attempt to be geographically comprehensive was made in the commissioning process, it proved impossible to find authors to write on some countries. What this volume can fruitfully do is provide a condensed introductory overview and regionally coordinated analytical account of a significant number of national/regional traditions in economics (28 chapters in total) that will facilitate comparisons across nations and between historical eras, something that has been lacking in the literature, at least within a single easily accessible volume.

This type of national/global world-view approach is especially relevant to the current period of a dramatic increase in the pace of economic globalization, which has been facilitated in part by technological changes such as the birth of the internet and the growth in affordable air travel, and in part by socio-political changes such as increased migration and heightened attempts at democratization in regions previously under autocratic rule. Not everyone agrees that globalization has entirely negated the nation-state as a socio-economic entity. Some have argued that advanced capitalist nations have gained increased power and autonomy from globalization, through the heightened control over their economies that the dissolving of existing nationally rooted relations of accumulation has enabled (Gritsch, 2005).

It is perhaps more accurate to say that globalization has simultaneously heightened and also negated national boundaries, but in various different ways. Together with increased economic and financial globalization, which is undoubtedly a real and a partly positive development, has gone a sense of an emboldened national consciousness in areas previously under forms of political subjugation that have been freed partly by globalizing cultural forces. But parallel with this there has also been a feeling of heightened threats to some national cultures in areas where this globalization has brought the most extensive changes to customs that have been long-lived and deeply embedded. As will be seen, such dramatic change is not only a very recent phenomenon.

However, there is an important difference between firstly the globalization of trading/technological links and fashion/popular culture, and secondly the globalization of economic ideas, business traditions and fundamental belief systems. The former does not necessarily require or produce the latter, although in some situations it might do so. As an example, the rise of the Chinese economy in international (capitalist) commerce is one of the most important developments in recent times, but it has not been accompanied either by China wholeheartedly adopting a purely free-trade/liberal economic ideology, or of contemporary Chinese-style state-led ideas being successfully propagated elsewhere. It could be argued that the Chinese economy has been so successful on the global stage in the very recent period in part because of the disconnection between its own domestic development ideology, and the 'liberal' economic ideas that have held sway in the more 'advanced' Western countries. These globalization relativities may change again in the future, but it is precisely these spatial/temporal and national/international relationships that can be more clearly understood by means of a local/regional approach.

This volume is therefore devoted in part to asking the question: how far has economic theory/discourse been globalized alongside the globalization of the world economy? Taking a long-view approach to this question by examining national trends over centuries will enable wider changes/patterns in the development of economic belief-systems to more clearly be discerned. But how did the idea of the nation-state develop in historical terms?

Nation-states and 'national character'

In his *Discourses on Titus Livius* of 1532, Niccolò Machiavelli suggested that 'nations preserve for a long time the same character; ever exhibiting the same disposition to avarice, or bad faith, or to some other special vice or virtue' (Machiavelli, 1950, 530). For Machiavelli, as men were always 'animated by the same passions', they always acted in the same way, although this could be modified by 'the nature of their education'. Is it so far from Machiavelli's 'national character' to John von Neumann and Oskar Morgenstern's 'accepted standards of behavior' within an 'established order of society' (1964, 41)? Game theory does not logically preclude the idea that the rules of a game may vary between different countries, as might the strategies commonly pursued within them. Consequently, one of the tasks of this volume is to investigate whether there are 'national characters' vis-à-vis economic understanding and business behaviour, to which no pre-ordained methods or structures have been applied by the editor. Each author was left entirely free to make their own judgments, and some very diverse conclusions have indeed been reached.

A 'naturalistic' variant of this topic was considered by Thomas Brown in his myth-busting *Enquiries into Received Tenets and Presumed Truths*, a mid-seventeenth-century treatise promoting the application of an empiricist scientific methodology to natural history. Brown declared that what he called national 'productions' were:

> . . . determined by the principles of place, or qualities of that region which admits them. And this is evident not only in gems, minerals, and metals, but observable in plants and animals; whereof some are common unto many Countries, some peculiar unto one, some not communicable unto another.
>
> (Brown, 1672, 356)

One example is the importance of precious metals in Indian culture, where gold and silver jewellery has for a long time had special significance. J.M. Keynes recognized this factor, which had exerted an important effect on the level and direction of international demand for silver (Barnett, 2013, 41), and indirectly on currency issues in India. Keynes was well aware of national financial particularities, explaining in *Indian Currency and Finance* that 'the British system' of currency operation was 'peculiar and is not suited to other conditions' (Keynes, 1971, 11). As the chapter on India in this volume shows, some Indian economists disagreed with Keynes on this issue fundamentally.

Consider another example, the Middle East. The Arabian Peninsula is a well-defined geographical entity including (today) the states of Saudi Arabia, Kuwait, Qatar, the UAE, Oman and Yemen, but Arabia as a single regional entity now has only a historical reality. Overlaid on the Arabian Peninsula as a geographical region are cultural forms of expression such as Arabic as a language and Islam as a religion. One contributor to this volume uses the term 'Arab-Islamic' to encompass and define a long-standing tradition in socio-economic understanding, which was perhaps most influential in a bygone historical era. Others have implied that this term is too wide-ranging, pointing out that some Persian (or even Azerbaijani) thinkers are sometimes illicitly included within this remit.

Persian scholars have certainly been influential in Arabic-speaking regions, in part because their works were translated into (or issued in) Arabic, but this does not make them more Arabic than Persian. Also some Muslim thinkers were neither Arabs nor Persians, writing in Turkish or even some Asian languages. In reality Persian culture is different from Arabic culture which can be distinct from Islamic culture, even though there is often a significant degree of overlap between these traditions.

It has been suggested that there is a 'clear distinction between Arabic and Moslem science' (Taton, 1963, 385): the problem is clearly defining this distinction. Is it more than simply Arabic is a language whereas Islam is a religion? Although classical Arabic is the language of the Qur'an, it had emerged as the dominant language in the Arabian peninsular long before the birth of Islam. Hence Arabic culture preceded the birth of the Muslim religion by a significant period, during which the Arabian economy (and Arabic science) developed without any influence from Islam. For example Mecca was an urban trading settlement in pre-Islamic Arabia. Thus, the link between the nation-state, regional geography and national culture/thought is a complex and evolving one.

'National traditions'

The idea of 'national traditions' in economic understanding has a notable if controversial history. Werner Sombart argued that the capitalist spirit was indeed universal, at least in Western civilization, but allowed that the national expression of this spirit would vary over time and place. These variations could involve the precise manner and intensiveness of expression, and also how different components of it were formulated. Each nation had within it the individuals with the personal qualities required for expressing the capitalist spirit, but in varying degrees. Thus the USA had this spirit to the utmost, whereas in France it was relatively under-developed (Sombart, 1915, 130, 217). Sombart located the birth of the modern capitalist spirit in the Europe of the early Middle Ages, but he allowed that it might have operated in the Ancient world also.

Perhaps the most well-known single work on 'national economy' in the history of economics corpus is Friedrich List's *The National System of Political Economy* of 1841. Given that mainstream economics has banished the protectionism rationale to a few special instances, List's approach to policy cannot be the model for this volume, but his distinction between national political economy and cosmopolitical or world-wide economy could conceivably be relevant (List, 1904, 98). If there are national against international interests, then might there also be national against international expressions of these interests in economic ideas? Wilhelm Roscher went even further than List, by defining economics as inherently national: 'By the science of national, or Political Economy, we understand the science . . . [of] the laws of the development of the economy of a nation' (Whittaker, 1943, 734). Perhaps the older term 'political economy' lends itself more readily to a national interpretation than does the modern term 'economics', which is (allegedly) national-politics-free.

There is more recent research on this topic that is worth considering. One well-known example is that by Geert Hofstede on how to measure 'national culture' using four dimensions of cultural expression: an individualism/collectivism scale, a power distance acceptance measure, an uncertainty avoidance measure, and a masculinity/femininity scale. The first refers to how far individuals look after themselves against their wider communities; the second refers to how far subordinates can express dissent to those higher up in a hierarchy; the third refers to how far ambiguity/uncertainty are tolerated; and the fourth refers to the degree to which assertiveness/aggression are valued over cooperation/friendliness. Hofstede's controversial results have been summarized as follows:

> Cultures tend to form around regions that also share common economic systems, history, or environmental characteristics. For example, free-market capitalist societies (e.g. the U.S., Western Europe) tend to have individualist, low power-distance oriented cultures. In contrast, developing nations, in particular those with the Confucian legacy (e.g. China, South Korea), tend to be collectivist and high power distance-oriented. In regions where harsh climates or other factors limit food supply, as in Scandinavian countries, feminine values of equality, harmony, and cooperation prevail. In contrast, societies where competition among people, rather than natural conditions, was the greater challenge, such as Southern Europe, developed masculine values of achievement. Finally, uncertainty avoidance is higher in societies characterized by political and economic volatility and oppression (e.g. Guatemala, Venezuela), while stability and personal safety increases tolerance for uncertainty. In summary . . . national and regional cultures are significantly and predictably different from one another.
>
> (Taras et al., 2011, 191)

The provider of this summary went on to argue that although these cultural differences were now being eroded by recent globalization trends, they still had some relevance to explaining regional economic characteristics and developments.

It would be easy to suggest that (for example) the masculinity/femininity axis employed by Hofstede illicitly draws upon gender stereotypes, which themselves are the products of particular patriarchal cultures rather than constituting their basic essences, but this volume is not the place to have this debate about fundamentals. What will be tested here is whether contributors see these types of national cultural features reflected in the national economic/business discourses that they are documenting. It has been suggested that 'Hofstede's framework of culture has helped generate an immense body of evidence that has been successfully utilized in business' (Taras et al., 2011, 190). If economists are found to disagree entirely with the notion of national culture, instead favouring universal laws and general mechanisms of market activity, then how can this incongruity be squared with the apparent fact that Hofstede's framework has been 'successfully utilized in business'? Can both approaches be true simultaneously?

Others problems identified with Hofstede's approach include that it appears to assume homogeneity within a nation, and is applied equally to very large and very small nations (e.g. Russia as against Slovakia). Might not the Western region of Russia differ from the Far East of Russia by just as much as Germany differs from Austria? Also, what about nation-states that have historically subsumed others, e.g. Great Britain versus England/Scotland/Wales? Or native American culture in the USA? Does the subsuming entity simply 'mix' the constituent parts equally, or is there some new meta-culture that is formed that is separate from the constituent elements?

There is some literature on the economics of the size of nations, which asserts a trade-off between the benefits and costs of varying size. Economies of scale may apply to the provision of public services in larger states, and large nations (or groups of nations such as the EU) are better able to assert their interests on the international stage. On the other hand, larger states often have more diverse populations which can lead to greater internal dissent or problems with national identity. Smaller more homogeneous states might be more stable internally in the long-run, especially in a world without tariff barriers or imperialist expansion (Spolaore, 2008, 519). In reality individual nations are rarely constructed on the basis of this type of optimizing calculation, although such considerations may play a role at key points in history. For example, consider the Unionist case during the US Civil War, or the decision of Scotland to join in a Union with England in 1706/07.

But what about any link between national size and national traditions in economics? It might be thought that larger and more powerful states are more able to project their intellectual traditions internationally, and hence the greatest link here is with the overseas dissemination of economics. In the twentieth century, the USA has become the most significant player, but this is not the only key factor: American Institutionalism was not very influential overseas after World War Two, despite it being an indigenous US tradition. And as China grows in economic importance, will Chinese economics take over the intellectual lead from American? Few might predict Asian dominance in economics, especially as the international dissemination process is 'a history of the flux of economic ideas, rendering any easy generalization difficult' (Kurz et al., 2011, 3). Economic ideas are often transformed through global propagation, sometimes even heavily distorted. There is also an important connection with language: English has become the *de facto* global language in very recent times, thus giving the nations where English is the first language a potential advantage in their global reach. On the other hand, given that translation software is now freely available to all with computer access, this factor may decline in importance in the near future.

Language, culture and thought

This particular aspect of culture deserves further consideration. Few would deny that linguistic diversity characterizes the world today, especially given that Noam Chomsky's universal 'deep structure' for all languages has been notoriously difficult to isolate. In terms of the influence of language on economic thought, there are two separate but related issues that require investigation. The first is the special terms used by economists (and business-people) in certain languages, and how they reflect long-standing national/cultural traditions, and also how they are then translated and/or interpreted in other cultures/languages.

For example, it is known that some key terms used today in Russian economics have had their own traditional equivalents in the Russian language for a long period of time, whereas other such terms are simply direct transfers of Western terms into Russian (Barnett, 1998, 2011). Thus, the Russian word for 'market' is '*rynok*', an indigenous term known in Russian from the beginning of the eighteenth century, whilst the Russian word for 'macroeconomics' is 'makroekonomika', a simple transliteration of the English-language term of recent origin. Why this is significant is that the indigenous term 'rynok' originally meant simply a place of trade (e.g. a market square); it only acquired the 'market mechanism' connotation at a later date. Similarly, when it was pointed out to Ragnar Frisch that the term 'econometrics' was first used by a Ukrainian economist (Pawel Ciompa) writing in German in 1910, he responded by accepting this fact in a purely terminological sense, but he then disputed that Ciompa had meant the same thing as he did: accounting rather than economic-mathematical modelling. The meaning of special terms can be lost (and also renewed) in translation.

Perhaps more significantly, some national business histories are embedded in now-standard English economics terms, Latin being particularly well represented. The terms capital, cartel, cash, coin, commerce, company, consumer, deposit, labour, revenue, salary and securities are all of Latin origin, either from single words, e.g. *cassa* (or box) for cash, or combinations of terms, e.g. *com* (or together) + *merx* (or goods) for commerce. Notable exceptions are the Greek word *oikonomia* (or household management) from which economics as a term derives, and the Arabic term *tarrif* (or notification) for tariff. It can be debated how important these linguistic origins actually are, given that the original meanings of the terms employed were often substantially modified or transformed in the adaptation process, but the fact that the Mediterranean region exerted an important influence on Western economics terminology through Latin and Greek has at the very least a definite symbolic significance.

The second and more fundamental issue is whether language influences or structures thought itself, i.e. the question of examining the potential implications of linguistic differences on actual thought patterns. The 'linguistic relativity hypothesis', that language bounds and directly affects thought, referred to as the Sapir-Whorf hypothesis after its two early twentieth-century advocates, has a controversial history. Even very recently, some have provided evidence for its relevance to economics. For example, a 'linguistic-savings hypothesis' has been proposed, which states that how a given language expresses the future in relation to the present affects some future-oriented economic actions, e.g. savings behaviour (Chen, 2013).

Those whose first language grammatically separates the future and the present very strictly, and therefore more strongly distinguishes between future and present states, save less on average than those whose first language does not formally and linguistically distinguish between the present and the future in such a rigid fashion. Another recent study concluded that the spatial metaphors contained in specific languages (e.g. 'time as quantity' versus 'time as distance') influences how users mentally conceive of time itself (Casasanto et al., 2004). Historically it has been suggested that Semitic languages 'tend towards shortened and abstract formulations': for example, Arabic is particularly suited to expressing exact scientific concepts (Taton, 1963, 403).

Some may remain sceptical about such linguistic/thought pattern associations, interpreting them as the result of long-standing cultural and historical factors rather than being the inherent consequences of linguistic structures (does language precede, develop simultaneously with or follow on from culture?), but it is evident that there is an important issue to consider regarding the relation between language and economic thought.

The origins of political economy

Another task of the volume is to see whether old-fashioned notions of the origins of the subject of economics, such as 'Political economy is in truth the creation of what has been called the European genius' (Nys, 1899, x), have any validity whatsoever, or are entirely imperialist constructs. Even in more modern formulation, such as that the dawning of the Renaissance unleashed the forces that created economics as a separate discipline (Rima, 1996, 23), the implication is that these forces were overwhelmingly European in origin/focus. An international perspective will assist in evaluating this issue further.

The Middle East again provides some illumination. It is conventional to highlight a 'golden age' in the Muslim world occurring roughly from the eighth to the thirteenth centuries, which was based at least in part on an expanding 'Islamic Empire'. This Empire included the various Muslim Caliphates and absorbed 'Persian culture in addition to the Hellenistic culture brought by Alexander' (Backhouse, 2002, 35). Muhammad had helped to establish a unified form of government in the Arabian Peninsula under Caliphate rule, although later the Sunni and Shia versions of Islam diverged over the function and status of the Caliph as ruler. But, as has been astutely outlined, the Muslim 'golden age' was not entirely Muslim:

> What was this 'golden age' . . . a surprising union of cultures which took place in the late eighth and early ninth centuries . . . The new Abbasid dynasty who ruled from Baghdad not only favoured trade, commerce, and public works (which, as usual, require mathematics at some level), but . . . saw a value in pure research . . . Scholars from what we can see as a melting-pot – Syriac, Greek and Arabic speakers, Christian, pagan, and Muslim – combined in the work of translation . . . a synthesis was essential.
>
> *(Hodgkin, 2005, 109–10)*

That mathematics was highly regarded is evident from the Arabic term '*al-jabr*' (restoration), the origin of the English term algebra, as found in the title of Al-Khwarizmi's *Book on Restoration and Balancing* from around 825 AD, which dealt with finding solutions to mathematical equations. Parallel with such intellectual developments, even up to the eighteenth century, 'the Islamic world did not appear economically underdeveloped to outside observers' (Kuran, 2008, 582).

But this positive understanding of Muslim history is partly a recent development. One contributor to this volume notes the disproving of the 'great gap' thesis advanced by Joseph Schumpeter. According to Schumpeter 'we may safely leap over 500 years to the epoch of St. Thomas Aquinas' (Schumpeter, 1954, 74), i.e. nothing much happened in economic thinking for half a millennium, during most of the Muslim 'golden age'. This echoes a previous quote on political economy being the result of European genius.

On this issue it is worth highlighting a relatively neglected yet rather interesting book entitled *Researches in the History of Economics* by Ernest Nys, which was first published in English in 1899. One interesting aspect of this book was that it treated economics more as culture than as pure theory. Another was that it highlighted the fact that:

> Musulman [i.e. Muslim – VB] culture gave to the mind the first impulse towards research and enterprise . . . Progress in the art of engineering and in the use of projectiles, development of the study of geography, medicine, botany, and mathematics, these were some of the effects of contact of the West with Arabs during the Crusades.
>
> *(Nys, 1899, xxiii–iv)*

Nys had evidently never heard of anything like a 'great gap' thesis. Obviously the natural sciences are not economics, but according to Nys, in the 'Arabo-Berber states' the 'Musulman governments' were based on religion in association with prosperous trading, as theorized by contemporary scholars such as Ibn Khaldun (1332–1406) of Tunisia, the author of a major work that 'wove together economic, political and social change' to explain the growth of civilizations (Backhouse, 2002, 38). That 'Arab-Islamic' economic thought did reach the West shows that while national cultures do exist, they are not immune from external influences, even from very different cultures and distant geographical regions.

Of course in the Middle Ages, the distinctions between natural, social and applied/practical knowledge were much less clear than they are today. Thus, in the Medieval Arab world 'biology was always considered a subsidiary branch of agriculture and medicine', yet 'Arabic agricultural texts were mainly derived from Greek sources' (Taton, 1963, 416). This is perhaps why one scholar has used the term 'Greco-Arab Islamic ideas' to describe early Arabic economic thinking. When considering such distant eras, it is sometimes difficult to be precise about cultural origins.

The contemporary Middle East region is very different from the period of the 'golden age' of Muslim culture: the period after 1973 could perhaps be termed a new 'black-golden age' of Arab economic power, but perhaps not of Arabic contributions to economics. A defining policy feature of the oil-rich Gulf States has been the existence of the OPEC oil cartel. Insiders within OPEC like Fadhil Chalaby, for some years its Secretary General, have documented the ineffectiveness of OPEC, arguing that it became a prisoner of its member states' budgets and the need to get maximum income in any given moment (Chalaby, 2011). It has thus provided lessons in the problems associated with managing a cartel when the interests of its members diverge, as had been predicted some years previously by a Nobel Prize-winning American economist (Stigler, 1964). But does this example signify that neoclassical price theory has been proved correct and applicable to all regions?

It is interesting to note that the OPEC oil cartel merits only one brief mention in Ingrid Rima's *Development of Economic Analysis*, where an economic technique for reducing OPEC's monopoly price is recommended (Rima, 1996, 536). It is also worth pointing out that although the collapse of the Soviet Union in 1991 put an end to central planning across Eastern Europe and Russia, in Saudi Arabia the ninth five-year plan was set in operation for the period 2010–14, and therefore neoclassical economics is not entirely triumphant in the region, despite the fact that OPEC has not always been successful in its cartel policies.

The major political issue in the contemporary Middle East is of course Israel and the Palestinians, and Judaic economic thought has a very long history, just like its Muslim counterpart (Sauer and Sauer, 2012). As with Islam/Arabia, Judaism as a religion is distinct from Israel as a nation-state, although there are obvious links between the two. However, while in the case of the link between Islam and Middle Eastern countries, Muslims identify themselves with various currently existing nation-states and only sometimes with a wider Islamic nation, in the case of Judaism this religious identity is linked to only one state: the complex links between economic ideas and the construction of a nation are revealingly explored in the chapter on Israel.

Nations and spacial regions

Another way to think about nation-states is as spatially defined regions of economic activity, i.e. as geographical territories. In this field various existing approaches have been developed with economics, such as location theory, optimal currency theory, market linkages theory, external/urbanized economies and so on. Nation-states as economic entities are unified in the sense that they have common cultural references, common political and legal systems, common currencies, common networks (e.g. transport and infrastructure) and common histories and institutions. According to Ludwig von Mises, the essence of nationality lay in language: all national conflicts were language struggles (von Mises, 1983, 37). This meant that, for Mises, England and America were part of the same nation, as they both had English as their first languages, but they were not part of the same state (44). The often-repeated truism that 'Britain and America are two countries separated by a common language' might suggest otherwise.

But can economics as the theoretical expression of business and trade be conceived as part of a common national history? Some recent research suggests this is a fruitful approach to pursue. For example, different approaches to financial accounting based on geographical associations have been identified: a continental European approach leading to either stock or flow models (assets-liabilities or revenues-expenses), and a US approach leading to either a proprietary theory or an entity theory, both of which are based on inquiring into the relations between enterprise and stakeholders (Biondi, 2013, 487).

Perhaps one basic way to differentiate here is to distinguish between economic theories that declare they are explicitly internationalist in application, i.e. maintain that that they are equally valid in the context of the USA or Cambodia, and economic theories which explicitly limit their application to a specific nation, region or a spatial geography. Most mainstream theories either implicitly (or sometimes explicitly) maintain a universalist position, whereas heterodox approaches tend to be more open in this regard. However, even many heterodox economists assume universal human behaviour exists internationally, they merely disagree with mainstream currents about what this behaviour is (i.e. more collectively oriented than individual maximization). It could be argued that a more radical critique of economics (both mainstream and heterodox) would suggest that business behaviour varies across nations and cultures, and perhaps even within them.

Another question is the link between economic regions and economic systems. The West (often defined to include Europe, North America plus so-called 'New World' countries like Australia) is often seen as essentially capitalist, while the East is sometimes seen as systemically distinct, either as non-capitalist (e.g. Russia until very recently) or more state-orientated (e.g. China today). The question of applying mainstream economic theory to non-capitalist states can be a confusing one. Even while accepting that the USSR was a type of socialist economy, some Western theorists applied 'conventional' economic theory to it, and came up with notions such as coloured markets (with differing degrees of legality), repressed inflation, and even shadow prices, as if underneath the planned economy of the USSR there existed a more fundamental level of reality, which was merely a distorted version of 'real' (i.e. market) economics.

The problem of this universalist view is clearly illustrated through the development of the post-Soviet economies after 2000. Russia, it has often been declared, now has a market economy. But if this is so, then how can Russia's ongoing political hostility to the West, and the development of its own unique brand of 'oligarch-capitalism', be convincingly explained? If market economics is universal, how come the contemporary Russian economy does not function in the same manner as that of Sweden? Surely, maintains the universal-economist, it cannot be due to cultural or historical factors, as economics is entirely separate from such contingencies. But what then has caused the distinctions? Perhaps the 'universal economy' notion itself is a chimera.

Those who accept the 'universal market' approach often refer to the lack of a stable legal framework or other institutions to explain the Russian economic 'anomaly', but this in itself requires an explanation. Could it be cultural factors generating this *lacuna*? If so, then economics is not quite as separate from cultural/national factors as some would have us believe. Recent book titles, such as *Varieties of Capitalism in Post-Communist Countries*, suggest that some recognition has taken place of the fact that factors outside of the purely economic can affect how economies operate (Lane and Myant, 2006).

Another interesting example is the concept of trade in American Aboriginal thought before any Aboriginal contact with Europeans. Trade certainly occurred in Aboriginal economic practice, but in addition to the conventional market function of facilitating economic gains from exchange, Aboriginal trade also had socio-political functions such as cementing alliances, buying-off enemies and settling non-economic disputes (Cicarelli, 2012, 101). These additional layers of meaning are usually absent from mainstream Western economics as it is constituted today, although this does not necessarily mean that in contemporary economic practice, trade does not sometimes serve this type of extra function as well.

Moreover, could national specificity help to explain why an original current in economics like the German Historical School was initially centred in Germany rather than in another nearby European state? And was it just an accident that the Cambridge school was developed at Cambridge University and not in (say) Oxford, or were the long-standing cultural traditions of Cambridge (not just its economics heritage) also important? J.M. Keynes famously straddled Cambridge and Bloomsbury (in central London), and *The General Theory* is sometimes seen as a mixture of the two traditions (weighted according to taste), but this further supports the idea of geographical impacts on economics.

Some historians of science accept a link between geography and scientific ideas very clearly. Cambridge University was described by Jagdish Mehra as a 'unique place in England' that enabled Paul Dirac's early *q*-number contributions to the development of quantum theory (Mehra, 1982, 24). Cambridge provided a very different environment from that experienced by German quantum pioneers like Werner Heisenberg, the originator of the distinct matrix mechanics formulation of quantum theory. If national culture influenced the creation of quantum mechanics to some degree, then it might also influence economic theory.

Marx on globalization

Marxists of course usually maintain that there are no nation-state boundaries for capital, and that when the idea of national culture comes up against the logic of capitalist expansion, then the latter always triumphs. For many Marxists the nation-state is a 'bourgeois' concept that creates false consciousness about divisions between peoples across the globe, when the real unifying factor is those that own the means of production versus those that are forced to sell their labour-power. But even within this framework, the 'false consciousness' idea of nationality cannot explain all the differences between and within capitalist economies, and why some non- or semi-capitalist systems differ from others. If capital has a universal logic, how come it still operates alongside the Communist Party in China, but does not do so any more in Russia?

Marx was not quite as unambiguous on globalization as some commentators have made out. His most recent biographer, Jonathan Sperber, declared while discussing the world market that 'Marx's own globalized views differed from those of a later era', i.e. from those of the twentieth and early twenty-first centuries, and 'when he thought about global politics, it was the Tsar's Empire that had his attention' (Sperber, 2013, 401). Sperber also showed Marx analyzing the 'positive' effects of British rule in India ('countering Oriental despotism' and the 'Asiatic mode of production'), illustrating how different the nineteenth-century understanding of imperialism was from the twentieth. In fact, it can plausibly be argued that in the early twenty-first century, it is precisely Marx's national-based commercial-globalization conception that is relevant to current trends, not the twentieth-century view of a bi-polar ideological-globalization into two opposed political camps.

In contemporary discussions, when globalization is being considered, it is not 'the entire world' that is being referred to, but the rise of previously less-important states like China, India and Tsar-Putin's commercial Empire, compared to the 'established' powers of Western Europe and North America. In this view globalization is 'merely' the rise (in international commerce) of some states alongside the relative decline of others, as it was in Marx's time and is also today.

Marx himself understood that the global search for new markets was always both controlled and bounded by nation-states, whilst at the same time being forced to erode the national differences within them. It was no accident that Marx and Engels wrote in *The Manifesto of the Communist Party* that: 'Modern industry has established the world-market, for which the discovery of America paved the way', i.e. capitalist internationalization was facilitated by new national developments (Marx and Engels, 1933, 4). In volume one of *Capital*, we read about 'the universal market, whose integral parts are the individual countries' (Marx, 1906, 612). In Marx's conception of 'capitalist globalization via the nation-state' it was the differences *within* the nation-states that were being eroded, not the nation-state/regional entities themselves.

Nation-states as historical constructs

Another question that requires consideration is that some may argue that the very idea of the nation-state is a historically specific construct, relevant only to a certain period (for example modern capitalism). According to Ludwig von Mises:

> Only since the second half of the eighteenth century did it gradually take on the significance that it has for us today . . . The word and concept *nation* belong completely to the modern sphere of ideas of political and philosophical individualism.
>
> *(von Mises, 1983, 34)*

In the Middle Ages, people identified more with local or regional identities rather than clearly-defined nations, and in the future the individual nation-state (it is alleged by some) will become ever more eroded, as economic globalization proceeds apace.

A famous article on this topic from the late nineteenth century entitled 'What is a Nation?' by Ernst Renan explained that:

> The modern nation is therefore a historical result brought about by a series of convergent facts. Sometimes unity has been effected by a dynasty, as was the case in France; sometimes it has been brought about by the direct will of provinces, as was the case with Holland, Switzerland, and Belgium; sometimes it has been the work of a general consciousness . . . as was the case in Italy and Germany . . . But what is a nation? Why is Holland a nation, when Hanover, or the Grand Duchy of Parma, are not?
>
> *(Renan, 1882)*

Renan's answer was that a nation was 'a soul, a spiritual principle', a unity of past legacy and present consent based partly on common ancestry and heritage, and partly on 'a daily plebiscite' of common agreement. This wide conception of national consciousness could encompass entities as disparate as twenty-first-century Germany within Europe and the nineteenth-century Zulu nation in Southern Africa. Obviously these two constructs were very different in many important ways, but they both had some variant of what Renan called 'a unity of heritage and legacy'.

Another very different conception of the nation-state proposed by contemporary Marxist dependency theorists such as Samir Amin is that 'the formation of what are today called nations is closely linked with the crystallization of a state and the centralized circulation at this level of a specifically capitalist surplus' (Amin, 2009, 256). That is, the nation-state is merely a 'bourgeois' class construct designed to control the surplus product generated by the global circulation of capital operating through trans-national companies. Although this 'nation = capitalist state' conception has some interest as a point of comparison, it cannot by itself explain the frequent coincidences between nation and language/cultural identity, except of course entirely as 'false consciousness', as opposed to the 'true universalism' or internationalism that is often hypothesized by Marxists in its place.

One problem among many with this 'true universalist' approach is that whenever it has been attempted in practice, it has invariably broken down along some previously existing cultural/religious/ethnic/national fault-line that had been assumed away by its advocates, but which turned out to be of greater resonance than the proposed comradeship of the globe. If national consciousness is merely false consciousness, then the crafty spell that has been spun to promote it is an unimaginably powerful one. Another argument against Amin's critique of what he calls 'Eurocentrism' is the actual geographical centre of the trans-national capital that he blames for under-developing the exploited periphery, which has for the second half of the twentieth century been located a whole continent away from Europe in the United States of America. Shouldn't 'late capitalism' be more accurately labelled as North America-centric?

But why examine economics within such disputed national bounds? One answer would be that the nation-state has for a long period been taken as the defining geo-political construct, either positively by nationalists or negatively by Marxists, despite there being periods before (and perhaps after) when it was/will be less important. Another answer might be that, as Joseph Schumpeter outlined, the birth of Western economic policy analysis was 'the problems of the rising National State' as capitalist evolution gathered pace (Schumpeter, 1954, 143). He also asked the question how far certain economists 'took account of national differences of economic behavior and of consciousness of nationality as a motive of economic behavior' (550).

Schumpeter's answer was that nationality affected the general social philosophy of economists more than their technical analysis, and that some classical economists like Nassau Senoir commented 'on the behavior of Dutchmen and Englishmen and Indians of Mexico' under the wider category of matters of observation (576). Once nationality becomes a matter of empirical observation, however, further issues then arise: how many Dutchmen must be studied to achieve a representative picture and over what period of time? Might the culture and traditions of Dutchmen evolve alongside the Dutch nation itself?

It should not be forgotten that, although it is not always emphasized by commentators, the most famous single work in political economy is entitled *An Inquiry into the Nature and Causes of the Wealth of Nations*, not *The Wealth of the World*. For Adam Smith the 'hidden hand' of the market was a universal mechanism, but the nations in which it operated were separate and distinct entities. And Joseph Dorfman began his magnum opus *The Economic Mind in American Civilization* with the statement that: 'In America as elsewhere, economic thought is an integral part of culture' (Dorfman, 1947, ix): it is clear from what followed that he meant American culture. The implicit contradiction of applying Smith's 'universal mechanism' within a 'disparate nations' approach is brought out clearly in a book entitled *British Economists*, which begins with the absolutely certain declaration that: 'Economics is a science, and in general science knows no national boundaries' (Hood, 1931, 1): the author then immediately adduces reasons why the focus will be exclusively on British economists.

Here is found a mirror image of Amin's paradoxical critique of international Eurocentrism: if a unified geographical entity called 'Europe' is really the power-base for global capital, as Amin suggests, then this would heighten the significance of national/continental identity, it would not prove it to be a mirage. Finally, not even Ptolemy could square this 'national versus international' circle, assertively declaring in his *Cosmographia* that he would treat the physical geography of nations by:

. . . spurning the multitudinous traditional farrago concerning the peculiar qualities of their different inhabitants, except that, in the case of qualities renowned by general report, we make a short and suitable note on the religion and manners.

So, not quite 'spurning the farrago' of peculiar national manners then. Despite these contentious issues, some of which remain unresolved, it is clear that understanding to a greater degree the national focus or national origins of economic ideas is potentially a very fruitful undertaking.

References

Amin, Samir. 2009. *Eurocentrism*. New York: Monthly Review.

Backhouse, Roger. 2002. *The Penguin History of Economics*. London: Penguin.

Barnett, Vincent. 1998. *Kondratiev and the Dynamics of Economic Development*. London: Macmillan.

Barnett, Vincent. 2011. *E.E. Slutsky as Economist and Mathematician*. London: Routledge.

Barnett, Vincent. 2013. *John Maynard Keynes*. London: Routledge.

Biondi, Yuri. 2013. *Accounting and Business Economics*. London: Routledge.

Brown, Thomas. 1672. *Enquiries into Received Tenets and Presumed Truths*. London: Crook.

Casasanto, Daniel, Boroditsky, Lera and Greene, Jesse. 2004. *How Deep are the Effects of Language on Thought?* At www.casasanto.com.

Chalaby, Fadhil. 2011. *Oil Policies, Oil Myths*. London: Tauris.

Chen, M.K. 2013. The Effect of Language on Economic Behavior. *American Economic Review*, 103 (2): 690–731.

Cicarelli, James. 2012. Economic Thought Among American Aboriginals Prior to 1492. *The American Journal of Economics and Sociology*, 71 (1): 77–125.

Dorfman, Joseph. 1947. *The Economic Mind in American Civilization*. London: Harrap. Vol. 1.

Gritsch, Maria. 2005. The Nation-State and Economic Globalization. *Review of International Political Economy*, 12 (1).

Hodgkin, Luke. 2005. *A History of Mathematics*. Oxford: OUP.

Hood, F.C. 1931. *British Economists*. London: Pitman.

Keynes, J.M. 1971. *Indian Currency and Finance*. London: Macmillan.

Kuran, Timur. 2008. Islamic Economic Institutions. In *The New Palgrave Dictionary of Economics*. London: Palgrave. Vol. 4.

Kurz, Heinz, Nishizawa, Tamotsu and Tribe, Keith. 2011. *The Dissemination of Economic Ideas*. Cheltenham: Elgar.

Lane, David and Myant, Martin (eds). 2006. *Varieties of Capitalism in Post-Communist Countries*. London: Palgrave.

List, Friedrich. 1904. *The National System of Political Economy*. London: Longmans.

Machiavelli, Niccolò. 1950. *The Prince and the Discourses*. New York: ML.

Marx, Karl. 1906. *Capital*. Chicago: Kerr. Vol. 1.

Marx, Karl and Engels, Friedrich. 1933. *The Manifesto of the Communist Party*. New York: Arrow.

Mehra, Jagdish. 1982. *The Historical Development of Quantum Theory*. New York: Springer. Vol. 4 Pt. 2.

von Mises, Ludwig. 1983. *Nation, State, and Economy*. Indianapolis: Liberty.

von Neumann, John and Morgenstern, Oskar. 1964. *Theory of Games and Economic Behavior*. New York: Wiley.

Nys, Ernest. 1899. *Researches in the History of Economics*. London: Black.

Renan, Ernst. 1882. *What is a Nation?* At www.cooper.edu.

Rima, I.H. 1996. *Development of Economic Analysis*. London: Routledge.

Sauer, Corinne and Sauer, R.M. 2012. *Judaism, Markets and Capitalism*. MI: Acton.

Schumpeter, Joseph. 1954. *History of Economic Analysis*. London: Unwin.

Sombart, Werner. 1915. *The Quintessence of Capitalism*. London: Unwin.

Sperber, Jonathan. 2013. Karl Marx the German. *German History*, Vol. 31 No. 3: 383–402.

Spolaore, Enrico. 2008. Size of Nations. In *The New Palgrave Dictionary of Economics*. London: Palgrave. Vol. 7.

Stigler, George. 1964. A Theory of Oligopoly. *Journal of Political Economy*, 72: 44–61.

Taras, Vas, Steel, Piers and Kirkman, Bradley. 2011. Three Decades of Research on National Culture in the Workplace. *Organizational Dynamics*, 40: 189–98.

Taton, Rene (ed.). 1963. *Ancient and Medieval Science*. London: Thames and Hudson.

Whittaker, Edmund. 1943. *A History of Economic Ideas*. New York: Longmans.

Part I

Europe

Part I

Europe

2

England

*Roger Middleton**

'English economics', if it ever existed, is a wholly historical entity, albeit one for which some distinction might be claimed in the round and for which, at various points, the existence or otherwise of 'English schools' has been the subject of scholarly enquiry. Thus, for example, we have the negative verdict in the original Palgrave that the 'English writers on political economy before Adam Smith do not at any time present the marks of a "school" properly so-called' (Bonar, 1894, 730); and, conversely, Schumpeter's (1954, 830) very positive assessment that there was a definite 'age of Marshall' which transformed economics, not just in England but internationally. Certainly, there is no such *current* entity as English economics, though there has been, and may still be in today's internationalised world of science, a 'British' economics.

'English economists' is a somewhat less problematic concept, at least historically, but even here we confront a general problem of geography and identity: from the Treaty of Union, 1707, Scotland has been part of the United Kingdom which also comprises England and Wales, with Ireland additionally part of that union from 1801 until 1922 when what is now the Republic of Ireland seceded, leaving only the province of Northern Ireland. Similarly, 'England' is problematic as, for centuries, England and Wales has operated as a single economic and political unit, although in the past 40 years or so Wales, and even more so Scotland, have achieved a measure of devolution. Amidst this complexity, we adopt an operational definition that 'English economics' is that produced by 'English economists', with these defined as those working (at least for a major part of their career) in England which, in turn, encompasses Wales and Ireland (Northern Ireland from 1923). Inevitably, given that English is a world language, economists are geographically mobile and their ideas even more so, and economics is a public discourse, the artificiality of the adjective 'English' means our subject inevitably becomes British economics as we approach the modern era, though the population dominance of England in the UK is considerably more pronounced now than in the past, when pre-famine Ireland was a significant component of the union.

Our account of the development and significance of English economics so defined is framed in terms of a market for 'economic knowledge', a concept broader than purely economic theory or economic doctrine so as to acknowledge, first, that in Britain, as typically elsewhere, 'professional economists do not have a monopoly of economic knowledge'; and, second, and here Britain is much more distinctive, that the market has *always* been highly contestable. Whilst it is axiomatic that the market mechanism lies at the heart of economics, it is also more than usually appropriate as a metaphor for British economics.

This market has had highly context- and time-specific supply and demand characteristics (Middleton, 1998, ch. 3). There is a long provenance to British political economy discourse being dominated by appeals to, or resistance against, the market (Middleton, 1996), and, much more recently, we have a 'new' history of economic thought paradigm 'with its concern for the relationship between the "high" political thought of theorists, the "medium" thought of officials, businessmen and commentators, and the "low" thought of daily life and experience (a formulation not without its problems)' (Daunton, 2011, 222). Current historiography on modern British history includes many contributions on how economic ideas have united (and often divided) civil society and commerce (for example, Rothschild, 2001 on Adam Smith and the Enlightenment; and Trentmann, 2008 on free trade). With widespread acceptance now that cultural norms matter for both the production and reception of economic ideas, and that modern internationalised economics is very much the product of Anglo-American cultural norms (Coats, 1997), an assessment of the development of English economics which foregrounds cultural and other non-economic concerns is very timely.

On the supply side of the market, the production of economic knowledge, historically, and still formally the case today, there are no barriers to entry to being an economist. For much of our period, no formal academic qualifications were required for being an academic economist, itself an inchoate profession, with canonical figures as late as J.M. Keynes (1883–1946) having no first degree in the subject (Keynes, as Marshall (1842–1924), was a Cambridge mathematics graduate), whilst doctoral training was relatively unusual until the 1960s. A measure of the demand side is provided by Peden's (1996, 171–2) five categories of economic knowledge sought in this market: first, information; second, practical experience; third, economic theory; fourth, informed opinion; and fifth what he calls, 'realities of political economy'. All are important, but only the third, economic theory, is routinely part of the academic history of economic thought, whilst the fifth category has an especial relevance, for it is conceived as 'A sense of the "art of the possible" in economic affairs . . . for ministers and their advisers' and, as we shall argue, the history of economics in Britain is intimately related to its public policy role. We thus follow Alex Cairncross (1911–98), a towering figure in postwar British economics, who operated 'as an intermediary in the market for economic advice . . . between theory and practice, between the theorists who seek to trap the inner secrets of the economy in their models and the practitioners who live in a world of action where time is precious, understanding is limited, nothing is certain, and noneconomic considerations are always important and often decisive' (Cairncross, 1985, 1).

Cultural and business traditions

The Scottish chapter begins rightly with that country's Enlightenment, with nascent political economy one product of the 'enlightenment philosophy' associated with David Hume (1711–76) and then Adam Smith (1723–90). Historians of England have generally concluded that there was no comparable English Enlightenment (but see Porter's 2000 notable dissent); indeed, in one much cited history of the British, Colley (1992, 123) has observed that in terms of intellectual contribution eighteenth-century 'Scotland was not England's peer but its superior'.

Certainly, relative to Scotland and to continental Europe, England's universities were under-developed – there was the duopoly of Oxford and Cambridge before the 1820s – with clear evidence that graduate production per thousand of population was significantly lower than these comparators, and geared more towards aristocratic/clerical priorities than intellectual enquiry.

On schooling, Daniel Defoe's observation of 1708 that England was a land 'full of ignorance' whilst in Scotland even the 'poorest people have their children taught and instructed' is still often cited, not least because nearly three centuries later the Scottish school system seems still to have the upper hand. These differences were reflected not just in England's lower literacy rate (though recent scholarship, Melton (2001, 82), has the gap closed by the mid-eighteenth century), but in the narrow ambition that underlay education which, in any case, was characterised by class-based, differential access, and significant religious discrimination against Catholics and dissenters (from the established Church of England). Nonetheless, between the 1850s and 1870s Oxford and Cambridge were both reformed to remove religious discrimination, though religion remained an important aspect of the story of nineteenth-century English economics as many leading figures were clerics (Thomas Malthus, 1766–1834) or turned to economics after having initially set forth on a clerical career, most famously Marshall.

Meanwhile, between the mid-seventeenth and mid-nineteenth centuries many dissenting academies were established (Ridder-Symoens, 1996, 260); those desiring a higher education often went to Scotland or abroad; the East India Company established in 1806 its college in which the teaching of political economy was provided by *inter alia* Malthus; and new universities were established, beginning with University College London (1826). Political economy, commerce and latterly economics were central to the development of these and subsequent higher education institutions (Kadish and Tribe, 1993). By the First World War, England had 17 universities (plus five colleges as constituents of a federal University of Wales) with all major cities embracing higher education, including the two significant industrial population centres of Birmingham (1900) and Manchester (1880), but with a concentration in London, notably University College and the London School of Economics (1895). By this point, the rise of the professions was very well established and the universities were transformed – if far from wholly for Oxbridge – from aristocratic and clerical preserves to effective, independent institutions for training an elite fusing upper and middle classes; additionally, they were also secularizing and, thereby, raising their scholarly standards. A century later, England has 91 universities (out of a UK total of 109).

Whilst an educational laggard, in most other respects England was in the vanguard of modernity as it experienced the great currents of change that were associated with commercialisation, cultural reorientation and the rise of the nation state. England, as Melton (2001) shows, was no laggard in the development of the 'public sphere' that is associated with the Enlightenment and which has an obvious resonance for both the demand and the supply side of the market for economic knowledge. Coffee houses, penny universities in eighteenth-century parlance, a well-developed press and intense public interest in Parliament – from 1707 London was the centre for politics – were all the marks of strong civic and political culture from an early point. The markers of Enlightenment, that of deductive reasoning (following René Descartes, 1596–1650) and empiricism (Francis Bacon, 1561–1626), are all evident.

Indeed, seventeenth-century England has been described as an 'age of great intellectual vigour, scientific curiosity and inventiveness' (Stone, 1997, 5), with Hutchison (1988, 12) claiming that leadership in what came to be the discipline of political economy lay with the English from 1662 to the early eighteenth century, with the work of William Petty (1623–87) the 'notable' advance from whom others followed. Petty, considered by Karl Marx (1818–83) as the 'founder of political economy' (McCormick, 2009, 1), has a central role in our historical account which emphasises a long-running practical, problem-solving imperative to English economics that is distinctive. Late seventeenth- and early eighteenth-century Britain was an age of deep and rapid change that was both stimulating and congenial to the further development of economic knowledge. Thus the traditional constraints upon rational thought, feudalism and religious fundamentalism, were both waning, though very far from being spent forces. Even so, the contemporaneous European 'scientific revolution' posed a broad challenge: confronting the 'dead hand and dead mind of orthodoxy'; provoking an 'intense struggle between rival natural philosophies . . . [which sought] liberation from hidebound orthodoxy' (Ridder-Symoens, 1996, 537); and, for figures like Petty, offering a vision of the potential of empiricism and rational enquiry – here the influence of Bacon is key (Stone, 1997, 18) – which was to prove profoundly fertile.

In governance and thence geo-political competition, the Glorious Revolution of 1688 is a conventional – albeit now somewhat contested (O'Brien, 2011) – waypoint, but certainly important as the developing fiscal-military state *inter alia* underpinned the growing demand for economic knowledge. With much English-language theorizing originating in Ireland and Scotland, suggesting that 'economic conditions underdetermine the content of economic theory' (Schabas, 2003, 173), it was nonetheless the case that the backdrop to these early English contributions was economic, social and political modernisation across a broad front (Mokyr, 2009). Whilst its population was dwarfed by its French neighbour, England's real GDP per capita was second only to Holland in the seventeenth century, and early in the next century would soon pull ahead as the market economy grew, was further integrated, and as a structural transformation that increased the output and employment shares of industry and services led onward to industrialising and urbanising Britain. International trade was central to this trans-formation, with openness here mirrored by domestic innovations affecting, for example, banking and the firm: notably, the Bank of England (established 1694) and the East India Company (established 1600), the world's first commercial multi-national company.

Amongst economic historians debate remains lively about why Britain was the first to experience an industrial revolution and the Great Divergence. For institutionalists, at least part of the answer lay with British superiority in matters of constitution and property rights. Recently, Mokyr (2009, ch. 16) has provided a persuasive analysis of how secure property rights and enhanced trust amongst economic agents ('politeness and manners') underpinned this further commercialisation of Britain. Of course, by further proclaiming the primacy of the market the challenge for nascent political economy was to reconcile sympathy and self-interest, the needs and rights of the individual and of society: cue the synthesis provided by Adam Smith and classical economics, albeit at the expense of his reading of mercantilism that gave it more coherence and unity than was warranted (Winch, 1996, 92–3).

With the old mercantilist-free market axis now discarded by serious historians of pre-Smithian economic thought, recent work, for example Dudley (2013), offers a construction of early eighteenth-century political economy as an ideological battle about the sources of wealth and appropriate degree and form of government regulation, this between a Whig party-inspired manufacturing and consumption version which triumphed over a re-exporting version associated with the Tory party. Appropriately, this brings us back to English/British distinctiveness: a concern about rent-seeking, the public role of economics and the characteristics of the market for economic knowledge.

Development of economic ideas over the long term

Before Adam Smith

The pre-Smithian roots of English economics can be traced to medieval churchmen, moralists and merchants. Indeed, antiquarian excursions into the 'history' of economic thought were a significant concern of Smith's followers, the founding fathers of classical economics. Letwin

(1963, vii–viii) perhaps overstates the case that, for James Mill (1773–1836) and J.R. McCulloch (1789–1864), 'Being inclined to view economic theory as a particularly elegant way of demonstrating the merits of *laissez-faire*, they concluded that whoever advocated free trade must be something of an economist, and they located several writers during the seventeenth and early eighteenth centuries who had advocated it so forcefully as to qualify them, in their eyes, as considerable economists'. Nonetheless, he made a wholly correct observation that 'economics has always been known. It is so vital to the life of merchants, moralists and statesmen that they could never have done their work without understanding its basic principles'.

The potential ahistoricism of seeking antecedents for then current wisdom need not detain us, for what is important from the pre-Smithian era is the fluidity and openness of the market for economic knowledge in all of Peden's five categories. McCulloch, generally considered the first historian of economic thought, but also perhaps the first Englishman to make his living as a teacher, journalist and professor of political economy, provided a broad listing of pre-Smithian figures (McCulloch, 1845). Of the proto-canonical figures, foremost was Petty. One-time personal secretary to Thomas Hobbes (1588–1679), in turn, a canonical figure (with Bacon) in developing some of the fundamentals of European liberal thought, notably that theory should set out the rational, pre-requisites for civil peace and material prosperity, Petty was a businessman, briefly an MP, founding member of Royal Society (established 1662) and, with his *Political Arithmetic* (written 1676, published 1690) a pioneer English empiricist (Stone, 1997, ch. 1).

Together with Gregory King (1648–1712), Petty laid the foundations for what will become a research programme in which English economists will be highly distinguished: notably Arthur Bowley (1869–1957) and Colin Clark (1905–89) during what was a transformation in national accounts between the world wars, culminating, of course, with Richard Stone's (1913–91) Nobel prize. Petty was a pivotal figure, if not inventor then at least progenitor of political arithmetic ('the art of reasoning by figures, upon things relating to government': Hoppit, 1996, 517 n.5), in which the central concept – the 'surplus' – became both the foundation of the classical theory of distribution (Aspromourgos, 1996) but, in effect, also an instrument of governance designed to meet the challenge the English then faced of a political entity comprising two monarchies, at least two religions and two significant colonial economies (Ireland and America) (McCormick, 2009).

Petty stood 'squarely in the progressive intellectual moment of his time' (Aspromourgos, 1996, 9), but it is important to emphasize that while there was a 'remarkable outpouring of thinking about economic issues' in the century before 1760, it was also the case that, in the round, this literature was thoroughly fluid, essentially inchoate, and that we should resist any simple framework of mapping individual contributions to either mercantilist or nascent political economy in furtherance of an essential Whiggish story that from these origins a late eighteenth-century Smithian synthesis would emerge (Hoppit, 2006, 79). Current work is very sensitive to the 'Whiggishness' that might be levelled at Letwin (1963) through Hutchison (1988), though the charge is perhaps unfair to the latter as Hoppit (2006, 80 n.5) acknowledges. Moreover, Petty combined, as did other contemporaries upon whom study has focused, other attributes of relevance for understanding pre-Smithian and later English economics.

For example, Letwin (1963, 48, 147, 183) focuses on a number of key figures across a range from Josiah Child (1630–99), the 'merchant economist', the 'epitome of the Restoration mercantile magnate', through John Locke (1632–1704), the 'philosopher as economist', but greater attention is undoubtedly given to those engaged in, or whose fortunes depended upon, commerce and international trade, though, and particularly in his account of Dudley North (1641–91), he is very careful to make clear that too often the writings of the mercantile class were as irrelevant to the development of scientific 'economic theory as an engineer's manual is to theoretical mechanics'. Nonetheless, with such a pivotal figure as Child, his 'economic doctrines were aimed at solving the economic problems that faced England during the decade after the Restoration' (Letwin, 1963, 3), with English contributions – pace the later Scottish Enlightenment – overwhelmingly 'oriented to immediate policy issues and [less] concerned to locate economic issues in a wider ethical and historical framework' (Brewer, 2003, 78).

The classical economists

Smith's reception in England and his influence over what came to be called the classical economists (with David Ricardo (1772–1823) and J.S. Mill (1806–73) the leading exponents) has been very well documented, with O'Brien (2004) the *locus classicus* but also, methodologically, a major step forward towards rational reconstruction and a comprehensive history of thought which ranged far beyond the canonical figures. Classical economics was the ruling body of economic thought from the onset of Britain's industrialisation and rapid population expansion in the second half of the eighteenth century through to the final quarter of the nineteenth century, at which point the marginalist challenge initiated by W.S. Jevons (1835–82) prevailed. Whist the classical economists' achievements are many and durable (so durable that they are still with us today in our understanding of the generalised operational superiority of markets over second-best alternatives), we begin our account of this era with a reminder from Schabas (2003, 174) that Smith defined 'political economy as the "science of the legislator", and thus subordinated his analysis of economic exchange and distribution to the broader questions of political stability and national well-being'. She continues: 'His greatness lay less in his specific insights into the theory of prices and distribution than in his overall comprehension of the subject'; indeed, 'Within the *Wealth of Nations* [1776] one can find discussions of virtually every branch of political economy as it has evolved up to the present'.

Economic growth is at the core of the *Wealth of Nations*, with subsequent classical theory focused on growth and development, and with the cardinal choice of government and/or the market a central preoccupation. The classical economists made advances both in, what we would now call, micro- and macroeconomics. This was a transformative phase for Britain's economy, one which was highly open and operating (save 1797–1821) within a gold standard monetary regime which, following Hume, had been shown to have self-adjusting properties. Thus classical theory developed in the areas of the balance of payments, banking, money and the price level. Additionally, whilst this was mostly a period of peace and uninterrupted international trade growth, the period of Napoleonic Wars (1793–1815) and its aftermath led to a high demand for, and supply of, economic knowledge on such traditional English preoccupations as the public finances (especially the national debt) and currency matters.

The achievements of the classical economists and the durability of their legacy might perhaps be thought the more remarkable for this era still being very much the pre-professionalisation stage of English economics. Thus, the two canonical figures, Ricardo and J.S. Mill were sometime MPs, writers, controversialists and, in the former's case, a spectacularly successful financial speculator. They did not hold university posts, though Ricardo's great exponent, McCulloch, was the founding professor of political economy at UCL in 1828 (the first professor of political economy in England was Nassau Senior (1790–1864) who was elected to the Drummond chair in political economy in Oxford in 1825). In this pre-professionalisation stage, the market for economic knowledge was highly contestable, with ample scope for non-university economists to have the highest influence, and for popular economics to produce original economic theories in advance of formal economics (as Kadish, 1996 has demonstrated with the wealth of writings associated with the free trade movement of the 1830s and 1840s).

Thus, whilst Senior has often been seen as the architect of the Poor Law Amendment Act, 1834, a key piece of legislation in which many classical economists made contributions (O'Brien, 2004, 4), the policy influence of Samuel Jones Loyd (1796–1883), Lord Overstone, is of at least equal interest. Overstone, a banker, MP, an early but not founding member of the Political Economy Club, the nearest to a scientific community that London economists had in this pre-learned society age, was one of the first economists to describe the trade cycle in detail but above all he was decisive in the then battle between rival schools (banking vs. currency) of monetary theorists that preceded the Bank Charter Act, 1844, which established an English monopoly of currency issue with the central bank. For the *Economist* magazine, founded in 1846, Overstone was 'one of the greatest figures in the world of banking and public finance in the early and middle nineteenth century'; indeed:

In an era rich in deep political economists, acute monetary and financial specialists, frenziedly polemical, theoretical disputes, Overstone as an all-rounder was a match for them all and more than a match for most. No one had a greater influence than he on shaping the major lines of monetary and fiscal policy between the 1830s and the 1860s.

[*Anon, 1972, 45*]

It is arguable that in the century or so from Smith to 1870 that English economists had more practical impact on public policy than they did during the so-called Keynesian era after the Second World War. Certainly, the range of policy areas was extensive and thoroughly modern: factory regulation; the machinery question; pauperism and poverty relief; education; trade unions; Ireland; and the colonies and emigration.

The last of these requires brief elaboration as the classical economists have been seen as playing a key role in the formative stage of the British Empire. O'Brien (2004, 345–9) presents a two-stage analysis, punctuated in the mid-1820s. This starts with Smith's attack on the '"savage injustice" of the mercantilist principle underlying the policies of European nations towards their colonies' (Winch, 1965, 6). This was not a critique of colonies *per se*, and when economic and political conditions changed it appeared to Smith's successors that there were mutual benefits in developing the colonies as an outlet for surplus population. It should be stressed that on this issue there was no one voice of the classical economists, though in terms of policy the influence of Edward G. Wakefield's (1796–1862) 'scientific colonisation' is well established (Winch, 1965, chs 6–7).

Wakefield's vision, of self-governing, settler societies with deep and enduring economic and cultural ties to the metropolis, did come to pass, but there were a plurality of motives behind the advocacy of colonial development. Had there not been so, in such a moral minefield, it would not have been possible for Jeremy Bentham (1748–1832) and later J.S. Mill to be such prominent supporters of colonial development, the former as the godfather of the 'colonial reform movement' with its emancipation aspirations, and the latter who matured from this being a solution to British social problems to his advocacy of the universal benefits: of civilization, peace, and prosperity. Modern scholarship denies that utilitarianism was an imperialist theory, and certainly Mill appears better to appreciate than most of his contemporaries the potential of what has come to be called the first era of globalisation.

In proffering advice and acting as policy entrepreneurs the classical economists, the 'earliest fully to appreciate the allocative mechanism of the market and the power, subtlety, and efficiency of this mechanism' (O'Brien, 2004, 328), now had a powerful analytical toolkit. Following Ricardo's modelling, policy problems could now be approached through abstraction; empiricism was applied routinely to a range of problems (Thompson, 2013 provides a recent demonstration of Petty's legacy for Peel's first income tax, 1799); and above all there was a ferment of ideas. The classical economists were not extreme advocates of *laissez-faire*. That was mainly confined to their popularisers, of whom there were many (Tribe, 2005). Nonetheless the 'caricature of the Classical economists as the die-hard defenders of extreme *laissez-faire* is one which has proved extremely persistent . . . Examination of the Classical writings on the role of government quickly reveals the misleading nature of the caricature' (O'Brien, 2004, 327–8).

With *laissez-faire* ideas occupying a central position well into the twentieth century, it is important to establish the precise inheritance for the agenda of government of the classical economists' policy prescriptions. As Robbins (1952, 12) had warned, 'you get an entirely distorted view of the significance of this [*laissez-faire*] doctrine unless you see it in combination with the theory of law and the functions of government which its authors also propounded; the idea of freedom *in vacuo* was entirely alien to their conception'. Thus, for the classical economists, the economic and political case for the market was not an ideal type; the agenda for government was much broader than a literal translation of *laissez-faire* would imply; and much energy was expended on the need for government to ensure that markets were able to function so as to maximise their potential benefits. Classical political economy was, above all, pragmatic in matters of policy.

The marginalist revolution and early professionalisation

Jevons, the first professor of political economy at what would become Manchester University, an appointment often taken as the beginning of university economics in England, is best known for his *Theory of Political Economy* (1871) and, somewhat less so, for *The Coal Question* (1865), though the latter was a milestone in applied economics research as well as raising the question of sustainability in a new way. Less well known is his 'Notice of a General Mathematical Theory of Political Economy' (1862), a pioneering work in the mathematisation of economics. Taken together, this trinity was both a challenge to English classical political economy and a foretaste of how modern economics would develop. For Jevons (1871, 3), if economics 'is to be a science at all, [it] must be a mathematical science', with much of the impetus here being contemporaneous developments 'in logic and physics rather than from problems internal to the discipline or from specific economic events' (Schabas, 2003, 181). That said, for Jevons, as for Marshall and most other contemporary economists, 'political economy was first and last a fruit-bearing subject concerned, above all, with the alleviation of real-world problems of poverty, insecurity and efficiency' (Hutchison, 1982, 366).

Typically, Jevons is taken as the first substantive English contribution to what has been called the 'marginalist revolution', in which classical value theory was questioned severely and a new generation developed both theory and policy prescriptions. We here stress English contributions for, as Hutchison (1978, ch. 3) has shown, contemporaneous continental European developments associated with Menger and Walras were largely unknown and there was at this time a certain intellectual insularity. This did not extend to the heterodox 'English historical economics': this was more cosmopolitan, using history to challenge classical political economy, and thereby developing an historical and inductive methodology for economics and which would greatly influence the development of the discipline of economic history (Kadish, 1989).

As it was, in practice the marginalist turn in England owed as much to Marshall, whose *Principles of Economics* (1890) brought together into a coherent whole the central concepts of demand and supply, marginal utility and costs of production, in the process establishing the first modern economics textbook and its author as the doyen of British economics (Groenewegen,

1995). Marshall's establishment of the economics tripos at Cambridge in 1903, the first three-year single honours economics degree programme, then set the seal on the development of English economics through to J.M. Keynes and beyond, making Cambridge a major centre for English economics until at least the 1970s (Middleton, 1998).

Marginalism coincided with the delayed professionalisation of English economics in an accelerated process of catch-up, and especially with the United States, between the 1880s and the First World War (Coats, [1980] 1993, 138–42). This was a period of national introspection as anxieties about economic decline (relative, not absolute) took hold (Middleton, 1996, chs 4–6), thereby increasing the demand for economic (and statistical) expertise to resolve the cardinal choice of government or market (Middleton, 1998, ch. 4). Concurrently, on the supply side the new universities were establishing degree and other economics teaching in a process of 'political economy to economics via commerce', as epitomised by developments in Birmingham and Manchester (Kadish and Tribe, 1993).

Marshall's influence, and that of his immediate successor to the Cambridge chair (Arthur Pigou, 1877–1959), affected profoundly the direction and content of English economics, both domestically and – through their training of the new generation as well as their own writings – abroad. This extended to the curriculum (economic history and the history of thought still integral to the discipline of economics) and to the public policy role of economists (most famously with Marshall and Pigou's protégé, J.M. Keynes). Both were greatly assisted by the final infrastructural development of this professionalisation stage: the establishment in 1890 of the British Economics Association (renamed the Royal Economic Society (RES) in 1902) as the learned society representing economists and the launch the following year of its journal, the *Economic Journal* (*EJ*). With F.Y. Edgeworth (1845–1926), in effect Marshall's counterpart at Oxford, as the first editor, and in post for thirty-four years (joined by Keynes, 1911–45), the *EJ* was by the First World War a significant international journal, as indeed it remains today a front-rank, general field journal (Hey and Winch, 1990).

The twentieth century

Professionalisation

This had many drivers, all more or less directly related to nature of the market for economic knowledge, now more than usually complex with the challenge posed by burgeoning socialist thought and agitation before and after the First World War. Much of the theoretical advances of the time related to the public policy potential of the new discipline, though that was far from being the sole impulse for research. A Cambridge approach to welfare is widely identified as being aggregative, based on utilitarianism with roots back to Bentham and particularly associated with Pigou, beginning with his *Wealth and Welfare* (1912) which established 'a strong sense that market failure is a rather pervasive problem and that governmental measures are necessary' (Medema, 2009, 64). That there was a specifically Cambridge approach is contestable (Backhouse and Nishizawa, 2010, ch. 1), but what is clear is the huge significance of Cambridge to prewar English economics.

Thus, we should highlight Pigou's *Unemployment* (1913), Hawtrey's *Good and Bad Trade* (1913) and Robertson's *Study of Industrial Fluctuations* (1915). The launch of the Cambridge Economic Handbooks series just after the war was also very significant, being edited by Keynes and with early volumes achieving large circulations, not least the first, Hubert Henderson's *Supply and Demand* (1922). Traditional English strengths in economics, such as banking, money, national accounts (with an increasing focus on income and wealth distribution), public finance and trade, were still very much to the fore but there was also a deepening of research which would bring forth such significant contributions as Joan Robinson's *Economics of Imperfect Competition* (1933) and, of course, with Keynes' *General Theory* (1936), the birth of what has come to be called macroeconomics.

Nonetheless, Cambridge dominance should not be overstated, and certainly not in terms of the production of economics graduates (Birmingham and Manchester were more important, though the majority took commerce degrees). Nor should the extent of professionalisation achieved by 1914, particularly if the test be Marshall's Organon:

> that economists should acquire an attribute, that of training in a body of theory which was rigorous and inaccessible to the uninitiated; be imbued with an attitude, an impartiality in politics which was buttressed by the scientific possibilities of applied welfare economics; and seek a consequent reward, that of a privileged position and voice in policy-making.
>
> *(Middleton, 1998, 106)*

Marshall's Organon is a tough test for 1914, but nonetheless English economists and university economics in particular had made significant steps towards professionalisation. Arguably, less than 25 individuals comprised the British economics profession by that date, of which half had English university posts (though not necessarily in economics or even political economy), with the remainder freelance writers and lecturers, MPs and civil servants. Almost all had written a monograph and more than a quarter a textbook; again almost all were involved in journalism, and approximately one half policy advocacy (especially the tariff reform campaign of the early 1900s) and a lesser number policy advice (Middleton, 1998, table 4.2).

In her comparative study of professionalisation in France, the US and UK, Fourcade (2009, 9–10) argued that:

> In Britain, the identity of economists has been historically shaped by a political culture centred on small, tightly knit elite societies that traditionally enjoyed great authority in producing public discourse and conducting the affairs of the nation, and by the nonprofessional, gentry tradition of the public service. This has produced a scientific field that is organized around the authority of elite institutions and personalities, but where the ability to communicate economic ideas in plain and eloquent language (through personal networks and contributions oriented towards the general public . . .) is also highly valued.

This public-minded elite, concentrated in the golden triangle of Oxbridge and London, would dominate English academic economics and the public policy activities of those economists until the 1970s, reaching its high point during the period from the 1930s to the 1960s, the Keynesian era. This view places much significance on Keynes and the advent of macroeconomics, and is often associated with the view that the period from the establishment of the tripos to the late 1920s was 'not the most exciting in the history of economics' (Collard, 1990, 164). Collard goes further to see Keynes as 'just one of a number of distinguished Cambridge economists of the period', but there is a different point to be made about the state of English economics and the market for economic knowledge before the so-called Keynesian revolution of the 1930s.

On the one hand, there is the Shackle (1967, 4–5) characterisation of the marginal revolution having produced a dominant neoclassical economics, a 'Great Theory or Grand System of Economics [of 'general, perfectly competitive, full-employment stationary (or better, timeless) equilibrium'], in one sense complete and self-sufficient, able, on its own terms, to answer all questions which those terms allowed' (see also Hutchison, 1953, ch. 25). On the other, there is the political economy that, for Britain, the First World War and its aftermath created on the demand side a major spur to English economists to be even more involved in solving contemporaneous economic problems, including assisting the political class on how to respond to the clamour for an increased welfare effort (and wider government intervention) borne of the rise of labour and modern democratic political competition. Incentives were thereby created for a discipline to become predisposed towards identifying market failures as endemic.

The rise and fall of Keynesian economics

In an influential assessment, Shackle (1967, 5–6) opined 'At the opening of the 1930s economic theory still rested on the assumption of a basically orderly and tranquil world. At their end it had come to terms with the relentless anarchy and disorder of the world of fact'. For him, as for many others, the long 1930s (his started with Sraffa 1926 and the state of value theory) represent the years of 'high theory'. Certainly, Cambridge was at the centre of high theory but did not have a monopoly, and as before its overall contribution to English economics has been overstated. Current research now focuses more on Oxford and provincial centres such as Manchester, which were both developing strengths in applied economics. Additionally, Oxford had finally inaugurated an economics degree in the form of Politics, Philosophy and Economics (PPE, which has come to have a central place in British public life) and was developing as a centre for pathbreaking theoretical research with the key figures Roy Harrod (1900–78), John Hicks (1904–89) and James Meade (1907–95) (Young and Lee, 1993).

The foremost rival institution, however, was the London School of Economics (LSE) which developed rapidly in size and reputation under Lionel Robbins (1898–1984) who, appointed as a professor in 1929, was famously against Keynes in the 1930s on many policy and theoretical grounds, and was instrumental in bringing Friedrich Hayek (1899–1992) and thus Austrian economics to the school in 1931. Additionally, Robbins (1932, 15) gave economics its most enduring definition as 'the science which studies human behaviour as a relationship between ends and scarce means which have alternative uses'.

The earlier, Cambridge-centred focus on the development of macroeconomic theory and policy has also been diluted in recent research; indeed, the breadth of contributions by English economists can be gauged from the nine British – here defined by nationality at date of award, with the problem thereby entailed of omitting 'non-British', who made significant contributions whilst employed in England – recipients (out of 74 individuals so awarded) to date of the Nobel Prize in economics:

- John Hicks for 'pioneering contributions to general economic equilibrium theory and welfare theory' in 1972 (Oxford);
- Hayek 'for pioneering work in the theory of money and economic fluctuations and for . . . penetrating analysis of the interdependence of economic, social and institutional phenomena' in 1974 (Freiburg);
- James Meade 'for . . . path-breaking contributions to the theory of international trade and international capital movements' in 1977 (Cambridge);
- W. Arthur Lewis (1915–91) 'for . . . pioneering research into development, with particular consideration of the problems of developing countries' in 1979 (Princeton);
- Richard Stone 'for having made fundamental contributions to the development of systems of national accounts and hence greatly improved the basis for empirical economic analysis' in 1984 (Cambridge);

- Ronald Coase (1910–2013) 'for his discovery and clarification of the significance of transaction costs and property rights for the institutional structure and functioning of the economy' in 1991 (Chicago);
- James Mirrlees (b. 1936) 'for . . . fundamental contribution to the economic theory of incentives under asymmetric information' in 1996 (Cambridge);
- Clive Granger (1934–2009) 'for methods of analyzing economic time series with common trends (cointegration)' in 2003 (UC San Diego);
- Christopher Pissarides (b. 1948) 'for . . . analysis of markets with search frictions' in 2010 (LSE).

English economics between the 1930s and the 1970s developed according to local factors and in response to the broader internationalisation ('Americanisation' for some, especially critics) of the discipline (Middleton, 1998, ch. 6). Academic economists were highly prominent in the policy debates of the 1930s, but it was during the Second World War that the demand schedule for economic knowledge rose significantly and economists were located right at the heart of government, not least Keynes, who was the intellectual father of the subsequent full employment policy and, with an American, joint architect of the Bretton Woods monetary system. University economics was somewhat disrupted as a consequence, but recovery was underway by the late 1940s and, from the 1960s, with the new universities was a significant growth subject. This was a time of innovation, with power and authority shifting from the golden triangle as Essex (which pioneered American-style postgraduate education) and other centres for economic research (for example, York) rose to the fore, with a number of departments (especially Essex and Warwick) aiming deliberately to Americanise, to be mid-Atlantic in their orientation (Backhouse, 1997, 36).

Whilst American influences were undoubtedly strong, there was also resistance to Americanisation, with much of this manifest in the development of British textbooks to rival Paul Samuelson's *Economics: an Introductory Analysis* (1948). At the national level, Richard Lipsey's *Introduction to Positive Economics* (1963) was pre-eminent but there were also interesting local experiments, including, at Cambridge, Joan Robinson and John Eatwell's *Introduction to Modern Economics* (1973) which sought to rescue Keynesianism and also radical political economy (King and Millmow, 2003). As it was, by the 1990s Backhouse (1997, 33) was to conclude:

> Though it retained many distinctive features, British economics is now undeniably international, exhibiting many of the features of what has been called American-style professional economics: students learn substantially the same theory as their counterparts in other countries, often using the same textbooks; graduate coursework is regarded as necessary preparation for research; university teachers are expected to have doctorates; frequent publication is essential to professional advancement; the journals in which people publish are essentially international; and there is an emphasis on mathematical theory and econometric technique.

This is to jump ahead somewhat, though it shows the destination of contemporary English economics. We can agree with Hicks (1963, 312) that with the end of the Second World War disciplinary leadership transferred from Britain to America, with the subsequent story told typically in terms of the British assimilation of the neoclassical synthesis associated with Samuelson: of American-style Keynesianism and of a particular analytical technique – general equilibrium – which drew inspiration from the natural sciences, and especially physics.

In Britain, as elsewhere, the charge was made that the neoclassical synthesis led to the empty formalism of an economics that had been incapacitated as a 'social science' (for example, Blaug, 1999a). However, the charge has also been made that it was the delayed Americanisation of English economics that hampered its scientific advancement (and produced poor policy advice). Foremost here was Harry Johnson (1923–77), a Canadian but with considerable experience of Cambridge, the LSE and other English universities (Moggridge, 2008). Johnson (1968) was scathing about the lack of professionalism in English economics, with particular ire directed at Cambridge and Keynes – 'an exceptional economist when he lived, but . . . a malevolent myth since he died' (1975, 226) – and at the British obsession with declinism, resulting in an 'economics . . . converted from a scientific subject into a species of political necromancy' (1973, 70). This last complaint followed on from the experience of a number of failed growth experiments in which leading British economists, notably Harrod and Nicholas Kaldor (1908–86), had been highly prominent, these failures undermining the reputation of academic economists vis-à-vis more sceptical economic journalists (now more prominent in an economic knowledge market grown even more competitive) and in the process compromising the Keynesian consensus of macro- and microeconomic policy activism (Middleton, 2004).

Later, Alan Walters (1926–2009), Thatcher's personal economic adviser, made the charge that British economists' professional norms were that 'free markets will perform in an unsatisfactory way and give rise to unemployment and exploitation, externalities and social costs, inefficiency and excess', such that 'Massive government intervention is needed in order to ensure full employment, fair rewards, and the efficient allocation of resources' (1978, 90). To this charge, O'Brien (1981, 64) then added that there was a 'presumption that pervade[d] most of the mainstream literature on the rôle of government in economic life – the imposed social welfare function, and the myth of the omniscient and impartial government'. These charges were made after a decade of theoretical and policy disputes, typically portrayed as Keynesians vs. monetarists in the 1970s and early 1980s, which were projected as a 'discipline in disarray'. In fact, for either charge to hold the British economics profession would need to have been substantially different from mainstream American economics. Yet, from survey evidence it was not: in 1971 'liberal economic orthodoxy' was clearly dominant in macro- and microeconomics, though Brittan (1973, 22–3) detected 'egalitarian concern[s] . . . greater than among economists in most other Western countries, and greater than that of almost any other British middle class professional group outside the social services'. These characteristics of the British profession were broadly mirrored in the later survey of Ricketts and Shoesmith (1990).

A concurrent debate about whether there was a distinctive 'European' economics yielded an unambiguous positive answer with respect to the US, but that 'the difference is more like that separating two dialects rather than completely separate languages' and that British economics 'can perhaps be taken to come from a home halfway, culturally, between the European and North American continents' (Baumol, 1995, 187). We might hypothesise that, during the Keynesian era, the median British economist was politically to the left of their American counterpart; there is evidence of greater British production and consumption of heterodox ideas; and that British economists have made particular contributions in such fields as the measurement of inequality and public economics (Backhouse, 1997, 58).

The hegemony of the neoclassical synthesis came under attack first in the US with the Keynesian paradigm initially questioned by a revival of monetary economics associated with Milton Friedman and associates, and then more substantially by new classical theory, with efficient market theories and the policy ineffectiveness proposition particularly significant. English economists engaged quickly with the monetarist challenge, both in terms of the defence of Keynesianism by Cambridge economists but also with emerging centres of research in monetary economics (Manchester with David Laidler and Michael Parkin) and a research network, the Money Study Group, in which Johnson played a key role, thereby linking Chicago with the LSE where he had a joint appointment (Moggridge, 2008, 308–11). Britain subsequently experienced a more extreme monetary policy experiment under the Thatcher governments than was the case in the US (Middleton, 1998, ch. 7), but in both neo-liberal ideas were in the ascendant by the 1980s in the wider market for economic knowledge. The end of the Keynesian era was marked spectacularly for British economists in March 1981 when 364 signed a letter to *The Times* protesting about the Thatcher government's deflationary policies at the very point that the recovery from the recession beginning in 1979 can be dated (Middleton, 1998, 34–5).

During the Keynesian era English economists responded to, and created the conditions for, the enlarged role of the state. Whilst English economics made distinguished contributions to macroeconomic theory, the long-run emphasis on economics as a practical science was also reflected in growing expertise in forecasting, not least the National Institute for Economic and Social Research (NIESR, founded 1938) which initiated its quarterly *National Institute Economic Review* in 1959; in public enterprise (for example, Ralph Turvey, 1927–2012) and tax reform (Kaldor and Meade, the latter for the Institute for Fiscal Studies (IFS) established in 1969 and by the 1980s unafraid of controversy but renowned for its objectivity). Normative egalitarian ideas were widely shared amongst English economists, though the works that were politically influential – Tawney's *Equality* (1931) and then Crosland's *Future of Socialism* (1956) – did not originate within academic economics. The English economics profession, however, was very far from homogenous with respect to Keynesianism. The Mont Pèlerin Society, created in 1947 by Hayek and others, formed an international forum for such dissent, and with Robbins a founding member, but domestically it was the establishment in 1955 of the Institute for Economic Affairs (IEA) that would provide the rallying point for those for whom Keynesianism undermined the free market (Cockett, 1994; Mirowski and Plehwe, 2009). This would be an important vector for a range of American academic work, and neo-liberal ideas more broadly, to be transmitted to English economists and thence into wider public debate.

Recent advances and trends

With the internationalisation of British economics came, as elsewhere, the triumph of the objectivist, deductivist mathematic approach to a discipline that increasingly was very far from resembling the human, social and historical 'moral science' that had been nascent economics, let alone political economy, as recently as the early twentieth century. The explosion in the scale of economic research brought forth the necessity for specialisation. Turvey's entry in Blaug (1999b, 1117) captures the flavour of the change for someone who got their first lectureship (at the LSE) in 1948: 'Started as an economic theorist in the days when it was possible to keep up with everything in economics, then gradually concentrated on' narrower fields. Specialisation then became a driver for disciplinary homogenisation. This, in turn, was buttressed by the narrowing of the English economic curriculum to exclude knowledge of economic history and the history of thought as essential to becoming an economist.

However, the most powerful driver of all was the consequence of British governments requiring that the quality and productivity of research in all disciplines be measured and improved: the Research Assessment Exercises (RAE, now the Research Excellence Framework, REF). Seven of these were conducted between 1986 and 2014, but serious concerns have been raised that the cumulative effects of these audits produced a homogenisation of mainstream economics that all but eliminated heterodox economics and which reinforced the dominance of a small group of universities: the top five in RAE2008 were – in ranked order – LSE, UCL, Warwick,

Oxford and Essex. They were all English and Cambridge is noticeable for its absence (Lee *et al.*, 2013, table 2).

In a major sense the internationalisation of English economics has kept English economists to the forefront as producers of economic knowledge. Thus, if citations be a good proxy for significance, then of the 1,082 leading living economists Blaug (1999b) identified as most frequently cited in 200 economic journals between 1984–96, predictably the US ranked first (65.5 per cent). The UK, however, did rank second (15.4 per cent, which translates to 167 leading economists, of which nearly half were in just five institutions, in rank order: Oxford and LSE, Cambridge, Warwick and UCL) but with the major European countries a very long way behind (France and Germany were ranked fourth and sixth respectively, with 2.3 and 1.9 per cent); indeed, the UK share was approximately double the aggregate of EU member states' share. If the English-speaking countries be aggregated (US, UK, Canada, Australia and New Zealand) the overall share of citations was 88.4 per cent.

Looked at from the perspective of RAE2008, the international significance of British economics is then further reinforced. Indeed, when viewed in relation to all subject results in that round of assessment, then economics and econometrics had the highest valuation as measured by the grade point average of publications (Gillies, 2012), which is somewhat ironic since this coincided with the widely discussed failure of economists generally to predict the implosion of the Great Moderation as financial collapse led to the Great Recession beginning in 2007–8, a crisis as yet far from resolved. Concurrently, the Economic and Social Research Council (ESRC) undertook an international benchmarking exercise for economics, broader in remit than the RAE: the report concluded 'that UK economics research is exceptional by international standards . . . second only to the United States'; a world leader in micro-econometrics and with 'significant strength and influence' in labour, public and development economics; and 'recognise[d] the high quality of applied work in the UK and the huge impact that this has had on policy and practice' (Vickers *et al.*, 2008, ii).

Whilst macroeconomics and PhD training were identified as requiring particular attention, overall the results were presented as highly favourable: good research quality; appropriate returns on investment; good research impact; and a profession with sustainable demographics – moreover one that was internationalising with overseas staff and students a growing proportion. However, whilst this was jointly organised with the RES and did solicit submissions from all of economics, the final report omitted economic history, heterodox economics, methodology and the history of economic thought, all areas in which English economists have significant international presence (Lee *et al.*, 2013, table 6). Such was the completeness of the Americanisation of mainstream English academic economics.

The ESRC benchmarking exercise was very positive about the 'healthy relationship between researchers and policymakers' and about broader research impact, especially the direct employ-ment of academic economists in such institutions as the Bank of England and the Treasury (Vickers *et al.*, 2008, 1, 26–7). Additionally, Britain has a very rich set of research institutes and networks, almost all policy-focused and now exploiting the facilities offered by social media, as for example VoxEU, the policy portal established by the Centre for Economic Policy Research. However, viewed in relation to the broader market for economic knowledge, on the supply side now much more populated by those who have a recent, narrowly specialised economics education, there are more disturbing trends.

These became very evident with the Great Recession after 2008, though even before concerns about the disjuncture between economic theory and lived reality were being expressed in many quarters by significant economists (for example, Marglin, 2008). One particular strand of emerging dissent was the campaign for a post-autistic economics. This had originated in France in undergraduate protests in 2000 (Bernstein, 2004), but very much continues today; it has become sufficiently mainstream that at UCL, following a launch at the British Treasury, a nine-country project 'Rethinking Economics' is underway in response to 'Economics students [who] have started to establish new student societies, which focus not on how to get a job in the City, but on the question "How can economics be used to understand the world better and improve it?"' (Carlin, 2012; Anon, 2013).

Whilst the Great Recession has been a spur to revisit the economics curriculum, the practical effects of reformism are not yet evident. The consequences of an economics profession, academic and non-academic, wedded to a version of neoclassical economics and neo-liberal, low regulation was all too evident in the failure to predict that a combination of permissive macroeconomic policies and financial liberalisation would make certain economies (the US and UK in particular) highly vulnerable to a good, old-fashioned banking crisis. The failure to predict events even attracted the attention of the head of state, with the so-called 'Queen's Question' posed upon a visit to the LSE in November 2008, some seven weeks after the Lehman Brothers' collapse (Gillies, 2012, 25). Even some four years later, the Governor of the Bank, Mervyn King (b. 1948), the first academic economist to hold the post, was projecting an orthodoxy that the answer to the 'Queen's Question' was 'extremely simple: no-one believed it could happen' (King, 2012, 4).

In fact, there were British economists who issued warnings and over a long period. Thus, beginning with the 'Cassandra of the fens', Wynne Godley (1926–2010), and his application of the sectoral financial balances approach to macroeconomic (in)stability (Godley, 1999, latterly picked up in Martin Wolf's (2012) influential *Financial Times* column), and then extending to City economists, such as Roger Bootle (2004) who warned of a housing bubble, and economic journalists such as Elliott and Atkinson (2007), there were attempts to correct the misidentification of the 1990s through to middle 2000s as a Great Moderation: not a NICE economy (Non-Inflationary Continually Expansionary) at all but a Great Complacence about the dangers facing contemporary capitalism (Engelen *et al.*, 2011). As it was, and perhaps remains so (Mirowski, 2013), the fate of orthodox economics in Britain vindicates the power of Prasad's (2006, 105) conclusion that why certain ideas become policy has 'everything to do with political interest' rather than economic theory.

The Great Recession illustrates a further aspect of contemporary British economics and the market for economic knowledge: on the demand side, policy-makers needed effective stabilisation policies to avoid the financial crisis and resulting downturn becoming a 1930s Great Depression, but what about the supply side? In fact, the quarterly peak-to-peak GDP loss between 1930.I and 1932.III at 6.9 per cent was slightly smaller than the 7.2 per cent loss between 2008.I and 2009.III, with both sharing the characteristic of being double dip, albeit that the pre-Great Depression GDP level was regained within 16 quarters whereas, with 21 quarters now elapsed (latest estimate is 2013.II), real GDP is still 3.3 per cent below the 2008.I peak (Middleton, 2013, table 8.1 updated by ONS ABMI series). Policy-makers faced a market for economic knowledge in which most academic economists were ignorant of the 1930s, or what they thought they knew about Keynes and policy would not be recognised as real knowledge by economic historians or historians of thought, while non-academic economists were no better equipped and probably worse on average.

Indeed, those working in the commercial world, either as business economists or economic commentators, were operating in the context of a media almost universally propagating a free market message which propounded austerity as the appropriate policy response. In the US, more so than in the UK, though not for want of trying (Crafts and Fearon, 2013), knowledge of the

Great Depression was used effectively to prevent catastrophe, and whilst austerity policies did prevail (more in the UK than US) the Keynesian automatic stabilisers were not, unlike 1930 and 1931, overridden. One leading US economist has gone so far as to say that 'economic historians have had a good crisis' in that positive lessons were learnt from the 1930s, transmitted to policy makers and then applied with beneficial effects. However, he also notes that 'The recent crisis . . . reminds us that the policy response is as much a matter of ideology and politics as it is a matter of economics' (Eichengreen, 2012, 289, 303). In Britain, that was all too evident, with those advocating radical fiscal contraction on the back of the expansionary fiscal contraction hypothesis which lacked empirical foundations. Finally, although the argument is typically oversimplified, there is a strong measure of truth that the Great Depression of the 1930s brought forth Keynesian macroeconomics. The more recent crisis does not appear as yet either to have impacted upon economics nor appear to have dented prevailing neo-liberalism.

The dissemination of national traditions overseas

English economics has had a profound influence on the development of all economics from the classicals through to the contemporary world. Initially, it was canonical figures that carried authority, but later – and here empire and its successor, the commonwealth, were important in the global reach – it was the English educational system that carried influence. From the 1850s the University of London BA could be examined overseas; by the 1920s, the London external degrees in economics and commerce were based on the LSE syllabus; and from the late 1930s we can date the modern university-level economics textbook (Frederic Benham's *Economics: a General Textbook for Students* (1938) is usually taken as the first), though textbooks and political economy manuals have a long provenance stretching back to the eighteenth century (Tribe, 2012).

From Smith through Keynes, and most recently Marshall (whose *Principles* (1890) became a disciplinary foundation globally (Raffaelli *et al.*, 2010)), the reception and enduring influence of English economists abroad has been much studied. Indeed, for Keynes it has become something of an industry so far as policy influence is concerned. In terms of the broader influence of the English tradition of economics education one has only to look at the yearbook of the Association of Commonwealth Universities (established 1913) to see how many Asian, African and Australian economics academics were UK-educated until well into the post-Second World War era. Staff exchanges were also important, though latterly, and in line with internationalisation, the US has been more the attractant for Commonwealth and aspiring academics.

There is a long history of economists' direct involvement in advising overseas governments about economic development and, much more recently, market reform. However, before this modern era, at the height of Empire, say *c*.1870–1950, a 'colonial economics' prevailed. Less the *laissez-faire* liberalism of the classical era and more about colonial exploitation for the benefit of the metropolis, albeit moderated by variable concerns about 'native welfare', English neoclassical economics was propagated through the colonial governing class. English imperialism was markedly economic in motive but also pragmatic, and thus when notions of development began to re-emerge in the 1940s, English economists were to be amongst the 'pioneers in development' (Meier and Seers, 1984, ch. 1).

As Empire turned to commonwealth, and development became the focus, English economists were then in the forefront of foreign aid, consultancy and international organisations (Coats, 1986). For many years Ian Little and James Mirrlees' *Manual of Industrial Project Analysis in Developing Countries* (1969) was the guide of choice for those in the field. More recently, as Collier's (2007) widely cited analysis of poverty amongst the global 'bottom billion' attests, English economists remain important in the field of development, both theory and practice. British economists have also been significantly involved in advising the successor states of the former USSR on how best to secure the transition to a market economy (the LSE's Centre for Economic Performance is particularly involved in Russia). Whilst this needs to be seen in the broader context of the Washington Consensus, as a consequence – and, of course, part cause – of the Thatcher governments' privatisation programmes and other market liberalisation programmes British economists have a significant expertise to offer to the global market for economic knowledge.

Finally, in terms of global impact today, English economics gains significantly from the global reach and authority of Britain's quality media, be it the BBC television and world radio service or print media, and especially the weekly *Economist* magazine and daily *Financial Times* newspaper, all of which are thoroughly internationalised in outlook and audience. However, it is difficult to separate out the advantage that the medium of English, the first global *lingua franca*, offers to English economists and other scientists. Certainly, the ability of the English to speak and write a language which approximates to American English must be incalculable.

Conclusion

If citations be the 'coinage of reward in academia' (Blaug, 1999b) then English economics has maintained its propensity to punch well above its weight, albeit with its influence diminished relative to its golden age of the nineteenth and first half of the twentieth centuries. It, like the British economy, has thus enjoyed unprecedented absolute growth and endured relative decline. Of course, despite a century and more of relative decline, the British economy is still the world's sixth largest, and as we have seen from Blaug (1999b) British economists – which means principally English residents – were the second most cited, achieving a share half that of the US but with less than one quarter of the national population.

Whilst English economists have this global profile and significance it is debateable whether a distinctive English economics has survived the pasteurisation that has been central to the Americanisation/internationalisation of the discipline. This is to raise very large questions about contemporary science, universities and indeed national identities in a global world, matters all beyond our scope here. As it is, English economics has not in recent years produced an economist of the significance of Marshall or Keynes, nor even economists who attained the public profile enjoyed by Kaldor and Balogh as late as the 1970s.

However, this is as much a result of the decline of 'donnish dominion' (Halsey, 1992) as the relative decline of English economics. Arguably, some very English preoccupations have endured, and are manifest in the weight and significance of a range of niche areas in Britain, from applied economics (multiple producers) through to very traditional distributional con-cerns (Tony Atkinson (b. 1944) on inequality). Like the British economy, where niche products prevail, and the so-called knowledge economy is the aspiration, the future of English economics is hopefully world-class general competence with appropriate specialisations according to academic comparative advantage. For some, who seek a post-autistic economics, the present feels a transitional time for the discipline. If so, it is appropriate to end with Hutchison (1978, xii):

> A fuller and clearer understanding of the past record over the last 200 years, in the first instance more widely disseminated amongst economists, might, or could, have a useful part to play in promoting a clearer grasp of the possibilities of economic knowledge.

Note

*   My thanks to Roger Backhouse and Keith Tribe for helping to fill in the gaps in my historical knowledge.

References

Anon (1972) 'Treasurer of the currency school', *Economist*, 8 January, 45–6.

Anon (2013) 'Keynes' new heirs', *Economist*, 23 November, 31–2.

Aspromourgos, T. (1996) *On the origins of classical economics: distribution and value from William Petty to Adam Smith*. London: Routledge.

Backhouse, R.E. (1997) 'The changing character of British economics', in A.W. Coats (ed.) *The post-1945 internationalization of economics*, 31–60.

Backhouse, R.E. (2000) 'Economics in mid-Atlantic: British economics, 1945–95', in A.W. Coats (ed.) *The development of economics in western Europe since 1945*. London: Routledge, 20–41.

Backhouse, R.E. and Nishizawa, T. (eds) (2010) *No wealth but life: welfare economics and the welfare state in Britain, 1880–1945*. Cambridge: Cambridge University Press.

Baumol, W.J. (1995) 'What's different about European economics?', *Kyklos*, 48.2, 187–92.

Bernstein, M.A. (2004) 'The pitfalls of mainstream reasoning (and teaching)', in E. Fullbrook (ed.) *A guide to what's wrong with economics*. London: Anthem Press, 33–40.

Blaug, M. (1999a) 'The formalist revolution or what happened to orthodox economics after World War II', in R.E. Backhouse and J. Creedy (eds) *From classical economics to the theory of the firm: essays in honour of D.P. O'Brien*. Cheltenham: Edward Elgar, 257–80.

Blaug, M. (1999b) *Who's who in economics*. Cheltenham: Edward Elgar.

Bonar, J. (1894) 'English school of political economy', in R.H.I. Palgrave (ed.) *Dictionary of political economy*. London: Macmillan, I, 730–6.

Bootle, R. (2004) *Money for nothing: real wealth, financial fantasies and the economy of the future*. London: Nicholas Brealey.

Brewer, A.A. (2003) 'Pre-classical economics in Britain', in W.J. Samuels, J. Biddle and J.B. Davis (eds) *A companion to the history of economic thought*. Oxford: Blackwell, 78–93.

Brittan, S. (1973) *Is there an economic consensus?: An attitude survey*. London: Macmillan.

Cairncross, A.K. (1985) 'Economics in theory and practice', *American Economic Review*, 75.2 (Papers and Proceedings), 1–14.

Carlin, W. (2012) 'How should macroeconomics be taught to undergraduates in the post-crisis era? A concrete proposal', 25 October <voxeu.org/article/how-should-macro-economics-be-taught-undergraduates-post-crisis-era-concrete-proposal> 04.12.13.

Coats, A.W. (1980) 'The culture and the economists: some reflections on Anglo-American differences', *History of Political Economy*, 12.4, 588–609. Rep. in A.W. Coats (1993) q.v., 134–54.

Coats, A.W. (ed.) (1986) *Economists in international agencies: an exploratory study*. New York: Praeger.

Coats, A.W. (1993) *British and American economic essays*, I: *The sociology and professionalization of economics*. London: Routledge.

Coats, A.W. (ed.) (1997) *The post-1945 internationalization of economics*. Durham, NC: Duke University Press.

Cockett, R. (1994) *Thinking the unthinkable: think-tanks and the economic counter-revolution, 1931–1983*. London: Harper Collins.

Collard, D.A. (1990) 'Cambridge after Marshall', in J.K. Whitaker (ed.) *Centenary essays on Alfred Marshall*. Cambridge: Cambridge University Press, 164–92.

Colley, L. (1992) *Britons: forging the nation, 1707–1837*. New Haven, CT: Yale University Press.

Collier, P. (2007) *The bottom billion: why the poorest countries are failing and what can be done about it*. Oxford: Oxford University Press.

Crafts, N.F.R. and Fearon, P. (eds) (2013) *The great depression of the 1930s: lessons for today*. Oxford: Oxford University Press.

Daunton, M.J. (2011) 'The future direction of British history: thinking about economic cultures', *History Workshop Journal*, 72.1, 222–39.

Dudley, C. (2013) 'Party politics, political economy and economic development in early eighteenth-century Britain', *Economic History Review*, 66.4, 1084–100.

Eichengreen, B.J. (2012) 'Economic history and economic policy', *Journal of Economic History*, 72.2, 289–307.

Elliott, L. and Atkinson, D. (2007) *Fantasy island: waking up to the incredible economic, political and social illusions of the Blair legacy*. London: Constable & Robinson.

Engelen, E., Ertürk, I., Froud, J., Johal, S., Leaver, A., Moran, M., Nilsson, A. and Williams, K. (2011) *After the great complacence: financial crisis and the politics of reform*. Oxford: Oxford University Press.

Fourcade, M. (2009) *Economists and societies: discipline and profession in the United States, Britain and France, 1890s to 1990s*. Princeton, NJ: Princeton University Press.

Gillies, D. (2012) 'Economics and research assessment systems', *Economic Thought*, 1.1, 23–47.

Godley, W. (1999) 'Seven unsustainable processes', <levyinstitute.org/pubs/sevenproc.pdf> 04.12.13.

Groenewegen, P.D. (1995) *A soaring eagle: Alfred Marshall, 1842–1924*. Aldershot: Edward Elgar.

Halsey, A.H. (1992) *Decline of donnish dominion: the British academic professions in the twentieth century*. Oxford: Clarendon Press.

Hey, J.D. and Winch, D. (eds) (1990) *A century of economics: 100 years of the Royal Economic Society and the Economic Journal*. Oxford: Basil Blackwell.

Hicks, J.R. (1963) *The theory of wages*, 2nd edn. London: Macmillan.

Hoppit, J. (1996) 'Political arithmetic in eighteenth-century England', *Economic History Review*, 49.3, 516–40.

Hoppit, J. (2006) 'The contexts and contours of British economic literature, 1660–1760', *Historical Journal*, 49.1, 79–110.

Hutchison, T.W. (1953) *A review of economic doctrines, 1870–1929*. Oxford: Clarendon Press.

Hutchison, T.W. (1978) *On revolutions and progress in economic knowledge*. Cambridge: Cambridge University Press.

Hutchison, T.W. (1982) 'The politics and philosophy in Jevons's political economy', *The Manchester School*, 50.4, 366–78.

Hutchison, T.W. (1988) *Before Adam Smith: emergence of political economy, 1662–1776*. Oxford: Basil Blackwell.

Jevons, W.S. (1871) *The theory of political economy*. London: Macmillan.

Johnson, H.G. (1968) 'A catarrh of economists?: From Keynes to Postan', *Encounter*, 30.5, 50–4.

Johnson, H.G. (1973) 'National styles in economic research: the United States, the United Kingdom, Canada and various European countries', *Daedalus*, 102.2, 65–74.

Johnson, H.G. (1975) 'What passes for economics in the English establishment', *The Banker*, 125. October, 1159–61. Rep. in E.S. Johnson and H.G. Johnson (1978) *The shadow of Keynes: understanding Keynes, Cambridge, and Keynesian economics*. Oxford: Basil Blackwell, 221–6.

Kadish, A. (1989) *Historians, economists and economic history*. New York: Routledge.

Kadish, A. (ed.) (1996) *The corn laws: the formation of popular economics in Britain*, 6 vols. London: Pickering & Chatto.

Kadish, A. and Tribe, K. (eds) (1993) *The market for political economy: the advent of economics in British university culture, 1850–1905*. London: Routledge.

King, J.E. and Millmow, A. (2003) 'Death of a revolutionary textbook', *History of Political Economy*, 35.1, 105–34.

King, M. (2012) 'BBC Today programme lecture', 2 May <bankofengland.co.uk/publications/Documents/speeches/2012/speech567.pdf> 04.12.13.

Lee, F.S., Pham, X. and Gu, G. (2013) 'The UK research assessment exercise and the narrowing of UK economics', *Cambridge Journal of Economics*, 37.4, 693–717.

Letwin, W. (1963) *The origins of scientific economics: English economic thought, 1660–1776*. London: Methuen.

Marglin, S.A. (2008) *The dismal science: how thinking like an economist undermines community*. Cambridge, MA: Harvard University Press.

McCormick, T. (2009) *William Petty and the ambitions of political arithmetic*. Oxford: Oxford University Press.

McCulloch, J.R. (1845) *The literature of political economy: a classified catalogue*. London: Longman, Brown, Green, and Longmans.

Medema, S.G. (2009) *The hesitant hand: taming self-interest in the history of economic ideas*. Princeton, NJ: Princeton University Press.

Meier, G.M. and Seers, D. (1984) *Pioneers in development*. Washington, DC: World Bank.

Melton, J. van Horn (2001) *The rise of the public in Enlightenment Europe*. Cambridge: Cambridge University Press.

Middleton, R. (1996) *Government versus the market: the growth of the public sector, economic management and British economic performance, c.1890–1979*. Cheltenham: Edward Elgar.

Middleton, R. (1998) *Charlatans or saviours?: Economists and the British economy from Marshall to Meade*. Cheltenham: Edward Elgar.

Middleton, R. (2004) 'Economists and economic growth in Britain, c.1955–65', in L.A. Black and H. Pemberton (eds) *Affluent Britain: Britain's postwar 'golden age' revisited*. Aldershot: Ashgate, 129–47.

Middleton, R. (2013) 'Can contractionary fiscal policy be expansionary?: Consolidation, sustainability and fiscal policy impact in Britain in the 1930s', in N.F.R. Crafts and P. Fearon (eds) *The Great Depression of the 1930s*, 212–57.

Mirowski, P. (2013) *Never let a serious crisis go to waste: how neoliberalism survived the financial meltdown*. London: Verso.

Mirowski, P. and Plehwe, D. (eds) (2009) *The road from Mont Pelerin: the making of the neoliberal thought collective*. Cambridge, MA: Harvard University Press.

Moggridge, D.E. (2008) *Harry Johnson: a life in economics*. Cambridge: Cambridge University Press.

Mokyr, J. (2009) *The enlightened economy: an economic history of Britain, 1700–1850*. New Haven, CT: Yale University Press.

O'Brien, D.P. (1981) 'The emphasis on market economics', in A. Seldon (ed.) *The emerging consensus?: Essays on the interplay between ideas, interests and circumstances in the first 25 years of the IEA*. London: IEA, 51–77.

O'Brien, D.P. (2004) *The classical economists revisited*. Princeton, NJ: Princeton University Press.

O'Brien, P.K. (2011) 'The nature and historical evolution of an exceptional fiscal state and its possible significance for the precocious commercialization and industrialization of the British economy from Cromwell to Nelson', *Economic History Review*, 64.2, 408–46.

Peden, G.C. (1996) 'Economic knowledge and the state in modern Britain', in S.J.D. Green and R.C. Whiting (eds) *The boundaries of the state in modern Britain*. Cambridge: Cambridge University Press, 170–87.

Porter, R. (2000) *Enlightenment: Britain and the creation of the modern world*. London: Allen Lane.

Prasad, M. (2006) *The politics of free markets: the rise of neoliberal economic policies in Britain, France, Germany and the United States*. Chicago, IL: University of Chicago Press.

Raffaelli, T., Becattini, G., Caldari, K. and Dardi, M. (eds) (2010) *The impact of Alfred Marshall's ideas: the global diffusion of his work*. Cheltenham: Edward Elgar.

Ricketts, M. and Shoesmith, E. (1990) *British economic opinion: a survey of a thousand economists*. London: IEA.

Ridder-Symoens, H. de (ed.) (1996) *A history of the university in Europe*, II: *Universities in early modern Europe (1500–1800)*. Cambridge, Cambridge University Press.

Robbins, L.C. (1932) *An essay on the nature and significance of economic science*. London: Macmillan.

Robbins, L.C. (1952) *The theory of economic policy in English classical political economy*. London: Macmillan.

Rothschild, E. (2001) *Economic sentiments: Adam Smith, Condorcet and the Enlightenment*. Cambridge, MA: Harvard University Press.

Schabas, M. (2003). 'British economic theory from Locke to Marshall'. In T.M. Porter and D. Ross (eds) *The Cambridge history of science*, 7: *The modern social sciences*. Cambridge: Cambridge University Press, 171–82.

Schumpeter, J.A. (1954) *History of economic analysis*, ed. E.B. Schumpeter. Oxford: Oxford University Press.

Shackle, G.L.S. (1967) *The years of high theory: invention and tradition in economic thought, 1926–1939*. Cambridge: Cambridge University Press.

Sraffa, P. (1926) 'The laws of returns under competitive conditions', *Economic Journal*, 36.4, 535–50.

Stone, J.R.N. (1997) *Some British empiricists in the social sciences, 1650–1900*. Cambridge: Cambridge University Press.

Thompson, S.J. (2013) 'The first income tax, political arithmetic and the measurement of economic growth', *Economic History Review*, 66.3, 873–94.

Trentmann, F. (2008) *Free trade nation: commerce, consumption, and civil society in modern Britain*. Oxford: Oxford University Press.

Tribe, K. (2005) 'Political economy and the science of economics in Victorian Britain', in M.J. Daunton (ed.) *The organisation of knowledge in Victorian Britain*. Oxford: Oxford University Press, 115–37.

Tribe, K. (2012) 'Economic manuals and textbooks in Great Britain and the British Empire, 1797–1938', in M.M. Augello and M.E.L. Guidi (eds) *The economic reader: textbooks, manuals and the dissemination of the economic sciences during the nineteenth and early twentieth centuries*. London: Routledge, 43–75.

Vickers, J. *et al.* (2008) *International benchmarking review of UK economics*. London: RES-ESRC.

Walters, A.A. (1978) *Economists and the British economy*. London: IEA.

Winch, D.N. (1965) *Classical political economy and colonies*. London: G. Bell & Sons.

Winch, D.N. (1996) *Riches and poverty: an intellectual history of political economy in Britain, 1750–1834*. Cambridge: Cambridge University Press.

Wolf, M. (2012) 'The balance sheet recession in the US', *Financial Times*, 19 July.

Young, W.L. and Lee, F.S. (1993) *Oxford economics and Oxford economists*. London: Macmillan.

3

Scotland

Alexander Dow and Sheila Dow

The history of Scottish economic thought holds a special place in the history of global economic thought since the central figure, Adam Smith, has been identified by many as the 'father' of modern economics. But Scottish economic thought consists of much more than the work of Smith, and Smith himself cannot be fully understood independently of his Scottish context. Further, while the eighteenth century saw the most important contributions to economic thought, the tradition of which Smith was a part continued for a time. It was then revived in the late nineteenth century, continuing through to the twentieth century, although with ever-diminishing impact on the discipline. In what follows, we set out the cultural and business background particularly in the seventeenth and eighteenth centuries in which the Scottish tradition was moulded. Special emphasis is placed on Scottish enlightenment philosophy, of which the newly emerging political economy was a product; David Hume and Adam Smith made their pioneering contributions to economics on the basis of their philosophy. We proceed to provide an account of the main economic ideas emerging from this tradition. But we emphasise particularly the approach taken to economics on the grounds that it is this which most clearly distinguishes the history of Scottish thought. Finally, we bring the account forward to the present day, with a separate discussion of how the Scottish tradition was disseminated elsewhere.

Cultural and business traditions

While for a long time major Scottish figures like Hume and Smith were considered isolated geniuses, it is now widely accepted that they were part of a more general phenomenon with a national character, the Scottish enlightenment (Campbell and Skinner, 1982; Broadie, 1990; Buchan, 2003), and that their economic thinking was a product of the particular political-economic environment. The Scottish enlightenment philosophy tradition, of which the Scottish political economy tradition was a product, is to be distinguished from other national enlightenment traditions. While, following Descartes, French enlightenment philosophy emphasised the sufficiency of deductive reason and, following Bacon and Newton, the English enlightenment emphasised empiricism, the Scottish enlightenment pursued a path which combined reason and evidence within a theory of human nature. This philosophical approach in turn was influenced by wider cultural and economic conditions in Scotland.

The cultural and economic conditions for the flowering of economic thought in Scotland in the eighteenth century were established at least as early as the seventeenth century. The court had moved to London when James VI also became James I of England in 1603; the removal of the political centre to London was cemented in 1707 with the Union of the Parliaments. The focus for public debate therefore had shifted away from politics and more towards issues concerning religion and moral issues more widely.

The context and character of such debate was coloured by the continuing presence of distinctive Scottish institutions: the Church of Scotland which is non-established, the legal system based on Roman law, and a national education system built on a foundation of general literacy. The aim to maximise access to good education meant that higher education was made available to students from all parts of the country at an early age. The structured approach to higher education played a crucial part in laying the foundations both for Scottish inventiveness in practical matters and for the development of Scottish enlightenment philosophy (Dow, Dow and Hutton, 1997). Disciplines were taught from a historical perspective, providing exemplars of systems of thought which had been suited to particular historical circumstances rather than one 'best' system. Further, the degree was structured such that students would be exposed at the start to moral philosophy, a subject within which topical issues would be debated.

The content of Scottish philosophy was subject to particular influence from continental Europe. Cultural and educational links with the continent were strong as a result of long-standing political forces, notably conflict with England. In particular, Pufendorf's application of natural law philosophy to economic questions, introduced to Scotland by Gershom Carmichael, was to prove highly influential in both the philosophy and the economics which developed during the enlightenment period. This continental influence on Scottish philosophy continued well into the eighteenth century, strengthened by extended stays in France on the part of Hume, Smith and Sir James Steuart. There was continuity also in the distinctiveness of non-governmental institutions in Scotland.

In the pre-enlightenment period, Scotland had been a relatively poor country, although already employing technical improvements. The scope for trade was restricted by England, but Scotland had long-standing trading and cultural ties with continental Europe. The eighteenth century saw not only a loss of government and the loss of a separate currency in 1707, but also a number of important socio-economic developments resulting from what we might encapsulate with the term 'commercialisation': the emergence of banking from 1695, the opening up of trade with England and English colonies, agricultural improvements and increasing migration into towns. There was further the cultural, economic and demographic upheaval associated first with the 1715 and 1745 Jacobite rebellions and then with the consequent suppression of Highland culture and economic organisation.

These developments brought to the fore a number of important questions. A particular focus for moral philosophy was the moral challenge of commercialisation. But further, there were practical issues surrounding the problem of promoting Highland improvement. This, together with issues related to the opening up of the New World and comparisons with the English economy, posed the 'rich-country poor-country problem': how to understand differences in economic advancement. Indeed it can be argued that the content not only of ideas on economic development, but also that of moral philosophy, were influenced profoundly by the history of Scottish culture and economic circumstances surrounding Highland-Lowland differences (see Dow, 2009a). In the absence of a parliament, civic humanism encouraged the formation of societies to address particular issues, such as the Honourable Society for Improvement in the Knowledge of Agriculture, founded in 1723, and its sequential successors, the Select Society, and the Edinburgh Society for Encouraging Arts, Sciences, Manufactures, and Agriculture in Scotland, whose membership included Hume and Smith.

An education system drawing more on Roman than Greek texts and covering a range of approaches which had been applied to different historical contexts was well-suited to addressing practical problems, leading to an impressive array of technical innovations in the eighteenth century. Indeed the epistemology underlying the structuring of education in Scotland arguably also paved the way for innovations in moral philosophy and its offshoots, including economics. In the spirit of this interdependence between ideas and real experience, Scottish enlightenment philosophy developed in such a way as to underpin these scientific advances with a new general theory of knowledge based on a science of human nature. The influence of continental philosophy on Hume (1739–40) encouraged him to grapple with the rationalism of the French enlightenment, only to conclude that reason was an insufficient foundation for knowledge. But evidence ('experience') was also inadequate given the problem of induction: since real processes are too complex for human understanding, there can be no assurance that past experience is a reliable guide to the future. Knowledge, rather, is built from social conventions with the aid of imagination, but any such knowledge is inevitably partial and open to challenge by experience. Hume and Smith thus employed the Scottish interpretation of Newton's experimental methodology, which was to draw inferences from experience which would be developed into theories and confronted with further experience. Unlike the axiomatic approach of Descartes, this was a method for deriving general principles which were provisional in the face of further evidence and likely to require adaptation to different contexts.

This science of human nature has had a lasting legacy in that it spawned a range of disciplines, such as psychology and sociology, in addition to economics. As far as Scottish philosophy itself is concerned, there was a complex range of currents, but there was sufficient continuity and commonality for a national enlightenment tradition to be identified in the modern literature (see Broadie, 1990). But in the post-enlightenment period, Hume in particular was interpreted very differently, both as a sceptic destructive of science and as the father of logical positivism. It could be argued, therefore, that Scottish enlightenment philosophy had its greatest lasting impact only through what many now regard as misinterpretation (Dow, 2002b).

Scottish philosophy was perpetuated within Scotland after the enlightenment through the continuing emphasis until the late twentieth century on history, moral philosophy and logic and metaphysics in higher education (in spite of strong arguments from Oxford in the early nineteenth century against the teaching of philosophy to undergraduates). Other Scottish institutions and culture also continued to be distinctive, although there has been a gradual process of homogenisation with the rest of the UK. The Scottish economy continued to flourish through trade and heavy industry until the early twentieth century, but then lost ground to the rest of the UK, only reviving through diversification in recent decades. The centrifugal political draw of Westminster (now reversed somewhat by the re-establishment of the Scottish parliament in 1999) has been mirrored in other areas (notably industry and academia), encouraging leaders in these fields to locate in or near London. This has reinforced the marginalisation in the UK of the traditional Scottish form of civic humanism and its philosophical underpinning.

The development of ideas over the long term

The literature on the history of Scottish economic thought is dominated by attention to the work of Adam Smith (see Ross, 1995 for a biography). Yet Smith was influenced by a range of others, from his precursors Carmichael and Hutcheson to his contemporaries such as Hume and Anderson. Further, his ideas should be considered in relation to the range of economic ideas put forward by others within the Scottish tradition: Smith was not an author generous in giving credit to others (see Dow, 1984). The key figures in the eighteenth and nineteenth centuries can be identified as Francis Hutcheson, David Hume, Adam Smith, Sir James Steuart, Adam Ferguson, Dugald Stewart, John Rae, Thomas Chalmers, W.S. Nicholson and William Smart. But there was a much wider range of contributors to economic debate over these two centuries, meticulously recorded by Rutherford (2012). We will discuss below the sense in which the approach taken to analysing economic issues followed a particularly Scottish tradition. But first we outline a selection of the main economic ideas and areas of debate within that tradition; a more comprehensive coverage would include additional areas, such as public finance, where Smith in particular made a pioneering contribution.

Stages approach to development

Before the enlightenment, indeed with origins dating back to ancient times, there had been discussion of change in the means of subsistence and associated modes of organisation by means of stages of development. But the eighteenth century saw a much greater focus on understanding economic history in terms of advance from one stage of development to another. Smith identified these stages as: hunting and gathering, pastoral and agricultural stages, leading to the final stage of commercialisation, while other Scottish writers suggested different ways of classifying the stages. In the French approach, notably that of Turgot, the emphasis was on agriculture, but Smith changed the focus to one of growth in prosperity once the fourth stage, commercialisation, had been reached. He introduced the idea, drawing on natural law philosophy, that such growth might be the normal condition for commercial societies. The Scottish analysis of the stages put primary emphasis on social organisation, identifying the development of human institutions with respect to property rights and the rule of law as a necessary condition for progression from pastoral to agricultural to commercial stages of development.

Moral issues with development

There was debate as to how far movement through the stages was to be interpreted as progress. Indeed the Scottish enlightenment studies of different 'savage' societies indicated a respect for their moral legitimacy. There was widespread concern (expressed particularly by Ferguson, 1767) as to how far commercialisation would challenge the moral fabric of society. The specialised nature of non-subsistence production methods raised a widespread concern at what we would now call worker alienation, justifying state-sponsored education as a means of alleviating the stultifying effects on the mind.

Yet Hume emphasised also the positive, transformative features of commercial employment, arguing that it was a civilising influence and encouraged the 'arts' leading to further productivity growth. But the population movements into towns associated with commercialisation, with its disruptive social consequences, was a further concern which gathered force into the nineteenth century. Chalmers (1821) argued for community-based moral education as the most effective means of promoting moral behaviour and alleviating poverty through self-help (as well as community-based income redistribution), in opposition to the monetary payments of the Poor Laws.

Population

The focus on moral, social, psychological and political forces is also evident in debates in eighteenth-century Scotland over the nature and causes of demographic change. These debates were given empirical grounding by early attempts at compiling population statistics for Scotland. Hume's concern in looking at changes in these forces over the very long term was to consider whether population had increased or decreased from ancient times. Of more contemporary concern, particularly in relation to the depopulation of the Highlands, was whether increasing population was to be welcomed as a symptom of growth and a spur to further growth, or alternatively regretted as putting undue pressure on limited resources. But Smith differed from his contemporaries in being more sanguine that population movements would respond to the demand for labour. Malthus credited several Scottish writers as having influenced his theory of population.

The division of labour

While the idea was anticipated by Hutcheson, the division of labour is the cornerstone of Smith's (1776) theory of economic development. Originally conceived by him in terms of an account of specialisation in philosophy, Smith drew on his extensive studies of different types and ages of society the general principle that commercial development arises from specialisation in production. Specialisation allowed for productivity gains, which in turn facilitated the build-up of capital for further investment. The range of application of this principle was debated in Scotland, and Smith himself accepted that the agriculture and manufacturing sectors might be developed in parallel. The principle encountered particular challenge when applied to Highland improvement, with Anderson (1777) for example arguing that diversification was preferable in geographically isolated regions. The theoretical foundations of the principle were later challenged by Rae (1834), who argued that invention was prior to the division of labour, so that growth should be understood as being built on invention and the necessary policy directed to promoting it.

Free trade

A direct implication of the principle of the division of labour is that it is limited by the extent of the market. As a corollary, free trade allows much more scope for the division of labour and thus for growth. Thus a central mechanism for encouraging growth, which could be observed to an increasing extent in Scotland in the eighteenth and nineteenth centuries, was international trade. This argument shifted the policy focus away from mercantilism, which had prioritised stocks of monetary wealth over the productive capacity of the economy. Not only did trade allow ever-increasing productivity, but trade had a dynamic effect on exporters and importers. Hume's (1752) price-specie-flow theory focused on the way in which foreign earnings spurred exporters on to ever-higher levels of inventiveness and thus productivity (the attendant money flows being part of the process, but not the causal mechanism). At the same time, imports of luxury goods into lower-productivity economies exposed the population to new products which encouraged new tastes and the development of local import-substituting production. It was through this mechanism that Hume saw the catching-up process operating, such that other economies would also develop.

Theory of value

The theory of value which emerged from Scottish enlightenment thought was prompted by moral concerns with commercialisation as well as the more practical considerations of exchange; what was a fair price given the effort and resources which went into a product and the nature and degree of its usefulness? Influenced by Hutcheson and natural law philosophy, Smith developed the notion of a natural price around which actual prices would fluctuate with changes in demand. The natural price was measured by the labour embodied in a product; by the same token, welfare was measured by labour commanded (Skinner, 2006a).

The invisible hand

One of the ideas most frequently drawn from Scottish economics is that markets are self-regulating, since self-interest is guided as if by an invisible hand to produce a socially optimal outcome. Smith had pointed out that commercial production would be aligned with demand by means of the price mechanism and the profit motive. But Smith's use of the term 'invisible hand' referred to a limited range of positive externalities (such as the tendency for capital investment to occur in the home economy), rather than as a general phenomenon. Indeed Smith warned of tendencies for market competition to be reduced (by monopolies or collusion), thus limiting the benefits of market forces. Nevertheless Smith's account of the benefits of market forces, based on a systemic analysis of markets, was one of the most influential Scottish economic ideas.

Institutions and approaches

A range of important economic ideas thus emerged and/or were developed in the Scottish enlightenment. There were disagreements about some of the key ideas, such as the division of labour. Nevertheless there is a commonality about economic discourse in Scotland which overrides these differences and which colours the way in which both concepts and analysis were understood or misunderstood. This commonality arose from the shared economic, political, social, cultural and intellectual background. This common Scottish approach was still evident up to the late twentieth century, in general public discourse as well as in economics. This approach arose from the Scottish enlightenment theory of knowledge, founded on a theory of human nature.

Political economy had become a university subject in its own right in the Scottish universities in the nineteenth century, after a period during which it was taught within the discipline of moral philosophy. The University of Edinburgh appointed the first Professor of Political Economy in the Scottish universities in 1871. Only in 1947 did the University of St Andrews do likewise, though from 1900 a Lectureship in Political Economy was instituted. (Incidentally the first incumbent of this Lectureship was William Scott, who invented the term 'Scottish enlightenment', and who became the second Professor of Political Economy appointed by the University of Glasgow in 1915.)

In effect the new university discipline reinvented the political economy of the Scottish enlightenment in Scotland to constitute the curriculum. History of thought was integral, and Smith figured centrally in the economic thought that was taught. The philosophical roots of the discipline were also respected and there was a concern for the practical, a desire almost that economic knowledge should be used to do good. In particular this tendency is to be found in the work of Smart, who was appointed in 1896 to be the first Professor of Political Economy at the University of Glasgow. He was a member of the UK Royal Commission on the Poor Law which reported in 1909. He drafted the Majority Report's chapter on a social insurance scheme which informed the scheme implemented by the Liberal government in 1911. In this he may have had an important input into the development of the British welfare state.

Indeed there was an 'applied economics' characteristic of much of the work undertaken by Scottish-based economists in the middle of the twentieth century (Dow, Dow and Hutton,

2000). Public service was an important contribution: the great exemplar of this approach was Sir Alec Cairncross, who had a career spanning public service and academic life. But William Smart, William Scott and Alec Macfie, likewise Professors in Political Economy at the University of Glasgow, shared this ethos, and served on many government committees as a result. Economic theory was used but not developed by the Scottish economists who founded (or revived if an earlier organisation is credited as predecessor) the Scottish Economic Society in 1954. But Macfie explicitly articulated their continuing commitment to the Scottish tradition in economic thought in 1955 (reprinted in Mair, 1990).

The main features of this Scottish political economy approach can be summarised as follows. First there was an awareness of the inevitability of more than one legitimate approach to knowledge, given the complexity of the subject matter and the basis of knowledge in human nature, and an acceptance therefore of the limitations of any theory and therefore of its provisional nature. There followed the need for persuasive argument based on recognition of the sociological and psychological aspects of theory appraisal. Theory was designed to address practical issues and to draw on several disciplines in an integrated manner. Arguments were developed from first principles (to be distinguished from axioms), and first principles were to be approached by discussing their contextual development, using a historical approach both to evidence of different contexts and as to ideas within their context. Finally, first principles were specified in terms of a non-individualistic representation of human nature, with an emphasis on conventional behaviour and moral issues.

On the basis of this theory of knowledge, whereby there was no scope for demonstrable truth, theories prevailed or not on the basis of persuasive discourse. The strength of the Scottish education system and the practical, policy focus of the economic ideas being developed meant that the range of individuals involved in this discourse was remarkable. As Rutherford (2012, 306) puts it: 'How they argued!'

Over the history of modern economics, the most influential figure in the development of economic ideas and the approach to economics within the Scottish enlightenment was Adam Smith. Given that many of his ideas can be traced to earlier figures and were also developed by contemporaries in Scotland, the reason for this influence is arguably the fact that, more than any of his contemporaries, he took an open-systems approach (Skinner, 1996). Developing his psychological theory of theory appraisal, Smith (1795) likened theories to 'imaginary machines', whose aesthetic appeal arose from being derived from a few principles and connecting in a novel way with existing conventional knowledge. But, as with Hume, real experience was to be the arbiter of theory, in contrast to the deductivist axiomatic theory of Descartes. Experience, in turn, was to be analysed using what Skinner (1965) terms 'analytical history', i.e. incorporating historical evidence into a (provisional) theoretical system. Steuart (1767), for whom a systems approach could only support short chains of reasoning applied to particular contexts, had much less influence than Smith.

Recent advances and trends

We now consider the influence of the history of Scottish economic thought on the development of modern economics. We will see that this influence has been coloured by the way in which Scottish ideas were interpreted, in terms of the Scottish approach, or in terms of alternative approaches.

As the impetus for theoretical development shifted away from Scotland during the nineteenth century, the emergence of new ideas from Scotland diminished. Instead we saw a consolidation of applied economics using the Scottish approach, where applied economics continues to be misunderstood in the wider discipline as something distinct from theoretical economics. It is, in fact, the philosophical and methodological approach to economics of the Scottish enlightenment, rather than particular theoretical ideas, which arguably has the most potential to contribute to modern debate. Yet this rich resource has largely gone unrecognised.

From the 1960s a range of different views have emerged about economics as a discipline, much of it in reaction to the growing dominance of the objectivist, deductivist mathematical approach, but in general without reference to Scottish economic thought. Kuhn promoted a view of the history of science in terms of successive paradigms, each with their own approach, none of which could be demonstrated as best. Skinner (1979) pointed out the way in which the Scottish enlightenment had laid the foundations for such an approach. The rhetoric approach revived interest in the persuasive element of the presentation of theories which Smith (1762–3) had pioneered. Further, while critical realist theory has been presented in opposition to Scottish enlightenment ideas, Dow (2002b) shows that Hume in fact provides a rich foundation for critical realist argument. More generally the approach taken in much of heterodox economics could benefit from more explicit recourse to Scottish enlightenment thought (Dow, 2009b).

Conclusion

Scottish economic thought had a profound influence on the development, first of classical economics and then of modern economics. It set the agenda for classical economics in terms of the analysis of the causes of economic growth and distribution, with an attendant focus on population, money, trade and public finance. The subsequent development of general equilibrium theory was presented as the completion of Smith's analysis of markets in terms of the invisible hand. For many years the social focus of the *Theory of Moral Sentiments* was contrasted with the self interest of the *Wealth of Nations*, implying a contradiction (the 'Adam Smith problem'). Now the consensus among Smith scholars is that the self whose interest Smith studied was a social self, conditioned by social norms. In the meantime, the wider political economy influence of Scottish thought had been acknowledged in an apparently disparate range of developments, such as in the founding of the United States and the work of Marx, Hayek and Keynes. More recently, experimental game theory has drawn new attention to Smith's (1759) theory of social relations.

Such disparate developments can be understood in terms of the different interpretations of Scottish thought, and in particular how far this thought was understood in terms of Scottish philosophy. The general equilibrium interpretation of Smith understood his system as something amenable to formalisation, yielding universal laws by means of deduction from axioms. Smith (1795) had himself understood the rhetorical power of deductivism. But the interpretation of Smith's system as an open historical process led to very different developments. Marx adopted the stages approach and much of the analysis of factors of production, while coming to different political conclusions. Hayek focused on Scottish enlightenment epistemology to support his methodologically individualistic analysis of market processes. Keynes similarly drew on Hume's organicism and the resulting epistemology for his theory of probability. As with Hayek, the implication was that deductive formalism was an inadequate basis for argument.

It is uncontroversial to identify Scottish history of thought as having had profound and widespread influence on economics. This applies particularly to the enlightenment period, although Scottish thinkers continued to make contributions after that period and the Scottish approach was revived with the establishment of the discipline in Scottish universities in the nineteenth century. But the alternative deductivist approach which had arisen from other traditions came to dominate the subject. The post-enlightenment contributions from Scotland therefore were misunderstood and devalued by the growing preference for formal mathematical modelling. While realist economic theory designed for application and applied economics continue to be regarded as second-class subsets of the discipline relative to formal deductivist economics, the philosophical grounding which could be provided for realist theory and applied economics by Scottish epistemology is largely ignored. Nevertheless new developments in methodology and theory outside the mainstream are increasingly referring to Scottish epistemology for grounding. While it is to theory that most literature on Scottish economic thought refers, it is the Scottish approach itself which has the potential to forge new developments in economic ideas.

Bibliography

Anderson, J. ([1777] 1968) *Observations on the Means of Exciting a Spirit of National Industry*. New York: Augustus M. Kelly.

Broadie, A. (1990) *The Tradition of Scottish Philosophy: A New Perspective on the Enlightenment*. Edinburgh: Polygon.

Buchan, J. (2003) *Capital of the Mind*. London: John Murray.

Campbell, R.H. and Skinner, A.S., eds (1982) *The Origins and Nature of the Scottish Enlightenment*. Edinburgh: John Donald.

Chalmers, T. (1821) *On the Christian and Economic Polity of a Nation, More Especially with Reference to its Large Towns*. Reprinted in *Chalmers' Works*, Vol. XIV. Glasgow: Collins.

Dow, A. (1984) 'The Hauteur of Adam Smith: An Unpublished Letter from James Anderson of Monkshill', *Scottish Journal of Political Economy*, 31(3): 284–5.

Dow, A. and Dow, S., eds (2006) *A History of Scottish Economic Thought*. London: Routledge.

Dow, A., Dow, S. and Hutton, A. (1997) 'Scottish Political Economy and Modern Economics', *Scottish Journal of Political Economy*, 44(4): 368–83.

Dow, A., Dow, S. and Hutton, A. (2000) 'Applied Economics in a Political Economy Tradition: The Case of Scotland from the 1890s to the 1950s', *History of Political Economy*, 32 (Annual Supplement): 177–98.

Dow, S. (2002a) 'Historical Reference: Hume and Critical Realism', *Cambridge Journal of Economics*, 26(6): 683–97.

Dow, S. (2002b) 'Interpretation: The Case of Hume', *History of Political Economy*, 34(2): 399–420.

Dow, S. (2009a) 'Hume and the Scottish Enlightenment – Two Cultures', *Revista de Economia*, 35(3): 7–20.

Dow, S. (2009b) 'David Hume and Modern Economics', *Capitalism and Society*, 4(1).

Ferguson, A. ([1767] 1995) *An Essay on the History of Civil Society*, ed. by Fania Oz-Salzberger. Cambridge: Cambridge University Press.

Hume, D. ([1739–40] 1978) *A Treatise of Human Nature*, ed. by K.A. Selby-Bigge and P.H. Nedditch. Oxford: Clarendon.

Hume, D. ([1752] 1985) *Political Discourses*. Edinburgh: A. Kincaid and A. Donaldson. Reprinted in *Essays Moral, Political and Literary*. Edinburgh: Cadell, Donaldson and Creech, 1777, and Indianapolis: Liberty Fund.

Mair, D., ed. (1990) *The Scottish Contribution to Modern Economic Thought*. Aberdeen: Aberdeen University Press.

Rae, J. ([1834] 1964) *Of Some New Principles on the Subject of Political Economy*. New York: Augustus M. Kelley.

Ross, I.S. (1995) *The Life of Adam Smith*. Oxford: Clarendon Press.

Rutherford, D. (2012) *In the Shadow of Adam Smith: Founders of Scottish Economics 1700–1900*. London: Palgrave Macmillan.

Skinner, A.S. (1965) 'Economics and History: The Scottish Enlightenment', *Scottish Journal of Political Economy*, 32(1).

Skinner, A.S. (1979) 'Adam Smith: An Aspect of Modern Economics?', *Scottish Journal of Political Economy*, 26(2): 109–25.

Skinner, A.S. (1996) *A System of Social Science: Papers Relating to Adam Smith*. Oxford: Oxford University Press.

Smith, A. ([1759] 1976) *The Theory of Moral Sentiments*, ed. by D.D. Raphael and A.L. Macfie. Oxford: Clarendon.

Smith, A. ([1762–3] 1983) *Lectures on Rhetoric and Belles Lettres*, ed. by J.C. Bryce. Oxford: Oxford University Press.

Smith, A. ([1776] 1976) *An Inquiry into the Nature and Causes of the Wealth of Nations*, ed. by R.H. Campbell and A.S. Skinner. Oxford: Clarendon.

Smith, A. ([1795] 1980) 'History of Astronomy', in W.P.D. Wightman (ed.), *Essays on Philosophical Subjects*. Oxford: Clarendon.

4

Ireland

Renee Prendergast

In 1977, J.K. Galbraith claimed that 'all races produced notable economists except the Irish'. Was Galbraith, with his Scottish ancestry, trying to copper fasten the claims of Adam Smith to be the true founder of political economy against the equally strong claims of the Irish-born Richard Cantillon, or did he have some inkling that the Irish relationship with political economy is disrespectful of its claims to be a universal science?

The present chapter argues that the peculiar feature of Irish involvement with political economy is that it contributed *both* to the construction of the edifice and to the undermining of its claims to universality. In order to understand how this came to be the case, we need to take account of Ireland's relationship with England, and the implications of this for Ireland's own development. In the sixteenth and seventeenth centuries, the English crown sought to secure its control over Ireland by embarking on a policy of land colonization by English and Scottish settlers. The last stage in this process was facilitated by a survey carried out by William Petty, who came to Ireland as the Physician in Chief to Cromwell's armies in 1652. It was finally consolidated following the victory by William of Orange over the Stuart armies in Ireland in 1690–1. This confirmed in power a Protestant landed elite of predominantly English descent. Adherents of the Stuarts amongst the old Irish and Hiberno-Norman elites such as the Cantillons departed for France or elsewhere in Europe.

As a result of the plantation of settlers, a tenure system superficially similar to that in England was imposed on Ireland. At the top were the Anglo-Protestant landlords many of whom were absentees residing in England, the middle tier were tenant farmers: in the North-East, these were mainly Scots Presbyterians but elsewhere largely Catholic. At the bottom of the pile were the catholic cottiers and agricultural labourers. This was the group most affected by the Great Irish Famine of 1845–9, as a consequence of which their numbers were greatly reduced through death and emigration. After 1880, a series of Land Acts led to the abolition of the landlord system so that, by 1920, the majority of farmers owned the land that they worked.

Agriculture was the dominant industry in Ireland until well into the twentieth century. Given the soil and climate, its natural advantages lay in the production of pastoral rather than arable crops, and pastoral products have tended to dominate. Potatoes were originally grown as a dietary supplement, but by the early nineteenth century they had become the main food of the poor.

Although this provided a nutritious diet, the dependence on a single source of nutrition left the poor vulnerable to malnutrition and starvation when the potato crop failed.

In the late seventeenth century, there was significant growth of output and exports in the linen and woollen trades. However, the Woollen Act of 1699 ended the export of woollen goods and finer woollen production began to be subject to competition from imports. Following a period of economic crises, recovery in the second half of the eighteenth century created demand for a broad range of manufactured goods. The 1780s saw the development of a partly mechanized cotton/calico printing industry, but this succumbed to competition from the Lancashire industry in the decades following the Union with Britain in 1801.

During the remainder of the nineteenth century, most industry outside Dublin and Belfast was geared towards the domestic market. Belfast became the main location for export-oriented industry with shipbuilding, textile machinery, tobacco and rope production joining linen as important industries. These differences in industrial structure carried into the twentieth century and were an important factor in Irish partition. After independence, attempts were made to nurture domestic industry using protective tariffs. However, the restricted domestic market meant that the policy met with only limited success. Following a period of economic crisis and high levels of emigration in the 1950s, there was a re-orientation of industrial policy towards attracting international investment. Partly because of the opportunities Ireland could provide through access to the single European market, this policy met with considerable success and contributed to the Celtic Tiger phenomenon of the 1990s. Meanwhile, in Northern Ireland, the 'troubles' and the inability to pursue independent industrial policy meant that there was insufficient new industry to compensate for the decay of traditional activities.

The development of economic ideas over the long term

With the exception of Petty (English) and Cantillon (Hiberno-Norman), most of the important contributors to economic thought in Ireland in the seventeenth, eighteenth and early nineteenth centuries came from members of Protestant elite. They were mainly educated at Trinity College, Dublin from which both Irish Catholics and dissenters – Ulster Scots Presbyterians – were debarred. Many achieved fame in other fields: Jonathan Swift in literature; George Berkeley and Francis Hutcheson in philosophy; Edmund Burke in politics. Some held high office in the established church, while others including Longfield, I. Butt, Hearn, J.E. Cairnes, T.E. Cliffe Leslie and C.F. Bastable had a background in law.

Prior to independence, Irish writers on political economy often resided and worked in England during part or all of their careers and could be regarded as forming part of a wider British economics community. Lurking in the background, however, were challenges to the official view and cautions that general maxims might not be applicable in the specific circumstances of Ireland. For some this pointed to the need for reforms that would make Irish institutions conform more closely to the English model. For others it pointed to the need for a different form of analysis and for institutions more in keeping with the culture of the people.

William Petty (1623–87) was the most important political economist of the seventeenth century, in Ireland or anywhere else. His contribution is foundational for a number of reasons. First, he sought to place political economy on a sound empirical footing by expressing himself 'in terms of *number weight* or *measure*' by using only 'arguments of sense', and by considering 'only such causes as have visible foundations in nature' (Petty, 1899: 244). Second, he conceived of the economy as an interrelated whole and, when he considered specific aspects such as foreign trade or monetary policy, he did so in the context of the wider system. Petty should also be credited for the first attempts to calculate national income and with initiating modern discussions of the division of labour including its dependence on the extent of the market.

It is commonplace nowadays to point out that, for all its appearance of objectivity, Petty's use of political arithmetic was a creative enterprise designed to sell ambitious economic, social and political projects whose objective in the Irish case was to secure British rule, and with it the security of Petty's own possessions (McCormick, 2009). In Petty's defence, it should be noted that there was little or no reliable data available at the time and if his estimates were sometimes rough and ready, they often provided a good starting point for analysis. *The Political Anatomy of Ireland* written in 1671–2 is a good example of the approach.

It starts by accounting for the lands of Ireland measured in Irish acres and classified according to quality and ownership. Petty then estimated the number of people classified by religion, national origin and occupation. This, in turn, allowed him to identify the extent of under- and unproductive employment which he regarded as a measure of development potential because, once employed productively, these 'spare hands' could add to local or universal (tradeable) wealth. Petty denied that Irish underdevelopment was due to disposition of the people and identified its main causes as constraints on Ireland's trade, an insufficiency of coin to drive the nation's trade, underdeveloped consumption patterns amongst the poor, perceived illegitimacy of rulers, rent-seeking and low population density (Petty, 1899).

The remedies proposed included restoration of trade with the plantations and England, regularisation of money, a bank based on landed property as security in order to reduce interest rates, reformation of the housing of the poor, application of some of the spare hands to the building of roads, bridges and harbours, union with England and later the transportation of large numbers from Ireland to England. Despite a suggestion that the nobility and wealthy citizens should by example discountenance the use of certain foreign commodities, Petty did not favour protection, arguing in *Political Anatomy* that the proceeds of exports would be more than sufficient to pay for imported products.

Petty's *Political Anatomy* was published posthumously in 1690 at a time of moderate prosperity which continued into the early decades of the eighteenth century. However, a quarter century punctuated by severe crisis and famine began around 1720. Initially the crisis was precipitated by the South Sea Bubble in England but it was exacerbated by problems of currency misalignment, the protection of the English market and poor weather conditions (Kelly, 1991). This evoked a response in the form of a steady stream of pamphlets from Molesworth, Prior, Browne, Hutcheson, Swift, Madden and Berkeley.

In many cases, the problems identified (lack of investment, trade restrictions, currency misalignment and lack of coin) and the remedies proposed did not differ substantially from Petty's. However, whereas Petty focused on problems associated with contested property rights in land, the later authors saw short leases as the main problem because tenants would not invest if they knew that rent would be raised in proportion to the improvements that they had made. Moreover, while Petty complained that Ireland being 'thinly peopled' was an impediment to its development, by the 1720s, unemployment and poverty had emerged as major problems, causing Jonathan Swift (1667–1745) to argue that (Petty's) maxim 'that people are the riches of a nation' did not apply in Ireland (Swift, 1925: 70).

Faced with the constraints placed by the British parliament on Irish trade, some, including Swift and George Berkeley (1685–1753), advocated the substitution of domestic products for imports as a means of developing domestic industry. Others, including Arthur Dobbs (1689–1765), who became governor of North Carolina in 1854, and John Browne, made the case that Britain's own interest would be best served by the promotion rather than restriction of Irish trade. Of the authors who urged the cultivation of domestic demand, Swift focused on the need to re-orientate the consumption patterns of the rich and to stem the leakage of demand due to absentee landlords. While Berkeley also saw potential in changing the consumption patterns of the rich even by way of a sumptuary law he, like Petty, emphasized the need to expand the wants of the poorer classes in order to create demand and to make them industrious.

During the early part of his career, spent in England, Swift showed himself to be more alive than most to the implications of the financial revolution for the transfer of political power from the landed gentry to the finance capitalists. In Ireland, he continued in this view and opposed the setting up of a National Bank (Swift, 1925: 27–30). By contrast, Berkeley saw the potential of the new financial instruments, arguing in his *Querist* that real wealth consisted in the plenty of the necessaries and comforts of life and the power to command the industry of others while money was simply a ticket or a counter for conveying or recording such power. As such, paper money and bank deposits were perfectly adequate and had some advantages over coin. This was a radical position at the time. Before Berkeley, John Law had argued for a purely fiduciary monetary system but with Law discredited following the collapse of the Mississippi Scheme, Berkeley's position was a minority one and was to remain so for three hundred years (Murphy, 2000).

One of those who made a fortune from Law's scheme was Richard Cantillon (1680?–1734), who became part of the Irish diaspora in Europe in the early eighteenth century. Alongside his great fortune, he acquired many enemies and was murdered in 1734. His *Essay on the Nature of Trade in General* was first published in 1755, but it had circulated in manuscript form and was extensively plagiarized both in England and in France. The first edition (issued in French but bearing a London imprint) is a great rarity of economics literature.

In his analysis, Cantillon completed the process, begun by Petty, of looking at the economy as an interconnected system. Starting with a hypothetical self-sufficient estate managed so as to best satisfy the owner's preferences, Cantillon showed that, rather than manage the estate himself, the owner could rent it to farmers and buy what he wanted from them. The farmers would have an incentive to work harder, and the operation of the price mechanism would force them to adjust their outputs in accordance with the desires of the landowner. Having explained the operation of the price mechanism using the concepts of intrinsic value and market price, Cantillon examined the flows of money between the different sectors and classes in Part II of the *Essay*.

He also provided a nuanced exposition of the quantity theory of money in which the impact of increased money supply on prices depends on the source of the increase, and of the price-specie flow mechanism which emphasized the long lags involved and the potential for policy intervention. The final part of the *Essay* extends the discussion of foreign exchange and considers issues relating to the role of paper money and the management of national debt. Cantillon's *Essay* does not appear to have been known in Ireland but was influential elsewhere. Quesnay's *Tableau Economique* builds on part II of the *Essay*. Cantillon may also have influenced Smith's theory of the market allocation of resources, though Smith unlike Cantillon has no role for the entrepreneur in the allocation process (Murphy, 2009: 81).

The last quarter of the eighteenth century saw the Irish Parliament secure a measure of legislative independence which enabled limited protection of the Irish market, although proposals for freer trade with Britain continued to be opposed by British manufacturing interests. However, by the union with Britain in 1801 there was a change in outlook as technical progress made English manufacturers confident of their commercial strength. Subsequently, British economists commented routinely on Irish affairs.

Despite some differences of emphasis, there was agreement amongst the likes of Ricardo, Malthus, Torrens and Trower that Irish agriculture was grossly inefficient and that improvements to agriculture would require the destruction of small tenancies. A system of agriculture more like the English one would produce the necessary food and raw materials more efficiently and release labour for employment in manufacturing. The problem was how to get from the existing situation to the new one. While some argued that Irish labourers needed to develop a taste for luxuries in order to create demand for local industry and increase their willingness to work, others warned that increases in consumption were more likely to be met by English imports. Yet others were concerned that the sequencing of development required the removal of labour from agriculture ahead of the provision of new sources of employment in manufactures and commerce.

This pointed to the need for a coherent set of measures such as poor relief, organized emigration or some measure of industrial protection. There was also some recognition that the problem arose at the level of institutions. Ricardo, somewhat optimistically, argued that if property was secure and contracts were reliably fulfilled, capital would flow into Ireland resulting in adoption of the most economical processes and abundant demand for labour. Nicholls, however, seems to have had a better appreciation of the self-reinforcing nature of the various problems: 'Want of capital produces want of employment – want of employment, turbulence and misery, – turbulence and misery, insecurity – insecurity prevents the introduction and accumulation of capital, and so on' (Black, 1960). Senior was even more categorical, identifying the insecurity of person and property arising from the detestation of Ireland's existing institutions by the mass of the people as the evil that creates or perpetuates all her other calamities. This Senior put down to ignorance – the lack of moral and intellectual education.

The provision of moral and intellectual education in the form of political economy was a mission of Senior's friend and former tutor Richard Whately (1787–1863), who following his appointment as Archbishop of Dublin in 1831 established the first Irish chair of political economy at Trinity College Dublin. More ambitiously, he sought to diffuse knowledge of political economy at every level of society and had a vehicle for doing so through his role as a commissioner for the national school system. Whately's *Easy Lessons on Money Matters* – a successful publication in its own right – was incorporated into the lesson books provided by the commissioners as a basis for the school curriculum and, reached a broad audience in Ireland and elsewhere (Boylan and Foley, 1992). Whately's approach was all about exchange. While labour could function as a measure of value, it was not its source. To be valuable goods had to be exchangeable, desired and scarce. Whereas in Ricardo's view, the interests of different classes could be opposed to one another, Whately's presumed a natural harmony of interests. Providence had so arranged things that, in an advanced state of society, self-interested and indeed selfish behaviour conduced to public prosperity.

Mountifort Longfield (1802–84), the first incumbent of the Whately chair, is recognised as having developed a proto-marginalist theory of value and distribution in opposition to the Ricardian view. The full extent of his anti-Ricardianism is subject to dispute, as is the extent to which his demand theory can be regarded as a forerunner of marginal utility theory. There is, however, agreement that Longfield developed a supply and demand theory of price, a marginal productivity theory of profit and a productivity theory of wages (Prendergast, 2010). Longfield viewed his analysis as showing that it was impossible to regulate wages by means of combinations or legislation, and that the only means by which the condition of the labourer could be improved was through an increase in productivity.

Although Longfield can be regarded as a harmony theorist who defended the status quo, he was one of the few economists to analyse the impact of absenteeism, and showed that it was prejudicial to the welfare of the community by worsening Irish terms of trade. Longfield also made important contributions in the currency controversies of the mid-nineteenth century and to the field of international trade (Black, 1971). Longfield's work on value and distribution was taken forward by his successors in the Whately chair – Isaac Butt (1813–79), James Anthony Lawson and William Neilson Hancock. However, their contributions were not influential as they were largely ignored by the leading economists of the day.

Afterwards, the intervention of the Great Irish Famine meant that later occupants of the Whately chair such as John Elliott Cairnes (1823–75) had very different pre-occupations. Cairnes' best known contributions are his book *The Slave Power* and his theory of non-competing groups. He was also a critic of *laissez-faire*, arguing that it amounted to an assumption that human interests were naturally harmonious – an assumption which neglected the reality of different class and interests. Cairnes' critique of *laissez-faire* had its origins in his consideration of the political economy of Irish land. According to Cairnes, the economic basis of property was the right of the producer to the fruits of his labour, while the basis for rent was that it consisted of excess returns over and above what was required to replace used capital and to provide normal profits. Cairnes argued that if the rights of the landlord were pushed beyond a certain point, they would come into conflict with the rights of the producer, which were actually more fundamental. In England and Scotland, it could be assumed that the competition between agriculture and other modes of investing capital was sufficient to ensure that actual rents did not exceed economic rents but this was not the case in most countries. Consequently, other means had to be found for ensuring the fairness of rents. Cairnes' conclusions can be summed as defending the right of the landlord to a 'fair rent' but imposing on the state the duty of determining what this 'fair rent' should be (Cairnes, 1873).

Arguments for reform of the land tenure system, for longer leases and for tenants' right to compensation for improvements had been put forward in the nineteenth century by Arthur O'Connor, William Conner, Thomas Davis and Gavan Duffy. However, it was only in the aftermath of the Great Famine that these proposals began to be treated seriously by economists of the stature of J.S. Mill and Cairnes. Their acceptance that it might be necessary for the state to intervene in the contracts between landlords and their tenants was a significant departure in itself but also had wider implications in that it undermined the notion that political economy was a body of immutable truths and therefore paved the way for the development of historical economics.

T.E. Cliffe Leslie (1826–82) of Queen's College, Belfast, who resided mainly in London and John Kells Ingram (1823–1907) of Trinity College, Dublin are widely regarded as leading members of what is often referred to as the English Historical School. Leslie carried out inter-disciplinary investigations into military systems and land tenure in Europe, including Ireland. Having attended some lectures by Henry Maine on historical jurisprudence, he sought to apply the approach within political economy arguing that 'political economy is not a body of natural laws . . . but an assemblage of speculations and doctrines which are the result of a particular history' (Leslie, 1888). Leslie also emphasized that political economy should be inductive rather than deductive. Deductive theories imposed an artificial homogeneity and took no account of the fact that the movement of the economic world was from simplicity to complexity and from the known to the unknown.

Ingram's book, *A History of Political Economy* was a wide ranging relativist account of the history of the subject in Europe and America. He cited Maine, Spencer and the German Historical School in support of his view that only the historical approach would yield an adequate under-standing of phenomena. Like Leslie, he was critical of the abstract, deductive approach but, as a disciple of Comte, he placed particular emphasis on the fact that the economy is imbedded in the wider social system so that a proper study of economic phenomena has to engage with this broader context. Ingram's book was translated into several European languages as well as Japanese. It was also influential in the United States where Ingram was made an honorary member of the American Economic Association in 1891.

Modern economics

Two important Irish-born economists of the late nineteenth and early twentieth centuries were Charles Bastable (1855–1945) and Francis Ysidoro Edgeworth (1845–1926), both educated in Trinity College, Dublin. Like his predecessor in the Whately chair, Bastable was an adherent of the classical approach to political economy and was also influenced by the historical approach of his compatriots Leslie and Ingram. His main contributions were in the fields of public finance and international trade, where he devised a stringent test of the conditions in which the infant industry argument applied (Boylan and Maloney, 2011).

Edgeworth's entire career was spent in London and Oxford. He became the first editor of the *Economic Journal* and made several foundational contributions to modern economics. Edgeworth is best known to students of economics as the originator of the Edgeworth box, which is commonly used in the explanation of general equilibrium theory. While Edgeworth identified the conditions in which a general equilibrium could exist, his own main interest was in the indeterminateness of contracts and not their perfect determination (Baccini, 2011). In addition to contract theory, Edgeworth also made contributions to international trade, monopoly pricing and to mathematical economics generally.

Berkeley had advocated import substitution as the only realistic option available in the absence of free trade. In the mid-nineteenth century, Butt (1846) showed that the protection of domestic industry would raise overall welfare in the conditions of widespread unemployment prevalent in Ireland. With the movement towards Irish independence in the early twentieth century, Arthur Griffith drew on Friedrich List to propose a programme of economic development based on protection of domestic producers until they were strong enough to meet international competition.

Bastable had earlier argued that such a strategy could be justified only where the discounted value of future cost savings exceeded the excess costs incurred during the period of protection. Others pointed to the small size of the market, the dangers of retaliation and the impact in terms of rising costs for exporting industries such as agriculture. Nonetheless, the advent of the Great Depression and a change of government in the 1930s saw the adoption of protectionist policies which were further intensified during World War Two. These remained in place until the late 1950s when a more outward looking industrial strategy was heralded by the publication of the *Economic Development* (Whitaker Report) (Boylan and Prendergast, 2008).

When Ireland achieved independence in 1922, its cadre of professional economists was small. The Statistical and Social Inquiry Society of Ireland (SSISI) (founded 1847) and its journal provided the main discussion forum for academic economists and government officials. Issues debated usually reflected the public interests of the time as perceived by the intellectual elite. They included agricultural efficiency, population, emigration, and the relevance of Keynesianism in the Irish context and the role of government in the economy. There were also major debates on industrial strategy in the 1950s and again in the 1980s.

Although George Duncan and T.J. Kiernan produced early estimates of Irish National Income, expertise in quantitative analysis was limited and influential economists such as George O'Brien adopted a largely literary approach. The Economic Research Institute (ERI) (later Economic and Social Research Institute (ESRI)) was set up in 1960 funded by a grant from the Ford

Foundation to rectify this deficiency. Its first director Roy Geary used his international contacts to recruit suitably trained staff and initiate a programme of training for young researchers. Although best known as a statistician, Geary himself had made important contributions to economics particularly the field of National Income Accounting. His innovations include the Stone-Geary utility function, the 'Geary' method of accounting for the trading gains or losses from changes in the terms of trade in estimating real income and the 'Geary-Khamis' method of computing purchasing power parities for conversion of national currency-denominated economic aggregates into a common, comparable currency unit (Spencer, 2011).

The present generation of Irish economists are more numerous and better trained than their predecessors in the early years of the twentieth century. Many are the products of graduate schools in the United States and in Britain. However, much of their research output relates to Irish problems and is published in Irish journals. Since the 1970s issues relating to Ireland's relationship with the European Community – the Common Agricultural Policy, the Single European Market, Regional Policy, the ERM, the Euro and more recently debt and stabilization – have been important topics for research. Work in the field of health economics has also become increasingly prevalent. A relatively small number of Irish economists have international reputations in their specialties: John Spencer, Queen's Belfast, for applied general equilibrium analysis; Peter Neary, University College Dublin, for his work on Dutch Disease; Kevin O'Rourke for his work on globalization and Philip Lane for his estimates of countries' foreign assets and liabilities.

As in earlier centuries, some of the most important work by Irish-born economists continues to be carried out in the United States and in Britain. Terence Gorman (1923–2003), who was educated at Trinity but spent his entire career at English universities, sought to develop tools to facilitate an understanding of the links between individuals' preferences and market behaviour. To this end, he carried out foundational work on the aggregation of preferences. He also explored the issue of separability in individual decision making, that is, the conditions under optimization problems can be broken into stages (Honohan and Neary, 2011). John Sutton, London School of Economics, has made important contributions on market structure. Canice Prendergast, University of Chicago, is a leading authority on incentives while Brian Arthur, Stanford and Santa Fe, has pioneered the new field of complexity.

International influences

In their introduction to *A History of Irish Economic Thought*, Boylan *et al.* (2011) indicated that while the questions that preoccupied political economists in Ireland were often the product of the particular conjuncture, there was no distinctly national Irish tradition of political economy. From Petty, Cantillon, Berkeley and Hutcheson through to Edgeworth and Gorman, writers from Ireland contributed significantly to the wider edifice of political economy. That said, the view that the maxims of political economy did not apply universally was a theme which was articulated not just by the post-famine historical economists but also by Jonathan Swift, who declared his contempt for those who proceed on general maxims, and by Edmund Burke, who warned that those who reason on abstract principles will be liable to the greatest errors imaginable (Prendergast, 2000).

As indicated above, Cairnes, Leslie and Ingram were particularly influenced by Maine or the German Historical School. Their recognition that the economy was imbedded in a wider legal and institutional framework which could not be ignored was influential in Britain and also in the United States where it was welcomed by the nascent Institutional school. R.D.C. Black in particular has noted the importance of the mid-nineteenth century debate on Irish land tenure, and the recognition of its non-contractual features, as modifying prevailing attitudes to markets and the role of government.

Irish ideas also travelled abroad as a result of emigration. Most emigration was economically motivated but for others it was motivated by political disagreement or the need to escape imprisonment. Thus, Mathew Carey (1760–1839), who had been active in the volunteer movement in Dublin at a time when the Irish parliament was taking steps to protect domestic industry, emigrated to America, where in his *Essays on Political Economy*, he was one of the first to articulate arguments in support of Hamilton's protectionist policy. Charles Gavan Duffy (1816–1903), editor of *The Nation* who had agitated for tenants' rights emigrated to Australia, eventually becoming Premier of the State of Victoria. William Hearn (1826–88), formerly Professor of Greek at Queen's College, Galway, also emigrated to Victoria where he became professor at Melbourne and authored *Plutology Or the Theory of the Efforts to Satisfy Human Wants*, in which he articulated a demand-oriented theory of value. Like Duffy, Hearn was a free-trader, but whereas Duffy advocated government intervention, Hearn was a strong believer in the efficacy of market forces (Moore, 2011).

Conclusion

While therefore, there can be no doubt about the major contribution of theorists such as Cantillon, Cairnes, Edgeworth, Geary, Gorman and Arthur to the development of the subject as a whole, and to this extent there was nothing specifically Irish about their contribution, it can also be argued that they did have one major characteristic in common. This is that their models and theories were never ends in themselves, but designed to facilitate an understanding of the real economy. In this, their Irish background, in an economy very different from that of England but also one which was in a very special relationship to it, made them particularly aware of both specific institutional features, and the dangers of general maxims.

References

Baccini, A. 2011. 'Francis Ysidro Edgeworth on the regularity of law and the impartiality of chance', in Boylan, Prendergast and Turner eds, *A History of Irish Economic Thought*, Abingdon: Routledge.

Berkeley, G. 1750. *The Querist*, 2nd edn, Dublin: George Faulkner.

Black, R.D.C. 1960. *Economic Thought and the Irish Question, 1817–1870*, Cambridge: Cambridge University Press.

Black, R.D.C. 1971. *The Economic Writings of Mountifort Longfield*, New York: Augustus M. Kelley.

Boylan, T. and Prendergast, R. 2008. 'Ireland, economics in', S. Durlauf and L. Blume eds, *New Palgrave Dictionary of Economics*. Basingstoke: Palgrave.

Boylan, T., Prendergast, R. and Turner, J.D. 2011. *A History of Irish Economic Thought*, Abingdon: Routledge.

Boylan, T.A. and Foley, T.P. 1992. *Political Economy and Colonial Ireland*, London: Routledge.

Boylan, T. and Maloney, J. 2011. 'Charles Francis Bastable on trade and public finance', in Boylan, Prendergast and Turner eds, *A History of Irish Economic Thought*, Abingdon: Routledge.

Butt, I. 1846. *Protection to Home Industry*, Dublin: Hodges and Smith.

Cairnes, J.E. 1873. *Essays in Political Economy*, London: Macmillan.

Cantillon, R. 1931 *Essai sur la nature du commerce en general*, edited and translated by Henry Higgs, London: Macmillan.

Carey, M. 1822. *Essays on Political Economy*, Philadelphia: Carey and Lea.

Daly, M.E. 1997. *The Spirit of Earnest Inquiry: The Statistical and Social Inquiry Society of Ireland, 1847–1997*, Dublin: Institute of Public Administration.

Edgeworth, F.Y. 1925. *Papers Relating to Political Economy*, 3 vols, London: Macmillan.

Galbraith, J.K. 1977. *The Age of Uncertainty*, London: BBC Books.

Honohan, P. and Neary, P. 2011. 'W.M. Gorman', in Boylan, Prendergast and Turner eds, *A History of Political Economy*, Edinburgh: Black.

Kelly, J. 1991. 'Jonathan Swift and the Irish economy in the 1720s', *Eighteenth Century Ireland*, 6: 7–36.

Leslie, T.E. Cliffe. 1888. *Essays in Political Economy*, 2nd edn, Dublin: Hodges & Figgis.

McCormick, T. 2009. *William Petty and the Ambitions of Political Arithmetic*, Oxford: Oxford University Press.

Moore, G.C.G. 2011. 'The Anglo-Irish context for William Hearn's economic beliefs and the ultimate failure of his *Plutology*', *The European Journal of the History of Economic Thought*, 18.1: 19–54.

Moss, L.S. 2011. 'Value and distribution theory at Trinity College Dublin, 1831–1844' in Boylan, Prendergast and Turner eds, *A History of Irish Economic Thought*, Abingdon: Routledge.

Murphy, A.E. 2000. 'Canons of monetary orthodoxy and John Law', in A.E. Murphy and R. Prendergast eds, *Contributions to Political Economy – Essays in Honour of R.D.C. Black*, London and New York: Routledge.

Murphy, A.E. 2009. *The Genesis of Macroeconomics: New Ideas from Sir William Petty to Henry Thornton.* Oxford: Oxford University Press.

Murphy, A.E. and Prendergast, R. 2000. *Contributions to Political Economy – Essays in Honour of R.D.C. Black*, London and New York: Routledge.

Petty, W. 1899. *The Economic Writings of Sir William Petty*, 2 vols, ed. C. Hull, Cambridge: Cambridge University Press.

Prendergast, R. 2000. 'The political economy of Edmund Burke', in A.E. Murphy and R. Prendergast eds, *Contributions to Political Economy – Essays in Honour of R.D.C. Black*, London and New York: Routledge.

Prendergast, R. 2010. 'Longfield' in N.F.B. Allington and N.W. Thompson eds, *English, Irish and Subversives Among the Dismal Scientists, Research in the History of Economic Thought and Methodology*, 28B: 349–72.

Ricardo, D. 1951–73. *Works and Correspondence of David Ricardo*, vols.II and VII, Cambridge: Cambridge University Press.

Spencer, J.E. 2011. 'Roy Geary' in Boylan, Prendergast and Turner eds, *A History of Irish Economic Thought*, Abingdon: Routledge.

Swift, J. 1925. *The Prose Works of Jonathan Swift*, vol.VII, *Historical and Political Tracts – Irish*, ed. Temple Scott, London: George Bell and Sons.

5

Italy

Pier Luigi Porta

Italy is the country where the *civic tradition* was born, although the term "civic" is preferably spelt "civil" in the Italian context. In Italy the "civil tradition" is the product of a special blend of lay and religious motives, which stems from the re-discovery, at the twilight of the Middle Ages, of antiquity or the pre-Christian world. That leads to a new taste for the earthly goods and pleasures, which is the substance of Humanism during the fifteenth century, a chemical fusion of classicism and Christianity. It is at that stage that we can see the roots of a new understanding of the relationship between market and society. The best contemporary author, analyzing Italian intellectual history along that line, is Eugenio Garin (1909–2004). More recently that same line of research on the civic tradition in Italy has been pursued by Bruni and Zamagni, who have launched the canon of the "civil economy" as characteristic of the Italian tradition of economic thought. We are today confronted with the big task of dusting off – as Bruni and Zamagni (2007, 13) write – "an Italian tradition of thought that began in the fifteenth and sixteenth centuries as Civic Humanism and continued up until the golden period of Italian Enlightenment, represented by the schools of Milan and Naples."

It should be mentioned that a considerable stream of contributions on the civic traditions in Europe and America, largely inspired by the works of J.G.A. Pocock (b. 1924), has given rise to new views on the Enlightenment during the past 30–40 years. That stream of historical thought has bordered on a new view of the rise of political economy. Indeed the Scottish Enlightenment has been a preferred object of study in some quarters, which has entailed giving rise to an important historiographic revision of Adam Smith. It is hardly surprising that the same stream of literature has also touched Italy, as is shown by the recent book by John Robertson on Scotland and Naples. "In the two different 'national' contexts of Scotland and Naples" – Robertson (2005, 377) wrote – "there emerged one Enlightenment . . . In both cases, the terms in which this objective was articulated were those of political economy."

Alberto Quadrio Curzio (2007) has also been using the same label, from the parallel angle of the theory of production. The phrase "civil economy" is taken from the outstanding treatise of Antonio Genovesi (1713–69). Genovesi is universally acknowledged as the pioneer of the Italian school of political economy ("civil economy" as he prefers to call the discipline) during the eighteenth century. He also was the first incumbent worldwide (1754) to an academic chair of the discipline at the University of Naples. It is imperative to re-visit the authors of the Italian tradition, in order to achieve a proper understanding of Adam Smith himself, so that the spell of *civil* life in shaping classical political economy can be properly understood.

Civil economy cannot accommodate the idea that self-interest is the only motivational drift to action for humans. The exclusive focus on self-interest – that would later turn into the hallmark of mainstream economics worldwide – is an idea that comes from an unduly pessimistic view of human nature and which was brought in contact with the economic discipline in the wake of the success of Hobbes' political philosophy and of Mandeville's view on achieving public virtue through private vices, of which self-interest is the common denominator. This view would conquer the field of political economy after Adam Smith and more explicitly during the latter part of the nineteenth century, but it was not dominant in the economics of the previous period. What we usually term classical economics should be kept separate, at least in its sources and early developments, from the subsequent developments of the discipline. The Italian tradition affords today a new appraisal of classicism in economics.

A reference to civil life, or *vita civile*, has been traced through a number of authors. Among them we mention here Leonardo Bruni (1370–1444), Matteo Palmieri (1406–75), Poggio Bracciolini (1380–1459), down to include Paolo Mattia Doria (1667–1746). They are only a few of the champions of a line of thinking leading to the idea, during the Enlightenment, that what is "civil" has to be directly and explicitly associated with the "economic" element. That is the achievement of Genovesi's *economia civile*. It is a successful move, also in view of its long-run effects, as the notion of *incivilimento* would continue to be pervasive in Italy especially during the first part of the nineteenth century and onwards.

A further force at work through the Italian tradition is given by the influence of the monastic culture, from the Middle Ages onwards, which – especially through Franciscanism – comes to shape the language of the market, property and forms of exchange: the contract, reciprocity, and gift. Monastic culture launched the early formative steps of a new economic and commercial language: on the other hand there were practical needs, for the abbeys were economic agents requiring new forms of accounting and management. Typically, once civil humanism had developed, the *montes pietatis* spread all over Italy, providing financial assistance and relief to the poor. Italy proved unable to achieve political unification at that stage, but had a strong civil culture with some considerable differences between north and south. Not surprisingly, between the seventeenth and the eighteenth centuries, Italian economists came forward with a theory of public happiness. Achille Loria (1857–1943), in his book on social justice (1904), would reach the conclusion that all Italian economists – from whatever regional background – differently from Adam Smith, were not intent on the wealth of nations, but on public happiness.

During the Napoleonic period, Pietro Custodi (1771–1842) published in Milan an important collection of economic writings of the Italian economists since the sixteenth century. The collection consisted of 50 volumes and was designed to show the richness of the Italian contribution. It is still reprinted today.

Economic ideas over the long-term

The age of mercantilism

After the age of humanism, modern political economy develops through the major schools of mercantilism, political arithmetic, physiocracy, and the classical school. In general terms modern political economy is focused on acquiring wealth: that reflects the fact that wealth – alongside with military strength and political skills – increasingly becomes a major pillar of political power.

Adam Smith's 1776 *Wealth of Nations*, as the best known title of modern political economy, effectively refers to that main issue. The different schools of political economy signal the fact that it proves difficult to agree on a definition of what wealth is and to have a consensus on policies, i.e. on the means for acquiring wealth. Mercantilism is in favor of state regulation and puts forward a view of economic growth based on monetary factors and on financial innovation. It is during the mercantilist age that the main institutions of money and finance – such as central banks, stock exchanges, public debts – are created. Physiocracy, on the other hand, reacts vigorously against mercantilist conceptions of wealth and policies for growth typified by Colbertism. Physiocracy goes to the opposite extreme by emphasizing the competitive market and the notion of *real* wealth acquired through rising real incomes. The classical school, especially with Smith, would later follow suit and put the accent on the division of labor and increasing returns in manufacturing.

Accordingly the Italians begin during the sixteenth century with the analysis of monetary factors. The first authors of the modern age are Gasparo Scaruffi (1519–84) and Bernardo Davanzati (1529–1606). Both write during the 1580s on money. It is here that the question of value and utility crops up in economics and the first attempts are made to overcome the so-called "paradox of value," which states that utility cannot be the source of value, simply because we see in practice that the most useful objects (air or water) have little value, while a number of superfluities (gold and diamonds) actually bear a high value. That is indeed a sophism, as many authors in Italy undertook to prove (notably Galiani). The Italians are basically supporters of metallism, i.e. the idea that the value of money depends on the value of the precious metal of which it is made. The Italians are also in the limelight in introducing the idea of what would (much later) be called the "quantity theory of money," in the form of a relationship between the quantity of money and the price level. During the mercantilist era the quantity theory was sometimes taken as a theory of prices, as just said, but it was also interpreted as a theory of the level of income. Other important authors in Italy developed the mathematical side of monetary theory: an outstanding example is given by Geminiano Montanari (1633–87).

Mercantilism is *not*, in itself, a typical Italian phenomenon. Nevertheless a mercantilist culture and a number of first rate intellectual contributions of a mercantilist character were offered by the Italians. Probably the best representatives in that sense are Antonio Serra – who in 1613 contributed a *Breve Trattato* or *Short Treatise*; the title of which draws attention to "the causes that can make kingdoms abound in gold and silver even in the absence of mines" – and Giovanni Botero (1544–1617). These two authors develop a fully fledged theory of development and of the wealth and poverty of nations. Botero also treats extensively the topic of population. They also criticize bullionism, i.e. the quasi-identification of wealth with gold.

Italian Enlightenment

The Italian Enlightenment is of one of the great intellectual achievements of Europe's *siècle des lumières*. It is also the greatest contribution of Italian culture to the development of a common European tradition of civil rights and enlightened governance. It shares with the French Enlightenment an interest in rational governance and with the Scottish Enlightenment a special focus on civil society. However, it is different from both of them in its attention to the interplay between legislation and moral sentiments, civic culture and economic development, fiscal technique, and social structure.

"The honors of the field" – Schumpeter wrote – "of pre-Smithian system production should go to the eighteenth-century Italians." "In intent, scope and plan" – Schumpeter perceptively added – "their works were in the tradition of . . . systems of Political Economy in the sense of *welfare economics*" (emphasis added). To the Italians "the old scholastic Public Good and the specifically utilitarian Happiness" came together "in their concept of welfare (*felicità pubblica*)." As noted by one of its greatest historians, Franco Venturi, the tension between utopia and reform is central to the Italian Enlightenment and explains most of its achievements. Echoing Antonio Genovesi's main title, we may add that the Italian Enlightenment is to a very considerable extent a *civil enlightenment* in the sense that it takes sociability as its starting point. At the same time the Italian Enlightenment is pragmatic and a large number of its contributions have to do with administrative and economic arrangements of a self-governing polity, and economics, justice, and legislation are addressed together both by the Milanese and by the Neapolitans, i.e. the two main branches of the economic school.

Among the many economists of the period we may single out, as the key figures of the Italian civil Enlightenment among the Milanese economists, Cesare Beccaria and Pietro Verri together with the Tuscan economist Pompeo Neri. From the Neapolitan school we mention Paolo Mattia Doria, Ferdinando Galiani, Antonio Genovesi, Gaetano Filangieri, and Mario Pagano. There are a number of other contributors in Italy which are not mentioned here, such as the Venetian monk Giammaria Ortes (1713–90). The Italian Enlightenment has recently become a focus of international interest with works for example by scholars such as John Davis, Anthony Pagden, and John Robertson.

Recent contributions (Bruni and Zamagni, 2007; Quadrio Curzio, 2007) argue that the tradition of economic thought in Italy has a characteristic expression in the form of *economia civile*, which is the result of the combination of three different elements: 1) a conception of the economic order based on *civil society* rather than based on state authority; 2) a view of the evolution of institutions through continued *reform*; 3) an emphasis on practical applications or *policy issues*. The resulting discipline has showed since the start a tendency to cluster around the following: a) a *social and ethical concern*, leading to a close analysis of institutions and the relation with extra-economic elements; b) an interest in *dynamic economics*; c) the adoption of Schumpeter's idea of *history of economic analysis*, considering a retrospective understanding of theory as an essential element of economic knowledge. These are the basic characters of the Italian tradition down to the present day.

The Neapolitan School

The phrase *economia civile* means a special approach to the discipline in the language of the intellectual leader of the Neapolitan School, Antonio Genovesi (1713–69). He is the heir of the previous generation of Neapolitan thinkers, Giambattista Vico, Pietro Giannone, and Paolo Mattia Doria, who lived under the spell of Cartesianism and neo-Platonism. Genovesi instead lived in an age of reforms with a strong drive to achieve independence through economic and civil development. Under another angle the scholastic notions of natural law and of *bonum commune* lay behind Genovesi's work: *Lezioni* (1765) is his main work. To Genovesi the idea of well-being is fundamental to explaining the functioning of the civil economy, together with relationships created by informal norms and conventions. This includes reciprocity, mutual friendship, confidence, and trust. Thus the idea of civil economy exhibits continuity with the humanist ideal. In Genovesi's system there are three levels of agency: the individual, civil society, and the state, whereas in Hobbes, civil society and the state are coincident. This tripartite scheme is reminiscent of Montesquieu's insistence on the significance of the *corps intermédiaires*: Montesquieu is a large influence on the Italian Enlightenment. Genovesi was convinced that culture, philosophy, and science must serve society and produce *felicità pubblica*, i.e. public happiness.

Genovesi's lectures (*Lezioni*, esp. ch. 10) contend that the desire for relationships with our fellow citizens stems from the natural (or "ontological") character of human being. Sociality is "an indelible feature of our nature." Genovesi argues that what is typical of man as an animal species is "reciprocal assistance," and maintains (ch. 1) that each person has a natural right to reciprocal assistance and a duty to provide it to others. In agreement with the Italian civic tradition, Genovesi understands economic relations, such as market exchange and production, precisely as relations of reciprocal assistance: in an economy, each agent is *helping* others to satisfy *their* wants in a way that presupposes reciprocal trust, and is virtuous *and* rational. His idea of rationality is quite different from the cold cynical idea used in rational-choice theory. The difference is mainly due to an emphasis on *we-thinking*. Social relations cannot be explained by instrumental rationality, for they are not just means of (or constraints against) pursuing self-interest. For Genovesi, the advantage of society is not only to be found in its production of material goods, but also in the enjoyment of social relationships. Finally, Genovesi puts forward a theory of *spontaneous order*, which can be summarized thus: 1) human beings naturally look out for their interests; 2) their *true* interest is happiness; 3) happiness means *eudaimonia*, full self-realization by means of *virtue*, i.e. the promotion of the happiness of others. He accepts as a universal law that it is impossible to make *our* happiness without facilitating the happiness of *others*; 4) if all people act with a view to happiness, they will be virtuous and *public happiness* will result.

Parallel to Genovesi, though considerably younger, Ferdinando Galiani (1728–87) is the other outstanding economist of the Neapolitan school. His treatise *Della Moneta* (1751) is one of the Italian glories. A metallist philosophy lies behind Galiani's idea of monetary reform. Galiani's book is famous for the complete solution it gives to the paradox of value (the "water–diamond paradox"). Together with monetary reform the important issue at the time was *laissez-faire* and competitive markets, particularly in the case of staple foods (the so-called problem of *annona*), to which Galiani devotes his second great work *Dialogues sur le Commerce des Bleds* (*Dialogues on the Grain Trade*) published in French in 1770. Differently from Genovesi, Galiani was not an academic but a learned intellectual who entered public administration and spent a number of years in Paris as the Secretary to the Embassy of the King of Naples during the 1760s. In the *Dialogues*, Galiani offers a great example of his dialectical skills and his (perhaps) opportunistic character, by changing sides (with respect to some of his previous treatments), and by producing a scathing attack on the physiocrats with a critique of free trade.

Though Galiani is currently described as a forerunner of the marginal utility theory of value, his value analysis was ignored by Adam Smith: the latter decreed that utility was only linked with value-in-use, and had nothing to do with value-in-exchange, which reflected labor commanded. That opened the way to the cost-of-production theory of value and, ultimately, to the labor theory of value espoused by David Ricardo and Karl Marx. Smith's choice thus inspired a line of analysis on value which became dominant through the subsequent period as a hallmark of classicism in economics. It must be stated that the Italians never nurtured any significant sympathy toward the labor theory of value. Even more radically, the very idea that value theory should be pivotal to economic analysis would later come under criticism by the Italians, their serious doubts leading them to pioneer the theory of equilibrium prices and discard any pretense to discover the "causes" of value. Along that critical line, which imbued both the marginalist camp *and* the classical and Marxian side, we shall find both Pareto and Sraffa, i.e. the top marginalist economist on one side and the best Italian economist close to Marxism on the other. To the present day the two of them, together with Galiani, form the top Italian trio of economists in terms of international reputation.

The Milanese School

The "School of Milan," as Voltaire called it, was established by Pietro Verri (1728–97). The notion of *felicità pubblica*, or public happiness, best conveys the meaning and the significance of the contribution of the Milanese School. Their concern was first of all about *happiness* and the utilitarian language becomes more explicit and richer in Milan. At the same time the *public* dimension becomes more prominent and intertwined with the practical needs for reform. Economists here are directly involved with the design and practical implementation of the Theresian Reforms in the Milanese territories. The predecessors of the generation of the Verris are Ludovico Antonio Muratori, who had put forward the ideal of public happiness and Pompeo Neri, the Tuscan economist and administrator who had worked on the practical side of the promotion of public happiness with his decisive contribution to the cadastral reform of the 1750s.

Pietro Verri also founded the Accademia dei Pugni (the *punching academy*, a curious name) and the periodical *Il Caffè* (the *coffee house*), a kind of Italian *Spectator*. Cesare Beccaria (1738–94), by far the best known name of the Italian economic school of the time, was one of his younger associates. Four main themes emerge from Verri's work: 1) money; 2) free trade, especially in staples; 3) pain and pleasure scientifically considered in order to measure happiness and public happiness in particular; 4) quantitative tools to analyse the economy and draw policy conclusions. The Italian School worked in parallel with the physiocratic school, but with a difference. Italian authors took up mercantilist themes – trade, money, public and private finance – in the context of a different agenda in which real growth, based on a concept of real production and income, takes the lead together with an emphasis on *creativity* in a context of *trust* and *sociality*. The competitive drive, not without exception, becomes the symbol of the abolition of privileges and obstacles. *Money* and *trust*, thereby sociality, are naturally bound together. At the same time the Italians, while they follow physiocracy on free trade (with qualifications), do not confine positive economic productivity to agriculture only. This is not so much a triumph of common sense against the excesses of rigor typical of the French economists, it is more a special sense of sociality which puts the emphasis on productive relations as a source of creativity.

The main follower of Verri certainly was Cesare Beccaria, by far the best known figure of the Italian Enlightenment, himself among the early Professors of Political Economy worldwide. Curiously he is sometimes *not* perceived as an economist, but more as a scholar on public law or a moral philosopher of a utilitarian breed. His reputation is almost entirely due to the pamphlet *Dei delitti e delle pene* (*Of Crimes and Punishment*) of 1764. In fact, Beccaria, ten years Verri's junior, had made his first significant contributions (published in *Il Caffè*) as a mathematical economist. He was still in his twenties when he acquired a worldwide reputation and his celebrated pamphlet on crimes and punishment became an explosive success. That is probably by far the best known works of the whole Italian Enlightenment. Beccaria, like Verri, was also a consultant administrator and a member of the Economic Council from 1771 in Milan. Both Beccaria and Verri contributed a number of reports, or *Consulte*, within the Council giving advice to the government. Beccaria also left a volume of his lectures in Milan at the Scuole Palatine: they were only published as *Elementi di Economia Pubblica* in Milano in the Custodi Collection in 1804.

The nineteenth and twentieth centuries

The age of marginalism

During the first part of the nineteenth century the civil economy tradition is continued by Giandomenico Romagnosi (1761–1835) and, more notably, by his pupil Carlo Cattaneo (1801–69). Cattaneo, in particular, enjoys a strong world reputation as a classical author in the field of federal studies, but he is almost totally ignored in his capacity as an economist. At the same time the German-born Historical School, or *Kathedersozialismus*, conquers Italy and it first triggers the mid-nineteenth century reaction of Francesco Ferrara (1810–1900). Later, in the final decades of the century, a much larger reaction would ensue with the rise of marginalism. Maffeo Pantaleoni and Vilfredo Pareto are the outstanding authors of Italian marginalism, along with Enrico Barone and Antonio De Viti De Marco. Schumpeter (1954: 855) rightly extols the achievements of the Italian marginalists. "The most benevolent observer" – he writes – "could not have paid any compliments to Italian economics in the early 1870s; the most malevolent observer could not have denied that it was second to none by 1914." Though the first part of the phrase endorses a malevolent commonplace, the second part is acceptable.

Core marginalism

Marginalism as a research program initially came to Italy through the works of W.S. Jevons and of Léon Walras, rather than Carl Menger, just to mention the founding fathers. Jevons's influence spread first and Pantaleoni (1857–1924) in his early years (differently from Pareto, to whom he was otherwise very close) found Jevons clearer compared to Walras. Pantaleoni was less mathematically inclined and he was able to combine, to some extent, Jevons with Marshall. It was only later that general equilibrium theory established itself as a leading influence on Italian economists, especially with Pareto (1848–1924) and his pupil Enrico Barone (1859–1924).

Both Jevons and Walras were rather promptly translated into Italian in the *Biblioteca dell'economista*, the series of texts of great economists launched by Ferrara in the mid-nineteenth century. Pantaleoni was the economist who first introduced in Italy the neoclassical approach, gradually turning into the mainstream after a considerable lapse of time. His book of *Principles* (1889) was influential and had an English translation before the turn of the century. Nevertheless, particularly compared to Pareto, his influence was mostly national. At the same time his work was not exclusively confined to economics, a distinctive character of the Italian tradition. Pantaleoni treated a number of themes typical of the formative stages of the Italian tradition, and came to develop a special kind of marginalism. Particularly in his treatment of economic dynamics he was far from the determinism and restrictive use of the economic principle prevailing elsewhere.

Pareto, no doubt, is the most important economist of the whole of the Italian economic tradition. He gave fundamental contributions to the construction of economic theory. His influence was strong in Italy (although his chair was in Lausanne, as the successor to Walras) but it was by no means limited to Italy. Gradually, also through the influence of a number of non-Italian economists (notably J.R. Hicks), his influence grew worldwide. At the same time his contributions are not limited to economics, though this happened in a way different from Pantaleoni. Pareto had strong views on economics as a positivistic science. At the same time economics was to stay confined to the analysis of *rational* actions. Irrationality was to be the domain of sociology, to which discipline also he gave first rate contributions. Moreover his work on political theory, on the circulation of the élites, is also well-known.

Dynamic analysis

Even during the marginalist era, dynamic analysis continued to be one of the preferred themes in the Italian tradition – despite the fact that (under the influence of the general equilibrium brand), a static approach became prevalent in principle. It is well-known that Schumpeter was the main critic of the approach dominated by the *Kreislauf* or the circular flow. No wonder that Schumpeter was widely read in Italy. Such authors as Luigi Amoroso, Giulio La Volpe, Marco Fanno, and above all Giovanni Demaria (1899–1998) gave significant contributions to dynamic analysis even if they *did not* abandon general equilibrium as their basic approach. This is true in particular of Demaria, who made dynamics the core issue of his research.

Socialism

Generally speaking, nineteenth century economics saw the triumph of value analysis, under the influence of Marx's labor-value on one side and of marginalism's utility-value in the opposite camp. Italy is different in that value analysis never was in the limelight at any stage, not even among Marx's followers. The best examples are Achille Loria and Antonio Graziadei's critical analysis of value. Piero Sraffa (1898–1983), among the greatest Italian economists of all time, is the outstanding scholar in the field. Sraffa became famous as the greatest critic of marginalism: he later revealed himself as the upholder of a *surplus* (rather than surplus *value*) approach to political economy, a theory of production and distribution of a clear Marxian inspiration. Sraffa is at the center of intense debate. Due also to his scanty publications and hermetic language, his economics still is insufficiently understood, while a lot is emerging from his remarkable unpublished writings, now under scrutiny by researchers. He remained an Italian citizen, but he spent most of his life (from 1927) at the University of Cambridge, where he was among the associates of J.M. Keynes. His work marked the origin of the so-called Anglo-Italian branch of the postwar Cambridge school of economics.

On the feasibility of a socialist economy Italy staged a debate which produced a famous article by Barone, who in 1908 published an essay on the application of the marginalist approach to a socialist economy. Even in the marginalist camp we should note that the emphasis on value theory faded away, as Pareto was uniquely interested in a theory of *price* which could support the analysis of rational choice based on preferences, and had soon abandoned any cardinalist pretences concerning utility.

Other features of the Italian style

An interesting strand of political economy in Italy, in line with the focus on policy and institutions, is given by the contributions on public economics. Political economy in Italy – as generally noted and analyzed in particular by James M. Buchanan – developed a special line of thought named *Scienza delle finanze* – a line of analysis on the economics of public choice. It should be mentioned that the very first contribution by Pantaleoni, bearing the signs of a marginalist approach, was precisely an article on the economic principles of public choice. The main figures among the founders of *Scienza delle finanze* were Antonio De Viti De Marco (1858–1943) and Francesco Saverio Nitti. Concerning the theory of *public goods* the early Italian contributions by De Marco and Ugo Mazzola are widely acknowledged.

During the so-called "years of high theory," "In Italy" – Schumpeter wrote (1954, 1157) – "scientific economics continued to move at . . . a high level, both within and without the Pareto school until the war. Barring war effects, there was no break and neither was there one after the fall of the regime." Among the main figures we mention Costantino Bresciani Turroni, Umberto Ricci, Pasquale Jannaccone, Gustavo Del Vecchio, and Giorgio Mortara. We add in particular the case of Luigi Einaudi (1874–1961), a typical independent scholar and mentor of many economists during that period, extending well into the post-war period. His *Lezioni di Politica Sociale* (1949) is an outstanding example of the teachings of the Italian school inspired by principles of liberalism and emphasis on the civilizing aspects of competitive markets. His opposition to the Keynesian doctrines was in line with the adverse judgment met by Keynes's economic philosophy all over the world. Italian economists would come to better terms with the Keynesian revolution with the younger generation including Ferdinando di Fenizio, Paolo Sylos Labini, Giorgio Fuà, Federico Caffè, Siro Lombardini, Pasquale Saraceno, Sergio Steve, Luigi Pasinetti, and Giacomo Becattini.

An important influence came also from Franco Modigliani (1918–2003), one of the founding fathers (together with Paul Samuelson) of the so-called "neoclassical synthesis," who had left Italy before the war and ended up as one of the most important figures at MIT. He became a US citizen after the war and he died in Cambridge, Mass., in 2003. He is the only Nobel Prize winner for economics of Italian origin. All the economists above were crucial in transforming Italian economic thought during the post-war period. They all share, in different ways, significant allegiance to liberal principles. Among them Paolo Sylos Labini (1920–2005), Pasinetti (b. 1930), and Modigliani should be singled out for their special worldwide reputation. In particular Pasinetti is prominent among the above-mentioned Anglo-Italian school originally at Cambridge, UK.

In the post-war period Italian economics has in part kept aloof from the temptations of "economic imperialism," common in certain quarters of the economic profession worldwide. The term was coined by George Stigler and it refers to the extension of the economic reasoning, based on "economic man," to the whole range of social and political sciences. An analogous kind of approach was the ambition of Marx's historical materialism from the mid-nineteenth century onwards. Marx's ambition was, however, based on a different kind of economic philosophy, identifying the economic principle with the analysis of the technical conditions of production prevailing at different stages of history. It is curious to find that same ambition turning up today under the new dress of quasi-libertarian principles. It becomes today the last word of a kind of "popular libertarianism," well signaled by the surge of *political economics*, a school of economics which has its main center of research in Italy at Bocconi University. With respect to our treatment of the Italian tradition, the line of research of political economics is sometimes criticized as reflecting a strategy of forced internationalization, leading perhaps to dispute the value of *any* national tradition as such.

At the same time the Italian tradition continues today in particular through the current revival of *civil economy* and its conception of the market. Contrary to political economics, Italian civil economists conceive of internationalization as a meeting point of the diverse traditions, which are enabled to communicate and enrich economic discourse through their varied approaches. Self-styled Libertarians, Chicago-boys, supporters of public choice, and general equilibrium theorists are present in the Italian context, a considerable number of economists share socially-oriented views and can be ascribed to the large stream of neo-Keynesians. Especially among the young, there is a split between the Bocconi-boys and the rest of the country. The former are almost as aggressively anti-Keynesian as the bloggers of NoisefromAmerika. They are also rather fierce supporters of the European strategy of austerity. Other groups argue in favor of rigorous reform but shun austerity.

Some would argue that Mario Monti, the leading economist and President of Bocconi, has recently put to test (as Prime Minister of Italy) the political credentials of the line of political economics upheld at Bocconi. But a vigorous reaction to the "excesses" of political economics is still far from appearing in the public arena.

References

Bartoli, H., 2003, *Histoire de la Pensée Économique en Italie*, Paris: Publications de la Sorbonne.

Barucci, P., 2009, *Sul Pensiero Economico Italiano (1750–1900)*, ed. by R. Patalano, Napoli: Istituto Italiano per gli Studi Filosofici.

Beccaria, C., 1984–continuing, *Edizione Nazionale delle Opere di Cesare Beccaria*, Milano: Mediobanca.

Bruni, L., and Zamagni, S., 2007, *Civil Economy. Efficiency, Equity, Public Happiness*, Oxford: Peter Lang.

Buchanan, J.M., 1960, "'La Scienza delle Finanze': the Italian Tradition in Fiscal Theory", in id., *Fiscal Theory and Political Economy. Selected Essays*, Chapel Hill, University of North Carolina Press, 24–74.

Custodi, P., ed., 1803–1815, *Scrittori Classici Italiani di Economia Politica*, Milano: Destefanis, 50 vols.

Einaudi, L., 1949, *Lezioni di Politica Sociale*, Torino: Einaudi.

Einaudi, L., 1953, *Saggi Bibliografici e Storici Intorno alle Dottrine Economiche*, Roma: Edizioni di storia e letteratura.

Faucci, R., 2014, *A History of Italian Economic Thought*, London and New York: Routledge.

Finoia, M., ed., 1980, *Il Pensiero Economico Italiano 1850–1950*, Bologna: Cappelli.

Garin, E., 1969, *Science and Civil Life in the Italian Renaissance*, Garden City, NY: Anchor Books.

Genovesi, A., 2005 [1765–7], *Delle Lezioni di Commercio o sia di Economia Civile con Elementi del Commercio*, M.L. Perna ed., Napoli: Istituto Italiano per gli Studi Filosofici. New ed. *Lezioni di Economia Civile*, 2013, ed. by Francesca Dal Degan, Milano: Vita & Pensiero.

Loria, A., 1904, *Verso la Giustizia Sociale*, Milano: Società editrice milanese.

Meacci, F., ed., 1988, *Italian Economists of the 20th Century*, Cheltenham: Edward Elgar.

Negri Zamagni, V. and Porta, P.L., eds., 2012, *Il Contributo Italiano alla Storia del Pensiero: Economia*, Rome: Istituto della Enciclopedia Italiana.

Pareto, V., 1964–continuing, *Oeuvres Complètes*, ed by G. Busino, Genéve: Droz.

Porta, P.L., 1997, "Italian Economics through the Postwar Years", in *The Postwar Internationalization of Economics*, ed. by A.W. Coats, Annual Supplement of *History of Political Economy*, vol. XXVIII, 1997, 163–81.

Porta, P.L., 2014, "Conquering Scarcity: Institutions, Learning and Creativity. The Italian Tradition", typescript accepted for publication in *Resources, Production and Structural Change*, ed. by M. Baranzini, C. Rotondi, R. Scazzieri (forthcoming 2014).

Quadrio Curzio, A., 2007, *Economisti ed Economia. Per un'Italia Europea: Paradigmi tra il XVIII e il XX Secolo*, Bologna: Mulino.

Reinert, S.A., ed., 2011, *Breve Trattato delle Cause, che Possono far Abbondare li Regni d'Oro, e Argento, dove non son Miniere* [1613], London: Anthem Press.

Robertson J., 2005, *The Case for the Enlightenment. Scotland and Naples 1680–1760*, Cambridge: Cambridge University Press.

Schumpeter, J.A., 1954, *History of Economic Analysis*, ed. by E. Boody Schumpeter, Oxford: Oxford University Press.

Venturi, F., 1991, *The End of the Old Regime in Europe, 1776–1789*, Princeton, NJ: Princeton University Press.

Verri, P., 2004–continuing, *Edizione Nazionale delle Opere di Pietro Verri*, Roma: Edizioni di Storia e Letteratura.

6

Greece

Michalis M. Psalidopoulos

After the Ottoman conquest of Constantinople in 1453, most Byzantine intellectuals, the bearers of Hellenic-Christian culture, emigrated to the West, mainly to Italy. Others stayed and became high-ranking state administrators and translators for the new rulers; they formed a distinct social group, the Phanariots. Greece became a Christian province of the Ottoman Empire and was excluded during the next 400 years from the technological and scientific breakthroughs of the early modern period. The Greek language was preserved through the reading and teaching of texts of the Eastern Christian Fathers of the Church dating from the third century AD. These texts called for a humble Christian life, a life of sharing surpluses in a closed community, of no luxury and of no taking-up of interest. Life generally ought to be non-materialistic, a stage of acquisition of properties by humans who qualified for paradise. This teaching was microeconomic as it applied to individual behaviour, but was also in tune with the macroeconomic maxims of Ottoman economic thought: provisionism, fiscalism and traditionalism (Psalidopoulos and Theocarakis, 2011).

According to this approach, the functions of government were the uninterrupted supply of goods to the internal market, particularly the urban population, the maximisation of treasury income in order to finance the state bureaucracy and the military, and a tendency to preserve existing conditions in economy and society. By the late seventeenth century these ideas and policies were in crisis. Extensive accumulation through the addition of new territories was no longer possible, and the extraction of an agricultural surplus made taxation harsh and arbitrary and the whole political and economic administration tyrannical. A fiscal crisis and the rise of nationalism in occupied regions led to the gradual decline of the empire. Mercantilist theories concerning the value of money, a favourable balance of trade and policies aimed at the strengthening of the state were, curiously, not transmitted or not fully understood among state administrators and officials of the late Ottoman Empire; the main belief among the peoples in the Balkans was that the state was entitled to intervene in the economy and shape society.

Commerce thrived in the eighteenth century with the 'Balkan Orthodox merchant' conquering new markets and obtaining profits, and balancing between state and church authority. Shipping also flourished. It was out of these merchant classes and ship-owners that sympathy for the Enlightenment and the French Revolution grew, and with them ideas associated with economic freedom and individual rights. Private property and individual freedom were regarded by them as the only way to welfare and to higher stages of civilisation.

On the eve of and immediately after the Greek Revolution encyclopaedias were published, and translations of books by Jean-Baptiste Say and Joseph Droz were widely read in Greece. The Greek Orthodox Church's hostility towards some of the Enlightenment teachings was a revisionist force that led to their retreat in the early 1830s (Henderson, 1970). However, the presence of Benthamites from Britain (Rosen, 1992), *économistes* from France (Vacalopoulos, 1977) and Bavarian administrators in Greece acted to disseminate in the country a liberal amalgam of thinking and policy-making that became dominant in the decades thereafter. The overthrow of the Ottomans and the creation of an independent Greece in 1830 did not bring about the immediate entry of the Greek state into modernity, as traditional, pre-modern patterns of government were abandoned only gradually, over several decades (Kostis, 2002).

In retrospect and by using as a criterion the institutionalisation of economics as a discipline, one can distinguish three distinct periods in the evolution of economic thought in Greece: a) from independence in 1830 to 1920; b) from 1920 to 1974; and c) from 1974 to today.

From independence in 1830 to 1920

During this first and longest period, the community of economists was very small. Economics was embedded in law, and the circle of economists in academia, parliament, business and public life consisted mainly of lawyers by training; most of the nineteenth-century economic policy-makers who sat in parliament and made decisions (Psalidopoulos and Syrmaloglou, 2005) had law degrees, and those who had studied abroad had gone to Paris or Pisa, and later Heidelberg or Munich. The influence of French economic thinking in Greece up to the 1880s was great, with German economic thought becoming more influential in the country around the turn of the century. After the development of romanticism and socialist ideas in the 1880s, Marxism also emerged (Kountouris, 1998).

British influences on economic thought remained minimal until the post-World War Two period. A possible reason for this lies in the policy-oriented approach of French economic theory and its considerable diversity as compared to the strictly analytical approach of British classical political economy, an analysis moreover based on the existence of three distinct social classes in the economy, classes not being so clearly defined in Greece at that time.

The dominant name in Greek economics in the nineteenth century was Ioannes Soutsos, the sole economics professor at the only Greek university, the University of Athens (he taught from 1835 to 1890). Soutsos was a liberal who placed great emphasis on the institutional reforms needed for the country to embark on a sustainable developmental path. Influenced by his Genevan mentor, Pellegrino Rossi, and by Say's approach to economics (Ithakissios, 1992), he participated actively in public life and wrote articles and pamphlets on economic policy issues (Psalidopoulos and Stassinopoulos, 2009). He rejected Ricardian rent theory, finding it inapplicable to the conditions prevailing in the Greek economy.

Despite their small number, Greek economists created a short-lived 'Society for the Freedoms of Trade' from 1865 to 1867, a group with close links to free trade associations in Belgium, Britain, Spain, Italy and the US (Psalidopoulos, 2005). Former judge turned economist and university lecturer Aristides Economos edited the monthly journal *Oikonomiki Epitheorisis* [Economic Review] from 1877 to 1890 and sat briefly in parliament. He criticised Greek economic policy as being incompatible with the postulates of classical economics (Psalidopoulos, 1996a).

What prevailed in the realm of ideas was liberalism of a South-East European variety. Liberal economic thought was seen as a complement to political democracy. Liberal ideas were at the service of social justice and hostile to the privileges given by an illiberal political class. The middle classes favoured liberalism as a weapon to defeat the higher echelons of power and policy-making, until then open only to a small group of people and the king. The realisation of nationalist goals demanded an active government in the economy, a potent military and good foreign policy relations, the last dependent on state contracts to British, French or German businesses. In short, economic policy was a tool to be used for political goals.

The first King of Greece, Otto, governed the country along cameralist lines and was expelled in 1862. His successor, George I, was made over the course of time to respect the will of Greek citizens. Government regulations and mistrust towards private initiative were the norm up to the 1870s. Property rights in agriculture remained confused until 1871 (McGrew, 1985); the infrastructure remained in a primitive condition until the 1880s; the enforcement of law and order in the countryside was inadequate; the tax system and its reform in 1881 were arbitrary; and the tariff systems of 1857 and 1884 neither induced growth nor were protective of local industry. To top it all, budget deficits and reckless public borrowing, especially after 1878, undermined efforts for sound monetary and fiscal policies. They led to the 1893 default and to the imposition of international financial control over state finances. This made Greek economists more accustomed to government regulation.

Throughout the nineteenth century and up to the 1970s, the Greek economy was mainly agricultural, but some sources of growth were shipping, commerce and the banking sector. Monetary issues were hotly debated among Greek economists (Stassinopoulos, 2000), as was fiscal policy (Syrmaloglou, 2007). After a century of moderate growth (Kostelenos, 1995), Greece almost achieved its foreign policy aspiration to expand its borders in order to include all Greeks living in South-East Europe after the end of World War One. However, due to foreign policy mistakes, in 1922 everything was lost with 1.2 million refugees from Asia Minor migrating to mainland Greece, a land of 4 million people.

From 1920 to 1974

The second period of Greek economics starts in 1920, when new universities and commercial schools were created and new economics professors were hired. Soon thereafter the number of academic economists rose from two to nine, and grew to thirty-seven by the late 1960s. This generation dominated economic discourse in the country until the fall of the dictatorship in 1974. Degrees in economics started being awarded from the mid-1920s, even if business studies and accounting were more popular, offering promising professional careers. In 1957 and 1960 respectively new graduate schools for industrial studies were established in Thessaloniki and Piraeus. The latter school published the journal *Spoudai* [Studies], the only such one still existing in Greece today. The curricula of studies, despite incorporating in the late 1960s such innova-tive elements as microeconomics, econometrics and development economics, remained orienta-ted to law. Only in the early 1970s did economics break free from law schools and take an independent path.

In general, out of the 37 economists who came to occupy university positions from the 1920s to the late 1960s, twenty had done their PhDs in Greece, 9 in Germany, 4 in France, 2 in the UK, 1 in the USA and 1 in Switzerland. After 1933 Germany lost its appeal as a place to study economics, and many PhDs began to be awarded by Greek universities. Three out of the 37 professors were already appointed in the 1920s; 4 became academics in the 1930s; 13 in the 1940s; 12 in the 1950s; and only 5 in the 1960s (Psalidopoulos, 2000). After World War Two, the Greek Society for Economic Sciences was founded and it had 25 members only, since membership was limited only to those holding a postgraduate degree in economics.

A decade later, the number grew to 123, 67 ordinary and 56 affiliated members, and the Society organised large conferences every three years. It was dissolved after the fall of the dictatorship.

During the interwar period the dominant approach to economics was interventionism and social reform. Interventionism reflected economic realities in the country. Economic policy-makers had to deal with the settlement and accommodation of refugees and had to find solutions to inflation after 1922. The increase in the supply of labour helped the industrialisation of the country, and the economy grew in the interwar years by a modest 1.8 per cent per year (Psalidopoulos, 1989). The Great Depression led to default in 1932 and to more regulation and protection. External economic relations, especially with the League of Nations, who intermediated for foreign borrowing, were based on the monetary orthodoxy of the day. Liberalism and Marxism clashed with the pragmatic interventionism of Greek economic policy but for different reasons.

The central figure in Greek economics in the interwar period was Andreas Andreades, Professor of Public Finance, who was active from 1901 to 1935. He was an eclectic liberal economist, who, as a senior academic, was appointed to all selection committees responsible for filling university positions in the 1920s. He believed that different schools of thought abroad were the products of certain political and philosophical ideas that had sprung out of the concrete historical and economic facts of foreign nations. Greek scientists should, in his view, apply these theories and test their relevance in their own country (Andreades, 1927: 237). This would assist them in creating a national economic theory suitable to the needs of the Greek economy in the future. He therefore followed a very pluralistic agenda and recommended the appointment of such economists as Xenophon Zolotas (University of Thessaloniki, 1928–32, and University of Athens, 1932–67), Demosthenes Stephanides (University of Thessaloniki, 1928–44, and University of Athens, 1950–65), Kyriakos Varvaressos (University of Athens, 1918–20 and 1923–45) and Demetrios Kalitsounakis (Athens Graduate School of Economics and Commerce, 1920–60).

The most important of the four proved to be Zolotas. He was a liberal follower of Gustav Cassel, who dismissed abstract theorizing as practised then by Ludwig von Mises and Friedrich von Hayek. He became governor of the Central Bank, the Bank of Greece, from 1955 to 1967 and from 1974 to 1981. Furthermore, he became prime minister in 1990. Stephanides was a historicist, who applauded National Socialism in 1939. Varvaressos was an interventionist who became minister of finance in 1932, a deputy governor of the Bank of Greece in the 1930s, its governor in exile, and a deputy prime minister in 1945. After his (early) retirement, he lived in the USA and worked at the World Bank. Kalitsounakis also favoured state intervention and was centre left in his political views.

Zolotas and Kalitsounakis were the editors of two economic journals, the *Epitheorisis Koinonikis kai Dimosias Oikonomikes* [Review of Social and Public Economics] 1932–43, and the *Epitheorisis Politikon kai Oikonomikon Epistimon* [Review of Political and Economic Sciences] 1947–67) and also the *Archion Economikon kai Koinonikon Epistimon* [Archive of Economics and Social Sciences] 1920–70. Whereas the 'Archive' defined economics in a broader social sciences setting the 'Review' placed emphasis only on economics and public finance, and the bulk of its contributions mostly followed the then prevailing mainstream neoclassical paradigm. Greek economists hotly debated such issues as public works and inflation in these journals and also in scientific clubs. Marxist authors, such as Pantelis Pouliopoulos and Seraphim Maximos, offered analyses close to those of the Third International. But the world economic depression led to a *de facto* acceptance of interventionism by liberal and interventionist economists alike.

When Keynesian economics became known in Greece, its framework of analysis was rejected by both liberals and interventionists. Keynes was known in interwar Greece as a monetary theorist and as an authority on international policy issues. His *Tract on Monetary Reform* and *The End of Laissez-Faire* were translated, his proposals for a managed currency discussed, and his objection to anti-deflationist policies as a way out of economic depression approved by Greek interventionists. However, and because of the absence of a British tradition in economic thought in Greece, his work was not comprehended as, at first, a continuation of and then a break from Marshallian economics.

In his review of *The General Theory of Employment, Interest and Money*, Zolotas condemned Keynes' attack on savings, the pillar of growth in his view. Other liberal academics disapproved of the new concepts introduced, the framework of analysis and the hypotheses put forward by Keynes. The conflict of Greek interventionists with *The General Theory* was explicitly articulated after 1945. The polarised political climate between conservatives and the left after the Civil War made such economists as Kalitsounakis and Professor Angelos Angelopoulos reject Keynesianism on the grounds that it espoused an interventionism that would preserve the free-enterprise economy centre-stage, whereas they both favoured an economy based on planning. This rejection of *The General Theory* in Greece did not change when Keynesianism established itself internationally after World War Two as the mainstream orthodoxy.

The same attitude was shown to Keynesianism by economic policy-makers in the 1950s, 1960s and 1970s, such as Minister of Economic Coordination Panagis Papaligouras, who served in the (conservative) governments of Constantine Karamanlis. For Papaligouras, nineteenth-century liberalism lacked a moral dimension and ignored social policy, whereas twentieth-century liberalism, the 'realist liberalism' he espoused, was a system where the administration intervened wherever the government felt it appropriate, in order to fix socially unacceptable circumstances for the poorest strata of society and the unemployed. The limits to such action were set by government revenue and productivity increases in the economy. Papaligouras had high esteem for Keynes as an economist, but objected to effective demand manipulation because of the peculiar problems facing the Greek economy: a scarcity of capital, the need to promote savings, balance of payments restrictions and the need to maintain price stability.

The opposing political party of these times, the Centre Union, on the other hand, with Andreas Papandreou, the son of its leader, as its main speaker, was committed to a different agenda, namely, structural reforms in the economy. With due respect to Keynes, his theories were regarded by the Centre Union as relevant to already developed countries, but not to Greece (Psalidopoulos, 1996b).

Greece fared well economically after World War Two and the Civil War, especially from 1955 to the late 1970s. Growth rates were around 7 per cent annually, and the inflation rate was as low as 1.8 per cent. The share of industry in GDP reached 30 per cent in 1970. Zolotas rose to the height of his fame in this period. In his *Monetary Equilibrium and Economic Development* (1964), he defined monetary stability as the primary goal of economic policy. Low inflation achieved after past hyperinflations had to be defended at all cost. The budget of the central government had to be balanced. Because the need for public investment was high, Zolotas recommended the introduction of a new account – the budget of public investment – that could run a deficit, but would be covered by foreign loans and public savings. Zolotas was a practical liberal, a moderate monetarist and a believer in sound regulation and oversight of the economy. The most prominent of his critics was Professor Andreas Papandreou, who, after a successful career at the universities of Harvard, Minnesota and California at Berkeley in the 1950s, served as a consultant to the (conservative) Greek government and raised money from Greek as well as US sources to create a Centre for Economic Research in Athens in 1961, which was renamed the Centre for Planning and Economic Research (KEPE) in 1964. The Centre invited many American and British economists to conduct research and give seminars to its young staff. These scientists introduced into Greece mathematical techniques, policy-orientated economic analysis and neoclassical-synthesis style Keynesianism.

The economic development of the country was the most important issue for Greek economists in the post-1945 era. Intertwined with economic development was the question of Greece's association with the European Economic Community (EEC) from 1962. In the early 1960s, as well as in the late 1970s, shortly before full Greek membership of the EEC in 1981, debates took place on whether Greece would sustain high rates of growth and its political independence if it became a full EEC member. In general, three schools of thought can be identified: liberal-dirigiste, structuralist-interventionist and Marxist.

The liberal camp considered economic development as an inevitable process, if the institutional framework of the Greek economy adjusted to the logic of markets. Reliance on foreign technical and financial assistance was important in the development process, because of the lack of native capital willing to invest in big, growth-inducing projects. However, Greek liberals always kept in the back of their minds the idea of strong government action in the economy, if needed. As expected, this liberal camp espoused Greece's association with and, later, full membership in the EEC, minimising in various degrees the possible negative effects of the gradual loss of protection of Greek industry and the right to autonomous economic action in future circumstances. A major figure in this camp was Zolotas.

The structuralist-interventionist group identified Greece not as a less-developed European country, but rather as a Third World one, finding itself in a vicious circle of 'political dependence on the Great Powers' and of economic underdevelopment. What was needed, according to these economists, was strong government action in all fields of social life and investment in human capital. External economic relations in this scenario were crucial, and this camp espoused the findings of Raúl Prebisch's study for the Economic Commission for Latin America: that the terms of trade between rich and poor countries favoured the former. Democratic planning on a large scale, it was claimed, could make the vision of a modern industrialised Greece a reality, rather than through joining the EEC. An important advocate of this camp in academia was Angelopoulos, editor of the monthly *Nea Oikonomia* [New Economy]. Papandreou, as a Centre Union politician in the 1960s, was close to these ideas.

The Marxist camp had nourished a whole generation with the idea that Greek under-development was due to the political dependence of Greece on foreign countries. In the early post-war period, Greek Marxists argued that there were enough financial sources and technical skills in Greece to build up heavy industry, provided that there was the political will to tame the bourgeois class that opposed the project. After the Communist defeat in the Greek Civil War, the Marxist camp was not in a position to articulate its views explicitly. *Synchrona Themata* [*Modern Issues*] was a Marxist review of letters and social sciences. Economic contributions therein applauded economic successes in 'real existing' socialism and were critical of all aspects of government policy in Greece. Consequently, Greek Marxists were vehemently opposed to Greece's association with the EEC, with the noble exception of the Eurocommunists, who voted in parliament in 1979 in favour of Greece's accession to the EEC.

From 1974 to today

After 1974, higher education in Greece was transformed from an elite system to a mass one. In 1982 a new university law specified requirements for university positions, and in the same decade four departments offering degrees in economics were established at the universities of Crete,

Patras, the Aegean and Ioannina. At the same time, economics departments were separated completely from political science. Generous government financing provoked an explosion in the number of appointments: there are approximately 300 academic economists in Greece today. In a final act of reform, in 1989, all existing graduate schools were renamed as universities, and new departments giving highly specialized first degrees, as for example in regional development, were introduced.

This enormous expansion changed the landscape of economic education in Greece completely. Within a short time, the curricula were changed to reflect the new situation. The internationalisation of post-war economics meant, primarily, the coming of age of UK- or American-trained economists in Greece (Psalidopoulos, 2000).

Since the 1980s, all schools of economic thought are represented more or less in every economics department, and the subject itself is taught (as it used to be) as an optional course in all universities. This plurality in numbers has destroyed the sense of community, for there is no longer a society of academic economists in Greece. Greek economists are members of foreign economic associations and societies, and publish both in Greek and other languages.

In the field of theorising and economic policy-making, a new (old) name grew in importance: Andreas Papandreou. His views shifted from the mainstream of the 1960s to more radical positions in the 1970s. Papandreou now opposed neoclassical theory and its approach to development. For him, underdevelopment could be best explained as a consequence of the dependency of some states on others. Imperialism was the means by which the industrialised nations held underdeveloped nations, such as Greece, in dependence. The global system was characterised by the contradiction between the countries of the Metropolis and the countries of the Periphery. Social planning in a truly democratic, participatory society had to be decentralised, with the region functioning as the key planning unit. Unequal exchange, the transfer of surplus from the Periphery to the Metropolis and the instruction of the economy of the Periphery by metropolitan decision-making had to be stopped (Psalidopoulos, 2010).

A very important concern for Papandreou was the popular support of any government wanting to implement 'change' in the Greek economy. In order to secure it, he wanted 'social consumption' to grow through big rises in wage income, especially in the public sector. The public sector was a tool to control the economy, to boost growth and to absorb the unemployed. Next to social consumption, the banking system had to be nationalised and supply the public sector, including public enterprises and agricultural cooperatives, with loans. Finally, foreign trade had to be centrally controlled in order for the national economy to remain immune from changes in international economic relations. The results of these policies were deteriorating for economic indicators: growth rates fell from 6.6 per cent in the 1960s, to 5.6 per cent in the 1970s, to 1.8 per cent in the 1980s, with rates in industrial output falling from 9.8 per cent, to 6.4 per cent, to 0.5 per cent respectively. The inflation rate averaged 16.2 per cent per year between 1983 and 1995. Industrial decline led in the 1980s to the take-over of 'ailing' firms by the government in order for unemployment to be kept to a minimum. Government expenditure rose from 30 per cent of GNP in the 1970s to 50 per cent in the late 1980s, and the debt to GDP ratio went from 20 per cent in 1979 to 110 per cent in 1990, creating a bubble waiting to burst.

It is ironic that during the 1980s, the decade of right-wing hegemony across most of the West, with Margaret Thatcher's and Ronald Reagan's governments applauding monetarism and supply-side economics, in Greece politics took a totally different turn. Papandreou's PASOK party was strongly influenced by dependency theory, which was put forward as a means of explaining particularly Latin American underdevelopment and was popularised by Paul Sweezy's *Monthly Review*. All prominent PASOK policy officials were committed to lines of economic management drawn up by Papandreou himself in his numerous publications. Eventually the rhetoric of a transition to socialism was abandoned for the sake of an economic administration that tried to fine tune poor economic performance with European Union integration and money transfers. Despite the opposition of neoclassical and Marxist economists, Papandreou's views found wide electoral support and popularised state-developmentalist thinking in Greece that dominated economic discourse for decades. Successive governments after 1995 did not challenge this prevailing economic paradigm; they tried to bring it in line with the country's European Union membership and the introduction of the euro. Low interest rates after 2002 added a further boost to foreign borrowing and led to crisis in 2010, when the actual state of Greek statistics was made public.

Economic thought in Greece is presently at a crossroads due to the ongoing economic crisis and distress. The economic downturn of the country and forced austerity led to wage cuts, reduction of the public sector, unemployment and heavy taxation, and has provoked many publications that try to analyse the current situation of the Greek economy. Neoclassical, Keynesian and Marxist writers and all other variants of economic thought compete to win the hearts and minds of the public and possibly influence the Greek electorate. Three different camps can be identified. One espouses a return to a national currency that would enable the country to regain through devaluation its international competitiveness; a variant in this camp is extremely nationalistic and xenophobic and espouses conspiracy theories to explain current conditions in Greece. A second camp calls for a new Marshall Plan of aid to Greece that would foster investment and growth and thus the repayment of public debt in the near future; this camp identifies the Eurozone crisis as stemming from a surplus North versus a deficit South divide and sees a solution in the issuing of Eurobonds, if this were possible. A third group agrees that austerity in the country is based on false premises, but believes that Greece ought to bring its finances back to order so that the country will be able in the future to renegotiate any changes to existing agreements from a position of economic solvency. Whatever the result will be, such a debate is a good and healthy sign. Economic thought in Greece still is, and needs to stay, pluralist in order to contribute to the welfare of the country.

References

Andreades, A. (1927), 'Griechenland', in H. Mayer (ed.), *Die Wirtschaftstheorie der Gegenwart*, Vienna: Springer, 236–46.

Henderson, G.P. (1970), *The Revival of Greek Thought, 1620–1830*, Albany: State University of New York Press.

Ithakissios, D. (1992), 'John A. Soutsos (1804–1890): Greece's First Academic Economist', *Quaderni di Storia dell Economia Politica*, 2: 136–48.

Kostelenos, G. (1995), *Money and Output in Modern Greece, 1858–1938*, Athens: Centre of Planning and Economic Research.

Kostis, K. (2002), 'The Formation of the State in Greece, 1830–1914', in M. Dogo and G. Franzinetti (eds), *Disrupting and Reshaping: Early Stages of Nation-building in the Balkans*, Ravenna: Longo, 47–64.

Kountouris, M. (1998), *The Development of Economic Thought in Greece, 1837–1942*, unpublished doctoral dissertation, University of Athens, Greece [in Greek].

McGrew, W. (1985), *Land and Revolution in Modern Greece, 1800–1881*, Kent: Kent University Press.

Psalidopoulos, M. (1989), *The Crisis of 1929 and the Greek Economists. A Contribution to the History of Economic Thought in Greece*, Athens: Foundation of Culture, Commercial Bank of Greece (in Greek).

Psalidopoulos, M. (1996a), 'Aristides Economos and the "Oikonomiki Epitheorisis": The Rise and Fall of an Economic Journal in 19th-century Greece', *History of Economic Ideas*, 4(3): 149–67.

Psalidopoulos, M. (1996b), 'Keynesianism across Nations: The Case of Greece', *European Journal for the History of Economic Thought*, 3(3): 449–62.

Psalidopoulos, M. (2000), 'Institutional Constraints and the Internationalization of Economics: The Case of Greece', in A.W. Bob Coats (ed.), *The Development of Economics in Western Europe*, London: Routledge, 227–45.

Psalidopoulos, M. (2005), 'The Greek "Society for the Freedoms of Trade" (1865–7): Rise, Activities, Decline', *Journal of the History of Economic Thought*, 27(4): 383–98.

Psalidopoulos, M. (2010), 'On the Interaction between Academic Economics and Politics: The Case of Andreas Papandreou', in M. Psalidopoulos (ed.), *Oikonomologoi kai Oikonomike Politike sti Sychrone Ellada*, Athens: Metamesonykties Ekdoseis, 341–59.

Psalidopoulos, M., and Y. Stassinopoulos (2009), 'A Liberal Economist and Economic Policy Reform in 19th-century Greece: The Case of Ioannes Soutsos', *History of Political Economy*, 41(3): 491–517.

Psalidopoulos, M., and A. Syrmaloglou (2005), 'Economists in the Greek Parliament (1862–1910): The Men and their Views on Fiscal and Monetary Policy', in M.M. Augello and M.E.L. Guidi (eds), *Economists in Parliament in the Liberal Age (1848–1920)*, Aldershot: Ashgate, 229–58.

Psalidopoulos, M., and N. Theocarakis (2011), 'The Dissemination of Economic Thought in South-Eastern Europe in the Nineteenth Century', in Heinz D. Kurz, Tamotsu Nishizawa and Keith Tribe (eds), *The Dissemination of Economic Ideas*, Cheltenham and Northampton, MA: Edward Elgar Publishing, 161–91.

Rosen, F. (1992), *Bentham, Byron and Greece: Constitutionalism, Nationalism and Early Liberal Political Thought*, Oxford: Clarendon Press.

Stassinopoulos, Y. (2000), *Monetary Theory and Policy in 19th-century Greece*, Athens: Typothyto [in Greek].

Syrmaloglou, A. (2007), *Taxation or Bankruptcy: Fiscal Policy in the Greek Parliament, 1862–1910*, Athens: Metamesonykties Ekdoseis [in Greek].

Vacalopoulos, C.A. (1977), *L'économiste Français Arthemond de Regny et son rôle dans l'Histoire Financière de la Grèce (1831–1841)*, Thessaloniki: Institute for Balkan Studies.

Zolotas, X. (1964), *Monetary Equilibrium and Economic Development. The Case of Greece*, Athens: Bank of Greece.

7

Spain and Portugal

José Luís Cardoso and Luis Perdices de Blas

Spain and Portugal went from being two maritime, colonial powers which carved up the newly discovered world through the treaty of Tordesillas in 1494, to being two member countries of the European Union from 1986 onwards. For a brief period in their history, between 1580 and 1640, they were united politically. In this chapter we aim to assess the main common features in the development of economic thought, as followed by the two Iberian countries, leaving aside national peculiarities. We shall also endeavor to point out and highlight some of the crucial moments in the evolution of economic thought in the two countries, during which we can find signs of innovation, as well as of original adaptation and appropriation, either in questions of a theoretical or doctrinal nature, or in issues related to their application in economic policy programs.

The sixteenth and seventeenth centuries

Spanish and Portuguese scholastics in the sixteenth and seventeenth centuries lived through a period when substantial change occurred in Western Europe – the emergence and consolidation of nation-states, the opening up of new routes for European-Asian trade, the discovery of America, and the colonization of new territories – when the Spanish Empire became the leading power in the world. There was a group of scholastics belonging mainly to the Dominican order, which made up the Salamanca school and studied or taught in the University there. Their undisputed master was Francisco de Vitoria. This School had a widespread projection, not only in Iberia, but also in South American colonies and in the main European countries. We can single out the following Spanish authors who were direct followers of Vitoria or influenced by him: Domingo de Soto, Martin de Azpilcueta, Juan de Medina, Diego de Covarrubias, Cristóbal de Villalón, Luis de Alcalá, Saravia de la Calle, Domingo de Báñez, Tomás de Mercado, Francisco García, Luis de Molina, Miguel de Salón, Juan de Salas, Francisco Suárez, Juan de Lugo, and Antonio Escobar.

The School was particularly influential in Portugal, in the universities of Évora and especially Coimbra, where a significant role was played by Azpilcueta, Mercado, Molina, and a few Portuguese such as Fernão Rebelo and Pedro de Santarém. Throughout this period the Salamanca School had a significant number of disciples and has influenced many theologians and jurists. Their works were highly quoted and were subject to several editions in Spain as well as in other European countries. For example *De iustitiaetiure* (1553) by Soto ran to twenty-six editions in the sixteenth century, seventeen of them outside Spain.

Scholastic contributions to economic theory were some of the side effects of their musings on the spiritual salvation of human beings in all their activities, especially those related with dangerous trading activities completely divorced from the honorable, virtuous life in the countryside. Stress has been placed on the fact that the main contribution of these scholastics was related to a new way of thinking of the role of institutions in the international sphere. In fact, theologians changed the principles on which the Spanish colonization of Latin America was based, insomuch as they bravely defended Indian rights before the Emperor Charles V. They were also concerned about slavery and the slave trade used by the Portuguese to provide a labor force for American colonies.

If we limit ourselves strictly to economic issues, they studied currency exchange, the working of Castilian fairs – which in those times rather than interchanging goods, were the focus of the activity of international financiers – and the functioning of banks and lending. Precisely in dealing with fair pricing, usury, and taxes, they had the opportunity to develop their approaches on the theory of value and prices, the morphology of the market, property rights, monetary theory, and taxation. It is important to underline the fact that, although the scholastics were determined to condemn the illegality of all acts leading to the acquisition of "excessive" or superfluous wealth, these authors provided arguments for the legitimacy of new economic practices which, under a rigorous canon law could be condemned as sinful and usurious. In this sense, the verification of situations where *lucrum cessans et damnum emergens* (loss of profit and emerging damage) could occur represented a basic criterion for legitimizing certain economic activities. The substantial increase of mercantile operations – a result of maritime and commercial expansion on a worldwide scale – gave rise to a new ethical attitude which decriminalized and legitimized practices involving money exchange and other banking and insurance activities.

Among all these contributions, special emphasis should be given to the presentation of the quantity theory of money and the idea of purchasing power parity, already clearly explained by Martín Azpilcueta in his *Comentario Resolutivo de Cambios (Commentary and Solution on Exchange)* in 1556, a decade before Jean Bodin. By means of the quantity theory, they explained that a general rise in prices was not the result of traders' speculative activities, but rather was caused by an increase in the amount of precious metals circulating in Spain after the discovery of rich gold and silver mines in America. In his analysis of price variations between different market places in Spain and Europe, Azpilcueta also gave a clear description of an initial version of the theory of purchasing power parity, a theory associated in the twentieth century with the Swedish economist Gustav Cassel, which related exchange rates between two currencies to the evolution of internal price levels in the two economies.

Similarly, Azpilcueta's theory of value, which impinged on the concepts of utility and scarcity, had an influence on European economists as diverse as Davanzati, Galiani, and Beccaria in Italy, Condillac, Turgot, and Quesnay in France, Grotius and Lessiusin in Holland and Belgium, Pufendorf in Germany and the Scandinavian countries, and Locke, Law, Hutcheson, and Adam Smith in Great Britain. Thus, some present-day economists from the Austrian School consider their subjective theory of value as stemming from Spanish scholastics.

The *arbitristas* were contemporaries of the scholastics and busied themselves with practical matters, leaving moral concerns out of their considerations. In the eighteenth century, the definition of the term *arbitristas* did not only refer to consultants and practical men offering suggestions on how to improve the fiscal and tax systems. The term meant also to include all those who proposed solutions to the increasingly severe economic problems in Spain and Portugal.

They were writers with a clear political aim who, on some occasions, were parodied by literary figures of the time, such as Miguel de Cervantes, for offering chimerical solutions to deal with economic difficulties. Among the Spanish *arbitristas* with the most coherent views we may mention Luis de Ortiz, Martín González de Cellorigo, Lope de Deza, Sancho de Moncada, Miguel Caxa de Lereuela, Francisco Martínez de Mata, and Álvarez Osorio y Redín. They did not influence other European authors, except an occasional Portuguese, as in the case of Moncada's influence on Duarte Ribeiro de Macedo. In Portugal, apart from this author, who became famous for the advice he gave and the influence he exercised in designing and implementing policies for fostering the arts and manufactures in the last decades of the seventeenth century (with a strong Colbertian influence), it is worth mentioning the names of António Vieira and Manuel Severim de Faria, who wrote their most significant texts in the period after the end of the dynastic union with Spain (around 1640). Both writers show a concern regarding the economic and financial recovery of the country, while also stressing the importance of the political process of building a nation-state. Like the *arbitrista* literature they were included in, the Portuguese testimonies contributed to the strengthening of this dimension of economic thinking on resource allocation and management, which involved the designing of a political strategy.

The *arbitristas* dealt with several particular matters such as the alleged depopulation problem, the malfunctioning of the monetary system, low levels of agricultural productivity, the uncompetitive nature of some manufacturing sectors, and the inadequate trade policy which should have moved towards protectionism and even the banning of imports. Moncada for example argued that the Spanish Empire had sufficient raw materials and population allowing for self-sufficiency. Nevertheless, the main subject covered by them was that of the decline of both Iberian countries, which had been prosperous in the sixteenth century and were being left behind. They came to the conclusion that "barren countries" (bereft of natural resources, such as Holland) were prosperous through being "hard-working," whereas Castile and Portugal, with raw materials and precious metals in abundance but being "not very industrious," were poverty stricken. On the back of a large population and given that riches were not associated with precious metals, although they criticized the despoiling of such metals and their transfer to Europe, they proposed the promotion of productive activities. Where differences appeared was in the relevance assigned to each of the productive sectors.

In Spain, authors such as Ortiz and González de Cellorigo referred to productive activities in general, whilst others opted for agriculture (Deza) or cattle breeding (Caxa de Lereuela). Finally, the "Toledo group," headed by Moncada, faithfully believed in the capacity of manufactures to definitively recoup the wealth of Castile and Spain. A similar position was adopted in Portugal by Macedo. Contrary to the main currents of thought, Faria chose the importance of internal colonization processes to establish the population in agriculture, while Vieira valued the importance of merchant capital raised from the Jews expelled from Spain and Portugal by the Inquisition.

The eighteenth century

There were many intellectuals and politicians who, from different parts of Spain and Portugal set out their economic ideas in the eighteenth century, particularly in the second half, and there were also several institutions, such as scientific academies and economic societies of friends of the country, who took upon themselves the task of spreading the basic principles of the emerging economic science. In the case of Spain, the Society in the vanguard of creating a chair of political economy was the Real Sociedad Económica Aragonesa de Amigos del País in 1784. Economists were also aware of the relevant contributions by foreign authors, such as the

French (Forbonnais, Herbert, the physiocrats, and Necker), the British (the political arithmeticians and Smith), the Austrian and Prussian (the cameralist literature), or the Italian (Galiani and Genovesi), not to mention the legacy from the Iberian *arbitristas*.

The most representative economists, and those whose writings were translated into other languages, were the following three: a) Jerónimo de Uztáriz, whose *Theorica y Práctica de Comercio y Marina* (*Theory and Practice of Commerce and the Navy*, 1724) was translated into English by John Kippax (1751 and 1752), into French by Forbonnais (1753), into Italian (1793), and also into German (1753); b) Pedro Rodríguez de Campomanes, whose *Discurso sobre el Fomento de la Industria Popular* (*Discourse on the Encouragement of Industry for the People*, 1778) was translated into Portuguese (1778), German (1778), Dutch (1780 and 1790), Italian (1787), and Tagalog (1793); and c) Gaspar Melchor de Jovellanos, whose *Informe* (*Report on the Agrarian Act*, 1795) was translated into French (1806 and 1808), English (1809), Italian (1815), and German (1816). The French and English editions were summarized by renowned economists such as James Mill and McCulloch. We can add another name to this trio of economists, someone who is half way between the eighteenth and nineteenth centuries, Juan López de Peñalver. In his *Reflexiones Sobre la Variación del Precio de Trigo* (*Reflections on Price Variations in Wheat*, 1812) López de Peñalver used mathematics and thus can be considered as one of the European forerunners of its application to the study of economic issues.

The main subject of debate of these economists was the Agrarian Act, the promotion of manufacturing, fiscal reform, and trade liberalization, both domestic and colonial. This latter question was of great importance and had as its starting point the criticism of the colonial regime, which during the reign of the House of Austria was a monopoly characterized by the centralization of all trade in just one port, Seville, and by a system of fleets which organized the entry and exit of two fleets, one for New Spain and the other for *Tierra Firme*. King Philip V, the first Spanish Bourbon, implemented a few modifications on imperial policy, which did not substantially disturb the traditional colonial system. The Consulate and the *Casa de Contratación* (Trade Contracts Tribunal) were transferred to Cádiz in 1717. In 1720 the regulations for fleets and galleons was published permitting one-off registers (that is, private individuals who joined up with the fleet or who could travel when convenient). The fiscal system was modified through the introduction of the right to "palmeo" (measurement by palms) as a replacement for "almoja rifazgo" (tax on exported goods). Finally, companies were created with trade privileges which limited the Cádiz monopoly.

Although Bernardo de Ulloa, José Campillo, and Bernardo Ward dealt with the colonial question in the first half of the eighteenth century, the economist who proposed a more radical change in imperial policy was Campomanes, who made a synthesis of his thought in a work written in 1762 and entitled *Reflexiones sobre el Comercio Español a Indias* (*Reflections on Spanish Trade with the Indies*). Inspired and influenced by a diversity of authors such as Joseph Child, Charles Davenant, Nicolas Barbon, Gregory King, John Carey, Mirabeu, Montesquieu, and Ulloa, Campomanes proposed in his *Reflections* a new arrangement of the relations between Spain and her colonies. He proposed a return to the free trade practices that had prevailed before 1543. He attributed the misfortunes of the colonies not only to a one-port monopoly, but also to some restrictions such as the setting up of trade companies. The aim of colonial trade should not be to obtain precious metals or fiscal benefits, but rather, to stimulate the economic development of the metropolis.

To achieve these new objectives, Campomanes made the following proposals: abolition of the exclusive right bestowed on the port of Cádiz, abolition of the system of fleets and galleons, setting up of a fleet of separate ships, reduction in the tariff for Spanish products and abolition of palmeo and tonnage taxes, and withdrawal of the privileges granted to commercial companies.

Campomanes' proposal influenced the more liberalizing regulation passed between 1765 and 1789. There was one author, Valentín de Foronda, who in his *Cartasobre lo Quedebehacerun Príncipe Quetenga Colonias a Gran Distancia)* (*Letter on the Obligations of a Prince with Far-Off Colonies*), written in 1800 and published in 1803, proposed the possibility of selling the Spanish colonies in America.

Eighteenth-century Spanish economists were aware of the writings coming from Europe and some of these works were translated into Spanish, as mentioned above. However, a gap began to appear as regards the quality and relevance of national contributions, when compared with the outstanding innovations made in other European contexts, which proved crucial for the development of modern political economy. Spanish authors kept a rather low profile on theoretical issues, showing a noticeable preference for studies on applied economics.

The nineteenth century

As far as Portuguese late eighteenth-century economic literature is concerned, the main contributions came from the activity of the Lisbon Academy of Science, which published between 1789 and 1815 a five-volume set of *Memórias Económicas*. This collection of essays offered a rigorous inventory of the resources of the kingdom and its colonies (particularly Brazil), with an attempt being made to define the most suitable orientations for developing the different sectors of economic activity. Starting from concerns inherited from the *arbitrista* tradition, the Academy's writers revealed a fundamental difference when compared to the previous century's economic literature, namely a belief in the virtues of private economic agents, in the market's ability to make a contribution to wealth creation, without a permanent need for state intervention. Domingos Vandelli, Guimarães Moreira, Álvares de Silva, José António de Sá, and Bacelar Chichorro, were some of the writers who contributed proposals for reforms in the economic and fiscal structure of the *ancien régime* society, and showed their enthusiasm for development models which would be sensitive to individualistic *laissez-faire* economic ideas. In their proposals they were influenced by physiocratic, French-influenced economic literature, Spanish authors (Campomanes and Jovellanos), and Italians (Galiani and Genovesi). Similarly to what occurred in Spain, the cameralist tradition made its presence felt in Portugal. Nonetheless, a difference between experiences in spreading economic thought produced in other contexts is worthy of mention: in Portugal, there were a very small number of translations of significant texts by foreign writers.

Another direct influence on Portuguese authors was Adam Smith, either on topics relating to the circulation of paper money, or particularly on subjects related to the extension of the domestic market, the elimination of barriers to the free circulation of goods, the reduction of the tax burden, and the liberalization of overseas trade. D. Rodrigo de Sousa Coutinho, minister for Overseas Dominions and Finance, was a distinguished politician particularly open to Smith's message, who tried to apply the teachings of political economy, that new science of the legislator, to the management of public affairs.

But the writer who showed the greatest zeal in his unconditional support of Adam Smith's system of political economy was José da Silva Lisboa, an author of Brazilian origin responsible for introducing the liberal economic language into the reform of colonial administration. His son translated the *Wealth of Nations*, which was published in Rio de Janeiro in 1811–12, and thanks to this type of influence it was possible to legitimize the process of economic autonomy of Brazil which would lead to its political independence in 1822. José da Silva Lisboa deserves outstanding mention for the theoretical polemic he carried on against Rodrigues de Brito, on the theoretical and doctrinal merits of the physiocrats and Adam Smith. In the books they published between 1803 and 1805, these two writers showed the importance of a public debate on questions of political economy, insofar as it is a basis for decisions and guidance for a country's economic development. Furthermore, they also showed some skill in making analyses, and engaging in profound debate on questions related to the theory of value and prices.

During the nineteenth century, in both Spain and Portugal, political economy and public finance were two disciplines which attracted interest and consideration in the public sphere. This was due to the process of institutionalization of their teaching in schools of commerce, technical schools and Law faculties. In the case of Spain, from 1807 onwards, when political economy was incorporated into university studies, there was a consolidation of economic studies which gave rise to the appearance from mid-century onwards of the subjects of political economy and public finance in the curriculum of all Law faculties. There was also a noteworthy effort from other non-university institutions in the diffusion of economic teaching, from the *Sociedad Librede Economía Política* (1856) and the *Real Academia de Ciencias Morales y Políticas* (1857), to *La Asociaciónpara la Reforma de Aranceles de Aduanas* (Association for Reform of Customs Tariffs, 1859), and also the consulates and boards of trade. To all of these we must add the numerous manuals published for the teaching of these disciplines, translations, and the work carried out by the press. In spite of all this, Spaniards were not noted for making relevant contributions on theoretical ground. In fact, the focus on production of economic theory was to be found in other countries.

In the Portuguese case, an identical process of institutionalization of economic theory could be observed, either through the creation of the first course in the Faculty of Law of the University of Coimbra in 1834, or even by creating political economy courses in the Trade Associations of Porto (1837) and Lisbon (1838). The manuals produced by Manuel de Almeida, José Ferreira Borges, António Oliveira Marreca, Agostinho Albano da Silveira Pinto, and Adrião Forjaz de Sampaio clearly show the capacity for spreading the basic principles of a science which could be shown as benefiting the modernization of Portuguese society. Beyond the precociousness of this process of institutionalization by means of teaching, it should be noted that the question began to occupy the attention of public authority in the Liberal Constituent Cortes of 1821–2, in which there was a specific discussion concerning the relevance of studying political economy for the civil training of state officials.

The principal classical economists received a very mixed reception in Spain and Portugal. The thoughts of classical French economists such as Say or Bastiat made a deeper impression than that of the British. Therefore Smith was more frequently read by the end of the eighteenth century and up to 1812, than in the nineteenth century. Ricardo was published in an incomplete translation of the third edition of his *Principles of Political Economy and Taxation* between 1848 and 1850. No edition of J.S. Mill's *Principles of Political Economy* appeared. Nor were there good editions of Marx's work before the last third of the twentieth century. On the other hand, much stress was made on applying the ideas of the philosopher Karl Krause to the economy, a task that did not contribute to economists improving the level of their arguments.

Furthermore, at the end of the nineteenth century, more confusion came about regarding the reception of different currents of thought originating in Germany, such as the Historical School, protectionism, the pragmatic interventionism of Otto von Bismarck, and *Katheder-socialism*. Marginalist economists, who were beginning to be quoted in Spain in the last third of the nineteenth century, did not establish themselves in monographs and manuals of the period. The low analytical level of Spanish, nineteenth-century economists can be judged in the arguments used in one of the main debates in which most of them took part, between proponents of free exchange rates and protectionists. The former were incapable of explaining clearly the theory of comparative advantage, and the latter were more influenced by private interests in preparing the tariffs than by economic ideas.

Nevertheless, we can single out some economists who played an important role in forming the economic ideas and debates of the nineteenth century over agrarian reform, trade policy, and tax and monetary reforms. Initially we should mention two economists from the first half of the century, firstly José Canga Argüelles. Outstanding among his works is the *Diccionario de Hacienda (Public Finance Dictionary)* published in 1826–7 during his exile in London. Secondly Álvaro Flórez Estrada, who published his *Curso de Economía Política* also in London in 1828, a manual clearly influenced by Ricardo, McCulloch, James Mill, Say, Storch, Sismondi, Richard Jones, Jovellanos, and Canga Argüelles. Then there was the Economist school, which was influential in the 1860s and to a lesser extent from 1870 onwards. The main members of this school were Luis María Pastor, Manuel Colmeiro, Laureano Figuerola, Gabriel Rodríguez, José Echegaray, and Segismundo Moret. They all defended free exchange rates, control of public spending, balanced budgets, free establishment of banking institutions, and the unrestricted functioning of markets. Among their main influences are economists from the classical school of political economy, but particularly Richard Cobden, Say, and Bastiat. Finally, though there is a consensus opinion that in the second half of the nineteenth century the quality of debate declined until the early decades of the twentieth, authors of the quality of Raimundo Fernández Villaverde, who took part in interesting public debates, should not be ignored. The most relevant debates were on tax reform and on monetary reform, the gold standard and the creation of the Latin Monetary Union.

Resistance to the faithful adoption of classical political economy was even more visible in the Portuguese case. No translation was produced of any of the works of the principal writers who contributed to the creation of the canon of this school of economic thought (Malthus, Say, Ricardo, Mill, and Marx). The Portuguese writer who was most familiar with the fundamental works of political economy was Francisco Solano Constâncio, who lived in exile in Paris till the beginning of the 1820s. He was responsible for the translation of the *Principles* of Malthus and Ricardo from English to French. However, in the texts he authored he distanced himself from supposedly universal principles of political economy, considering that they did not give sufficient importance to national motivations for economic development, using a similar argument to that used in American protectionist literature (Carey and Hamilton), and very close to that which would be adopted by List in Germany. Another aspect which attracted Constâncio's critical attention was that classical economists paid little attention to the 'evil' social consequences of economic growth, coming close to the critique elaborated by Sismondi.

Despite the protectionist inclination prevailing in debates on questions of economic policy throughout the second half of the nineteenth century in Portugal, the French liberal school had some impact, particularly in the ideological field. Cláudio Adriano da Costa and Carlos Morato Roma – the latter being the author of an interesting project for the creation of a single European currency at the beginning of the 1860s – deserve a reference for the exceptional quality of their contributions. But the characteristic element which was so noticeable in Portuguese economic literature in the second half of the nineteenth and early decades of the twentieth century is the lack of any theoretical developments anchored in orientations which were known in neoclassical economics following the marginalist revolution and later consolidated in the Marshallian tradition.

In fact, Portuguese authors had limited themselves for a long time to polemics on subjects of economic policy and the organization of sectors of activity, or to producing eclectic, not very up-to-date manuals of descriptive teaching on basic economic notions. The first signs of following modern thought only became visible after 1949, when an important reform of higher education took place in the fields of economics and finance. At this level the contributions of neoclassical microeconomics were assimilated, accompanied by a new macroeconomic vision inspired by Keynes. In an atmosphere very marked by corporatist ideology and by the suspicion that free competition would not help to bring about the much-desired social harmony, the Keynesian appeal for greater state intervention was a boon to the aims of a group of economists and engineers who in Portugal, after the Second World War, tried to challenge the conditions and instruments to promote economic and social growth.

The twentieth century

In Spain, the early decades of the twentieth century saw an incipient renovation of economic studies carried out by Antonio Flores de Lemus, José María Zumalacárregui, and Francisco Bernis. The disciples of the first two were the contributors to the creation of the Faculty of Political and Economic Sciences in Madrid in 1943, the first of its kind in Spain. This first breakthrough of the 1940s led to a total of 74 centers for the study of Economic and Business Sciences being in existence at the end of the century. The spread of economics was also due to the creation of non-university institutions such as the Servicio de Estudios of the Banco de España (1930), the Instituto de Estudios Políticos (1939), the Instituto de Economía Sancho de Moncada (1949), or the Instituto de Estudios Fiscales (1960). Of similar importance was the effort put in by both scholarly journals in economics and the specialized media on economic affairs.

The reception given to foreign economists in the first half of the century was fluid, ranging from marginalism (Stackelberg taught in the above-mentioned Madrid faculty created in 1943) to Keynesianism, which was not always well received by highly qualified economists such as Manuel de Torres or Luis Ángel Rojo. In the second half of the twentieth century – when the economy was emerging from a long period in which it was closed to the outside, from 1890 till the 1940s – there was an important flow of economic ideas imported from the United States, with the adoption of a great variety of schools of thought with different ideologies and methodological approaches. These ranged from the institutionalists to the Chicago and Austrian schools, from Keynesianism and neo-Keynesianism to the new classical macroeconomics, from mathematical economics to new approaches to human behavior, and from public choice theory to the political economy of regulation.

Spanish economists were also receptive to the ideas put forward by other European economists, mainly from Germany (Röpke and the members of the Freiburg School such as Eucken), France (Perroux and planning economists), and Italy (Einaudi), as well as from Latin America (Raul Prebisch, Celso Furtado, and the economists associated to the Economic Commission for Latin America). This importation of theories, doctrines, and policy orientations was produced by means of translations, the reading of works in the original language, a brain drain to foreign universities, and the presence of some of the most important foreign economists in Spain. An identical movement of transmission and adaptation of ideas and recommendations in political economy occurred in Portugal throughout this period.

All the facts mentioned gave rise to a consolidation of economics in the second half of the twentieth century, both in Spain and Portugal, not only as a university discipline but also as a profession. Economists gave proof of their professional expertise by participating in the integration and assimilation processes undertaken by the Spanish and Portuguese economies, from the early stages of the opening up and reform of institutions at the end of the 1950s to the formal entry into the European Union in 1986.

After integration the most important challenge for Portuguese and Spanish economists has been the adherence of both countries to the European Monetary System and their permanence in the Euro. Before 2002 opinion leaders were able to persuade the public sphere on the advantages of belonging and accepting the European rules and targets on inflation, public debt, and budget deficit. However, in the aftermath of the 2008 crisis, it has been difficult to explain the rigorous austerity and recession measures imposed by the European Union, the European Central Bank, and the International Monetary Fund, especially in the case of Portugal. The economists' inability to explain the causes of the crisis and the measures to be implemented to overcome it contributed to the negative reputation of those who were supposed to provide answers and solutions. It is nevertheless clear that the economics profession is not to be blamed for the consequences of the Great Recession initiated in 2008. In this sense, the process of diffusion and assimilation of economic theories and practices has been sustainable enough to produce a general framework of understanding and a common language and precepts guiding discussion and decision making in international contexts.

References

Almodovar, António, and Cardoso, José Luís (1998). *A History of Portuguese Economic Thought*. London and New York: Routledge.

Cardoso, José Luís (2001). *Dicionário Histórico de Economistas Portugueses*. Lisboa: Temas e Debates.

Fuentes Quintana, Enrique (dir.) (1999–2004). *Economía y Economistas Españoles*, 9 tomos. Barcelona: FUNCAS, Círculo de Lectores-Galaxia Gutenberg.

Grice-Hutchison, Marjorie (1978). *Early Economic Thought in Spain, 1177–1740*. London: Allen and Unwin.

Perdices de Blas, Luis, and Reeder, John (2003). *Diccionario de Pensamiento Económico en España (1500–2000)*. Madrid: Editorial Síntesis-Fundación ICO.

8

Germany

From sciences of state to modern economics

Erik Grimmer-Solem

A good starting point for understanding the historical contours of German economic thought is the fact that Germany as a modern nation-state only came into being in 1871, so that much of the history of the German lands was defined by disunity and particularism. This created a variety of universities and encouraged a plurality of approaches to the discipline of economics. Until 1866 Austria, along with Prussia, was one of the most important influences upon the other German states and so must be considered in any survey of the cultural, administrative, and business traditions that shaped German economics.

In the eighteenth century German economics grew out of *Staatskunst* (statecraft) into *Staatswirtschaft* (state economy), an administrative discipline that had evolved alongside the needs of enlightened absolutist rulers, the political order that defined the courts of Austria, Prussia and many of the lesser German states following the catastrophe of the Thirty Years War (1618–48). As such, it was a field preoccupied with the practical administrative needs of the court, namely management of royal domain lands, forests, mines, and military and luxury industries, as well as royal finances. While many of the German states were open to new economic ideas coming from the French and Scottish Enlightenments, notably the ideas of Du Pont, Mirabeau, Quesnay, Turgot, and especially Adam Smith, the political, social, and economic conditions in Germany (estate order, guilds, remnants of serfdom) made their application difficult until the Napoleonic invasions and the modernizing reforms they forced on the German states, most prominently the Stein-Hardenberg reforms in Prussia after 1807.

Even as Adam Smith's ideas began to inform German understandings of the economy as an autonomous component of civil society, the administrative legacy of cameralistic *Staatswirtschaft* remained prominent in modern German conceptions of economics. As such the economy, even an ostensibly free economy, was conceived as something ordered by law and institutions and requiring administrative guidance. Inspired by Smithian ideas, Prussian civil servant reformers introduced a liberalization of customs and tolls (1818) and then the German Customs Union (1834),which enabled a national division of labor among the German states for the first time and which would later spur the rapid industrial development of Germany in the 1850s and 1860s.

Under Prussian leadership the North German Confederation (1867–71) and German Empire (1871–1918) introduced freedom of navigation on inland waterways, a modern commercial code, uniform weights and measures, a common currency, and a central bank. Even before unification, various competing German states had developed outstanding systems of public education that assured near universal literacy by the early nineteenth century, and individual states invested heavily in systems of vocational, technical, and higher education, including major polytechnic schools and research universities that conducted cutting-edge applied and theoretical research in the natural sciences. The state also played a key role in developing and administering the system of universal health, accident, and old-age insurance pioneered in Germany in the 1880s.

Beyond the important role of state and federal governments, other key institutions in the German economy have been universal banks, employers' organizations, and trade unions. Germany's rapid industrial development in coal, iron, steel, railroads, machinery, chemicals, and electrical equipment meant that banking institutions emerged which combined the functions of commercial and investment banks in order to pool deposits into direct lines of credit and raise the needed investment capital by underwriting bond and stock issuance for very heavy investments in plant and machinery. The so-called "D-banks" (large joint-stock banks so named because they happened to have names starting with the letter D: Darmstädter Bank, Deutsche Bank, Disconto-Gesellschaft, and Dresdner Bank) not only lent directly to firms but also often became their major shareholders and subsequently took an unusually direct role in advising business strategy and guiding long-term investments.

German employers, who faced a literate, organized, and increasingly social democratic workforce, were quick to organize themselves into employers' organizations (*Arbeitgeberverbände*) which negotiated with organized labor to avoid disruptive striking and lobbied their interests to government. A similar process of interest organization and advocacy also emerged in the agricultural and handicrafts sectors. Cartels and syndicates in such industries as iron, coal, and chemicals became a notable feature of this uniquely German form of "organized capitalism," a development often encouraged by the close ties between banks and firms. Partly to escape the strictures of cartels and partly to gain the scale economies needed in certain industries to reduce unit costs, many German firms developed a strong export orientation, often in highly specialized niches where they would come to hold monopolies or near monopolies, a strategy that defines the German *Mittelstand*, the medium-sized, family-owned firms that form the backbone of the German economy to this day.

Even with such powerful institutions as stabilizers in the German economy, economic policy was highly contentious and saw frequent breakdowns in the twentieth century. The Revolution of 1918 and the Weimar Republic gave organized labor a prominent political role, a time which also witnessed catastrophic hyperinflation and an expanded welfare state. This sparked a backlash from employers and conservative politicians during the Great Depression that enabled the rise to power of the Nazis. Hitler came to power at a time of ruinous deflation and unprecedented mass unemployment in 1933. He violently "coordinated" organized labor and then mobilized Germany's prodigious industrial resources to rearm and launch a war for *Lebensraum* (living space) in the east, which Hitler and the Nazis imagined would solve Germany's social and economic problems once and for all. Instead, total war and genocide followed, culminating in the devastation of much of Germany and Europe.

With the birth of the Federal Republic in 1949, a more durable economic policy consensus formed which managed to balance the legitimate claims of both organized labor and employers, a consensus that enabled a stable currency and internationally competitive firms while also sustaining heavy investment in infrastructure, education, housing, and social services. This mix of policies, commonly referred to as *soziale Marktwirtschaft* (social market economy), has not always been uncontested, but it has been flexible enough to survive stagflation in the 1970s and the challenges of German reunification in the 1990s. Remarkably, most of the key institutional features of German capitalism (with the exception of cartels) remain in place in reunified Germany today, despite two destructive world wars and Cold War division in the twentieth century. Heavy investment in R&D, high levels of technical skill, and a strong orientation toward quality remain defining features of the modern German industrial economy. That said, the traditional focus on investment (producer) goods means that the consumer economy, the service sector and newer industries like IT have been somewhat starved of investment and lag behind in competitiveness. Consumer credit is likewise remarkably underdeveloped in Germany, and labor participation rates for women are comparatively low. With barriers to entry in most sectors high due to trade and employers' organizations, rather rigid systems of vocational and professional certification, and the dominant position of powerful banks, not much of a tradition of active entrepreneurship and venture capitalism has yet developed in Germany. Most employment in the German private sector today is in older firms pursuing long-term investments in established product markets.

The development of economic ideas

The first German university chairs in cameralism were created at Halle and Frankfurt an der Oder in 1727, and by the late eighteenth century nearly every German and Austrian university had followed suit. Cameralism evolved into a systematic administrative discipline that came to be called *Staatswirtschaft* through the lecturing and textbooks of J.H.G. von Justi and Joseph von Sonnenfels. Von Sonnenfels, who was active in Vienna and well-informed of the work of the French Physiocrats, defined *Staatswirtschaft* in his *Grundsätze der Polizey, Handlung und Finanz* (1787) as a science of government comprising three main fields: *Polizeiwissenschaft* (police science, concerned with maintaining moral order and internal security); *Handlungswissenschaft* (the science of economic action, focused on raising agricultural and labor productivity); and *Finanzwissenschaft* (financial science, devoted to raising royal revenues). The aim of *Staatswirtschaft* was fulfilling human need, and the model at its core was the Aristotelean householder, with the royal subjects seen as children in an extended household who required the active management and policing of royal administrators. A large, submissive and flourishing agricultural population that could be taxed effectively was perhaps the single most important metric of successful *Staatswirtschaft*.

With the disruptions of the French Revolution and French invasions of the Holy Roman Empire, profound changes were imposed upon the German lands which made much of *Staatswirtschaft* obsolete. The single most influential economic thinker in the German states in the first two decades of the nineteenth century was Adam Smith, and his idea of an unfettered division of labor came to be understood as *Nationalökonomie* (national economy) and/or *Volkswirtschaft* (people's economy), both of which were synonymous with the English term "political economy" in the classical sense. Nevertheless, many aspects of the administrative heritage of *Staatswirtschaft* were retained and combined with *Nationalökonomie* to form the new umbrella discipline of *Staatswissenschaften* (sciences of state). This combined classical political economy with finance, money and banking, economic administration, technology, and many fields of law and became conventional in the discipline through Karl Heinrich Rau's influential textbook, *Lehrbuch der Politischen Oekonomie* (1826–37).

The backlash against French occupation, the upheavals of the Napoleonic wars, and the anxieties over ongoing German disunity after 1815 did fuel considerable nationalist criticism of the cosmopolitan orientation of Adam Smith's political economy, most prominently in Friedrich List's *Nationale System der Politischen Oekonomie* (1841). However the analytical basis of List's critique of Smith drew almost exclusively on American sources that List had studied over his many years in the United States, notably Alexander Hamilton. The growth of German nationalism in the first half of the ninteenth century was also marked by an intense interest in the national past which culminated in the formation of the modern discipline of history in Germany (Leopold von Ranke). This "historicism" would have a profound impact on both the study of law (Friedrich von Savigny and Karl Eichhorn) and the field of political economy for the remainder of the nineteenth century, finding its way into the curriculum of *Staatswissenschaften* through the most influential textbook of the time, Wilhelm Roscher's *System der Volkswirtschaft* (1854).

It is customary to distinguish between an "older" and "younger" German historical school of political economy, the older of which included – in addition to its leading figure, Wilhelm Roscher – Bruno Hildebrand and Karl Knies. While Roscher was inspired by the application of historical method to law, in his work history was used merely to illustrate classical economic theory and not as a new economic method per se. Of the three, only Hildebrand worked with what could accurately be described as a historical method. He went so far as to deny natural economic laws and aimed to turn political economy into discipline devoted to understanding the process of economic development. Beyond programmatic statements, however, this never took on any concrete form.

In the 1850s and 1860s the impulse for more statistical work in political economy came from the various statistical bureaus in German states, most notably those in Saxony and Prussia. The director of the Royal Saxon Statistical Bureau, Ernst Engel, made one of the major discoveries in economics (1857) by observing that the share of the household budget spent on food rose as household income fell. Conversely, as household income rose, a smaller relative share of the household budget was spent on food, even as expenditure on food increased in absolute terms. This relationship, which became known as Engel's Law, was one of the first functional economic relationships ever discovered using quantitative techniques, and as such, its discovery marks the beginnings of econometrics (Engel's Law and Engel curves are today a fundamental part of microeconomic price theory).

Major advances in laboratory science at the time in numerous fields such as physics (Hermann Helmholtz), chemistry (Justus Liebig), and medicine (Rudolf Virchow), as well as the Darwinian revolution unfolding in biology, lent great credibility to empiricism in economics, for which history and statistics seemed the most closely approximate tools. Indeed, so powerful were these natural scientific models that an empirical, descriptive, and statistical orientation tied closely to practice (i.e. policy) would predominate in all of German *Staatswissenschaften* for the next 50 years, of which the "younger" historical school was but one, if the most influential, strand.

The "younger" historical school went further in rejecting the universal claims of classical political economy to also criticize its inadequate psychological foundations and misuse of abstract deduction. They also criticized what they saw as the role of classical political economy as a dogmatic bulwark of *laissez-faire* capitalism and thus the policy status quo, which in light of the grave tensions emerging in Germany as a consequence of rapid industrialization, urbanization, and the rise of organized labor and socialism (the "social question"), they held to be untenable. Their call to action resulted in the creation of the Verein für Socialpolitik (Association for Social Policy, founded 1873) and a mobilizing text of sorts of the "younger" historical school and their commitment to reform was Gustav Schmoller's *Übereinig Grundfragen des Rechts und der Volkswirtschaft* (1875). In other words, the "younger" historical school was motivated as much by the desire for social reform as a reform of political economy. Beyond their commitment to reform, most of the "younger" historical school's research energy was devoted to detailed studies of economic history which highlighted the role of values, conventions, laws, and institutions in shaping economic processes. The most prominent figures associated with this group beyond

Gustav Schmoller were Lujo Brentano, Karl Bücher, Georg Friedrich Knapp, and Werner Sombart. Sombart was notable for his receptiveness to Marxism, one of the very few economists of any influence in an academic position with such an interest in Germany before 1918.

The priority given to statistics and economic history by members of the historical school over the development of general economic theory was not without criticism. One of the sharpest of these was launched by the Austrian economist Carl Menger in his *Untersuchungenüber die Methode der Socialwissenschaften* (1883). While the resulting dispute between Menger and Schmoller was ostensibly over the best economic methodology, strong personal animosities overshadowed the dispute from the very beginning and drew artificial lines between empirical-statistical research and analytical-deductive theoretical work which proved to be sterile and counterproductive over the longer term. Schmoller's faith in a grand theoretical synthesis emerging inductively from economic history proved to be as misplaced as Menger's insistence that analytical-deductive theorizing could be permanently insulated from empirical measurement and testing. The dispute between them became as hostile as it was also because it was situated in then current political questions about the desirability and possibility of state intervention in the economy, which Schmoller advocated and Menger rejected.

While the historical school remained very influential in Germany up until the First World War, it should not be overlooked that many other prominent German economists of the nineteenth century continued to embrace deductive theorizing and worked to refine classical political economy, some of whom took it in directions which would anticipate twentieth century neoclassical economic theory. Economists who worked in this vein included Karl Heinrich Rau, Hermann Heinrich Gossen, Friedrich Hermann, Karl Knies, and H.K.E. von Mangoldt. Carl Menger's work in developing a neoclassical theory of value based on subjective valuation (marginalism) introduced in his *Grundsätze der Volkswirtschaftslehre* (1871) was strongly indebted to many of these predecessors, most notably Rau, Hermann, and Mangoldt. Likewise, it has been shown that Heinrich Gossen anticipated William Stanley Jevons' work in this direction in Britain by many years. Other German economists who continued to work using classical and neoclassical theory before the First World War included Albert Schäffle, Adolph Wagner, Johannes Conrad, and Heinrich Dietzel, though in their work the empirical and encyclopedic orientation toward political economy typical of this time can certainly also be seen. Two important milestones in the work of organizing and systematizing economic knowledge were the *Handwörterbuch der Staatswissenschaften* (8 vols. 3rd edn. 1910) and the *Grundriss der Sozialökonomik* (9 vols. 1914–30).

Another major strand of German economic thought not tied to the historical school is *Raumwirtschaft* (the economics of space). Heinrich von Thünen's path-breaking work *Der Isolierte Staat* (1842–63) laid the foundation for a rigorous formalized (mathematical) treatment of the economics of space using Ricardian rent and price theory in his analysis of the land use patterns of a hypothetical town and its surrounding lands. The cultivation patterns that he surmised from his abstracted "isolated state" were the result of differential land rents that obtained on soil of uniform fertility at varying distances from a central town as determined by demand for various food products, the intensity of cultivation, the barter ratios of the respective products, and transportation costs. Thünen's work was built upon by Roscher and Schäffle and then developed further by Wilhelm Launhardt and Alfred Weber, who focused on the practical and theoretical geometry of optimally locating industrial plant and transport routes (location theory). Weber was himself one of the first to analyze economies of agglomeration.

Following Germany's defeat in the First World War and the experience of catastrophic hyperinflation in 1923, much (though not always deserved) blame was placed on members of the "younger" historical school for having abandoned economic theory, this allegedly having led to economic mismanagement and leaving Germans ill-equipped to face the profound economic dislocations and challenges of the postwar period. In any case, the 1920s were a time when German economics as a discipline became self-consciously more international and when methodologies were much in flux. One example of this was the success of new foreign textbooks, notably Gustav Cassel's *Theoretische Sozialökonomie* (1918), which by 1932 had gone through no fewer than five German editions. As another indicator, the Austrian theorist Joseph Schumpeter was called to a prominent chair in economics at the prestigious University of Bonn in 1925 and spearheaded important reforms in teaching, methodology, and research focus, thus helping to bring Germany closer to the international mainstream.

Given the economic disorder of the 1920s and early 1930s, business cycles became one of the most active areas of research in the Weimar Republic. Particularly prominent in this field was Ernst Wagemann, who headed the Reich Statistical Office as well as the state-sponsored Institute for Business Cycle Research. Wagemann's significance to the history of economic thought is tied to his early development of an equation of exchange that amounted to a circular flow of aggregate economic activity in which the value of production equaled production costs and profit, which in turn was equivalent to total national income. In other words, there are strong indications that Wagemann developed the rudiments of national income accounting in Germany and must be counted alongside Keynes as one of the fathers of macroeconomics. German location theory and the economics of space also developed rapidly after the First World War and began to exercise greater influence on German urban and regional planning during the Weimar Republic and under National Socialism. Of those working in this area during this time was the economic geographer Walter Christaller, who developed what would become his influential "central place theory" to explain the economic hierarchies between towns and cities. This would later provide a template for Nazi plans to systematically resettle and develop annexed territories to the east.

In the 1930s/40s a group of German liberal economists around Walter Eucken, Franz Böhm, and Hans Grossmann-Doerth at the University of Freiburg were alarmed by the legacy of hyperinflation and the many other examples of arbitrary state intervention in the economy during the Weimar and Nazi years. They committed themselves instead to restoring a liberal free market system with a strong legal and institutional framework to sustain a competitive economic order and individual freedom. Though the influence of these "Ordo-Liberals" on postwar German academic economics was limited, they did influence Chancellor Konrad Andenauer and the first West German Economics Minister, Ludwig Erhard, who established an independent central bank and a hard currency, and engaged in limited countercyclical demand management via fiscal and monetary policy. West German economic policy and particularly the policies of the Bundesbank, were guided by these Ordo-Liberal ideas for much of the postwar era.

By contrast, American and British economic thinking dominated postwar German academic economics, which was defined in many ways by the reception of the Keynesian-neoclassical synthesis in macroeconomics, a steady formalization (mathematization) of microeconomic theory, and the introduction of probability theory in econometrics. The most important figure in the reception of Anglo-American economics and leading light in the discipline in the immediate postwar period was Erich Schneider, who was later made director of the influential Institut für Weltwirtschaft (Institute for the World Economy) at the University of Kiel in 1961. His textbook *Einführung in die Wirtschaftstheorie* (1947–9) was widely used to train postwar economists in West Germany.

For much of the postwar period, Kiel was the leading center of empirical research and "free-market" economic policy thought, with a particular focus on the analysis of structural change led for many years by Herbert Giersch, who succeeded Schneider in 1969. The University of

Bonn, by comparison, developed a reputation for working on the theoretical frontiers of microeconomics with very high levels of formalization. Reinhard Selten, who taught there for many years, shared the 1994 Nobel Prize for his contributions to game theory. Selten was also a pioneer in experimental economics. Two other important postwar centers of research emerged at the Universities of Mannheim and Cologne. Mannheim developed strengths in general equilibrium theory and time series analysis, while Cologne became an important center for empirical work tied closely to policy at its Institut für Wirtschaftspolitik (Institute for Economic Policy). This was due in no small measure to the strong ties that developed between its faculty and federal ministries in Bonn. The Verein für Socialpolitik continued to function as the professional body of academic economists, and most of the German economic journals that were founded in the ninteenth century continued publication in the postwar period.

Postwar German economic research was also shaped by the plethora of "acronym" research institutes funded by state and federal government agencies, employers' organizations, private firms, and foundations. Among the more influential of these was the Ifo-Institut in Munich, the ZEW in Mannheim, the IW in Cologne, the DIW in Berlin, and the HWWA in Hamburg. Much of this research focused on economic growth and the business cycle.

Recent advances and trends

The leading centers of economic research in Germany today continue to be Bonn, Cologne, Kiel, and Mannheim (not necessarily in that order), though very strong centers have also emerged in Berlin, Karlsruhe, and Munich. The Anglophone influences in the German economics profession today are pervasive, having created a thoroughly international discipline that extends to virtually all areas, whether it be pedagogy, methodology, research fields, language of publication, professional journals, or academic networks. Nearly all German economic journals today publish in English, and it is now common for young aspiring academic economists to have publications in the leading American journals. As a result, some of the distinctly "German" features of economic thinking, notably the historical and Ordo-Liberal strands, have been pushed to the margins. Yet in a country where powerful institutions have long played such a pre-dominant role in the economy and where heterodox economic thought has a long and proud tradition, it is not surprising that institutional, experimental, and evolutionary approaches have emerged in recent years. Evolutionary economics has been cultivated at the Max Planck Institute for Economics, founded in Jena in 1993. The Verein für Socialpolitik has also been open to these newer heterodox trends.

Since well before the Euro's formal introduction in 1999, prominent German economists were critics of the single currency for the distorting impact it would have on competitiveness within the EU due to the wide productivity, wage, and price disparities within Europe. More recently they have criticized the resulting accumulation of Euro-denominated debt in less competitive Eurozone countries and the Euro's inadequate institutional foundations, notably the lack of harmonized taxation and public spending to counterweigh these distorting effects. They have also pointed out that the Euro was and is a political project and that their expert advice was routinely ignored by the European and German politicians behind its creation. Due to the outsized influence of the German Bundesbank on the European System of Central Banks (ESCB), the monetary policy of the European Central Bank (ECB) has had a distinctly deflationary bias, something that has been criticized by many economists outside of Germany. Some prominent German economists, led by Hans-Werner Sinn of the Ifo-Institut, have recently panned proposals for a European banking union and been sharply critical of the ECB bond purchases undertaken to combat the Eurozone debt crisis which emerged after the "Great

Recession" of 2008–9. Others such as Kai Konrad of the Max Planck Institute for Tax Law and Public Finance have proposed that Germany leave the Euro in order to save the EU.

Dissemination and reception overseas

The most prominent overseas influence of German economics was probably in the United States. This was due to the fact that before American universities developed their own PhD programs in the late ninteenth century, it was very common for aspiring American academics to complete PhDs in Germany. Before the First World War many of the leading economists in the United States had studied in Germany, including John B. Clark, Richard T. Ely, Arthur T. Hadley, Simon S. Patten, E.R.A. Seligman, and Frank Taussig. That influence made itself felt less in the development of historical and institutional approaches to economics (though that was one observable trend), but more in the organization of the discipline around the American Economic Association (founded by Richard T. Ely in 1885), which was consciously modeled on the German Verein für Socialpolitik.

Likewise, the development of academic journals with peer review (*American Economic Review*, founded 1911), the seminar system of education at the graduate level, the insistence on original research in graduate training, and the founding of public and private economic research institutes like the Bureau of Labor Statistics (1884) and National Bureau of Economic Research (1920) were all unmistakably German features of American higher education in economics and economic research that continue to this day. This does not begin to exhaust the many other lines of contact that linked German economics with the emergence of newer disciplines like Business Administration, Sociology, Social Work and Public Administration in the United States, or the many reform initiatives of the Progressive Movement which involved American economists either trained or strongly influenced by German economic thought. Later in the mid twentieth century, the German economics of space and location theory would have an impact on the development and formalization of economic geography and regional science in the United States, such as in the work of Walter Isard.

It is perhaps less widely known that a parallel transfer of German ideas and institutions occurred in Meiji-era Japan, where German teachers and government advisers were active. Those who took up the study of economics in Germany in the Meiji era included Wadagaki Kenzō, Kanai Noboru, Kuwata Kumazō, Takano Iwasaburō, Seki Hajime, Fukuda Tokuzō, and Kawakami Hajime. It was this first cohort of Japanese students in Germany, and particularly Kanai, who introduced the term *shakaimondai* (from German *soziale frage*, "social question") to Japan through a number of publications, *Shakaimondai* (1892) among them. Kanai, Kuwata, Fukuda, and others would also form the Nihon shakaisei sakugakkai (Japanese Social Policy Association) in 1896, modeled on the German Verein für Socialpolitik. The range of Japanese scholarship influenced by German training in economics was wide and spanned the political spectrum, including the trade unionism and social democracy of Takano, the revisionist Marxism of Kawakami, and Takano and Kawakami's extensive early involvement with the Ohara Institute in systematic collection of social statistics. As in the United States, many German-trained Japanese economists were active as social reformers.

Bibliography

Balabkins, Nicholas W. *Not by Theory Alone . . .: The Economics of Gustav von Schmoller and Its Legacy to America.* Berlin: Duncker & Humblot, 1988.

Barkai, Avram. *Nazi Economics: Ideology, Theory and Policy.* Translated by Ruth Hadass-Vashnitz. New Haven and London: Yale, 1990.

Blaug, Mark, ed. *Gustav Schmoller (1838–1917) and Werner Sombart (1863–1941)*. Aldershot: Edward Elgar; Brookfield, VT: Ashgate, 1992.

Brentano, Lujo. *The Relation of Labor to the Law of To-Day*. Translated by Porter Sherman with an introduction by the translator. New York: G.P. Putnam's Sons, 1898.

Bücher, Karl. *Industrial Evolution*. Translated from the 3rd German edition by S. Morley Wickett. New York: A.M. Kelley, 1968.

Christaller, Walter. *Central Places in Southern Germany*. Translated from *Die Zentralen Orte in Süddeutschland* by Carlisle W. Baskin. Englewood Cliffs, NJ: Prentice-Hall, 1966.

Eucken, Walter. *The Foundations of Economics: History and Theory in the Analysis of Economic Reality*. Berlin & Heidelberg: Springer, 1992.

Grimmer-Solem, Erik. *The Rise of Historical Economics and Social Reform in Germany 1864–1894*. Oxford: Clarendon Press; New York: Oxford University Press, 2003.

Herbst, Jurgen. *The German Historical School in American Scholarship: A Study in the Transfer of Culture*. Ithaca, NY: Cornell University Press, 1965.

Knapp, Georg Friedrich. *The State Theory of Money*. Abridged edition translated by H.M. Lucas and J. Bonar. London: Macmillan, 1924.

Koslowski, Peter, ed. *The Theory of Capitalism in the German Economic Tradition: Historism, Ordo-Liberalism, Critical Theory, Solidarism*. Berlin: Springer, 2000.

Lindenfeld, David F. *The Practical Imagination: The German Sciences of State in the Nineteenth Century*. Chicago and London: University of Chicago Press, 1997.

List, Friedrich. *The National System of Political Economy*. New York: A.M. Kelly, 1966.

Menger, Carl. *Principles of Economics*. With an introduction by F.A. Hayek. New York: New York University Press, 1981.

Nicholls, Anthony James. *Freedom with Responsibility: The Social Market Economy in Germany, 1918–1963*. Oxford: Clarendon Press; New York: Oxford University Press, 1994.

Peacock, Alan, and Hans Willgerodt. *Germany's Social Market Economy: Origins and Evolution*. Basingstoke: Macmillan for the Trade Policy Research Centre, 1989.

Roscher, Wilhelm. *Principles of Political Economy*. 2 vols. From the 13th (1877) German edition. Chicago: Callaghan, 1877.

Schmoller, Gustav. "The Idea of Justice in Political Economy." *Annals of the American Academy of Political and Social Science* 4 (1894): 697–737.

Schmoller, Gustav. "The Historical Development of the Enterprise." In Frederic C. Lane and Jelle C. Riemersma, eds., *Enterprise and Secular Change: Readings in Economic History*, 3–24. Homewood, IL: R.D. Irwin, 1953.

Shionoya, Yuichi. *The Soul of the German Historical School: Methodological Essays on Schmoller, Weber, and Schumpeter*. New York: Springer, 2005.

Sombart, Werner. *Economic Life in the Modern Age*. Edited by Nico Stehr & Reiner Gudermann. New Brunswick, NJ: Transaction, 2001.

Tooze, J. Adam. *Statistics and the German State, 1900–1945: The Making of Modern Economic Knowledge*. Cambridge & New York: Cambridge University Press, 2001.

Tribe, Keith. *Governing Economy: The Reformation of German Economic Discourse, 1750–1840*. Cambridge & New York: Cambridge University Press, 1988.

von Thunen, Johann Heinrich. *Von Thünen's Isolated State. An English Edition of Der Isolierte Staat*. Edited by Peter Hall. Oxford: Pergamon, 1966.

Weber, Alfred, *Theory of the Location of Industries*. Translated by Carl J. Friedrich. Chicago: University of Chicago Press, 1957.

9

Sweden

Lars Magnusson

Sweden is a thinly populated country in northern Europe, out-stretched with a concentration in its southern part up to its capital Stockholm, situated by the lake Mälaren. Its political and economic history has largely been influenced by its position between Western and Eastern Europe, and its long coastline along the Baltic Sea. When Sweden was formed as a state in the eleventh century, it served as an exchange post – also as a producer of iron – in the lively trade with silver, slaves and goods between Western Europe and Imperial Persia. During the late Medieval period the main Swedish harbour cities became entangled within the great Hanseatic League, and its predominantly trade with iron was in the seventeenth century dominated by Dutch Merchants.

In the eighteenth century, the trade hegemony of Amsterdam was replaced by England as a main importer of iron and steel – which was also a major factor behind the first wave of industrial breakthrough in the 1850s, stimulated by an upsurge of demand for Swedish saw-mill as well as iron and steel products. Around the turn of the century (1900) industrialisation had become self generated, with the establishment of many new firms, especially in the mechanical engineering industry (Ericson, Alfa Laval, SKF, Atlas Copco). Also a growing domestic market helped to increase economic growth and income. However, still in the early 1920s agriculture was dominating in terms of employment. The 1930s saw the rise of the Swedish welfare state and growth rates peaked during the 1950s and 1960s, making Swedish per capita income one of the highest in the world. After a period of sluggish growth and structural problems following its major 1990s crisis, Sweden has emerged once again as one of the wealthiest countries in the world, with a high profile concerning welfare and high levels of employment.

Although being one of the oldest centralised states in Europe with a rather homogenous ethnical composition, its position between west and east, but also connecting to central Europe in the south, has been a strong influential factor concerning its intellectual development in general and perhaps economic thinking and writing in particular. For Sweden as well as elsewhere the word 'influence' must be used with caution. Certainly, Sweden was open to new ideas and modes of writing and thought originating from outside. However, such imports can not be regarded as immediate reflections but should rather be understood in terms of an active process of translation in which concepts and theories were transformed and changed according to the peculiar political, social and economic institutions formed through history. Hence influences came from different corners, and what might look like bleak imports from abroad should rather be looked upon as adaptations making sense in a specific institutional and cultural context.

The eighteenth century

The first printed works which might be defined as 'economics' only arrived in the early eighteenth century. Moreover, the first chair in the economic sciences was established at the University of Uppsala in 1741. Then a chair was created in Åbo (Turku) in 1747 and Lund in 1750. However, already during the seventeenth century books and tracts were published which might be recognised as examples of the so-called *Hausvater-literatur* widely spread in Europe at the time. For example, in Per Brahes' *Oeconomia eller Huuszholdsbook för ungt Adelsfolk* (1581) and Schering Rosenhanes' *Oeconomia* (1662), it is demonstrated how a large estate in the countryside should be managed in order not only to make a profit, but also to keep up its owner's social position and status: 'economics' at this time was defined in its Aristotelian meaning as an Art of Household Management.

The noblemen Brahes' and Rosenhanes' works were never printed but spread in hand-written copies in small circles of land-estate owners. The fate of not being printed was also alloted to a work of a different kind, certainly also influenced by Aristotle, a longish manual written by Johan Risingh (of which a fraction was published as *Itt Uthogh om Kiöphandelen eller Commercierene* in 1669). Instead of agriculture it dealt with foreign trade and commerce and how these should be regulated in order to gain the most income for the state. Risingh is mainly referred to as a cameralist, but his focus is less on taxation than on commerce and he seems close in his thinking to Johan Joakim Becher, the councillor of commerce in Vienna at the court of the Habsburgs. Risingh was a leading official in the Collegium of Commerce set up in 1651 to enhance Swedish foreign trade – not least in order to lift the dominance of the Dutch.

The first printed economic treatise in Sweden was Anders Bachmansson's (later Nordencrantz) *Arcana Oeconomiae* (1730). It followed on the same theme as Risingh: how to make Sweden richer through capture of foreign trade. In the 1720s Nordencrantz had been a Swedish *envoyé* posted in Lisbon where he had learned several foreign languages, but also read economic treatises and handbooks on commerce. He was well acknowledged by English writers such as Josuah Child and Charles Davenant, as well as with early French *economistes*. Besides propagating for more foreign trade on Swedish keel-boats, he also saw the benefits of a larger population through an improved *policey*, including the possibilities for foreigners (especially French Hugenots) to migrate to Sweden. The same messages can also be found in the textbook published in 1747 by the first professor in Uppsala (Anders Berch, *Inledningen til Almänna Hushåldningen*). In its structure the book closely followed the example of Justus Christoph Dithmar, appointed professor (1727) in Frankfurt an der Oder, in dividing the text into three parts, the sciences of *Kameral, Policey* and *Oeconomia*. However, in contrast to his German college he treated the sources and methods of taxation rather hastily. Instead he proposed means to increase the population, reforms to improve agriculture, the establishment of manufactories and the most beneficial methods to regulate trade, both domestic and foreign.

It has been customary to portray Bachmansson, Nordencrantz and Berch's works as 'mercantilist'. Although especially Berch refers to something he called the 'balance of trade', it is not so easy to discern what he meant by using the concept. No doubt, he was not making the mistake which Adam Smith accused the 'mercantile' or 'commercial' system of making: confusing wealth with gold and silver. Rather he defines the 'balance of trade' in the same manner as English writers at the end of the seventeenth and beginning of the eighteenth century, as a balance making it advantageous for a state to export value-added and import raw products. Such an emphasis on the need for more manufactories, greater employment of handicrafts and worked-up production is a general theme in much of the lively economic discussion in Sweden from around 1730 up to the end of the 'Age of Liberty' in 1772, with the *coup d'état* of Gustav III ending a long period of a high degree of freedom of the press. As with Berch, many of these texts were highly *dirigiste* in tone and particularly supported so-called manufacture policies that had been established in the 1730s, which included both subsidies to the sector as well a plethora of privileges.

In general, however, such policies led to financial speculation and inflation, which in the early 1760s ended with a big financial crash. Inflation soured into deflation and the economic writers turned away from *dirigisme*. This change was more apparent in public discussion than in the universities, where a mixture of commercial law, agricultural improvements and policies in order to increase the population still prevailed. But from outside, a number of writers appeared who were ready to condemn early regulations as violations against 'natural law'. In order to increase economic wealth and happiness, they argued, trade must be unregulated and more freedom of enterprise allowed. Only by pursuing its own interest and seeking the best opportunities can the whole prosper, argued for example the radical clergyman Anders Chydenius from the distant Ostrabothnia in Finland. While this perhaps does not make him – as has been proposed – a predecessor of Adam Smith, he was clearly inspired by the general discussion on natural rights which spread through Europe at the time. In a small pamphlet from 1765, *The National Gain*, he effectively argues for deregulation of (foreign) trade, with arguments based upon the notion of an invisible hand. This was not uncommon at the time and was not – of course – invented by Smith. But is perhaps remarkable for its time how Chydenius was able to use individual liberty as an argument for more economic freedom.

However, Chydenius' main inspiration did not stem directly from foreign sources but rather from someone he himself called his teacher, Anders Nordencrantz. Since we first encountered him in 1730, he had been nobled as Nordencrantz instead of Bachmansson, had made a career as an (eventually defaulted) iron mine owner, politician and a vitriolic writer condemning the old *dirigisme* in stark language. His intellectual influences came from reading British and French moral philosophers such as Mandeville, Hume and Helvetius. His main outlook was pessimistic: men were at heart 'knaves and rogues', he said. They were passioned, self-interested and likely to be corrupted when provided with power. Only republican rule, or even better a constitutional monarchy, could remedy the situation, thus assuring that 'individual vices' would turn into 'public benefits'. In his economics he – like Chydenius – was well-read on the arguments for a free grain trade, reforms in agriculture, more free trade, less privilege, etc. put forward by the French *economistes*, particularly Melon (whose works were translated several times during the Age of Liberty), but also Mirabeau and Turgot.

At least one Swedish economic writer at this period was clearly influenced by Quesnay and the Physiocratic School, the nobleman and politician Carl Fredrik Scheffer. However, in his own translation of some of the school's main texts, including Quesnay's *Maximes*, the majority of its most important exclusivities were left out. While agreeing that the *net produit* for a country could only be achieved in agriculture, he did not characterise the other sectors as sterile. Moreover according to his plan for new taxation, he made a plea for the old feudal estate owners and ignored the middle-farmers, the *fermiers*. Most likely this reflected the situation in the Swedish countryside during the middle of the eighteenth century, with the absence of 'capitalist' farmers.

The nineteenth century

After the *coup d'état* of Gustav III in 1772, there was a standstill in the public discussion on economic matters, mainly as an effect of wars, pestilences, famines, the assassination of Gustav III in 1792, the dethroning of his son Gustav IV from power in 1809 and eventually the loss of Finland the same year. Berch's increasingly dated textbook from 1747 continued to be read to Uppsala students, and was only replaced in 1829 by Professor Lars Georg Rabenius' *Lärobok i National–ekonomien*. His book was an eclectic mixture of teachings from classical political economy (particularly Say) and contemporary German cameralism. While naming the subject 'National Economy' from the German *Nationalökonomi* (still a term used in Sweden), he identified three different 'economic systems', the mercantile, agricultural and industrial system. The first two of them had been surpassed by history, he thought. The third one, the 'industrial' system, he connected with Adam Smith. According to Rabenius the base of this system was not individual liberty or the benefits of the invisible hand, but an insistence upon industry as the major generator of wealth. To support industry was thus a main task for the state and government.

This dominance of German *Nationalökonomi* mixed up with a little Say was not shaken until the middle of the nineteenth century. The main translator of Say's economics for a Swedish economic audience was the Professor of 'Economics and Botany' from 1812 to 1834, Carl Adolph Agardh in Lund. During the semester of 1821–2, he followed Say's lectures in Paris, and in his *Granskning af Statseconomiens Grundläror* (1829) he says that he adheres to Smith's views – but only to a certain degree. His caution lay in that Smith gives a much too passive role in economic matters for the state. Practical men and politicians have already abandoned this 'utopianism'. Moreover, Smith put too much emphasis on the role of labour for economic wealth and neglected the role of natural resources. In Sweden during the nineteenth century both Ricardo and Malthus were looked upon with suspicion. Their gloomy predictions concerning a declining marginal rate of rent on land and population increase were regarded as not adaptable (like with the USA) to a country with a small population and ample natural resources.

Perhaps not surprisingly the impetus for change came from outside academia. The liberal reform era of dismantling the old *dirigiste* economy started in the 1840s and included an abolition of guilds and freedom of enterprise. In the public discussion many of the old truths were questioned, but there is no evidence that they were particularly based upon economic theories (although the finance minister J.A. Gripenstedt had read Cobden and some French 'harmony' economists). The first academic writer of a more principal *laissez-faire* stance was G.K. Hamilton, who held a chair in National Economy and Administrative Law in Uppsala. In his *Om Politiska Ekonomins Utveckling och Begrepp* (1858) he seems clearly inspired by Frédéric Bastiat.

Another important *importeur* of French *laissez-faire* economics was Wolter Arnberg, a reader in national economy in Uppsala with his small booklet, *Om Arbetets och Bytets Frihet* (1864). Moreover, with the establishment of *Nationalekonomiska föreningen* in 1877 – with its mixture of academic economists and businessmen – the ground was laid for a more liberal economic discourse. However, there was a twist to Arnberg and the others' liberalism. De-regulation should not be carried too far, they argued. The visible hand of the state should help to introduce good regulations in order to promote economic growth. They proposed pragmatic liberalism, and one of the most vocal followers of Bastiat in Sweden, the finance minister Gripenstedt, did not hesitate to create a state-owned railway system in Sweden, as well as to save private banks from defaulting with public means.

The twentieth century

The breakthrough for neoclassical academic economics in Sweden is most often connected with three names: David Davidsson, Knut Wicksell and Gustav Cassel. When David Davidsson (1854–1942) in 1899 started *Ekonomisk Tidskrift*, this was the first step in the professionalisation of modern academic economics in Sweden. However, Davidsson was never a neo-classicist. In his early days he was clearly inspired by the German *Katheder-sozialisten* and even in old age he did not altogether abandon his fondness of the Marx/Ricardo labour theory of value. His chair was placed partly in the Faculty of Law and partly in the Faculty of Philosophy, and the bulk of his teaching was in economic law and the history of economic thought.

Seen in perspective the most outstanding of the threesome was most probably Knut Wicksell (1851–1926). He started his career as a radical student in Uppsala and became known as neo-Malthusian propagating for birth control. He was also a republican and critical of the established state church, which he mocked especially for its teachings on the immaculate conception – in an essay which sent him to jail for two months in 1909. After becoming a doctor he was refused the *Docent* title in Uppsala (probably because of his radicalism). Instead he moved to Lund where he received a chair in *Nationalekonomi och finansrätt* in 1901. Later on he was used as an expert by different Swedish governments on taxation and he sat in many parliamentary committees. While never being a socialist, his social reform views made him an ally of the emerging Social Democratic party.

While studying abroad in the early 1890s, Wicksell came into contact with the Austrian school and especially the works of Carl Menger and Eugen von Böhm-Bawerk. Already in 1892 he had published an essay *Kapitalzins und Arbeitslohn* where he presented a rough sketch of what later became his marginal productivity theory of distribution. It was followed up by a number of original works – influenced by the Austrians, but also including a number of innovative ideas on the use of marginal analysis in different fields of economics – such as *Uber Wert, Kapital under Rente* (1893, translated into English in 1954 as 'Value, Capital and Rent') and *Geldzins und Guterpreise* (1898, translated as 'Interest and Prices' in 1936). For his doctorate he dug deep into the theory and practice of fiscal policy, and in 1896 he received a doctorate *magna cum laude* for the first part of *Finanztheoretische Untersuchungen*. In Sweden his position as the leading economist of his time was established after the publication of the first part of his *Föreläsningar i Nationalekonomi* (1901, 1906), which for a long time became the standard academic textbook introducing the new neoclassical theories into the Swedish universities.

However, Wicksell was more than a compiler of new theories on marginal analysis. What has made him so attractive to later generations of neoclassicals, such as J.R. Hicks and others, was his mix of Austrian theories of production and capital with a Walrasian general equilibrium theory. His ability to synthesise especially showed in his paper *Om Inkomstfördelningen* (1901), in which he elegantly presented his version of the marginal cost theory later developed by Cobb and Douglas, which remained standard for many years to come. However, in Sweden he became most known for his analysis of what he called 'natural rent' (where no inflation occurred), where the rent of money equalised the interest on capital. His contribution here paved the way for what some decades later would become known as 'the Stockholm school' with its emphasis on disequilibrium and the impact of prices.

The third of this first wave of new professional economists, Gustav Cassel (1864–1944) has remained a controversial figure. Receiving a chair in Stockholm 1904 – after a passing flirt with the Historical School and social reform – he became an enigmatic Walrasian. However, what was problematic was that he was eager to emphasise that his version of general equilibrium theory was the original one, rather than Walras's. Later generations have been less convinced, or for that matter that his *magnum opus*, *Teoretisk Socialekonomi* (1914) was as innovative as Cassel thought it to be. Outside Sweden, after the First World War he became something like an international monetary expert travelling to different countries in order to give advice on how to adapt to the reintroduction of the Gold standard, as well as making vocal his ideas within the international conference on monetary stabilisation in Genoa in 1922.

The birthplace of the so-called Stockholm school of economics has been located to a meeting with the Stockholm-based *Nationalekonomiska klubben* in 1928, where a number of young Turks of the younger generation of economists – including Gunnar Myrdal (1898–1987), Erik Lindahl and Dag Hammarskjöld (who later became Secretary general of the United Nations) – aggressively attacked the older generation, particularly Cassel, Sven Brisman and Eli Heckscher (1879–1952). Heckscher was at heart an economic historian, but together with Bertil Ohlin (1899–1979) he had formulated the so-called Heckscher-Ohlin theorem of comparative advantage in 1919. Although Ohlin was not present at the meeting, he surely also belonged to this group.

Partly inspired by the 'new economics' stemming from J.M. Keynes, but more fundamentally from their reading of Wicksell's theories on the 'natural rate of rent', this group of young economists started out from the assumption that the older generation's faith in the inevitability of general equilibrium in the long run was a false start. Especially in Myrdal's dissertation, *Prisbildningsproblemet och Föränderligheten* (1927), its message was formulated: that the old micro-based and static theories had little to say about such phenomena as slumps, crises and mass unemployment. In his dissertation Myrdal especially discussed the role of expectations and the dynamics between *ex ante* and *ex post*. It was not self-evident that an economy, having fallen into problems, would automatically readjust itself and reach equilibrium. Taking off where Wicksell had ended with his discussion on cumulative disruption over time, Myrdal, Ohlin, Hammarskjöld and others developed an analysis of the business cycle which, in contrast to Keynes' *General Theory*, was of a dynamic kind. Perhaps Erik Lundberg in his *Studies in the Theory of Economic Expansion* (1936) went furthest in this direction, and also highlighted the weakness of the whole group. Instead of contributing to a reconciliation between micro and macro theory – which seemed a necessary task for 'Keynesian' economists after 1945 – the work of the Stockholm school led into opposite and, for standard economic theory, dire directions.

Two themes appear once the Stockholm school is up for discussion. First its relation to Keynes, and here it seems clear that Wicksell instead was the school's main source of inspiration. Secondly, the impact of both Keynes and the Stockholm school on the crisis policies developed in Sweden during the 1930s has been discussed vividly. Also in this case, Keynes' influence on the Stockholm school was minimal. Already in 1932 Myrdal and Ohlin formulated the new fiscal policies which would be the hallmark of the new Social democratic government coming to power the same year. When Keynes' *General Theory* appeared in 1936, such policies in order to stimulate demand were standard procedure. More important for Myrdal and Ohlin had been the general discussion during the 1920s on public works formulated by liberals and social democrats both in Britain and Sweden.

While the Stockholm school in the 1930s seemed to provide an alternative road to Keynes for macroeconomics, this would not become the case. Why? There are several reasons for this. First, of course, Keynes' theories were easier to model with – and to combine with the old micro fundamentals – than Stockholm's complex and dynamic case-study approach, which offered few if any equilibrium points. Secondly, many of the leading Stockholm economists went into politics or administration: Myrdal first went to the USA to write *An American Dilemma* (1944) concerning race problems, and then after the war became a minister in the social democratic government; Ohlin became the leader of the liberal *Folkpartiet*. Thirdly, this meant that they did not raise a second generation of Stockholm economists in the universities. Rather, their influence waned and after 1945 Keynesianism was also adopted as an orthodoxy in Sweden.

As in most other Western countries, the dominance of Anglo-Saxon economics and the neoclassical synthesis became strongly felt after the Second World War. When economics at the universities grew in importance during the 1960s/70s, macro- and microeconomics *à la* Paul Samuelson were taught and explicated. When the Institute for International Economics was started at Stockholm University in 1967 this was where Sweden's leading economists gathered. Up to the 1970s economists such as Erik Lundberg and Assar Lindbäck were defending orthodox Keynesianism – but always seeking to combine macro with micro, and emphasising the role of the market instead of the visible hand of the state. However in the 1980s there was a breakthrough for new theories. The influence of Hayek, Friedman, and also the Public Choice School became remarkably strong. This reflected what was going on elsewhere, but was perhaps reinforced in Sweden by the establishment in 1968 of the Swedish Central Bank Nobel Memorial Prize, which most probably has led to a certain trendiness within the Swedish economic establishment. At the same time the neoclassical orthodoxy has prevailed very strongly among Swedish economists. In recent years the subject in Sweden has been divided up into a number of sub-fields: particularly strong have been labour market economics, general macroeconomics, taxation and game theory.

Bibliography

Heckscher, Eli F., 'A survey of economic thought in Sweden 1875–1950', *Scandinavian Economic History Review*, vol.1:(2), 1953.

Jonung, Lars (ed.), *The Stockholm School of Economics Revisited*. Cambridge: Cambridge University Press, 1991.

Magnusson, Lars, *An Economic History of Sweden*. London: Routledge, 2000.

Magnusson, Lars, *A Tradition of Free Trade*. London: Routledge, 2004.

Sandelin, Bo (ed.), *The History of Swedish Economic Thought*. London: Routledge, 1990.

10
Russia and Ukraine

François Allisson

Russia and Ukraine, although they are now politically independent of each other, share a long common history. The first state of Rus' was established in Kiev between the ninth and the twelfth centuries, and ruled the territories of today's Ukraine, Belarus and Western Russia. The city was entirely destroyed in the thirteenth century by a Mongol invasion. The capital of the state accordingly moved from Kiev to Moscow: Muscovy succeeded Kievian Rus'. From this moment and periodically, there were demands for the return of the capital to Kiev, as well as separatist movements. Moscow managed to remain the capital of this new state until the early eighteenth century. In 1713, Peter the Great transferred the capital of his Empire to Petersburg (later known as St. Petersburg, Petrograd, Leningrad and back to St. Petersburg). The capital was transferred back to Moscow in 1918 by Soviet leaders.

In the meantime, from the thirteenth to the twentieth centuries, the territory of Ukraine underwent several foreign dominations: Polish, Lithuanian, Ottoman, Tatar and eventually the Russian tsarist regime. Ukraine was thus under Russian hands before the 1917 revolutions and soon engaged in a war of independence, and was run by several independent Ukrainian governments from 1917 to 1920. Eventually, Soviet Russia took Ukraine back and, at the birth of USSR in 1922, Russia and Ukraine both became Soviet Socialist Republics: Moscow was the capital of Soviet Russia, and Kiev of Soviet Ukraine. But Moscow remained the capital of the USSR. After the fall of the USSR, Ukraine regained its independence vis-à-vis Russia. Although it was not perceived alike, Russia also gained its independence in 1991 (see Plokhy, 2010).

A key difference between contemporary Russia and Ukraine is their external orientations. Russia has always been torn between the West (Europe) and the East (Asia). If the Western turn, initiated by Peter the Great, has tipped the balance (at least that of the government) in the last three centuries, it can still change. The current strength of the Eurasian movements recalls the unique position of Russia: neither Europe, nor Asia. On its side, Ukraine is in Europe. But Ukraine hesitates about its relationships with Western Europe on one side, and with Russia on the other. The versatile reactions of Europe and of Russia towards Ukraine explain these hesitations. It should be remembered that many Russians live in Ukraine, and that many Ukrainians live in Russia. Both languages are similar, and the cultures are as well. Having this in mind, the present study considers Russia and Ukraine together, as having a common tradition of economic thought, even if we are aware of the shortcomings of such approach.

The Russian and Ukrainian economies

The Russian and Ukrainian economies have long been peasant economies characterised by inefficient paths of communication, which restricted trade to major cities, where markets were held (once a year in the biggest of them, Novgorod). Cities were not industrial centres; small handicraft work was done in the countryside. The numerous enemies of the state (Tatars, Mongols) rendered both money and taxes necessary, either to pay tributes, or to finance wars.

Sources of information on the Russian and Ukrainian economies were scarce until the nineteenth century, and then things radically changed. At the beginning of the century, the Tsar invited foreign scholars to travel through the country for a few months or years, each with the eventual aim of delivering a *tableau statistique* based on their observations. The most striking examples were C. von Schlözer and A. von Haxthausen. By the end of the century, local *zemstvo* statistics, central statistical bodies and scientific societies were far more effective.

Most indigenous economic thought in the nineteenth century was based around conflicting views on the *obshchina*, the traditional rural institution of collective landownership. Was it an archaic institution impeding economic development *or* a genuine basis for a higher socialist world? A minority defended the first point of view, including B.N. Chicherin, I.V. Vernadsky and L.N. Litoshenko and B. Brutzkus during the early Soviet period. The second point of view was the most popular, defended by authorities like N.G. Chernyshevsky, M.M. Kovalevsky and N.F. Danielson. For the government, the *obshchina* guaranteed stability through strong social cohesion (peasants bound to their land, a life confined to tradition), but at the same time, it was perceived as a low productivity system, responsible for economic backwardness. Various reforms to abolish the *obshchina* were attempted at the beginning of the twentieth century with controversial success. It nevertheless legalised the (already on-going) rural exodus, and significantly contributed to increasing it. The fate of the new city dwellers was to feed the emerging industrial system.

Industry had two roots in Imperial Russia. First, there was a centralised state-controlled and state-sponsored industry devoted to the extraction of raw materials and to military equipment. Second, there was a decentralised craft industry in the countryside, either a landlord's small factory employing serfs or an association of workers who increased their income after fieldwork in the *artel* – a production cooperative. Russian cities were unlike European cities: they were almost exclusively centres of consumption of luxury goods imported for the aristocracy, where private factories were largely missing until the 1880s. Many efforts had been made by the state to extract Russia out of its industrial lethargy: Russian ministers of finance, among others, attempted to create the conditions for an industrialisation of Russia: monetary and credit reforms, extension of the railroad network, attraction of foreign investments and active foreign policies. But – and the famines of 1891, 1892 and 1902 recalled it – industry could not develop without a strong agriculture. With P.A. Stolypin's reforms at the turn of the 1910s, for the first time the agricultural and industrial sectors seemed to develop together. Industrialisation was not abandoned after the revolution; on the contrary, it was a highly debated topic with huge practical consequences.

The various actors of the economy restlessly debated these industrial and agricultural issues. Under the old regime, society was divided into several social groups, or *sosloviye*, grouped under four titles: the nobility, the clergy, the urban dwellers and the peasants. These groups, while they might have had a direct connection with some empirical reality up until the first half of the nineteenth century, were not able to grasp the on-going stratification of society. A popular Russian proverb said, 'God is in His Heaven and the Tsar is far away'. Popular wisdom captured well the fact that the Tsar was no longer the intermediary between God and the people: there were many intermediaries between the Tsar and his peasants, including new economic actors and economic thinkers. Whatever the names given to these groups (*raznochintsy, intelligentsia*), they represented those who swelled the cities but did not fit into the traditional *sosloviye*: the new professionals (merchants, industrialists, bankers), journalists, publicists, writers, artists, ruined landlords, and the growing bodies of civil servants and academics, statisticians and economists, among others, whose expertise were needed by both local and central levels of government.

Before the nineteenth century: Kievian Rus', Muscovy and Petersburg

The first articulated economic theories appeared on the territories of the present Russia and Ukraine in the nineteenth century. However, many texts involving economic ideas in more general reasoning, mostly legal, political and religious, appeared during the late seventeenth and the whole eighteenth century. And even in earlier periods, since the ninth century, some documents, often official, sometimes letters from counsillors, documenting the policies of successive Tsars, reached us. Tales and popular texts also often included economic considerations.

The Tsars' public policies provided indication on the issues of concern to the government. Military and religious problems predominated, but economics issues often derived from them. The art of war required tax collection, which implied the existence of a surplus, and knowledge of it. Thus, fiscal issues were frequently crucial. Foreign trade, with imports of luxury goods and needed raw materials against exports of agricultural goods, raised the question of tariffs. Among the frequent issues, the ownership of land and the fate of peasants were as important as the scarcity of metals for coinage (mainly copper and silver). Some particularly interesting debates, such as whether tax should be paid in nature (i.e. corn) or in coins, or on the ownership of the Eastern Orthodox Church in line with its relationship with the power, came as well.

In contrast to the military needs, the Russian economy was insufficiently productive at the beginning of the seventeenth century. The productivity of the peasant economy is explained by the low level of education of the serfs, the exorbitant transportation costs due to the lack of commercial roads and the low handicrafts activity. The tax burden heavily weighed on the peasantry, who would revolt on several occasions (the Pugachev revolt of 1773–4 being a lustrous example). The Tsar, helped by a few councillors, and annoyed by some pamphleteers, was aware of the situation and tried to reform the country. Essentially under the reigns of Peter the Great (1682–1725) and Catherine the Great (1762–96), Russia underwent profound changes: development of large state-owned (but also private) manufactures, exploration for locating natural resources, development of the mining industry, of trade, maritime roads, etc. The first institutions dedicated to knowledge appear: the first museum, the Academy of Sciences (under Peter the Great), the universities of Moscow and St. Petersburg, the Free Economic Society (under Catherine the Great). This modernisation was carried out in the name of Westernisation and at the cost of the peasant world.

The attraction exerted by liberalism, by the French enlightenment philosophy, by the Physiocrats (e.g. on D.V. Golitsyn) and by the ideas of Smith (which were taught at the University of Moscow by two of his students, S.E. Desnitsky and I.A. Tretyakov) took place within an autocratic environment. Any liberal reform that threatened state power was suppressed and many pamphleteers, because they dared touch taboo issues (absolute power and serfdom in particular) were imprisoned.

Among the documents of significant importance in this vast period up to the eighteenth century, let us mention four. The *Russkaia Pravda*, the old legal code of the Kievian Rus' (whose origin goes back to the ninth and tenth centuries, but our knowledge of it dates from the dozens of different versions of the thirteenth century), which explained among others the existing social relations and serfdom. The *Domostroi*, a sixteenth-century guide for the management of the household, explaining in every domain of private life (religion, education, agriculture, cooking, etc.) the good (i.e. moral and useful) way of doing things. I. Pososhkov's *Book on Poverty and Wealth* (1724) evaluated Russian society and gave advice for the management of the social economy. On every aspect of the Russian economy (agriculture, trade, taxes, money, mining, fishing), he explained 'what causes useless poverty', he fought injustices and gave advice on how to increase wealth. Finally, A.N. Radishchev's *Journey from St. Petersburg to Moscow* ([1790] 1958) inaugurated an economic and systematic denunciation of serfdom.

The nineteenth century: Imperial Russia

The imprint of political power on the Russian economy is significant during the whole nineteenth century. The Tsars wanted at the same time to maintain the autocracy, which implied *status quo* policies, and to fight on equal terms with the other European powers, which implied major reforms of the economy and consequently of the whole society. Within this dilemma, nineteenth-century tsarist policies look like political business cycles measuring conservatism and reform. The general trend, however, is characterised by an accumulation of reforms. The reign of Alexander I (1801–25) started with a relative burst of liberalism. He was replaced by Nicholas I (1825–55), who inaugurated his reign by the suppression, through bloodshed, of the Decembrist revolt in 1825. Meanwhile, during half a century, the Russian economy was kept unchanged.

In contrast, the reign of Alexander II (1855–81) was decisive as an attempt to modernise both society and its economy. The most important reforms were: the abolition of serfdom (1861), the establishment of local governmental bodies (*zemstva*, 1864), a judiciary reform (1864), the establishment of municipal *dumas* (1870) and various measures to boost industrialisation and the railway network. The reforms of Alexander II were driven less by the desire to meet the growing demand of radical factions of society than by the fear of social unrest, and the recognition of the backward state of Russia after the military disappointment of the Crimean war. And indeed, Alexander II's reforms were clearly not enough to answer the aspirations of the society. After several miscarried attempts, the Tsar Alexander II was assassinated in 1881. The reign of Alexander III (1881–94) was characterised by a return to authoritarianism, with measures specifically aimed at fighting terrorism and strengthening the autocracy (creation of the *okhrana*, the political police and the re-establishment of precautionary censorship). It marked a break in the reforms. The last Tsar, Nicholas II (1894–1917), initiated numerous reforms, often as a response to the troubles of the time. In particular, his ministers S.Yu. Witte and Stolypin conducted reforms to modernise and boost, respectively, industry and agriculture.

Within this political landscape, political economy flourished when it could, at the whim of censorship. At the beginning of the nineteenth century, for instance, there was a fad for Smith. The ideas of the classical school were dominant. There were fewer economic discourses up until 1870. From the 1870s onward, stimulated by the reforms, economists and publicists acknowledged the reception of several foreign currents: Marxism (especially by N.I. Ziber, among the first readers of K. Marx, and G.V. Plekhanov) and the German Historical Schools (I.K. Babst, A.I. Chuprov). After a time of assimilation of these theories, the 1890s inaugurated what was called the 'golden age of Russian political economy'. Russian revisionism in Marxism (i.e. Legal Marxism) was stimulated by the import of neo-Kantian philosophy and of Austrian marginalism (P.B. Struve, M.I. Tugan-Baranovsky, S.N. Bulgakov).

Mathematical economics developed often with a Walrasian inspiration (V.K. Dmitriev, E.E. Slutsky, N.N. Shaposhnikov, L.N. Yurovsky). The theory of probability entered in statistics thanks to economists (Yu.E. Yanson, A.A. Chuprov, L. von Bortkiewicz). F. List was invoked in tariff issues (Witte, D.I. Mendeleev). But, more crucial for the Tsarist economy, on *the* practical issue, i.e. the economic development of Russia (and its sub-issues: industrialisation, reforms in agriculture, the role devoted to the *obshchina*, capitalism versus socialism, etc.), two main camps confronted each other: the Populists and the Marxists.

The Populists (*narodniki*) were a considerable social movement born in the 1870s. They inherited a Slavophile heritage, which implied a faith in the *obshchina* and in the Russian *muzhik* (peasant), and a rejection of the Western path of development (industrialisation and capitalism). Their master philosopher was Chernyshevsky, supplemented by Marx's critique of capitalism. The movement was very broad, from very conservative to socialist, revolutionary and terrorist members. The most famous economists in the movement were V.P. Vorontsov and Nikolai-on (i.e. Danielson, the translator of Marx in Russia). Populists theorised the possibility for Russia to jump from archaic communism to the higher agrarian socialist stage, without having to cross 'painful' capitalism. This argument was strongly disputed in the 1890s by the Marxists, which were also a broad movement. Almost every anti-Populist was a Marxist. It included the future Bolsheviks (V.I. Lenin) and Mensheviks, Liberal authors and all those who believed in the ineluctability of capitalism in Tsarist Russia. Marx found as nowhere else such a remarkable circle of followers. There were of course other movements besides Populists and Marxists: anarchists, liberals, followers of early French socialists, etc. And the influence of the German Historical School was colossal. In order to give a picture of turn of the twentieth century Russian economists, here are two examples: A.I. Chuprov and Tugan-Baranovsky.

A.I. Chuprov (1842–1908) was perhaps the most characteristic Russian economist of his time. A student and follower of Babst (the translator of W. Roscher in Russia and thus a bringer of the German Historical School to Russia), he was professor of political economy at the University of Moscow, where his manual of political economy was used by several generations of students. At the same time, Chuprov adopted Marx's theory of value, was an active promoter of *zemstvo* statistics and had sympathies with the Populists' doctrines. Chuprov's example does not suggest that all Russian economists were historicists, but most of them shared a historical approach.

Tugan-Baranovsky (1865–1919) was a socialist economist. He had special connections with both Ukraine and Russia: born in Ukraine, he studied first in St. Petersburg in the 1880s, but was then exiled in Kharkov in Ukraine, where he pursued his studies. He further studied in Moscow in the 1890s, and taught in St. Petersburg from the mid-1890s. He was once again exiled in Ukraine at the beginning of the twentieth century. Back in St. Petersburg in 1905, he left Russia finally in 1917 for the nascent independent Ukraine. Fascinated by Marx, I. Kant and by the marginalist school, he made path-breaking contributions combining historical research with highly theoretical constructions (he was the first to make an analytic use of Marx's schemes of reproduction and later to suggest market socialism).

He also contributed to revision of Marxism with a synthesis in value theory, combining a labour theory of value with a marginalist theory of price (see Allisson, 2012). He worked on the history of Russian industry, on socialism, cooperatives and monetary circulation. But he is world-renowned for his theory of business cycles developed in his 1894 masterpiece *Industrial Crises in Contemporary England, their Causes and Influence on National Life*. In this theory, crises occur endogenously because of disproportions in branches of production, and their recurrence as phases of the business cycles is explained by fluctuations in free loanable capital. On this latter point, his influence on Western business cycles theorists (A. Spiethoff, A. Aftalion, J.A. Schumpeter, W.C. Mitchell, D.H. Robertson, J.M. Keynes) was important. And in Russia and Ukraine, Tugan-Baranovsky's influence on economists active under the New Economic Policy (NEP) was tremendous.

The USSR and beyond

The revolutions of 1917 gave various new directions to economic thought in Russia and Ukraine. There was no initial rupture, and much continuity can be observed. The people suffered from World War One, and the policies of War Communism (1918–20) – shock therapy in the vanguard – did not help to recover the situation. Lenin announced NEP (1921–9), bringing back temporarily the market in the developing USSR.

The 1920s were a period of intense theoretical stimulation for economic thought. Communism was to be built. Research was mainly organised around institutes and administrative bodies. N.D. Kondratiev's Conjuncture Institute – where E.E. Slutsky, N.S. Chetverikov, T.I. Rainov and Shaposhnikov worked, among others – was a place where business cycles, price movements and monetary circulation were studied in a pioneering manner.

Slutsky (1880–1948) was an economist and statistician, established in Kiev until 1926, when he had to leave Ukraine, due to him not mastering the Ukrainian language. He then joined Kondratiev's Conjuncture Institute in Moscow. Slutsky is famously known in economics for two contributions. The first, 'On the Theory of the Budget of the Consumer' (1915), was originally published in Italian and went unnoticed for several years. It was rediscovered as a path-breaking mathematical development of Paretian ordinal utility theory, in particular of his distinction, similar to J.R. Hicks's later one, of the budget and substitution effects of the consumer's demand subsequent to a variation of price. This contribution is the only one, out of this history, to be included in all contemporary mainstream economic textbooks. The second, 'The Summation of Random Causes as the Source of Cyclic Processes', first published in Russian in 1927, then in 1937 in English in *Econometrica*, is concomitant with similar efforts in the West to formalise business cycle theory. He was the first to show that stochastic errors may by itself cause a cyclical process (see Barnett, 2011).

Kondratiev's Conjuncture Institute also worked on the development of emerging econometric techniques, and on methodological issues related to economic equilibrium and to planning. Agriculture was the speciality of the Institute of Agriculture Economy, directed by A.V. Chayanov. The Central Statistical Directorate, headed by P.I. Popov, provided innovative methods for the establishment of a balance of the national economy. The People's Commissariat for Finance, among others things, worked hard in stabilising the ruble, with Yurovsky. The Marx-Engels Institute published, under the editorship of D.B. Riazanov and I.I. Rubin, the works of Marx and F. Engels and high-quality Marx studies. Closer to the centre of the political power, economists like N.I. Bukharin, Ye.A. Preobrazhensky, A.A. Bogdanov and V.A. Bazarov were directly involved in the debates on *the* direction to take, while Gosplan (State Committee for Planning), where V.G. Groman and S.G. Strumilin worked, became the heart of Soviet economic policies from the first five-year plan (1929–33).

Stalinism had disastrous consequences on the fate of Soviet economic thought. The 1920s developed under the banner of economic pluralism. The 1930s, inaugurated by a series of trials involving many of the mentioned economists, established a single-minded world of ossified Marxism-Leninist dogma. Many economists (Bukharin, Kondratiev, Yurovsky, Chayanov, Riazanov, to name only a few) were executed during the Stalinist purges of 1937–8. But besides physical liquidations, Soviet economic thought lost even more. Many economists worked only for themselves, since they were not allowed to publish their work (this was the case of L.V. Kantorovich, the future and only Soviet Nobel Prize in economics, whose works could be published only after J. Stalin's death). Others would simply substitute economics for another discipline (geophysics for Slutsky). Eventually, many chose (or suffered) exile, like W. Leontief, S.N. Prokopovich and Brutzkus. This represented an enormous loss of human capital. In the meanwhile, a massive collectivisation in agriculture (far away from the old *obshchina*) and an accelerated industrialisation were occurring, while Soviet economic thought was at half-mast. For instance, Stalin commissioned in 1936 what was to become the first Soviet manual of political economy, but its conception implied difficult debates, in which Stalin himself intervened. The first and only manual was eventually published in 1954.

The death of Stalin in 1953 released some of the pressure, and Soviet political economy began to revive. But the blow to Soviet science remained visible: for instance, teaching (at universities) was separated from research (at the Soviet Academy of Sciences). Moreover, the ideological framework provided by the Soviet manual of political economy prevented any theoretical research at the core of socialist political economy. Research was therefore confined to applied issues, or engaged in comparing the Soviet economy with other countries. However, Kantorovich, V.S. Nemchinov and V.V. Novozhilov made an achievement in the field of linear programming, recognised abroad, with mathematical techniques of optimisation for economic planning. As in Tsarist times, the importation of ideas from abroad had a huge impact. In this context of intellectual stagnation, the arrival in the 1980s of copies of the work of Janos Kornai (*The Economics of Shortage*) had a decisive influence on a new generation of economists (an example among others): those involved, like A.N. Yakovlev, in the internal reforms under M.S. Gorbachev's *perestroika*, and those involved, like Ye.T. Gaidar, in the transition to a market economy.

The post-Soviet transition to a market economy in the independent Russia and Ukraine was anew the battleground for different camps, representatives of several currents of economic thought. Today the old Marxists, supporters of the former regime, still resist. The young liberals, seduced by the Western neoclassical market model, brought the first liberal reforms. But a third group challenges their dominance. This heterogeneous *third way* consists of economists with (either) neo-institutionalist, evolutionary, nationalist (or Eurasian) ideas, seeking the optimal path of economic development for their respective countries. These economists returned to the debates that inflamed economic thought in the late-nineteenth century on the same issue. Thus, at the beginning of the twenty-first century, contemporary Russian/Ukrainian economic thought is also fed by the history of economic thought, perhaps more so than in the West.

Global influences and impacts

From Kievian Rus' to post-Soviet times, Russia and Ukraine were often integrated in global currents of thought. The Eastern Orthodox Church, which came from Rome after successive schisms, or the modern Cyrillic alphabet, which results from successive adaptations from the Greek alphabet, are perfect examples of the ubiquitous importance of the circulation of ideas. In their first centuries, Russia and Ukraine mostly borrowed ideas and techniques. And it was done in a way of adapting them to local conditions.

Economic thought in Russia and Ukraine was for a long time (as elsewhere) encompassed in broader social thought and very little differentiated from the latter. But the desire, at the beginning of the nineteenth century, to imitate developments in Western Europe produced a different story. Political economy was rapidly institutionalised; chairs were established at universities, scientific societies were inaugurated. But, the autonomy of the discipline had not even started. This explains in large part the fact that, during the nineteenth century up to the first decade of the twentieth century, the import of knowledge from Europe had such an impact in Tsarist Russia. Books were imported and translated. But also professors were imported (Germans were at that time considered the most erudite, while in the eighteenth century it would have been the French and English). From the 1890s, things began to change. Original ideas were exported (Tugan-Baranovsky's and Kondratiev's works on crises and cycles for instance). During the 1920s, many academic exchanges took place between the Soviet Union, Germany and the USA. With Stalin and after, there was a reversal of the trend: ideas were no longer imported. The USSR and USA were cautiously watching each other, but didn't exchange ideas any more, except with émigré economists: Russian professors were welcomed in German universities (the reverse situation, 150 years after) and in the USA. With the fall of the USSR, Russia and Ukraine strongly started again the importation of Western economic ideas, with always the same question: are these theories good for us?

Many lively discussions were driven, and continue to attract the finest scholars, over the issue of whether there is (or is not) a Russian and a Ukrainian economic thought. The two extreme positions are the following. The first believe that the science of political economy was born in Russia in 1802–06 with the first translation of Smith's *Wealth of Nations*. They think that political economy is, if not universal, at least a Western affair, although Russia and Ukraine may benefit from these ideas. The second think that there is genuine indigenous economic thought going back to well before the arrival of classical political economy (or the Physiocrats or Mercantilists) on Russian and Ukrainian soils. This indigenous thought should be traced back in the specificities of the indigenous economy: the *obshchina*, the Eastern Orthodox Church, the characteristics of the Russian *muzhik*, etc.

In the Soviet Union, there was an official position stating that, while the Russian bourgeois only imitated Western economists, there was a genuine non-bourgeois Russian economic thought that owed nothing to Western ideas: instead of catching up with their Western colleagues, genuine Russian socialists were actually far beyond them (see the papers in *Problems of Economic Transition*, 2002, 9–10). The truth is probably in between the two extremes. To sum up, Russian and Ukrainian economic thought was often fed by foreign ideas, which were adapted to local conditions. In a few occasions (in the 1890s, the 1920s and with Kantorovich's Nobel Prize in economics in 1975) the balance of trade of economic thought showed a surplus of exports.

Bibliography

This bird's eye view would have been impossible to write without relying on works previously published by historians whose works are listed below. A special mention is due to the efforts of Russian scholars in editions of the works of past Russian economists, such as P.N. Klyukin. This chapter draws on chapter one of my doctoral dissertation (Allisson, 2012).

Akhabbar, Amanar and François Allisson (eds.). 2014. 'Utopia, political economy and social engineering in Russian economic thought', *OEconomia – History | Methodology | Philosophy*, 4(1), Forthcoming special issue.

Allisson, François. 2012. *Value and Prices in Russian Economic Thought (1890–1920)*. PhD Dissertation. University of Lausanne.

Ananin, Oleg, Vladimir Avtonomov and Natalia Makasheva. 2013. *Istoriâ èkonomičeskih učenij (History of Economic Thought)*. Moscow: Infra.

Barnett, Vincent. 2005. *A History of Russian Economic Thought*. London: Routledge.

Barnett, Vincent. 2011. *E.E. Slutsky as Economist and Mathematician*. Abingdon: Routledge.

Barnett, Vincent and Joachim Zweynert (eds.). 2008. *Economics in Russia: Studies in Intellectual History*. Aldershot: Ashgate.

Campbell, Robert. 2012. *A Biobibliographical Dictionary of Russian and Soviet Economists*. London: Routledge.

Ellman, Michael. 1973. *Planning Problems in the USSR*. Cambridge: Cambridge University Press.

Jasny, Naum. 1972. *Soviet Economists of the Twenties*. Cambridge: Cambridge University Press.

Kingston-Mann, Esther. 1999. *In Search of the True West: Culture, Economics and Problems of Russian Development*. Princeton, NJ: Princeton University Press.

Kornai, Janos. 1992. *The Socialist Economic System*. Oxford: Clarendon Press.

Korniychuk, L.Â. *Istoriya Ekonomichnoi dumky Ukrainy*. Kiev: KNEU.

Koropeckyj, I.S. (ed.). 1984. *Selected Contributions of Ukrainian Scholars to Economics*. Cambridge, MA: Harvard University Press.

Lieven, Dominic, Maureen Perrie and Ronald Grigor Suny (eds). 2006. *The Cambridge History of Russia*. 3 vols. Cambridge: Cambridge University Press.

Mespoulet, Martine. 2001. *Statistique et Révolution en Russie: Un Compromis Impossible (1880–1930)*. Rennes: Presses Universitaires de Rennes.

Pashkov, A.I. (ed.). 1955–66. *Istoriâ russkoj ekonomičeskoj mysli (History of Russian Economic Thought)*. 3 vols in 5. Moscow: Socekgiz.

Plokhy, Serhii. 2010. *The Origins of the Slavic Nations: Premodern Identities in Russia, Ukraine, and Belarus*. Cambridge: Cambridge University Press.

Pososhkov, Ivan Tikhonovich. 1724. *Kniga o Skudostii Bogatstve (Book of Poverty and Wealth)*, (eds.) A.P. Vlasto and L.R. Lewitter. London: Athlone, 1987.

Radishchev, A.N. [1790] 1958. *A Journey from St. Petersburg to Moscow*. Cambridge, MA: Harvard University Press.

Slutsky, E.E. 1915. 'Sulla teoria del bilancio del consumatore', *Giornale degli Economisti*. In George J. Stigler and Kenneth E. Boulding (eds.), *Readings in Price Theory*, 27–56. London: Allen and Unwin.

Spulber, Nicolas (ed.). 1964. *Foundations of Soviet Strategy for Economic Growth*. Bloomington, IN: Indiana University Press.

Stanziani, Alessandro. 1998. *L'économie en Révolution: Le cas Russe. 1870–1930*. Paris: Albin Michel.

Sutela, Pekka. 1991. *Economic Thought and Economic Reform in the Soviet Union*. Cambridge: Cambridge University Press.

Tugan-Baranovsky, M.I. 1894. *Promyšlennye krizisy v sovremennoj Anglij, ih pričiny i vliânie na narodnuûžizn'*. St. Petersburg: Skorohodov. 'Periodic Industrial Crises', *Annals of the Ukrainian Academy of Arts and Sciences in the United States*, 1954, III(3): 745–802.

Zlupko, S.M. 2000. *Ekonomichna Dumka Ukrainy: Vid Davnyny do Suchasnosti*. Lviv: Lviv University.

Zweynert, Joachim. 2002. *Eine Geschichte des Ökonomischen Denkens in Russland. 1805–1905*. Marburg: Metropolis.

Part II
The Americas

11

United States of America

J.E. King

In 2013 there were almost 317 million people living in the United States, or slightly less than 5 per cent of the world's population. In 1700, more than two centuries after Columbus's voyage of discovery, the population of the continental United States was approximately 1 million, or 0.17 per cent of the world total. By 1914 it had risen to almost 100 million (already 5.5 per cent of the world total), as a result of both a high rate of natural increase and mass immigration – over 20 million in the century beginning in 1820. Some of this was involuntary, although the 399,000 slaves imported from Africa were much less important than natural increase in the slave population (which had reached 4.5 million by 1860) and were dwarfed by the almost 9 million slaves transported to the rest of the Americas. The total US population continued to grow at least twice as fast as that of Western Europe, with a further net migration of more than 31 million between 1913 and 1998 (see Maddison, 2006 for details). At the start of the new millennium, 10.4 per cent of the population was foreign-born, up from a low of 4.8 per cent in 1970 but still well below the peak of 14.7 per cent in 1910. Three in every four Americans now lived in urban areas (Hughes and Cain, 2011, 358).

Rapid population growth was accompanied by even faster expansion in output, which grew at annual rates of almost 4 per cent in the periods 1820–1913 and 1950–73, and almost 3 per cent in both 1913–50 and 1973–98. In consequence the United States' share of world GDP rose from a miniscule 0.1 per cent in 1700 to a peak of 27.3 per cent in 1950; in 2001 it still accounted for 21.4 per cent of world output. In terms of GDP per capita, the US had moved from fifth place in 1820, when it lagged behind Belgium, the Netherlands, the UK and Switzerland and was barely ahead of the Western European average, to lead the world in 1950, with output per head more than double that of Western Europe. By 1998 the gap had closed a little, but the US still had a 35 per cent advantage over the second richest nation (Japan) and a slightly more than 50 per cent lead over Western Europe (again see Maddison, 2006).

This remarkable growth in output was not entirely smooth or continuous, being interrupted by cyclical downturns of variable length and severity (the most dramatic being the Great Depression of the 1930s), and the benefits were very unevenly distributed between rich and poor. It was made possible by the profound structural changes that transformed a predominantly agricultural economy into the world's greatest industrial power (responsible for half the world's manufacturing output in 1945) and then into its most advanced post-industrial nation. The primary sector (agriculture, forestry and fishing) still employed 37.5 per cent of the working population in 1910; by 1950 this had fallen to 11.9 per cent, and by 2007 to a mere 0.7 per cent. The share of secondary employment (manufacturing, construction and transport) peaked at 41.0 per cent in 1950 and more than halved over the next half century, falling to 22.6 per cent in 2007 (Hughes and Cain, 2011, 567). By this time the tertiary (service) sector accounted for 76.8 per cent of total employment, and the largest US enterprises (in terms of stock market valuation) were no longer steel companies or car manufacturers but Information Technology corporations like Microsoft and Google.

There were equally profound social changes. In 1500 the Native American inhabitants were predominantly nomadic hunter-gatherers, although there was a significant settled agricultural population in some areas. By 1861 the native inhabitants had been almost completely displaced by European settlers, who were themselves divided between three quite distinct (though closely connected) modes of production: capitalism, simple commodity production (mainly by independent farmers) and slavery. In contrast with Europe, there was of course no landowning feudal aristocracy. In the next half century, with slavery abolished in 1865 at the end of the Civil War and the frontier now closed, the US had become an overwhelmingly capitalist country, in which the great majority of the population were legally free but had no alternative means of subsistence other than the sale of their labour power in waged employment. From about 1890 there was a rapid expansion of large corporations with substantial market power, initiating what is sometimes described as the 'monopoly stage' of US capitalism, which on some accounts has persisted until the present day.

The very distinctive economic and social development of the US is reflected in the prevailing ideology, which combined 'the idea – derived from initial Puritan settlement – of a nation enjoying divine favour, imbued with a sacred calling; and the belief – derived from the War of Independence – that a republic endowed with a constitution of liberty for all times had arisen in the New World'. The result was 'a *complexio oppositorum* of exceptionalism and universalism. The United States was unique among nations, yet at the same time a lode-star for the world: an order at once historically unexampled and ultimately compelling example to all' (Anderson, 2013, 6).

This pervasive American exceptionalism has exercised an extremely important influence on the development of the social sciences, including economics (Ross, 1991). It has induced a long-standing and persistent hostility to all forms of socialism, and has also encouraged resistance to government intervention in the economy. For this reason the US is sometimes seen as the leading example of a 'Liberal Market Economy', in contrast to the 'Co-ordinated Market Economies' of Northern and North-Western Europe. Certainly the US has always had a significantly smaller government sector, as can be seen from the ratio of government expenditure to GDP, which in 1913 was 8.0 per cent, compared with a 12.0 per cent average in four European countries (France, Germany, Netherlands, UK). By 1999 it had risen to 30.1 per cent, but the four-country European average was now 45.9 per cent (Maddison, 2006, 135).

Economic thought in the long-term

The pre-Columbian inhabitants left no documentary records, but their thinking on economic matters has been reconstructed by anthropologists and is summarised by Cicarelli (2012). It included some remarkably modern themes, including the need to live modestly but purposively, in harmony with nature, and to be content with satisfactory rather than optimal outcomes. The new European population also took a strong interest in political economy in the pre-Civil War period, as can be seen from the 987 pages devoted to this period in the first two volumes of

Joseph Dorfman's monumental history of economic ideas in the United States (Dorfman, 1965–9; see also Emmett and Madison 2006, which is an indispensable source of information on all US economists of any significance). Some of the early writers were natives, like Benjamin Franklin (1706–90). New ideas also came regularly with the immigrant ships from Europe. Friedrich List (1789–1846) arrived in 1825 and spent seven years in the United States before returning to Germany, where he advocated protection for the country's infant industries. The Ricardian Socialist John Francis Bray (1809–97) was born in Washington D.C. but lived in England from 1822 to 1842, writing his influential *Labour's Wrong's and Labour's Remedy* (1839) there. Bray settled in Michigan in the early 1840s and continued to promote the socialist cause until his death (King, 1988, ch. 4). But his ideas had little impact. The prevailing American exceptionalism required that an explicitly anti-socialist approach be taken to political economy, emphasising the freedom and equality of opportunity that working people enjoyed in the United States and the grounds for optimism about the future. Thus Henry Carey (1793–1879), who was deeply influenced by the British classical economists, nevertheless criticised David Ricardo harshly for his emphasis on the conflict of interest between landlords and other classes. Like List, Carey also repudiated the Smith-Ricardo case for free trade as inappropriate to late industrialisers like Germany and the United States.

None of these writers had much influence in Europe, though Carey did attract criticism from John Stuart Mill. Along with the relatively obscure George Opdyke (1805–80), Carey and Bray were the only American economists cited by Karl Marx in the three volumes of his *Theories of Surplus Value* (1862–3; first published 1905–10), which was easily the most comprehensive history of economic ideas to have been written at the time. The first US economist to attract significant international attention was the journalist Henry George (1839–97), who won enormous popular support for his attack in *Progress and Poverty* (1879) on the 'unearned increment' represented by the rent on unimproved land. George's adaptation of Ricardian rent theory (in a direction that its author never contemplated) struck a chord not only with Americans worried at the closing of the frontier but also with radicals in Britain, who had always been hostile to their country's hereditary landed aristocracy, and in Australia, where the 'squattocracy' had a morally even more dubious claim to the land. Despite his call for 'common ownership' of the land, which appealed to many socialists, George opposed nationalisation and argued instead for the replacement of all existing taxes by a 'single tax' on rent to capture the unearned increment for the community (King, 1988, ch.5).

George was self-taught in economics, and it is notable that for much of the nineteenth century, Americans who wanted postgraduate education had to go overseas for it, most frequently to Germany; in 1880 there were only three professors of economics in US universities. This contributed to the considerable influence of the German Historical School in the US and probably slowed the diffusion of the new 'marginalist' or 'neoclassical' economic theory associated with William Stanley Jevons, Alfred Marshall, Carl Menger and Léon Walras. There was, however, a massive expansion of American universities in subsequent decades. The number of students increased twenty-fold between 1870 and 1928, and by 1900 there were already 51 professors of economics and a well-developed system of graduate schools offering PhDs in the discipline (Fourcade, 2009).

The first American neoclassical theorist of any stature was John Bates Clark (1847–1938), who made a genuinely original contribution to marginalist theory. In *The Distribution of Wealth* (1899) he identified capital as a factor of production on a par with labour and land, whose contribution to production could in principle be measured. The marginal product of capital determined the return to its owners, he maintained, in the same way that the wage rate was set by the marginal product of labour, and rent was determined by the marginal product of land.

Again there was a political dimension to this analysis, since Clark had repudiated his earlier socialist sympathies and used the new theory to provide an explicit defence of the ethical legitimacy of the interest and profit income that was derived from the ownership of capital.

Hostility to socialism was a constant theme in US social thought, in both the 'Gilded Age' (1865–95) and the 'Progressive Era' (1895–1920). Indeed, it became stronger after 1865, when the evident existence of a large and rapidly growing class of permanent wage labourers turned the relations between capital and labour into the central social problem. This was 'the crisis of American exceptionalism' (Ross, 1991, 172). These concerns intensified in the 1880s, with the emergence of radical trade unionism and a mass socialist movement. When the American Economic Association was established in 1885, its platform drew on the German Historical School in calling for urgent social reform and greatly increased state intervention in economic life. However, this platform was soon watered down, under pressure from pro-capitalist interests.

Repression of socialist ideas in the academy was a recurring phenomenon (Lee, 2009, ch. 2), extending even to moderate social reformers like Richard T. Ely (1854–1943) and John R. Commons (1862–1945). It damaged the career of Thorstein Veblen (1857–1929), the author of *The Theory of the Leisure Class* (1899) and *The Theory of Business Enterprise* (1904), though in his case there was also an element of punishment for his extra-marital affairs. In his economic writings Veblen drew a sharp distinction between 'workmanship' and 'predation', the former associated with the technicians and engineers who contributed to efficient production and the latter benefiting the unproductive financiers and absentee owners who profited from it. But he was also highly critical of Marxian socialism, believing that emulation of one's social superiors was a stronger source of motivation than class solidarity. Veblen was equally hostile to neoclassical economics – a term that he invented – and argued that rational calculation was less important than habit and custom in motivating economic behaviour, and that economics should base itself on evolutionary biology, rather than on mechanics. Veblen is the only American economist of this era who continues to attract strong critical interest today; a new book devoted to his ideas has appeared almost every year in the twenty-first century.

By 1920 a distinct Institutionalist School of Economics had emerged, drawing on Veblen but also emphasising the priority of empirical research – above all, the collection of data – over abstract theoretical work. Its strongholds were Johns Hopkins, Wisconsin and Columbia Universities, with Harvard and Chicago dominated by neoclassical ideas (Morgan and Rutherford, 1998; Yonay, 1998).

Commons was the dominant force at Wisconsin, where he influenced the state's progressive social legislation and wrote the important text, *Legal Foundations of Capitalism* (1924), stressing the importance for economic theory of collective action by the state and also by a range of voluntary associations, including corporations and trade unions.

This emphasis on collective rather than individual behaviour served to distinguish the Institutionalists from the neoclassical economists. But the boundaries between the two schools were not at all clear-cut, either politically or methodologically. Thus Wesley Mitchell (1874–1948), author of a major book on *Business Cycles* (1913), expressed his support for capitalism in almost Panglossian terms, while John Maurice Clark (1884–1963), the son of John Bates Clark, attempted to reconcile the neoclassical and Institutional approaches. With the exception of Irving Fisher (1867–1947), who made important contributions to mathematical economics and to the theories of capital, value and money, the American neoclassical theorists were relatively undistinguished, in the 1920s and beyond.

The evident pluralism of economics during the 'Roaring Twenties' did not extend to toleration of Marxian political economy, which remained underdeveloped in the United States and was entirely absent from the academy. In fact the most prescient critics of unregulated capitalism were amateur economists: the professor of English William Trufant Foster (1879–1950) and the banker Waddill Catchings (1879–1967), who in their best-selling book *Profits* (1925) pointed to the danger of a crisis of underconsumption, since consumer expenditure tended to lag behind the growth of production. But Foster and Catchings failed to convince the academic economists, and right down to the Wall Street crash in 1929 all neoclassicals and many Institutionalists retained their faith in the market.

The Great Depression shattered this faith. It hit the US economy especially hard: between 1929 and 1933 output fell by 30 per cent, more than anywhere else in the developed world except Canada, and significantly more than in Germany, where the economic collapse brought Adolf Hitler to power. The percentage of Americans who were unemployed peaked in the high or low twenties, depending on whether the large numbers working on temporary government relief projects are counted as being in genuine employment. No prominent economist, neoclassical or Institutionalist, had predicted the collapse. The business cycle seemed to have been abolished, and steady growth with very low inflation appeared to be a permanent achievement of what was rapidly becoming the world's greatest economy. There are striking parallels between the 'Roaring Twenties' and the so-called 'Great Moderation' of 1992–2007. Irving Fisher was the most prominent, but by no means the only, academic economist to lose everything in the Wall Street crash.

Fisher redeemed himself, intellectually if not financially, by setting out a 'debt-deflation' explanation of the Depression in his *Booms and Depressions* (1932). When the price level falls sharply, Fisher argued, as it did in the Great Depression, the real value of debt increases, forcing many debtors into bankruptcy and compelling many others to reduce expenditure in order to meet their financial commitments. There was a fundamental asymmetry between debtors and creditors: the former could be forced to reduce their spending, while the latter were under no compulsion to increase theirs. Thus a falling price level was a major part of the problem, not part of the solution to a cyclical downturn.

These lessons were learned for a while – they were repeated (without acknowledgement) in chapter 19 of John Maynard Keynes's *General Theory* – only to be forgotten in the inflationary decades after 1945, when American economists began once more to maintain that debt was irrelevant and falling prices and money wages would be sufficient to eliminate unemployment of labour and capital. In the 1930s, however, Fisher's arguments had some influence on Franklin Delano Roosevelt's New Deal, which included provisions (later struck down as unconstitutional) legalising price-fixing agreements and encouraging the growth of trade unions and the determination of wages through collective bargaining.

Roosevelt's macroeconomic policies, however, were unstable and inconsistent, reflecting the confusion that prevailed among economists over the causes of the Depression and the potential remedies. The New Deal was, in fact, a series of improvisations, concocted by advisers who were sometimes sympathetic to Keynes, like Harry Dexter White and Marriner Eccles, and sometimes hostile. Among the latter was Henry Morgenthau, who was responsible for the disastrous attempt to restore 'sound finance' in the austerity budget of 1937 that triggered a brief but extremely sharp fall in output and employment in 1937–8. The Second World War, however, served as 'an incomparable laboratory demonstrating that deficits do cause prosperity' (Lekachman, 1969, 121). Keynes's own *How to Pay for the War* (1940) proved that the *General Theory* was not merely the economics of depression but was equally relevant to a situation of excess aggregate demand, when inflation had become the crucial policy issue.

By the early 1940s the influence of Keynes was beginning to grow, with the new ideas being accepted rapidly by a younger generation of American economists (Colander and Landreth,

1996). A particularly important older convert was Alvin Hansen (1887–1975), whose *Fiscal Policy and Business Cycles* (1941) provided a teaching version of the *General Theory* with detailed statistical applications for the US economy. The statistical appendix was supplied by the young Paul Samuelson (1915–2009), who had already published a mathematical model of the business cycle in the same vein, synthesising the accelerator principle and the Keynesian multiplier and whose *Foundations of Economic Analysis* (1948) was a landmark in the development of mathematical economics in the United States. After the war the new ideas found their way into the introductory textbooks, though not without resistance from conservative politicians and businessmen who regarded government demand management as dangerously close to socialism. Samuelson was again an important influence, his *Economics* (1948) making Keynes both accessible and respectable for first-year undergraduate readers; it is still in print, the eighteenth edition appearing in 2010.

Unsurprisingly, the influence of Marxist ideas also increased substantially in the wake of the Depression, and the first genuinely original and distinctively American work on Marxian political economy was produced by Paul Sweezy (1910–2004), whose *Theory of Capitalist Development* (1942) contains one of the best summaries of Marx's economic thought ever written, together with a comprehensive account of developments in European Marxism in the sixty years since Marx's death. In the final part of the book Sweezy set out his own ideas, which were often described (though not by him) as 'Left Keynesian'. In the monopoly stage of US capitalism, and above all in the Roaring Twenties, corporate profit margins had widened, real wages had lagged behind productivity, and there was a chronic tendency for consumption to grow too slowly relative to output. This explained the severity of the Great Depression, and it made any sustained recovery unlikely. In essence Sweezy (like Hansen, but for very different reasons) was a stagnationist.

The Great Depression and the New Deal were only two of the forces that transformed American economics after 1933. Equally important were the flood of refugees from Hitler's Germany, the huge expansion of the military in the Second World War, and the rapidly increasing use of mathematical models and advanced statistical techniques. These developments were closely related. First, there were the European immigrants. Two of the most notable figures arrived before the establishment of the Nazi regime. Joseph Schumpeter (1883–1950), author of *Business Cycles* (1939, two volumes) and the posthumously published *History of Economic Analysis* (1954), spent the last two decades of his life at Harvard. The Hungarian-born polymath John von Neumann (1902–57), who was based at Princeton but worked extensively for the US government, made important contributions to mathematics and computing as well as to economics. Von Neumann's *Theory of Games and Economic Behaviour* (1944), co-authored with another émigré, Oskar Morgenstern (1902–77), was not fully appreciated for some years but eventually established game theory at the very heart of microeconomic analysis.

Between 1933 and 1941 a steady stream of Europeans arrived in the US. The authoritative two-volume study edited by Harald Hagemann and Claus-Dieter Krohn (sadly not translated into English) has entries on over 300 German-speaking refugee economists, many of whom ended up in the United States. Many of them left a mark on the development of American economics, including the development economists Albert Hirschman (1915–2007), Bert Hoselitz (1913–95) and Paul Rosenstein-Rodan (1902–85); the public finance theorists Gerhard Colm (1897–1968) and Richard Musgrave (1910–2007); the trade theorists Gottfried Haberler (1900–95) and Wolfgang Stolper (1912–2002); and the economic historian Alexander Gerschenkron (1904–78). Outside the mainstream, there were the Austrian subjectivists Fritz Machlup (1902–83) and Ludwig von Mises (1881–1973) and a number of Marxists, including Paul Baran (1910–64) and Adolph Lowe (1893–1995).

Probably the most important of all the Europeans, however, were the mathematical theorists and econometricians Jacob Marschak (1898–1977), Gerhard Tintner (1907–83), Tjalling Koopmans (1910–85) and Abraham Wald (1902–50). As Director of the Cowles Commission, which was based first at Chicago and then at Yale, Marschak was especially important in developing the foundations of econometrics and in encouraging the formalisation of economic theory. His team at Cowles included the future Nobel laureates Kenneth Arrow (b. 1921), Tryge Haavelmo (1911–99) and Lawrence Klein (1920–2013). These radical changes in the nature of American economics were profoundly affected by the Second World War and the Cold War that soon followed it. The new techniques of linear programming, activity analysis and decision theory were extremely useful to the US military, and the work of the economists who developed them was often financed by the federal government and its agencies (Mirowski, 2002).

All this foreshadowed the future of American economics. The reality at the end of the war was still very different, as can be seen from the contents of a typical issue of the *American Economic Review* (*AER*), then (as now) the country's leading academic journal. The September 1944 *AER* was a relatively slim volume. Just over 100 of its 250 pages were taken up by six main papers. The lead article was devoted to a pressing policy issue, the disposal of surplus war property. Then there was an analysis of the national output at full employment in 1950, which involved the use of descriptive statistics and informal projections, and an empirical and descriptive article on the future economic prospects of Palestine. The remaining two papers were contributed by Leon Trotsky's former secretary, the Russian émigrée Raya Dunayevskaya (1910–87). One was her translation of a 30-page article on the teaching of economics in the Soviet Union, from the Russian-language journal *Under the Banner of Marxism*, and the other was her own analysis of this 'new revision of Marxian economics'. The editors promised further discussion of the Soviet article in the December issue.

None of these six main articles was concerned with neoclassical economics, and none contained a single equation or diagram. The same was true of three of the four brief 'communications', which dealt with the official British White Paper on full employment and the work of the US Labor Board. Ironically, the only theoretical piece in the entire issue was contributed by Kenneth Boulding (1910–93), whose later career revealed that his sympathies lay with evolutionary and Institutional rather than neoclassical economics. Boulding's brief note on the incidence of profits taxation did include two elaborate diagrams, but there were no equations. It was followed by no less than 80 pages of book reviews, and the issue concluded with 48 pages of lists, covering new books, the contents of new periodicals, and recent doctoral dissertations in economics. This final list demonstrates just how different the US PhD programme was in 1944; extended, book-length dissertations had yet to succumb to the twenty-first-century formula of compulsory coursework plus three (possibly unrelated) short articles.

This is, of course, not the only contrast. The December 2013 issue of the *AER* was the latest available to me as I completed the first draft of this chapter. It ran to a massive 470 pages, but there were no book reviews or lists of journal articles, which had long been relegated to the *Journal of Economic Literature*, established by the AEA in 1969 to release space in the *Review* for more articles. Books were in any case much less important than they had been in 1944, and were often ignored altogether by the increasingly influential citation indices. The entire issue of the *AER* consisted of 12 main articles, averaging more than 30 pages in length, and five shorter pieces. All were entirely mainstream in content and presentation, all included formal modelling, usually with many equations, and the empirical articles all used elaborate econometric techniques.

In 1944 the use of the term 'mainstream' would have been premature and anachronistic. Twenty years later, however, it would have been an entirely accurate description of the economics that was taught in all the major US universities and formed the basis of publications in all the leading journals. By the early 1960s, the core of mainstream microeconomics in the United States was provided by the Arrow-Debreu formalisation of Walrasian general equilibrium theory, set out in a series of journal articles and in Debreu's *Theory of Value: An Axiomatic Analysis of Economic Equilibrium* (1959). Gérard Debreu (1921–2000) was born and educated in Paris, where he was strongly influenced by the Bourbakist movement, a group of French mathematicians who attempted to reformulate mathematics on strictly axiomatic foundations (Weintraub, 2002). He came to the United States on a Rockefeller Scholarship in 1948 and made a permanent move in 1950, working first at Cowles and then at Berkeley; Arrow was nearby, at Stanford.

This was high theory, produced on the American seaboard, in California and also on the East Coast, at Harvard and MIT; it was sometimes described as 'saltwater economics'. The 'freshwater economics' taught at the University of Chicago was less abstract and more overtly political. Here Milton Friedman (1912–2006), George Stigler (1911–91) and their colleagues made the case for corporate capitalism, arguing that even the most concentrated product markets behaved in practice as if they were perfectly competitive, and denying the need for government regulation. Their free market liberalism was reinforced by the British-born Ronald Coase (1910–2013), who demonstrated that, on certain (somewhat implausible) assumptions, external costs and benefits could be internalised in voluntary contracts between the affected parties, eliminating the need for either regulation, or Pigovian taxes and subsidies. The Coase Theorem subsequently became a key element in neo-liberal economics.

Friedrich Hayek (1899–1992), who arrived at the University of Chicago in 1950, played a significant role in establishing the Mont Pèlerin Society, which was based in Switzerland and, beginning in 1947, brought together American and European neo-liberals to promote the cause of the free market (Van Horn and Mirowski, 2009). Hayek's own interests were already moving away from economics to political philosophy and psychology, and he was never really a core member of the Chicago school. By 1970, however, there was a distinct Austrian school of economics in the United States, in which Israel Kirzner (b. 1930) and Murray Rothbard (1937–96) were prominent. These American Austrians were firmly subjectivist in orientation, stressing the role of entrepreneurship, the importance of competitive market processes, the irrelevance of equilibrium outcomes and the futility of macroeconomic modelling. Although they were strong supporters of unregulated markets, their hostility to mathematical formalism and econometric research rendered them very uncertain allies of the neoclassical mainstream in microeconomics.

In macroeconomics, a neoclassical-Keynesian synthesis came to dominate teaching, research and eventually (in the Kennedy-Johnson administrations of the 1960s) US government policy. It had three components. The first was the IS-LM model that established the equilibrium levels of real income and the rate of interest, with output potentially constrained by effective demand rather than by supply conditions, requiring active fiscal and/or monetary policy to guarantee full employment. This, however, applied only to the short period. The second component of what came to be known as the Old Neoclassical Synthesis was the neoclassical growth model published in 1956 by Robert Solow (b. 1924), which assumed full employment of both labour and capital. Finally, the inflation rate was determined in the labour market by reference to the Phillips Curve, which related the rate of money wage inflation to the unemployment rate. Like IS-LM, first devised by the English theorists J.R. Hicks and James Meade, this was another analytical import from the United Kingdom (the New Zealander A.W. Phillips was based at the London School of Economics).

In this theoretical framework, changes in the stock of money affected the rate of interest but not (directly) the inflation rate. This drew strong criticism from 'monetarists' like Milton

Friedman, who insisted on the continuing relevance of the Quantity Theory, as formalised by Irving Fisher; on the importance of inflationary expectations; and on the need for the Federal Reserve to apply a strict zero-inflation rule limiting the rate of growth of the money stock to the expected rate of growth of real output. In *A Monetary History of the United States, 1867–1960* (1963), Friedman and Anna J. Schwartz explained the severity of the Great Depression in monetarist (and clearly anti-Keynesian) terms, as the result of the Fed's inaction in the face of the bank failures of the early 1930s, which had led to a sharp and damaging contraction in the money supply. Until the acceleration of inflation in the late 1960s, however, monetarism remained a minority position, and as late as 1971 the Republican President Richard Nixon declared himself to be a Keynesian.

Very different objections to the Old Neoclassical Synthesis came from Sidney Weintraub (1914–83), his former student Paul Davidson (b. 1930) and Hyman Minsky (1919–96), who complained that the new orthodoxy was inadequate in its treatment of money and finance and also neglected the cost-push (and especially the wage-push) dimension of inflation. From *Money and the Real World* (1972) through to his *Post Keynesian Macroeconomic Theory, Second Edition* (2011), Davidson consistently stressed the role of fundamental uncertainty in Keynes's own thought, and the need to reject the three fundamental axioms that the neoclassical Keynesians took for granted: the neutrality of money, its gross substitutability for all other commodities, and the ergodic (that is, predictable) nature of economic phenomena. Minsky's *John Maynard Keynes* (1975) set out a rather different, original and idiosyncratic version of Keynesian macro-economics, focussing on the financial fragility created by the relaxation of lending standards in the upswing phase of the business cycle and the need for vigilant regulation of the financial system to prevent a repetition of the Great Depression. By the late 1970s these ideas formed the theoretical core of a new 'Post Keynesian' school.

There was also some life elsewhere outside the mainstream. The emergence of an American school of Austrian economics has already been mentioned. One or two of the surviving Institutionalists were also prominent. Clarence Ayres (1891–1972) taught at the University of Texas for almost forty years. Drawing heavily on Veblen, Ayres distinguished 'techno-logical' and 'ceremonial' forms of behaviour and stressed the interplay of institutions and technology, which he contrasted with the neoclassical emphasis on individual wants and scarcity. At least one Institutionalist exercised real influence over public policy in the postwar era. This was Arthur F. Burns (1904–87), who was President of the AEA in 1959 and served both the Eisenhower and Nixon administrations, first as Chair of the Council of Economic Advisers (1953–6) and then as Chair of the Board of the Federal Reserve (1970–8). Burns is a salutary reminder that the Institutionalist/neoclassical divide was not also unambiguously a division between left and right, for he was a Republican and an associate of the strongly pro-market American Enterprise Institute. Compare his political persuasions with those of the neoclassical stalwart Paul Samuelson, who was a liberal Democrat and served the Kennedy and Johnson administrations.

Also on the left was John Kenneth Galbraith (1908–2006), who combined Institutionalist and Keynesian themes in a series of influential books, including *American Capitalism: the Concept of Countervailing Power* (1952), the best-selling *The Affluent Society* (1958) and *The New Industrial State* (1967). He argued that the highly unionised, big-government, corporate capitalism of the post-1945 period was fundamentally different from the nineteenth-century owner-managed, competitive, liberal capitalist market system on which neoclassical economic theory was based, and therefore required a very different type of economic analysis. Galbraith drew on the ideas of many earlier thinkers, including Veblen, the technocrats of the 1920s and Adolph Berle's and Gardiner Means's Institutionalist classic, *The Modern Corporation and Private Property* (1932).

He may also have been influenced by the ex-Trotskyist James Burnham's *The Managerial Revolution* (1941), which maintained that Nazi Germany, Stalin's Russia and corporate America were converging to a post-capitalist managerial dystopia. In his *Capitalism, Socialism and Democracy* (1943), Galbraith's Harvard colleague Joseph Schumpeter had taken a rather similar line. Although Galbraith was a brilliant writer and was respected sufficiently by the profession to be elected President of the AEA in 1970, his ideas were by this time a very long way outside the mainstream of US economics.

There was also a small (and declining) Marxist residue, which was subject to severe repression in the heyday of McCarthyism (Lee 2009). In the 1950s Paul Baran was the only tenured Marxist professor of economics in the United States (King, 1988, ch. 8). In 1958 Baran published *The Political Economy of Growth*, a powerful attack on US imperialism that attributed the continuing poverty and slow growth of the underdeveloped global South to exploitation by the rich capitalist countries of the North. The poor countries did produce an economic surplus, Baran argued, but much of it was extracted in the form of super-profits and most of the rest was squandered on luxury consumption by parasitical ruling classes subservient to overseas capital. He was already working with Paul Sweezy on *Monopoly Capital* (1964), which applied the concept of the economic surplus to the United States, in an ambitious application of Marx's analysis of productive and unproductive labour. Baran and Sweezy set out a 'law of the rising surplus', according to which a steadily increasing proportion of economic activity was wasteful, or surplus-absorbing. This included expenditure on advertising and product differentiation, much civilian government spending, and the ever-increasing military budget.

None of these heterodox groupings had any significant influence on teaching or research in Ivy League universities or on the activities of the major research foundations. But this began to change in the late 1960s, with the re-emergence of political radicalism, especially among students (where a crucial role was played by opposition to the Vietnam War), industrial workers (with a wave of strikes, and an increasingly serious problem of 'wage-push' inflation), and women (with the emergence of a 'second wave' of feminism). There was a rediscovery of Marx, again with a distinctively American flavour; the beginnings of a consciously feminist economics; the revival of Institutionalist ideas; and the emergence of a self-proclaimed Post Keynesian macroeconomics that rejected the neoclassical synthesis. New organisations were established: the Association for Evolutionary Economics in 1965 and the Union for Radical Political Economics in 1968. New journals began to appear: the *Journal of Economic Issues* in 1967, the *Review of Radical Political Economics* in 1969, the *Journal of Post Keynesian Economics* in 1977 and (surprisingly delayed) *Feminist Economics* in 1995.

Neoclassical economics was now being criticised for its excessive abstraction and formalism, for its neglect of the social, psychological, political and gender dimensions of economic behaviour, and (not least) for its political apologetics. Serious logical defects in the Clarkian theory of capital had been identified by the Cambridge (UK) economists Piero Sraffa and Joan Robinson, which undermined both the marginal productivity theory of distribution and the neoclassical growth model. Samuelson, Solow and other theorists based in Cambridge (MA) attempted unsuccessfully to rescue neoclassical analysis, before Samuelson conceded defeat in 1966 (Harcourt, 1972). When John Kenneth Galbraith was elected president of the American Economic Association for 1971, and invited Robinson to give the keynote Richard T. Ely lecture at the AEA's annual meeting at the end of that year, opponents of the mainstream had some reason to believe that they were in with a chance of supplanting it, or at least of bringing about substantial change.

Intermezzo: the Americanisation of economics

The third quarter of the twentieth century saw the rapid and comprehensive 'internationalization' of economics (Coats, 1996). Actually this term is a polite euphemism for Americanisation. The increasing dominance of the United States can be seen in every aspect of the discipline, from the pinnacle of research achievement to the structure, content and graphic design of first-year undergraduate textbooks. Thus 63 of the 74 Nobel Prizes in economics awarded between 1969 and 2013 went to Americans, either native-born or long-term permanent residents; between 1980 and 2013, it was 49 out of 56 (http://nobelprize.org/nobel-prizes/economics).

A substantial number of the very best economists from all over the world came to work at the best American universities, only now as free agents, not as refugees. Publication in US journals (and therefore in English) was increasingly seen by overseas scholars as essential in order to establish their professional standing and influence public policy. By 1989, 20 of the top 27 economics journals were published in the United States (Lee, 2009, 45). It might be objected that this is not an unbiased statistic, since its compiler, Art Diamond, was himself an American, but this is precisely the point: no such list compiled by someone outside the United States would have carried such (global) authority.

Additional influence was exercised through the graduate schools, which increasingly attracted the brightest and best of the world's students; by 2000, 54 per cent of those enrolled in US PhD programmes in economics came from overseas (Fourcade, 2006, 173). American dominance was evident in almost every element of postgraduate education, from the now-universal requirement of a PhD as a pre-condition of academic employment to the introduction of a substantial coursework element in the degree (neither being generally found even in Anglophone countries such as Australia or the United Kingdom until late in the twentieth century). Last, but not least, was the Americanisation of undergraduate education in economics, with Samuelson's *Economics* and its many imitators making massive inroads into the national textbook markets of almost every country on the planet and encouraging lecturers, tutors, course designers and university managers to adopt the American approach to the teaching of economics.

To a considerable extent, the Americanisation of economics was a rather straightforward consequence of the hegemonic position of the United States at the end of the Second World War; it was one important dimension of the nation's overwhelming 'soft power'. This was not confined to popular culture, though jazz and the Hollywood cinema were important elements in it. The economic strength of the United States at the end of the Second World War was simply overwhelming; the economy had doubled between 1938 and 1945, now accounting for half the world's industrial output and three-quarters of its gold reserves. Its intellectual dominance had been strengthened by the influx of European refugee economists after 1933, which contributed (as we have seen) to the triumph of neoclassical formalism over what now appeared to be an outdated and parochial tradition of American Institutionalism.

Globalisation also played a part. The cost of transport and communications fell steeply and continuously after 1945, making the movement of people and ideas much easier, and this, too, disproportionately benefited the global hegemon. English became the global language, in academic life no less than in finance, trade and industry. Thus when the European Society for the History of Economic Thought was set up in 1996 it adopted English as its *lingua franca* from the start, while the *European Journal of the History of Economic Thought*, with editors drawn from Austria, France, Ireland and Portugal, rarely publishes papers or book reviews in any other language.

But the Americanisation of economics was also the result of deliberate action by private and public sector organisations. This included the provision of fellowships and scholarships, by the Rockefeller and Ford Foundations and by federal government agencies, to enable the brightest and best of overseas economists to visit the United States. It was also significant that the two crucial Bretton Woods institutions, the International Monetary Fund and the World Bank, had their headquarters in Washington, where they had close links with the US Treasury and its Wall Street connections. It was thus no accident that the neo-liberal policy prescriptions imposed on many developing countries in the 1980s and 1990s came to be known as the 'Washington Consensus'. Often they were implemented by local officials with Ivy League PhDs in economics, who had apparently studied American economic life more closely than the country's democratic political system: the 'Chicago Boys' in Pinochet's Chile, for example, and the 'Berkeley Mafia' in Suharto's Indonesia.

Late in the century, US military and political power seemed to be in irreversible decline, as argued by the historian Paul Kennedy in his influential *The Rise and Fall of the Great Powers* (1988). But the nation's cultural and ideological hegemony remained largely intact, and it could indeed be seen as increasing, with the growing acceptance of neo-liberal ideas around the world, not least (after 1991) in the former Communist countries of Eastern Europe. In Western Europe, the former Co-ordinated Market Economies were increasingly coming to resemble the Anglo-Saxon Liberal Market Economies, with the increasing power of finance enforcing 'shareholder value' – short-run profit maximisation – as the only sustainable objective of the large corporation. In some ways, then, the 'soft power' of the United States was still growing. Certainly there was no evidence that the Americanisation of economics was under serious threat.

US economics in the age of neo-liberalism

The neo-liberal age dawned with the election of Margaret Thatcher in Britain in 1979 and Ronald Reagan as US President in the following year. It took another decade for the high inflation of the 1970s to be brought under control, ushering in a period of faster growth, somewhat lower unemployment and very much lower inflation that came to be known as the 'Great Moderation' of 1992–2007. Until the onset of the Global Financial Crisis – otherwise known as the 'Great Recession' of 2007–? (Mirowski, 2013) – it was possible to believe that improvements in macroeconomic management had made a return to the crisis years of 1973–92 impossible. A similar illusion had prevailed in the 1920s, as we have seen.

In microeconomics, the rise of Walrasian equilibrium modelling had culminated in the canonical *General Competitive Analysis* (1971) by Arrow and the Cambridge (UK) theorist Frank Hahn. Very soon, however, the entire general equilibrium project was undermined by the demonstration, by Debreu and two colleagues, the American Hugo Sonnenschein (b. 1940) and the Yale-trained Argentinian Rolf Mantel (1935–99), that almost nothing could be said *a priori* about the excess demand functions that were generated by such models, and therefore there was no reason to expect the existence of a unique equilibrium. The Debreu-Mantel-Sonnenschein theorem, sometimes described as the 'anything goes theorem', was so influential that by the end of the 1980s general equilibrium models had been quietly abandoned by the great majority of US microeconomists, just as (ironically) they were being incorporated into the core of macroeconomic theory. General equilibrium was rapidly replaced by game theory as the principal theoretical framework for the analysis of microeconomic problems. It shared the most important characteristics of Walrasian modelling, above all the assumptions of methodological individualism, instrumental rationality and certainty-equivalence, so that goals and constraints were known, at least probabilistically, and the standard procedures of constrained maximisation could be applied.

The range of problems to which neoclassical microeconomics appeared to offer solutions was steadily expanding. Under the leadership of the Chicago theorist Gary Becker (1930–2014), economists now invaded what had previously been considered the domain of the other social sciences, which (it was claimed) were being driven out of the occupied terrain by the irresistible advance of the new 'economics imperialism'. Thus neoclassical economic modelling was applied to education (via the concept of 'human capital'), political behaviour (in 'public choice' theory), crime (since the criminal could be seen as a rational, utility-maximising entrepreneur) and the family (with the popular metaphor of the 'marriage market' being taken literally and feminists being enraged by the idealisation of male domestic tyranny). In this way, inter-disciplinary cooperation gave way to invasion tactics. But the imperialists were often fiercely resisted, and with considerable success; neoclassical models were indeed sometimes used in political science, sociology, anthropology and social psychology, but only on the disciplinary fringes.

Perhaps the most important new field for the employment of neoclassical modelling techniques was provided by financial theory, which proved to have extremely large and wide-ranging real-world applications. Without the Capital Asset Pricing Model developed by Fischer Black (1938–95), Harry Markowitz (b. 1927), Merton Miller (1923–2000), William Sharpe (b. 1934) and others, there would have been no explosive growth of the market for financial derivatives, and without the Efficient Market Hypothesis articulated by Eugene Fama (b. 1939) the New Deal regulatory structure would not have been dismantled in the 1980s and 1990s to permit the explosive and very largely unregulated growth of those markets. Thus mainstream microeconomics played an important part in constituting the new economic world of financialised neo-liberalism.

The political context was, as always, extremely important. The neo-liberal credo was that all social problems had a market solution, and where markets did not exist they had to be created. The Coase Theorem was interpreted (though not, perhaps, by its creator) as implying that government failure was always worse than market failure. Taken in conjunction with the notions of rent-seeking behaviour and regulatory capture, it allowed mainstream economics to be used to advocate light regulation, self-regulation and thoroughgoing deregulation of labour markets and utilities as well as the financial sector.

Economics imperialism now extended its reach from the academic journals into popular culture and ideology. Chicago was again at the centre of this movement, with the best-selling book by Milton Friedman and his wife, Rose Friedman (1910–2009), *Free to Choose* (1980), being used as the basis for an influential television series promoting neo-liberal ideas. This is the epoch when 'economics goes to the movies', and also to the television studios. Galbraith's 'Age of Uncertainty', televised in 1977, presented the history of economics from a broadly social democratic, Keynesian perspective, but it was much less influential than the Friedmans' programmes, which were made in reaction to it. It was not long before the first successful Hollywood film was made starring an economist. This was Ron Howard's *A Beautiful Mind* (2001), featuring the brilliant but deeply troubled game theorist John Nash (b. 1928), whose eponymous theorem was one of the most influential products of the post-von Neumann era in game theory. Nine years later, Charles Ferguson's *Inside Job* (2010) took a much less sympathetic look at the prominent macroeconomic theorists who had given a clean bill of health to the Icelandic banking system just before what, with hindsight, was its inevitable collapse. Back in 1872 Marx had already described those responsible as 'hired prize-fighters of the bourgeoisie'.

Macroeconomic theory had changed dramatically since the heyday of US Keynesianism. The stagflation of the 1970s had deeply undermined faith in the Old Neoclassical Synthesis, in macroeconometric modelling, and in the sort of fine-tuning of macroeconomic policy that this intellectual apparatus had been used to design and implement. There was a rapid shift in policy towards the adoption of a single target, output price inflation, and a single instrument, the stock of money and (when this failed) the rate of interest. The so-called Taylor rule, named after the

Stanford theorist John B. Taylor (b. 1946), required the Federal Reserve to increase the base interest rate whenever inflation rose above a two per cent target rate, or real GDP rose above its trend level, and to reduce it when the reverse was true. This was a *de facto* (though unacknowledged) acceptance of the Post Keynesian proposition that the money supply was endogenous, but without any recognition of the need to target employment (except indirectly, through the relation between actual and trend GDP), asset price inflation or the stability of the financial system. And there was no longer any scope for fiscal policy or incomes policy, let alone financial market regulation, as useful policy instruments.

These developments in macroeconomic policy were accompanied (and indeed largely caused) by a radical shift in macroeconomic theory, and in the methodological arguments used to justify this shift. Monetarism had always been rather light on theory, with the Quantity Theory defended mainly on empirical grounds: the velocity of circulation was roughly constant, Friedman claimed, and in the Equation of Exchange ($MV = PT$) causation ran principally (though not exclusively) from left to right, so that changes in the money stock (M) caused changes in the price level (P). Friedman also claimed, correctly, to have something in common with Keynes, since both men did their macroeconomics from the top down, not from the bottom up.

The second generation of Chicago monetarists, led by Robert Lucas (b. 1937), did it the other way round, insisting on the provision of 'microfoundations' for macroeconomic theory. If macroeconomic models were not based on the assumption of rational, utility-maximising behaviour by individuals, there could be no guarantee that these relationships would be stable over time, no reason to have confidence in econometric estimates of the relevant parameters, and hence no grounds on which to expect policies based upon such estimates to be successful. This was especially important for the analysis of inflation, since it led to the replacement of the old monetarist assumption of 'adaptive expectations' by the new assumption of 'rational expectations', first articulated in 1961 by John Muth (b. 1930) and vigorously advocated by Lucas and other self-proclaimed New Classical theorists like Thomas Sargent (b. 1943), Finn Kydland (b. 1943) and Edward Prescott (b. 1940).

As already noted, the macroeconomists of the neo-liberal era took up general equilibrium modelling just as it was being discarded by their colleagues in microeconomics. The new Dynamic Stochastic General Equilibrium (DSGE) models focussed on individual consumers of a very particular type: representative agents with rational expectations, who maximised lifetime utility in an economic environment that was characterised by random shocks. By the 1990s these RARE microfoundations were very widely accepted by mainstream macroeconomists, including many of those who described themselves as 'New Keynesians'. The New Classicals saw unemployment as voluntary in nature, since it resulted from the free decisions of rational individuals who had chosen leisure in preference to paid employment. The New Keynesians, like Paul Krugman (b. 1953) and Joseph Stiglitz (b. 1942), argued instead that labour and product markets were imperfect, so that prices and money wages tended to be sticky downwards. Involuntary unemployment was the most important consequence of the asymmetries in information that gave rise to imperfect markets. There were good reasons why profit-maximising employers might not offer work to unemployed people who were prepared to undercut their existing workforce.

These arguments constituted an important element of the New Neoclassical Synthesis that had emerged by the late 1990s. Post Keynesian critics like Davidson and Minsky always maintained that this was a travesty of Keynes, who had maintained in chapter 19 of the *General Theory* that downward flexibility in prices and wages should be discouraged. The great majority of New Classicals and New Keynesians, however, now agreed on the need for RARE microfoundations, accepted the Taylor Rule as the basis for macroeconomic policy, and at least implicitly rejected Keynes's irreducibly macroeconomic principle of effective demand.

Thus the insights of Post Keynesians like Davidson and Minsky were marginalised, along with the contributions of other heterodox economists from the Institutionalist and radical-Marxist traditions. It became increasingly difficult for non-mainstream economists to publish in the leading journals, and their own students were less and less likely to find employment in the leading universities. Some formerly heterodox economics departments were besieged and overrun by the mainstream – Rutgers in the mid-1980s, Notre Dame 20 years later – leaving only a handful of institutions still offering heterodox PhD programmes. By 2014 only the New School in New York City, the University of Massachusetts at Amherst, the Levy Institute of Bard College at Annandale-on-Hudson in New York and the University of Kansas City-Missouri remained. Individuals could still find jobs in less prestigious state universities and in liberal arts colleges, but at the expense of heavy teaching loads and limited access (if any) to research funding (Lee, 2009, chs. 4–5). The 'second crisis of economic theory' that Joan Robinson had foreshadowed back in 1971 had not worked out as she had hoped.

By the beginning of the new century, however, some observers were pointing to an entirely new phase in the evolution of American economics, with emerging research paradigms that posed a real challenge to neoclassical theory. The former mainstream, they claimed, was now fragmenting. The new research programmes included evolutionary economics, behavioural economics, evolutionary game theory, behavioural game theory, experimental economics, neuroeconomics and agent-based complexity economics (Colander *et al.*, 2004). The last-named provides a good case study. Complexity economics is a branch of the science of complexity, centred on the Santa Fé Institute and largely financed by Citibank. Its fundamental conception is of an economic system dominated by evolutionary processes of change that are adaptive and self-organising and that generate non-linearities, path dependence, emergent properties that cannot be reduced to their component parts, and increasing returns to scale. Complexity economics only became possible with advances in information technology that allowed the numerical simulation of dynamic equation systems for which analytical solutions could be obtained.

These developments not only represented a new pluralism in American economics, it was argued, but also provided clear evidence of *reverse* imperialism, with economics importing new ideas, techniques and research agendas from biology, neuroscience and cognitive psychology. In the process, the new 'dissenters', or 'heterodox mainstreamers', were abandoning much of the intellectual apparatus of the old mainstream. They recognised that individuals are socially embedded, not atomistic; accepted that economic processes are evolutionary rather than mechanical; and acknowledged that individuals and socio-economic structures are mutually dependent, so that the quest for 'microfoundations' was bound to fail. Thus critics from the old heterodox schools were becoming increasingly irrelevant in their continuing attacks on what was now a straw man.

The heterodox economists, however, maintained that the new ideas were being absorbed into mainstream theory in ways that ensured that no threat was posed to its core tenets. A process of 'bastardization' was under way, similar to that which had accompanied the incorporation of Keynes's macroeconomics into the mainstream of American economics in the 1940s. This could be seen in all the new streams of thought, perhaps most clearly in the case of behavioural economics. Here the 'old behaviourism' of Herbert Simon (1916–2001) had been edged aside by the 'new behaviourism' of Daniel Kahneman (b. 1934) and Amos Tversky (1937–96), which was essentially individualistic and carried the comforting implication that in many cases economic agents needed only to be 'nudged' in the right direction for something approaching the instrumentally rational behaviour postulated by traditional neoclassical theory to be obtained.

Increasing concern is at last being shown over the growth of inequality in income and wealth that has occurred in the United States since the 1970s, and which has had a social and political no less than an economic impact. This has been recognised by mainstream economists like Stiglitz, in *The Price of Inequality* (2012), and Jeffrey Sachs, in *The Price of Civilization* (2011). But it has not been adequately explained by mainstream theory, since narratives that focus exclusively on the consequences of labour-saving technical change are not convincing. Changes in social and (especially) political power are a crucial part of the explanation for the growth in inequality, which suggests that there may well be some mileage left in the (old) Institutionalism and in radical and Marxian political economy. This conclusion is reinforced by the after-math of the Global Financial Crisis, which only failed to repeat the catastrophe of the Great Depression because of the adoption of old-fashioned Keynesian stimulus measures, in the United States and elsewhere. Although there was a short-lived increase in interest in Post Keynesian and Marxian ideas after 2007, and the work of Hyman Minsky was often cited, there seems to have been little or no reduction in the influence of the core ideas of mainstream economic theory (Mirowski, 2013).

To conclude: the course of economics in the United States has been influenced by factors both internal and external to the discipline. Most important among the internal influences after 1945 was the strong commitment to formal modelling, which reinforced the tendency towards economics imperialism but also provoked criticism of the economists' inappropriate 'scientism' – mindless imitation of the methods of the natural sciences – and, even more pejoratively, of their 'physics envy'. The external influences included the pervasive American exceptionalism that had been a common element in all the social sciences from the earliest days and included a strong anti-socialist orientation that was strengthened after 1945 by the onset of the Cold War. For much of the twentieth century, academic economics in the United States had very close links to both business and the state, providing practical instruments and techniques for use by government, corporations and courts of law (Fourcade, 2009). It relied on four sets of patrons: universities, governments, business and foundations (Goodwin in Morgan and Rutherford, 1998). While the academy was never merely a creature of the other three patrons, it was never entirely independent of them, either. What the future holds for economics in the United States will of course be decided by its academic practitioners, but their decisions will be conditioned and constrained, as they always have been, by outside political and financial interests.

Bibliography

Anderson, P. 2013. 'American foreign policy and its thinkers', *New Left Review*, n.s., 85, September–October, 5–167.

Cicarelli, J. 2012. 'Economic thought among American aboriginals prior to 1492', *American Journal of Economics and Sociology*, 71 (1), January, 77–125.

Coats, A.W. (ed). 1996. *The Post-1945 Internationalization of Economics*. Durham, NC: Duke University Press.

Colander, D, Holt, R.P.F. and Rosser, J.B. 2004. *The Changing Face of Economics*. Ann Arbor, MI: University of Michigan Press.

Colander, D. and Landreth, H. 1996. *The Coming of Keynesianism to America: Conversations with the Founders of Keynesian Economics*. Cheltenham: Edward Elgar.

Dorfman, J. 1965–9. *The Economic Mind in American Civilisation*, five volumes. New York: Kelley.

Emmett, R.B. and Madison, J. (eds). 2006. *The Biographical Dictionary of American Economists*, two volumes. Bristol: Thoemmes Continuum.

Fourcade, M. 2006. 'The construction of a global profession: the transnationalization of economics', *American Journal of Sociology*, 112 (1), July, 145–94.

Fourcade, M. 2009, *Economists and Societies: Discipline and Profession in the United States, Britain and France, 1890s to 1990s*. Princeton, NJ: Princeton University Press.

Harcourt, G.C. 1972. *Some Cambridge Controversies in the Theory of Capital*. Cambridge: Cambridge University Press.

Hughes, J. and Cain, L. 2011. *American Economic History*, eighth edition. Boston, MA: Addison Wesley.

King, J.E. 1988. *Economic Exiles*. Basingstoke: Macmillan.

Lee, F. 2009. *A History of Heterodox Economics: Challenging the Mainstream in the Twentieth Century*. London: Routledge.

Lekachman, R. 1969. *The Age of Keynes*. Harmondsworth: Penguin.

Maddison, A. 2006. *The World Economy*. Paris: OECD.

Mirowski, P. 2002. *Machine Dreams: Economics Becomes a Cyborg Science*. Cambridge: Cambridge University Press.

Mirowski, P. 2013. *Never Let a Serious Crisis Go To Waste: How Neoliberalism Survived the Financial Meltdown*. London: Verso.

Morgan, M.S. and Rutherford, M. (eds). 1998. *From Interwar Pluralism to Postwar Neoclassicism*. Durham, NC: Duke University Press.

Ross, D. 1991. *The Origins of American Social Science*. Cambridge: Cambridge University Press.

Van Horn, R. and Mirowski, P. 2009. 'The rise of the Chicago School of economics and the birth of neoliberalism', in P. Mirowski and D. Plehwe (eds), *The Road from Mont Pèlerin: the Making of the Neoliberal Thought Collective*. Cambridge, MA: Harvard University Press, 139–78.

Weintraub, E.R. 2002. *How Economics Became a Mathematical Science*. Durham, NC: Duke University Press.

Yonay, Y.P. 1998. *The Struggle over the Soul of Economics: Institutionalist and Neoclassical Economics in America between the Wars*. Princeton, NJ: Princeton University Press.

12

Canada

Robin Neill

Canada is an independent political unit, or as independent as a small country can be in a post-modern, globalized world. It does not have an independent economy: its economy is a region in the Euro-American economy. Accordingly, in so far as economics is a derivative of the circumstances of a nation and the policies adopted to cope with circumstances, economics in Canada is a distinctive derivative of a region in the Euro-American economy, which is not to say a derivative of economics itself in France, Britain or the United States.

A measure of its derivation is the number of Canadian economists who have migrated to the United States. We can start with the economic historian Norman Gras, who challenged F.J. Turner's Frontier Hypothesis by asking the question, frontier of what? Gras, born in Toronto, graduated from the University of Western Ontario, but ended his career in 1950 at Harvard. William Ashley is a lame example. He migrated from Britain to the University of Toronto, staying only four years before moving to Harvard in 1892. Jacob Viner was born in Montreal in 1892, took his first degree at McGill, but spent the rest of his life at Chicago, Stanford, Yale, and Princeton. Of course there is J.K. Galbraith, born at Iona Station in Ontario in 1931, he received his first degree at the Ontario Agricultural College and spent the rest of his life in the United States. Harry Johnson perhaps never really left Canada, but his career was in the United States and the United Kingdom. Other examples would include Craufurd Goodwin at Duke University, and perhaps Randall Wright, a graduate of the University of Manitoba, who in 2012 was a leading light at the Wisconsin School of Business. No doubt still other examples could be given, William H. Lazonick, who finished at Harvard, and Dan Usher, who finished at Chicago (Groenewegen, 2000, 81), but this is enough to give substance to Harold Innis' comment, "Canada becomes a headless nation with its brains scattered over other countries" (Innis, 1946, xi).

Canada is not a derivative of Euro-American civilization: it is a part of it. Its economics is not a derivative of economics in Europe or the United States: its economics is derivative of that part of Euro-American civilization that is Canada. Of course, there has been contrary opinion. Melville Watkins referred to Harry Johnson's work as derivative, alleging Johnson had not escaped "the dilemma of the colonial intellectual" (Watkins, 1978, S89). Watkins is to be forgiven. He was responding to an equally tendentious debating point.

Referring to a number of Western Marxist, Canadian nationalists, Daniel Drache, Stephen Hymer, James Laxer, Abraham Rotstein, and Melville Watkins, Johnson wrote,

> [T]he temptation of Canadian academics with either insufficient academic competence by standards or a taste for easy popularity among the masses to take the easy route of imitating and regurgitating the unscholarly [sic] and rabble-rousing pseudointellectual [sic] outpourings of their opposite numbers in foreign countries . . . It would be extremely difficult to discern from the shallow and frequently near-psychotic writings of some Canadians employed in otherwise reputable economics departments, on such subjects as American investment in Canada and the destruction of pollution of the environment, that serious Canadian economic scholars have achieved world-wide professional recognition for their contributions to the economics of resource utilization and the multinational corporation.
>
> *(Cited in Moggridge, 2008, 332)*

Johnson is also to be forgiven. Watkins had said some damning things about Johnson and his friends (Watkins, 1970).

Further, with respect to the "derivative" nature of things, the first economic regime in Canada was an incidence of the feudal Custom of Paris. Canada's First National Policy of tariffs and a fiat currency, announced by the Prime Minister in 1878, was a copy of practice in the United States. The Second National Policy, unannounced but in place by 1896, was manifestation of the New Imperialism as it took shape in Britain's global band of railways and steamships. The Third National Policy, written into a 1944 Government White Paper and Green Book, presented a Canadian version of British Keynesian policy. Finally, the Fourth National Policy, control of inflation, free trade with the United States, and the neo-conservative downsizing of government, mimicked policy in the United States. Harold Innis would have referred to this as "wholesale borrowing." On this showing, Canada itself has been simply a derivative of France, Britain, and the United States.

Evidently, authoritative assertions of the derivative nature of economics in Canada are easy to find. The only full length history of economics in Canada concluded to a "common North American discourse" (Neill, 1991). Writing at the close of the first 25 years of the Canadian Economics Association, Anthony Scott asserted: "It is . . . difficult to show that the Canadian economics profession is not merely a pocket of the larger profession" (Scott, 1992, 36).

It is difficult to show, but it can be shown there is a characteristic of "Canadian economics" that makes it distinct. In his intellectual biography of Harry Johnson, Donald Moggridge stated: "There was a certain nihilism in Harry's work" (Moggridge, 2008, 150). As Richard Lipsey put it, "Harry's work on pure trade in the 1950s [his most original contribution according to W. Max Cordon (1984)] . . . consisted of a series of case studies [often of a small, open economy] in which an extremely ingenious and subtle mind found exceptions to virtually all of the qualitative 'laws' of international Economics with which he was presented" (Lipsey, 1978, S37). But Lipsey insisted Johnson's contribution to economics was not "nihilistic" (ibid.). It was not a rejection of neoclassical theory, it was a qualification.

From the beginning

The first example of this kind of nihilism in Canadian economics appeared in John Rae's *New Principles* (1833–4), in which he took precisely the position attributed to Johnson. Specifically, Adam Smith's argument against tariffs would hold only if certain assumptions about conditions on the ground were made (James, vol.II, 1965, 384), and, in general, theory without empirical reference is no guide to policy (ibid., *passim*).

An analysis of Canadian economic thought in the nineteenth century must start with Craufurd Goodwin's account (Goodwin, 1961). Before the nineteenth century there was some economics in Canada, but very little (Neill, 1991). What one finds in Goodwin is a repeated assertion that most of what was to be found in nineteenth-century Canadian economic thought was too primitive to be called economics, and what was not primitive was borrowed from Britain and the United States. Still, Goodwin draws an interesting conclusion.

> During these years [1867 to 1900] the principles of classical economics were generally accepted both in Great Britain and the Colonies, and Canadians were convinced that any use of economic science as a guide to policy would require compliance with doctrinaire laissez faire and the subordination of long run economic, social, and political goals of their policies of tariff protection, railway subsidy, and western land disposal to searching analysis because they feared that examination of means would lead to condemnation of ends. Governments hesitated to consult or to employ professional economists; avenues of publication were closed to amateurs; and in the face of public disapproval universities were reluctant to offer extensive economic training. The ground was fertile in this period for growth of a distinctly Canadian "protectionist" economics, but no Friedrich List or Henry Carey appeared.
>
> *(Goodwin, 1961, 203)*

But John Rae had appeared and was cited by Prime Minister Macdonald when the National Policy was proclaimed in 1877. Further, Goodwin himself devoted six pages specifically to John Rae (122–7), in addition to a lengthy chapter (42–68) to other advocates of tariff protection, particularly Isaac Buchanan whose organization, the Association for the Promotion of Canadian Industry, under one name or another, was largely responsible for the fiscal half of the 1877 National Policy.

This is not a criticism of Goodwin's account. Goodwin defined economics as normative theory, what Richard Lipsey called "qualitative" theory, and Goodwin was not explicitly addressing the question posed here. Though much more could be said with respect to the nihilism of economic thought in nineteenth-century Canada, it is time to move on to the first decade of the twentieth century, to Gilles Paquet's accounts (Paquet, 1987; Neill and Paquet, 1983) and to Harold Adams Innis.

But before continuing, it is necessary to point out that there is a real difference in economics in the different regions of Canada, as I have detailed in my *A History of Canadian Economic Thought*. The reader must understand, however, that the delicate political position of French-speaking Quebec in the Canadian federation has generated a mindset that privileges that element in national discourse. *Pensée économique* has no more influence on the discipline in general in Canada, than has the economics produced in any other region. Indeed, major advances in the discipline have not originated in Quebec or in any other region.

Paquet answers the question, "What has been distinct about economics in Canada?" right off. Economics in Canada, particularly in Quebec, has been "heretical," which is something beyond nihilistic, where "nihilistic" means "a considered qualification of qualitative theory." A nihilistic reading of Canadian economics in general leads to a more moderate judgement (Neill, 1991, 39–56, 149–71). Etienne Parent wrote with Adam Smith and the nineteenth-century political economists in a supporting background, but was ready to abandon their theory for the sake of "national" survival. Antoine Gerin-Lajoie and his son, Léon Gerin, wrote in the shadow of the French sociologist, P.G.F. Le Play, not of the "marginal revolution" in economics. Over the turn-of-the-century, Robert Errol Bouchette had J.K. Robertus in the background of his economics. Robertus was something of a socialist and opposed to what one might designate mainstream, qualitative political economy. I do not mean to imply that Paquet's use of the word "heretical" was totally off the mark. What was distinct about the work of Robert Errol Bouchette, Édouard Montpetit, and François-Albert Angers (to unconscionably shrink the list) was not their economics, it was their being *economist esengagées*.

Bouchette, particularly in his first book, *Emparon nous de l'Industrie* (1901), moved nationalism in Quebec away from agriculture to commerce and manufacturing where it was anchored by Édouard Montpetit. In his three-volume published works, *La Conquête Économique* (1939–42), Montpetit constructed economics to include values beyond those expressed in prices, specifically the values of French Canada. Angers was nihilistic in the Johnsonian sense.

> Let us not forget that we have, within the past half century, witnessed the political bankruptcy of two theories in which our modern world, or at least certain parts of it, had placed its hopes – the liberal theory of economic equilibrium and the quantitative theory of money in its mathematical form . . . They leave behind them principles and experiences which are definite acquisitions for human knowledge and wisdom, but nothing to defend their integral application as policies.
>
> *(Angers, 1956, 297)*

Pensée économique, in one respect, was typically Canadian. The principal development in turn-of-the-century qualitative theory was the "marginal revolution," particularly as embodied in Marshall's *Principles*. The influence of even Marshallian economics, let alone of Marshall himself, was diffuse and weak in Canada before Keynesian Marshallian economics came on the scene (Dimand and Neill, 2010, 56–7). The influence of the Historical School, with its emphasis on empiricism rather than theory, was everywhere evident. Economics in Quebec, though having a historical bent, was not of the Historical School, but neither was it Marshallian.

This brings the story to Harold Adams Innis, commonly thought to have been the salient figure in "pre-war" economics in Canada. Innis certainly began by rejecting the boundaries of qualitative theory. Simply put, he chose American Institutionalism over Marshallian static micro economics:

> Veblen has waged a constructive warfare of emancipation against the standardized static economics which has become so dangerous on a continent with ever increasing numbers of students clamouring for textbooks on final economic theory. He attempted to outline the economics of dynamic change and to work out a theory not only of dynamics but of cyclonics . . . The conflict between the economics of a long and highly industrialized country such as England and the economics of recently new and borrowing countries will become less severe as the theory of cyclonics is worked out.
>
> *(Innis, 1929, 56)*

Innis began looking for a theory of growth in a new satellite economy. What he sought was not at all like the theory of growth that emerged at the time of Keynesian macroeconomics, nor was it simply a "vent for surplus" theory of expansion in a small, resource exporting economy as presented in the neoclassical formulations of Wynne Plumptre (1936), Archibald Currie (1942), or Richard Caves (1971). Certainly it was not at all like W.A. Mackintosh's early Keynesian version (1936, 462–3) or the later Melville Watkins' Marxist theory of the staple trap (1977).

The point is not that these formulations were empirically questionable, as Ken Buckley (1958) and Chambers and Gordon (1966) suggested. The point is the staple theory presented by Innis was based on the "very long run" consequences of new "all-purpose technologies," not the "short and long run" considerations featured in qualitative theory.

But evidently, there is another point to be made here. There was a reaction to Chambers and Gordon's counter factual, nihilistic questioning of the Staple Theory (Bertram (1973); J.H. Dales, J.C. McManus, and M.H. Watkins (1967); R.E. Caves (1971)). The point to be made is by mid-century, even without reference to the emerging high fashion of Keynesian macroeconomics, and even with respect to what has been touted as Canada's contribution to economics (the Staple Theory), there was more in Canadian economics than can be found in Innis' nihilistic approach.

The recent period

Within a decade of Innis' untimely death, his student, Harry Gordon Johnson, though not a resident (*cf.* Anthony Scott, 1992) in Canada, had taken Innis' place in the Canadian economics establishment. He soon passed judgment on his colleagues:

> There are four broadly defined areas in which I think Canadian economists have made or are making significant contributions to the scientific discipline of economics. These are the economics of natural resources, monetary economics, public finance and especially the theory of federal finance, and international economics.
>
> *(1968, 141)*

These are fields of economics of particular interest in a small, open, regionalized economy. Actually Johnson stated that Canadians had dominated the field of international economics with major contributions to the subject on the world stage, but his concern was only with the role of resident Canadians, thereby ruling out himself. He named major contributors: Ed Safarian, Paul Wonnacott, and Harry Eastman and Stefan Stykolt on international economics, Tony Scott and H. Scott Gordon on resource economics, and Albert Breton on a neoclassical construction of a federal system of government.

Johnson was pointing to Canadian contributions, not to the general trend of economics in Canada. In fact there were three major components of the trend in the second half of the twentieth century: the Keynesian vision and its evolution into Monetarism, the "formal revolution" that mathematized economics, and positivist econometrics. In this information environment, with the Canadian economics profession multiplying in expanding university departments, and the *Canadian Journal of Economics* emerging from the *Canadian Journal of Economics and Political Science*, we find Harry Johnson and his entourage at the University of Manchester, the University of Chicago, and the London School of Economics.

It would be rash to attempt yet another summary of Johnson's contribution to the content of the discipline of economics (*cf. Canadian Journal of Economics*, vol.11, no.4, Supplement, 1978; *Journal of Political Economy,* vol.92, 1984, 565–711; Donald Moggridge's biography, 2008). In any case, his major contribution may have been of a different sort. He was a giant in the economics profession of his day, bridging the Atlantic Ocean by teaching at the London School of Economics and the University of Chicago at the same time. He exploited the divide between the "Post Keynesian" Joan Robinson and the Monetarist Milton Friedman, between socialists and neoconservatives, and between "nationalists" and "continentalists" in Canada. He rejected the post-Keynesianism of Cambridge, UK, but never totally accepted the Monetarism of Chicago.

He promoted free trade, though he showed that the qualitative arguments underpinning it were not proof against all historical conditions. He was a masterful teacher and a support for promising students. He was not resident in Canada, but he religiously attended the annual conference of the Canadian Economics Association, and he was the *eminence gris* in the development of the Economics Department at the University of Western Ontario.

His students and associates were prominent in the Canadian economics profession into the twenty-first century: particularly Christopher Archibald, Michael Parkin, Richard Lipsey, and David Laidler, but also others whom he encountered in Manchester, Chicago, and London. David Laidler (*cf.* Leeson, 2010) and Richard Lipsey, who, when history is written will stand among his best students, did have a certain nihilism in their work. Like Johnson, Laidler used the history of thought as an entry into current debate. He began as a Monetarist but eventually moved away from that position in matters of policy. Richard Lipsey will be remembered most for his "General Theory of the Second Best" (1956), and for his monumental *Economic Transformations* (2005), both of which proclaim the proposition, either read in or read into Harry Johnson's opera, that whatever qualitative theory might have to say, historical circumstance determines historical outcomes. *Economic Transformations* brings to mind Johnson's comment at the end of a book on contemporary growth theory, "Abstraction is an indispensable element of scientific investigation ... but not abstraction from the problem at hand" (Kraus and Johnson, 1974, 335).

Clearly, however, I am making a case on the basis of a few, however outstanding, members of the profession. The period also encompassed "old Keynesians," for example Pierre Fortin, and new style growth theorists, for example the internationally respected Peter Howitt. There were old Keynesians who were quite able to defend their view even in the presence of hostile company (Dimand, 2010). There were many others, and an opinion on their general character was put forward in the late Johnson era:

> On the whole Canadian economists seem to be quite supportive of the price mechanism as an allocative devise, and convinced of the powers of market forces in delivering outcomes. The more highly educated the economist, the more likely he or she was to accept the role of markets ... [Canadian economists are] not asinclined as American and European economists to accept Keynesian propositions regarding the stabilization functions of government. An astoundingly high 97 percent of Canadian economists accepted the view that tariffs and quotas reduced the general level of welfare ... on the whole Canadian economists are less disposed to support interventionist policy than are their American counterparts ... Canadian economists [are] slightly more supportive of the redistributive role of government.
>
> *(Black with Walker, 1988, 148–9)*

Of course, this does not necessarily mean they were rigid adherents of qualitative theory.

Perhaps this was also true of economics in French-speaking Quebec. After François-Albert Angers, value-oriented economics, what Angers designated as truly "*pensée économique*" seemed to disappear (Fortin, 1984; Paquet, 1985). One would work hard to find the New Institutionalism of Migué or the conservative Currency School neoclassicism of Roger Dehem to be nihilistic in the Johnsonian sense. The attack on neoclassical economics by the purveyors of Western Marxist *Sociologie Économique* was anything but Johnsonian. A possible explanation of this state of affairs may be found in Innis' assertion that demands of publication required a more standard view and non-Canada-specific topics (Innis, 1946, xi); and in Tony Scott's comment on the twenty-fifth anniversary of the Canadian Economics Association: "For it is mostly senior Canadian economists who can develop a commitment to Canadian issues or policies" (Scott, 1993, 34). However, it was a "senior economist" who displayed a penchant for criticism of the discipline in general:

> Monetarists, neo-Keynesians, and New-Classicists passionately debate the respective merits of their views . . . [but] there is no generally agreed statement of their major theories . . . A science where, after decades of hypothesis testing, no one can agree on the precise specification of the hypotheses already subject to prolonged testing is a very dismal discipline indeed.
>
> *(Lipsey, 1983, 367)*

The post-recent period

Beginning with Laband (1985) and Black with Walker (1988), if not before, the profession in Canada took account of itself as an institution: the number and character of its members, the number and quality of its publications, the leading Departments of Economics. The Canadian Economics Association's twenty-fifth anniversary summation of Economics in Canada focused attention on the institutional development of the profession (*Canadian Journal of Economics*, 1993, vol.26, 1–76). Lucas (1995), Davies, Kocher and Sutter (2008), and Simpson and Emery (2012) kept a running score into the twenty-first century. These works, too, from a different point of view, say something about the nature of economics in Canada.

Concern with methodology continued beyond the twentieth century. Though not in the spirit of Johnson, Lawrence Boland (2003) continued his critique of neoclassical economics. Arthur Robson (2007) took a very different route to defend the principles of neoclassical economics, presumably against the emerging behavioralists. Tom Courchene can be taken to represent the legions who labored in the service of so-called objective research institutes. His publications, well into the twenty-first century, have been as numberless as have been the publications of his counterparts in other research institutes. Courchene began as something of a monetarist, but, like his ilk, he has not taken up a single-minded pursuit of economic theory. Rather he has served in the trench war over current policy. Perhaps that is "capital using" rather than "capital building" as Johnson said, but, there is something Johnsonian, even Innisian, in a focus on conditions on the ground rather than on abstractions.

In the last years of the twentieth century, feminist economics arrived in Canada (Wooley, 1993; Phipps, 1999). It was openly nihilistic, insisting on the importance of institutions and the fluidity of preferences. Like Johnsonian nihilism, feminist economics, as it appeared in Canada, qualified rather than rejected qualitative theory. Frances Wooley and Shelley Phipps continued their critique of Gary Becker's economics of the family well into the twenty-first century.

In the last two decades of the twentieth century, New Institutionalism, behavioral economics, and game theory did not go unnoticed in public sector economics (Boadway, 1997), in industrial organization (Green, 1987), and in international trade theory (Harris, 1995). In a species of nihilistic economics, Timothy Hazeldine (1990) tied the new departures together. Both behavioral economics and game theory began as qualifications of qualitative theory. The same could be said of the New Institutionalism when it was still in the hands of Ronald Coase. New departures continued into the twenty-first century. Richard Harris turned his attention to elements of happiness economics in a series of first decade reports for the Canadian Institute for Living Standards. John Helliwell also turned to happiness economics. Robin Boadway (2012) continued producing in the general field of public sector economics. New departures notwithstanding, international trade and public finance were still fields in which contributions to the discipline in general were being made. But this may overstate the distinctive character of economics in Canada. Clearly, much of this qualification of neoclassical economics is to be found elsewhere in the Euro-American information environment.

Before concluding it would be a mistake not to mention two internationally successful Canadian historians of economic thought, Robert Dimand and Samuel Hollander, who also continued their seemingly endless contributions to the discipline into the twenty-first century.

The first decade of the twenty-first century saw innumerable quantitative studies in the details of every field of economics, but no new overall hypothesis was forthcoming. Economists in Quebec were still interested in the economic possibilities of a politically separate state for *francophones*. In the optimism surrounding telematics in the late twentieth century, the future held promise (Hamel and Belanger, 1992). In the Great Recession, however, the promise of support for independence was unfulfilled (Joanis and Godbout, 2009). Given the nation's continued reliance on primary product exports, particularly petroleum products, the Staple Theory had not lost its explanatory value. Richard Lipsey's *Economic Transformations* looked like the beginning of a new paradigm in the general discipline, but it was received with the enthusiasm with which the 1820s received John Rea's *New Principles*.

Economics in Canada is a mature part of economics in the Euro-American information environment. Its nihilism is less a distinctive characteristic in the twenty-first century. No leading figure with the stature of Rea, Innis, Angers, or Johnson has appeared, but no reincarnation of Marshall, Veblen, Keynes, or even Friedman has yet analyzed the Great Recession. There is no new overarching theory to be foiled by the conditions of a small, open, regionalized economy.

References

Angers, François-Albert, 1956, [Quebec] *Report* Royal Commission of Enquiry on Constitutional Problems, Government of Quebec, Quebec.

Bertram, Gordon W., 1973, "The Relevance of the Wheat Boom in Canadian Economic Growth", *Canadian Journal of Economics*, vol.6, 545–6.

Black, W. with Walker, M., 1988, "Entropy in the Canadian Economics Profession: Sampling Consensus", *Canadian Public Policy*, vol.14, 137–50.

Boadway, Robin, 1997, "Public Economics and the Theory of Public Policy", *Canadian Journal of Economics*, vol.30, 753–72.

Boadway, Robin, 2012, *From Optimal Tax Theory to Tax Policy: Retrospect and Prospective Views*. MIT Press, Cambridge, MA.

Boland, Lawrence A., 2003, *The Foundations of Economic Method: A Popperian Perspective*, Routledge, London.

Buckley, Kenneth, 1958, "The Role of Staple Industries in Canada's Economic Development", *Journal of Economic History*, 1958, vol.18, 439–50.

Caves, Richard E., 1971, "Export Led Growth and the New Economic History", in J.N. Bhagwati *et al.*, *Trade, Balance of Payments and Growth*, North Holland, Amsterdam, 403–42.

Chambers, Edward J. and Gordon, Donald, 1966, "Primary Products and Economic Growth, an Empirical Measurement", *Journal of Political Economy*, vol.74, 315–32.

Cordon, W. Max, 1984, "Harry Johnson's Contributions to International Economics", *Journal of Political Economy*, vol.92, 564–9.

Currie, Archibald W., 1942, *Canadian Economic Development*, Nelson, Toronto.

Dales, J.H., McManus, J.C., and Watkins, M.H., 1967, "Primary Products and Economic Growth: a Comment", *Journal of Political Economy*, 1967, vol.75, 876–80.

Davies, James B., Kosher, Martin, and Sutter, Mathias, 2008, "Economic Research in Canada: a Long Run Assessment of Journal Publications", *Canadian Journal of Economics*, vol.41, 22–45.

Dimand, Robert, 2010, "David Laidler's Contribution to the History of Monetary Economics", in Robert Leeson (ed.), *David Laidler's Contribution to Economics*, Palgrave Macmillan, Basingstoke, St. Martin's, New York, 60–84.

Dimand, Robert and Neill, Robin, 2010, 'The Reception of Marshall in the US', in Tiziano Raffaelli, Gioacomo Becattini, Katia Caldari, and Marco Dardi (eds), *The Impact of Alfred Marshall's Ideas: The Global Diffusion of his Work*, Edward Elgar Publishing, Cheltenham, UK, and Northampton, MA, 53–8.

Fortin, Pierre, 1984, "La Récherche Économique dans les Universites du Québec Français: les Source de Ruppture ave le Passée et les Défis de l'Avnir", in G.-H. Levesque, *Continuité et rupture, les science sociales au Québec*, PUM, Montreal, vol.1, 161–71.

Goodwin, Craufurd D.W., 1961, *Canadian Economic Thought*, Cambridge University Press, London.

Green, Christopher, 1987, "Industrial Organization Paradigms, Empirical Evidence, and the Economic Case for Competition Policy", *Canadian Journal of Economics*, vol.20, 483–505.

Groenewegen, Peter, 2000, Review of *Exemplary Economists of the Twentieth Century* http://www.hetsa.org.au/pdf/32-RA-1.pdf

Hamel, Pierre, and Belanger, Yves (eds), 1992, *Québec 2000: Quell Développement?* Presses de l'Université du Québec, Sillery.

Harris, Richard, 1995, "Trade and Communication Costs", *Canadian Journal of Economics*, vol.28, S46–S75.

Hazeldine, Timothy, 1990, "Why Do the Free Trade Gain Numbers Differ So Much? The Role of Industrial Organization in General Equilibrium", *Canadian Journal of Economics*, vol.23, 791–806.

Innis, H.A., 1929, "A Bibliography of Thorstein Veblen", *Southwestern Political and Social Science Quarterly*, vol.10, 56–68.

Innis, H.A., 1946, *Political Economy in the Modern State*, Ryerson Press, Toronto.

James, R. Warren, 1965, *John Rae, Political Economist*, University of Toronto Press, Toronto.

Joanis, Marcelin and Luc Godbout (eds), 2009, *Le Québec Économique*, 2009, Les Presses de l'Université Laval, Québec.

Johnson, Harry G., 1968, "Canadian Contributions to the Discipline of Economics since 1945", *Canadian Journal of Economics*, vol.1, 129–46.

Kraus, M.B. and Johnson, H.G. (eds), 1974, *General Equilibrium Analysis*, George Allen and Unwin, London.

Laband, David N., 1985, "A Ranking of the Top Canadian Economics Departments by Research Productivity of Graduates", *Canadian Journal of Economics*, vol.18, 904–7.

Laidler, David N., 1988, "Taking Money Seriously", *Canadian Journal of Economics*, vol.18, 686–713.

Leeson, Robert (ed.), 2010, *David Laidler's Contributions to Economics*, Palgrave Macmillan, New York.

Lipsey, Richard G., 1978, "Harry Johnson's Contribution to the Theory of International Trade", *Canadian Journal of Economics,* vol.11, November Supplement, S34–S54.

Lipsey, Richard G., 1983, Review of *Macro-Economics: First Canadian Edition* (Dornbush, Fischer, and Sparks), *Modern Macroeconomics* (Parkin), *Macroeconomics: Theory and Policy in Canada* (Wilton and Prescott), *Canadian Journal of Economics*, vol.16, 362–71.

Lipsey, Richard G., and Lancaster, Kevin, 1956, "The General Theory of Second Best", *Review of Economic Studies*, vol.24, 11–32.

Lipsey, Richard G., Kenneth Carlaw, and Clifford Bekar, 2005, *Economic Transformations, General Purpose Technologies and Sustained Economic Growth*, Oxford University Press, Oxford.

Mackintosh, William A., 1936, "Some Aspects of a Pioneer Economy", *Canadian Journal of Economics and Political Science*, vol.2, 457–63.

Lucas, Robert F. 1995, "Contributions to Economic Journals by the Canadian Economics Profession", *Canadian Journal of Economics*, vol.28, 945–60.

Moggridge, Donald, 2008, *Harry Johnson: A Life in Economics*, Cambridge University Press, Cambridge.

Neill, Robin F., 1972, *A New Theory of Value: the Canadian Economics of H.A. Innis*, University of Toronto Press, Toronto.

Neill, Robin F., 1991, *A History of Canadian Economic Thought*, Routledge, London.

Neill, Robin F., 2008, "The Passing of Naive Neoclassicism, *or Not*: Economics in Canada, 1977–2007", presented at the 35th annual meeting of the History of Economics Society, June 27, York University, Toronto.

Neill, Robin F. and Paquet, Gilles, 1983, "L'Économie Hérétique: Canada to 1967", *Canadian Journal of Economics*, vol.16, 3–13.

Paquet, Gilles, 1985, "La Fruit Dont l'Ombre est la Saveur: Reflections Aventureuse sur la Pensée Économique au Québec", *Récherches Sociographiques*, vol.26, 356–98.

Paquet, Gilles, 1987, "*La Pensée Économique au Québec Française*", Association canadienne-français pour l'avancement des sciences, Montreal.

Phipps, Shelly, 1999, "Economics and the Wellbeing of Canadian Children", *Canadian Journal of Economics*, vol.32, 1135–63.

Plumptre, A.F. Wynne, 1936, "The Nature of Economic and Political Development in the British Dominions", *Canadian Journal of Economics and Political Science*, vol.3, 488–507.

Robson, Arthur, with Hillard Kaplan, 2007, "The Evolution of Intertemporal Preferences", *American Journal of Economics*, vol.97, 496–500.

Scott, Anthony D., 1993, "Does Living in Canada Make One a Canadian Economist?", *Canadian Journal of Economics*, vol.26, 26–38.

Simpson, W. and Emery, J.C., 2012, "Canadian Economics in Decline: Implication for Canada's Economics Journals", *Canadian Public Policy*, vol.38, 445–70.

Watkins, Melville H., 1970, "The Dismal State of Economics in Canada", in Ian Lumsden, *Close the 49th Parallel*, University of Toronto Press, Toronto, 284–302.

Watkins, Melville, H., 1977, "The Staple Theory Revisited", *Journal of Canadian Studies*, vol.12, 83–96.

Watkins, Melville H., 1978, "The Economics of Nationalism and the Nationalism of Economics", *Canadian Journal of Economics*, vol.11, no.4, Supplement, November, S87–S120.

Wooley, Frances R., 1993, "The Feminist Challenge to Neoclassical Economics", *Cambridge Journal of Economics*, vol.17, 485–500.

13

Mexico and Central America

Richard Weiner

Despite the fact that there are indigenous peoples in Mesoamerica today who contend that they are still resisting the European conquest, Mexico and Central America have had a long history of connections to the West. Indeed, Mexico's National University (founded 1551) is one of the Western hemisphere's oldest European-influenced universities. Thus, Western thought and culture have been influential in the sphere of economic ideas. But contrary to the claims of those who critiqued Mexicans and Central Americans for imitating imported economic ideas that did not fit local conditions (e.g. dependency theorists such as André Gunder Frank, who charged that Latin American elites blindly adhered to wrong-headed free market ideals during the nineteenth-century export boom), foreign ideas have not been thoughtlessly adopted. Rather, they have been reformulated and adapted to fit the local and national contexts. This refashioning is partly a consequence of the distinct histories and cultures of the region. For example, a history of revolt and concern with unrest has helped to make social liberalism prominent in Mexico. Similarly, the region's proximity to the United States has inspired anti-imperialist discourse. Refashioning has also been inspired by politics. Foreign concepts have been "nationalized" by incorporating national symbols to give them greater credibility.

Despite the fact that there are groups that adhere to divergent philosophies, some of which are shaped by certain Mesoamerican ideals and others that are influenced by strands of Western thought, there is a prominent materialist ethic in Mexico and Central America. This contention clashes with much of the earlier writings on the subject by contemporary actors and scholars. Colonial and national-era elites complained about natives' lack of individualism and materialism. Nineteenth-century liberals lamented about the Catholic Church's non-materialist philosophy and influence. Similarly, scholars have argued that a Protestant work ethic accounts for the United States' material progress and a lack of that ethic explains Latin America's sub-par performance. However, recent historical scholarship on ethno-history, the Church's economic role in society and comparative histories of the Western Hemisphere has challenged the idea that a non-materialist philosophy predominated in Mexico and Central America.

Another similarity is that trends in economic ideas have evolved in related ways in both regions. Nevertheless, public economic discourse and academic economics are much more developed in Mexico than Central America. Indeed, leading twentieth-century Latin America economic journals, such as *Trimestre Económico* [*Economic Quarterly*], and publishing houses for economic texts, e.g. Fondo de Cultura Económica [Collection in Economic Culture], are Mexican. This contrast between the regions is largely a consequence of the fact that intellectual culture (the press, the arts, etc.) and academia are more established in Mexico than Central America, a difference stemming from the two regions' contrasting development. Despite the fact that both have high degrees of inequality, Mexico is one of the wealthiest parts of Latin America (today some predict it will shoot ahead of Brazil in coming decades), and Central America, which is comprised of several small nations, is one of the poorest.

The development of ideas over the long-term

In the aftermath of the Conquest of Mexico (1519–21), mercantilism and the experience of the Reconquista (711–1492) shaped general Spanish attitudes about the economic value of the New World, when Mexico became the jewel of Spain's empire. Shaped by mercantilist ideals, during three centuries of colonial rule (1521–1821), Mexico was valued mostly for its precious metals. Columbus's "discovery" took place during an intellectual age when bullion was held in very high regard. It was said to boost international trade, create jobs, and alleviate social problems. Some writers (e.g. Thomas Mun) used biological metaphors to illustrate the social and economic importance of the circulation of money in society, explaining that a healthy body (i.e. society) needed "blood" (i.e. bullion). Unsurprisingly, Columbus's reports emphasized bullion.

So did the writings by noted Conquistadors of Mexico (e.g. Fernando Cortés and Bernal Díaz del Castillo). Columbus and Conquistadors also stressed another economic resource: native populations. The Reconquista revealed that conquered subjects could be utilized as workers (i.e. coerced labor drafts called "encomiendas") and sources of revenue (since subjects were required to pay a head tax). From this perspective, Mexico proved to be very valuable, owing to the fact that the Aztecs were the largest sedentary civilization in the New World. Since it had limited precious metals and its Mayan kingdoms proved difficult to conquer, Central America was a backwater for most of the colonial era. Spain's economic success in Mexico inspired imitators. At the start of the seventeenth century the British Virginia Company hoped to find precious metals and large sedentary civilizations in North America.

Evolving seventeenth- and eighteenth-century mercantilist thought that highlighted the importance of manufacturing informed an economic critique of Spanish colonialism (e.g. Mun critiqued Spain in the early seventeenth century). From this perspective, Spain's abundance of bullion was its downfall since precious metals impeded industrialization. French thought was influential, especially the ideas of Jean Baptiste Colbert regarding the significance of manufacturing. Spain's eighteenth-century modification of the colonial system, known as the Bourbon Reforms, which were enacted in part to derive more economic benefits from the colonies, were informed by this new thinking. Spanish Visitor General José de Gálvez was in charge of developing and implementing these reforms in New Spain, which Mexico and Central America were part of.

Spain's reforms – informed by mercantilist and liberal ideals – were contradictory, leading scholars to label them a form of "enlightened despotism." Mercantilism informed reforms that stimulated Spanish manufacturing to achieve a favorable balance of trade. In keeping with the English model, the ideal was to make the colonies sources of raw materials for Spanish manufacturing and also consumers of Spanish industrial goods. Colonial industries that competed with Spanish ones, e.g. wine, were prohibited, and colonial raw materials deemed useful to Spanish manufacturing industry were stimulated. This enhanced Central America's significance since its indigo and cochineal were utilized in European textile industries. This pro-industrial perspective also inspired a critique of Spain's merchants' guilds. Critics charged that monopolies favored foreign imported goods, and therefore they needed to be weakened in the quest for Spanish industrialization.

Economic liberalism informed reforms that sought to boost agricultural production. Spanish economist Gasper de Jovellanos's *Informe sobre la Ley Agraria* [*Report about the Agrarian Law*, 1795], a text influenced by Adam Smith and the Physiocrats, proved influential. Jovellanos maintained that clerical estates, entailed estates, and unoccupied public land impeded production. Influenced by the English enclosure movement, he promoted individualism and private property to enhance production. Influenced by Jovellanos, Gálvez promoted secularizing Church missions and distributing land to families. He also promoted mixed-race agricultural colonies, which would remove Indians from their isolated condition and out of the clutches of the Church and make them productive subjects. Liberal ideals, albeit with mercantilist elements, also informed trade: the new policy of "free trade" allowed greater freedom in the name of increasing commerce, but it had to be within the confines of the Spanish Empire. In Mexico and Central America some found this appealing since it provided autonomy from the colonizing power (and in the case of Central America, from Mexico too).

During the age of independence another reformist economic discourse that had strong liberal tendencies and proved influential was Alexander von Humboldt's *Political Essay on the Kingdom of New Spain*, which originally appeared in French in 1811 and was quickly translated into English, Spanish, and German. The fact that his work was authoritative, encyclopedic, highly optimistic, relied on and cited New Spain authors, and appeared at a time when global interest in Spain's new world Empire was high, helps to explain *Political Essay*'s great popularity. In nineteenth-century Latin America, the tremendous influence of a single work is unique to Mexico. Humboldt's study was broad (covering politics, economics, defense, demography, etc.) and thus cannot be characterized as a work of political economy. Nevertheless, he focused heavily on economics and was influenced by Adam Smith, the Physiocrats, and William Petty's political arithmetic.

Humboldt depicted New Spain as favored by nature owing to its large size, fertile soil, varied climate (in which countless products could grow), and advantageous commercial location between the Atlantic and Pacific (which destined it to be a leader in world trade). Showing Smith's influence, Humboldt critiqued colonialism, maintaining that Spain's restrictive economic policies impeded Mexico's material progress and industrialization. Humboldt's downgrading of the economic significance of silver also revealed Smith's influence. But Humboldt departed from Smith by arguing that agriculture and mining reinforced one another. Humboldt's high praise for agriculture (he defined it as the most important sector) was partly informed by Physiocratic thought. His socio-economic critique also highlighted agriculture. He maintained that farming for local consumption was most significant since it sustained the population, a socio-economic preoccupation that was also reflected in Humboldt's severe critique – influenced by the Mexican cleric Manuel Abad y Queipo – of inequality and poverty in Mexico.

Humboldt's *Political Essay* influenced and stimulated classical economists' analysis (e.g. that of David Ricardo, Malthus, John Cairnes, and perhaps J.S. Mill) on the relationship between institutions, resource endowment, and development. It was also very influential in Mexico, shaping ideas about the region's potential, the importance of natural environment, economic sectors, policy, and socioeconomic analysis. Humboldt's text helps to explain the great optimism that Mexican and Central American leaders had about their nations' economic futures in the early national era.

This optimism is more surprising for Central America since in the Mexican case Humboldt merely statistically confirmed Mexicans' assumption that their nation was naturally rich. Part of

Central Americans' optimism was rooted in the idea that constructing a canal through the isthmus would bring prosperity, something Humboldt (and numerous writers before him) had promoted. Mexican Tadeo Ortiz de Ayala was strongly influenced by Humboldt. Ortiz echoed Humboldt by emphasizing Mexico's natural advantages, and by promoting colonization (something Gálvez previously championed) and the construction of a transport system to exploit Mexico's vast agricultural potential. Some Central American intellectuals, who championed building a transportation infrastructure and attracting foreign agricultural colonists, had a similar vision.

In the 1830s and 1840s noteworthy liberal and conservative ideologies emerged in Mexico. José María Luis Mora articulated a liberal vision with a socio-economic component, influenced by French thought, Humboldt, and colonial antecedents. Following Humboldt, Mora conceived of Mexico as naturally rich, but identified impediments to the exploitation of wealth. Mora focused on socioeconomic issues, particularly the inequitable distribution of property, above all, the dilemma of the vast holdings of the Church and (to a lesser degree) Indian villages (Mora's "monasteries of Indians"), socio-economic problems Jovellanos and Abad y Queipo had previously identified. Mora's push for social equality differed from the European moderate liberals (e.g. Francois Guizot) who did not promote the interests of labor and champion equality. Scholar Jesús Reyes Heroles argues that the fact that Indians played a large role in Mexico's war of independence helps to explain this preoccupation within equality in Mexican liberal thought.

In fact, before independence Humboldt had warned that inequality in Mexico might inspire a revolt like the 1780s Peruvian Tupac Amaru rebellion. If Humboldt influenced Mora in some ways, in others Mora departed, relying more on the abstract ideas of the "economists," particularly regarding international trade. David Ricardo's works were not prominent in Mexico. Smith, Jean Baptiste Say, and Álvaro Flórez Estrada circulated far more widely, especially the latter's *Curso de Economía Política* [*Manual of Political Economy*, 1828], which championed the international division of labor. From this theoretical framework Mora emphasized products that Mexico had a comparative advantage in, which discounted some of Humboldt's laundry list of natural riches. Mora's focus on comparative advantage, leading him to conclude industrialization was not an option, departed from Humboldt's industrial vision.

Lucas Alamán, the leading Mexican conservative thinker of the era, articulated a competing vision. He rejected the "economists'" abstractions and advocated a historical and empirical perspective. Influenced by the Spanish colonial bureaucrat Fausto de Elhuyar, he initially favored mining as the motor of the Mexican economy. But he later championed industrialization (following the eighteenth-century ideas of Spaniard Pedro Rodríguez Campomanes) for the sake of national independence, and promoted a national development bank to finance manufacturing. Despite Alamán's critique of the liberal economists, he followed Smith in the sense that his vision stressed the division of labor and the importance of capital and labor in generating wealth.

A variant of Mora's liberal economic vision – carried on by a new generation of leading liberal thinkers – Mariano Otero, José María Iglesias, Miguel Lerdo de Tejada, and Guillermo Prieto – won out in the 1850s, during a period known as the Mexican Reform, when Liberals confiscated and sold the Church's landholdings, separated Church and state, passed legislation that set the stage for privatizing Indians' villages, and attacked corporate privileges. In keeping with earlier social concerns, there was an emphasis on individual liberties (especially the freedom of labor) and equality (a yeoman farmer vision).

A parallel development took place in Central America, for around mid-century, liberals also won out, defeating their conservative opponents. Furthermore, the economic ideals of the competing sides were broadly analogous, with the liberals adhering to liberal economic theory and championing comparative advantage and conservatives promoting protectionism. There were minor differences, however. Central American conservatives sought to protect existing crafts industries rather than promote manufacturing, as was the case in Mexico. Central American liberals may not have been as committed to social liberalism as Mexican liberals.

Despite familiarity with contemporary economic thinkers (e.g. J.S. Mill), Comte's positivism, social Darwinism, and material developments proved more consequential for late nineteenth century economic discourse in Mexico and Central America than did economic theorists. Departing from classic economic liberal constructs, positivists conceived society as an evolving social organism rather than a collection of individuals. Sometimes positivist rhetoric fit with classic liberal economic goals. For example, Mexican economist Pablo Macedo justified abolishing taxes on interstate trade by asserting that different "tribute systems" within the same "social organism" resulted in "chaos." Other times, it did not: positivists maintained that, since the civil society was weak, state tutelage, not *laissez-faire*, propelled the "social organism." Another departure was a turn away from a focus on economic liberty (e.g. the ideals of Frederic Bastiat and the French Liberal School). Following the Comtean motto "order and progress," individual rights and freedoms became less of a focus, for production for the booming export economy became the main concern. Scientific racism played a role in this shift. Elite discourse suggested that "Indians," the main labor force, needed to be coerced to work since they did not respond to material incentives. Furthermore, social Darwinism made national material progress paramount to sovereignty.

In "Porfirian" Mexico (Porfirio Díaz ruled from 1876–1910, so the era is called the "Porfiriato"), Justo Sierra, a leading intellectual and member of the *científicos* [scientists], a small but powerful political clique, proved influential. Sierra critiqued his Reform-era predecessors' economic liberalism from a Comtean angle, complaining that it was abstract and deductive, and countering that economic analysis should be inductive and empirical. Sierra was familiar with the German Historical School, and perhaps it, too, informed his critique. Positivism, Darwinism, and evolutionism influenced *científicos'* ideas about international trade and industry. True, there were adherents to the international division of labor (e.g. economists Alberto María Carreño and Enrique Martínez Sobral) who embraced Mexico's comparative advantages and condemned introducing "exotic" and "artificial" industries. Nevertheless, *científicos* strongly promoted manufacturing. During the "export boom" they did not reject traditional exports, but simply asserted that manufacturing was important too. This industrial ideal was rooted in evolutionism and social Darwinism more than economic theory. *Científico* Francisco Bulnes predicted that Mexico would evolve to the industrial phase (Bulnes followed the Physiocrats' stages) and maintained that manufacturing was essential to sovereignty.

Similarly, *Semana Mercantil* [*Commercial Weekly*] and *El Economista Mexicano* [*The Mexican Economist*], Mexico City's top financial weeklies, maintained manufacturing would free Mexico from dependence. Rather than rely on the market, *científicos* ascribed a significant role to the state in the industrial process. *Científicos'* predilection for manufacturing was also revealed in Sierra's lament that Mexico was rich in silver rather than fossil fuels. The downgrading of silver was also a consequence of its declining international value. Silver's fall and the shortage of fossil fuels partly inspired Sierra's critique of the Humboldtean legend of riches. Sierra surveyed Mexico's physical environment and concluded that the nation was naturally poor. Further reflecting this waning optimism, *científicos* had less faith in the colonization project – Mexico couldn't attract foreigners because it didn't have much to offer.

Sierra's critique complemented *científicos'* analysis of what generated wealth, an analysis rooted more in observation than theory. *Científicos*, who lived in the heyday of the second industrial revolution and were enamored with science, stressed the primacy of technology in production. Some of their economic writings read like histories of technology, highlighting the ways the technological advances made by Liebig, Hellriegel, Winotradsky, and others enhanced productivity. Stressing technology's significance, *científico*-economist Carlos Díaz Dufoo countered economic theory by contending that capital trumped all other factors in the generation of wealth. *Científicos'* charge that their predecessors wrongly believed that nature created wealth also revealed the importance they placed on capital. A generation later, Mexican economist Daniel Cosío Villegas contended that Díaz Dufoo was overly optimistic about technologies' transformative power. Whatever the case may be, Díaz Dufoo's technology-driven analysis fit with *científicos'* critique of Mexico's natural environment: technology overcame natural obstacles and generated wealth.

Opponents of the Díaz government critiqued *científicos*. A socioeconomic critique informed by social liberalism (articulated in liberal press, e.g. *El Comillo Público*, *El Paladín*, *El Hijo de Ahuizote*, and *Regeneración*) and social Catholicism charged that *científicos* emphasized material progress but neglected social progress. European social Catholicism, especially Pope Leo XIII's 1891 encyclical Rerum Novarum, influenced Mexican Trinidad Sánchez Santos. Sánchez Santos's tirade against classical economic liberalism and its excessive freedoms followed the Pope, but did not accurately portray the *científicos'* positivist-infused liberal discourse. There was also a nationalist critique, which charged that the Mexican–American War (1846–8) had been a military defeat, but now there was a "peaceful conquest" via American investment, trade, and loans. Despite this latter charge, there was a strong nationalist element in *científicos'* discourse. Finance Minister José Limantour invoked sovereignty to justify the Mexicanization of American railroads.

The twentieth century

The Mexican Revolution (1910s) and Reconstruction (1920s–1930s) had an impact on Mexican economic thought. While there may have been some foreign influence, many ideas were rooted in Mexican history and experience. Cosío Villegas observed that the Mexican Revolution was the last one with no "isms" attached to it. Reflecting this, despite the fact that Mexican anarchists (e.g. Ricardo Flores Magón) were active, their impact was limited. In contrast, Andrés Molina Enríquez, a Porfirian/Revolutionary bureaucrat, proved important since his ideas influenced Revolutionists, particularly Luis Cabrera. Molina Enríquez advocated overturning liberal ideals by returning to aspects of the Spanish Colonial legal heritage. His ideas of restoring the *ejido* (Indians communal village lands, which had pre-Columbian antecedents) and returning the subsoil rights to the nation (as part of the national patrimony) were enshrined in the 1917 Constitution. Revolutionary agraristas' calls (e.g. Emiliano Zapata) for returning *ejidos* to Indians also influenced thought. *Científicos* Díaz Dufoo and Bulnes severely attacked these nationalist and redistributionist aspects of the 1917 Constitution on economic grounds.

There was an intensification and modification of these revolutionary ideals in the 1930s, when President Lázaro Cárdenas came to power. He nationalized foreign (American and British) oil in 1938. Nationalism stemmed from a labor dispute between Mexican workers and foreign owners (reflecting the Constitution's progressive position on labor rights), not a vision of national development based on state control over the energy sector. The *ejido* program accelerated under Cárdenas, but it shifted by conceiving *ejidos* as a permanent form of land tenure (for Molina Enríquez they were a temporary solution) and by promoting collective rather than individual *ejidos*, revealing the influence of socialist ideas. This focus was in keeping with the social economics that predominated in Mexico (loosely informed by Karl Marx's critique of capitalism), with its promotion of redistribution of wealth and social wellbeing in the countryside.

Cosío Villegas, for example, loosely echoing Humboldt's critique of silver, maintained that the agrarian sector was the most significant since it provided sustenance to the population, and the oil sector only enriched foreigners. This social concern also inspired Cosío Villegas's social critique of Porfirian material progress, and separated revolutionists from *científicos*. Nevertheless, there were continuities. Following Sierra, revolutionaries critiqued the Humboldtean legend of riches. But they did so for distinct ends: cultural nationalism. Economist Jesús Silva Herzog maintained Indians did not cause Mexico's backwardness; rather, natural impediments were the culprit.

The influences of the Mexican and Russian Revolutions along with the collapse of the international economic system and the subsequent Depression influenced Central American thought, posing a challenge to economic liberalism. Some trends from revolutionary Mexico – especially nationalism, agrarian reform, and redistribution of wealth – were echoed in Central America. There was a direct connection between Mexico and Nicaraguan nationalist Augusto Sandino, for he spent some time in Mexico in the 1920s. Sandino protested American intervention in Nicaragua, but his resistance was cut short in the 1930s when the Nicaraguan National Guard killed him. Nevertheless, his influence lived on since a group of Nicaraguan revolutionaries took his name – the "Sandinistas" – and came to power in 1979. More closely paralleling the Mexican model, nationalist-agrarianist-redistributionist reformers with socialist leanings came to power in Guatemala in the 1940s and 1950s, expropriated the American United Fruit Company, and carried out significant land reform.

An industrial ideology emerged in the post-Second World War era. Raúl Prebisch, the Argentine economist who played the leading role in the United Nation's Economic Commission on Latin America (ECLA), influenced Mexican and Central American thought, but ECLA had more of an impact on policy in the latter. Prebisch visited Mexico in the 1940s and gave presentations, attended conferences, and published in *Trimestre Económico*. He also served on the journal's board. Furthermore, Víctor Urquidi, head of ECLA chapter in Mexico, directed the journal (Juan Noyla Vázquez was another prominent chapter member). Prebisch's structuralist analysis challenged the theory of comparative advantage. Departing form classic liberal constructs, Prebisch first used the terms "core" and "periphery" in print in his publications in Mexico. He also discussed the dilemma of declining terms of trade, and "unequal exchange" between the core and periphery. The solution: industrialization. Prebisch also departed from classic liberal economic theory by asserting that the state and governmental planning were central to industrialization.

Mexicans and Central Americans were in agreement that *laissez-faire* was not the road to industrialism, but their interventionist ideas were distinct. In Mexico, two perspectives emerged. One, influenced by German industrial planning, called for rational state planning. Technocrats at The Bank of Mexico's Office of Industrial Research (OII), e.g. Gonzalo Robles, advocated this strategy. J.M. Keynes, too, influenced OII technocrats. They cited him to support their assertion that the state could bolster capitalism. Spanish translations of Keynes' articles and *The General Theory of Employment, Interest, and Money* appeared in Mexico in the early 1940s. The other position, championed by Mexico's National Chamber of Manufacturing Industry, called for a more prominent role for the private sector, with the state intervening on behalf of business, since the latter was driven by profit and was the creator of wealth. The ECLA strategy for Central America called for cooperation in the form of a Central American Common Market. Collaboration would overcome smallness and provide the basis for industrialization.

An intellectual controversy generated by scholar Frank Tannenbaum, the famed foreign scholar and supporter of Mexico's agrarian Revolution, clearly illustrates the prominence of the industrial ideal. In 1950, with the so-called "Mexican miracle" of rapid industrialization speeding forward, Tannenbaum published *Mexico, The Struggle for Peace and Bread*. It argued that the industrial model was doomed to failure and that Mexico should revert to an agrarian economy that focused on local markets. Tannenbaum argued that Mexico had inadequate industrial resources, financing industrialism would be too costly, and the industrial model would create a privileged minority of industrial workers and an impoverished agrarian majority that was forced to purchase overpriced shoddy goods.

Mexican intellectuals loudly attacked Tannenbaum in the daily press, monographs (e.g. Manuel German Parra) and journals (*Problemas Agrícolas e Industriales de México* [*Industrial and Agricultural Problems*] dedicated an issue to refuting Tannenbaum). The influence of structuralism and dependency was evident in some critiques, which condemned Tannenbaum as a tool of foreign imperialists who sought to relegate Mexico to exporter of raw material and importer of finished goods in the international division of labor. Political Scientist Pablo González (whose writings influenced Frank's "Dependency" analysis) charged that Tannenbaum's strategy was akin to European theories of "free trade" that supported European industrial exports to America.

Debates notwithstanding, if manufacturing was more extensive in Mexico than Central America, so too were academic economics. The idea of developing academic economics in Mexico can be traced back to the early nineteenth century, when Mora championed the idea. Guillermo Prieto, influenced by the French Liberal School, wrote the first comprehensive Mexican economics textbook in the 1870s. Today, the most important academic economics programs in Mexico are at the Autonomous National University of Mexico (UNAM) and the Autonomous Technical Institute of Mexico (ITAM). Social economists, including Cosío Villegas, founded the former in the 1930s. The latter was inspired by business interests to counter what it perceived as the anti-business perspective of the UNAM program.

The way philosophies of academic programs have evolved mirrored broader trends in Mexican economic thought. In the 1930s social economics and rural agrarian concerns dominated. In the 1940s, concerns about growth held sway over preoccupations with development, and in the 1950s state interventionism predominated. Marxism became more prominent, at least amongst radical economists at UNAM, in the 1960s, and neo-liberalism has predominated in recent decades, especially at ITAM. For most of its history, Mexican academic economics has been eclectic; borrowing what it saw fit and placing its own Mexican stamp on it. Thus, while Marx was most cited in the 1930s, it was to critique capitalism rather than adhere strictly to his ideology.

Similarly, while Keynes was widely read around mid-century, Mexican interventionists cited him more as an afterthought than a blueprint. Perhaps the exception to this trend of autonomy is Mexican neo-liberal thought, which has been heavily influenced by the United States. Methodologies in Mexico have followed trends in the discipline, with mathematical models becoming more prominent since the 1950s (especially at ITAM), as well as the tendency to study small isolated problems (eschewing the earlier style of economist-philosophers who tackled larger social and economic issues). Economists have increased their influence in Mexico over time. Since the inception of the profession in the 1930s economists have worked as bureaucrats. But in recent decades their role has been expanded in national discourse, as it is not uncommon for economics experts to write opinion pieces for newspapers.

Recent advances and trends

Mexico and Central America, in keeping with trends in the rest of Latin America, parts of Europe, and the United States, took a neo-liberal turn in the 1980s and 1990s. In contrast to some parts of Latin America (including some Central American countries), which have turned slightly away from neo-liberalism since the new millennium, Mexico has remained committed to it. Critics of Mexican neo-liberalism have labeled it "neo-Porfirian," disparaging the ideals of the current era by associating them with economic ideology in the age of Díaz. This comparison misses the mark, for current neo-liberalism is more individualist and has a stronger dose of social liberalism than its Porfirian counterpart. While no historical comparison entirely fits, the structure of the current brand of Mexican neo-liberal discourse is closer to the early nineteenth-century variant articulated by Mora and other liberals in the sense that both promoted dismantling the existing system – for Mora, the colonial heritage; for neo-liberals today, Mexican state capitalism, which ballooned over the course of the twentieth century – and replacing it with a system that promoted economic freedom.

Some scholars have located the roots of Mexican neo-liberalism in Friedrich von Hayek since he spent some time in Mexico around mid-century. The impact of the US, however, appears to have been far more influential, as many Mexican economists and politicians have studied business, public administration, and economics in the United States. The three successive Mexican presidents most instrumental in Mexico's shift to neo-liberalism in the 1980s/1990s – Miguel de la Madrid, Carlos Salinas, and Ernesto Zedillo – all earned advanced degrees at either Harvard or Yale.

Despite the fact that Mexican neo-liberalism has been strongly influenced by the United States and adheres to economic principles, its articulation is strongly rooted in the national context. Consequently, in keeping with historical antecedents, there is a strong nationalist element in Mexican neo-liberal discourse. In the realm of commerce, for example, Mexico's rejection of bilateralism and protectionism and embrace of multilateralism and free trade was couched in nationalist rhetoric that maintained that the demise of the Soviet Union demonstrated that sovereignty rested upon rapid market opening. In the post-Cold War globalized era, strengthening world ties via free trade enhanced sovereignty. Another major neo-liberal policy shift – the privatization of the *ejidos* – echoed Mexican nationalist and social liberal traditions. Salinas maintained that the *ejido* land tenure system stifled national development and repressed Mexicans since it made them dependent on government. Thus, privatization was associated with nationalism and strengthening Mexican citizenry.

Salinas also invoked Revolutionary "Indianism" by associating *ejido* privatization with the tradition of Zapata, the leader of agrarian reform in Revolutionary Mexico. The irony is that for most Mexicans Zapata is a symbol of defense of the *ejido* system. Relying on the more conventional symbolism, Indians protesting neo-liberal reforms named themselves "Zapatistas." There are other naysayers. Today, there is a national debate about reforming the energy sector by altering Article 27 of the Constitution to allow private interests to have a greater role in the oil industry. The leading opponent to reform is none other than Cuauhtémoc Cárdenas, the son of the famous president who nationalized Mexican oil in the 1930s. His discourse, associating national control over resources with sovereignty, harks back to that of his father.

Bibliography

Babb, Sarah. *Managing Mexico: Economists from Nationalism to Neoliberalism*. Princeton: Princeton University Press, 2001.

O'Toole, Gavin. *The Reinvention of Mexico: National Ideology in a Neoliberal Era*. Liverpool: Liverpool University Press, 2010.

Reyes Heroles, Jesús. *El Liberalismo Mexicano*. 3 vols. Mexico City: Fondo de Cultura Económica, 1974.

Weaver, Frederick Stirton. *Inside the Volcano: The History and Political Economy of Central America*. Boulder: Westview Press, 1994.

Weiner, Richard. *Race, Nation, and Market: Economic Culture in Porfirian Mexico*. Tucson: University of Arizona Press, 2004.

Woodward, Ralph Lee Jr. *Central America: A Nation Divided*. 3rd Edn. Oxford: Oxford University Press, 1999.

14

The Caribbean

Mark Figueroa*

The island states and European/US-controlled territories, situated within (or contiguous with) the Caribbean Sea and the mainland units usually classified with them: Belize, Guyana, Guyane, and Suriname, constitute this region. For its size, it has exhibited great diversity in geography and micro-climates, colonial and post-colonial history, constitutional arrangements, official and vernacular languages, economic prosperity, political stability, and social differentiation.

Archaeologists identify settlements in the region from before 4000 BCE, with agriculturalists appearing after 500 BCE and Taino chiefdoms from about 1200 CE. The business models, introduced by the Europeans after arriving in 1492, sought the rapid extraction of economic values with little regard for the indigenous peoples or their economic practices. Despite this, the latter have left a mark in terms of the use of technologies in indigenous crops, and more broadly in areas such as fishing and small farming.

Mercantilist notions drove the Europeans to prioritize precious metals but little was found. Salt, timber, guano, and non-precious ores were subsequently of greater significance, and plantation agriculture provided greater wealth. Colonial trading monopolies, which Spain, Britain, and France sought to impose, were another element of mercantilism. Exclusive rights to engage in particular enterprises were standard, although frequently evaded, with mainly Dutch free ports providing an alternative. The latter received praise from Adam Smith, who criticised the prevailing mercantilism perspectives and provided economic arguments against colonialism.

Exploitation, racism, and use of state power by vested interest pervaded. Indigenous and African slave populations were so brutalized that they failed to reproduce at self-sustaining rates. The racism which justified this brutality later hampered certain groups' entry into lucrative employments and business ventures; race, color, and ethnicity remain important up to the present. The propertied classes imposed tax and other regimes to strengthen their pre-eminence, limit prospects for smaller property owners, and undercut the bargaining position of the laboring classes. Wide disparities in income distribution often resulted. Caribbean women have faced patriarchal challenges similar to other regions, but gender relations have had distinctive features; for example, women and men worked side by side in the fields under slavery.

Absentee ownership was significant in some countries, and its negative effect was compounded by the metropolitan merchants' control over trade, and mercantilist opposition to certain types of production in the colonies. Varied topographies and patterns of settlement impacted the degree to which agriculture thrived, peasantries developed, markets in local products flourished, businesses catering to local needs prospered, and mercantile-plantation elites exercised hegemony; but even with respect to the latter, there were differences. For example, in Barbados locals maintained control, but in Cuba, Guyana, and Jamaica, US or British trans-national firms came to dominate agricultural production and/or trade in the twentieth century. Trans-nationals controlled the mining and refining of minerals such as bauxite, nickel, and petroleum, and entrenched themselves in the financial sector, and later, tourism. Manufacturing, outside of agricultural processing, developed slowly based on local markets, but by the 1940s states were promoting its growth. US businesses used Puerto Rico as a base for exports to their home market, but elsewhere new industries were mainly protected, finishing operations for local markets. Soon after the 1959 revolution, state enterprises became the norm in Cuba and grew significantly in some countries from the 1970s. Caribbean economies are open and, in many cases, the main production units have been plantations and/or branches of vertically integrated trans-national firms. National business cultures dominated by margin gathering, based on import-export trade, are common. Where this is the case, production-oriented innovation is not highly developed. By privileging an academic orientation and professions such as law and medicine, education systems have often re-enforced this tendency. Migration by all classes (forced, free, or partially free) has been a constant feature of Caribbean life. From the end of the nineteenth century, this has increasingly involved circuits of migration and return.

Traditional export agriculture has declined in most countries, while food imports have grown. Uncompetitive manufacturers have shut down and services have become more important. The oil and gas sector has prospered, although refining and transhipment of oil has declined in some non-oil-producing countries. Other minerals have had mixed fortunes with precious stones and gold being most buoyant. Trans-nationals often continue to dominate in the minerals, tourism, and financial (including offshore) services sectors. Some have taken over long established activities such as the production of alcoholic beverages. Where it still exists, large scale agriculture varies as to the prevalence of state, local, or foreign ownership. National enterprises have done better in merchandising and in small scale production and services for the local market. Some local firms have developed to be major players in national or regional manufacturing, and more so hospitality, tourism, and finance, where some have extended beyond the region. Services are provided to the Caribbean diaspora in North Atlantic countries; notably, for the transfer of remittances on which many countries depend.

Although under reform, the state sector remains paramount in Cuba. It also retains a strong presence in some other countries or in particular sectors, such as transport. The pervasive informal sector is an area where women have long had an entrepreneurial presence, notably in trading. Failure to comply with regulatory frameworks and/or corruption are common in some countries but not uniformly so. The level of national policy consensus varies widely, and conflict in some countries is exacerbated by racially or ethnically based divisiveness. Criminal businesses have prospered in the drug trade and in extortion, cyber-crime, and other scams in some countries, especially where links between criminal business, legal business, and the political and state systems are evident. Environmental degradation is common. Natural hazards including droughts, floods, volcanoes, earthquakes, and hurricanes are a constant concern, as is vulnerability to external economic shocks. In addition to previously established ministries, planning offices, and development corporations, new agencies have emerged; for example, to regulate privatized utilities, financial services, and competition. New offices have also arisen under the anticorruption, good governance, and transparency banners, and the business classes often complain of excessive regulation.

One indicator of the region's diversity is the date when national/central banks were established: ranging, for example, from the 1820s for the Dutch Islands to the 1980s for Belize and the English-speaking Eastern Caribbean. Geopolitical shifts have diminished bilateral North Atlantic institutional interest in the independent countries (post-2010 earthquake Haiti is an exception), but dependent territories are better able to secure transfers. National debts are generally large and there have been recent defaults. The region is not well integrated, especially across language communities, but various efforts have been made at political, economic, and functional cooperation. A shift towards strong internal ties, long advocated by regionalists, has not emerged, but there have been recent changes in external relations. Here, China is most significant, but Venezuela (especially under Hugo Chávez) and Brazil have also been important.

Regional diversity can be seen in founding dates for national universities which are even more varied than those noted above for Central Banks. Compare, for example, Dominican Republic, 1538 (closed during most of the nineteenth century); Cuba, 1728; Puerto Rico, 1903 with Haiti, 1942; English-speaking Caribbean (Jamaica campus), 1948; Suriname, 1966; and French Caribbean, 1982. Yet this indicates nothing of the diversity in the nature of the universities or the existence of earlier tertiary institutions. There was some teaching of political economy in the nineteenth century, but economics was generally first introduced from the 1940s or 1950s or later, and is still only taught as part of the business curriculum in some cases. With or without institutions, there was awareness of the development of political economic ideas. For example, Smith's *Wealth of Nations* was read in Jamaica within a year of its publication, and in Cuba the Sociedad Económica de Amigos del País maintained between 1818 and 1824 the first political economy chair utilizing, as a text, the work of Jean Baptiste Say.

From mercantilism to the abolition of slavery

In the mercantilist struggle for wealth, the sixteenth-century Caribbean represented a significant hope for Spain. This changed after precious metals were identified on the mainland and the looting of the wealth of the indigenous peoples had begun. The Caribbean islands then became secondary way stations. For Spain's rivals, the initial method for acquiring mercantile wealth was licensing pirates to steal bullion from Spanish ships. It was not until the seventeenth century that the other pillar of mercantilism began to transform the Caribbean. By the middle of the eighteenth century, the entire region had been colonized and trade in tropical crops was well established. The generation of wealth expanded rapidly, especially with the introduction of sugar production based on the labor of slaves captured on the West Coast of Africa.

Caribbean development proceeded unevenly, even where sugar came to be a main crop. This can be seen in the shift from crops like tobacco, which were grown by small settlers utilizing their own labor, to sugar, which requires production on a large scale. Examples of such a shift in principal export crops can be seen in Barbados in the middle of the seventeenth century and the Dominican Republic at the end of the nineteenth century. Differential development is also evident in dates for the final abolition of slavery; starting with the Haitian revolution, 1804, and ending in Cuba, 1886. Economic thought during these years is often found in works of writers who focused more on historical, philosophical, political, sociological, or literary matters. Alternatively, it is seen in the debates around policy issues which took place in local representative institutions or in newspapers, journals, and pamphlet literature. For concerns of the ordinary citizens one needs to examine the reports of the officers whose responsibility it was to record them, or to follow the demands associated with revolts, riots, and other mass protests which contributed to significant changes during Caribbean history. These included the abolition of slavery and modifications of constitutional arrangements.

The rights of the colonies vis-à-vis the metropolitan governments, including the powers of local councils where they existed as against those of the colonial officials, was a major issue. Taxation was a common source of dispute, as was the trading monopoly imposed by the mother country. In British colonies, such issues were a source of friction between the governors and the assemblies; in Spanish colonies they led to demands for autonomy and ultimately independence. The latter calls were often associated with abolitionist ideas. Associated with abolitionist thinking throughout the region were works which sought to vindicate persons of African heritage from the racist slurs which were deployed in an effort to restrict their progress. A variety of other issues also received attention in the nineteenth century; for example, the viability of post-slavery economies; application of new technologies; development of new ventures including those for the local market; and regionalism. The latter included proposals by Spanish Caribbean writers for an Antillean Confederation focused on the Greater Antilles; while Britain promoted federal arrangements in the Eastern Caribbean, but faced opposition from local assemblies.

The twentieth century and the professionalization of economics

The most prominent trends in political economy/economics have had their adherents within the Caribbean. Mercantilism exerted its effect throughout society, leaving long-term expectations of state intervention to ensure economic prosperity and promote social welfare. The emergence of classical liberalism also had an influence but it must be recalled that while the main classical political economists were writing in Britain, the majority of the people of the Caribbean were slaves. In addition, the actual practice of liberalism in Europe was quite limited. The political, social and economic turbulence of the nineteenth century did not provide a fertile soil for economic liberalism, although the idea of being able to trade with nations beyond the mother country had its appeal. For the Caribbean, liberalism also received a blow in the latter part of the nineteenth century when European nations increasingly subsidized beet sugar production at the expense of Caribbean producers. Special trading relationships with colonial and neo-colonial partners persisted throughout the twentieth century, and were only finally undermined in the aftermath of the formation of the World Trade Organization in 1995, which ruled against them.

Neoclassical economists would later have their influence as economics became increasingly professionalized in the twentieth century, and in as far as colonial/occupying governments sought to impose such policies. Despite this, it must be noted that even among professional economists, support for a *laissez-faire* approach was often constrained by the presence of Marxist, Keynesian, and developmentalist thinking. In addition, some of the regimes that emerged, while by no means socialist, did not promote a climate of business freedom. The most dramatic of these was that of Rafael Trujillo, who ruled the Dominican Republic from 1930 until 1961 when he was killed. Despite being credited by some with exercising a modernizing influence on the economy, his policies were directed at repressing all opposition and ensuring that he (and his associates) owned all new industries developed.

The twentieth century was a turbulent period with two major wars which impacted the region; depressions and recessions; commodity crises; tightening control on Puerto Rico, domination of Cuba, occupation of Haiti and the Dominican Republic, and other overt and covert interventions by the US; constitutional suspensions, coups and attempted coups; labor rebellions and general strikes; contestations with respect to the issue of race; transformations in gender relations; demands for constitutional reform leading ultimately to the emergence of many new independent nations; and the various developments relating to the Cuban revolution.

Economics students tended to stick (but not exclusively) with their former colonial power or language area, with a shift mainly towards the US as it became more important in economics and within the region. Given the training that Caribbean economists have received, it is not surprising that the majority outside of Cuba have remained within fairly orthodox lines, but extreme neo-liberalism never achieved unquestioned dominance within the Caribbean. It had its adherents especially among US-trained economists, with Chicago-trained former Haitian Minister of Finance Leslie Delatour being a good example. The Washington Consensus institutions impacted sections of the public sector, but their outlook did not take hold of the consciousness of the citizenry, more or less, regardless of their station in life. Many economists defended a developmentalist perspective and the shift from "get the prices right" back to "institutions matter" and "development is a multi-dimensional process" has generally been welcomed.

Particular Caribbean contributions

Suriname, while not producing any economists whom I would mention, is distinctive in terms of extent to which developmentalist ideas have involved planning, including infrastructural planning whether successfully implemented or not. This no doubt reflects traditions from The Netherlands but it has parallels elsewhere. In Puerto Rico, the main architect of its industrial-ization plan, Teodoro Moscoso, was not an economist; while Cuba's planning derived from a Marxist perspective which prevailed during debates in the early 1960s.

Such debates among Marxist economists in Cuba were not new as they had been plying their trade long before the revolution, starting with Rubén Martínez Villena and Antonio Guiteras, who provided the first Marxist analysis of the deficiencies of the Cuban mono crop economy, following the sugar crisis of 1921. Elsewhere, Marxist ideas have also been important although sometimes more in politics than economics. For example, the Peoples Political Party (PPP) was put out of office based on concerns regarding its Marxist-influenced policies on two occasions, in colonial British Guiana (Guyana). In 1953, the British intervened militarily and suspended the constitution, and in the early 1960s, the US CIA used covert means to remove the PPP from power. When the PPP returned to power in 1992, the Cold War was over and any intentions it had of implementing its earlier program had dissipated.

In the Dominican Republic Marxist historiography is one of the tendencies which blossomed after Trujillo's demise. Its commitment to the working class propelled it to counter his anti-Haitian-ism which sought to erase the African presence from Dominican history; a presence which was most evident amongst the workers. The strength of such tendencies has meant that heterodox economic ideas have retained a place in the Dominican Republic. One of Haiti's best known economists, Gérard Pierre-Charles, was also a Marxist. In the English-speaking Caribbean, Marxist economists influenced the People's Revolutionary Government in Grenada, critiqued International Monetary Fund (IMF) programs, and warned of the "debt trap" in Jamaica from the 1970s. Among the Marxist economists, Guyanese author C.Y. Thomas produced what was probably the most widely cited text: *Dependency and Transformation*. Marxist ideas also played a significant role in the French Caribbean where the Communists led by Aimé Césaire won the 1945 elections in Martinique. Despite the strength of the Communists in Martinique, there was no possibility of a Marxist-conceived effort at transformation (even if Césaire had not broken with them) as in 1946 France chose to integrate the French Caribbean as overseas departments.

An analysis of the resulting situation has led Martinique-based Fred Célimène to apply the notion of a rent-seeking economy to the French sub-region. He projects that given the weak productive base, local groups pressure the metropolitan government through their local councils. Subsidies result, in keeping with a commitment to help less developed regions and because of the relatively low cost to the national budget. Nothing is demanded in return in terms of production or productivity. A disconnect results as consumption is high despite the absence of corresponding production, and there is no issue of balance of payments. Similar concerns have been raised regarding production and productivity in economies which depend heavily on remittances, and Dennis Pantin applies a related idea of the rentier state in oil- and gas-rich Trinidad and Tobago. He suggested that the focus is not on production and productivity but on getting a share of the state's mineral rents. This analysis can be linked to what came to be known in the 1970s as the "Dutch Disease," but which was identified for mineral exporting countries within the greater Caribbean by W. Arthur Lewis and Dudley Seers in the early 1960s.

Both US "Samuelson" and British "Cambridge" type Keynesianism have had their adherence in the Caribbean. For example, in 1950s' Cuba, Keynesian analysis influenced the economic policy of the Batista regime. This period provided an example where various schools of thought contended, including the Keynesian (Julián Alienes, a Spanish national), neoclassical (Felipe Pazos), and Marxist (Carlos Rafael Rodríguez). Questions were raised as to the application of Keynesian policy in an open economy, especially where investment decisions were in the hands of foreigners and there was corruption. Given the sympathy for state action among much of the Caribbean intelligentsia, it is not surprising that many of the more mainstream economists were drawn to Keynesianism. This meant that the issue as to its application in an open economy required exploration, a theme pursued by British economist Charles Kennedy while in Jamaica, and C.J. Bruce in Trinidad.

The use of multi/interdisciplinary approaches and the applications of structuralism, and subsequently dependency thinking, have had a wide influence on Caribbean economists. The Cuban Regino Boti was a founding member of CEPAL (UNECLAC) under the leadership of Raúl Prebisch in 1948. The Martinican economist Jean Crusol studied under Celso Furtado at the Sorbonne and interacted with like-minded English-speaking Caribbean economists from the 1960s. Most of the 1950s/1960s generation of academic English-speaking Caribbean economists, including some of those who made extended visits to the region, such as Dudley Seers and Kari Levitt, utilized structuralist approaches.

In the 1960s, a radical tendency associated with the journal *New World* emerged. It was made up of pan-Caribbean nationalists who wished to overcome what they saw as the integration of individual production units with foreign, often trans-national corporations, to the benefit of the latter, and replace this with a programmed economic integration of the entire Caribbean basin, for the benefit of its people. While not primarily socialist in orientation, they took the view that the only local institution which had the capacity to facilitate the necessary transformation was often the state. Some of their ideas were reflected in the policies pursued by Caribbean governments in the 1970s. Norman Girvan, who analysed the Bauxite sector and the role of trans-nationals, is significant not just for his work but because he stands out for his early adoption of new media and his continued maintenance of an active website.

Within *New World*, there was a distinctive sub-grouping which focused on the impact that the historical, institutional, and structural conjuncture associated with plantation agriculture had had on Caribbean economies. Levitt credits Alister McIntyre as being involved in its early development, but it was she and Lloyd Best who documented the plantation economy perspective, and George Beckford's *Persistent Poverty* is the most cited work from this school. For these economists, Caribbean economies suffered from enclavism typified by the plantation, which had more links abroad and responded more to foreign than to local demand.

Plantation type economies were therefore externally propelled and lacked an internal dynamic. A transformation was required to relocate decision-making within the local economy, link plantation type units with locally oriented sectors, and thereby create an integrated economy, which could achieve self-sustained development.

The English-speaking sub-region also produced W. Arthur Lewis, the Caribbean economist who is by far the most cited. In 1979, he shared the Nobel Prize for helping to create development economics. His analysis also had a structural element and he adopted a multidisciplinary approach. He wrote on industrial economics, planning, and world trade, as well as on race, education, and political systems. Unfortunately, he is best known for the "Lewis model" which, although inspired in part by his most famous 1954 article on "Economic Development with Unlimited Supplies of Labour," was created by John Fei and Gustav Rannis, and deviates significantly from his original work. In the Caribbean, his 1950s' proposals for development in the sub-region were often caricatured by later writers who disagreed with his promotion of foreign investment and his analytic reference points. Given these circumstances, misunderstandings of his perspective are frequent. His main goals were to identify how economies shifted to a high growth path; what determined their participation in international trade; and hence the development policies appropriate for the tropical world, which he saw as lagging behind the temperate world since the latter part of the nineteenth century.

For him, the key issue was labor productivity in food produced for the home market, noting that Britain had become the most developed country following the first industrial revolution, based on a prior agricultural revolution. Productivity in this sector also determined the factoral terms of trade and hence the benefits accrued therefrom. Land-rich countries (Ghana) needed to resolve social issues in the organization of agriculture which hindered productivity, and get the latest technology to farmers, thereby effecting an agricultural revolution. In over-populated countries (the Caribbean), the two revolutions needed to proceed simultaneously. Agricultural productivity needed to be raised using the same methods outlined for under-populated countries, but this would not be possible without reducing surplus labor on the land, where the productivity of the last additional worker in agriculture (and other traditional subsistence sectors) approximated to zero. Hence, industrialization was necessary to create the jobs to absorb surplus labor.

Only rapid accumulation in a modern capitalist sector could make this possible. This required the creation of a capitalist class whether within the state, from the local propertied classes, or initially by importing foreign capitalists to kickstart the process until the locals could take over. For the Caribbean, Lewis emphasized the last option as the small market size meant that new jobs would need to be in export manufacturing, and there was little relevant local expertise. Foreign capitalists were to be attracted to relocate light manufacturing industries in the Caribbean, based on the availability of workers who could be transferred from the overcrowded sectors at relatively low wages. This was to be facilitated by the state which would ensure that, with the growth of incomes and knowledge, locals would eventually take over the process. From the 1940s, when he worked with the British Colonial Office, Lewis was at the forefront of the ideological struggle against racist and other narrow views which suggested that the peoples of the tropical world should concentrate on primary production. In this he was not alone, but at that time he had one of the boldest visions for a Caribbean transformed, in a generation or two, as subsequently took place in a number of Asian countries; but he favored a social democratic framework, based on voluntary consensus and a liberal political system.

Between the trends and tendencies there have often been more polemics and sharp critiques than dialogue. These have involved wide-ranging differences surrounding methodology, role of the state, planning, and industrial policy; foreign investment and capabilities of local capitalists, significance of small size, and value of regionalism; importance of trade and value of export orientation versus import substitution; land reform and agricultural policy, technology and technological transfer; and pricing, exchange rate, and monetary as well as labor, social, and welfare policy. All of this is in addition to a range of differences on more political questions.

The contemporary scene

Issues relating to the creation of self-sustaining growth in Caribbean economies are very much on the agenda. In Cuba, this takes the form of identifying an appropriate reform path given its past. Elsewhere, some question whether, in the drive for growth, sustainability will be a casualty. Attention is therefore being paid to adaptation to climate change and related environmental matters. The debt and associated tax and exchange rate issues (sometimes connected to pressures to adopt IMF-type programs) are being faced in many countries. Divisions are notable between governments and central banks which have insisted on fixed exchange rates and those which have adopted a managed float. Rightly or wrongly, citizens in the latter countries often look at those in the former with envy. In Haiti the issue of the role of aid and aid agencies is of particular interest given that country's special situation. Here and elsewhere, questions relating to poverty and inequality remain a significant concern.

The negotiations around the European Partnership Agreement in which most regional governments have participated also saw significant disagreements with respect to industrial and trade policy, as well as the value of regionalism and the extent to which special and differential treatment remains valid on the grounds which it is demanded, many relating to the vulnerability of the small island developing states (SIDS). Questions have also been raised regarding the space which the new globalization permits to Caribbean economies, which seek to maintain sectors as varied as local manufacturing and offshore financial services. The role of micro-, small-, and medium-sized businesses and the nature of the informal economy and/or how it can be drawn more into the formal economy, continue to receive attention as does the revival of the agricultural sector in some countries.

Credence must be given to the region's vulnerability as economies have been devastated by a single natural event. At the same time, many economists would argue that popular sentiment favors contradictory policies which would support high wages, low prices on locally produced and imported goods, fixed exchange rates, protected national industries, low taxes, and high government spending. The business classes often only differ from the masses with respect to wages. They favor incentives for their own operations and government expenditure which benefits them, but are more willing to see other expenditure curtailed. In the past there have been debates as to the interaction between the economy and society, and where the problems had to be addressed first. Currently there is growing appreciation for the importance of achieving social consensus as an important element in creating the conditions for economic development.

Economists continue to disseminate their work through international and regional channels, including a range of annually held conferences within the region and Caribbean journals which are increasingly available through electronic databases or through online versions. Websites which provide accessible information on Caribbean economics are also emerging. There is a fairly well established network of academic institutions but many students still have to go abroad to do doctoral studies. Economics has been a male-dominated profession but this has been changing at varying paces in different countries, and when the history of the next two generations of economics is written I expect that this shift will be evident.

Note

* In preparing this chapter, I have benefited from the assistance of colleagues working throughout the region, including Maribel Aponte-García, Jean Casimir, Miguel Ceara Hatton, Graciela Chailloux, Charles Clermont, Romain Cruse, Macklenan Hasham, Peter Jordens, Winston Ramautarsing, and Pedro Rivera Guzmán, whom I acknowledge and thank, while absolving them of responsibility for any errors. Histories of economic thought are yet to be written for most Caribbean countries.

Bibliography

Caribbean Studies. University of Puerto Rico, Rio Piedras.

Journal of Business, Finance and Economics in Emerging Economies. Caribbean Centre for Money and Finance. The University of the West Indies (UWI), St Augustine.

Journal of Eastern Caribbean Studies. Sir Arthur Lewis Institute of Social and Economic Studies (SALISES), UWI Cave Hill.

Figueroa, Mark. 2004. W. Arthur Lewis versus the Lewis Model: Agricultural or Industrial Development?. *The Manchester School of Social and Economic Studies*, 72 (6): 736–50.

Figueroa, Mark. 2008. George Cumper and the Critical Tradition: Common Themes in post-World War II Caribbean Thought. *Social and Economic Studies*, 57 (2): 162–87.

Monlino, Ernesto. 2007. *El Pensamiento Económico en la Nación Cubana*. Havana, Editorial de Sciencias Sociales.

New West Indian Guide. Royal Netherlands Institute of Southeast Asian and Caribbean Studies.

Social and Economic Studies. (SALISES), UWI, Mona.

Sorhequi Ortega, Rafael Antonio, Graciela Chailloux Laffita, Tamarys Bahomonde Pérez, Silvia Odriózola Guitart and Magaly León Segura (eds). 2008. *Antología del Pensamiento Económico Cubano*. Havana, Editorial Felix Varela.

15

Spanish-speaking South America

Politicized economic thought

Verónica Montecinos

No comprehensive history of economic thought in Latin America exists, despite its long-term, weighty sway over the region's domestic and international affairs. This chapter focuses on Spanish-speaking South America as a region whose economic and geopolitical history is distinct from that of Mexico and Central America and dissimilar from that of Brazil. References to the larger Latin American region, however, are unavoidable. Latin American professional economists, as well as their predecessors since colonial times, have often spoken with an idiosyncratic and somewhat contentious voice, being at once, integral and peripheral to evolving notions of the modernizing West. Thinkers from the region have never been too isolated from their counterparts in Europe and the United States but never fully absorbed by external influences either.

At different times, a uniquely politicized internationalism appears as the hallmark of Latin America's economic thinking, hardly distinguishable from overall conceptions of power hierarchies. Relative to other areas of the world, economic ideas in Latin America seemed more intentionally sharpened into political tools, overtly framed in struggles over regional identity and autonomy. Two hundred years after independence, the essence of colonial controversies over economic relations with the outside world still informs strategies to deal with the region's subordinate position in global systems of domination. Very high levels of class, ethnic, and other forms of inequality introduce another layer of politicization to Latin America's economic thinking. Distributive questions can rapidly transform the most technical controversies into ideological confrontations. Strategic conflicts over the pace and timing of economic policy reforms have more than once altered the course of democracy. Indeed, economic issues have torn the heart of Latin American politics more than language, religion, or any other social cleavage.

In transnational economic debates, only a few major figures from Latin America have received a hearing commensurate with their merit. In country after country one finds examples of originality and cosmopolitanism but a world map of economic thought would come out in chiaroscuro, with the Anglo-American zone in starkest relief. By and large, economic knowledge produced in Latin America and in other non-English-speaking areas remains unnoticed, particularly when articulated in a language that is less theoretical and more eclectic than usage within the world's most prestigious academic centers. Comparative studies in the history of economic ideas have never been enthusiastically cultivated, although intercontinental comparisons that include Latin America can be found in the works of Love (1996) and Coats

(1997). As the hegemonic canon of economics spread since the mid-twentieth century, those studies were further devalued.

Recent generations of Latin American economists, more attuned to universalist claims in professional and disciplinary norms, came to lose sight of what their more regionalist and nationalist forbearers had sought to accomplish by challenging the ideas and interests of world powers, in some cases with innovative flare and fame. The younger elites of the profession in this region, typically trained abroad, aspire to prestige and employment in the worldwide market for economic expertise by publishing and participating as full constituents of mainstream economics. The career trajectories of current economic ministers and central bankers as well as the most distinguished academic economists illustrate this convergence trend, with notable variations across and within countries (Montecinos and Markoff, 2009).

While policy regimes have oscillated from market dominance to state dominance and back, a recurrently debated theme is whether imported economic doctrines are biased in favor of external interests and whether those doctrines adequately account for the contextual and historical specificities of what has been called Latin American peripheral capitalism (Prebisch, 1981). In simplified formulation, two opposing views condense major disputes: an orthodox camp in favor of free markets that recognizes a unified body of economic ideas, and a heterodox camp that supports state intervention, disciplinary pluralism and distinctively Latin American economic interpretations. In reality, a more complex pattern of orthodoxies and heterodoxies have coexisted at various times (Ocampo, n.d.).

History

In a brief summary of economic approaches in the region, several main stages can be identified. During the early expansion of capitalism, pre-colonial indigenous civilizations were devastated and much of the continent emerged as a rich field for imperialist plunder. The distant, centralized administrative authority of Spain and its trading monopoly established a colonial export economy ruled according to mercantilist principles, in contrast with the liberal model of British colonialism associated with free markets (Lange, Mahoney, and vom Hau, 2006). For centuries, Spain focused on the extraction of silver and gold, maintaining agriculture as a subsistence activity. Indeed, it was the peripheral and poorest areas of the empire, with smaller indigenous populations, that tended to become later the most developed. This hierarchy of relative affluence continued in the post-colonial period and is evident to this date (Mahoney, 2003).

In the eighteenth century, mercantilism was revitalized during the Bourbon administrative and commercial reforms aimed at reversing Spain's economic decline. The changes reduced the significance of metals in favor of agricultural exports, strengthened trade restrictions for other European powers while partially liberalizing commercial ties among the colonies. But not until the second half of the nineteenth century did the ideology of economic liberalism become dominant in the former Spanish dominions. This happened as international trade resumed following the period of economic dislocation linked to independence. New export activities emerged while countries grew increasingly dependent on external lending. Foreign merchants and bankers, often British, invested in communications and infrastructural projects to ease integration into the world economy. For decades free trade ideas had been stifled by the legacy of Spanish mercantilism, intra-elite conflict between liberal-minded groups, and landed interests intent on preserving semi-feudal structures supported by military and other conservative and nationalist groups.

Subsequently, when the old vulnerabilities of export economies were reconstituted in neocolonial ties with Britain and then the United States, adherence to the creed of national industrialization gained strength across the region. Particularly after the 1930s, broad political and class coalitions supported development projects with some resemblance with Keynesianism but that evolved into what came to be known as structuralism, the most distinctive school of economic thought in Latin America (http://prebisch.cepal.org/en/project). By the 1980s, the heavily indebted region was reverting to export-led strategies, reclaiming the theory of comparative advantage to strengthen international competitiveness and regain creditworthiness in financial markets. In fact, the Washington Consensus policies were implemented first in Latin America and more fully than in other world areas. As in the past, however, the transnational propagation of prevailing economic doctrines involved adaptive emulation and resistance to outright convergence. More recently, a new framework, appropriately labeled neo-structuralism, represents an effort to rebalance markets and state and restore the maligned legacy of Latin American structuralism (Sunkel, 1993; Bielschowsky, 2009).

The transmission of economic ideas during the neo-liberal age was again a multidirectional process, with Latin Americans actively deploying their own versions of market fundamentalism. Peru, for example, was the source of the international celebrity for the idea that the keys to innovation and development were hidden in the state-strangled entrepreneurship of informal, underground markets, rendered invisible by inefficient and corrupt bureaucracies (de Soto, 1989). The thought that the previously protectionist Chilean state was a theoretical and practical world model for economic revival entered the revolutionary rhetoric of free market advocates after that country privatized, among other things, its social security system, promising that every worker would become a financially empowered small capitalist. Although the debt crisis of the 1980s forced policy adjustments throughout the region, there were also episodes of heterodoxy in which macroeconomic reforms were combined with anti-inflationary efforts to reduce growing income disparities, as in Argentina with the Austral Plan and Peru with Plan Inti.

While discontent with the excesses of dominant *laissez-faire* grew in Latin America and elsewhere, the history of economic thought seemed again in vogue, at least in some circles. In an unprecedented move, for example, the European Society for the History of Economic Thought and Latin American colleagues recently began meetings in Latin America. Parallels with the Great Depression were invoked after 2008. Changes in mainstream economic thinking were then advocated to avert other devastating crises. Some thought that if the marketization fervor eroded in the United States, the hub of world economics where economists were publicly questioned about their involvement in the financial meltdown, Latin America would follow suit, just as the collapse of international trade in the 1930s had brought doctrinal revision, with the region changing the "outward-orientation" of its economies. At the turn of this century, leftist governments coming to office in several South American countries gave credence to these beliefs. Although the issue is far from settled, market orthodoxy seems weakened (Flores-Macías, 2012).

Because of variation in national politics and intellectual traditions, much needs to be understood about how and why diverse roots influenced the history of economic thought in different countries within the same region. Few scholars have considered the connections among autochthonous traditions of economic knowledge in different parts of Latin America. Few comparative analyses have explored the broader ideational context of pre-professionalized economic essayists of the nineteenth and early twentieth centuries. Even less is known of economic ideas in older systems, such as the Inca Empire, which effectively covered a vast territory but lacked money and markets. Oreste Popescu's *Studies in the History of Latin American Economic Thought* (1997) is a rare effort to present a longer term perspective (sixteenth to the twentieth century), including Spanish Scholasticism – considered a precursor of modern economics.

Occasionally, fragments of these overlooked indigenous thought systems did resurge within Latin American mixed streams of Catholic, positivist, Marxist and populist ideas, adding to the syncretism of Latin American economic thought. Lacking place and worth in many strictly Euro-centric academic worldviews and the narrowly defined disciplinary jurisdiction of economics, the study of those doctrinal currents was left to historians and other social scientists. Currently, a call for "epistemological decolonization" has surged, along with Latin American indigenous movements fighting for greater control over increasingly privatized lands and natural resources (Stavenhagen, 2011).

The 2007 Bolivian constitution and the 2008 Ecuadorian constitution, for example, adopt as a central principle the concept of *sumak kawsay* ("good living" in Quechua), in order to recognize the significance of Andean heritage and non-Western systems of thought. The Ecuadorian strategic plan proposes a moratorium of the word "development" to promote greater harmony with nature. The question of whether these epistemic shifts will eventually affect the boundaries of modern economics or future approaches to the history of economic thought in Latin America still remains open.

Regionalism

In this multicultural continent still trying to forge a disputed sense of cultural homogeneity, independent nation-states emerged relatively early. The liberation movement was partly inspired by the Enlightenment and revolutions in France/the United States, but Simón Bolívar's leadership went further. He articulated a pragmatic defense of economic sovereignty, admitting the need for open trade, especially with Britain. His unrealized vision of regional unity remains inspirational because the region's thwarted economic potential is often attributed to the early political fragmentation of the former colonial domains. By 1825, instead of forming a confederation, Spanish America had become a cluster of separate independent republics.

Various approaches to regional cooperation have been fostered by a defensive posture toward adverse external circumstances and inequalities in international trade. Regionalism, reframed more than once, has centered narrowly on trade issues and more overtly on geo-political designs and anti-imperialism. A current classification distinguishes between mid-twentieth century closed regionalism – corresponding to inward-looking strategies of development with economies of scale in enlarged protected markets – and open regionalism, seeking international competitiveness in liberalized markets.

Regional schemes have proliferated, either as a form of economic nationalism, as a defensive mechanism against the protectionism of rich countries or as unrestricted insertion in global markets. One of the unfulfilled attempts to advance a Latin American community of nations was proposed in the 1920s by the Peruvian Haya de la Torre to increase autonomy and socialist solidarity in the face of expansionist policies from the United States. A more technocratic approach was tried in the 1960s, with the Latin American Free Trade Association (ALALC) that envisioned a common market modeled after European integration. This was followed by sub-regional trade agreements, such as the Andean Pact (1969) and MERCOSUR (1980s).

More recent examples of regional solidarity have emphasized political associations. ALBA (Bolivarian Alliance for the Peoples of Our America) was put forward by the Venezuelan president Hugo Chávez in 2004 as a counter-hegemonic project against the wave of market-oriented trade agreements and policies. A more ambitious invocation of "Bolívar's dream" is UNASUR, the Union of South American Nations, born in a treaty signed by twelve nations in 2008. CELAC, the Community of Latin American and Caribbean States, launched in 2011 and excluding the United States, is another initiative to enhance self-rule over regional affairs.

The desire to join forces to elevate the status of Latin America in the international system by speaking with a single voice can be traced to early denunciation of colonial officials and missionaries. This was followed with critiques of foreign bankers and academics for resorting to coerced compliance with this or that system of taxation, tariffs, or budgeting. Academic and professional networks, political movements as well as waves of political exile energized dynamic cross-border dialogues that reinforced the cosmopolitanism of Latin American intellectual elites.

At times, conflicting economic visions from both world centers and Latin America led to a boomerang effect. The United States answered the challenges of redistributive reforms from the region with the Alliance for Progress in the 1960s. The World Bank's *2006 World Development Report* stressed the complementary of equity, economic efficiency and growth long after the Economic Commission for Latin America (ECLA) introduced the widely used slogan of "productive transformation with equity" in the early 1990s. Much older illustrations include Spain's attempt to address the mistreatment of indigenous labor with the Laws of Burgos in 1512 in response to the anti-slavery advocacy of Antonio de Montesinos, a Dominican friar sent to support the empire in the Americas. The Jesuit order was expelled from Spanish dominions in 1767 for its renowned economic experiments in Paraguay, which lasted well over a century. Jesuits, it was said, had created an "Empire within the Empire."

Catholic and technocratic approaches

The extensive power of the Catholic Church declined with secularizing crusades in the post-independence period but the influence of the church on economic thought remained sturdy. The 1891 papal encyclical *Rerum Novarum*, which took a critical stance on capital-labor relations and the excesses of liberal capitalism, had strong echoes among Latin Americans taking part in transnational debates on state responses to rising class conflicts.

A technocratic bent in policymaking was manifest when several countries in the region became early adopters of social insurance programs promoted by the International Labor Organization and other agencies of the incipient international policy system. Reformist elites of the early twentieth century were still influenced by the weighty presence of positivism, which in Latin America constituted a *sui generis* school of thought with important national variations (Guadarrama, 2004). Faith in science and in state action, typical of positivism, led to new understandings of the realities of Latin America and facilitated participation in cross-national expert networks concerned with the spread of revolutionary ideologies.

Compared with the stature of the anti-clerical left, increasingly shaped by Marxism, and religious conservatism sustaining the old oligarchic order, the political significance of progressive Catholicism was limited when a new encyclical, *Quadragesimo Anno*, was issued in 1931. The papal document resonated with Catholic intellectuals and politicians because it condemned individualism and collectivism, taking a moralist middle path for improvement in working conditions. The Cold War propelled Christian Democratic parties to successfully occupy the political center, especially in Chile and Venezuela. While in office, these party platforms referenced Catholic economic doctrine and development economics in redistributive programs to lessen the concentration of income and land. Their policies received significant support from Catholic organizations in Latin America and Europe, the United States government, and international development agencies. This type of technocratic reformism offered an appealing alternative to the swell of radicalizing trends after the revolution in Cuba.

Dissatisfaction with the pace of change, however, moved Catholic groups further left to liberation theology, an internationally influential movement most famously associated with the Peruvian priest Gustavo Gutiérrez. For a while, the region's ecclesiastical hierarchy endorsed this "Preferential Option for the Poor," an approach that in part claimed the heritage of Bartolomé de las Casas, the sixteenth-century Dominican friar who advocated indigenous rights. Marxist ideas merged with progressive Catholicism in the ideological effervescence of the 1960s, with reformist and revolutionary paths fracturing multiple arenas. Liberation theology, after years of Vatican hostile scrutiny for its excessive politicization and anti-capitalist overtones, is being revalued under the recently elected Argentinean Jesuit pope, the first non-European in 1,300 years, who defines himself as a champion of the poor.

Nowhere has the cosmopolitan outlook of Latin American economic thinkers been stronger than among economists after the discipline became institutionalized in the region's universities in the 1940s. The promise of locally developed economic expertise, allegedly more appropriate to the particularities of local circumstances and constituencies, has repeatedly clashed with the propensity of external advisers to generalize prescriptions in unfamiliar contexts. Latin America's lengthy experience with visiting economists (Bianchi, 2011) and foreign "money doctors" (Drake, 1993) suggests that outside experts play an eminently political role, despite claims of unbiased technical advice.

Courcelle-Seneuil, a French finance specialist appointed counselor to the Chilean government in the 1850s, is still signaled as a precursor of economic orthodoxy and a prototypical crusader for economic liberalism. The externally validated professional credentials of foreign advisers typically constitute a power device in doctrinal disputes and in negotiations over the terms of foreign investments and loans. Sometimes, money doctoring varied in style and content, as shown in comparisons of the standard recommendations offered by the orthodox Edwin Kemmerer in his missions to several Latin American countries in the 1920s, and the more varied and heterodox proposals made by the Keynesian Robert Triffin in the 1940s, most famously in Paraguay (Helleiner, 2010).

Structuralism and dependency

The most elaborate critique of the universality of economic theory formulated in Latin America, and the most thoroughly explored original contribution to economic thought from the perspective of developing countries, came out of the United Nations Economic Commission for Latin America (ECLA) after 1948. ECLA is now known as ECLAC, Economic Commission for Latin America and the Caribbean. Cold War factors pushed the United States to try merging the new agency with the Organization of American States in an unsuccessful move that would have averted ambitions of intellectual independence. The ability of ECLA to speak with an independent voice was seen as a threat as it surged as a significant force among a variety of governments, inspiring the first generations of Latin American economists. Hundreds received training in ECLA headquarters in Santiago, Chile.

ECLA defended the need to elaborate a Latin American economic theory based on observations of the specific conditions of the region and thus more suitable to explain its distinctive problems and development goals. ECLA structuralism shared some arguments with the structuralism of early development economics in its affinity with Keynesianism. Both schools of thought promoted the need for planned industrialization, recognizing the need to overcome structural obstacles in heterogeneous less developed economies. Both currents criticized the neoclassical theory of comparative advantage, but their analytical reach and methodologies differed. Latin American structuralism placed more emphasis on history and institutions, and it was unique in stressing the differences and asymmetries between economies in the center and the periphery of world capitalism (Sanchez-Ancochea, 2007).

Latin American structuralism also shared some insights with the earlier North American institutional school of economic thought associated with Thorstein Veblen, Clarence Ayres, J.R. Commons and W.C. Mitchell as both challenged the narrow tenets of neoclassical economics and emphasized issues of power and history. Institutionalists, however, rarely addressed the reality of developing countries (Street and James, 1982; Mallorquín, 2001).

In the late 1960s, dependency theory emerged within the cosmopolitan circles of Santiago that included a group of prominent Brazilian exiles. Elements of ECLA structuralism were transformed into more radical explanations for the obstacles to development. Intrinsic inequalities in the world capitalist system were conceptualized as originating in the extraction of surplus from the periphery that went to finance capital accumulation in metropolitan centers. Dependency gained significant influence beyond the region partly because it evolved in different directions and a variety of formulations. Some of its variants were infused with Marxist categories that emphasized chronic economic stagnation and massive poverty. Others called attention to the potential for industrial advance and wider consumer markets. By making explicit the linkages between international inequalities and class structures within the dependent periphery, authors in this perspective moved to a more interdisciplinary framework, addressing the nature of decision-making, income distribution and consumption patterns, industrial policies, and the treatment of foreign capital investments.

Neo-liberalism

Raúl Prebisch, born in Argentina, the first leader of ECLA and its main theoretician (Vernengo, 2013), had been an early critic of the excesses of protectionism in import-substitution industrialization. In addition, Latin American economists had been ardently divided over the treatment of inflation. However, a radical paradigm shift came only after a series of military coups, in Chile and Uruguay in 1973 and in Argentina in 1976. A new group of economists in high office then proclaimed that decades of policy mistakes, failed statist and populist experimentation ought to give way to "good economics" and scientific rationality (Edwards, 1995).

When the Chicago school of economics was first brought to Chile in the mid-1950s it was regarded with skepticism or disdain for its strict allegiance to economic orthodoxy (Valdés, 1995). Yet shortly after the *coup d'état* in 1973, Chicago-trained economists were firmly in control of comprehensive policy reforms. Sergio de Castro, Pablo Baraona, Sergio de la Cuadra, among others, occupied key ministerial posts in the post-Allende government. Arnold Harberger, a member of the initial Chicago mission and a long-time mentor of economists from the region, later praised the "catalytic role" that his Chicago alumni played in the transformation of economic education in the region, and in the economic liberalization of Latin America more generally (Harberger, 1997). Harberger had in the early 1960s published a study of inflation in Chile, following on from Milton Friedman's earlier work on the quantity theory of money, which was taken by Friedman to confirm the link between changes in the quantity of money in circulation and prices (Friedman, 1969, 276).

Free market ideas were then re-exported from the Friedman-certified economic success of Pinochet's Chile, receiving added traction from Margaret Thatcher's privatization efforts in the UK after 1979 and Reagan's policies in the United States. The famous monetarist economist, who visited the country and met with the General in 1975, remained enthusiastic even when a massive crisis confirmed flaws in the model: "Chile is an economic miracle," Friedman wrote for a mass audience (Friedman, 1982). The Washington Consensus subsequently spread the privatization agenda from Latin America to Eastern Europe and other world regions (Montecinos, 2012).

Assertions of universalism and epistemic objectivism notwithstanding, political repression had made it possible for neo-liberalism to find its cradle in the Southern Cone of Latin America. The politicization of economic expertise was undiminished and the Chicago legacy, backed by well-funded conservative think tanks and the most dynamic segments of the entrepreneurial class, solidified after Latin American dictatorships collapsed. It was surprising, for instance, that in Argentina under Menem, a Peronist, the privatization policy recommended by the Washington Consensus was followed closely (Stokes, 2001). Perón's nationalization of British-owned railroads in the 1940s had been at the core of his nationalist program. In Argentina as well as most countries, privatized state firms remain in private hands, some in the control of the same reformers who decried the arbitrariness and self-interest of state bureaucrats. The administrative support for economic planning created in the 1960s is now defunct. Among other institutional reforms, central bank independence was firmly established across the region during the 1990s.

Currently, the virtues of unregulated markets so dogmatically extolled at the height of neo-liberalism seem less attractive. The need for state action, however, is seen as part of a commitment to fiscal discipline and efficiency, even by many of those convinced that poverty and inequality should decline and that the region should guard itself against the unsustainable commodity boom fueled by China's growth. Historically, economic populism, defined as broad redistributive policies implemented at the expense of budget deficits and inflation, has been tried under a variety of political regimes, especially in Argentina, Chile, and Peru, and more often than in other world regions. Leftist populism has come back recently, most clearly in Bolivia, Ecuador, and Venezuela, whose leaders see themselves as "twenty-first-century socialists," but the general climate for this type of economic thinking is inauspicious. The policies adopted by left-wing governments since the late 1990s ranged from moderate, market-friendly reforms in Chile and Uruguay to more radical rejections of neo-liberalism in the Bolivarian Alliance. In all cases, however, the left faces identity dilemmas and globalization constraints and is no longer defined by the kind of revolutionary pursuits attempted in the 1960s and 1970s (Weyland, 2010; Panizza, 2005).

Mainstream economics education in its increasing homogeneity and credentialism is accepted in the region's centers of academic excellence. With some national variations, central banks and other top government institutions now employ economists with prestigious foreign degrees and the political influence of mainstream economists has steadily increased. Yet standardized professional norms (economics curricula, publications, conferences, and policy measures) remain a subject of dispute and are often tailored to regional and country-specific historical and political circumstances. This is not really surprising in a region with such a long history of searching for economic ideas fit to its own contours.

References

Bianchi, Ana Maria, "Visiting-Economists through Hirschman's Eyes," *European Journal of the History of Economic Thought*, vol.18, no.2, 2011, 217–42.

Bielschowsky, Ricardo, "Sixty Years of ECLAC: Structuralism and New-Structuralism," *CEPAL Review*, 97, 2009.

Coats, A.W., ed., *The Post-1945 Internationalization of Economics*, Annual Supplement to Vol. 28, *History of Political Economy*, Durham, NC and London: Duke University Press, 1997.

de Soto, Hernando, *The Other Path. The Invisible Revolution in the Third World*, New York: Harper & Row, 1989.

Drake, Paul W., *Money Doctors, Foreign Debts, and Economic Reforms in Latin America from 1890s to the Present*, Wilmington: A Scholarly Resources Inc. Imprint, 1993.

Edwards, Sebastián, *Crisis and Reform in Latin America. From Despair to Hope*, New York: The World Bank, published by Oxford University Press, 1995.

Flores-Macías, Gustavo A., *After Neoliberalism? The Left and Economic Reforms in Latin America*, Oxford and New York: Oxford University Press, 2012.

Friedman, Milton, *The Optimum Quantity of Money*. Chicago: Aldine, 1969.

Friedman, Milton, "Free Markets and the Generals," *Newsweek*, 25 January 1982.

Guadarrama González, Pablo, *Positivismo y antipositivismo en América Latina*, La Habana: Ciencias Sociales, 2004.

Harberger, Arnold C., "Good Economics Comes to Latin America, 1955–95," in A.W. Coats, ed., *The Post-1945 Internationalization of Economics*, Annual Supplement to vol.28, *History of Political Economy*, Durham, NC and London: Duke University Press, 1997, 301–11.

Helleiner, Eric, "The Culture of Money Doctoring. American Financial Advising in Latin America in the 1940s," in Jacqueline Best and Matthew Paterson, eds, *Cultural Political Economy*, New York: Routledge, 2010, 91–110.

Lange, Matthew, James Mahoney and Matthias vom Hau, "Colonialism and Development: A Comparative Analysis of Spanish and British Colonies," *American Journal of Sociology*, vol.111, no.5, March 2006, 1412–62.

Love, Joseph L., *Crafting the Third World: Theorizing Underdevelopment in Rumania and Brazil*, Stanford: Stanford University Press, 1996.

Mahoney, James, "Long-Run Development and the Legacy of Colonialism in Spanish America," *American Journal of Sociology*, vol.109, no.1, July 2003, 50–106.

Mallorquín, Carlos, "El institucionalismo norteamericano y el estructuralism latinoamericano: Discursos compatibles?," *Revista Mexicana de Sociología*, vol.63, no.1, January–March 2001, 71–108.

Montecinos, Verónica and John Markoff, *Economists in the Americas*, Cheltenham and Northampton, MA: Edward Elgar, 2009.

Montecinos, Verónica, "Washington Consensus," in George Ritzer, ed., *The Wiley-Blackwell Encyclopedia of Globalization*, West Sussex: Blackwell Publishing, 2012, 2194–202.

Ocampo, José Antonio, "Seis décadas de debates económicos latinoamericanos," http://policydialogue.org/files/events/SEGIB-PNUD_Ocampo-final.pdf.

Panizza, Francisco, "The Social Democratisation of the Latin American Left," *Revista Europea de Estudios Latinoamericanos y del Caribe*, 79, 2005, 95–103.

Popescu, Oreste, *Studies in the History of Latin American Economic Thought*, New York: Routledge, 1997.

Prebisch, Raúl, *Capitalismo Periférico. Crisis y transformación*, Mexico: Fondo de Cultura Económica, 1981.

Sanchez-Ancochea, Diego, "Anglo-Saxon vs. Latin American Structuralism in Development Economics," in Esteban Pérez Caldentey and Matías Vernengo, eds, *Ideas, Policies and Economic Development in Latin America*, New York: Routledge, 2007, 208–27.

Stavenhagen, Rodolfo, "Repensar América Latina desde la subalternidad: el desafío de Abya Yala," in Francisco Rojas Aravena and Andrea Álvarez-Marín, eds, *América Latina y el Caribe: Globalización y conocimiento. Repensar las Ciencias Sociales*, Montevideo: UNESCO, 2011, 167–96.

Stokes, Susan C., *Mandates and Democracy. Neoliberalism by Surprise in Latin America*, Cambridge: Cambridge University Press, 2001.

Street, James H. and Dilmus D. James, "Institutionalism, Structuralism, and Dependency in Latin America," *Journal of Economic Issues*, vol.XVI, no.3, September 1982, 673–89.

Sunkel, Osvaldo, ed., *Development from Within. Towards a New Structuralist Approach for Latin America*, Boulder: Lynne Rienner, 1993.

Valdés, Juan Gabriel, *Pinochet's Economists. The Chicago School in Chile*, New York: Cambridge University Press, 1995.

Vernengo, Matías, "Raúl Prebisch: A Peripheral Economist at Centre Stage," *Development and Change*, vol. 44, no. 5, 2013, 1207–19.

Weyland, Kurt, "The Performance of Leftist Governments in Latin America. Conceptual and Theoretical Issues," in Kurt Weyland, Raúl L. Madrid and Wendy Hunter, eds, *Leftist Governments in Latin America: Successes and Shortcomings*, New York: Cambridge University Press, 2010, 1–27.

16

Brazil

A very big and complicated country

Patrice Franko

Brazilians have a habit of tacking *ão* onto a word to signify its enormous size or importance. *Gordo*, or fat, becomes *gordão*, a really big fat person, or the 2005 corruption scheme of monthly payments to congressmen became dubbed the *mensalão*. Brazil itself might be nicknamed *Brazilão* – a really big complicated country that is difficult to categorize and understand: in the famous words of Tom Jobim, Brazil is not for beginners.

There are multiple Brazils. One can find abject poverty in the largely rural North and North-west and visitors can become lost in the maze of upscale shopping malls in the Southeast. It is extraordinarily rich in resources – a top global exporter of soya, iron ore, petroleum, and poultry. Yet it is also rather parochial and insular, often inwardly focused on domestic concerns. Like its iconic samba parade at Carnival, it is full of color and sound that may appear chaotic on the surface, but also has a discipline, rhythm, and creativity carrying it forward. Brazil is highly complex and multifaceted.

This chapter explores both the economic ideas and the economic policies of this tropical country with global ambitions. We begin by delving into some of the distinctly Brazilian cultural practices that shape business and policy-making. We then look back to how Brazil's economy evolved to respond to domestic and international pressures, and in relation to the various economic plans that were developed in order to improve it. Rather than a dismal foreshadowing in the joke "Brazil is a country of the future – and always will be," we can see some causes for optimism in the structural changes in the Brazilian economy that have propelled it to become the eighth largest in the world (The World Factbook, 2013). But we close on a cautious note. If Brazil does not push deeply into a new round of reforms – largely in its micro-foundations – it may find its rise to the top of the league tables of global economic players to be short-lived.

Samba and seriousness

Carnival in Brazil invites all to participate in the celebration of sound and dance. Offspring of Portuguese, Italian, Spanish, German, Lebanese and Japanese immigrants mix with the descendants of slaves forced from Western Africa – and a not insignificant number of tourists – to celebrate the pre-Lenten festival. Of course, Brazilians don't need the spirit of carnival to display their warmth and generosity, as it is a relational society. Identity is defined by a web of extended family and friends. The country clubs of major cities are populated by people with shared backgrounds in high school and university; it is less common than in the USA to permanently move across state lines. Although an air bridge now served by discount airlines connects Rio and Sao Paulo, the traditional *Carioca* and *Paulista* rivalries remain.

Brazilians invest their time in others. Weekends will find families and friends gathered, often at cafes lining coastal landscapes or in chic malls, shooting the breeze over a well-chilled *chope* or beer. That Brazil has become one of the most networked societies as measured by participation in Facebook or its domestic Orkut is not surprising; Brazilians connect to those they call friends. A foreigner is welcome – and a token of a reciprocal willingness to reach out to become a little bit Brazilian is most appreciated.

Do not, however, allow the late social dinners and the lazy Sundays of *futbal*, or soccer, fool you into thinking that Brazilians don't have a hardworking streak. Both the poor in the informal sector and the professional class put in long hours at work. If a Brazilian is late for a meeting it is more likely attributable to a broken-down bus or long traffic jam than it is to inattention to time. The warm mixing of social classes on a Copacabana beach also belies the rigid stratification in society. Yale trained Edmar Bacha (b. 1942) first coined the phrase *Belindia* in 1974 to capture the notion of a country divided by the elite standards of Belgium entangled with poverty as experienced in India. Although contemporary lines are blurring with the emergence of a new middle class and recent attention has been paid to race as a criterion for access to university, what is often portrayed as a racial democracy is highly segmented along lines of color. A quick visual survey of skin tone on a bus anecdotally confirms that Brazil is the largest African nation outside of Nigeria. Although the sociologist Gilberto Freyre (1900–87) tried to recast modern Brazil as a racial mixing bowl, skin-tone has long been a major determinant of economic class (Skidmore, 2010, 105).

The Brazilian State has historically acted as a broker of the complexities of *Brazilão*. Geographic, economic, and social fragmentations are managed by a state that attempts to drive consensus among widely disparate Brazilians. Finding a way – or as it is called, *jeitinho* – of bridging divides falls to both state and federal agencies. States are powerful in this federal system; through a byzantine system of taxes called the ICMS (Impostosobre Circulação de Mercadorias e. Serviços), states retain resources to proffer regional solutions and garner power. The federal government layers over local solutions with a federal glue, making Brazil one of the highest tax environments in the world. Brokering the different needs of industrial clusters, mega-cities, agricultural breadbaskets, energy wells, and deep rural poverty, the state is often over-reaching its capacity to effectively manage economic transformation. One can also observe a high degree of "leakage," as the state churns European-level taxes, yet glaring gaps appear in the delivery of education, health, or transportation services. *Corrupção* is on the lips of most Brazilians as they explain abysmal outcomes in the social sector or national infrastructure, when improved social well-being fails to materialize.

Economic ideas with a mixed/tropical flair

Brazilian economic policy prescriptions tend toward a pragmatic design. Some countries can be seen as more consistently market oriented, others embrace an active role for the state across the economy. Brazil is less rigid; it often chooses a third way that tries to maximize market returns but with a firm hand of government. Hybrid ideas and policies feature regularly in economic strategies. In taming inflation in the 1980s/1990s, both orthodox and heterodox economic tools were employed – sometimes in the same package. The military regimes (1964–83) employed orthodox macroeconomic tools but embraced state intervention for developmental, nationalist ends. In the face of a collapse in investment, a financial crisis and a balance of payments crunch, the inflation stabilization plan implemented by Finance Minister Luiz Carlos Bresser-Pereira in 1987 attacked both aggregate demand and also froze prices – strong doses of monetarist and heterodox approaches (Bresser-Pereira, 1990). Brazilian policy blazes a third way.

Bresser's work gives a flavor of the distinctive Brazilian approach. He was born in 1934, and received his doctorate from The Getulio Vargas Institute in Sao Paulo in 1972, where he advanced (when not active in government) through the ranks to honored emeritus. His pragmatic blend of understanding markets as situated within states has led him to advocate a hybrid paradigm known as social developmentalism (Bresser-Pereira, 2013). As Bresser explained, developmentalism is a form of social organization of capitalism wherein the state plays a moderate but strategic role in regulating markets and coordinating the economic system. It first appeared historically under the name of mercantilism, which was also the era that gave birth to capitalism; it appeared for the second time in the thirty "golden years" of capitalism (1946–73). It is associated with structuralist development economics and with Keynesian macroeconomics. As Bresser's approach suggests, Brazilians seem to have an ability to function under a high degree of ambiguity. Unlike more rigid neo-liberal strategies employed in Chile, or the more "purist" socialist revolution in Venezuela, Brazilian programs to promote growth borrow from a flexible toolbox of economic ideas that responds pragmatically to changing internal and external conditions.

As the multifaceted nature of the Brazilian economy intersects with domestic interest groups and international opportunities, it is not surprising to observe frequent shifts in policy orientation. For example, the construction firm Odebrecht is a major player in Africa and Latin America. The formerly state-owned but now privately managed Embraer has soared to the third spot among aircraft manufacturers. Like these more modern Brazilian multilatinas, the orientation of the Brazilian economy historically shifted in response to tensions at home and opportunities abroad. Favorable conditions in the external market inflated the prospects of the commodity lottery in the country's early period. Gold drew prospectors to colonial cities such as Ouro Preto; the coffee economy was integrally woven with both Brazil's insertion into the global economy, as well as its darker association with the transatlantic slave trade (Skidmore, 2010).

In response to the contraction of global markets post-World War One and the Great Depression, a policy of import-substitution industrialization (ISI) took hold. Brazil turned inward during this period to develop its industrial and technological backbone. ISI employed a toolbox of protectionist trade policies with active state engagement in the productive sector. High tariff walls were set to protect infant domestic industries. Somewhat paradoxically, these protective measures also encouraged foreign companies to establish subsidiaries to access the large internal market. During this period multinationals such as General Motors and Ford invested in large production bases in Brazil. As described in the work of Tom Trebat, state owned enterprises were established in the bedrock industries to promote investment in complementary infrastructure such as electricity or telecommunications (Trebat, 1983). Private capital was partnered with state financing through the national development bank BNDES. The expanding role for the state placed economists as protagonists in policy circles. As agencies were created in the service of industrialization, they served as on the job training for a cadre of engineers, lawyers, and other technocrats put in the service of economic policy-making (Loureiro, 2009, 100–41).

The foundations of ISI in Brazil were partly orchestrated conceptually and in practice by Celso Furtado (1920–2004). A PhD in economics from the Sorbonne, in his seminal book *The Economic Formation of Brazil* of 1959 (translated into English as *The Economic Growth of Brazil* in 1963), Furtado outlined the basic elements of structuralist economic thought for the region. Consistent with the work of Argentine Raúl Prebisch and A.O. Hirschman, Furtado advocated the application of state resources to unleash domestic industrialization. Planning was seen as critical in order to overcome ongoing underdevelopment and to promote structural transformation (Furtado, 2011). The automobile cluster in the greater Sao Paulo area was, among others, a targeted investment to break the bottlenecks on the road towards broader industrialization. The aircraft producer Embraer was founded during this time, adjacent to the Air Force's ITA or Aerospace Technical Institute. Lead by the indefatigable retired Coronel Ozires Silva, its launch as a state firm assembling Piper aircraft in Brazil quickly outpaced the US partner to develop a family of aircraft particularly well-suited for the tropical environment.

Furtado rejected the dominant monetarist model that privileged the market as an engine of growth. Rather than a staged progression of exiting feudal agriculture and entering labor-intensive capitalist development, he identified that states could harness technology to leapfrog to strategies driven by heavy industry. In counterpoint to existing approaches, he explained economic underdevelopment as the full utilization of available capital without the complete absorption of the available workforce. The heterodox twist – this time on a Marxian rejection of center country control – was partnering with multinational capital for its control of technology in the service of autonomous development in the periphery. With a cost/price structure determined exogenously by powerful center countries, industrial development exacted a delicate management of expensive imported technology originally designed for European or US markets. Beyond technology, Furtado cautioned that the industrial center dominated demand patterns were often inconsistent with the needs of developing countries. Underdevelopment in countries like Brazil was thus not simply a temporary stage on the road to oncoming developed status, but an economic trap from which it was difficult to exit.

However, in keeping with his Brazilian origins, Furtado's approach to understanding the nature of underdevelopment was often more moderate and pragmatic than writing of other structuralist/dependency theorists from Latin America; it therefore found great policy acceptance. Furtado also wrote more wide-ranging works in economic theory such as *The Myth of Economic Development* (1974), which argued that it was a myth to think that economic development, and all its individual benefits, would some day reach everyone in the world through the magic of the Western capitalistic model of development. As an early harbinger of the modern environmental movement, he warned that natural resource or space limitations would not allow all people in the world to reach the highest standard of living. Foreshadowing the miles-long pileups in cities like Sao Paulo, he suggested that if everyone on the planet owned a car, then gridlock would ensue in many cities.

But Furtado's work on development was not unanimously accepted, even within Brazil, and Brazilian government policies were by no means straightforward applications of his ideas. Thus, in addition to the mix of state and multinational capital, Brazil employed a range of macro-tools to meet its industrialization objectives. Under the guidance of Roberto de Oliveira Campos (1917–2001) as Minister of Planning in the staunch pro-market anti-communist military government of Castello Branco, institutions such as the central bank, the workers' pension fund and the national housing bank were formed to aid market maturation (Espinoza, 2002). Although developmentalists gained sway with the expansion of state enterprises, monetarist economists, largely centered in the conservative FGV (Getulio Vargas Foundation) mounted an orthodox counter-attack advocating caution in monetary policy (Loureiro, 2009, 111–13). With scarce foreign exchange, the central bank had kept the Brazilian currency persistently over-valued to allow for the import of critical intermediate components to industrialize. With relatively abundant global liquidity, the pragmatic combination of structuralist state intervention with conservative macro-strategies gave rise to the so-called Brazilian miracle, managed in part by Antônio Delfim Netto (b. 1928), an economist who was Minister of Finance between 1969–74.

The end of ISI and inflation

Brazil's expansion was debt-led, with foreign liabilities largely issued in dollar-denominated assets. ISI created pressures on the balance of payments, as the irony of import substitution was an initial surge of imports of intermediate capital to fabricate the finished product. At the time Brazil was also dependent on oil imports, so the quadrupling of oil prices in the 1970s weighed heavily on its external balance. Given the large internal market, industries responded to the incentives under ISI and the economy grew at robust rates nearing 8 percent until 1980.

Engineer and self-taught economist Mário Henrique Simonsen (1935–97) helped preside over the robust growth engineered by successive military governments by marrying market commitments with statist intervention (Schroy, 2013). Two of Simonsen's most important contributions to economics were a cash-in-advance model of the demand for money, and the novel concept of inertial inflation. Both were at least partly linked to the experience of the Brazilian economy. Inertial inflation referred to the "feedback element" of the inflationary process, as opposed to other more conventional autonomous components such as supply shocks or excess demand. Inertial inflation could be generated by adaptive expectations, indexation processes, or as developed by Simonsen, a reduction in the inflation adjustment interval as price changes gathered pace.

Simonsen broke inflation down into three components: autonomous (picking up exogenous shocks), demand (including government policy), and a feedback variable where past inflation fueled current rates (Cabello, 2013). Simonsen cast Brazilian inflation dynamics in a structuralist light. Rather than simple rational expectations approaches to inflation, he observed that various parties – government, labor and industry – began acting in an uncoordinated fashion to raise interest rates, wages, and prices in anticipation of inflation. Therefore an increase in the interest rate could have unintended effects that debilitated traditional monetary policy. In a normal case an interest rate rise should signal a tightening of the money supply and a subsequent reduction of inflation. But the observed interest rate was seen by Simonsen as having two parts: real plus expected inflation. In this case an increase in interest rates was not a mark of monetary tightening but its opposite, an inflationary momentum. With inertial inflation, agents instead interpreted this as a signal that the central bank was trying to protect returns.

Simonsen also applied game theory models to the wage/income indexation processes at work in inertial inflation. He appreciated the cash-in-advance microeconomic model which posited that money was demanded because it was the only means of purchasing some goods. The paradox in high inflation economies like Brazil was that holding cash was a guaranteed means of losing wealth. The wealthy therefore kept their money in interest bearing "overnight" checking accounts, whereas the poor lost purchasing power due to lack of access to banks.

The high Brazilian comfort-level with theoretical contradictions, such as Simonsen's "monetarist-structuralist" approach to inflation, allowed some conservative economists to ally with nationalists in the military government, to expand the role of the state in defending free market ideology. Unfortunately, the tensions within the mixed model turned out to be too great when hit with external shocks in the 1970s and 1980s. To counter the predictable problems with the balance of payments from an import bias, the government only auctioned the strong cruzeiro currency to the industries deemed strategically important. Not surprisingly, this led to problems with dual exchange rates and prompted hard currency shortages to support the overvalued rate.

In the early 1980s, conditions closed off opportunities for further industrialization using ISI tools. In response to rising inflation in the United States, Federal Reserve chair Paul Volcker pursued a contractionary policy that reined in the global oversupply of dollars. From negative real interest rates in 1978, the rapid monetary shock of an additional 10 percent on debt due was crippling. When the Mexican call of "can't pay, won't pay" reverberated in the global financial system in 1982, the external spigots financing intensive industrialization rapidly closed off. The Brazilian Central Bank attempted to compensate for the drought in external financing by making capital more available at home, but this fueled inflationary flames. Among others, Maria da Conceição Tavares (b. 1930), a naturalized citizen from Portugal, was a vociferous critic of the adoption of neo-liberal International Monetary Fund (IMF) policies that forced tough medicine of adjustment on Brazil.

Inflation was the dominant concern in the lost decade of the 1980s and the first part of the 1990s. At times, Brazil attempted to combat rapidly rising prices by orthodox means, cutting the money supply and raising the interest rate to reduce circulating currency; but these attempts failed as inertial inflation had become ingrained in Brazilian institutions. Key interests were protected by an intricate web of indexing. As Albert Fishlow describes, over a hundred laws circumscribed the process of managing inflation in Brazil (Fishlow, 1974). Wages, rents, bus fares, and electricity were adjusted monthly to inflation. Checking accounts were protected by interest paid to pace inflation; no one with access to banks held cash. Private retailers joined the indexation game by printing daily *tabelas* corresponding to changing prices. Clothing was not tagged by price but rather coded to match the latest rise in the price table. Oligopolistic conglomerates passed on price increases to consumers. Taxes, too, were indexed, albeit at a slower rate. But the poor suffered the most, as informal sector wages were not indexed and those living in crowded *favelas* rarely were banked. Each pay period was marked by fraught lines in stores as people obtained all the staple goods they could buy before prices increased.

The newly elected democratic government tried to slow this inertial inflation by lagging the pace of indexing behind actual inflation. People came to distrust the government-published inflation indices, clamoring for higher wages to cover rising consumer costs – a spiral passed on at the checkout counter. Investors also began to read interest rate changes as harbingers of future inflation. Rather than observe rising interest rates as evidence of credible contractionary monetary policy, investors interpreted these as signals that the government expected higher future inflation. Those with the capability to invest abroad began to diversify portfolios, choosing to purchase safe assets overseas.

There were many economic plans to tackle the unintended consequences of living with inflation. After failed trips to the IMF in the early 1980s and paralleling the transition from military rule to civilian democracy, José Sarney implemented the cruzado plan in 1986 to shock Brazilians out of their addiction to inflation. Wages and prices were frozen; he deputized Brazilians as *fiscais*, empowering them to arrest store managers who violated the price freeze. Sarney reformed the weak cruzeiro by slashing three zeros off and renaming it the cruzado. These heterodox measures were accompanied by a contractionary monetary policy (Roett, 2011, 88).

At first, Sarney's plan worked; inflation stopped, albeit temporarily. People were encouraged by the new buying power of the cruzado – and made postponed purchases from hyperinflationary times. As domestic consumption spilled into imports, the current account deficit bulged and foreign reserves weakened. Investors reasoned if the government had devalued before, then it could do it again, and so moved money offshore. Expecting the collapse of the cruzado, those with commodities that wouldn't perish hoarded them. As cattle were not slaughtered, meat shortages erupted. These measures were further strained by the new demands of the emerging democratic state. In 1987 the Bresser plan introduced new adjustments into the cruzado strategy, but markets and consumers were not convinced and hyperinflation resumed.

New hope for political and economic change came with the 1990 election of Fernando Collor de Mello. Committed to clean government and slaying the tiger of inflation with a single bullet, Collor enacted a mega-liquidity shock to wrest inflation from the Brazilian economy by freezing all bank accounts in excess of $1,000. Consistent with orthodox monetary theory, a sharp and credible cut in the quantity of money in circulation rapidly squeezed inflation out of Brazil. The architect of this radical Collor plan was University of Sao Paulo Professor Zelia Cardoso de Mello (b. 1953) (Zelia Mello: Executive Profile and Biography, 2013). Enacted on Collor's first day in office, the plan also engaged aggressive liberalization and privatization in the economy. The problem was in restarting growth. Investment craves capital; Brazilians learned to work around the financial restrictions and money flowed back into the market. Credibility destroyed, inflation crashed back. With a government weakened by corruption scandals, tarnished Collor left the presidency two years after assuming office.

Once again a Vice President found himself in charge. Itamar Franco, a seasoned politician from the powerful state of Minas Gerais, assumed office amidst yet another crisis. Breaking ranks with the market-driven policies of Collor, he saw a more nuanced role for the state in development. He called upon Fernando Henrique Cardoso (or FHC, b. 1931), his finance minister and successor as president, to introduce a quintessentially Brazilian package – a bit orthodox, a dash of heterodox, targeted toward the uniquely Brazilian environment. FHC had begun as a typical dependency theorist, but had become increasingly critical of the simplistic leftist interpretation of the idea of dependency that applied rigid Marxist "ruling class" terms. Moving to a more Weberian understanding of class, he distinguished between the different contexts of individual underdeveloped countries, and allowed for more positive aspects to the capitalist "modernization" of the periphery, rather than simple dependency on the center.

In some daring policy engineering, a group composed of FHC, together with the Berkeley economist and former Minister of Finance Pedro Sampaio Malan (b. 1943) and Harvard-trained Gustavo Franco (b. 1956), invented a new unit of account, the urv or unit of real value. This was envisaged as a super index – the big index to out-index all of the indexation that was contributing to inertial inflation. While providing a key function of a currency – a stable unit of value – it wasn't a currency, simply a denominator. After an adjustment to cover declining purchasing power, all other indexes were disbanded. As people began to trust in this unit of measure, a new currency called the real was launched. After over a decade of straining under inflationary pressures, Brazilians swallowed hard budget cuts and the successful new currency propelled Cardoso into the presidency. A great big adjustment had managed to gain control of *Brazilão*.

From stabilization to inclusion

Gaining control of inflation in Brazil required steadfast commitment. As president, FHC struggled with reducing fiscal outlays to meet strict monetary objectives, but confidence in the real had unintended effects as consumers discovered stable buying power. Increasing liberalization allowed imports to outrun exports. When contagion from the 1997/8 Asian financial crisis reached the real, the fixed currency anchor was ended. Monetary stability was maintained through a measurable inflation target managed by the Central Bank. Although Brazil ran primary fiscal surpluses, FHC was unable to engineer deep reforms in pensions and formal sector entitlements.

Market confidence was cultivated by Princeton-trained Arminio Fraga (b. 1957), who served as Governor of the Central Bank of Brazil from 1999 to 2002; his deft hand guided Brazil toward macroeconomic stability (Committee Member Profile: Arminio Fraga, 2013). Fraga argued that factors external to a developing country's domestic fundamentals frequently drove the flow of funds to and from the country. When monetary policy was loose in the main financial centers of the world, developing countries tended to have easy access to capital. Conversely, developing countries faced problems following a Federal Reserve tightening, or negative global shock. In periods of loose monetary policy when capital was too easily available this caused complacency in the developing country's financial sector, associated with loan growth that outstripped real GDP growth several times over, which in turn produced financial fragility in the developing country. The danger signal for investors was the excessive accumulation of short-term debt, which eventually led to crisis when external monetary policy tightened. Fraga's suggestion that capital in an underdeveloped country could sometimes come "too easily" illustrates how far the hybrid model in Cardoso's government was from traditional dependency theorists.

Brazil's hallmark inequality became more apparent as Brazil began to benefit from opening to global markets. Globalization favored the skilled or those tied to commodities in demand from China; those in the informal sector fell behind. After three unsuccessful runs, the election of Luiz Inácio Lula da Silva as president was a tacit acceptance by Brazilian elites of the need to promote social inclusion. Markets were jittery but accepted Lula's domestic populism. Ever the pragmatist, Lula had appointed largely conservative economists to build confidence (Loureiro, 2009, 132). While an experienced team managed monetary and exchange rate policies, he crafted a widening policy space for social supports. His "family purse" became a regional prototype for conditional cash transfer (CCT) approaches. Families received payments to Bolsa credit cards if their children met 85 percent of school attendance norms and completed health checkups. Combined with increases in the minimum wage and healthy GDP growth, Brazilian poverty was cut in half and inequality declined for the first time anyone could remember.

Lula deployed his political skills to build global coalitions among emerging market partners, fortifying not only the South American common market Mercosur but also reveling in the BRICS denomination. Strong macroeconomic fundamentals maximized the opportunities created by attending to the Chinese market for minerals and food. Mining giant Vale brandished its global reach while highly productive agricultural producers created truck queues bringing soya to the Asian market. Large firms such as Gerdau in steel, Odebrecht in construction, or Embraer in aerospace flourished, but SMEs without easy access to preferential capital offered by BNDES, the national development bank, suffocated under high logistics costs and oppressive taxes.

Weaknesses in microeconomic foundations plagued Dilma Rousseff, Lula's successor to the Worker's Party governing mantle. Although Brazil had escaped severe damage from the global financial crisis due to self-insuring reserves of capital, restarting growth was problematic. Asian demand drivers weakened, cooling off commodities. Brazil had not capitalized on the window of strong global growth to improve competitiveness, and the environment to start/expand enterprises remained one of the worst in the world. When the United States infused the world with dollars through quantitative easing to combat its domestic recession after 2008, uncompetitive Brazilian firms were squeezed by a strengthening real.

When other countries joined in this competitive devaluation process, this was dubbed the "international currency wars" by Finance Minister Guido Mantega (b. 1949) in 2010, a USP Sao Paulo-trained economist with a PhD in sociology (Profile of Guido Mantega, 2010). These "currency wars," a phrase which quickly became popular, were the result of divergent policy goals. As the USA printed cash to stave off domestic depression, global capital markets channeled some of this liquidity to Brazil. With an ample supply of dollars relative to reals, the Brazilian currency rapidly strengthened. In counterpoint to the received orthodoxy at the time, Mantega used currency controls to fight appreciation and maintain competitiveness in the Brazilian economy. This policy helped international financial institutions to an appreciation of the effectiveness of currency controls in the global economy (IMF, 21 April 2012).

But the currency intervention used to moderate competitiveness effects on the real exchange rate wasn't enough to overcome the lack of structural competitiveness. The two combined to deliver a *golpão* – a huge punch in the gut – to Brazilian industrial growth. Dilma made gestures toward investment in high technology and innovation but the neglect of infrastructure and education strangled success. Trained by another female economist, Maria da Conceição de Almeida Tavares, Dilma's heart is in the structuralist model of state intervention. The straight-jacket of globalization, however, requires that state capitalism be moderated by capital-friendly policies. Brazil's star rating in capital markets became tarnished.

Just as Brazil had begun to anticipate the global stage of the World Cup in 2014 and the Olympics in 2016, the microeconomic pressure cooker blew open. Linked by social networks, Brazilians took to the streets to protest against massive investments in athletic complexes while infrastructure decayed. Middle class aspirations veered toward improving education and health services – not a sports party that only elites could afford. Dilma recovered her former self as student protestor imprisoned by the military, and managed new initiatives for the social sector. But the complexities of *Brazilão* make such band-aid solutions fragile.

Brazil faces tough tradeoffs. Rent-seeking behavior on the part of elites must diminish to create fiscal space for inclusive growth. The Brazilian state cannot continue to provide early pensions for formal sector workers while its public school students cram into two or three poorly-staffed sessions a day. People and businesses cannot continue to suffer the tax on productivity exacted by hours each day wasted in traffic or attending to bureaucratic regulations. Without a burst in productivity growth rates, Brazil will remain in the middle income trap. But engineering these changes in *Brazilão* is a formidable challenge. No intellectual leader – neither politician nor economist – appears poised to guide Brazil in this tenuous transition toward sustainable, inclusive growth.

Bibliography

Bresser-Pereira, Luiz Carlos. "Brazil's Inflation and the Cruzado Plan, 1985–1988." In *Inflation: Are we Next? Hyperinflation and Solutions in Argentina, Brazil and Israel*, edited by Pamela Falk, 54–7. Boulder: Lynne Rienner, 1990.

Bresser-Pereira, Luiz Carlos. "Developmental Capitalism and the Liberal Alternative." Prepared for the 1st International Symposium "Growth, Crisis, Democracy: The Political Economy of Class Coalitions and Policy Regime Change," Waseda University, December 17th, 2013.

"Committee Member Profile: Arminio Fraga." http://www.claaf.org/portugues/Members/Fraga.html.

Espinoza, Rodolfo. "The Man Who Knew Too Much." http://www.brazzil.com/component/content/article/54-november-2001/6804.pdf.

Felippe Cabello, Andrea. "Reaching a Broader Audience: Simonsen's International Career." Prepared for XLI Encontro Nacional de Economia, Foz de Iguaçu, Brazil, December 10th–13th, 2013.

Fishlow, Albert. "Indexing Brazilian Style: Inflation without Tears?" *Brookings Papers in Economic Activity* 1, 1974: 261–82.

Furtado, Celso. "When the Future Arrives." In *Brazil: A Century of Change*, edited by Ignacy Sachs, Jorge Wilheim and Paulo Sergio Pinheiro, 291–99. Chapel Hill: UNC Press, 2009.

Loureiro, Maria Rita. "Economists in the Brazilian Government: From Developmentalist State to Neoliberal Policies." In *Economists in the Americas*, edited by Veronica Montecinos and John Markoff, 100–141. Cheltenham, UK: Edward Elgar, 2009.

"Profile of Guido Mantega." http://www.walkersresearch.com/profilepages/Show_Executive_Title/Executiveprofile/G/Guido__Mantega_100021107.html.

Roett, Riordan. *The New Brazil*. Washington, DC: Brookings Institution Press, 2011.

Schroy, John Oswin. "Mario Henrique Simonsen, Midea S-N, and the Rio De Janeiro Stock Exchange." http://www.capital-flow-analysis.com/investment-tutorial/case_1q.html.

Skidmore, Thomas E. *Brazil: Five Centuries of Change*. New York: Oxford University Press, 2010.

Trebat, Thomas. *Brazil's State-Owned Enterprises: A Case Study of the State as Entrepreneur*. New York: Cambridge University Press, 1983.

"The World Factbook." https://www.cia.gov/library/publications/the-world-factbook/rankorder/2001 rank.html?countryname=Brazil&countrycode=br&regionCode=soa&rank=8#br.

"Zelia Mello: Executive Profile and Biography." http://investing.businessweek.com/research/stocks/people/person.asp?personId=128035790&ticker=EGE:CN.

Part III

The Middle East

17

Turkey and the Turkic linguistic zone

The case that doesn't quite fit

Eyüp Özveren

When one speaks of a linguistic zone, it is often assumed that the zone in question is likely to display a stronger unity than that of a mere cultural zone. For example, the Chinese cultural zone includes many peoples and countries that do not share Chinese as their language, and therefore possesses its own potentially divisive sub-zones. In contrast, the German linguistic zone brings to mind a whole geography, much of which was occupied by the Austrian Empire as well as what would become Germany by way of unification. Politically divided, this zone nevertheless has had a lot in common culturally. If economic thought developed with a strong Historical School accent in Germany while the Austrians launched their own version of the marginal revolution, there was significant interaction, in fact a *Methodenstreit* across the border. Without one, the other would not have been the same. This is most true when the methodological sophistication of Austrian economists vis-à-vis other neoclassical economists is taken into consideration.

This is what we might refer to as the linguistic zone effect in this particular case. If we take the German linguistic zone as a model, we will observe that the Turkic linguistic zone deviates from it significantly. What defines the loose unity of the Turkic linguistic zone are, first, the preponderance of a family of related languages that display important variations, and second, the occasional interaction of physically mobile and ethnically related populations. This zone did not constitute an integrated economic space, even though it had been en route to historic long-distance links that helped diffuse a certain culture of business practices, usually correlated with diaspora ethnic and/or religious communities. As it will become clear from the rest of the discussion, as far as economic thought is concerned, the dissemination and interaction of economic ideas across this geography remained rather limited, and whenever it occurred, far from being direct, it was mediated through a zone of greater influence, be that Russia – with its rich intellectual heritage in general and its experience with the dissemination of European economic ideas in particular (Barnett and Zweynert, 2008) – or the contemporary global political economic order – with its straightjacket. In other words, either the field of interaction was external or the influence and interaction were indirect. In this sense, here we are faced with a case that does not quite fit. Even so, approaching the issue from this viewpoint casts a different light on the case under study that sharpens certain features that would otherwise have been easily overlooked in a standard national narrative that takes as its geographical reference South Eastern Europe of which Turkey is a natural extension.

The Republic of Turkey as a sovereign nation-state was founded in 1923 as the major successor of the multi-ethnic and multi-religious Ottoman Empire, the foundation of which as an offshoot of a tribal Turkic principality (*beylik*) bordering the Byzantine Empire is dated back to 1299. It was only after the conquest of Istanbul in 1453, that the imperial status of this formation became incontestable. Before then, it was an heir to both Central Asian nomadic tribal and Middle Eastern Islamic imperial traditions. After 1453, it also became the heir to the Eastern Roman Empire. As such, its ancient and medieval Mediterranean characteristics became all the more pronounced. Its institutions were hybrid in many ways (Köprülü, 1931), and its structure highly complex, not only because it was an heir to variegated imperial traditions, but also because it was territorially much expanded to cover a vast geography. The Roman heritage was also of critical importance for differentiating the Ottoman Empire from the rest of the Turkic zone.

Whereas Central Asia has been home to the successive rise and fall of short-lived tribal nomadic empires, in sharp contrast, the Ottoman Empire changed its character thoroughly after 1453 and persisted well into the twentieth century because of this "Roman" input. The Ottoman Empire was classified as a world power during the latter part of "the long sixteenth century" when it contested its archrival the Habsburg Empire over Mediterranean hegemony. During its classical period, the Ottoman state was relatively strong vis-à-vis society and center (Istanbul) prevailed over the vast periphery. One could conceive that the Ottoman Empire combined a feudal-like social and economic structure with a centralized and strong state. This meant a primarily feudal-like agrarian economy that was nevertheless monetized in conjunction with a strong long-distance trade. Moreover, this economic system relied on the import of precious metals that served as means of exchange. During this period, economic life was subject to rules and regulations designed according to social and political needs. Economic policy favored long-distance trade over industry, whereas the main source of wealth and political and military power was vested in land. The territorial expansion of the Ottoman Empire brought with it greater economic wealth (İnalcık, 1970; Braudel, 1984). Economy was embedded not only in society but also remained as an ancillary to state's ultimate expansionary ends.

Development of economic ideas over the long-term

Classical economic thought as expressed in advisory treatises written for Sultans emphasized the need for the maintenance of the so-called Circle of Justice according to which the Sultan and his men were entitled to taxes as true holders of title to the land, which they used to pursue further conquest as well as introducing law and order in the country. The vast rural population consisting of subjects could work these lands, prosper, and produce greater total output as long as tax revenues were used appropriately (Darling, 1996; Ermiş, 2013). However, once the Ottoman Empire reached its natural frontiers, beyond which expansion could no longer be realized, together with this system of accumulation, the classical age came to an end.

As of the seventeenth century, Ottoman scholars endeavored much to come to terms with stagnation and the long-term destabilizing effects of the sixteenth-century inflation (Kafadar, 1995). Economic thought favored fiscalism in tune with the above conception, but also traditionalism over innovation in industry, and provisionism over free trade (Genç, 1989). The last principle meant that the day-to-day provisioning of the capital of the Ottoman Empire, with its vast population wavering between 400,000 and 1,000,000, was the first concern. This implied that the import of necessities for subsistence be tolerated, if not outright encouraged, at a time when exports were seen as a potential threat to the livelihood of the domestic population. At a time when European cities still had moderate populations and states practiced mercantilism, the Ottoman Empire was practically anti-mercantilist in both economic thought and policy.

This did not, however, mean that trade was left on its own. On the contrary, it was highly and minutely regulated. As hinted above, this system could function well as long as territorial expansion remained geographically and economically feasible. Ottoman economic thought of the seventeenth and eighteenth centuries addressed practical problems and sought to elaborate an existing body of thought and practice that were hard pressed by increasingly unfavorable circumstances (Aksan, 1993; Ağır, 2013). The search for piecemeal adjustment and elaboration prevailed over a thorough overhaul of the system in mind and at work. The dominant trend in the Ottoman lands over these two centuries became in favor of decentralization. Demographic stagnation combined with this trend brought about the fragmentation of the domestic market. Against this backdrop, any genuine concern with productivity as the key to surplus expansion and commercialization in the rural sector *pace* some sort of physiocratic doctrine became redundant. In this way, as long as land-labor ratios remained high, Ottoman economic thought successfully avoided not only mercantilism but also physiocracy as essentially irrelevant well into the nineteenth century.

It is only with the nineteenth century, the parameters of which were designed by the paradigmatic British Industrial Revolution and the French Revolution, that the need for a more profound reshaping of Ottoman economic thought arose. As wars became more likely yet came with spiraling costs, the Ottoman statesmen were forced to modernize and maintain an army and navy by recourse to new revenues. Of critical importance were the worldwide disequilibrium effects of the Napoleonic Wars. The French expedition to Egypt demonstrated the vulnerability of the Ottoman Empire as well as exposing local populations to modernity. Muhammed Ali Pasha (1769–1848) of Egypt, an enlightened despot with industrialization ambitions, rebelled against the Sultan in 1831 and waged a decade-long war that extended well into Anatolia, the Ottoman heartland from where most of the soldiers that set off for first conquest and then the defense of the tri-continental empire originated. For this reason, Karl Marx identified it as the real seat of power (Marx, 2006: 4).

However, the Balkans, "Turkey in Europe" as it came to be known in Marx's time, had always been the true domain of the exercise of this power since the conquest of Istanbul, and was of critical economic and strategic importance for the imperial capital. The Empire survived well as long as it retained its Balkan possessions and disintegrated within a decade once it lost them with the Balkan Wars (1912–13). It is no surprise that the Ottoman Empire could survive the rebellion but not the Balkan Wars. Whereas Muhammed Ali Pasha enjoyed French support, the Ottomans, frightened by both the rebellion at home and the threat posed by Russian advances into the Black Sea in the North, turned to Britain for assistance. Britain offered support for the preservation of the integrity of the Ottoman Empire in return for the adoption of reforms conducive to free trade. With the Anglo-Ottoman Commercial Treaty of 1838, the Ottoman Empire officially entered a new economic course. Restrictions over trade would be abolished and free trade be embraced. In a nutshell, this free trade policy would encourage the export of raw materials and the import of manufactures. Manufactures would greatly originate from Britain and to a lesser extent France, to which the bulk of Ottoman raw material exports were destined. The destructive effect of this major policy shift on traditional local manufactures was imminent.

This long-term context paved the way for the development and persistence of two rival camps in Ottoman economic thought. Be that as it may, with the nineteenth century, the rules of the game had thus changed. In the realm of economic thought, a conceivable rupture with the past had occurred. Neither of the contesting parties sought continuity with their immediate predecessors. They turned instead to Europe for ammunition to wage their intellectual battles. As of then, Ottoman economic thought was subject to the influence of European ideas and policies. The rival camps of European economic thought thus inadvertently helped to develop, albeit with a delay, their extensions on the Ottoman soil.

Of the two rival camps, advocates of free trade doctrine and the classical theory behind it appeared first. According to them, the Ottoman Empire had vast resources, the inventory of which attested to a favorable inscription into the international division of labor as an exporter of primary materials. Exports would generate wealth and help afford imports of manufactures thereby giving a new shape to Ottoman economy and society. This position was advocated by resident foreigners with a vested interest in commerce such as Alexander Blacque and David Urquhart, minorities as well as certain Ottoman statesmen with intellectual credentials. The primary instruments of spreading these optimistic Smithian ideas were newspapers, pamphlets, and occasionally books as in the case of David Urquhart's *Turkey and its Resources* (1833), that attracted much criticism from Marx (2006, 25). The classical approach penetrated via French linguistic and educational intermediation as was the case with Serandi Arşizen, the author of an early introductory manuscript and a student of Pellegrino Rossi in France (Özgür and Genç, 2014).

In opposition, there emerged a group that was excited with the devastating effects on domestic manufactures of imports and the growing disparity between the Ottoman Empire and the West who turned increasingly to protectionism as a way of self-defense. These included Ottoman dilettanti, statesmen, and ambassadors. Among the first to call attention to the unfavorable consequences of the Anglo-Ottoman Commercial Treaty were Ahmed Fethi Pasha, Sadık Rıfat Pasha, Kostaki Bey, Ahmed Cevdet Paşa, Namık Kemal, and Ziya Pasha. This opposition was not only protectionist but also understandably productionist at a time when the prospects of free-trade blinded many an eye.

Whereas the classical paradigm looked more consistent and squarely rounded-off with its universal credentials, its alternative in-the-making was piecemeal, ad hoc, and at best reminiscent of mercantilism and cameralism, even though the channels of dissemination of ideas, in case there were any, remained obscure. The classical approach found its best expression in the works of Sakızlı Ohannes Pasha (1830–1912). His work was a compendium of then current European economic ideas filtered through French-language sources. The scope of his reading had been vast, and so was his *magnum opus*. The emphases he put on certain themes of immediate relevance for the Ottoman circumstances made his work a true adaptation rather than mere translation and compilation. Whereas the next step in line ought to have been the infiltration of the marginal revolution, somewhat paradoxically, it was not (Sayar, 1986). This was because it was far too abstract and impractical to address immediate policy concerns.

The successor to Ohannes Pasha was Cavit Bey (1875–1926) and the line of succession worked through *Mekteb-i Mülkiye*, a school designed to raise statesmen – elevated in 1877 to the status of a school of higher learning – which provided the first hospitable environment for the institutionalization of political economy as a discipline in the Ottoman Empire. Cavit Bey's work updated and replaced the text of Ohannes Pasha. It served for instruction during a critical period when economics gained popularity and recognition. Cavit Bey was a consistent and sound economist who was not only an academic but also an actual policymaker in his capacity as the influential Minister of Finance for most of the period after the Young Turk Revolution of 1908. Having already gone bankrupt as officially recognized by the infamous Decree of Muharrem (1881), the Ottoman economy was subject to important constraints, such as that imposed by the very existence and authority of the Public Debt Administration that left no room for policy improvization, at least until the outbreak of the First World War. Against this backdrop, Cavit Bey set the tone for the last decade of Ottoman policymaking as a committed liberal. The ideas of classical liberalism would hence continue to dominate the scene, and Bey was aloof to neoclassical economics. Where the classical approach served well, marginalism failed because it could not help to explain how things functioned, but to come to that stage, the Ottoman economy needed the deployment of pro-active policies first.

It was as of the 1870s that the rival approach to that of classical orthodoxy gained a new impetus when Ottomans like Mehmet Şerif Effendi and Hayreddin Pasha introduced the name of Colbert as a source of inspiration. Mercantilism had thus finally come to the Ottoman Empire with a vengeance. But this *déjà vu* mercantilism could not suffice, something more was needed. It is no coincidence that the oppositional ideas developed fast into a Historical School *alla turca*. For example, Ottoman patriot Namık Kemal (1840–88), a victim of the Hamidian despotism (1878–1908), rejected the classical approach while developing a neo-mercantilist alternative by making use of mercantilism as it was (mis)represented in the texts of the classical school, physiocracy and Malthus. The inferences he drew were reminiscent of those of the German Historical School. Here we are faced with a case of theoretical independent (re)discovery.

Ahmed Midhat Effendi (1844–1912) was a popular and prolific writer of the Hamidian era. Just like his predecessors, he turned to Colbert for inspiration in his *Ekonomi Politik* that deserves at least as much attention for its simple and straightforward title that heralds a new era. More importantly, he delved into the investigation of Ottoman character relative to the conception of *homo-economicus*. In his view, Ottomans behaved differently because of cultural reasons. Even so, he insisted that a new approach to economic affairs could be cultivated. In this way he brought to the foreground the issues of rationality and character-traits of economic agents. This is how the question of individualism arrived on the Ottoman scene. The fact that Midhat Effendi concentrated on individual behavior may have had to do with the repressive character of the Hamidian regime. He advocated hard work, entrepreneurial gist, and frugality in his didactic literary works and in many ways anticipated, albeit in a crude form, the Protestant-ethic thesis of Max Weber. This was yet another instance of simultaneous independent discovery.

Fostered by a set of multiple independent discoveries, yet handicapped by its relative ignorance of the then contemporary European scholarship, the critical alternative approach was further elaborated during the last quarter of the nineteenth century. This alternative was theoretically squared off and thus evolved out of a naïve *alla turca historismus* with the works of Akyiğitzade Musa Bey (1865–1923) who taught at the prestigious Military Academy in Istanbul. He advocated temporary protection for nascent industries in a way reminiscent of Friedrich List (1789–1846) within a "national economy" perspective (Çavdar, 1992, 131). Musa Bey was originally from Kazan, a thriving city of the Russian Empire populated by the Tatars, who were in many ways linked with the Ottoman culture and acted as a bridge to the more backward Russian Muslims of Central Asia, thereby spreading the urge for an enlightenment via education as advocated by Ismail Gaspıralı (known also as Gasprinskii, 1851–1914), the equivalent of Midhat Effendi as the "Teacher of the Nation" (Baldauf, 2001, 87). The economic development then under way in Kazan attracted much attention, including that of Max Weber, who felt compelled to qualify his position concerning the relationship between a religion and economic action: "Industrialization was not impeded by Islam as the religion of individuals – the Tartars in the Russian Caucasus are often very 'modern' entrepreneurs –, but by the religiously determined structure of the Islamic *states*, their officialdom and their jurisprudence" (Weber, vol.II, 1978, 1095). It must have been in Russia that Musa Bey came to know List and *Historismus* (Berkes, 1972, 52–3).

Hence German influence over Ottoman Turkish economic thought worked, at least in part, by way of Russian mediation. In this respect, there was also Alexander Israel Helphand

(1867–1924), a Russian Jew brought up in Odessa, who had obtained a doctorate degree in economics and finance in Basel (1891) before seeking refuge in the Ottoman Empire as of 1910. He published extensively under the pen-name of Parvus from 1912 to 1914 and exerted an influence on the Young Turks. Parvus insisted that indigenous economic development should start off with the peasantry (Sencer, 1977, 22, 22n) – a thesis disclosing his affinities with the Russian debates – whereas Yusuf Akçura (1876–1935), again originally from Kazan, the prominent precursor of Turkish nationalism, proclaimed that the foundation of a modern state ought to be the national bourgeoisie nurtured by a modern national economy; a policy objective embraced soon by the Young Turks and the nascent Turkish nationalists (Berkes, 1978: 461–2) such as Tekin Alp (the Jewish convert Moiz Kohen, 1883–1961) and Ziya Gökalp (1876–1924), who helped popularize Musa Bey's economic ideas and policy preferences.

Gökalp, posthumously named as the father of Turkish sociology, was in fact of critical importance in transmitting the economic thought of the late Ottoman Empire to the leading cadres and the first generation of the Turkish Republic. If industrialization became a major concern in the Republican era, it was because of Gökalp, who endorsed it wholeheartedly. Otherwise, the last decade of the Empire had witnessed how the debate between the primacy of agriculture and industry had remained unresolved. To the very end, there remained those like Ethem Nejat (1883–1921) who believed that investment in agriculture and commerce via education (human capital) and infrastructure would be more fitting to trigger sustained economic development in the Ottoman Empire. Gökalp identified in industry a transformative social force, much in the spirit of List. It should be noted that the alternative approach was thus rounded off only when Listian political economy was consciously integrated to the naïve and *sui generis* Ottoman historical approach. The circumstances of a war economy as dictated by the outbreak of the First World War in which the Ottoman Empire was allied with Germany, only helped the fortunes of this ultimate synthesis and its rising popularity among the Ottoman-Turkish intelligentsia (Toprak, 1982). This was all happening at a time when these debates found outlets in the first academic journals and associations of economists, while economics education found increasing room in the traditional university of Istanbul then known as *Darülfünun*.

Convergence and divergence during the twentieth century and the further flow of ideas

The Republic of Turkey was internationally recognized with the Treaty of Lausanne in 1923. The same treaty had economic stipulations that set a transitional period as far as trade and monetary policies were concerned. This meant that the Republican governments were practically deprived of certain policy instruments throughout the 1920s. A full-fledged overhaul of economic policy had thus to await the 1930s. Thanks to the further impetus provided with the Great Depression, the liberal interregnum of the 1920s was easily terminated for good. This encouraged critical economic thought to pick up from where it had left off.

The *Kadro*, published between 1932 and 1935 in Ankara, was a short-lived but highly influential journal in this respect. The mentor of the journal was Şevket Süreyya Aydemir, and his economics-minded colleagues included Vedat Nedim Tör, İsmail Hüsrev Tökin and Burhan Asaf Belge. Şevket Süreyya and İsmail Hüsrev had been to post-revolutionary Moscow in the early 1920s in order to pursue studies in an exemplary party school, whereas Vedat Nedim and Burhan Asaf had studied in postwar Germany. Vedat Nedim had stayed in Berlin and did his PhD (1922) under the supervision of Werner Sombart. In their view, the Great Depression, by crippling the metropolitan economies and international trade, offered a golden opportunity for countries like Turkey to appropriate Western technology and to institute it within the context of a planned mixed-economy. They envisaged *étatisme* as an economic policy to this end. They argued that one could overcome by such an active policy the kind of underdevelopment fostered by the unequal exchange-ridden international economic division of labor (Özveren, 1996). They developed "the most articulate and authentic Turkish school of political economy … that prefigured post-Second World War dependency approaches" (Özveren, 2002, 141–2). There is also a strong parallelism if not outright continuity between the Third Worldist revolutionary Sultan Galiyev (1892–1940) of the Russian Muslims and the *Kadro* authors. It is no surprise that *Kadro* enthusiasts of industry also held a theoretically sound position on the agrarian question; a theme of great import for the Russian debates.

At about the same time, Turkish government, on the verge of reforming *Darülfünun* into modern Istanbul University, launched a program to recruit ex-German academics in Turkey. Among the recruits to the would-be Faculty of Economics, the first of its kind in Turkey, were Wilhelm Röpke (1899–1966), Fritz Neumark (1900–91), Gerhard Kessler (1883–1963), Alexander Rüstow (1885–1963), Josef Dobretsberger (1903–70), and Alfred Isaac (1888–1956). There was also Umberto Ricci, the Italian (Fındıkoğlu, 1946; Neumark, 2008). In retrospect, Neumark came first in terms of influence. Hence this was also a period when the "dissident" German influence over Turkish economic thought was at its highest level.

As of the 1930s, in line with the *Kadro*'s expectations, the new regime initiated an ambitious national economic development program along the line of import-substituting industrialization. The realization of such an economic plan required foreign financial and technical assistance that came forth from the Soviet Union as a friendly neighbor. As such, there occurred a convergence of economic interests. This brief but critically important period lasted until the Second World War which disrupted the industrialization effort. Nevertheless, preferences of both the Soviet Union and Turkey in favor of economic planning with the state assuming an active role implied also a convergence among Turkey on the one side and the Turkic republics of the USSR on the other. Policy preferences might have cultivated a stronger structural resemblance if only the Second World War was not succeeded by the Cold War. In any case, the period of 1878–1945 witnessed the closest rapprochement and interaction among the Russian and Turkish spheres of influence that could not have left the intermediate Turkic republics unaffected.

The Cold War placed Turkey and the Turkic republics in hostile camps and made any further contact, even via Russian intermediation, impossible. Hence convergence of the 1930s gave way to the protracted divergence that lasted until the fall of the Berlin Wall. After the Second World War, Turkey turned to the West. This also reflected itself in the reorientation of economic policy and economic thought. The preference for a mixed economic system was practical given the achievements of the previous economic planning phase. The heyday of Keynesianism until the 1970s by way of the neoclassical synthesis had its repercussions in Turkey. After the war, students and young academics were sent to the UK and the USA. They came back with a Keynesian formation. Sabri Ülgener from Istanbul University and Sadun Aren from Ankara University went to Harvard and Cambridge respectively (Sayar, 1998; Aren, 2006). They played a key role in the dissemination of Keynesian ideas among Turkish academia. Gülten Kazgan of Istanbul University was a third name important not only because she went for research to the USA but also because she became the first female academic economist, who trained generations of students until recently (Kazgan, 2009).

Visits by economists such as Gunnar Myrdal, Nicholas Kaldor, and Jan Tinbergen during the 1950s and 1960s prepared the political establishment to receive these ideas well. In this context, the 1960s/early 1970s in Turkey witnessed a synthesis of Keynesian, neoclassical, and pro-developmental economic ideas and policies. During this period, an American-inspired university, the Middle East Technical University (1956) came into the academic scene and brought fresh air to economics education, along with the voluntarily nationalized Robert Academy that became Boğaziçi University (1971). Even so, the total number of universities had not yet exceeded ten.

The picture was made more complex with the outbreak of the world economic crisis of the 1970s. As Keynesianism fell from grace, neoclassical economics started to speak with the accent of Friedman and Hayek. A few high quality Turkish academics such as Sencer Divitçioğlu and Yılmaz Akyüz in turn turned to Marxian and Sraffian political economy. It is no coincidence that Divitçioğlu gained recognition with his controversial work on the so-called "Asiatic mode of production," which linked the fortunes of Marx and Central Asian history via the Faculty of Economics at Istanbul University. In general, Turkish academic economists came into contact with heterodox economics as of the late 1970s. Akyüz moved to Europe in the 1980s and became noted for publications in development macroeconomics. In conjunction, the same period witnessed the development of a certain interest in mathematical economics. Based in Boğaziçi University, Murat Sertel gained international recognition and became the most prominent figure in this respect. Mathematical economics found a favorable reception, not only because of winds blowing from the West, but also because it had always been strong in the Soviet Union to which some Turkish academics looked for inspiration because of their political leanings. Given the circumstances, this was as much as Turkey and some Turkic Republics could come close only indirectly.

The worldwide economic crisis of the 1970s coincided with the domestic crisis of import-substituting industrialization strategy in Turkey, which triggered a political crisis in turn. The subsequent shift to an export-oriented growth strategy coupled with a trade liberalization regime renewed popular interest in the prospects and priorities of economics as a profession. The initiation with Bilkent University (1984) of a wave of foundation-supported private universities gave a new turn to the Americanization of economics education. In general, on the one side, increasing adherence to International Monetary Fund and World Bank policy recommendations helped streamline economics education after the Anglo-American model promoting neoclassical economic analysis. The universalism of the dominant theory facilitated the task of academics and policymakers alike.

On the other side, dissatisfaction with the social consequences of economic policies cultivated an interest in academic dissidence. As Marxism itself fell into disrepute with the decline and fall of the Soviet Empire, heterodox leaning economists increased in number and felt all the more liberated from the deadweight of orthodoxy. Consequently, among Turkish academics, names like Karl Polanyi and Joseph Schumpeter gained a new following. The quality of followers outweighed their quantity. In this sense, one can safely infer that during the last three decades both mainstream economic analysis and its more promising heterodox rivals gained strength. This means an enrichment of the spectrum of economics. This has been helped by the progress of graduate level economics education in general. The crisis of 2008 and the Great Recession initiated an interest in Keynes's economics manifest in a number of workshops and conferences leading to publications defying the international orthodoxy.

After the 1990s, the strengthening of ties with the Turkic republics after a long interval arose much enthusiasm. The greater circulation of goods and services along with populations did not bring about a corresponding enrichment of economic thought through interaction and cross-fertilization. On the contrary, economics curriculum and thought in the Turkic republics remain a bizarre combination of discredited Soviet topics and mainstream economics of the worst sort. As global recipes of shock therapy, gradual gradualism, privatization, and development *pace* the neo-liberal Washington Consensus penetrated into this hitherto protected Russian domain (Papava, 2005), economic thought and policy seem to have fallen prey to these new shortsighted orthodoxies. It seems unlikely that further cultural and intellectual exchanges among Turkey and the Turkic republics will bear any fruits in the realm of economic thought in the foreseeable future.

Poles apart, both parties will remain subject to influx of further foreign economic ideas and practices. Originality will be wanting in the first place. Be that as it may, the quality of mainstream economics and economists may still experience a certain improvement albeit unevenly as the standardization of curricula and professionalism is spread. This is indeed an optimistic forecast given the inflationary rise in the number of institutions of higher learning, most of which amount to little more than dubious backyard operations. In Turkey alone, there exist now some one hundred universities with programs in economics. It is more realistic to anticipate that Turkey will be further integrated as a peripheral end to European circuits, while the rest will wait for yet another wind of change.

References

Ağır, Seven (2013). "The Evolution of Grain Policy Beyond Europe: Ottoman Grain Administration in the Late Eighteenth Century," *Journal of Interdisciplinary History*, 43: 571–98.

Aksan, Virginia (1993). "Ottoman Political Writing, 1768–1808," *International Journal of Middle East Studies*, 25, 1: 53–69.

Aren, Sadun (2006). *Puslu Camın Arkasından*. Ankara: İmge.

Baldauf, Ingeborg (2001). "Jadidism in Central Asia within Reformism and Modernism in the Muslim World," *Die Welt des Islams*, New Series, 41, 1: 72–88.

Barnett, Vincent and Zweynert, Joachim, eds. (2008). *Economics in Russia: Studies in Intellectual History*. London: Ashgate.

Berkes, Niyazi (1978). *Türkiye de Çağdaşlaşma [Secularism in Turkey]*. Istanbul: Doğu-Batı Yayınları.

Berkes, Niyazi (1972). "Ekonomik Tarih ile Teori Açısından Türkiye de Ekonomik Düşünün Evrimi, [The Evolution of Economic Thought in Turkey from the Viewpoint of Economic History and Theory]," in Fikret Görün, ed., *Türkiye de Üniversitelerde Okutulan İktisat Üzerine [On Economics Thought at the Universities in Turkey]*. Ankara: Orta Doğu Teknik Üniversitesi, 39–55.

Braudel, Fernand (1984). *The Perspective of the World*. New York: Harper & Row.

Çavdar, Tevfik (1992). *Türkiye'de Liberalizm (1860–1990)*. Ankara: İmge.

Darling, Linda (1996). *Revenue Raising and Legitimacy: Tax Collection and Finance Administration in the Ottoman Empire, 1560–1660*. New York: E.J. Brill.

Ermiş, Fatih (2013). *A History of Ottoman Economic Thought: Developments Before the Nineteenth Century*. London: Routledge.

Fındıkoğlu, Ziyaeddin Fahri (1946). *Türkiye'de İktisat Tedrisatı Tarihçesi ve İktisat Fakültesi Teşkilatı*. Istanbul: İsmail Akgün Matbaası.

Genç, Mehmet (1989). "Osmanlı İktisadi Dünya Görüşünün İlkeleri," *İstanbul Üniversitesi Edebiyat Fakültesi Sosyoloji Dergisi*, 3, 1.

İnalcık, Halil (1970). "The Ottoman Economic Mind and Aspects of the Ottoman Economy," in M.A. Cook, ed. *Studies in the Economic History of the Middle East*. London: Oxford University Press, 207–18.

Kafadar, Cemal (1995). *Between Two Worlds: The Construction of the Ottoman State*. Berkeley: University of California Press.

Kazgan, Gülten (2009). *Bir İktisatçının Tanıklıkları*. Istanbul: Bilgi Üniversitesi Yayınları.

Köprülü, Fuat (1931). "Bizans Müesseselerinin Osmanlı Müesseselerine Tesiri Hakkında Bazı Mülahazalar," *Türk Hukuk ve İktisat Tarihi Mecmuası*, 165–313.

Marx, Karl (2006). *The Eastern Question*. London: Frank Cass & Co. [1897].

Neumark, Fritz (2008). *Boğaziçi'ne Sığınanlar: Türkiye'ye İltica Eden Alman Bilim, Siyaset ve Sanat Adamları (1933–1953)*. Istanbul: Neden.

Özgür, M. Erdem ve and Genç, Hamdi (2014). "Sarantis Archigenes (Serandi Arşizen), Pellegrino Rossi and the Spread of the Classical Approach in the Ottoman Empire," *The European Journal of the History of Economic Thought*, 21, 3: 421–47.

Özveren, Eyüp (2002). "Ottoman Economic Thought and Economic Policy in Transition: Rethinking the Nineteenth Century," in Michalis Psalidopoulos and Maria Eugénia Mata, eds., *Economic Thought and Policy in Less Developed Europe: The Nineteenth Century*. London: Routledge, 129–44.

Özveren, Eyüp (1996). "The Intellectual Legacy of the *Kadro* Movement in Retrospect," *METU Studies in Development*, 23, 4: 565–76.

Papava, Vladimer (2005). "On the Theory of post-Communist Economic Transition to Market," *Post-Communist Economic Transition*, 32, 1–2: 77–97.

Sayar, Ahmed Güner (1998). *Bir İktisatçının Entellektüel Portresi: Sabri F. Ülgener*. Istanbul: Eren.

Sayar, Ahmed Güner (1986). *Osmanlı İktisat Düşüncesinin Çağdaşlaşmı*. Istanbul: DerYayınları.

Sencer, Muammer (1977). "Parvus'un Yaşam ve Kişilik Dialoğu," his introduction to Parvus Efendi, *Türkiye'nin Mali Tutsaklığı*. Istanbul: May Yayınları, 7–26.

Toprak, Zafer (1982). *Türkiye'de "Milli İktisat," (1908–1918)*. Ankara: Yurt Yayınları.

Weber, Max (1978). *Economy and Society*, vol.II. Berkeley: University of California Press.

18

Israel

Yuval Yonay and Arie Krampf

Unlike other new nations, Israel is a new society. It was erected by Jewish immigrants who arrived since the 1880s and aspired to develop a Jewish homeland in Palestine. Building a new society (separate from the local Palestinian society) required a vision of what this society would be like, and the new immigrants relied upon the liberal and socialist ideas brought by them from Europe. Most immigrants came from Eastern Europe, and their academic training was either acquired in Central Europe or in Eastern Europe in universities under German influence. The encounter with new conditions and unscripted challenges in Palestine obliged the leaders of the political forces in the emerging Jewish community to adjust their visions and invent new solutions. In this chapter we present the history of economic ideas of the new Jewish community, first as a settler's society in Ottoman and British Palestine, and later as an independent state. Our aim is to trace the evolution of economic ideas in the context of changing economic conditions and challenges, the reception of economic ideas originating in other countries, and the ensuing economic policy-making discourse.

The Zionist movement

The modern Jewish society in Palestine/Israel is the outcome of the Zionist movement that emerged in Eastern Europe in the last quarter of the nineteenth century. The economic ideas/views that guided Israel's early business community, party members, and leaders can therefore be tracked back to the brewing intellectual and ideological environment of Central and Eastern Europe in 1870–1939 (Alroey, 2014).

In 1897 Theodor Herzl (1860–1904) convened numerous and diverse Zionist activists and established the World Zionist Organization (WZO) as the formal body overarching the project of establishing a Jewish national home. The ambitious goal of building a Jewish homeland from scratch unavoidably raised stern economic questions: Should the Zionist project be guided by the laws of the market and rely on private enterprise, or should the emerging economy be planned and run by national bodies in order to overcome market laws (Metzer, 1979)? Should the economy be agrarian as part of the return to the land or industrial and technologically advanced as in modern nations (Krampf, 2010b; Troen, 2003)?

The first wave of Jewish immigrants to Palestine (1880–1900) was driven by a bourgeois vision of making their own farms in the "Land of the Fathers." They established private farms but a lack of experience and harsh conditions brought them to the brink of bankruptcy, forcing them to rely heavily on turn-of-the-century Jewish financial moguls, Maurice de Hirsch and Edmond James de Rothschild, for aid. This reliance on financial aid obliged the farmers to adopt rationalized production according to market forces. The Jewish settlements were accompanied by a liberal vision of a Jewish homeland in Palestine that evolved among the Zionist intellectuals. Herzl believed that the Jewish homeland, unfettered by a powerful landlord class, would be built according to the vision of liberal Europeans. Herzl's *Altneuland* (1919), *The Old New Land*, a utopian novel published in 1902, is considered the utopia of the Zionist movement; it is also a utopia of a modern capitalist welfare society.

At the beginning of the Zionist movement, socialism and Zionism offered competing visions for solving the problems faced by Jews in Eastern Europe. Many Jews and many socialists thought that the "Jewish problem" would disappear in a post-revolutionary, classless society. Changing views among socialists toward notional aspirations in Europe at the end of the nineteenth century convinced many Jewish socialists to join the Zionist movement and to advance the Jewish homeland as a socialist project that would solve the Jewish problem and also be a model for a just society. Since the Second Zionist Congress (1898), socialist factions have become a major force within the Zionist movement, and since the beginning of the twentieth century they were also the major force among Zionist immigrants to Palestine. Yet socialist Zionists were divided over the exact nature of the desirable socialist society and on the strategy of reaching the aspired goal, especially how to cooperate with non-socialist Zionists.

Two of the intellectual leaders of socialist Zionism were Nachman Syrkin (1868–1924), who got a PhD in philosophy from Berlin University, and Dov Ber Borochov (1881–1917). They represent two general trends typical in turn-of-the-century socialism. Syrkin was influenced by the Utopian socialists and the Russian reformers such as Herzen and Tolstoy and endorsed a conciliatory approach of cooperation with bourgeois Zionism and the advancement of communal forms of enterprise (Syrkin, 1935, 1939; Pilowski, 1974). Borochov represented a more orthodox Marxian view including the idea of class struggle; socialist Zionists should take part in building a capitalist economy, which when mature would lead to a socialist revolution (Borochov, 1928, 1937, 1972). Other Zionist thinkers saw the idea of cooperatives as especially fitting a society in the making. A major exponent of this view was Franz Oppenheimer (1864–1943), one of the major champions of cooperatives (1932, 1933, 1938, 1942–4).

The national logic of collective settlements

While some European and American leaders argued that settlements should be judged by strict economic criteria, the socialist Zionists understood that such an approach could not work in the economically unattractive conditions of Palestine. WZO leaders accepted this view, as is evident in the strategy adopted by Arthur Ruppin (1876–1943), the head of the WZO office in Palestine, who led the settlement project of the organization. Ruppin, a German-Jewish sociologist, demographer, and political-economist, studied in Berlin and Halle and imported the ideas of German economic nationalism to the Zionist project. He understood the need to coordinate the efforts of nation building in order to use the scarce resources that the Zionist movement could muster and promoted collaboration between the WZO and the socialists. The WZO provided the capital and the socialist factions provided the *Halutzim* (pioneers) who established new collective settlements (Gorny and Greenberg, 1997; Kimmerling, 1983; Penslar, 1991, 2001).

Agriculture was crucial in this strategy for several reasons. First, agrarian settlements were a tool to establish a claim on the land (Shilo, 1988). Second, following prevailing economic theories of the time, the country's "absorptive economic capacity" was believed to be determined by the number of its farmers (Krampf, 2010b). Third, agricultural physical labor was regarded as part of the revival of the Jewish nation and for the creation of the "New Jew" (e.g. Ruppin, 1913, 1973). The objective of the Zionist movement was not only to establish a Jewish state, but also to correct that sociological "anomaly" of the Jewish people, that is, to shift Jews from "unproductive" occupations in *luftgeschäft* to "productive" jobs in agriculture (Bloom, 2007, 2011).

The collective settlement strategy suited well the ideological aspirations of the *Haluzim*, but its implementation might owe more to its service to the national purpose: it was an instrument to drive a wedge between the Jewish and the Arab economies. Lacking financial resources to buy their own land and lacking experience in agricultural work, the cooperative strategy was a way by which unskilled Jewish farm hands could survive the competition with the local and far more skillful Arab farmers. In free-market conditions the Jewish settlements would not have any chance of surviving, as they were far less "efficient." Hence, the collectivist approach was also a means to create a "dual economy," consisted of two separate Jewish and Arab sectors (Metzer, 1998; Penslar, 1991).

Industrial development was still part of the Zionist project and private enterprise was therefore essential for its success. Consequently, the socialist leaders had an incentive to maintain labor relations under control. At the same time, private capital was limited and did not provide enough jobs. The solution adopted by the socialist leadership was the expansion of the responsibilities of trade unions. The General Federation of Workers in Israel, established in 1920 and known as *The Histadrut* ("The Federation"), became much more than merely a labor union. It also provided social services (education, health, housing, welfare) to its members, and established its own economic enterprises to secure work for its members. The *Histadrut* played a pivotal role in the development of a Jewish community in British-ruled Palestine, playing in many senses the role of the state.

National planning for a Jewish state

In the late 1920s the conflict between the Jewish and Arab communities escalated and the Jewish leadership in Palestine decided to concentrate on establishing a Jewish majority in Palestine. The agrarian paradigm could not support this aim, because land acquisition and settlement were slow. Simultaneously, due to the rise of Nazism in Germany and spread of anti-Semitism and political unrest in Central Europe, a wave of middle-class Jews immigrated to Palestine and boosted the development of urban areas and private enterprise. The agrarian strategy was doubted and an alternative was sought (Krampf, 2010b).

Following the "success" of planned economies during World War One and the failure of the market during the Great Depression, many European and American interwar economists adopted the view that, due to the changing nature of advanced capitalism, governments should play a much bigger role in producing sufficient demand and keeping the economy functioning (Yonay, 1998). This idea of demand-led growth was exploited by Zionist economists into the idea that immigration might stimulate development rather than be dependent on suitable conditions in the absorbing country (Halevi, 1983).

Following the establishment of the state and the 1948 war, the Jewish population in Palestine more than doubled to 1.5 million in less than two years, and continued to rapidly increase in the following years. The government faced huge problems of providing employment, housing, and other services to the newcomers. The government employed a policy of "employment at any cost," paying little attention to economic constraints and efficiency considerations: direct involvement in the allocation of resources, subsidizing investment indiscriminately, and extensive professional training. This strategy could work for a short period but it soon created a huge problem in the balance of payments. In facing this challenge, economists played a more significant role than ever, which is why we turn now to the realm of ideas and theories at that period.

Ideologies and academics

Although many Jewish immigrants to Palestine came due to economic opportunities and lack of better opportunities, many others came due to their commitment to the Zionist idea of a Jewish homeland and forsook more promising immigration destinations. For many, the future character of the Jewish homeland was an essential part of their vision, and therefore the small Jewish community that emerged in Palestine was engaged in lively and prolific discussion of social and economic problems. The numerous political factions, the various kibbutz movements, the numerous offices of the *Histadrut*, and many other bodies published a plethora of pamphlets and translations of European thinkers in Hebrew from all nations and of all stripes.

Outside the political arena there were very few other institutions in which economic debates could take place. Most noticeable was the absence of academic studies of the economy. Indeed, the establishment of a university was a central idea in the Zionist program since its inception, and the first university, the Hebrew University (HU), was officially opened in 1925. It fascinated many Jewish scholars worldwide as is evident in the membership of Albert Einstein and Sigmund Freud on its Board of Trustees. Growing anti-Semitic and Fascist trends pushed many salient scholars out of Europe, most notably from Germany after the rise of the Nazi party in 1933; a few went to the HU.

Yet this development missed the social sciences, and during its first quarter of a century the university had only two faculties: humanities and natural sciences. Without constant state funding, and in a small and poor Jewish community (in 1931 there were only 175,000 Jews in Palestine), budgetary constraints limited the number of new appointments, and outside funding was necessary to secure a new position. Several times during the 1930s/1940s attempts were made to establish chairs in social science, including economics. Prominent Jewish economists were contacted to solicit names of suitable candidates, including Richard Kahn from Cambridge and Adolph Löwe, a German Jew who was fired from Frankfurt in 1933 and eventually taught at The New School in New York. Abba Lerner and Michael Kalecki were two candidates who were considered to lead the economics studies at HU, but the work conditions offered were not attractive enough, and the HU was unwilling to compromise on less prominent nominations (Gross, 2005). Sally Herbert Frankel, a prominent development economist from South Africa, considered an invitation to teach at HU but eventually preferred a career at Oxford. His objection to the collectivist approach to economic development was probably a factor.

With funding from the Jewish National Fund (JNF), the HU did have a chair in agrarian economics. This was Boris-Dob Brutzkus (1874–1938), a specialist on Jewish agrarian settlement in Russia who taught in St. Petersburg (1907–22) and worked in the Russian Scientific Institute in Berlin until 1932 (Brutzkus, 1935). His death in 1935, three years after his nomination, left HU again with no nomination in economics. Economics was taught, however, by an adjunct lecturer at the Department for Islam Culture (and later in the Agricultural Institute as well) by Alfred Bonne (1889–1959), a German Jew who got a PhD in economics from the University of Munich (1923) and left an academic career in favor of the Zionist project. He was the head of the Statistics Office of the JNF and headed the Economic Research Institute of the Jewish Agency. Bonne studied Palestinian economics and his book (1932) on that topic was quite successful in Germany (Gross, 2004; Michaeli, 2005). When a Social Science Department was established at HU in 1944 (headed by Martin Buber), Bonne taught "the descriptive-institutional aspects of Palestine [Eretz-Israel] and Middle-East economies" (Michaeli, 2005, 3).

The void created by the absence of social science at HU was filled by a public research institute and a private enterprise of academic education.

In 1935 Ruppin persuaded the WZO that a body for economic research would be useful in advancing the rational development of a Jewish community in Palestine. The result was the Economic Research Institute (ERI; Ruppin, 1968, 240–1), a unit whose objectives were to "investigate methodically economic life in Palestine, examine the possibilities of its development, and provide Executives [of the Jewish Agency] the necessary material for its economic and practical operation" (Ruppin, 1922, 809). ERI had an independent budget, and its structure granted Ruppin an autonomous space relatively free of political pressures. Ruppin assembled a group of young economists who arrived in Palestine from Germany, and their studies helped the Zionist leadership in its bargaining with the British rulers, but following Ruppin's death in 1942 the ERI lost its influence and was eventually dismantled.

In 1937 the Higher School of Law and Economics (HSLE) was established in Tel Aviv and responded to the growing need of professional training for the burgeoning industrial economy. The school absorbed several European-educated economists, who often worked also in the service of the Jewish Agency, the *Histadrut*, and other public bodies. The head of the economics wing of the school was Benjamin Ziv (1879–1948), a Lithuanian Jew, who got his PhD from the University of Königsberg and worked in commercial banks and in the Russian and Latvian Treasuries, and wrote for local newspapers. Gershon Cyderovich, a Lithuanian Jew, who got a PhD in economics from University of Berlin, worked in a state research center on business cycles in Berlin, and left Germany after the Nazis took power. In addition to teaching, he worked in the Economic Research Center of the Jewish Agency and, after independence, advised government offices and the *Histadrut*.

Another prominent teacher at HSLE was Peretz (Fritz) Naphtali (1888–1961), a prominent economic columnist and editor in Weimar Germany (see Naphtali and Kahn, 1930). He served as the head of the economic research institute of the federation of German unions. In Israel he served as the Director-General of the *Histadrut*-owned Bank Hapoalim, one of Israel's largest banks, a Member of the Knesset, and a Minister in several governments (Naphtali, 1962; Riemer, 1991). Walter Preuss (1895–1984), another German Jew who got a PhD in 1921 in Germany, was among the founders of the Higher School (Preuss, 1936, 1960). He also founded the Statistic Department of the *Histadrut*. Fanny Ginor (1911–2007), another lecturer at the School, was one of the first female economists in Israel. Due to the Nazi rise to power she had to complete her studies at Basel (under Edgar Salin). She was an economic advisor of David Horowitz in the Jewish Agency, Ministry of Finance (MOF), and the Bank of Israel (BI), and served as a member of Israel's UN delegation (Ginor, 1959, 1979).

The above researchers studied at German universities and worked in research units of the Jewish Agency and the *Histadrut*. Their main topics of research were labor relations, unionization, cooperatives, and income distribution, but the topics taught included political economic theory (including the major schools from mercantilism to Marxism), business cycle theory, and finance. Some of the teachers published their courses as textbooks and thus produced the first Hebrew textbooks in economics. Ziv, for example, published the first book on political economy theory

(1938), a book on the business cycle (1945), and a book on public finance (1937). He also translated in the early 1940s J.S. Mill's and Ricardo's famous treatises on political economy, the first (to the best of our knowledge) Hebrew publications in Palestine (Israel) of *non-socialist* classics in political economy. This heritage notwithstanding, the contributions of the above economists has been forgotten. This fact owes much to the dominance of Don Patinkin and the Department of Economics at HU that he led upon his arrival in Israel in 1949.

Don Patinkin

The establishment of an Economics Department in 1949 constitutes a watershed in the practice of economics in Israel as it signals the shift from European-type institutional-historical approach to the American type of abstract mathematical analysis of maximization decisions. The key figure in this process was Don Patinkin, who got his PhD from the University of Chicago. Although young and inexperienced, Patinkin shaped the department at HU and economics training in later-established institutions in Israel (Gross, 2004; Michaeli, 2005), the same way his generation shaped economics teaching in American research universities at the same time. His success demands an explanation. Here is a young man, 27 at the time of his nomination, arriving at a foreign country, full of European-trained economists and steeped in socialist thinking and Marxian analysis, and yet his leadership has created a free-market oriented economic profession that has played a major role in determining Israeli policies from the 1950s to this day. Patinkin's exceptional aptitude and charisma undoubtedly played a major role, but such a revolutionary change could not happen without the demand in the government for the type of economic knowledge Patinkin championed.

Although Patinkin was a novice, he was designated to lead the new department, although the veteran Alfred Bonne was appointed as the Department Chair, a position he held until his death in 1959. During the last four years he served also as the Dean of the new Kaplan School of Economics and Social Sciences. Due to interest in development economics during the postwar period, Bonne suddenly enjoyed international recognition as an original researcher and thinker (Bonne, 1960, 1948, 1957) but Patinkin was still designated for intellectual leadership (Gross, 2004, 2005; Michaeli, 2005).

Patinkin offered for the first time the analytical courses that became the trademark of the postwar American version of neoclassical economics (Yonay, 1998). Patinkin's book (1956) brought international reputation and secured his academic influence at the HU. More importantly, he used his reputation and connections in the US to secure fellowships to fund the studies of his brightest students at the best universities, and they were nominated as lecturers upon their return. Those students – e.g. Michael Michaeli, Haim Barkai, Nissan Leviathan, Nadav Halevi, Reuben Gronau, and Menachem Yaari – became the "founding fathers" of the economic profession in Israel as it is seen today. They gained high reputation in the US and continued Patinkin's very close relationships with the American profession. Today this is common in many countries, but in the case of Israel it started as early as the 1950s and contributed to its prominence in economics to this day.

Although Patinkin bolstered the American side of the new department, for several more years other directions were present at the department. Bonne and his student Hershlag (1914–99) taught economics of the Middle East and Israel using the historical-institutional approach. Bonne saw Hershlag as his successor, but Patinkin did not like his style of research and tried to block the approval of his dissertation first and his nomination later (Gross, 2004), and indeed Hershlag did not become a lecturer at HU and the Bonne tradition of histor-ical and institutional studies did not have a continuation. He did develop a successful career, however, at the defunct Department of Developing Countries at Tel-Aviv University, and published several well-regarded books on Middle East economics and especially on Turkey (e.g. 1964, 1958).

In the early 1950s the university nominated another prominent European economist, Edmond Silberner (1910–85; PhD Geneva) to teach economic history (EH) and history of economic thought (HET) (Michaeli, 2005; Gross, 2004). Until the triumph of mathematical economics in the 1960s, HET and EH were required courses in many undergraduate and graduate programs in the US, and in Europe it has continued to be required. HU leaders were aware of this fact and brought Silberner (1939, 1946, 1962) to teach these courses. Yet Silberner failed to make these courses a mainstay of the economic training program at HU. He remained part of the faculty until his retirement but failed to have an influence on the direction of the department. As in most major American universities, HET disappeared, but EH has survived due to the works of Nachum Gross (1972), Gur Ofer (1973), Jacob Metzer (1998), and, currently, Nathan Sussman (Mauro, Sussman, and Yafeh, 2006).

During the 1950s there was an attempt at establishing chairs in labor movement history and cooperative theory. The idea was pushed forward by top *Histadrut* leaders and by Jewish union leaders from the US who pledged funding for this goal. Between 1950 and 1956 three nominations were made in this field, but none of them led to permanent positions: Harry (Zvi) Viteles, a specialist on cooperatives (1966–70) and a manager of a bank founded to support cooperatives; Ferdynand Zweig (1896–1988), a Polish lawyer who taught political economy at Krakow University before World War Two on labor relations and continued to conduct research in London and Manchester University, and published 13 books prior to his nomination (e.g. 1959, 1975); and Henrik F. Infield, an expert on cooperatives who got his PhD from the University of Wien in 1925 (1944, 1947, 1955).

Gross (2004) and Michaeli (2005) write about the eventual failure of the above scholars – Hershlag, Silberner, Viteles, Zweig, Infield – as unavoidable given their inept scholarship. But looking from the outside one can suspect that the reason is different. All of them were considered experts in their fields and published plentifully, but their approach differed from Patinkin's, and Patinkin set the standards for what was considered "good economic research" at HU. Approaches that deviated from his were either abandoned or pushed to other disciplines such as sociology and history.

The "Patinkin boys" and the Americanization of Israeli economics

Patinkin was a firm believer in market forces and the price mechanism as the best way to allocate resources. Like his teacher, Henry Simons, he believed the only role of the state is to defend the market economy (Simons, 1948). As a mathematical economist, Patinkin held a universalist view regarding the functioning of modern economies and rejected institutional views according to which institutional differences between economies justify the use of different policies (Krampf, 2010a; Mehrling, 2002). Patinkin also turned the Maurice Falk Institute for Economic Research into an extension of the Economics Department, providing funding for its faculty and graduate students. At the early days of the Institute, Simon Kuznets was involved in its activities and tried to keep it open to various kinds of economic research, but Patinkin insisted on direct control of the Institute. As a consequence the copious harvest of the Institute reflected the Department's theoretical and empirical pursuits (Krampf, 2010a).

The graduates of the economics department at HU – often called, affectionately or ironically, "Patinkin boys" – were placed in key positions in the MOF, BI, other government ministries and agencies, and big (private, state, and *Histadrut*) corporations (Kleiman, 1981). Key policy makers – e.g. Levi Eshkol (Minister of Finance, 1952–63; Prime Minister 1963–69) and David Horowitz (first MOF Director-General, 1948–52; first BI Governor, 1954–71) – needed the new economic knowledge to regulate the economy, avoid special interests' pressures, and fight economists who represented workers' interests within their own party. The MOF Director-General from 1954 was Yaakov Arnon, an economist by training (from the Netherlands) whose top priority was the establishment of "mechanism for orderly economic thinking" within the Ministry of Finance (Michaeli, 2005, 10). In 1952 he founded and headed the Budgets Department that has become the central place for economic planning within the government and absorbed many HU graduates. The BI also employed many graduates, especially in the Research Department, which was established by David Kokhav, a graduate of the first cohort of the Department (Michaeli, 2005, 10). The young graduates had little esteem toward the economists of the older generation and saw them as partisan experts, serving ideological and political interests. They perceived themselves as "pure professionals," providing policy makers and the business community with objective analyses based on scientific research (Michaeli, 2005, 9).

The dominance of the economics department at HU determined the direction that younger departments assumed. When the department was established, there was only one more institution of higher education where economics had been taught: The Higher School for Law and Economics (HSLE). It was a private school that provided professional training for the developing economy but lacked the academic reputation. In 1959 the HSLE merged into the HU and became its Tel-Aviv branch in an attempt of the HU to block the development of a competing university in Tel-Aviv, and although several senior HSLE faculty got nominations at the HU, the curriculum of the HU prevailed and became standard at the Tel-Aviv branch. Difficulties in running the branch and political pressures from the government led eventually to the transfer of the branch from the HU to the Tel-Aviv University (TAU; 1968). The Department of Economics became independent and within a few years gained prestige and influence similar to its older sister, but the two departments were similar in their programs and theoretical directions (Gross, 2009). One lecturer from HSLE, Isaac Guelfat, a specialist on cooperation and on economic thought, taught at the Jerusalem main campus and was mentioned by several of the department graduates. He published many books, and was a specialist on Soviet economic thinking. Interestingly, Abba Lerner served as the first Dean of Social Science at Tel Aviv University (1965–66). Lerner had been previously a visiting lecturer at HU (1954–6) and an adviser to the government and BI (1953–6). His international reputation notwithstanding, Lerner did not have management skills and had little impact on the faculty, and after two years returned to the US.

There are today four other departments of economics at research universities in Israel. They were established either by graduates of the HU and TAU departments, often after getting a PhD in the US, or immigrants from the US. They were all shaped from the beginning according to the norms that characterized American economics since 1960 and depended on the more established faculties of the HU and TAU for approval and recognition. Thus, even if each department had its own uniqueness, none could threaten the hegemony of the economic training established at the HU, and the programs of studies are quite homogeneous. Economists of the older generation continued to conduct research and promote their ideas within the *Histadrut*. They viewed the "Patinkin boys" as a group that served the capitalists and their allies within the government. But the *Histadrut* gradually lost its power, and even within the *Histadrut*, there was not much demand to the ideas and theories of the older schools. More importantly, since all training grounds in economics have been held by the mathematical neoclassicists, older approaches to economic research petered out with their European-trained carriers.

Israeli economics departments rank high in various lists of departments. In 2003 all the six research universities in Israel were included in the top 200 economics departments worldwide, with Tel Aviv and Hebrew University among the top 50 (nos. 25 and 48, respectively; they ranked third and eighth among European universities; Kalaitzidakis, Mamuneas, and Stengos, 2003). Among the 1,931 top 5 percent most-cited authors in the IDEAS database, 30 teach in Israeli universities, putting Israel at eleventh place in contributing to this list. Given Israel's small population this is an extraordinary achievement. Many Israeli economists got their PhDs in the best departments in the US, and many Israelis teach in those departments. Given Israel's fixed salaries scales for all universities and all disciplines, economics departments find it hard to compete with salaries in the US and maintain their reputation by hiring the best Israeli economists as before. At least some of the most-cited economists have taught in Israel in the past. This brain drain is an adversity Israel shares with many other countries.

Israel's excellence is expressed most obviously within game theory, which alone accounts for more than a third of the 30 Israeli most-cited economics authors. The Israeli success in this field is related to its excellence in mathematical research. Since the arrival of Abraham Halevi Fraenkel to the budding HU in 1929, Israel could boast numerous outstanding mathematicians, some born in Israel and others migrating from other countries. One of the latter is Robert John (Yisrael) Aumann (b. 1930), the Nobel laureate in economics in 2005, who was born in Germany but grew up in the US, got his PhD from MIT but made his career at the HU (Aumann, 2000). The single arrival of Aumann due to ideological reasons might have had a large impact through many of his students, including David Schmeidler (b. 1939) and Sergiu Hart (b. 1949) who made important contributions of their own. Aumann can claim also important intellectual "grandchildren" such as Itzhak Gilboa (b. 1963; 2009, 2010) who studied and worked with Schmeidler (Gilboa and Schmeidler, 2001). Many other Israeli game theorists teach in Israel and abroad, and Israel is considered a superpower in this field. Just for illustration, 7 out of the 124 of the 5 percent most cited authors in this field according to IDEAS teach in Israel.

Another Israeli contribution to economics came from psychology. Amos Tversky (1937–96) and Daniel Kahneman (b. 1934) are two psychologists who taught at the HU before moving to North America. Since the early 1970s the two collaborated in a series of experiments about human decision-making, judgments, and biases, and developed what they called prospect theory. This work, which brought Kahneman the Nobel Prize in 2002 (Tversky passed away six years earlier), was very influential in the development of behavioral economics, one of the rising sub-fields in economics. While there are other prominent Israelis who have excelled in this field, e.g. Eldar Shafir and Uri Gneezy, there is no evidence that there is an "Israeli connection." Shafir studied in the US since his undergraduate studies, and Gneezy got his PhD at the Center for Economic Research at Tilburg University. Moreover, although Gneezy had taught for a short while in economics departments in Israel before moving to the US, there is no tradition yet of experimental or behavioral economists in Israel.

Although game theory and behavioral economics are obviously related to each other – both are concerned with interactive decision-making – they are based on very different epistemic principles and involve very different research practices. It is therefore hard to see any causal connection between the two successes. Yet there might be some recent connection in the unique Center for the Study of Rationality at the HU (est. 1991), where game theorists, psychologists, biologists, philosophers, mathematicians and others cooperate in exploring "the rational basis of decision-making." It is also tempting to look for a link to Israel's strategic behavior in the Middle East conflict, but there is little evidence of formal ties between the academic practitioners and the defense establishment, and Ariel Rubinstein constantly warns against attempts to translate game theory insights into policy recipes.

From full employment to export-oriented development

The strategy of rapid development during the first decade after independence was designed to address the urgent need to absorb hundreds of thousands of Jews within a very short period of time. The government allocated resources to labor intensive industries and subsidized enterprises on the basis of job creation. The prioritization of job creation over productivity hampered the competitiveness of the Israeli economy in the global economy and hence this policy put a strain on the balance of payments. Professional economists in the government and BI shared the same response to this problem: reducing the intervention of the government in the labor market, giving up the goal of full employment, and promoting export through subsidies and the devaluation of the Israeli shekel (Kleiman, 1981; Levi-Faur, 2001; Krampf, 2014).

This position was led by the leading economist in the country, Don Patinkin. In 1960, in his lone book on the Israeli economy (Patinkin, 1960), he was not enamored by Israel's rapid growth, around 10 percent annually, arguing that this growth was fueled by massive import of capital. The Israeli economy, he argued, remained uncompetitive and dependent on foreign aid. Unemployment was structural rather than frictional, and therefore Keynesian policies would be ineffective. Patinkin thus backed the MOF and BI's policy with his academic authority, paving the way toward a policy paradigm change in Israel. After several failed attempts to implement this policy and worsening balance of payment deficits, a recession policy was implemented (1964). The academic economists played a key and active role in legitimizing this planned recession that ended only due to the 1967 war. A traumatic scar in the collective memory as it is, the recession does mark the seizure of control by professional economists belonging to the postwar orthodoxy, control that has nothing but solidified ever since.

The neo-liberal triumph

During the 1980s and the 1990s the Israeli economy went through a rapid and drastic structural as well as a policy paradigm change in the direction of privatization and liberalization (Aharoni, 1991; Ben-Basaṭ, 2002; Ben-Porath, 1986), and academic economists have, again, played a crucial role in this process. The shift started in 1977 when, after three decades of hegemony of the labor movement, the Likud center-right party took over the election. The Likud government immediately liberalized the foreign exchange market but without concomitant fiscal restraints, the outcome was a hyperinflation of up to 435 percent (in 1984). The crisis created an opportunity for a deep structural change in the economy. The Stabilization Plan of 1985 was designed by several top Israeli economists, interestingly helped by American economists (most notably, Stanley Fischer, who later became the Governor of the BI, and Herbert Stein). It included several steps necessary to stop the inflationary spiral but, in addition, and exploiting the public's eagerness to get out of the crisis, included major revisions in the mechanisms of economic policy-making (Mandelkern, 2010). These revisions opened the way towards liberalization, privatization, and fiscal consolidation.

The Stabilization Plan was followed by more changes made later in order to bolster the power and autonomy of professional economists. For example, the Bank of Israel Law was amended, barring the government from funding the deficit by printing money (Maman and Rosenhek, 2009). The MOF has received much more power to restrain government expenses, many state-owned companies were privatized, and welfare services have been out-sourced. In short, the Israeli economy merged with neo-liberal trends that gradually engulfed almost the entire globe during the 1980s/1990s. Nevertheless, either due to the Israeli policy legacy, or due to its security conditions, the Israeli economy still retains some features of its collectivist past. The economic discourse is highly national, the state supports certain economic branches, especially in the military industry, and appeals to national considerations to favor several large firms (Shalev, 1998).

The neo-liberal turn shed the many past socialist vestiges of a country built, not exclusively but primarily, by socialist pioneers and led for decades by at-least-formally socialist parties. The economists have been the midwives of this transformation. In the 1930s and 1940s they helped policy makers to move from obsolete agrarian fixation and utopian collectivist settlement toward ideas of nation-building based on private enterprise, but regulated and controlled by the national interest. In the 1950s, 1960s, and 1970s they helped the state quell mounting demands from various sectors and conduct its affair rationally, and in the 1980s and 1990s they pulled the state and the society as a whole towards the neo-liberal pole.

Bibliography

Aharoni, Yair. 1991. *The Israeli Economy: Dreams and Realities*. London: Routledge.

Alroey, Gur. 2014. *An Unpromising Land: Jewish Migration to Palestine in the Early Twentieth Century*. Stanford: Stanford University Press.

Aumann, Robert J. 2000. *Collected Papers*. vols.1 and 2. Cambridge, MA: MIT Press.

Ben-Basaṭ, Avi (ed.). 2002. *The Israeli Economy, 1985–1998: From Government Intervention to Market Economics*. Cambridge, MA: MIT Press.

Ben-Porath, Yoram (ed.). 1986. *The Israeli Economy: Maturing through Crises*. Cambridge, MA: Harvard University Press.

Bloom, Etan. 2007. "What 'The Father' Had in Mind? Arthur Ruppin (1876–1943), Cultural Identity, Weltanschauung and Action." *History of European Ideas* 33 (3): 330–49.

Bloom, Etan. 2011. *Arthur Ruppin and the Production of Pre-Israeli Culture*. Leiden: E.J. Brill.

Bonne, Alfred. 1932. *Palastina: land und Wirtschaft*. Leipzig: Deutsche Wissenschaftliche Buchhandlung.

Bonne, Alfred. 1948. *State and Economics in the Middle East: A Society in Transition*. London: Kegan Paul, Trench, Trubner.

Bonne, Alfred. 1957. *Studies in Economic Development: With Special Reference to Conditions in the Underdeveloped Areas of Western Asia and India*. London: Routledge and Kegan Paul.

Bonne, Alfred. 1960. *On the Late Alfred Bonne: Speeches for the Sheloshim to His Death*. Jerusalem: Magnes.

Borochov, Dov Ber. 1928. *The Class Struggle and the National Question*. Jerusalem: The Borochov Publishing. (Hebrew)

Borochov, Dov Ber. 1937. *Nationalism and the Class Struggle: A Marxian Approach to the Jewish Problem*. New York: Poale Zion-Zeire Zion of America.

Borochov, Dov Ber. 1972. *Nationalism and the Class Struggle: A Marxian Approach to the Jewish Problem*. Westport: Greenwood.

Brutzkus, Boris. 1935. *Economic Planning in Soviet Russia*. With a Foreword by F.A. Hayek. London: Routledge.

Gilboa, Itzhak. 2009. *Theory of Decision Under Uncertainty*. New York: Cambridge University Press.

Gilboa, Itzhak. 2010. *Rational Choice*. New York: Cambridge University Press.

Gilboa, Itzhak and David Schmeidler. 2001. *A Theory of Case-Based Decisions*. Cambridge: Cambridge University Press.

Ginor, Fanny. 1959. *Political Economy*. Tel-Aviv: Tel-Aviv University Students Union.

Ginor, Fanny. 1979. *Socio-Economic Disparities in Israel*. Tel-Aviv: David Horowitz Institute for the Research of Developing Countries, Tel-Aviv University.

Gorny, Yosef and Yitzhak Greenberg. 1997. *The Israeli Labor Movement: Ideational Basis, Social Trends, and the Economic Method*. Tel-Aviv: Open University Press.

Greenwald, Carol Schwartz. 1972. *Recession as a Policy Instrument: Israel 1965–1969*. London: C. Hurst.

Gross, T. Nachum. 1972. *The Industrial Revolution in the Habsburg Monarchy, 1750–1914*. London: Collins Clear-Type.

Gross, T. Nachum. 2004. "The Department of Economics at Hebrew University during the 1950s." http://economics.huji.ac.il/Uploads/Contents/documents/GrossHistory.pdf, retrieved 24.1.2014. (Hebrew)

Gross, T. Nachum. 2005. "Social Science at Hebrew University until 1948/9: Plans and Beginnings." In Hagit Lavsky (ed.), *The History of the Hebrew University: Plans and Beginnings*, 1st vol. Jerusalem: Magnes. (Hebrew).

Gross, T. Nachum. 2009. "The Hebrew University and Its Branches in Tel-Aviv, 1950–1970." *Iyunim Betkumat Israel* 19L 93–119. (Hebrew).

Hachoen, Dvora. 1994. *Immigrants in Turmoil*. Jerusalem: Yad Ben-Zvi Press. (Hebrew).

Halevi, Nadav. 1983. "The Political Economy of Absorptive Capacity: Growth and Cycles in Jewish Palestine under the British Mandate." *Middle Eastern Studies* 19(4): 456–69.

Hart, Mitchell Bryan. 2000. *Social Science and the Politics of Modern Jewish Identity*. Stanford: Stanford University Press.

Hershlag, Zvi Yehuda. 1964. *Introduction to the Modern Economic History of the Middle East*. Leiden: E. J. Brill.

Hershlag, Zvi Yehuda. 1958. *Turkey: An Economy in Transition*. The Hague: Uitgeverif van Keulen.

Herzl, Theodor. 1919 [1902]. *Altneuland: Roman*. Berlin: B. Harz.

Infield, Henrik F. 1944. *Cooperative Living in Palestine*. New York: Dryden.

Infield, Henrik F. 1947. *Co-Operative Communities at Work*. London: Kegan Paul, Trench, Trubner.

Infield, Henrik F. 1955. *Utopia and Experiment: Essays in the Sociology of Cooperation*. New York: Praeger.

Kalaitzidakis, Pantelis, Theofanis P. Mamuneas, and Thanasis Stengos. 2003. "Rankings of Academic Journals and Institutions in Economics." *Journal of the European Economic Association* 1: 1346–66.

Kimmerling, Baruch. 1983. *Zionism and Economy*. Cambridge, MA: Schenkman.

Kleiman, Efraim. 1981. "Israel: Economists in a New State." *History of Political Economy* 13(3): 548–78.

Krampf, Arie. 2010a. "Economic Planning of the Free Market in Israel during the First Decade: The Influence of Don Patinkin on Israeli Policy Discourse." *Science in Context* 23(3): 507–34.

Krampf, Arie. 2010b. "Reception of the Developmental Approach in the Economic Discourse of Mandatory Palestine, 1934–1938." *Israel Studies* 15(2).

Krampf, Arie. 2014. "Between Private Property Rights and National Preferences: The Bank of Israel's Early Years." *Israel Affairs*.

Levi-Faur, David. 2001. *The Visible Hand: State-Directed Industrialization in Israel*. Jerusalem: Yad Ben-Zvi Press. (Hebrew).

Maman, Daniel and Zeev Rosenhek. 2009. *The Bank of Israel: Political Economy in the Neoliberal Era*. Jerusalem: Van Leer Jerusalem Institute and Hakibbutz Hamuchad. (Hebrew).

Mandelkern, Ronnen. 2010. *Professionals Struggling for Reform: Economists and Power in Israel's Political-Economic Liberalization*. Jerusalem: Thesis Submitted for Degree of Doctor of Philosophy, The Hebrew University.

Mauro, Paolo, Nathan Sussman, and Yishai Yafeh. 2006. *Emerging Markets and Financial Globalization: Sovereign Bonds Spreads in 1870–1913 and Today*. Oxford: Oxford University Press.

Mehrling, Perry. 2002. "Don Patinkin and the Origins of Postwar Monetary Orthodoxy." *European Journal of the History of Economic Thought* 9(2): 161–85.

Metzer, Jacob. 1979. *National Capital to National Home, 1919–1921*. Jerusalem: YadItzhak Ben-Zvi. (Hebrew)

Metzer, Jacob. 1998. *The Divided Economy of Mandatory Palestine*. Cambridge, MA: Harvard University Press.

Michaeli, Michael. 2005. "The Department of Economics at Hebrew University – Early Days from a Personal Perspective." http://economics.huji.ac.il/Uploads/Contents/documents/Early%20Days.pdf, retrieved 24.1.2014. (Hebrew)

Naphtali, Fritz (Pere(t)z) and Ernst Kahn. 1930. *Wieliest man den Handelsteileiner Tageszeitung?* Frankfurt am Main: Frankfurter Societats.

Naphtali, Fritz (Pere(t)z) and Ernst Kahn. 1962. *Economic Democracy: Selected Writings*. Tel-Aviv: Davar. (Hebrew)

Ofer, Gur. 1973. *The Service Sector in Soviet Economic Growth: A Comparative Study*. Cambridge, MA: Harvard University Press.

Oppenheimer, Franz. 1932. *Weder Kapitalismusnoch Kommunismus*. Jena: Gustav Fischer.

Oppenheimer, Franz. 1933. *Weder so-noch so: Der Dritte Weg*. Potsdam: Alfred Drotte.

Oppenheimer, Franz. 1938. *Das Kapital, Kritik der Politischen Ökonomie: Ein Kurzgefasstes Lehrbuch der Nationalökonomischen Theorie*. Leiden: Sijthoff.

Oppenheimer, Franz. 1942–4. "A Post-Mortem on Cambridge Economics." *American Journal of Economics and Sociology* 2(3): 369–376, 2(4): 533–541, and 3(1): 115–124.

Patinkin, Don. 1956. *Money, Interest, and Prices: An Integration of Monetary and Value Theory*. Evanston: Row, Peterson.

Patinkin, Don. 1960. *The Israel Economy: The First Decade.* Jerusalem: Falk Project for Economic Research in Israel.

Penslar, Derek Jonathan. 1991. *Zionism and Technocracy: The Engineering of Jewish Settlement in Palestine, 1870–1918.* Bloomington: Indiana University Press.

Penslar, Derek Jonathan. 2001. *Shylock's Children: Economics and Jewish Identity in Modern Europe.* Berkeley: University of California Press.

Pilowski (Bar-Shalom), Varda. 1974. *N. Syrkin: A Political and Intellectual Biography (1868–1898).* PhD Dissertation, Hebrew University. (Hebrew).

Preuss, Walter. 1936. *Die Jüdische Arbeiterbewegung in Palastina.* Wien: Fiba.

Preuss, Walter. 1960. *Co-Operation in Israel and the World.* Trans. from German by Shlomo Barer. Jerusalem: Rubin Mass.

Riemer, Jehuda. 1991. *Fritz Perez Naphtali – Sozialdemokrat und Zionist.* Gerlingen: Bleicher.

Ruppin, Arthur. 1913. *The Jews of To-Day.* London: G. Bell.

Ruppin, Arthur. 1922. *Economic Activities in Palestine: Report submitted to the XIIth Zionist Congress held at Carlsbad.* Jerusalem: Zionist Organization.

Ruppin, Arthur. 1968. *Pirkei Hayay.* vol.3. Tel Aviv: Am Oved. (Hebrew).

Ruppin, Arthur. 1973. *The Jews in the Modern World.* The Jewish People: History, Religion, Literature. New York: Arno Press.

Shalev, Michael. 1992. *Labour and the Political Economy in Israel.* Oxford: Oxford University Press.

Shalev, Michael. 1998. "Have Globalization and Liberalization 'normalized' Israel's Political Economy?" *Israel Affairs* 5(2–3): 121–155.

Shilo, Margalit. 1988. *Experiment in Settlement.* Jerusalem: Yad Yitzhak Ben Zvi. (Hebrew).

Silberner, Edmund. 1939. *La Guerre dans la Pansee Economique du XVIe au XVIIIe Siecle.* Paris: Librairie du Recueil Sirey.

Silberner, Edmund. 1946. *The Problem of War in Nineteenth Century Economic Thought.* Princeton: Princeton University Press.

Silberner, Edmund. 1962. *Sozialistenzur Judenfrage: EinBeitragezue Geschichte von Anfang des 19. Yahrhundretscis 1914.* Berlin: Colloquium.

Simons, Henry C. 1948 [1934]. "A Positive Program for Laissez-Faire." In *Economic Policy for a Free Society,* edited by Henry C. Simons, 40–77. Chicago: University of Chicago Press.

Syrkin, Nachum. 1935. *Essays on socialist Zionism.* New York: Young Poale Zion Alliance of America.

Syrkin, Nachum. 1939. *Writings.* Collected and Edited by B. Katznelson and Yehouda Koffman.

Troen, S. Ilan. 2003. *Imagining Zion: Dreams, Designs, and Realities in a Century of Jewish Settlement.* New Haven: Yale University Press.

Viteles, Harry (Zvi). 1966–70. *A History of the Cooperative Movement in Israel: A Source Book in 7 Volumes.* London: Vallentine, Mitchell.

Yonay, Yuval. 1998. *The Struggle Over the Soul of Economics: Institutionalist and Neoclassical Economists in America Between the Wars.* Princeton: Princeton University Press.

Ziv, Benjamin. 1937. *Finance Theory.* Tel-Aviv: The High School for Law and Economics. (Hebrew).

Ziv, Benjamin. 1938. *Political Economy Theory.* Tel-Aviv: The High School for Law and Economics. (Hebrew).

Ziv, Benjamin. 1945. *Business Cycle Theory [Torat Hakonjunktura].* Tel-Aviv: Yavne. (Hebrew).

Zweig, Ferdynand. 1959. *The Israeli Worker: Achievements, Attitudes and Aspirations.* New York: Hertzl.

Zweig, Ferdynand. 1975. *Labour, Life and Poverty.* Wakefield: EP.

19

Arab-Islamic economics

S.M. Ghazanfar

The primary purpose of this chapter is to provide a survey of economic thought originating with some Arab-Islamic scholars whose writings extend over several (medieval) centuries. The term "Arab-Islamic" is to be broadly interpreted. Several Islamic scholars had their origins in Persia (part of the Seljuk Dynasty, 1038–1194), others in Abbasid Baghdad, and yet others in the Mediterranean Al-Andalus (Islamic Spain). The word "Arab" may be viewed not so much as relating to a scholar's geographical origins, conceived in terms of the nation-states that now exist in the contemporary Middle East, but more to the fact that Arabic was the main language of their scholarship. Aside from being the language of the Holy Qur'an, Arabic was the lingua franca of the era, "the main vehicle of culture" (Sarton, II, 109). Even several Jewish scholars wrote their major works in Arabic (e.g. Moses Maimonides, 1135–1204; Ibn Gabirol, 1021–58).

Specifically, the chapter will focus firstly on four such scholars who wrote on economic matters during the pre-Renaissance period, before the emergence of Latin scholastic economics typically associated with St. Thomas Aquinas (1225–74). Then the chapter will discuss some salient features of what has come to be known as Islamic economics, much in discussion in recent decades.

It is appropriate to note the notion of the historical "gap" that has been promoted in intellectual history, which has been the stimulus for several papers on the subject (Ghazanfar, 1991, 2003). Joseph Schumpeter propounded the "great gap" thesis in his *History of Economic Analysis*. After arguing that the "study of doctrinal history" is "historically conditioned," he suggested that while "economic thought started with the Greeks" over 2,000 years ago, "many centuries within that span are blanks," until Latin-Scholasticism emerged with St. Thomas Aquinas (Schumpeter, 1954, 4–6, 52). That is, for over 500 years, nothing of any significance to economics was discussed anywhere else. As one scholar noted, such a stance is "all the more disappointing," as Schumpeter "must have been well aware of the fascinating process of cultural diffusion" between the Arab-Islamic civilization and Europe (Bernardelli, 320). Thus, Schumpeter perpetuated a well-embedded tradition in the literature: a denial of literary history to the rest of the world, specifically to the early Islamic world, although lately there is some acknowledgement of Muslim scholars' economic thought in mainstream texts (Landrem and Colander).

Early Arab-Islamic economic thought

While there has been, until recently, almost uncritical acceptance of the "gap" thesis, there is an exception to be noted. Joseph Spengler wrote a paper about 50 years ago, in which he explored the economic thought of a late-medieval, "post-blank centuries" Arab-Islamic scholar, Ibn Khaldun (1332–1406). He noted, "One is compelled to infer from a comparison of Ibn Khaldun's economic ideas with those set down in Muslim moral-philosophical literature that the knowledge of economic behavior in some circles was very great indeed" (Spengler, 1964, 304). Another scholar referred to Ibn Khaldun as "among the fathers of economic science," but he concluded that he was an "accident of history without predecessors and without successors" (Boulakia, 1118, n. 3). Yet, Ibn Khaldun was in the news during the Ronald Reagan era; the Laffer curve, identified with supply-side economics, is derived from Khaldun's writings and one scholar called it "the Khaldun curve" (Siegel). Also the mainstream media published articles linking Ibn Khaldun's analysis to Reaganomics (Hardcastle).

Be that as it may, by and large, the general tendency has remained one of a complete *lacuna* over intellectual evolution elsewhere during those centuries. Illustratively, one prominent text on the subject noted "it is inconceivable that there was no 'economic thought' over so many centuries – even in the Dark Ages" (Newman, et al., 15): yet no attempt to explore further.

As the main task, while 30–5 Arab-Islamic scholars can be identified writing on economic issues during the "blank" centuries, this chapter will focus on four such early medieval scholars (M.N. Siddiqui, 1981). These are: (1) Abu Yusuf (731–98); (2) Alberuni (973–1048); (3) Al-Ghazali (1058–1111); and (4) Nasir al-Din Tusi (1201–74). It may be noted that these scholars wrote within many diverse fields of knowledge, and their writings, as those of their European-Latin counterparts, emphasized the integrative, holistic approach to learning. Thus, their scholarship, highly normative but with major positive themes, was not dominated by the economic aspects of life, though some Arab-Islamic scholars did write separate volumes, or had separate chapters, devoted to economic issues. Further, several economic concepts and principles identifiable in their writings are remarkably similar to those found in the works of the Latin-European scholastics and their later European successors.

Abu Yusuf (AD 731–98)

While there were other Arab-Islamic scholars and jurists who wrote on economic issues almost from the inception of Islam, one of the earliest is Abu Yusuf. He lived during Baghdad's Abbasid Caliphate of Harun al-Rashid (763–806) and served as his chief justice. He addressed a long narrative to the Caliph, later to become known as *Kitab al Kharaj* (*The Book of Taxation*). Relevant to economics, his main interests were public finance and taxation, distribution and cultivation of land, regulation of prices, economic responsibilities of the state, and usurious transactions. Abu Yusuf's works have been studied by several writers (Tuma, Fariq, M.N. Siddiqui, B. Siddiqi, and Haq).

While discussing agricultural activities, Abu Yusuf favored a proportional tax on agricultural produce, rather than a fixed rent on land. This, he thought, would not only be just, but also conducive to larger revenue by providing incentives to bring more land into cultivation. He also offered insights concerning the administration of agriculture in new territories, agricultural estates, their cultivation and distribution, tenancy conditions, problems relating to water supply, fisheries, forests and pasture lands, and general public works (such as roads and bridges, and canals for irrigation and transportation).

A controversial point in Abu Yusuf's economics relates to price controls. He was generally against price-fixing or price controls on the part of rulers, but he distinguished between conditions when such controls may or may not be permissible. He talked of an abundance of grain not being the reason for low prices nor scarcity the reason for high prices. One commentator points out that this assertion does not mean a denial of the role of market forces in determining prices; rather, it reflects something that Abu Yusuf observed around him – the possible coexistence of abundance and high prices, and of scarcity and low prices (M.N. Siddiqui, 1964, 86). Elsewhere, Tuma has noted that during the period when Abu Yusuf wrote, the rulers generally solved the problem of rising prices not by price controls, but by increasing the supply of food grain. Economic discourses as well as the practices at the time leaned heavily in favor of allowing the free play of market forces. However, there was also emphasis on ridding the markets of hoarding, monopolies, and other corrupt practices (Tuma, 1965, 14).

The main strength of Abu Yusuf, however, lies in the area of public finance. Aside from the principles of taxation and the responsibilities of the state concerning the welfare of the society, he provided discussion on promoting economic development, especially in agriculture, by building socio-economic infrastructure. Further, guided by his deep concern for the common good, he exhorted the rulers to work toward eliminating oppression and promoting social justice (Fariq, 24). In discussing taxation, Abu Yusuf also delineated certain principles which anticipate those proposed several centuries later by Adam Smith as the "four canons of taxation" (equity, certainty, convenience, and economy). He talked of easing the burden on taxpayers by taking into account their ability to pay, and convenience regarding time, place and manner of payment. He also discussed the distribution of tax revenue and various types of taxes such as taxation of agricultural land and commodities, death duties, and taxes on imports. He favored centralized tax administration, with strictly supervised salaried tax collectors, so that corruption is prevented (see Siddiqui and Ghazanfar, 2001).

Abu Al-Raihan M. Ibn Ahmed Alberuni (973–1048)

Alberuni was "one of the greatest scholars of medieval Islam, and certainly the most original and profound" (Spengler, 1971a, 93), and "one of the very greatest scientists of Islam and, all considered, one of the greatest of all times" (Sarton, vol.I, 407). Like several other Arab-Islamic scholars (e.g. Ibn Mishkawail, Ibn Sina, Fakhr al-Din Razi, Nasir al-Din Tusi), Alberuni was born in Persia (Iran); all of them, however, are generally identified with Islamic civilization, and Arabic was the primary language of their discourses.

Two of Alberuni's most famous works, both edited and translated by Edward C. Sachau, are *Alberuni's India* (2 volumes, 1887), and *Chronology of Ancient Nations* (1879). More relevant to our topic is *Alberuni's India*. Two major, interrelated themes are identifiable here, and both have significant implications for economics. One pertains to the concept of "Social Darwinism," with its self-interest, unbridled market implications; and the other, perhaps more important, relates to the "population–food" dilemma, usually associated with the name of Thomas Malthus (1766–1834).

Writing in 1943, a Russian scholar, T.I. Rainow, argued that one may find the "whole theory of Darwinism already expounded more than eight hundred years before the publication of the theory of natural selection." Rainow is quite emphatic:

> Thus, in modern language we could express this thought of Alberuni as follows: Nature performs natural selection of the most adequate, well-adapted being through the extermination of others, and, in this case, it proceeds in the same way as farmers and

gardeners. We see, therefore, that Darwin's great idea of natural selection through the struggle for life and survival of the fittest was already reached by Alberuni approximately eight hundred years before Darwin. It is true that he seized it in the most general outlines only, but, curiously enough, even the very meaning and the way in which he came to it were the same as Darwin's. The latter, as we know, discovered natural selection by observation of the methods of artificial selection, as applied by animal breeders.

(quoted in Wilczynski, 459)

Several arguments in Alberuni's writings, according to Rainow, pre-echo the "theory of evolution," "natural selection," and "survival of the fittest" themes of Charles Darwin (1809–1882) – concepts which "influenced some, but by no means all, of the streams and schools of economic thought" (Oser, 373).

Alberuni talked in terms of "selectivity" and "evolution" with respect to plants, animals, and human beings. According to Wilczynski, similarities with Darwin's idea are detected in the following paragraphs:

When a class of plants or animals does not increase any more in its structure, and its peculiar kind is established *as a species* of its own, when each individual of it does not simply come into existence once and perish, but besides procreates a being like itself or several together, and not only once but several times . . . Nature proceeds in a similar way; however, it does not distinguish, for its action is under all circumstances one and the same. It allows the leaves and fruit of the trees to perish, thus preventing them from realizing that result which they are intended to produce in the economy of the nature. It removes them so as to make room for others.

(Alberuni, vol.I, 400)

Thus, Alberuni suggested that the pressure of increasing numbers would give rise to natural selection, though not to selection so favorable as that conducted under human guidance. Wilczynski cautiously concludes that "some views resembling the basic principles of Darwin's future doctrine are undeniably to be found" in Alberuni (Wilczynski, 466). Spengler acknowledges that arguments such as these "led some to look upon Alberuni as a precursor of Darwin" (Spengler, 1971a, 95–96).

The other closely related theme, the "population–food" dilemma, emanates from this astute observation by Alberuni: "The life of the world depends upon sowing and procreating. Both processes increase in the course of time, and this increase is unlimited, whilst the world is limited" (Alberuni, vol.I, 400). Alberuni was clearly talking in terms of the effect of excess (unlimited) reproduction on the limited area of the world, reference being to the "limited resources/unlimited needs" premise of economics. This "finite world/infinite needs" dichotomy persuades Wilczynski to acknowledge that "this corresponds to the central idea of Malthus on the disproportion between the increase in the rates of reproduction and means of subsistence" (Wilczynski, 460). As with the theories of Darwin, Alberuni seems to be a forerunner of Malthus.

Not only is Alberuni aware of the aforementioned dilemma, but he also provides an early version, or at least an awareness, of the law of diminishing returns:

The agriculturalist selects his corn, letting grow as much as he requires and tearing out the remainder. The forester leaves those branches which he perceives to be excellent, whilst he cuts away all others. The bees kill those of their kind who only eat, but do not work in their beehive.

(Alberuni, vol.I, 400)

According to Spengler, "Alberuni points out that since the growth of man's numbers is limited by the capacity of the environment to provide support, the earth could become overpopulated and in need of a thinning of its numbers" (Spengler, 1971a, 96). Spengler concludes that Alberuni failed "to put forward a rational explanation and to postulate [a] natural corrective mechanism." However, borrowing from Plato's *Laws* and *Timaeus*, Alberuni discussed demographic situations and unavoidable disasters which destroy communities and force survivors to begin anew, bringing civilization and its accompanying evils and vulnerabilities back into existence. Thus, it is clear that Alberuni does provide some economic–demographic implications of the shrinking economic base.

With respect to the population theory, Spengler concludes that Alberuni recognized (1) "the growth of anything is limited by the environment accessible to it," and (2) "since the capacity of growth of a species is unlimited, its actual growth is restrained by limited and (apparently) almost exclusively external agents." Then, Spengler argues that Alberuni "did not seek to identify, as did Malthus, the natality-curbing as well as the mortality-curbing checks" on population (Spengler, 1971a, 101). However, upon closer scrutiny, one finds that Alberuni does discuss some of these checks ("deluge or an earthquake," "contagious and other diseases, pestilence, and more of the like"). Furthermore, he must have been aware of the only natality-curbing check known at the time ("coitus interruptus") which had been condoned by Judeo-Christian-Islamic traditions centuries earlier. Eight hundred years later, Malthus talked in similar terms, including marital postponement, celibacy, etc. Interestingly, Spengler acknowledges that "Alberuni expressed himself much as did Malthus nearly a millennium latter, though without anticipating Darwin" (Spengler, 1971b, 160).

Further, one must speculate if Alberuni's works were available to Malthus and Darwin as background for their discourses, just as Malthus' work was accessible to Darwin (Spengler, 1971a, 95). Certainly, much of Arab-Islamic scholarship was translated into Latin during the "age of translation" covering the tenth to thirteenth centuries. There is evidence that Adam Smith had numerous volumes of Greek heritage in his own library (Lowry, 1979, 72), and he makes numerous references to Arabs in his *Wealth of Nations* (1776). It is quite possible that Darwin and Malthus had access not only to the Greek literature via Arab mediation, but also to the Arab-Islamic literature via their Latin translations.

Abu-Hamid Al-Ghazali (1058–1111)

This eleventh-century Arab-Islamic scholastic has been "acclaimed as the greatest . . . certainly one of the greatest" (Watt, 1963, vii), and "by general consent, the most important thinker of medieval Islam" (Bagley, 1964, xv). Al-Ghazali was born in Tus (in Persia) but then lived for a time in Baghdad and Damascus, before returning again to Tus. While the influence of numerous Arab-Islamic writers upon European scholastics is well-known, Al-Ghazali's role is especially significant in the following respect. According to Myers, "since Al-Ghazali placed science, philosophy, and reason in position inferior to religion and theology, the Scholastics accepted his views which became characteristic of most medieval philosophy" (Myers, 40). Further, Al-Ghazali's "work was paralleled by Thomas Aquinas in the discourse on Christian doctrine and in other portions of the *Summa Theologica*" (Jurji, 313).

Much of Al-Ghazali's discourses on economics are to be found in his four-volume *Ihya Ulum al-Din (Revival of the Religious Sciences)* and his contribution to economics is remarkably sophisticated and similar to what we find in contemporary discussions (Ghazanfar and Islahi, 1990). Incidentally, the *Ihya* volumes "were translated into Latin before 1150" (Myers, 39). Al-Ghazali's economics begins with a rather well-defined social-welfare function, based upon specific socio-economic goals as well as guidelines for the "prioritizing" of individual and social needs (material and non-material). He discusses a hierarchy of needs-necessities, conveniences or comforts, and luxuries, reminiscent of the Aristotelian tradition.

More specifically, Al-Ghazali's scholarship reveals deep understanding of a voluntary market-exchange that "naturally" evolves among free individuals guided by self-interest and mutual necessity, in an environment where there is competition as well as cooperation. He shows rather astute awareness of the operation of markets and price-determination through the forces of demand and supply, including shifts in them due to factors other than price. Further, he develops a detailed code of ethics concerning participants' market behavior. And, while warning against worldly evils, Al-Ghazali acknowledges – indeed, mandates – the need for economic pursuits, both private and public (Ihya n.d., vol.II, 60, 83). In fact, he accords such activities an aura of piety and nobility by constant reminders as to their religious sanctity – a "calling" (Ihya n.d.,vol.II, 63, 249).

When discussing productive behavior, Al-Ghazali provided a tripartite hierarchy of production activities: basic industries (agriculture), ancillary (manufacturing), and complementary (processing and services). He talked in terms of interdependence as well as stages and linkages in production – e.g., anticipating Smith, "the farmer produces grain, the miller converts it into flour, the baker prepares bread from the flour" (Ihya n.d., vol.IV, 128). And, he recognized the need for a division of labor and specialization in all economic endeavors: analogous to Smith's pin-factory example seven centuries later, Al-Ghazali elaborated these concepts by using the example of a needle (Ihya n.d., vol.IV, 119).

Al-Ghazali began with a barter-system in discussing voluntary-exchange behavior, and then identified associated problems such as the lack of double-coincidence of wants, indivisibility of goods due to lack of a common denominator, and limited specialization (though he did not use such contemporary terms). He defined various functions of money, much as one finds currently, the most important being the medium of exchange. Then he discussed the use of gold and silver coins, and after arguing that money itself was "useless," he criticized its conversion into other objects. Further, he discussed the harmful effects of counterfeiting and currency debasement, anticipating similar observations by Nicholas Oresme during the fourteenth century, and Thomas Gresham, Richard Cantillon, and others much later. Indeed, Al-Ghazali developed an early version of the "Gresham's Law" ("bad money drives out good"). Further, as with other Arab-Islamic and European-Latin scholars, Al-Ghazali condemned usury, for it causes money to deviate from its key function – i.e. a medium of exchange.

Al-Ghazali wrote a special treatise on the role of the public sector in the economy. He discussed the topics of public finance-taxation, spending, and even borrowing. He considered the state as a necessary institution, not only for the proper functioning of society's economic activities but also for the fulfillment of social-welfare objectives. Further, in order to promote economic prosperity, the state must establish justice, peace, security, and stability. He even insisted on a state institution, quite common in the Islamic civilization, called "al-Hasbah," meaning "accountability." The official who enforced accountability was called "mohtasib" (the closest English term would be "ombudsman"), whose main function was to check any harmful activities of markets. As for the conduct of the ruler, Al-Ghazali recommended ten "principles of justice and equitable treatment of the subjects" (Counsel, 13–31), and each is discussed not only from the Islamic perspective, but also with illustrations from the Torah, the Bible, and other historical sources (including Chinese). And he relied on the inherited Greek heritage, frequently referencing Plato and Aristotle.

When discussing taxation, Al-Ghazali advocated the well-known ability-to-pay principle of tax justice, although he was aware of the benefits-received concept. He was critical of malpractice and corruption in tax administration. With regard to public expenditures, he discussed various functional categories (though not in the manner one finds in contemporary texts) not simply for promoting social welfare, but also to promote economic development. He suggested several items of public expenditure, usually labeled as "socio-economic infrastructure" in present-day terms. And, he was aware of the need for efficiency in the use of public funds, for they are a "public trust." Indeed, given the hierarchy of society's needs, Al-Ghazali suggested guidelines for "prioritizing" public expenditure (Ghazanfar and Islahi, 1992).

Nasir al-Din Tusi (1201–74)

Nasir al-Din Tusi is credited with a treatise focusing on public finances (*Risala-e-Maliyat*, or *Treatise on Public Treasury*). Tusi argued that the encouragement of economic enterprise requires that the burden of taxation on society should be kept to a minimum. Further, he emphasized that the foundation of economic prosperity was agriculture, trading and other activities being secondary, and argued for moderate expenditure and against conspicuous consumption (B.H. Siddiqi, 571).

Another well-known book by Tusi (originally written in Persian, but also available in Arabic, Urdu and English) is *Akhlaq-e-Nasiri*, or *The Nasirean Ethics*, a book on practical "domestic and political disciplines." Tusi devotes a special chapter, entitled "Siyasat-e-Mudun," to discussing economic issues for a "civic society": the first word ("siyasat") means "politics" and the second ("mudun") means "cities and their economic structure." Thus, Tusi's focus is the "political economy" of society. It is often argued that the term "political economy" originated with Antoine de Montchretien's *Traite del'Oeconomie Politique* published in 1615 (Lowry, 65). However, Tusi's analysis clearly locates the concept in the twelfth century.

This emphasis becomes evident from his discussion, and in order to appreciate Tusi's economics, a part of his text follows:

> If every person had to remain occupied in producing his own food, clothing, shelter and tools respectively. He could not have survived because of becoming foodless during the long period required (for supplying the above things). However, since people cooperate with each other and everyone adopts a particular profession, producing more than what is sufficient for his own consumption, and since the laws of justice take care of the matters pertaining to the exchange of one's surplus output with the products of other people, economic means and goods become available to all. Thus God diversified people's activities and tastes so that they might adopt different professions (to help each other). It is this division of work which brings into existence international structure and mankind's economic system. Since human existence does not acquire a shape without mutual cooperation, and since this cooperation cannot take place without social contact, hence man by nature is dependent upon society. It is this dependence of man on society which we call as "tamaddun" (or "mudun," i.e., cities or economy). The word "tamaddun" is derived out of "madina" which implies an assemblage of persons who cooperate with one another by adopting various crafts and industries in order to provide comforts of life. This is exactly the meaning of the statement that man by his very nature is social.
>
> However, if we were to leave every person to do whatever he liked, there may be no cooperation and the strong one may subdue the weak one and the greedy person may collect all the things for himself, and so because of the quarrels people may start exterminating each other. Hence it is necessary to take practical steps to ensure that every man gets his due share, is content with what he deserves, does not encroach upon the

rights of others and pursues his own interest in a spirit of cooperation. Taking of such steps is called "siyasat," or politics.

From all this it is clear that "political economy" is a science which studies uniform laws of public welfare, meant to encourage mutual cooperation for attaining real progress, and that its subject-matter is that structure of society which emerges out of the assembling of human beings and which serves as a source of their activities directed towards the perfection (of their occupations). Thus, every craftsman (or producer) concentrates on his craft, not because it is good or bad, but due to the fact that he belongs to it (i.e., has specialized in it according to social requirement).

(Tusi, 1952, 241–6)

The purpose of reproducing this lengthy quotation is two-fold: to demonstrate that the term "political economy" had been clearly defined by this Arab-Islamic scholar as early as the twelfth century, and to indicate that Tusi took considerable interest in explaining the conception of the discipline that this term represented. His definition lays emphasis on two key themes – the division of labor/specialization, and the promotion of public welfare through the political structure of society.

Dissemination of Arab-Islamic ideas overseas

Apart from these early medieval Arab-Islamic scholars, there are several others who wrote on economic issues, and whose works had wider impact. Some of these, along with some of their major works in which discourses on economic issues are to be found, are noted below:

1. Yahya bin Adam al-Qarshi (d. 818), *Kitab al-Kharaj* (*Book of Taxation*);
2. Abu Obaid al-Qasim bin Sallan (d. 839), *Kitab-al-Amwaal* (*A Treatise on Wealth*);
3. Qudamah Bin Jafar (d. 947), *Al-Kharaj-wa-Sana'at-ul-Kitabah* (*A Treatise on Taxation and Industry*);
4. Abu Nasir al-Farabi (d. 950), *Siyasat-al-Madaniyah* (*Politics of Civic Society*, or *Political Economy*);
5. Abu Jafar al-Dawudi (d. 1012), *Kitab-al-Amwaal* (*A Treatise on Wealth*) (Sharafuddin);
6. Abu Ali al-Husayn Ibn Sina (d. 1036), *Kitab-al-Shifa* (*Book of Healing*): this book discusses economics as one of the six practical disciplines;
7. Abul Hasan al-Mawardi (979–1058), *Al-Ahkam al Sultaniyah* (*Principles of Public Administration*) (Amedroz);
8. Shamsuddin al-Sarakhsi (d. 1090) *Al-Mabsut* (*The Complete Book*): discusses various areas of knowledge, including economics;
9. Nizam al-Mulk Tusi (1018–1092), *Siyasat Nameh* (*Book on State Politics*);
10. Abul Fadl Jafar bin Ali al-Dimashqi (*c.* eleventh century), *Kitab al-Isharah ila Mahasin alt-Tijarah wa Ma'rifat Jayyid al-A'rad wa Radi'iha wa Ghushush al-Mudallisin fiha* (*A Guide to the Merits of Commerce and to Recognition of Both Fine and Defective Merchandise and the Swindles of Those Who Deal Dishonestly*);
11. Taqi al-Din Ahmad 'Abd al-Halim, known as Ibn Tammiyah (1263–1328), *Al-Hisbah fi'l-Islam* (*Public Duties in Islam*) and *al-Siyasah al-Shariyah fi Islah al-Rai wa'l-Raiyah* (*Public and Private Laws in Islam*) (Ghazanfar-Islahi, 1992);
12. Shams al-Din Abu Abdullah Muhammad bin Abi Bakr Al-Zari, known as Ibn Qayyim (1292–1350), *al Turuq al Hukmiyah* (*Governing Methods and Rules*) (Ghazanfar and Islahi, 1997).

It should be highlighted as well that much of the knowledge on various disciplines, including economics, emanating from the Islamic civilization was transmitted to Latin-Europe during the eleventh and twelfth centuries. Indeed, there is hardly any medieval Latin-European scholar who was not, directly or indirectly, influenced by Arab-Islamic scholarship. Briefly, there were several different mechanisms for such transmission.

First, travels by scholars, many of whom learnt Arabic, who brought back knowledge to Europe. Second, translations *en masse* – "the real contact with the Arabic culture was made by twelfth-century translators in Spain; it was then and there that dykes were opened and stored-up experience of the ages began to pour in upon the medieval West" (Goldstein, 113). Third, oral transmission, which, over "eight or more centuries of such intimate contact (via Islamic Spain particularly) is, in itself, quite persuasive an argument for cultural interaction and continuity" (Chejne, 120). Fourth, the development of trade and commerce, leading to the diffusion of economic institutions and practices: "Italian cities . . . in the wake of the Crusades . . . had established relations with the traders of the Near East and had adopted various institutions and devices which were at variance with the rigid pattern of medieval social and economic organization" (Pribram, 21; see also Heaton). Fifth, the Crusades, whose central importance was that "they helped shape European attitudes, feelings, and values" (Ferruolo, 136), "stimulated intellectual life in Europe" (Izzedin, 42), and represented "the strongest influence on development of medieval trade and industry" (Krueger, 72).

There were also other miscellaneous sources of transmission: students "from Italy, Spain and southern France [who] attended Muslim seminaries" (Sharif, 2, 1367); monasteries, whose libraries housed voluminous translations of Arab-Islamic scholarship; cathedral charter schools: "to them was brought most of the science and philosophy from the Byzantines and the Saracens" (Artz, 229); royal courts, which were "as brilliant and refined a center of Arab learning as any in the Middle East or in Spain" (Menocal, 75); missionaries – "Islamic culture was known in Europe partly through the commercial markets, sometimes through the travels of Christian missionaries in the East" (Sauvaget, 228); and the growth of cities – many cities/towns, especially in southern France and Italy, originated in the "footsteps of trade" with the Mediterranean Arab-Islamic world (Krueger, 69).

Recent Islamic economics

It is appropriate to discuss a subject that has generated considerable literature in recent decades: contemporary Islamic economics. As a distinct discipline, Islamic economics emerged in the 1960s, but the subject has been an intrinsic component of Islam ever since its inception. The fundamental sources of the Islamic order emanate from the Holy Qur'an, but also from *Sunnah* (teachings and traditions) of Prophet Mohammad, comprehensively called the *Shari'a*. Further, while there are substantial similarities between the Islamic paradigm and modern free-market (capitalist) economics, there are also some differences. Indeed, there is considerable literature that persuasively argues that the origins of "rational capitalism" lie in the early Islamic world (see Ghazanfar, 2009; Banaji, Gran, Heck, Robertson, Rodison, and Weaver): "The great cause of the rise of rational capitalism was not Christian at all – it was a secular scientific development taken over by Western Europeans from Muslim Arabs and Syrians" (Robertson, 45). Further, Islamic economic concepts provided the rationale that empowered medieval Europe to escape its centuries-old experiment with "Dark Age economics" (Heck, 9).

Islamic economics may be described as a qualified extension of mainstream economics, but consistent with Islamic principles. While self-interest is a key component of the incentive/ motivation structure, it alone must not rule. Economic pursuits must not be the ultimate ends;

the means–ends dichotomy of economics does not go far enough. So, unlike mainstream economics, Islamic economics is not independent of moral-ethical values. It follows that, as a social science, Islamic economics is a composite of positive as well as normative content; both are critical in analyzing economic phenomena and in deriving social goals and policy objectives. Thus, the Islamic scriptures suggest that the "homo-islamicus" is more than mere "homo-economicus." In addition to guiding utility-maximizing behavior, individual behavior must encompass social utility as well. And in this process, the state must actively promote socio-economic justice, a goal not to be left as a byproduct of the free-market or "invisible hand" – i.e., the "trickle-down" alone approach is not acceptable. Islamic economy is a voluntary-exchange economy, but exchange must be a "humanized" blend of markets and morals. In that sense, Islamic economics is part of the integrative, holistic, interdisciplinary Islamic social order.

Given this broad definition, what are the underlying assumptions and premises of Islamic economics? Viewed as mutually reinforcing, these may be noted as follows:

(a) Private ownership of property and humans are "free to choose." However, private ownership is not absolute; a balance between individual freedom and social good is essential, and extreme individualism must be tempered by Islamic ethical principles. Such balance, though less well-known, is what even Adam Smith called for; he visualized the "invisible hand" functioning within a moral-ethical framework, guided by Providence (see Davis).

(b) Scarcity and needs/wants – as with mainstream economics, the means–ends dilemma is also fundamental to Islamic economics, but conditionally. The argument is that scarcity in relation to human wants and needs must be understood in the light of "holistic" rationality, inclusive of both economic and non-economic motivations.

(c) Desirability of economic enterprise – unlike early Christianity, working for a living is exalted throughout the Scriptures; it is part of the "calling," a duty and an obligation. The work ethic is emphasized in the Holy Qur'an.

(d) Encouragement of material progress – within the prescribed constraints of private gain and social good, no amount of material progress is viewed as detrimental to society. But, material gain is not the ultimate goal. Yet, the pursuit of goodness and a virtuous life does not mean asceticism or denial of material gain.

(e) Cooperation and competition – the Holy Qur'an says: "Then strive together (as in a race) towards all that is good" (Holy Qur'an, sura 2, verse 148). Pursuit of economic activities in a voluntary, competitive environment is part of one's "calling," but it is a means to living, not life itself. The notion of human brotherhood implies that the proper pattern of relationships must be based on cooperation and mutual responsibility.

(f) Interpretative flexibility of Scriptures – in economic matters, as in others, Islam provides considerable latitude and variety of interpretations. Indeed, the Holy Qur'an, as an evolutionary message, does not lay down an immutable system in economics, or in any other sphere of affairs. Aside from certain broad principles, all details are for society to determine, according to evolving socio-cultural conditions, subject to *Ijtihaad* ("dynamic reasoning," literally means "interpretative struggle," derived from the verb *jahd*, "to struggle," and *jahaad*, "the struggle") and *Ijma'* (social consensus).

Furthermore, in an Islamic social order, humans are judged by their moral and spiritual excellence and not just by material affluence. Thus, there is no scope for a social arrangement based chiefly on economic possessions, and the concept of human brotherhood transcends any socio-economic stratifications. For the purpose of achieving a just social order, Islamic economics calls for several institutional arrangements, including (a) the institution of *Zakah*, (b) inheritance laws, (c) voluntary charity (*sadaqat*), (d) prohibition of interest (*riba'*), (e) role of the state, and (f) guidelines for appropriate economic activities and conditions governing ownership and use of private property (Ghazanfar, 2009).

How viable is Islamic economics in practice? While there appears to be a broad consensus among proponents as to its theoretical validity, there are divergent opinions as to operational efficacy. Such concerns are evident in a substantial critical literature that emerged in recent years. As early as the 1960s, an eminent Muslim scholar expressed reservations as to the prohibition of *riba'*; he argued, akin to the debates in early Christianity, that *riba'* meant *excessive* interest, or usury, which may lead to exploitation, and thus, is forbidden; it does not refer to interest as practiced in modern financial institutions (Rahman, 1964; Weiss).

Similarly, a Western scholar of Islam has argued that "a modern progressive income and property tax system includes in essence more *Zakah* than the Islamic injunctions intended," and those modern tax systems may achieve the goal of an equitable income-wealth distribution, as part of an Islamic fiscal system (Weiss, 55). Further, some Muslim scholars warn that introducing *Zakah* and abolishing interest cannot be equated with establishing an Islamic economic system. These same scholars point out that policy-makers' concentration "on just the two elements of *Zakah* and interest-free banking to the exclusion of the fundamental structural elements of Islamic reform" amounts to a "mixed-economy with some Islamic whitewash" (Weiss, 56, quoting from Naqvi, et al., 1984). Another scholar argues that we must "abandon" the "obsession" with the "mythical" elements of Islamic economics, and "pay greater attention to issues of poverty alleviation, redistribution of wealth and resources, and Islamic forms of government" (Muqtedar, xvii).

Among the strongest critics of Islamic economics, however, is Timur Kuran, a recent "modernist," trained in the West but with roots in Turkey. He argues that "mainstream Islam has been, and remains, supportive of markets, technological creativity, and material prosperity." Yet, he suggests "economic globalization has benefited the West and harmed vast segments of the Islamic world," thus the arguments for "economic separatism" and "mistrust of Westernization, even into antagonism to modernity" (Kuran, 2002). Among Kuran's works is a recent book, entitled *Islam and Mammon: The Economic Predicaments of Islamism* (2004). Essentially, he argues "that the doctrine of Islamic economics is simplistic, incoherent, and largely irrelevant to present economic challenges" (Kuran, xi). Further, he asserts, "the real purpose of Islamic economics has not been economic improvement but cultivation of a distinct Islamic identity to resist cultural globalization" (Kuran, v).

Conclusion

This chapter has presented a survey of the economic thought of four Arab-Islamic scholastics, who provided rather sophisticated discourses during the early medieval period, descriptive as well as analytical, on numerous economic issues, during the Schumpeterian "blank centuries." The content of their discussions, positive as well as normative, is quite similar to that found in the writings of subsequent European-Latin scholastics of the late medieval period, especially so with respect to Al-Ghazali.

Much of the literature of these Arab scholastics was available to the European scholastics (e.g. Albertus Magnus, 1193–1280; St. Thomas Aquinas, 1225–74; Raymund Lull, 1232–1315; Duns Scotus, 1265–1308), directly or through translations and other avenues during the tenth to thirteenth centuries, from Arabic to Latin, just as there were extensive translations earlier into Arabic once the Greek heritage was re-discovered in the eighth century. Our modest effort provides evidence to support what Spengler suggested, in that, unlike the claim of "blank centuries," economics occupied a distinct place in the writings of earlier Arab-Islamic scholars. The status of contemporary Islamic economics, with its blend of the sacred and the material, is more problematic when viewed from a Western modernist perspective, but has important influence across some regions of the world.

References

Ahmad, Khurshid (ed.), *Studies in Islamic Economics: A Selection of Papers presented at the First International Conference on Islamic Economics*, Jeddah, Saudi Arabia; the Islamic Foundation, Leicester, UK; 1980.

Alberuni, A., *Kitab fi Tahqiq ma li'l Hind (Alberuni's India)*, edited by Edward C. Sachau; Trubner and Company, London; 1971; original, 1887.

Al-Beruni, A., *The Chronology of Ancient Nations*; translated from Arabic by C. Edward Sachau, William H. Allen and Co., London; 1879.

Al-Ghazali, Abu Hamid, *Book of Counsel for Kings (Kitab Nasihat al-Muluk)*, translated from Persian by F.R. Bagley, Oxford University Press, Oxford; 1964.

Al-Ghazali, A. n.d., *Ihya Ulum al Din.* [*Revival of the Religious Sciences*], 4 volumes; Daral Nadwah, Beirut, Lebanon.

Artz, F.B., *The Mind of the Middle Ages, AD 200–1500: A Historical Survey*, Alfred A. Knopff, New York; 1953.

Bagley, F.R., *Book of Counsel for Kings*, translated from Persian, *Nasihat al Muluk*, original by Abu Hamid Al-Ghazali. Oxford University Press, New York; 1964.

Banji, Jarius, "Islam, the Mediterranean, and the Rise of Capitalism," *Historical Materialism*, 15: 47–74; 2007.

Bernardelli, H., "The Origins of Modern Economic Theory." *Economic Record* 37: 320–38; 1961.

Bosch, K.G., "Ibn Khaldun on Evolution." *Islamic Review* 385: 26–34; 1950.

Boulakia, J.D., "Ibn Khaldun: A Fourteenth Century Economist." *Economic Record* 79:5; 1105–18; 1971.

Chapra, M. Umer, *The Future of Economics: An Islamic Perspective*; The Islamic Foundation, Leicester, UK; 2000.

Chapra, M. Umer, *The Economic System of Islam*; University of Karachi, Pakistan; 1971.

Chejne, A., "The Role of Al-Andalus in the Movement of Ideas Between Islam and the West." In *Islam and the West: Aspects of Intercultural Relations*, edited by K.I. Semaan. State University of New York Press, New York; 1980.

Choudhury, Masudul Alam, "Islamic Economics as a Social Science," *International Journal of Social Economics*, 17:6; 35–59; 1990.

Davis, J. Ronnie, "Adam Smith on the Providential reconciliation of individual and societal interests: is man led by an invisible hand or misled by a sleight of hand?" *History of Political Economy*, 22:2; 341–52; 1990.

Fariq, K.A., *Qadi Abu Yusuf ki Kitab al Kharaj.* [*Qadi Abu Yusuf's Book of Taxation*], Burhan, Delhi, India; 1956.

Ferruolo, S.C., "The Twelfth Century Renaissance." In *Renaissance Before the Renaissance: Cultural Revival of Late Antiquity and the Middle Ages*, edited by Warren Treadgold; 114–43; Stanford University Press, Stanford, CA; 1984.

Ghazanfar, S.M., and A.A. Islahi, "Economic Thought of an Arab Scholastic: Abu Hamid Al-Ghazali 1058–1111." *History of Political Economy* 22: 2, 381–403; 1990.

Ghazanfar, S.M., "Scholastic Economics and Arab Scholars: The 'Great Gap' Thesis Reconsidered," *Diogenes: International Review of Humane Sciences*, 154: 117–40; 1991.

Ghazanfar, S.M. and A.A. Islahi, "Explorations in Medieval Arab-Islamic Economic Thought: Some Aspects of Ibn Taimiyah's Economics." In S. Todd Lowry (Editor), *Perspectives on the History of Economic Thought: Selected Papers from the History of Economics Society Conference 1990*, vol.7; 45–63; Edward Elgar, Brookfield, VT; 1992.

Ghazanfar, S.M. and A.A. Islahi, "Explorations in Medieval Arab-Islamic Economic Thought: Some Aspects of Ibn Qayyim's economics." *History of Economic Ideas* III: 1; 7–25; 1997.

Ghazanfar, S.M. (Editor; Foreword by S. Todd Lowry), *Medieval Islamic Economic Thought: Filling the 'Great Gap' in European Economics*; Routledge, London and New York; 2003.

Ghazanfar, S.M., "Capitalist Tradition in Early Arab-Islamic Civilization," *Journal of Oriental and African Studies*; 18; 139–57; 2009.

Goldstein, Thomas, *Dawn of Modern Science*; Houghton Mifflin, Boston; 1988.

Gran, Peter, *Islamic Roots of Capitalism, Egypt 1760–1840*; Syracuse University Press, Syracuse, New York; 1998.

Haq, Z., *Landlord and Peasant in Early Islam*. Islamic Research Institute, Islamabad, Pakistan; 1977.

Hardcastle, Bruce, "The Supply Side Meets the 14th Century: Reagan's Ibn Khaldun." *The New Republic*; October 28, 1981.

Heaton, H., *Economic History of Europe*, Harper and Brothers, New York; 1948.

Heck, Gene W., *Charlemagne, Muhammad and the Arab Roots of Capitalism*; Walter de Guyter Publishers; 2006.

Ibn Khaldun, Abdel Rahman (1332–1404), *The Muqaddimah*, 3 vols, translated by Frank Rosenthal; Routledge and Kegan Paul, London; 1987.

Izzedin, N., *The Arab World: Past, Present, and Future*, Henry Regency Company, Chicago, IL; 1983.

Jurji, E.J., "Islam." In *The Great Religions of the World*, edited by E.J. Jurji; Princeton University Press, Princeton, NJ; 1946.

Khan, M.A. Muqtedar, "Mythology of Islamic Economics and Theology of the East Asian Economic Miracle," *American Journal of Islamic Social Sciences*, 16:4, Winter 1999; v–xviii.

Krueger, H.C., "Economic Aspects of Expansionary Europe." In *Twelfth Century Europe and the Foundations of Modern Society*, edited by Marshall Claggett, Gaines Post and Robert Reynolds, 59–76; University of Wisconsin Press, Madison; 1961.

Kuran, Timur, "The Religious Undertow of Muslim Economic Grievances." In Craig Calhoun, Paul Price, and Ashley Timmer (Eds), *Understanding September 11: Perspectives from the Social Sciences*; New Press, New York, 67–74; 2002.

Kuran, Timur, *Islam and Mammon: The Economic Predicaments of Islamism*, Princeton University Press, Princeton, NJ; 2004.

Landreth, H., and David C. Colander, *History of Economic Thought*, South-Western College Publications, Boston, MA; 4th edition; 2001.

Lowry, S.T., "Recent Literature on Ancient Greek Economic Thought," *Journal of EconomicLiterature*; 171: 65–86; 1979.

Mannan, M. Abdul, *Islamic Economics: Theory and Practice*, Shaikh Mohammad Ashraf Publishers, Lahore, Pakistan; 1970.

Menocal, M.R., "Pride and Prejudice in Medieval Studies: European and Oriental," *Hispanic Review*, 53: 61–78; 1985.

Moss, L.S., ed., *Joseph A. Schumpeter, Historian of Economics: Perspectives on the History of Economic Thought – Papers from the History of Economics Society Conference, 1994*; Routledge, London; 1996.

Myers, E.A., *Arabic Thought and the Western World: A Survey of Islamic Scholars' Influence on Western Scholars and Culture*; Frederick Ungar Publishing Co., New York; 1964.

Naqvi, Syed Nawab Haider, H.U. Beg, Rafiq Ahmed and M.M. Nazeer, *Principles of Islamic Economic Reform*; Islamabad, Pakistan; 1984.

Newman, P.C., A.D. Gayer, and M.H. Spencer, eds., *Source Readings in Economic Thought*; W.W. Norton and Co., New York; 1954.

Oser, J., *The Evolution of Economic Thought*, Harcourt Brace and World, New York; 1954.

Pribram, K., *A History of Economic Reasoning*, Johns Hopkins University Press, Baltimore, MD; 1983.

Rahman, Fazlur, "Riba' and Interest," *Islamic Studies*, 3:1, March 1964; 1–43.

Rainow, T.I., *Wielikije Uczenyje Usbecistana IX-XI bb. [The Great Scholars of Uzkebistan IXth to XIth centuries]*. Tashkent, USSR: Ousphan; 1943.

Robertson, H.M., *Aspects of the Rise of Economic Individualism: Criticism of Max Weber and His School*; University Press, Cambridge, UK; 1933.

Rodison, Maxime, *Islam and Capitalism*, Pantheon, New York; 1973.

Sachau, E.C., *Alberuni's India*, W.W. Norton & Company, Inc., New York; 1971.

Sarton, George, *Introduction to the History of Science*, 3 volumes; Williams and Wilkins, Baltimore, MD; 1927–48.

Sauvaget, J., *Introduction to the History of the Muslim East: A Bibliographic Guide*, 2nd Edition; University of California Press, Berkeley, CA; 1965.

Schumpeter, J.A., *History of Economic Analysis*, Oxford University Press, New York, 1954.

Sharif, M. M. ed., *A History of Muslim Philosophy*, 2 volumes, Harrassowitz, Frankfurt; 1966.

Siddiqi, B.H., "Nasiruddin Tusi" in *A History of Muslim Philosophy*, edited by M.M. Shariff. Harrassowitz, Frankfurt; 1966.

Siddiqui, M.N., "Abu Yusuf ka Ma'ashi Fikr." [Translation from Urdu: Economic Thought of Abu Yusuf]. *Fikr-o-Nazar*, 1964; 66–95.

Siddiqui, M.N., *Muslim Economic Thinking: A Survey of Contemporary Literature*, The Islamic Foundation, London; 1981.

Siddiqui, M.N. and S.M. Ghazanfar, "Early Medieval Islamic Economic Thought: Abu Yousuf's (731–798 AD) Economics of Public Finance," *History of Economic Ideas*, IX: 1; 2001; 13–38.

Siegel, Barry N., "Thoughts on The Tax Revolt," International Institute for Economic Research, Los Angeles, CA; Green Hill Publishers; Occasional Paper 21; 1979.

Spengler, Joseph J., "Economic Thought of Islam: Ibn Khaldun," *Contemporary Studies in Society and History*, VI: 3; 1964.

Spengler, Joseph J., "Alberuni: Eleventh Century Iranian Malthus?" *History of Political Economy* 31; 1971a; 92–104.

Spengler, Joseph J., *Indian Economic Thought: A Preface to History*, Duke University Press, Durham, NC; 1971b.

Tuma, E.H., "Early Arab Economic Policies," *Islamic Studies*, 1965; 10–18.

Tusi, N., *Akhlaq-e-Nasiri*. [*The Nasirean Ethics*], Punjab University, Lahore, Pakistan; 1952.

Watt, W.M., *Muslim Intellectual: A Study of Al-Ghazali*, Edinburgh University Press, UK; 1963.

Weaver, H.G., *The Mainspring of Human Progress*, Foundations for Economic Education, Irvington-on-Hudson, New York; 1953.

Weiss, Dieter, "The Struggle for a Viable Islamic Economy," *The Muslim World*, 74: 2, January 1989; 46–58.

Wilczynski, J.Z., "On the Presumed Darwinism of Alberuni Eight Hundred Years Before Darwin," *ISIS*, 50: 459–66; 1959.

20

Persia/Iran

Hamid Hosseini

While we can accurately regard modern economics as predominantly a Western social science, and cannot ignore the contributions of ancient Greeks to this science, we should by no means ignore the contributions of non-Western civilizations to this old branch of social thought. This is particularly true of medieval Muslims in general and medieval Persian-speaking (Iranian) scholars in particular. As this chapter will demonstrate, medieval Persian scholars contributed a great deal to the development of economics when few such ideas were being generated in Christian Europe.

This absence of economic analysis in medieval Europe, and a lack of emphasis on economic gain by medieval Christian Europeans, is evident in George O'Brien's book on the economic aspect of medieval Europe. Quoting his contemporary French scholar Jourdain, who had studied the economic thought of numerous medieval European thinkers, O'Brien writes:

> he carefully examined the work of Alcuin, Robanas, Mauras, Scouts, Erigenus, Hinkmar, Gerbert, St. Anselm, and Abeland – the greatest light of theology and philosophy in the early Middle Ages – without finding a single passage to suggest any of these authors suspected that the pursuit of riches, which they despised, occupied a sufficiently large place in the national as well as individual life to offer to the philosopher a subject fruitful in reflection and results.
>
> *(1920, 14)*

Although modern Iranians have been rather active, contributing to both secular and Islamic economics, the contributions of medieval Iranians to the development of economics was tremendously more significant than those active at the present. As the works of medieval Persian scholars indicate, their understanding of economic processes was substantial. Persian-speaking Muslims anticipated many economic concepts discussed centuries later in Europe, and influenced Europeans as economic theorizing began to emerge in modern times. Although political economy as an independent branch of social thought is attributed to Adam Smith, and the first use of the term "political economy" is traced to the writings of French author Antonine Montcretein in 1615, medieval Persian philosopher/ethicist/astronomer Nasir Tusi discussed the need for such a science, the science of urban life, in his *Nasirean Ethics*, and provided a modern-sounding definition of economics.

After introducing three distinct groups of Iranian scholars in medieval times, this chapter will illustrate their contributions to different aspects of economics, and will demonstrate how they influenced European scholastics and perhaps other Europeans later. Then the contributions of modern Iranians to both secular and Islamic economics will be discussed.

Persian-speaking Iranians in medieval times

Persia came under Islamic/Arab domination after the defeat of Sassanid Persian Empire by the second Islamic Caliph Omar in the year 651. As Muslims, medieval Iranian scholars made substantial contributions, not only to the development of Islamic intellectual history, but also to the advancement of science, mathematics, and philosophy. Medieval Iranians not only had inherited the great achievements of Pre-Islamic Persian civilization, they had also inherited the scientific achievements of the Ancient Greeks and Indian Sciences. Interestingly enough, during the medieval centuries, most of the best of medieval Muslim philosophers, scientists, physicians, and theologians were Persian-speaking Iranians, even if they published their writings in Arabic which, as the language of the Quran, had emerged as the language of theology, philosophy, science, and communication among diverse Muslims during those centuries.

The fact that many Persian scholars wrote mostly in Arabic has caused much confusion among non-Iranians, who often refer to Persian-speaking Iranians as Arabs. During those golden centuries, Persia also gave rise to some of the best poets/writers in the world, including giants such as Rumi, the epic poet Ferdousi, Nezami, Saadi, Hafiz, and Omar Khayyam, who created classical Persian poetry/prose which became models for literature from contemporary Turkey all the way to Indonesia.

The following three different groups of medieval Persian-speaking Iranians demonstrated a tremendous understanding of the economic process:

(1) Medieval Persian-speaking Muslim philosophers/ethicists who were inspired by Greek thought, after Abbasid Caliph Mammon had ordered the translation of the philosophic/scientific works of the Greek masters. Persia, which was also ruled by the Greeks after its defeat by Alexander, had access to Greek thought long before this. In fact the Persian University of Jundi Shapur, according to many the oldest university in the world, had numerous Greek teachers.
(2) Persian-speaking Muslim theologians who were inspired by Islamic teachings, which were very friendly to economic gain and the market.
(3) Persian-speaking writers of Islamic mirrors for princes, who were inspired by a realistic/economically friendly body of pre-Islamic Persian mirrors. Islamic mirrors consisted of a body of medieval "Islamic" thought – in Persian, Arabic, and later in Turkish – that emerged in the Muslim world after a Muslim convert (from Zoroastrianism), Ibn Moqafah, translated a pre-Islamic book of wisdom titled *Kellileh Demneh* from Middle Persian to Arabic. This translation gave rise to numerous mirrors in the above languages that provided advice to political leaders.

Of course, these scholars could not have made those contributions had it not been for two other factors: the mercantile roots of Islam, and the fact that a rudimentary form of capitalism had emerged in much of the Islamic world when European lands were under feudalism, and the fact that Christian scholars did not advocate economic gain.

The medieval Persian/Muslim view of wealth and economic activity was much closer to Adam Smith's than those of the Ancient Greeks, or even medieval Christian scholars. After all,

Islam had mercantile roots: Prophet Muhammad had been a merchant, and had married a merchant (Khadijeh) prior to his claim of receiving revelation. The Quran and Hadith (reported words and acts of the Prophet, and for Shiites also of several Imams) were pro-trade, and Persians also had a positive view of wealth and economic activity on the eve of the rise of Islam. Furthermore, Muslim scholars were equipped with the rationalism they had inherited from the Greeks. Besides, both the Quran and Hadith are anti-ascetic and advocate moderation in worldly affairs. In fact, production and trade are pictured in the Quran and Hadith as noble practices and merchants are favorably portrayed (Essid, 1987). These main sources of Islamic teaching encourage trade and economic activity, and "the early Muslims of Mecca and Madina continued in trade" (Zubaida, 1972). It is no wonder that economic historians Subhi Labib, Elias Tuma, A. Udovitch, and Maxim Rodinson have emphasized the pro-market aspects of Islam, and the French scholar Goitein speaks of the rise of an Islamic bourgeoisie in Islamic lands during the first six centuries of Islamic history.

Thus, being influenced by their pro-market environment and Persian tradition, plus the inherited Greek rationalism, the realism of the mirrors with pre-Islamic Iranian roots, and responding to the requirements of the early form of capitalism, these three groups of medieval Islamic scholars made substantial contributions to understanding the economic process, and influenced various European scholars, including Thomas Aquinas. These contributions to economics appeared in several areas: in their appreciation of the significance of wealth and economic activity; in their knowledge of division of labor and its usefulness; in their acknowledgement of the roles of demand, supply and the market; in understanding the evolution and functions of money; in their appreciation of public finance and the need for government; and their anticipation of the population theory as expressed by Thomas Malthus centuries later.

The main themes of medieval Persian economics

In contrast to many medieval Christian scholars, medieval Muslim Iranian scholars respected economic activity and gain, as well as wealth accumulation. This approval can be observed in the writings of all three groups of Iranian/Persian scholars listed above. For example, Iranian theologian Ghazali (1058–1111) in his seminal encyclopedic works *Ihya-al-Ulum-al-Din* (*The Revival of Religious Sciences*, from here on *Ihya*), while explaining human nature writes: "Man loves to accumulate wealth and possessions of all kinds of property. If he has two valleys of gold, he wants to have a third" (Quoted by Hosseini, 1996). Elsewhere in the same book, this important theologian views wealth accumulation as a religious obligation.

Medieval Persian Nasir Tusi, in his Nasirean *Ethics*, also viewed wealth accumulation as significant. In his own words: "The intelligent man should not neglect to store up provisions and property" (Hosseini, 1998, 118). Asaad Davani, another medieval Persian philosopher/ ethicist, also viewed wealth accumulation as an attribute of human nature. Kai Kavus, a brilliant eleventh-century author of the famous Persian mirror for princes *Qabus Nameh*, advocated both wealth accumulation and its maximization. He also understood what is now called utility. Kai Kavus wrote: "My son, do not be indifferent to the acquisition of wealth, assure yourself that everything you acquire shall be the best quality and is likely to give you pleasure/satisfaction" (ibid.).

Historians of economic thought attribute the origin of the assumption of self-interest to Adam Smith's *Wealth of Nations*. While this assumption is accurate in terms of modern economics, it is not accurate historically. In fact, various medieval Persian scholars, in addition to viewing human beings as self-interested, even advocated self-interest as a logical human attribute. This advocacy of the notion of self-interest can be seen in the writings of the Persian philosopher/ethicist Ibn Myskaway and Nasir Tusi: it can also be observed in Kai Kavus's *Qabus Nameh*. About self-interest, Ibn Myskaway writes: "The creditor desires the well-being of the debtor in order to get his money back rather than his love for him. The debtor, on the other hand, does not take great interest in the creditor" (Hosseini, 2003, 36). Or, addressing his son in *Qabus Nameh*, Kai Kavus writes: "never in anything you do lose sight of your interest – to do so is superfluous folly" (ibid.). Both wealth and profit maximization are obvious in the following statement in Nasir Tusi's *Nasirean Ethics*: "all those who engage in a profession or craft should seek perfection and maximization there in, not showing contentment with an inferior degree of acquisition" (1985, 212). Similar arguments can also be found in the writings of Asaad Davani.

Historians of economic thought have identified at least three types of division of labor – the social division of labor, division of labor in the household, and division of labor within the factory which is also called technical/manufacturing division of labor. According to these economists, the social division of labor was first discussed by ancient Greek thinkers particularly Plato and Xenophon. According to Peter Groenewegen, the first scholar to acknowledge the division of labor in the household was the English economist Thomas Hodgskin in his 1829 book *Popular Political Economy*. And those historians who view the division of labor in the factory as central to Adam Smith's analysis of economic growth believe that the concept had been considered before 1776 by English writers such as William Petty. However, medieval Iranian scholars discussed various types of division of labor and its significance centuries before.

Of course, those contributions were unknown (if not ignored) by historians of economic thought until recently. This explains why, for example, Vernard Foley's 1974 article traces the roots of Adam Smith's, and William Petty's, division of labor to Plato, or Paul McNulty's 1975 article traces Smith's notion of division of labor to French Encyclopedie and the writings of Joseph Harris, John Locke, Sir Thomas Mun, and Bernard Mandeville. Or, Todd Lowry's 1979 article, which cites Smith's substantive economic analysis of the manufacturing/technical division of labor in the *Wealth of Nations'* illustration of the pin factory, also acknowledges its discussion by Joseph Harris in his 1757 work *An Essay Upon Money and Coins*. However, Smith's example of a pin factory had been used by the eleventh-century Persian Ghazali (Algazel in Latin) in his discussions of the needle factory.

Various medieval Persian scholars – as philosophers and ethicists, theologians, and the writers of medieval (Islamic) mirrors – discussed and contributed to the above-mentioned types of divisions of labor. A few examples will demonstrate this claim.

Let us begin with social division of labor. The medieval Persian-speaking philosopher Farabi (870–950) – one of the first Greek-inspired Muslim philosophers – discussed divisions of labor and their significance in his famous book *Good City*. In that book he writes: "A human being is a creature who, obtaining his/her means of subsistence and building his character, requires the achievement of certain tasks that he/she cannot achieve alone. These tasks must be done by a group which he/she is only a part of" (Farabi, 1982, 251).

The medieval Iranian Nasir Tusi discusses the social division of labor in several parts of his *Nasirean Ethics*. For example, in the course of defining civilization (*Tamdon* in Persian), Tusi writes: "The term is derived from Madina which means the assemblage of persons who cooperate with one another by adopting various crafts in industries in order to provide the comforts of life. This is exactly the meaning of the statement that humans by their very nature are social." Elsewhere in the same book, Tusi writes: "Thus every craftsman/producer concentrates on his craft because he has specialized in it according to social requirements."

Peter Groenewegen attributes the household division of labor to Hodgskin's 1829 work. However, numerous medieval Persian-speaking (Muslim) Iranians discussed this concept centuries before Hodgskin. For example, the noted Persian-speaking philosopher/scientist/ physician Ibn Sina (Avicenna) discussed this concept in his short book *Todbir Manzel* (*Household Management*). In this eleventh-century Persian book Ibn Sina writes: "To protect what he has accumulated, man needs a partner. The partner he chooses must be trustworthy and reliable. Only a wife is worthy of this relationship, since God has granted her these qualities. Thus man is obligated to marry."

In this book, Ibn Sina also writes: "As far as the means of subsistence are concerned, kings and subjects, masters and servants are alike. Man needs a house to protect from burglars, what he has accumulated, and a place as shelter and to rest. He also needs a wife to protect his assets and the house. Man also needs children to help him in times of need, to attend to his chores when he is old, and to protect and revive his good name after he dies."

Nasir Tusi too devoted the Second Discourse of his *Nasirean Ethics* to the application of the division of labor to the household. In fact, Tusi viewed this notion of division of labor as a necessity and as needed for efficiency, and tried to prove this as follows:

> Whereas mankind needs food for the preservation of the individual, and the food needed for the human species cannot be produced without adhering to the economic tasks of sowing, harvesting, cleaning, pounding, kneading and cooking; and the arrangements of such processes cannot conceivably be effective without the collaboration of those who help, and the application of toils . . .
>
> *(1985, 205)*

Given the limitations of their pre-industrial age and writing before the rise of the modern factory, medieval Iranian scholars' understating of the manufacturing division of labor was substantial. In fact, this type of division of labor and its usefulness was understood by several Persian scholars. For example, medieval Iranian Ethicist Asaad Davani stated that: "Philosophers have a saying that there are a thousand things to be done before anyone could put a morsel of bread in his/her mouth" (1946, 320).

Or, Iranian theologian Ghazali, understanding that, to produce a good, various tasks should be assigned to different workers. In the *Ihya*, centuries before Adam Smith, he writes: "If one inquires, one will find that perhaps a single loaf of bread takes its final shape with the help of perhaps one thousand workers." Ghazali explained this complex process as follows:

> You should know that the plants and animals cannot be eaten and digested as they are. Each needs some transformation – cleaning, mixing, and cooking, before consumption. For bread, for example, first the farmer prepares and cultivates the land, and then bullocks and tools are needed to plough the land. Then the crop is harvested and grains are cleaned and separated. Then there is the milling into flour before baking. Just imagine how many tasks are involved; and we have mentioned only a few. And, imagine the number of people performing these various tasks.
>
> *(Ghazali, 1985)*

Adam Smith made a similar argument about the woolen coat some seven centuries later.

Another similarity between eleventh-century Persian Ghazali and eighteenth-century Smith is that both writers saw a relationship between division of labor and exchange. As Ghazali argues in his *Ihya*:

> Perhaps farmers live where farming tools are not available; blacksmiths and carpenters live where farming is absent. So, the farmer needs blacksmiths and carpenters, and they in turn

need farmers. Naturally, each will want to satisfy his needs by giving up in exchange a portion of what he possesses. But, it is also possible that when the carpenter wants food in exchange for tools, the carpenter does not need the tools. Or, when the farmer needs tools the carpenter does not need food. Therefore, pressure emerges leading to creating trading places where tools can be kept for exchange and also warehouses where the farmers produce can be stored.

(Hosseini, 1998, 672)

As stated before, Smith's substantive economic analysis of manufacturing division of labor appears with his celebrated illustration of the productivity of the pin factory. However, Smith's pin factory example was almost identical to an example provided by Persian Ghazali some seven hundred years before when providing an example of a needle factory. Discussing the division of labor Ghazali wrote: "Even the small needle becomes useful only after passing through the hand of needle makers about twenty five times, each time going through a different process" (ibid., 673).

Long before the modern application of the division of labor to the international economy, various medieval Iranian scholars had understood and discussed that application and its benefits. This can be seen in Farabi's *Good City* (1982, 25), in which all societies are portrayed as imperfect, since each is endowed only with certain resources and goods. Farabi maintains that a perfect society can only be achieved when domestic, regional and international exchange all take place.

The benefits of international and inter-regional exchange were also appreciated and understood by Iranian Kai Kavus in the *Qabus Nameh*. This Persian Prince understood that international trade/exchange can be very valuable to society, since each country/region has certain goods/resources while lacking others. Praising the positive role of merchants engaging in international trade, in the eleventh century Kavus wrote: "To benefit the inhabitants of the west they (merchants) import the products of the east, and for those of the east the products of the west, and by doing so become the instruments of world's civilization" (1951, 156). The usefulness of the international division of labor and international trade is also emphasized by theologian Ghazali in the *Ihya*.

Centuries before the emergence of modern economics, medieval Persian scholars also understood the barter system, its problems, and the evolution and functions of money. This is in particular true of Ghazali. While discussing voluntary exchange in volume four of *Ihya*, Ghazali discusses the evolution of money and its roots in the barter system. Understanding the problems associated with barter, such as what we now call the lack of double coincidence of wants, indivisibility of goods due to lack of a common denominator, and limited specialization, Ghazali demonstrates the evolution of money and its utilization in the exchange process. He understood the functions of money as discussed today, in particular emphasizing that money is a means of exchange.

It is interesting that medieval Persian scholars even understood that money is only one asset people can own, and that, to mitigate risk, a person's total assets should be diversified. This can be seen in the writings of both Nasir Tusi and Asaad Davani. For example, according to Asaad Davani: "It is advisable to have part of our property in money and species, and part in land, establishments . . . in order that if anything occurs to unsettle one kind, it may be made up by another." The same argument was also made by Tusi in his *Nasirean Ethics*: "It is advisable to have part of one's property in cash and part in the proceeds of merchandise, part in commodities, furnishings . . ." (1964, 159).

Medieval Persian scholars had a substantial understanding of market processes and their significance centuries before Adam Smith. Their understanding and advocacy of the market far exceeded those of Greek scholars, and even anticipated some developments in Western Europe during and after the rise of capitalism. It is interesting that for those scholars both domestic and international exchange were rooted in the profit motive and the satisfaction of consumer needs. This explains why Ghazali, in the *Ihya*, described the cause of international exchange as follows: "The motive behind all these activities is the accumulation of profits" (327).

In *Qabus Nameh*, and long before Alfred Marshall, Kai Kavus understood that demand, supply, and markets had their own, albeit imperfect, laws. Kavus writes: "My son, although commerce is not an occupation which can with complete accuracy be called a skilled craft, yet, properly regarded, it has laws" (*Kavus*, 1951, 156). In providing his son advice for purchasing a house, Kavus understood how housing markets function: "If you wish to buy a house, buy one in a street where prosperous people reside and not on the outskirts. Also, look first at all your neighbors, not closing the bargain/deal until the land had been valued and is free of doubtful qualities." In a modern sounding statement in *Qabus Nameh*, he advised his son that: "When you make purchases, buy nothing which has not been seen by you or displayed to you and, if you wish to sell goods, first inform yourself of the market rate/price and sell according to proper conditions and contract, and avoid any litigation and dispute."

Various other statements in *Qabus Nameh* are indicative of Kavus' understanding of the market process. For example, in an aphorism that he attributes to a pre-Islamic Persian King, i.e. Anu Shiravan the Just, Kavus provided the following two statements: "Do not buy at any price, so that you may not be compelled to sell at any price" (ibid.). And: "The most profitable merchandise, let it be clear to you, is that which is bought in wholesale quantity and sold retail by the dram – the worse being the opposite" (ibid., 158).

An understanding of the market mechanism by medieval Persian scholars is also evident in the writings of Iranian theologian Ghazali. His understanding of what we now call the law of supply is obvious from his statement in the *Ihya* that, "If the farmer does not get a buyer for his produce then sells at a very low price." In fact, Ghazali seems even to have understood what we now call price elasticity of demand. This is evident in his argument in the *Ihya* that a cut in profit margins by a price reduction may cause an increase in sales, and thus total profits. Long before the emergence of classical economics, Ghazali understood various aspects of the market mechanism and demand/supply as we understand them today.

In the following quotation from *Qabus Nameh*, Kai Kavus demonstrates his understanding of demand, supply, competition, and even the need for marketing and sales promotion by businesses:

> If you are a craftsman (business person) in the bazaar, whatever your craft, let your work be quick and worthy of praise, so that you may acquire many patrons; and whatever work you are engaged in, let it be better than that of your fellow craftsmen. Be content with a modest profit, for while you sell at eleven a single article which costs you ten, you may sell two at ten and a half a piece. Do not drive customers away importuning and over-insistence; thus you will gain a livelihood from the practice of your craft and more people transact business with you. In the course of selling an article exert yourself to say "my friend," "my dear sir," or "my brother," and to make a show of humanity, and with all your strength . . . contain yourself from harsh and foul language. By your gentleness the customer will shame from bargaining/haggling and you gain your object.
>
> *(1951, 237–8)*

Although historians of economic thought attribute the concept of the just price to the thirteenth-century Christian scholar Thomas Aquinas, this concept too had been discussed by Persian writers several centuries before its discussion by Aquinas. This is in particular true of Muslim theologians such as Ghazali, and to some extent philosophers/ethicists like Ibn Myskaway. Ghazali discusses this concept in his Persian book *Kimya-Ye-Saadat* (unlike *Ihya*, which was in Arabic), where he proposes a series of ethical guidelines that would lead to a just price. Among these guidelines is the following: "The seller must not praise the commodity beyond what it is worth. Otherwise it would be deceitful, cruel, and sinful . . . the seller must not conceal the defects of the commodity being sold. The seller must be frank; otherwise he is guilty of fraud, cruelty, and sinfulness" (from the 1940 edition, 273–9).

In the first few decades of Islamic history, Muslims assumed that only God was entitled to set market prices. According to Yassine Essid, this was taken to imply that the market corresponds to God's will (1987, 81). However, later on, Islamic society became much larger and more complex than the time of the Prophet. As Muslim societies expanded to include numerous non-Arab lands, that view of the market was modified. This can especially be seen in works by Persian writers. For example, Ghazali, who still believed in free markets, and generally opposed price controls, came to support price controls in times of emergency like wars and famine, and if price increases had occurred as a result of monopolization of markets and hoarding. This type of view resulted in the rise of the institution of *hisbah*, which allowed politico-religious authorities to control prices under the above circumstances.

While many Persian Muslim scholars believed in free markets, however, they did not support the Smithian notion of the invisible hand. Interestingly enough, medieval Iranian Asaad Davani, as if responding to Smith's argument that self-interest will necessarily lead to public interest, stated that: "men must not be left to their own natures . . . for each, in pursuing his/her own advantage/interest, would be injuring the rest; this must lead to dissension, till they fell to hurting and destroying one another. Some provisions therefore must evidently be made . . . now this provision is termed supreme government" (Hosseini, 1996).

Like modern economists, medieval Iranian scholars, in particular in several mirrors for princes they composed, also understood that governments are needed to provide peace and stability in the market/society; also, they saw government as a necessary institution to construct infrastructure – like canals for irrigation and transportation. As an example, several chapters of Kai Kavus' *Qabus Nameh* dealt with government and its functions in the economy/society. For example, in the chapter on being a king, the author views government as a useful institution necessary for the proper functioning of the market/society. Kavus, believing in what we now call government activism, encouraged the government's role in promoting economic development.

Another very important mirror by a medieval Iranian scholar dealing with the role of government and public finance was *Siasat Nameh* by Nezam-al-Mulk, the wise *wazir* of two Persian Seljuk kings. In that mirror, as a wise practitioner of politics, Nezam-al-Mulk truly understood public finance issues and the proper function of the government. For example, in chapter fifty of this seminal work, while discussing the difficulties facing the country and budget and tax policies, Nezam-al-Mulk describes the king's role in the budgetary process and the proper way to collect taxes. Believing that government should seek a balanced budget, he proposed a golden rule for the king according to whom the country's budget, while seeking the maximum welfare of the subjects, should also avoid being extravagant and wasteful.

Influences outside Persia

Wilczynski (1959) and Joseph Spengler (1971) have brought to our attention that medieval Persian scholar/scientist Abu Rayhan Biruni, who lived some nine centuries before Thomas Malthus and Charles Darwin, can be regarded as their precursor in the book he wrote on India. According to Spengler, Biruni had acknowledged that: "since the growth of man's numbers is limited by the capacity of the environment to provide support, the earth could become overpopulated and in need of a thinning of its numbers." According to Biruni's book on India, the growth of anything is limited by the environment accessible to it. And, since the capability for the growth of a species in number is unlimited, its actual growth is restrained by limiting and almost exclusively external agents. As suggested by Spengler, Biruni observed, as did Darwin upon reading Thomas Malthus, that the pressure of increasing numbers will give rise to natural selection.

Biruni was not the only medieval Persian-speaking Muslim scholar with a "Malthusian" population theory centuries before Malthus. In fact, all the three Persian ethicists, i.e. Ibn Miskaway, Nasir Tusi, and Asaad Davani, held similar views after Biruni. In fact, these three ethicists even utilized mathematical calculations to demonstrate their population theories.

As the previously mentioned statement by George O'Brien indicates, medieval Christian/ Western European scholars did not contribute very much towards economic analysis. Beginning with the British economist William Ashley in the late nineteenth century, many historians of economics, ignoring the contributions of Iranians, assumed that economic analysis which, to them, had ended with the demise of the golden age of Greek civilization, was revived in Western Europe beginning with the genius of Thomas Aquinas, in his seminal book *Summa Theologica*.

However, while no one can deny the significance of *Summa Theologica*, it is also undeniable that he and other Christian scholars were very much influenced by medieval Muslims, in particular by Persian scholars. After all, as suggested by the historian of the Middle Ages P. Hitti (1943), medieval Muslim scholars, in particular Persian-speaking ones, were: "bearers of the torch of culture and civilization throughout the world" (ibid., 143). In fact, medieval Persian-speaking scholars such as Ibn Sina, Farabi, and Ghazali, along with the medieval Spanish Muslim Ibn Rushd (Averroes), influenced pre-Renaissance European scholars in various ways, including by introducing them to Greek/Aristotelian rationalism, which had been preserved by Muslim thinkers.

In fact, as W.M. Watt has argued, Aquinas and other European scholars had to learn all they could from medieval Persian and other Muslim scholars before they could make further advances in various fields of inquiry (Watt, 1972, 43). According to Abbas Mirakhor (1988), many medieval Christian scholars borrowed, explored, assimilated, and elaborated the writings and teachings of medieval Persian and other Muslim scholars. Robert Hammond (1947) has demonstrated the extent of this borrowing/assimilation by placing some of the arguments of Thomas Aquinas opposite those of Persian-speaking Farabi and showing that they are virtually the same (ibid., 41). The translations of the works by Persians and Arabs had a substantial influence on West-European thinkers. This explains why Gordon Leff has noted that: "Intellectually, the difference between the twelfth and thirteenth century was, at its broadest, the difference been isolation from the Islamic world and contact with it" (1958, 141).

Philosopher of science S.H. Nasr (1970) has demonstrated the influence of particular medieval Persian-speaking Muslims on Europe that affected further developments in various sciences. For various reasons those influences were even greater regarding economic ideas. According to Abbas Mirakhor, if those ideas of Persian/Arab Muslims:

> in philosophy and science reached the scholars through the translation of their works, the economic ideas had two other channels of entry into the medieval way of life. One such channel was trade and the other was the cultural diffusion of Muslim economic institutions and processes into European medieval societies.
>
> *(Mirakhor, 1988, 329)*

The last century

Obviously, the contributions of present-day Iranians to economics, as compared to those of modern Western economists or of medieval Persian scholars, are relatively insignificant. Persia declined tremendously and lost its preeminence overall, including in intellectual pursuits, in the modern centuries, joining the ranks of many less-developed economies. However, having a tremendously significant intellectual history, it has seen a great deal of progress in various areas since the introduction of modernization at the beginning of the twentieth century – in literature, the sciences, and economics in particular as compared to many other less-developed societies.

While most Iranian economists today are secular economists, some have been relatively active in a branch of Islamic social thought known as Islamic economics. Perhaps because of Islam's opposition to interest in banking, what has become known as Islamic economics began as an alternative to secular economics in the mid-twentieth century, and was created by three Islamist activists – Pakistani Islamist thinker A.A. Mamdudi (1903–79), Egyptian writer/activist and one of the early leaders of the Egyptian Islamic Brotherhood Seyyed Qutb (1906–66), and Iraqi Shiite cleric Mohammad Bagher Sadre (1931–80). These three founding fathers of Islamic economics were joined by various other true believers – both Sunni and Shiite – that have included those with secular economics training, and even those without it. For proponents of Islamic economics, the moral teachings of Islam provide the ethical guidelines needed for effective control of economic behavior, believing that both orthodox and heterodox paradigms in economics are inadequate for or incapable of explaining the real economic problems of the modern world.

Although several secular-trained Iranian economists, such as Abbas Mirakhor, have been active in Islamic economics since the 1980s, by far most active secularly trained economists engaged in that type of economics have been Pakistani, Bengali, Arab, and Indian Muslim economists. Interestingly enough, Iranians active in this type of economics have mostly been non-economist Islamic activists. In fact, these Iranian writers began their work in Islamic economics in the 1970s, when Iranian Islamist activists joined the left and the nationalist forces in their opposition to monarchy.

Iranians become active in the field of Islamic economics during the 1970s mostly for political reasons, due to the fact that in pre-1979 Iran, Marxism-Leninism, along with Mossadegh's brand of progressive/secular nationalism, had a great deal of appeal among Iranians. Marxism's appeal in pre-1979 Iran influenced Iranian Islamist activists in two different ways. On the one hand, left-leaning Islamists/organizations (the so-called Islamic Marxists), like proponents of Liberation Theology in Latin America, incorporated a great deal of Marxist-Leninist themes and concepts into their beliefs/ideological stands, arguing that these had also been emphasized by Shiite Islam.

The second group, what I call the reactive group, included more religious individuals who, disliking communism and Marxism, tried to provide responses to Marxian themes from an Islamic perspective. Those involved in the reactive group, with some exceptions like Iran's first Islamic President Bani Sadre, were typically theologians. It is interesting that all those writers usually began their essays/books with an Islamic critique and explanation of certain Marxian themes, rather than explaining their own thoughts about economics. As a result of the affinity of Iranian intellectuals with Marxism-Leninism, even the reactive group tried to incorporate some Marxist-Leninist themes in their writings/slogans. Examples are Ayatollah Khomeini's use of the (Leninist) themes of imperialism and oppressed/exploited classes, or Bani Sadre's statement in his *Divine Economics* that: "Islamic view of ownership is not in harmony with ownership under various class societies, and as will be shown below, Islam ended all forms of exploitation, and oppression aimed at usurping the fruits of the labor of workers . . ." (1979, 118).

Although such mixed ideologies are not always to be read literally, given the contemporary conflict over Iran's position in the Middle East, a greater understanding of the long and important history of Persian/Iranian economics is essential to fostering international dialogue.

References

Bani Sadre, A. Hassan, 1979, *Divine Economics* (in Persian), Tehran, Iran.

Davani, Asaad, 1946, *The Akhlaq-e-Jalali* (translated from the Persian), London, W.M. Thomas.

Durant, Will, 1950, *The Age of Reason*, vol.4, New York, Simon and Schuster.

Essid, Yassine, 1987, "Islamic Economic Thought", in Todd Lowry (ed.), *Pre-Classical Economic Thought from the Greeks to Scottish Enlightenment*, Boston, Kluwer Academic Press.

Farabi, Abu Nasr, 1982, *Good City*, in Persian.

Foley, Vernard, 1974, "The Division of Labor in Plato, and Smith", *HOPE*, 6(2), 220–42.

Ghazali, Abu Hamed, 1940, *Kimiya –ye-Saadat* (in Persian).

Ghazali, Abu Hamed, 1989, *Ihya –al –Ulum-al-Din*, the Persian translation.

Ghazanfar, S.M., 2000, "The Economic Thoughts of Abu Hamed Ghazali and St. Thomas Aquinas", *HOPE*, 32, no.2.

Ghazanfar, S.M. and Azim Islahi, 1992, "Exploration in Medieval Arab-Islamic Economic Thought", in Todd Lowry (ed.), *Perspectives on the History of Economic Thought*. Cheltenham, Elgar.

Goitein, S.G., 1957, "The Rise and Fall of Middle Eastern Bourgeoisie in Early Islamic Times", *Journal of World History*, 3, 583–604.

Groenewegen, Peter, 1987, "Division of Labor", in vol.1, *The New Palgrave: A New Dictionary of Economics*, New York, Stockton Press.

Hammond, Robert, 1947, *The Philosophy of Al-Farabi and Its Influence on Medieval Thought*, New York, Hobson Book Press.

Hitti, P., 1943, *The Arabs: A Short History*, Princeton, NJ, Princeton University Press.

Hosseini, Hamid, 1988, "Notions of Private Property in the Literature of Islamic Economics in Iran", *International Journal of Social Economy*, 15, 15–36.

Hosseini, Hamid, 1995, "Understanding the Market Mechanism before Adam Smith: Economic Thought in Medieval Islam", *HOPE*, 27(3), 359–71.

Hosseini, Hamid, 1996, "The Inaccuracy of the Schumpeterian Gap Thesis: Economic Thought in Medieval Persia (Iran)", in Laurence Moss (ed.), *Joseph Schumpeter: Perspectives on the History of Economics*, Routledge, New York.

Hosseini, Hamid, 1998, "Seeking the Roots of Adam Smith's Division of Labor in Medieval Persia", *HOPE*, 40(4), 653–81.

Hosseini, Hamid, 2001, "Medieval Islamic (Persian) Mirrors for Princes Literature and the History of Economics", *Journal of South Asian and Middle Eastern Studies*, 14(4), 13–37.

Hosseini, Hamid, 2003, "Contributions of Muslim Scholars to the History of Economics and Their Impact: A Refutation of the Schumpeterian Great Gap", in W. Samuels, J. Biddle, and J. Davis (eds), *A Companion to the History of Economic Thought*, New York, Blackwell.

Ibn Miskaway, 1968, *Tahdhib-al-Akhlaq* (The Refinement of Character), Beirut, Lebanon.

Ibn Sina, 1940, *Tadbir Manzel* (Household Management), in Persian, Tehran, Iran, Ibn Sina Publications.

Kai Kavus, 1951, *Qabus Nameh* (A Mirror for Princes), English Translation by R. Levy, New York, Dalton.

Leff, G., 1958, *Medieval Thought*, Chicago, Illinois, Quadrangle Books.

Lowry, Todd, 1979, "Recent Literature on Ancient Greek Economic Thought", *Journal of Economic Literature*, 27 (March), 65–86.

Mannan, M.A., 1980, *Islamic Economics: Theory and Practice*, Lahore, Pakistan, Ashraf Publishers.

McNulty, 1975, "A Note on the Division of Labor in Plato and Smith", *HOPE*, 7(3), 372–78.

Mirakhor, Abbas, 1988, "Muslim Scholars and the History of Economics: A Need for Consideration", (in English), in *Islamic Banking*, Tehran, Iran, Iranian Central Bank. This paper had originally been Presented in the United States, in 1983, during the Annual Meetings of South-West and Mid-West Economic Associations.

Nasir Tusi, 1985, *Nasirean Ethics*, in Persian, Tehran, Iran, Minavi Publishers.

Nasr, Seyyed Hosseini, 1970, *Science and Civilization in Islam*, Cambridge, MA, Harvard University Press.

Nezam-al-Mulk, 1960, *Siasat Nameh* (English Translation by Hubert Darke), London, Routledge.

O'Brien, George, 1920, *An Essay on Medieval Economic Teaching*, London, Longmans Green.

Schumpeter, Joseph, 1954, *History of Economic Analysis*, NY, Oxford University Press.

Smith, Adam, (1976) 1985, *An Inquiry into the Nature and Causes of the Wealth of Nations*, NY, Modern Library.

Spengler, Joseph, 1971, "Alberuni: Eleventh Century Iranian Malthus", *HOPE*, 3(1), 92–104.

Watt, W.W., 1972, *The Influence of Islam on Medieval Europe*, Edinburgh, Edinburgh Press.

Wilczynski, Jan, 1959, "On the Presumed Darwinism of Alberuni Eight Hundred years Before Darwin", *ISIS*, vol.50, 459–66.

Zubaida, S., 1972, "Economic and Political Activism in Islam", *Economy and Society*, 1(3), 308–37.

21

North Africa

From boom to bust to revolution

Hamed El-Said

North Africa (NA) includes the six Arab states of Algeria, Egypt, Libya, Morocco, Tunisia and Sudan. In recent years, NA has attracted a great deal of attention. First, it was the birthplace of Arab nationalism and state-led development in the post-independence period. NA has also been the pioneer of market-oriented reforms in the Arab world after 1980. Finally, NA is the birthplace of the Arab Spring, which erupted first in Tunisia in late 2010 before spreading to the rest of the Arab world. This chapter focuses on factors affecting the choice of economic ideologies in relation to the evolution of economic policy, and the individuals/institutions behind such choices, throughout North African history.

NA is not a homogenous region. Although NA is overwhelmingly Muslim, diversities exist in terms of geographic and demographic size, per capita income, natural endowments, political systems and ethnic backgrounds. Libya and Algeria are rich in hydrocarbons (exporters), while Morocco and Tunisia are classified as oil-gas-importers. Although Sudan is endowed with water, large fertile land and other natural resources, it lost its oil resources to the South after 2010 but continues to access rents from oil transportation through its territories. Prolonged conflict has turned Sudan into one of the poorest states in the world. Egypt is the largest NA country, with more than 75 million people in 2005, followed by Algeria whose population grew to 32 million in 2005. Taken together, NA makes more than 60 per cent of the Arab world. Events and attitudes in NA therefore, as has been seen since the Arab Spring, can be representative of the wider Arab world.

The Ottoman Empire

At the beginning of the twentieth century, much of the Arab world was still subjected to the control of the Ottoman Empire, an Empire that dominated the world for almost 400 years prior to the First World War. Although the Empire's main centre of gravity (population, revenue, land and army) was its European provinces, it controlled large segments of land in the Arab world, including what is today known as Jordan, Syria, Palestine, Iraq, Lebanon and North Yemen. In North Africa, the Ottomans held strong presence in Tripoli and Benghazi in Libya, Algeria, Egypt and Tunisia. Morocco was the only North African country that managed to resist direct Ottoman control, and was ruled instead by the Alaouite Dynasty (Owen, 1992, 8).

The Alaouite Dynasty succeeded the Saadi Dynasty in Morocco in 1631. It has been ruling the country since then. It is therefore the oldest ruling family in the world. Both the Saadi and the Alaouite Dynasties are believed to be descended from the Prophet Muhammad through his daughter Fatima and her husband the fourth Caliph Ali. This longevity, and religious authenticity, has added a sense of continuity and legitimacy, enabling the royal family to endure through the Ottoman Empire and through European colonial rule. It was not before the second half of the eighteenth century that the Alaouite Dynasty was able to unify the country and reorganize its administration, as the Berbers and local tribes opposed their rule. The Alaouite Dynasty created a very centralized government system known as the *Makhzan*, and ruled as an absolute monarchy for most of its period. Despite the weakness of its authority, the Alaouite Dynasty distinguished itself in the eighteenth and nineteenth centuries by maintaining Morocco's independence while other states in the region succumbed to Turkish, French or British domination.

Little is known about the economic thinking of the centralized Alaouite state, apart from its monarchial absolutism. In 1777, however, Morocco was the very first state to recognize the sovereignty of a newly independent USA. The consolidation of the power of the ruling dynasty in the second half of the eighteenth century led to more attention being paid to economic policies. Following the recognition of US sovereignty in 1777, the Moroccan *Makhzan* began relying less on mercantilist policies and promoted instead an open trade policy, particularly with the US and European countries. It also worked to modernize the army and administrative infra-structure to control Berber and Bedouin tribes. However, in the latter part of the nineteenth century, Morocco's weakness and instability invited European intervention to protect threatened investments and to demand economic concessions. This led to Morocco falling into European control (French and Spanish) in 1912 until 1956 (Library of Congress, 2006).

With regard to other NA countries, their importance to the Ottoman Empire varied, with Egypt, Tunisia and Algeria occupying special significance. This was due to their geo-strategic location, trade and sources of revenue. In general, the Ottomans ruled NA through 'governors who owed their ultimate allegiance to Istanbul' (Owen, 1992, 8). At the head of the system of government was the sultan, who maintained his rule through a grand Vizir, regarded as having absolute power beneath the ruler (Sultan). Under the grand Vizir there were a number of Vizirs, who controlled the provisional governments and key state positions, including finance and economy. The grand Vizir and his Vizirs met regularly in the palace's *diwan* (council) to decide economic policy in coordination with Istanbul. They made all decisions regarding economic policy, and were supported by a bureaucracy of two groups; the secretaries who drew up documents – orders, regulations and replies to petitions – and those who kept the financial records, the assessment of taxable assets and how much was collected/used and surpluses/deficits (Hourani, 1991, 261–7).

Most of the Vizirs came from the Empire's centre, and Istanbul also provided most of the economic and political input for the rest of the Empire. In fact, most appointments to key state positions were based on personal relations rather than merit. Loyalty to Istanbul was a key criterion in those appointments, and most appointees came from the family of the governor or his close circle. NA received most of its economic input from Istanbul and became so dependent on policy input from the centre to a point where it became 'difficult for them [Arabs] to imagine a world without the Ottoman Sultan as their political and . . . religious leader' (Owen, 1992, 9).

The Ottoman Empire followed a mixture of Keynesian-style and liberal economic policies. On the one hand, it encouraged free trade with the rest of the world and left interest rates to be determined by supply and demand factors. It also introduced a new land registry and property rights system to improve private investment and boost the role of the private sector, and broadened the existing tax system in former Muslim states. In addition, the Ottoman Empire improved documentation, recording and tax assessment and expenditure systems. On the other hand, the state was encouraged to invest in public works and provide jobs to the local population through such projects as roads, railways, irrigation, dams and technology transfer. In each large city, a provincial government was created and became a central one in miniature, the 'governor had his elaborate household, his secretaries and accountants, and his council of high officials meeting regularly' (Hourani, 1991, 217).

In NA, only 'modern Egypt was built up from the beginning (starting with Viceroy Mohamed Ali) by its aristocracy, which gradually became aristocratic bourgeoisie (or a capitalist aristocracy)' (Amin, 2012, 6). Ali had conceived and undertaken a huge programme of renovation and modernization for Egypt. That experience took two-thirds of the nineteenth century and ran out of steam in the 1870s. Its failure culminated in Britain's military occupation of Egypt in 1882 (ibid., 16). During the last hundred years of their reign, the Ottomans devoted more resources and energy towards defending their Empire and possessions in the Arab world from increased European threat. During the second half of the eighteenth century, the Ottoman Empire introduced various reforms (*tanzimat*). The political reforms aimed at upgrading its military and power structure. Economically, several important legal and administrative practices, which endured in the Arab world long after the end of the Ottoman Empire, were introduced. This did little to preserve the Empire.

Long before the First World War, most North African countries were under European domination. Egypt and Sudan were under British control between 1882 and 1952, and 1899 and 1956 respectively. Algeria was the first North African country to be subjected to French control from 1830 to 1956. Tunisia and Morocco followed suit in 1882–1956 and 1912–56 respectively. Libya was colonized by Italy from 1912 to 1943, before falling under British control from 1943 to 1952. Autonomous economic policy was prevented from emerging in NA by the colonial authorities. Except in Egypt, where the British authorities were forced to grant qualified political independence in 1922 following a revolt in 1919, North Africans played a minimum role in running their own affairs. The colonial authorities blocked the emergence of other institutions with potential economic clout and policy influence.

This colonial management style was best described by Owen (1992, 17–18) where he stated that the constraints of the colonial management style:

> left little money for development . . . colonies were also subject to a particular type of fiscal and monetary regime, with their currency tied to that of the colonial power and managed by a currency board in the metropolis . . . they were not allowed a central bank, which could have regulated the money supply or moved the rate of interest in such a way as to expand or dampen local demand. Meanwhile, throughout most of the Middle East the new states remained subject to 19th-century commercial treaties, which until they ran out round about 1930, prevented them from setting their own tariffs. The result was the creation of more or less an open economy, subject to influences stemming from the metropolis and the world at large, over which the state had little or no control.

To facilitate their grip on the countryside, the colonial authorities created alliances with large landowners, rich peasants and conservative tribal sheikhs, which controlled most rural areas (Amin, 2011). This not only led to the emergence of large landholdings, but also fostered what Richards and Waterbury (1996, 154, 172) described as 'bimodalism', which 'refers to a land tenure system that combines a small number of owners holding very large estates with a large number of owners holding very small farms'. In NA, the best agricultural land was seized by foreign conquerors.

This dispossessed millions of indigenous Arabs, forced them into more marginal land, and relegated them to subsistence farming or wage labour (Richards and Waterbury, 1996, 154–5; Smith, 1975; Abun-Nsr, 1971). Thus the colonial tenure system fostered poverty, social inequalities, and impeded human capital formation.

The rise and fall of socialism

NA emerged from colonization as poor, uneducated, underdeveloped and, in the case of Algeria radicalized socially and ideologically. The 'politics of decolonization' and the legacy of backwardness, poverty and underdevelopment played a key role in shaping the evolution of economic thinking in NA in the immediate post-independence period (Richards and Waterbury, 1996, 174). In almost every North African country, save perhaps Libya before 1969, nationalist leaders drawn either from the army or national liberation movements emerged to shape the post-colonial order.

Strong leaders emerged in Egypt (Gamal Abd al-Nasser, 1952–70), Algeria (Houari Boumediene, 1965–78), Tunisia (Habib Bourguiba, 1956–88), Morocco (Mohammed V, 1956–61) and Libya (Colonel Muamer Gaddafi, 1969–2011). These nationalist leaders, except Nimiri and Gaddafi in Sudan and Libya, not only architected their countries' political independence, but also the economic/social revolutions that followed. All NA leaders shared a vision of autonomous, equal, prosperous and strong states. They were determined to change the status of their nations and to rid them of the legacies of underdevelopment. It was against this background that a new model of development, specific to the Arab world, emerged after independence first in NA, before spreading to the rest of Arab Middle East. The literature refers to this new model of development as 'Arab Socialism', the 'Arab socialist model' or ASM (Kadri, 2012, 1).

The ASM first emerged in Egypt and was shaped by the ideas of its president, Gamal Abd al-Nasser, before spreading to NA and other Arab states. As Ayubi (1996, 289, 310) noted, the policies that emerged in the Arab world after independence were influenced 'by the Egyptian transfer of their own experience to the rest of the Arab World ... the impact of the Egyptian model ... as an exemplar' model of development was imitated in the entire Arab world, 'regardless of size, politico-institutional history, wealth or socio-political doctrine'. In fact, the Egyptian model of Arab Socialism (AS), it can reasonably be argued, shaped the evolution of economic thinking, not only in the Arab world, but also in other emerging economies in Asia and Africa. As Hayashi (2007, 81) wrote: 'In 1954, at Bandung, leaders of the Egyptian revolution were encouraged to talk with the leaders of the Afro-Asian countries who were struggling against the same conditions'.

Nasser was born on 15 January 1918 in Alexandria, Egypt. He was one of the key army officers who led the military Junta, known as the Free Officers, that deposed King Farouk and terminated British control in 1952. His main ambition was to modernize Egypt and create a secular Arab Empire in North Africa and the Middle East. He put his ideas into a book in 1954 entitled *The Philosophy of Revolution* (Cairo, Information Department). Here Nasser distinguished between AS and other forms of socialism, including nineteenth-century European socialism, in several ways. Nasser based AS on the Arabs' own history and experience, and it was not simply an attempt to imitate the experiences of others. Since nations' history and circumstances varied tremendously, Nasser asserted, it was not suitable to import models of development from other regions.

There were important differences, of course, in the models of governing that emerged after independence in NA. But all NA countries followed similar policies, and created/used a single party as a mechanism to oversee economic strategies and to mobilize support. Regardless of size, wealth, form of governing, history or political doctrine, all Arab states embraced strong government intervention in the economy, state-led development and a large public sector. As Ayubi (1996, 290) wrote:

> In the economic sphere the expansion of state policies has been most remarkable and has included practically all Middle Eastern countries regardless of size, politico-institutional history, wealth or socio-political doctrine . . . all the Arab countries had a very large public sector.

Richards and Waterbury (1996, 174–5) elaborated on the rationale behind government intervention in the post-independence NA era:

> it is more the politics of decolonization and development than history and culture that account for the interventionist, organic state in the Middle East. The caretaker states of the colonial era . . . have logically evoked their opposites, states that impinge upon all aspects of their citizens' lives. Moreover, the postcolonial state has seen as its duty the reparation of all the economic damage resulting from colonial policies. It has had to mobilize human and material resources on an unprecedented scale . . . The leaders of the state saw the need for intervention in order to avoid wasting scare resources . . . A more equitable distribution of assets became a universal goal throughout the area.

In addition, the assumed weakness of the private sector and the bourgeoisie class in most North African countries on independence also encouraged state-led development and heavy state investment. The 'Private sector might be tolerated, but nowhere . . . did they enjoy legitimacy. Reliance on private entrepreneurs and on the law of supply and demand to allocate resources would be wasteful . . .' (Richards and Waterbury, 1996, 175).

NA's AS and developmental approach relied on several strategies to achieve its objectives. The first step was to elevate the state to the position of the only policy-making body and controller of natural resources. The aim was to harness the surplus to be redeployed in national development projects. 'Economic planning and government intervention in relative autarky represented the means by which the foremost binding constraint of underdevelopment, which is the financing needed to galvanise national resources, was to be overcome' (Kadri, 2012, 6). This was followed by nationalisation of large-scale financial and industrial institutions. Planning and intervention in the economy were implemented in tandem with large-scale land reform to redistribute wealth and to limit the power of the landlords, seen as collaborators with the colonial powers. Hostility towards the private sector was taken most radically in Algeria, Egypt after the 1956 Suez crisis, and Libya after 1969. The fourth strategy followed by NA to promote industrialization was based on the ideas of the English economist, John Maynard Keynes.

Keynes argued that, in order to overcome depression in an economy, state inducement was needed. This can take either the form of lowering interest rates or state investment in infrastructure, or both. This injection of state capital, Keynes argued, leads to more general spending in the economy, which in return stimulates more investment and production, generating even more income and spending (Keynes, 1936). In the immediate post-independence era, NA lowered its interest rates and its national currencies circulated without any intervention from or consultation with international financial institutions (IFIs). In fact, several interest and exchange rates were at play to attenuate the impact of foreign exchange shortages on the national issue of currency. Investing heavily in infrastructure and industry represented other important state inducements in NA in the post-independence era. The current account real and capital balances were also devised in order to promote industrialization (Kadri, 2012, 6; Ayubi, 1999; Richards and Waterbury, 1996; Owen, 1992; Hayashi, 2007).

Typically, North African regimes supported an import-substitution industrialization strategy (ISI) based on a large public sector and public sector enterprises. ISI is based on the premise that a country should reduce its dependency on foreign imports by 'replac[ing] commodities that are being imported, usually manufactured goods, with domestic sources of production and supply' (Todaro, 1989, 435). The strategy is first to erect tariff barriers or quotas on the importation of certain commodities, then to set up local industry to produce these goods. It is thus a state-induced strategy to achieve rapid industrialization. While the initial cost of production may be higher than the former imported prices, the rationale for ISI is that either the industry will be able to reap economies of scale and reduce costs of production (the infant industry argument), or that the balance of payments will improve as a result of fewer imports, or a combination of both.

It has been suggested that ISI was first advocated by the mercantilist school of economic thinking in Europe between the sixteenth and eighteenth centuries, which supported protection of the economy in order to industrialize, reduce imports and attain favourable terms of trade (ibid.). Ha-Joon Chang (2002, 1) argues that almost all of today's developed countries used such policies when they were developing. As Chang stated, policies associated with ISI based on government intervention:

> were used by the developed countries when they themselves were developing countries. Contrary to the conventional wisdom, the historical fact is that the rich countries did not develop on the basis of the policies and the institutions that they now recommend to, and often force upon, the developing countries . . . Almost all of today's rich countries used tariff protection and subsidies to develop their industries. Interestingly, Britain and the USA . . . are actually the ones that had most aggressively used protection and subsidies.

In the 1930s, 'ISI was initiated in many Latin American countries as a response to the disruption caused by World War I, the economic depression of the 1930s and World War II . . . but ISI became more widespread in the post-1945 world' (Colman and Nixon, 1986, 282).

From the 1950s onwards, ISI was incorporated in the works of such structuralist economists as Raul Prebisch and Hans Singer. The Prebisch-Singer thesis 'concerned the long-term deterioration of poor countries' terms of trade. It analysed why, in the long run, the price of primary products tended to decline relative to that of manufactured goods. [Their] conclusion was that the benefits of trade were distributed unequally between the countries that imported agricultural commodities and those that exported them, to the disadvantage of the exporters' (*The Economist*, 2006). The Prebisch-Singer thesis became the basis of dependency theory 'developed in the late 1950s under the guidance of the Director of the UN Economic Commission for Latin America, Raul Prebisch . . . and his colleagues [who] were troubled by the fact that economic growth in the advanced industrialized countries did not necessarily lead to growth in the poorer countries . . . Such a possibility was not predicted by neoclassical theory, which had assumed that economic growth was beneficial to all (Pareto optimal)' (Ferraro, 2008).

In NA, ISI started first in Egypt after the end of the Second World War and continued until at least 1974, when Sadat introduced his *infitah* (open door) policy. It was replicated in Algeria (1962–89), Tunisia (1962–86), and Morocco (after independence until 1983). Although ISI started after independence in Sudan, it was accelerated after Ga'afar Nimeri seized power in 1969 (1969–84). ISI fitted perfectly the objectives of AS, which sought political and economic liberation and de-linking of economic ties to former colonial power (Ayubi, 1999; Richards and Waterbury, 1996).

The transition to neo-liberalism

'Most observers agree that import substitution industrialisation in a large number of developing countries . . . has for the most part been unsuccessful' (Todaro, 1989, 439). Colman and Nixon (1989, 292) explained why:

> Perhaps the most crucial problem of the ISI process is its apparent inability in the long run to continue to reduce the import ratio and thus to sustain a growth rate of GNP in excess of the growth in the capacity to import. In other words, ISI generates a high rate of growth in its initial stages but such growth is short lived . . . And the economy experiences stagnation at a low level of development once ISI opportunities appear to have been exhausted and the foreign exchange constraint once again becomes dominant.

ISI in NA was no exception. All NA states came to face similar challenges associated with the internal contradictions of ISI. By the late 1970s, almost all NA countries were suffering major macroeconomic instabilities, including large trade and current account deficits, large fiscal deficits, a high volume of foreign debt, low level of foreign reserves, high unemployment, and high inflation (Harrigan and El-Said, 2009a, 2009b).

The call for reform, consistent with a tradition of centralized decision-making processes in the region, came from the leadership itself. North African leaders began publicly acknowledging the flaws of state-led development strategies. Egypt, the first Arab state to embark on state-led development, was also the first to begin dismantling its socialist policies. This came from Nasser himself, who began openly criticising his government's social policies by the mid-1960s. Nasser started a programme of economic liberalisation based on encouraging private and foreign investment. Following Nasser's death in 1970, his successor, Sadat, continued to open up the Egyptian economy and pioneered the *infitah* (open door) policy in 1974. *Infitah* continued Nasser's focus on reducing the role of the public sector and promoting the role of the private sector in the economy.

Similarly, Bourguiba in Tunisia began doubting his state-led development strategy as early as 1969. Similar processes also began in both Algeria and Morocco in the late 1970s, when the leadership embarked on similar reforms to Egypt, aimed at reducing the size of the public sector and boosting the private sector (Ayubi, 1999). Even Libya, despite the country's oil reserves, faced a balance of payments crisis in the early 1980s, emanating from both economic mis-management coupled with a slump in the oil market. Nowhere, however, did reforms in NA go far enough, or were even sustainable to restore macroeconomic balance and obviate the need for resorting to the kind of conditionality associated with neo-liberal reforms promoted by the IFIs, particularly the International Monetary Fund (IMF) and the World Bank.

Criticism of state-led development came not only from the North African leadership, but from several economists too. One such Egyptian economist was Galal Amin, a Professor of Economics at the American University in Cairo. Amin received an undergraduate degree in economics from the Cairo University (1955) and an MSc (1961) and PhD (1964) from the London School of Economics. He is the author of many books in Arabic and English on economic developments in Egypt and the Arab world, including *Egypt's Economic Predicament* (London, 1995). While urging Arab regimes to carry out badly needed economic reforms, Amin was very critical of neo-liberal reforms promoted by IFIs, warning against the implementation 'of the

Structural Adjustment programme of reform, which constitutes modern conventional wisdom' (Amin, 1995). Amin argued:

> A liberalization policy is valid at a time of growing world economy, high flow of foreign investment, and relatively stable political climate. On the other hand, a higher degree of protection would make much more sense . . . when the country is faced with a depressed world economy, a sluggish flow of foreign investment, and highly volatile political climate.
>
> (El-Naggar, 1987, 16)

Amin neither adhered to unfettered free market economics nor to an autarkic intervention. His views were closer to Keynesianism, namely to guide an economy out of depression through careful government intervention.

Another prominent North African economist is the Moroccan Bachir Hamdouch, Professor of Economics at the Faculty of Law and Economics (Université Mohamed V Agdal, Raba). Like Amin, Hamdouch has also been very critical of neo-liberal free market reforms in the context of developing countries. Hamdouch completed his Diplôme in Economics and Finance in 1969 (de l'Institut d'Etudes Politiques de Paris), Master in Economics (1969, University of Paris I Panthéon – Sorbonne), and Doctorat d'Etat in Economics (1974). His best known work was 'The Open Door and Underdevelopment of Morocco' (University of Paris I Panthéon – Sorbonne). Hamdouch criticised the neglect of the social aspect of reform under IMF and World Bank lending, and the implementation of economic policies that failed to take into account the level of development and institutional capacity in reforming countries. He argued that reforms promoted by IFIs:

> suffer from certain limitations both with respect to design and implementation . . . excessive importance attached to external balance at the expense of growth and development. The economic and social cost involved cannot be underestimated . . . [IFIs'] policy has coincided with zero development, which means that there has been hardly any progression in the average standard of living . . . the lowest income groups have suffered in particular.
>
> (El-Naggar, 1987, 22–3)

Hamdouch wondered how long a developing country like Morocco could sustain adjustment without development.

However, and as *The Economist* (2011) once stated, 'being famous is not the same as being influential. Neither means that you are worthy'. The point is that, although some North African economists acquired the status of 'Prominent economist[s] and author[s]' in their respective countries, this does not mean that they were influential in shaping their countries' economic ideas (Saleh, 2013). As argued earlier, the kind, timing, pace and quality of reforms in NA were determined by the leaders of the region. These leaders, by the early/mid-1980s, found themselves with little choice but to resort to IMF/World Bank financial assistance, or policy-based lending. They could no longer postpone reforms as their foreign debt, fiscal and trade deficits, as well as inflationary pressures, all reached alarming levels. North African leaders were also alarmed by the overthrow in 1984 of the Numeri regime in Sudan, following a period of instability caused by the avoidance of reform.

Morocco was the first North African state to sign a Stabilisation Agreement (SBA) and Structural Adjustment Lending Programme (SAL) with the IMF and World Bank in 1981 and 1990, followed by Sudan. Tunisia followed suit in 1984, as well as Algeria. Since 1987, Egypt has also had four economic programmes that were supported financially by the IMF, totalling

SDR1.1558 billion ($1.850 billion) (Harrigan and El-Said, 2009a, 2009b). The IMF SBA is a sub-set of IMF and World Bank programmes aimed at assisting countries facing economic crises to respond to their balance of payments problems and external financial needs, and initiate structural change in the economy in favour of external markets and globalization (Mosely *et al.* 1991). SBA and SALs are the IMF's and World Bank's 'workhorse lending instrument' through which they are able to influence reforms and economic policies in 'emerging and advanced market countries'. SBA and SALs are thus financial and technical assistance in return for reforms; assistance is conditional upon reforms.

In the 1980s, the IMF and World Bank lending reforms were reorganized as a 'set of ideas' evolving around the so-called 'Washington Consensus', which is 'both the political Washington of Congress ... and the technocratic Washington of the international financial institutions' (Williamson, 2004, 2). The Washington Consensus became a framework that the US government and the IFIs 'believed were necessary elements of first stage policy reform that all countries should adopt to increase economic growth. At its heart is an emphasis on macroeconomic stability and integration into the international economy – in other words a neo-liberal view of globalization' (WHO, 2014).

Williamson, who coined the term 'Washington Consensus' in 1989, listed ten key policies that were accepted by the 'Consensus' as necessary to solve developing countries' macroeconomic imbalances. They included: austerity and fiscal discipline aimed at controlling the money supply to reduce the fiscal deficit and rein in inflation; tax reform that combines a broader tax base with marginally higher tax rates to speed up reduction in fiscal deficit; reordering public expenditure through provision of a more targeted subsidy system and switching expenditure in a more pro-growth and pro-poor way; financial liberalization, particularly interest rates; reforming the exchange rate, meaning devaluations to boost exports; trade liberalization to increase domestic competition and opening up markets for foreign investors; privatization aimed at shifting the structure of ownership; and deregulation, which 'focused specifically on easing barriers to entry and exit, not on abolishing regulations designed for safety or environmental reasons' (Williamson, 2004, 3–4).

The performance of North African economies during the transition to neo-liberal policies since 1980 has arguably been disappointing. El-Said and Harrigan (2014) have recently shown how the social and economic performances of the socialist era outperformed the transition to neo-liberal policies after 1980. Not only did economic growth and per capita income during the socialist era outperform those achieved after 1980, but poverty reduction improved much faster than it did after 1980. In 2006 the World Bank acknowledged these shortcomings:

> By 2000, the region's average per capita output had ... not fully recovered to its 1985 level ... Very little progress was made on the poverty front. The region's average poverty rate fluctuated between 20 and 25 percent during the entire decade of the 1990s. By 2001, approximately 52 million people were poor, an increase in absolute numbers of approximately 11.5 million people, compared with the situation in 1987.
>
> *(Iqbal, 2006, xix)*

Pressure for neo-liberal reform in NA should be seen in light of the failure of ISI to achieve its original objectives. Neo-liberal policies did not come from the emergence of new regimes committed to a free market economy, or as a result of a newly found conviction in the superiority of neo-liberal approaches to economic growth. This led Richards and Waterbury (1996, 231) to interpret the reforms as a 'classic case of survival strategy', one aimed at restoring the legitimacy of the incumbent regimes by improving economic performance, and reducing the debt burden and the fiscal deficit. Jane Harrigan (2011, 11–12) has also explained these reforms in NA in a similar fashion: 'Despite the nuanced differences, a common assessment is that the reforms actually undertaken can be seen as a process whereby the state, rather than retreating from economic activity, simply repositions itself to safeguard the positions of its major interest groups'.

The Arab Spring

The social impact of the neo-liberal era was not favourable, with poverty and unemployment remaining relatively high and inequalities sharpening. Although the IMF and the World Bank provided a more positive picture, there was a widespread negative perception of the impact of neo-liberal reforms in the NA region by the majority of the population. But more than neo-liberal economics, the widespread nature of corruption, nepotism and rent seeking, as well as repression, have contributed most to negative perceptions. There was little open criticism of economic policies implemented by the incumbent regimes before the Arab Spring. What were criticized most openly were the perceived injustices, large inequalities, widespread corruption, nepotism, and rent seeking activities that failed to create a level playing field and benefited most the 'establishment's elite' and the 'establishment's' insiders' (UNDP, 2012).

Most Egyptians did not riot in 2011 against the IMF and the World Bank as they did in the mid-1970s. But they opposed and criticized openly 'The corruption of the Egyptian government', the fact that 'Mubarak's . . . younger son Gamal, a former investment banker had filled the cabinet with his inner circle of businessmen friends', that 'Mubarak's cronies were seen to be the beneficiaries' of neo-liberal reforms, and 'The wish of his wife to have her son succeed Mubarak is what really led to his downfall'. The fact that neo-liberal reforms 'failed to alleviate poverty' and that the growth rate 'widened the gap between rich and poor' did not help. All of this led 'Ultimately [to] a sense of economic injustice [that] helped create the conditions for the 18-day uprising that unseated Mubarak' (Knell, 2013). The neo-liberal reforms were also implemented undemocratically, following a long tradition of centralized economic activity and decision-making processes.

Islamists were a main beneficiary of the Arab Spring, although they played a small role in its initiation. In Tunisia, Morocco, and Egypt until President Mohammed Morsi, who won elections in June 2012, was removed from office in July 2013, Islamists went as far as winning elections and constituting governments for the first time in their history. The arrival of political Islam to power in Tunisia, Morocco, and Egypt led some to speculate regarding the emergence of an 'Islamic economy' in the region, which would place morality, equity, the well-being of society, an open trade system, and stability as key policy objectives (Arab News, 2014).

As one source explained, Islamic economics is 'that branch of knowledge which helps to realize human well-being through an allocation and distribution of scarce resources that is in conformity with Islamic teachings without unduly curbing individual freedom or creating continued macroeconomic and ecological imbalances' (Islamic Economics, 2013). Islam is a religion that was initially born in a territory with limited agricultural potential. This led to more emphasis on generating commercial possibilities, such as trade and finance. Commerce acquires a special significance in Islam and is considered a blessed activity. This is because the prophet himself, many of his companions, and several eminent Muslim scholars were successful businessmen. In many ways the Islamic economic system 'is very close to today's free market . . . or liberal economy' (Islamic Economics, 2013).

However, Islamic economic thought is different from neo-liberal economics in that Islam is not just a religion, but also a way of life. Islamist economists list five points which distinguishes their system from other economic ideologies: Forbidding interest (usury or *riba'* in Arabic);

forbidding earnings from gambling, lotteries, and the production, sale, and distribution of alcohol; forbidding hoarding food and other basic necessities; Muslims must pay *zakat* (alms-giving); and Muslims are encouraged to give constantly to charity. The arrival of political Islam after 2010 raised possibilities of introducing an Islamic economic system along these lines.

However, the outbreak of the Arab Spring did not usher in a new era of 'Islamic economics', one that could compete with or substitute neo-liberal economic policies. On the contrary, there has been a continuation of past pro-market policies. The Moroccan Justice and Development Islamic Party, the Tunisian al-Nahad Party and the Egyptian Muslim Brotherhood all continued collaboration with the IMF and World Bank, and did not sever relations with them, as some had predicted. Egypt had been negotiating with the IMF for three years over a proposed $4.8bn loan, and President Morsi continued to negotiate and held the Fund responsible for delays in implementation. These developments should not come as a surprise, as Islamists are not anti-free market economics in general. Islamist movements in the Arab world lacked a distinctive economic development ideology to promote in place of neo-liberalism. As Kadri (2012, 2) recently wrote: 'The neo-liberal phase of development has not ended with the beginning of the Arab Spring. If anything, many of the dispossessing policies of the past have gained momentum under newly elected Islamic governments'. However, all NA states have re-introduced some form of social protection since the eruption of the Arab Spring.

Conclusion

NA's economic decision-making is characterized by a long history of centralization and a top-down approach. During the Ottoman Empire, economic policy-making was interested to a grand Vizir, aided by a number of Vizirs who controlled all key state positions, received their policy input from Istanbul, and were loyal to the Sultan. This changed somewhat during European control, which followed a more free market approach but with little input from the colonies. NA began its post-dependence era with a heavy dose of nationalism and socialism, based on state-led development and public sector enterprises. In the early 1980s, NA had to abandon its state-led development and was forced by IFIs to return to the fold of countries dominated by the neo-liberal formula. The outbreak of the Arab Spring seemed to have caused a change of policies in some areas but without leading to alternative economic thinking or a new development paradigm.

The experience of the NA region suggests that the impact of economic ideas as pure theory has (at least in the short-run) been limited, and that changes in government economic policies are most often generated by factors outside the economics profession, even though the work produced by this profession is often used to bolster or negate certain existing tenets of belief. The impact of a single leader can be determinate on the economic policies selected, if not on the outcome of these policies, as can external bodies with sufficient power, but economic theory in itself is only moderately influential at best.

References

Abun-Nsr, Jamil (1971). *A History of the Maghreb*, Cambridge, Cambridge University Press.
Adams, Richard and Page, John (2003). Poverty, Inequality and Growth in Selected Middle East and North African Countries, 1980–2000, *World Development*, 31(12), 2027–48.
Amin, Galal A. (1995). *Egypt's Economic Predicament: A Study in the Interaction of External Pressure, Folly and Social Tension in Egypt, 1960–1990*, London, Brill.
Amin, Samir (2011). An Arab Springtime? In *Monthly Review*, June 2. http://monthlyreview.org/commentary/2011-an-arab-springtime.

Amin, Samir (2012). *The People's Spring: The Future of the Arab Revolution*, Dakar, Pambazuka Press.

Arab News (2014). Knowledge, expertise in Islamic economy to dominate WIEF sessions, January 19. http://www.arabnews.com/news/469956.

Ayubi, Nazih (1996/1999). *Over-Stating the Arab State: Politics and Society in the Middle East*, London, I.B. Tauris.

Badawi, Nada (2013). Morsi's adviser says "IMF responsible" for loan delay, *Daily News*, June 10.

Cardiff, Patrick (1997). Poverty and Inequality in Egypt, in Pfierer, Karen (ed.), *Research in Middle East Economics*, Volume II, Stamford, CT, JAI Press.

Centre for International and Regional Studies (CIRS) (2012). Food Security and Food Sovereignty in the Middle East, Georgetown University, School of Foreign Services Qatar, Working Group Summary Report, No.6.

Chang, Ha-Joon (2002). Kicking Away the Ladder, *Post-Autistic Economics Review*, no.15, September 4.

Colman, David, and Nixon, Frederick (1986/1989). *Economics of Change in Less Developed Countries*, London, Philip Allan.

Deutsche Bank (2013). Two Years of Arab Spring: Where are We Now? What's Next? *Current Issues Emerging Markets*, January 25.

El-Naggar, Said (ed.) (1987). *Adjustment Policies and Development Strategies in the Arab World*, Washington, D.C., IMF.

El-Said, Hamed, and Barrett, Richard (2011). Radicalization and Extremism that Lead to Terrorism, in Harrigan, Jane and El-Said, Hamed (eds). (2011). *Globalisation, Democratisation and Radicalisation in the Arab World*, London, Palgrave-Macmillan, 199–235.

El-Said, Hamed and Harrigan, Jane (2006). Globalisation, International Finance and Political Islam in the Middle East and North Africa, *Middle East Journal*, 60(3), 236–51.

El-Said, Hamed and Harrigan, Jane (2014). Economic Reform, Social Welfare, and Instability: Jordan, Egypt, Morocco, and Tunisia, 1983–1984, *Middle East Journal*, 68(1), 99–121.

Ferraro, Vincent (2008). Dependency Theory: An Introduction, in *The Development Economics Reader*, ed. Giorgio Secondi, London, Routledge, 58–64.

Gaddafi, Moammar (2013). *The Green Book: the Solution of the Problem of Democracy*, online English translation: http://www.mathaba.net/gci/theory/gb1.htm.

Gammeltoft, Peter (2002). Remittances and Other Financial Flows to Developing Countries, *International Migration*, 40(5), 180–211.

Harrigan, Jane, Wang, Chengang and El-Said, Hamed (2006). The Economic and Political Determinants of IMF and World Bank Lending in the Middle East and North Africa, *World Development*, 34(2), 247–70.

Harrigan, Jane and El-Said, Hamed (2009a). *Aid and Power: the IMF and World Bank Policy Lending in the Middle East and North Africa*, London, Palgrave.

Harrigan, Jane and El-Said, Hamed (2009b). *Economic Liberalization, Islamic Social Capital and Social Welfare Provision*, London, Palgrave.

Harrigan, Jane (2011). The Political Economy of Aid Flows to North Africa, World Institute for Development, United Nations University, Working Paper No. 2011/72, November.

Hashemi, Nader (2013). The Arab Spring Two Years On: Reflection on Dignity, Democracy, and Devotion, *Ethics International Affairs*, May 13.

Hayashi, Takeshi (2007). On Arab Socialism, in the Developing Economies, Online Library, 2(1), 78–90. http://onlinelibrary.wiley.com/doi/10.1111/j.1746–1049.1964.tb00671.x/pdf.

Hourani, Albert (1991). *A History of the Arab People*, New York, Warner Books.

IMF (2010). Sudan: Article IV Consultation – Staff Report; Debt Sustainability Analysis; Staff Statement; Statement by the Executive Director, MF Country Report No. 10/256.

Iqbal, Farrukh (2006). Sustaining Gains in Poverty Reduction and Human Development in the Middle East and North Africa, World Bank, Washington, DC.

Islamic Economics (2013). What is Islamic Economics? April 17, http://islamiceconomy.net/what-is-islamic-economics.

Kadri, Ali (2012). Revisiting Arab Socialism, MEI/NUS. http://werdiscussion.worldeconomicsassociation. org/wp-content/uploads/Arab_socialism_version_one_.pdf.

Keynes, J.M. (1936). *The General Theory of Employment, Interest and Money*, Cambridge, Cambridge University Press.

King, Stephen (2009). *The New Authoritarianism in the Middle East and North Africa*, Indiana, Indiana University Press.

Knell, Yolande (2013). The complicated legacy of Egypt's Hosni Mubarak, BBC News, 5 January. http://www.bbc.co.uk/news/world-middle-east-21201364?print=true.

Korayem, Karima (1998). Causes of Poverty in the Arab Countries: An Economic Perspective, in Poverty and Social Exclusion in the Mediterranean Area, the Comparative Research Programme on Poverty (CROP), Bergen, Norway.

Library of Congress (2006). Country Profile: Morocco, Federal Research Division, May.

Lofgren, Hans and Richards, Alan (2011). Food Security, Poverty, and Economic Policy in the Middle East and North Africa, TMD Discussion Paper, No. 111.

Lubeck, P.M. (1998), Islamist Response to Globalization: Cultural Conflict in Egypt, Algeria, and Malaysia, in *The Myth of Ethnic Conflict, Economics and Cultural Violence*. Berkeley: University of California Press, 293–319.

Manar, Mohammad (2013). The Justice and Development Party's Experience of Governance in Morocco, Arab Centre for Research and Policy Studies, September 3.

Messkoub, Mahmood (2008). *Economic Growth, Employment and Poverty in the Middle East and North Africa*, Geneva, ILO.

Middle East Online (2012). Assessing the Mood on the Arab Street, August.

Mosely, Paul, Harrigan, Jane, and Toye, John (1991). *Aid and Power: the World Bank Policy-based Lending*, London, Routledge, Volume 1.

Osman, Osman M. (1997). Development and National Poverty Reduction Strategies in Egypt. Case study presented at the Second Workshop on 'Knowledge Networking on Poverty Reduction', UNDP, New York, 11–12 September 1997.

Owen, Roger (1992). *State, Power and Politics in the Making of the Middle East*, London, Routledge.

Pfiefer, Karen (1999). Parameters of Economic Reform in NA, *Review of African Political Economy*, no.82, 441–54.

Ravid, Barak (2011). Netanyahu: Arab Spring Pushing Mideast East Backward, Not Forward, *Haaretz*, November 24.

Richards, Allan and Waterbury, John (1996). *A Political Economy of the Middle East*, London, WestPress.

Saleh, Mohamed (2013). IMF may have required Islamic Sukuk, *Daily News Egypt*, January 16.

Skousen, Mark (2009). *The Making of Modern Economics*, New York, M.E. Sharp Inc.

Smith, Tony (1975). The Political and Economic Ambitions of Algerian Land Reform, 1962–74, *MEJ*, 29(3).

Stiglitz, Joseph (2002). *Globalization and its Discontents*, London, Penguin Press.

Teal, Francis (1995). Does 'Getting Prices Right' Work? Micro Evidence from Ghana, Centre for the Study of African Economies, Institute of Economics and Statistics, University of Oxford, WPS/95–19.

The Economist (1999). A survey of Egypt: The IMF's model pupil, March 18.

The Economist (2006). Sir Hans Singer, development economist, died on February 26th, aged 95, March 9.

The Economist (2011). Influential Africans: They might be giants, June 7.

Todaro, Michael (1989). *Economic Development in the Third World*, New York, Longman.

United Nations (UN) (2009). Arab Human Development Report 2009, Challenges to Human Security in the Arab Countries, Geneva.

UNDP (2011). Response Strategy and Framework of Action: Towards an Inclusive Development Path Within a New Arab Social Contract Between State and Citizen, New York, UNDG.

UNDP (2012). Rethinking Economic Growth: Towards Productive and Inclusive Arab Societies, New York, UNDG.

WHO (2014). Washington Consensus http://www.who.int/trade/glossary/story094/en/.

Williamson, John (2004). A Short History of the Washington Consensus, Paper commissioned by Fundación CIDOB for a conference 'From the Washington Consensus towards a new Global Governance', Barcelona, September 24–25.

Part IV

Africa

22

West Africa

Gareth Austin and Gerardo Serra

Much has been written on economic values and attitudes in West Africa, from pre-colonial times to the present, as well as on the importance of Africa as a 'testing ground' and site of discovery in the history of economic theory and the social sciences (Collier, 1993; Rimmer, 2000; Sichone, 2003). Yet, West Africans' contributions to economic thought have been neglected. This chapter offers, to the best of our knowledge, the first long-run historical overview. We understand 'economic thought' broadly, to include not only the analytic outlook associated with professional economists (who in West Africa emerged as a distinguishable group only in the terminal phase of colonial domination), but also expressions of what Joseph Schumpeter called 'economic vision', in which the understanding of economic reality is explicitly shaped by 'pre-analytic' moral or political considerations. It is worth noting, at the outset, that the works of Adam Smith and David Ricardo have not been translated into West African languages, and their direct reception by West African writers appears to have been mainly by professional economists.

Economic culture and policies in the pre-colonial nineteenth century

Considering that the supply of cultivable land was rarely a constraint on the expansion of production, the extent of the social and economic commitment to the market in fifteenth- to nineteenth-century West Africa was remarkably high. It went beyond absolute advantage, which was illustrated by the salt trade, from desert and coast sites to areas that could not produce it, to include comparative advantage and consumer taste, notably in cotton textiles. Over much of the region, ethnic-cum-religious diasporas, usually Muslim, organised trade across political and cultural boundaries. Judging from an 1881 dictionary, the Akan language, spoken in much of the forest zone of what is now Ghana, included words for a range of economic concepts, including *dwetiri*, 'a capital or stock of money to begin trade with; a fund employed in business or any undertaking' (Hill, 1963, 215, quoting Christaller, 1881).

Some scholars have emphasised a mercantilist tendency in late pre-colonial kingdoms. In the case of the Asante kingdom (centred in the northern part of the forest zone of what is now Ghana), Ivor Wilks went further, proposing parallels with the policies of the first president of independent Ghana, Kwame Nkrumah. One was a sustained attempt during the nineteenth century (before British occupation in 1896) to avert the growth of a private merchant class autonomous from the state. Another was the attempts of Asante rulers in the 1880s and early 1890s, facing British imperialism, to promote economic development through state intervention. Uniting both parallels was a third: a willingness to allow a major role to foreign enterprise, whether African Muslims or Europeans, rather than promote the indigenous private sector (Wilks, 1989, 684–6, 720–3). A revisionist analysis disputes the view of the Asante state as repressing domestic private enterprise, except briefly under Asantehene Mensa Bonsu, whose heavy taxation provoked the revolution that overthrew him in 1883 (Austin, 1996). Meanwhile the Sokoto Caliphate, the largest state of nineteenth-century West Africa, generally encouraged private enterprise, which flourished in textile production and long-distance trade, assisted by generally low taxes on these sectors, especially in the central emirates (Lovejoy, 2006).

In Asante, the achievement of self-made wealth was lauded with official celebrations and honours: on condition that the newly rich shared his wealth with the state (Wilks, 1993). In 1894, Asante exiles, in British territory, proclaimed an ideology of self-made wealth in two tracts, attacking the tax and death duties of the 'thief Kings' of Asante, and welcoming the prospect of unhindered *laissez-faire* following what they hoped would be the imposition of British control. They proclaimed 'In this vast country, Gold alone is King. If any get that wealth he is King. We are all free aborigines of this country' (quoted in Wilks, 1993, 180–1).

The evidence about attitudes to wealth in the animist cultures of the forest societies hardly suggests respect for the poor. But that position did not always go unchallenged, at least within West Africa as a whole. A notable example comes from the mainly Muslim societies of the interior savanna. Early in the colonial period, c.1923, al-Hājj 'Umar of Kano (commercial centre of the former Sokoto Caliphate), Salaga and Kete-Krachi (in northern Ghana) wrote a long, powerful poem in Hausa, *Talauci* ('Poverty') (translated by I.A. Tahir, 1969: published in Goody, 1982: 194–203). With excruciating precision, ranging over sex, food and perceptions of wisdom and honesty, 'Umar satirised the hypocrisy of elite and popular worship of wealth and contempt for poverty. Certain verses were even theologically provocative: 'None but God loves the poor man./ He who created him in his dire condition' (Goody, 1982, 198).

Pan-African and nationalist economic thought during the colonial era

In colonial West Africa, land remained overwhelmingly under African control and occupation. In the case of the large British colonies, Nigeria and what is now Ghana, this was to a great extent the result of African success in export agriculture, out-competing European planters in Ghana and rendering European plantations against the interest of colonial treasuries and British merchants. The effect was to permit greater opportunities for African enterprise in farming and trade than in the settler and plantation colonies characteristic of southern and central Africa. This context was a premise of the writings we discuss in this section. Given limited space, we concentrate here on three authors: Edward Wilmot Blyden (Liberia, 1832–1912), Winfried Tete-Ansah (Ghana, 1889–1941) and Nnamdi Azikiwe (Nigeria, 1904–96). Among these, Tete-Ansah published least, being primarily a businessman: and even his writing, though framed in general African terms, was geared to advertising his companies and encouraging investment in them. Blyden and especially Azikiwe were politicians as well as writers. Tete-Ansah's concern was entirely with commerce; for the others, economic arguments were just part of broader visions. All of them had interesting ideas on the economic future of Africa. For all three, perhaps the fundamental issue was African destiny in a world dominated by the West. Was the best response to assert and maintain the distinctiveness of African civilization, or to adopt Western methods in the hope of emulating Western material achievements? In this context, what should Africans expect from the African diaspora in the Americas: comradeship in difference, or partnership in playing the whites at their own game?

The West Indies-born Blyden landed in Liberia, from the USA, at the age of eighteen and became a politician in the African-American dominated republic, the only part of West Africa to escape European rule. A leading advocate of the return of African-Americans to Africa, his conception of African culture could hardly be more different from that of the Asante dissidents quoted above. In *African Life and Customs* (Blyden, 1908a) he characterised 'the African system' as 'socialistic and co-operative', based on 'collective ownership by the tribe of all the land and water' (Blyden, 1908a, extracted in Lynch, 1971, 167). He added 'The property laws of Africa in intention and in practice make for the widest distribution of wealth or well-being and work steadily against concentrating the wealth of a community, either of land or production in the hands of a comparatively small number of individuals' (Blyden, 1908a, extracted in Lynch, 1971, 170). Blyden, along with others among the westernized West African elite of the late nineteenth century, had called upon Britain to establish a protectorate over much of West Africa, as a means of stimulating Africans onto the world stage (Lynch, 1971, 315). Writing deep in the colonial era, Tete-Ansah gave much of the space in *Africa at Work* (Tete-Ansá, 1930), his only book, slim and self-published, to reproducing statements by liberal colonial officials. This was apparently in the hope of assuring African-American readers that West Africa was indeed making material progress. Like Blyden, he called upon diasporic Africans to come to the help of what he called 'the Race' as a whole: but not through socialism but by joint action for self-enrichment; by investing their capital in Africa, rather than necessarily coming to live there in large numbers (Tete-Ansá, 1930). For Blyden (whose position was described by Craufurd Goodwin (1967, 443) as 'the pinnacle of African institutionalism'), 'the political economy of the white man is not our political economy, his moral philosophy is not our moral philosophy; and far less is his theology; and wherever he has been successful in forcing these upon us there has been atrophy and death' (Blyden, 1908b, extracted in Lynch, 1971, 122). Blyden's struggle for an authentically African political economy, his appeal to (a version of) the pre-colonial past and his plea for Pan-Africanism anticipated important tendencies of the postcolonial era.

In contrast, Tete-Ansah seems not to have doubted that whites and blacks shared the same political economy. But, whereas the Asante exiles thought an absence of taxation would be sufficient for hard-working individuals to prosper, Tete-Ansah recognised the problem of European monopolies. He accused 'foreign corporations, mostly European' of 'attempting to monopolize the marketing by creating a vicious barrier between the producers and the consumers abroad through organized systems of banking and trading which practically deny those facilities required in an international exchange of commodities' (Tete-Ansá, 1930, 63). In colonial Ghana cocoa brokers and farmers thought so too, countering the formation of successive European cocoa-buying cartels with organised 'hold-ups' of their exports and boycotts of imports. Tete-Ansah's contribution was to make and act on the case for African adoption of European business forms, notably limited liability companies and banks (Hopkins, 1966). In contrast to Blyden, Tete-Ansah firmly believed that Western forms of economic organization should be adopted by Africans. European monopolists should be challenged by 'mutual organization' among Africans and, he earnestly hoped, African-Americans (Tete-Ansá, 1930, 63). He himself founded three limited liability companies, most notably the Industrial and Commercial Bank Limited, which he based in Nigeria. All, however, foundered sooner rather than later: the bank did so in 1930, the same year as his book appeared (Hopkins, 1966).

Azikiwe, too, was willing to criticise African economic practices in comparison to Western ones. He was especially harsh on what he described as the preference of African businessmen for working alone, rather than pooling financial resources. One-man businesses 'will work out temporarily, but [a] time will come when that one man will face problems which require many heads to solve' (Azikiwe, 1937/1968, 132). 'Because of this' single-handedness, and in contrast to European firms, 'the average African business liquidates with the death of the owner' (Azikiwe, 1937/1968, 133). Putting his words into practice, Azikiwe himself joined the Nigerian indigenous banking movement in the 1940s, buying what eventually became the African Continental Bank. In 1954 he formed the first elected regional government in Eastern Nigeria. Meanwhile the bank was struggling to meet stringent regulations imposed by the 1952 Banking Ordinance in Nigeria. Controversy arose when his government injected funds into the bank: though he had disclosed his interests and resigned from its management, he remained the major shareholder. Both his career and the bank survived, he becoming the first president of Nigeria (1963–66), while the bank was one of only three of the more than twenty indigenous banks founded in the colonial period in Nigeria to survive the early decades of independence.

Leaders at independence: Kwame Nkrumah and his contemporaries

Between 1957 and 1960 most of West Africa moved from the periphery of European empires to sovereign statehood. Nationalist leaders who, during the struggle for decolonization, had learnt the importance of ideas as a weapon of political struggle (Falola, 2001, 27) were now actually responsible for the economic and social welfare of their populations as heads of state. Most of them shared a commitment to economic modernization, a usually hostile attitude towards indigenous business, and the assumption, quite common at the time – especially in Francophone writing (Hugon, 1993), but far from exclusively so – that the state had to play an active role in promoting economic development. Yet, given the ideological context of the Cold War, it is possible to draw a line between more 'socialist' and more 'market oriented' governments. Leading examples of the former were Kwame Nkrumah's regime in Ghana, especially from 1961, Ahmed Sékou Touré's in Guinea and Modibo Keita's in Mali; while the latter approach was championed by Felix Houphouët-Boigny in Ivory Coast. An intermediate, if not openly ambiguous, position was occupied by Leopold Sedar Senghor's Senegal. While Houphouët-Boigny (1905–93), who ruled Ivory Coast from independence in 1959 until 1990, thought that a qualified economic liberalism was the appropriate model for the development of his country, Senghor (1906–2001), a distinguished poet and intellectual, provided a highly original inter-pretation of African socialism: 'the object of socialism is not the economy, as too many Marxists now believe, but concrete, living man, in his totality, body and soul' (Senghor, 1964: 108). Senghor's humanism, based on the concept of *Négritude*, was aimed principally at developing a distinctive African epistemology that could embody an alternative to both Western individualism and scientific rationalism. Though these themes recur in the work of postcolonial African philosophers, Senghor's ideas never shaped significantly the thought of economists and economic reformers.

Ultimately it was Kwame Nkrumah (1909–72) who emerged from the first generation of postcolonial West African politicians as the most systematic and influential writer on economic matters, anticipating many insights that would characterise the work of radical African scholars in later decades. Nkrumah's economic thought, which developed as a blend of socialism and Pan-Africanism, was largely based on Lenin's theory of imperialism (Lenin, 1917/1947). Although Lenin referred to the Scramble for Africa, and noted that 'capitalism's transition to the phase of monopoly capitalism, to finance capital is bound up with the intensification of the struggle for the partition of the world' (Lenin, 1917/1947, 131), his treatment of imperialism was mostly concerned with the concentration and spread of industrial and financial capital in the West. In contrast, Nkrumah identified in the Scramble for Africa and European colonization not only a necessary stage of the evolution of capitalism, but the prime cause of Africa's contemporary underdevelopment. In his view the gap between political independence and economic dependence (noted by Lenin, 1917/1947, 144–6), with reference to Argentina's and Portugal's reliance on British capital) was the main feature of the stage in the history of global capitalism experienced by post-colonial Africa, that of 'neo-colonialism'. The essence of neo-colonialism was that 'The State which is subjected to it is, in theory, independent . . . In reality its economic system and thus its political policy is directed from outside' (Nkrumah, 1965/1970, ix). The 'subtle and varied' (Nkrumah, 1965/1970, 239) means through which neo-colonialist agents (including former colonial powers, international organizations and multinational corporations) imposed their will on African states included the manipulation of primary product prices in international markets, the use of high interest rates, multilateral aid, and such tools of cultural policy as evangelism and American cinema (Nkrumah, 1965/1970, 239–54).

Although an ardent Pan-Africanist, Nkrumah's vision had little to do with the African-American diaspora discussed by Blyden, representing instead an attempt to achieve fuller political and economic integration on African soil for African benefit. According to Nkrumah, the most effective way for Africa to regain its economic and political freedom was the formation of a socialist African continental political union, which could plan its development 'centrally and scientifically through a pattern of economic integration' (Nkrumah, 1963/1970, 170). Meanwhile Nkrumah rejected the Tete-Ansah project of economic development led by African private enterprise. While he was willing to work with foreign companies bringing large-scale capital and industrial technology, his view of the economy had little place for indigenous capitalists (Nkrumah, 1961/1997). Following his overthrow in 1966, Nkrumah spent the last years of his life in exile, as honorary vice-president in Sékou Toure's Guinea. During these years his ideas showed a marked radicalization, adopting class struggle as a key analytical concept (Nkrumah, 1970/1999). Thus embracing more closely the tenets of orthodox Marxism, rather than his own version of 'African socialism', he now called for armed struggle against neo-colonialism.

Development/professionalisation of economics in West Africa

Development economics emerged in the 1940s as a specialised branch of economic science studying growth, inequality, poverty and institutions in the economies of Asia, Africa and Latin America. Downplaying the neoclassical obsession with allocative efficiency, and appealing instead to the lessons of the great classical political economists on capital accumulation, technical progress and distribution in the long-run, by the time of West African independence the new sub-discipline had reached a consensus on several key points, such as the importance of capital formation as a growth engine, the need to adopt import substitution strategies and the general need for the state to plan development in order to promote industrialization. The fulfilment of these ambitious goals was thought to depend on the availability of technocratic experts who could analyse real economies and modify them according to human design: economics had come to increasingly resemble a form of social engineering. Regardless of their position on the socialism-capitalism continuum, the new African nations needed indigenous elites of academics and civil servants trained in economics and statistics. From the 1940s on, many influential economic ideas in West Africa came from professional economists.

The professionalisation of economics can be understood in an institutional constellation comprising universities, professional associations, academic journals and policy-making bodies.

The University College of the Gold Coast (later University of Ghana) established the first Department of Economics in West Africa in 1948, followed by the University College of Ibadan in 1957. Francophone colonies took longer to establish universities, as the tendency lingered for African students to complete their education in France. The creation of economics departments in West African universities led to the constitution of professional associations and the foundation of academic journals like *The Economic Bulletin of Ghana* (*EBG*) and *The Nigerian Journal of Economic and Social Studies* (*NJESS*).

Admittedly, foreign economists continued to be important in West African policy-making. Perhaps most notably, W. Arthur Lewis served as Ghana's Chief Economic Advisor in 1957–8, and Nicholas Kaldor was the architect of Ghanaian fiscal reform in 1961. The striking adherence of economic policies implemented under Nkrumah between 1960 and 1966 to the prescriptions of the first generation of development economists led Tony Killick (2010) to define Ghana a case of 'development economics in action'. The preparation of the first development plan in independent Nigeria fell on the shoulders of Austrian Wolfgang Stolper. Meanwhile Mali and Guinea relied on the expertise of imported Marxists: the Egyptian Samir Amin and the Frenchman Jean Bernard in the case of Mali, and the Frenchman Charles Bettelheim in the case of Guinea. But West African economists were increasingly involved in the tasks of policy-making and nation-building, and started staffing what in the West African context were fairly recent institutions like central banks, planning commissions and statistical offices. For example, Sierra Leonean economist David Carney (b. 1925) authored in 1962 the first postcolonial development plan for his country. Jonathan Frimpong-Ansah (1930–99) started working in the Ghanaian Office of the Government Statistician and then served as Deputy Governor or Governor of the Bank of Ghana under four regimes until 1973.

In postcolonial Nigeria the advice of indigenous economists was increasingly sought by the government for issues as different as tax reform, wage and income policy, financial regulation, and land policy (Tomori, 1979, 44–9). The career of Nigerian Pius Okigbo (1924–2000) embodies the nexus of technical expertise and political skills which came to characterise many influential West African economists: the first African to receive a PhD from North-Western University, Okigbo became also the first Nigerian ambassador to the European Economic Community and, during the Nigerian civil war (1967–70), the first economic advisor to the short-lived Republic of Biafra, as well as chairman of the Federal Planning Committee of Nigeria, chairman of the UN Panel of Experts of the African Development Bank, and member of the UN Conference on Trade and Development (on the life and work of Okigbo, see Guyer and Denzer, 2005). Yet development policy was now also a supranational enterprise with the World Bank, the International Monetary Fund and the United Nations. The UN Economic Commission for Africa, created in 1958, became an important institutional platform used by West African economists to discuss and implement policies of economic integration. A striking example is Nigerian Adebayo Adedeji (b. 1930) who, after serving the Nigerian government for several years, became in 1975 the Executive Commissioner of the Commission. Another important example is the UN African Institute for Economic Development and Planning, located in Dakar (Senegal), whose directors have included Senegalese Mamadou Toure (1964–7) and Gambian Jeggan Senghor (1990–9).

While West Africa provided the setting for much influential research in development (classic works include Bauer (1954) on trade and marketing boards, Hill (1963) on cocoa farmers and indigenous capitalism in Ghana, and Hart's (1973) notion of the 'informal economy') West African economists in the 1960s attached primary importance to empirical work rather than the construction of theoretical models. In his 1962 presidential address to the Nigerian Economic Society, J. Amadi-Edina (1962, 3) urged Nigerian economists to 'Spend little time in theorizing

. . . [and] engage more in fact finding . . . spend less time in abstractions, more in observation, less time in analysis and model making'. Indeed, many articles published in *EBG* and *NJESS* in the 1960s tackled problems of specific economic and social statistics, provided new estimates, and presented suggestions on how to improve the effectiveness of planning machinery (see for example Aboyade, 1965 on Nigeria and Omaboe, 1963 on Ghana). The collection of economic data was not simply an intellectual exercise: better data were considered vital to successful development planning. Despite their diversity, development plans shared a pivotal political significance in the eyes of African policymakers as representations of national sovereignty and rationality.

Despite its apparent lack of theoretical ambition, the collection of useful and reliable information about African economies required in many cases a partial re-conceptualization of the categories adopted in industrialized countries. Thus one of the main contributions of West African economists in the 1960s was to provide a more solid basis for policy by their work at the intersection of local realities and imported templates. An important part of this task was assessing the limits of existing information, and introducing more useful distinctions and more realistic assumptions in the conceptual frameworks inherited from colonial regimes or the new international organizations. Okigbo, for example, under the auspices of the Federal Ministry of Economic Development, published in 1962 a lengthy study of Nigerian national accounts which, drawing on a large number of government sources and introducing useful conceptual distinctions, marked an improvement over Prest and Stewart's (1953) 'colonial' study of Nigerian national income in 1950–1 (Okigbo, 1962).

This empirical focus does not imply that economists were not questioning once again the utility of 'Western' doctrines for economic analysis and policy in West Africa. In his presidential address to the Economic Society of Ghana, J.H. Mensah, a LSE-trained Ghanaian economist and the main author of the seven-year plan intended to transform Ghana into a socialist economy under Nkrumah (and which was abruptly abandoned following the 1966 coup), discussed the relevance of Marxian economics for Ghana's development. Mensah noted that Marxism emerged as a system of thought to explain economic evolution in the West, and argued that the notion of class struggle was useless in the African context because a 'country like Ghana cannot afford the luxury of not utilising some of its available trained manpower' (Mensah, 1965, 15). Thus socialist thought 'ought to move from the concept of class conflict and increasingly emphasise the concept of nation building through the joint efforts of all citizens' (ibid.). Certainly the relationships between rulers and African top planners were often far from simple. Mensah, who was accused by Nkrumah of lacking ideological purity and invited to put his commitment to socialism into writing (Tignor, 2006, 185), was also imprisoned from 1975 until 1978 by the military government of I.K. Acheampong, while Okigbo was jailed for eighteen months for his role in the secessionist project of the Republic of Biafra. Yet, the work of the first generation of West African economists could not be easily disentangled from the tasks of nation-building and modernization which, regardless of ideological differences, loomed large and accounted for most economic research.

On the other hand, professionalisation and research in post-colonial West African economics were accompanied by the development of 'local' intellectual traditions. In the case of Nigeria, for example, the so-called 'Ibadan School' from the 1960s through the 1980s developed a distinctive approach to public finance. Given the vast size of Nigeria and the fierce struggles over the federal structure and the distribution of public revenues, it is not surprising that economic research was shaped significantly by problems of taxation and redistribution among different levels of government. While holding different beliefs on many important issues, the Ibadan school was united by the extensive use of calculation and statistical evidence to construct new tools and operational concepts to understand and improve the complex reality of Nigerian fiscal machinery (Adebayo, 1990, 245–6).

The articles published in the *NJESS* in the 1970s and early 1980s reveal that the Ibadan school were part of a broader tendency in West African economics to increasingly employ quantitative methods. While West African economists in the 1960s were discussing the quality of official statistics, in the following decades 'numbers' were increasingly accepted and used in a number of articles using tools derived from econometric analysis and linear programming. In the *NJESS* the proportion of articles using statistical methods increased from 25 per cent in 1962–70 to 42 per cent in 1971–6. Similarly, papers using mathematical methods increased from 17 per cent in the 1960s to 35 per cent in 1971–6 (calculations based on Adamu, 1979, 86). It is possible that West Africans' progressive embrace of quantitative analysis was related to the worsening conditions experienced by many local universities. Indeed from the 1970s, and even more so in the 1980s, 'migration' became the context of much African academic writing in the social sciences (Falola, 2001, 287). In particular, an increasing number of scholars migrated to the United States. Apparently the first multi-probit model published in *NJESS* was from a PhD thesis submitted by the author at Cornell University (Falusi, 1974, 3).

Intellectual change from Left and Right, 1970s/early 1980s

The 1970s and early 1980s marked a difficult phase in the economic and political history of much of West Africa: statist policies did not bring the expected transformation, and by the late 1970s most of West Africa – Ivory Coast was a spectacular exception – was facing stagnant or negative growth. Meanwhile many West African countries were plagued by military coups. This situation led to a divide in development thinking, with the strengthening of Marxist-inspired scholarship and dependency theories on one hand, and the rise of a new free market consensus, based on neoclassical economics, on the other hand. While they differed on both diagnosis and cure, radical political economy and free market economics shared, in stark contrast with much research published in the 1960s, a deep sense of pessimism about the capacity of African nation-states to promote economic development. These positions also shared an adherence to what Albert Hirschman (1981, 3, 14–19) called 'the mono-economics claim': namely that, in contrast with many accounts from the 1950s and 1960s, there was one body of economic theory (whether neoclassical or Marxist) that had universal applicability, and thus did not require significant modifications before it could be applied to developing countries.

The disappointments of 'statist' development policies were felt on both sides of the political spectrum. On the left, 'dependency theory' arrived on African campuses mainly in the form of Walter Rodney's *How Europe Underdeveloped Africa* (1972), followed by the numerous publications of the Senegal-based Egyptian writer Samir Amin (for example Amin, 1973). Following broadly in the tradition of Andre Gunder Frank and other Latin American 'dependentistas', Rodney and Amin argued, with particular reference to Africa, that the development of the West and the 'underdevelopment of the Rest' were necessarily the same historical process, which continued today in the form of neo-colonialism. In their view, the socialism of early-independence governments had been too limited to make the decisive break with the world capitalist system that Africa needed.

These ideas found a strong echo in the work of West African political economists. The work of West African neo-Marxists was deeply entrenched in a dependency reading of history: imperialism, the notion at the centre of their approach, could not be understood as an abstract category, but only in its historical evolution (Onimode, 1982). Consequently, the failure of postcolonial African states to modernise was explained by the inheritance of the 'extractive features' characterising colonial economies, which in turn had been shaped by the expansion of capitalist production in the industrializing world (Ake, 1981, 88–9).

Furthermore, unlike the first generation of development economists, as well as African socialists like Nkrumah (up to 1966), Marxist writers of the 1970s and 1980s rejected many of the claims made about the 'exceptionalism' of developing countries: Nigerian Bade Onimode (1944–2001), for example, claimed that 'Class struggles have been an integral part of the process of economic development in Nigeria since the pre-capitalist era. Though the social classes are embryonic relative to the classical ones of Western Europe and North America', their development was 'clearly visible with respect to the usual criteria of Marxist class analysis' (Onimode, 1978, 507). To think otherwise meant to introduce 'bourgeois distortions' reflecting 'the unscientific methodology of imperialist social science' (ibid.). The acknowledgement of the global and historical nature of African underdevelopment called in turn for a radical solution: 'structural disengagement from the international capitalist system' (Onimode, 1982, 240).

Nearly a decade after Dependency theory, neoclassical economics emphatically reasserted itself in Africa through the 'policy door'. In Africa the 'counter-revolution in development theory and policy' (Toye, 1987) is usually dated to 1981, when the World Bank published *Accelerated Development in Sub-Saharan Africa: An Agenda for Action*, better known as the Berg Report. The report stated that the main cause of the political and economic crisis was the inconsiderate action of postcolonial governments. Protectionist policies, overvalued currencies, price and capital controls, and excessive state intervention in all aspects of social and economic life was what had turned ordinary price fluctuations into an economic tragedy. The solution was straightforward: the adoption of 'Structural Adjustment Policies' (SAPs hereafter), which replaced administrative allocation of resources with the price mechanisms through abolishing price controls, floating the currency, and cutting public expenditure. The overarching slogan was 'getting the prices right'.

For their part, a few West African economists produced works that resonated with a free market vision. Within Ghana, the intellectual case for general economic liberalization was hardly made in public at the time that the self-described 'revolutionary' government of J.J. Rawlings, confronted with a steadily falling GDP, reversed course by embarking on the progressive abandonment of price controls and the adoption of Structural Adjustment. The policy changes began to be implemented in 1983. A rare exception to the absence of a public argument for economic liberalization in advance of the event was the appearance in the early 1980s of occasional, usually anonymous, articles criticising aspects of the price and quantity controls in a small-circulation journal, *The Legon Observer*. This was published within the University of Ghana, many of whose scholars at the time were more associated with the Left.

Meanwhile a Ghanaian expatriate in North America, James Ahiakpor (b. 1945), an economist who had received his education in Ghana as well as Canada, was developing a scorching critique of dependency theories (Ahiakpor, 1985, 1986). If underdevelopment was in the interests of the West, queried Ahiakpor, why had foreign investment in Ghana been shrinking as the economy declined, whereas in Ivory Coast it was the other way around (Ahiakpor, 1986)? Ahiakpor claimed that the appeal of dependency theories to politicians in developing countries was partly because it did 'not require an understanding of neoclassical economic analysis', whose logic appeared counterintuitive, but was ultimately correct (Ahiakpor, 1985, 538). Neoclassical economics had less political appeal because it left 'the impression that development is a slow process, requiring difficult choices' (ibid.). Before Rawlings' about-turn, state-led development policies in Ghana, consistent with Dependency theory, had included currency overvaluation, price and capital controls and protectionism which 'severely reduced the incentives for production, savings, investment, and increased productivity' (Ahiakpor, 1985, 549). Another Ghanaian, Frimpong-Ansah (1991), incorporating ideas from rational-choice institutionalist political economy, presented the dismal performance of postcolonial Ghana as the cumulative outcome of policy decisions to satisfy the unproductive urban constituencies (bureaucracy, trade unions and the army) that, it hoped, would guarantee their political survival: as it did, until 1983 at least.

Against and beyond Structural Adjustment

Resistance to free market economics at the policy level was expressed in 1980, on what proved to be the eve of Structural Adjustment, in the ideas and suggestions contained in the Organization of African Unity (OAU)'s *Lagos Plan of Action for the Economic Development of Africa 1980–2000*. The Lagos plan, arguably 'the first continent-wide effort by Africans to forge a comprehensive unified approach to the economic development of their continent' (Asante, 1991, 60), largely reflected a development strategy designed by Nigerian economist Adebayo Adedeji. Although the Lagos Plan of Action echoed some of the radicals' concerns about the impact of neo-colonialist forces in holding back Africa's development (OAU, 1981/1982, 3), Adedeji was not a revolu-tionary calling for disentanglement from the capitalist world system, or advocating the formation of a socialist continental political union. Instead, rather like Raúl Prebisch when he was Executive Secretary of the Economic Commission for Latin America in 1950–63, Adedeji was expressing his scepticism about the benefits that developing countries could obtain by placing overwhelming emphasis on market mechanisms and engaging in free trade following the doctrine of comparative advantage (Asante, 1991, 51–5). The key pillars of the comprehensive strategy contained in the document, ranging from agriculture to environmental policy, were self-reliance in food and agricultural production, coordination through economic planning, the building of a stronger industrial base at both national and supra-national level, and the creation of an African common market (OAU, 1981/1982).

Despite the unanimous political support of African leaders, the Lagos Plan of Action was never implemented, with virtually the whole of West Africa agreeing over the following few years to adopt SAPs. The conflict between the World Bank's SAPs and OAU's Lagos Plan, and the former's victory, was a crucial confrontation of two developmental paradigms in the political arena, and a reminder of the extent to which the fate of economic doctrines is dependent on the institutional arrangements and power structures supporting them.

Reactions to SAPs and the neoclassical principles which underpinned them have inspired yet another stream of literature written by West African political economists. In contrast with the grand-unified historical narratives advanced by Marxist scholars, as well as the 'one policy fits all' approach advanced by the World Bank in the 1980s, economists like Nigerian Charles Soludo (b. 1960) stood up against what they saw as harmful reductionism. Indeed, claiming that economic development 'is quintessentially a political process' (Mkandawire and Soludo, 2003, 15), Soludo and the Malawian economist Thandika Mkandawire, argued that reform should have addressed 'a broad range of fundamentals: macro-economic stabilization funda-mentals; proactive, supplyside (production) fundamentals; and sociopolitical [sic] fundamentals' (Mkandawire and Soludo, 1999, 94). The work of these authors needs to be understood within the broader experience of the Dakar-based Council for the Development of Social Sciences Research In Africa (CODESRIA), founded in 1973. Through a wide range of educational and research activities (exemplified by their journal *Africa Development*), CODESRIA has tried to give voice to African scholars to countervail the dominance of institutions like the World Bank in matters of social science and development policy.

Putting indigenous culture and institutions to work

The mere contraposition of Marxism and free market economics hides the existence of other alternatives to free market economics, and (as we saw with the Ibadan School), the emergence of local traditions in post-colonial economics. The role of 'traditional' African culture in shaping economic behaviour fostered heated debates among Western social scientists in the decades following independence, but remained largely outside the work of most West African economists. In contrast with some early economic historiography which saw indigenous institutions as assisting economic development (Hill, 1963), West African economists shared with former colonial masters, nationalist leaders and Cold War partners the assumption, partly derived from modernization theory, that pre-colonial knowledge and institutions mostly represented an obstacle to economic progress.

Yet the perceived failure of imported development models, whether capitalist or socialist, has occasionally led West African economists to seek an authentically 'African' way to diagnose and cure the continent's economic and political malaise. Given the imposition of colonialism from Europe, it is not surprising that the source for the authentic voice of Africa had to be identified in the pre-colonial past, interpretations of which vary. Sometimes this implied a rediscovery of ethnicity: Okigbo stated that, given their distinctive values such as 'work ethic, enterprise, innovativeness in times of adversity . . . a dedication to fair competition and merit' there was 'ample room for the Igbo to bring to bear on the solution of Nigerian economic and political problems some unique contribution' (Okigbo, 1986/1993, 143). Far from being the 'modernizing' social engineers envisaged in the 1950s and 1960s, social scientists were, by virtue of their training, the best qualified to 'identify the decline in elemental values' (Okigbo, 1981/1987, 14) and correct it for the good of society at large.

A later contribution on the role of indigenous knowledge and institutions comes from the Ghanaian economist George Ayittey (b. 1945), who, like Ahiakpor, was trained partly at the University of Ghana and partly in Canada. Unlike many West African economists, Ayittey criticized SAPs from a free market perspective, maintaining that most SAPs amounted to 'reorganizing a bankrupt company and placing it – together with a massive infusion of capital – in the hands of the same incompetent managers who ruined it' (Ayittey, 1991, n.p.). Ayittey largely explains the failure of statist policies implemented from the 1960s on as the consequence of a perverse adoption of values which do not fit African indigenous tradition. In his view, in line more with the rhetoric of the Asante exiles of 1894 than with Blyden's diasporic nostalgia, pre-colonial institutions were the highest expression of an individualistic economy, where means of production were privately owned, the 'profit motive was present in most market trans-actions' and 'Free enterprise and free trade were the rule' (Ayittey, 2005, 350). The lessons of free-market pre-colonial Africa are not only limited to economic institutions, but could be extended to the political domain. In striking contrast with the postcolonial African experience, dominated by tyrants, generals and presidents for life, in Ayittey's account pre-colonial Africa offered examples of democratic institutions, where chiefs and elders could be 'destooled' by their subjects. The appeal to pre-colonial values does not conflict with support for Pan-African co-operation: an alliance of Pan-Africanism and indigenous wisdom, in contrast with Nkrumah's centralised socialist model, for instance, would lead to the adoption of a confederal system with a higher degree of decentralization of power (Ayittey, 2010, 100).

Conclusion

The quest for economic development, itself a historically complex notion, emerges from this overview as the core of the intellectual endeavours of West African economic thinkers in the long run. While this is to some extent true for most parts of the world, in the West African context the search for economic development was pursued in a distinctive fashion: as part of a struggle to define the identity of Africa vis-à-vis the West (affirming, denying or at least delimiting difference), as the expression of a will to expand the political boundaries imposed by circumstances under the ever-changing label of Pan-Africanism, and as an attempt to come to terms with the legacies of history. The past seems simultaneously to offer valid explanations for today's underdevelopment and recipes for the future: part of the differences among West African visions of the economic future are grounded in contrasting interpretations of pre-colonial history.

On the other hand the evolution of West African economic thought should be understood also as part of a global history: specifically, as another encounter in the intellectual and political battle over the proper roles of the state and the market. In West Africa, as elsewhere, economic analysis detached itself (or rather, some economists sought to detach it) from the surrounding moral and political issues, developing into a 'science' increasingly dominated by the practices of formal modelling and statistical testing. Yet, much further research is required in order to write a genuinely global history of economic thought, in which West Africa is more than a laboratory, no matter how 'living' (Tilley, 2011), for the West.

References

Aboyade, O. 1965. 'Problems in Plan Revision.' *NJESS* 7:2, 121–30.

Adamu, S.O. 1979. 'Quantitative Content of *The Nigerian Journal of Economic and Social Studies*.' *NJESS, Special Issue* 21: 1–3, 67–88.

Adebayo, A.G. 1990. 'The "Ibadan School" and the Handling of Public Finance in Nigeria.' *Journal of Modern African Studies* 28:2, 245–64.

Ahiakpor, James C. 1985. 'The Success and Failure of Dependency Theory: The Experience of Ghana.' *International Organization* 39:3, 535–52.

Ahiakpor, James C. 1986. 'The Profits of Foreign Firms in a Less Developed Country: Ghana.' *Journal of Development Economics* 22:2, 321–35.

Ake, Claude. 1981. *A Political Economy of Africa*. Harlow: Longman.

Amadi-Edina, J. 1962. 'Presidential Address.' *NJESS* 4:1, 1–6.

Amin, Samir. 1973. *Neo-Colonialism in West Africa*. New York: Monthly Review Press.

Asante, S.K.B. 1991. *African Development*. London: Hans Zell Publishers.

Austin, Gareth. 1996. '"No Elders were Present": Commoners and Private Ownership in Asante, 1807–96.' *Journal of African History* 37:1, 1–30.

Ayittey, George N.B. 1991. 'Why Structural Adjustment Failed in Africa.' *Trans Africa Forum* 8:2, 22 pages (no page numbers), accessed online.

Ayittey, George N.B. 2005. *Africa Unchained: The Blueprint for Africa's Future*. New York: Palgrave Macmillan.

Ayittey, George N.B. 2010. 'The United States of Africa: A Revisit.' *Annals of the American Academy of Political and Social Science* 632, 86–102.

Azikiwe, Nnamdi. 1937/1968. *Renascent Africa*. London: Frank Cass.

Bauer, P.T. 1954. *West African Trade*. Cambridge: Cambridge University Press.

Blyden, Edward Wilmot. 1908a. *African Life and Customs*. London.

Blyden, Edward Wilmot. 1908b. *'The Three Needs of Liberia'. Lecture delivered at Lower Buchanan, Grand Bassa County, Liberia, 26 March 1908*. London.

Christaller, J.G. 1881. *A Dictionary of the Asante and Fante Language called Tshi*. Basel: Basel Evangelical Missionary Society.

Collier, Paul. 1993. 'Africa and the Study of Economics.' In Bates, Robert H., V.Y. Mudimbe and Jean O'Barr (eds.) *Africa and the Disciplines*. Chicago: The University of Chicago Press, 58–82.

Falola, Toyin. 2001. *Nationalism and African Intellectuals*. Rochester: University of Rochester Press.

Falusi, Biodun. 1974. 'Multivariate Probit: Analysis of Selected Factors Influencing Fertilizer Adoption Among Farmers in Western Nigeria.' *NJESS* 16:1, 3–16.

Frimpong-Ansah, J.H. 1991. *The Vampire State in Africa: The Political Economy of Decline in Ghana*. London: James Currey.

Goodwin, Craufurd D. 1967. 'Economic Analysis and Development in British West Africa.' *Economic Development and Cultural Change* 15:4, 438–51.

Goody, Jack. 1982. *Cooking, Cuisine and Class*. Cambridge: Cambridge University Press.

Guyer, Jane I. and Denzer LaRay (eds). 2005. *Vision and Policy in Nigerian Economics*. Ibadan: University of Ibadan Press.

Hart, Keith. 1973. 'Informal Income Opportunities and Urban Employment in Ghana.' *Journal of Modern African Studies* 11:1, 61–89.

Hill, Polly. 1963. *The Migrant Cocoa Farmers of Southern Ghana*. Cambridge: Cambridge University Press.

Hirschman, Albert O. 1981. *Essays in Trespassing*. Cambridge: Cambridge University Press.

Hopkins, A.G. 1966. 'Economic Aspects of Political Movements in Nigeria and in the Gold Coast 1918–1939.' *Journal of African History* 7:1, 133–52.

Hugon, Philippe. 1993. 'Les trois temps de la pensée francophone en économie du développement.' In Choquet, C., O. Dollfus, E. Le Roy and M. Vernières (eds.) *État des savoirs sur le développement*. Paris: Karthala, 43–74.

Killick, Tony. 2010. *Development Economics in Action*. London: Routledge.

Lenin, V.I. 1917/1947. *Imperialism, The Highest Stage of Capitalism*. Moscow: Foreign Languages Publishing House.

Lovejoy, Paul E. 2006. *Slavery, Commerce and Production in the Sokoto Caliphate of West Africa*. Trenton: Africa World Press.

Lynch, Hollis R. 1971. *Black Spokesman: Selected Published Writings of Edward Wilmot Blyden*. London: Frank Cass.

Mensah, J.H. 1965. 'Presidential Address: The Relevance of Marxian Economics to Development Planning in Ghana.' *EBG* IX: 1, 3–15.

Mkandawire, Thandika and Charles C. Soludo. 1999. *Our Continent, Our Future*. Trenton: Africa World Press.

Mkandawire, Thandika and Charles C. Soludo. 2003. 'Introduction: Toward the Broadening of Development Policy Dialogue for Africa.' In their (eds.) *African Voices on Structural Adjustment. A Companion to Our Continent, Our Future*. Trenton: Africa World Press, 1–16.

Nkrumah, Kwame. 1961/1997. 'Dawn Broadcast: April 8, 1961'. *Selected Speeches of Kwame Nkrumah, Volume 2*, compiled by Samuel Obeng. Accra: Afram Publications, 58–66.

Nkrumah, Kwame. 1963/1970. *Africa Must Unite*. New York: International Publishers.

Nkrumah, Kwame. 1965/1970. *Neo-Colonialism: The Last Stage of Imperialism*. London: Heinemann.

Nkrumah, Kwame. 1970/1999. *Class Struggle in Africa*. London: Panaf.

Okigbo, P.N.C. 1962. *Nigerian National Accounts, 1950–1957*. Enugu: Federal Ministry of Economic Development.

Okigbo, P.N.C. 1981/1987. 'Social Analysis and the Crisis of Values.' In *Essays in the Public Philosophy of Development*, vol.1: Enugu: Fourth Dimension Publishing, 1–17.

Okigbo, P.N.C. 1986/1993. 'Toward a Reconstruction of the Political Economy of the Igbo Civilisation.' In *Essays in the Public Philosophy of Development*, vol.2: *Change and Crisis in the Management of the Nigerian Economy*. Enugu: Fourth Dimension Publishing, 119–48.

Omaboe, E.N. 1963. 'Some Observations on the Statistical Requirements of Development Planning in Less Developed Countries.' *EBG* VII: 2, 3–11.

Onimode, Bade. 1978. 'Economic Development and Class Struggle in Nigeria.' *NJESS* 20:3, 477–512.

Onimode, Bade. 1982. *Imperialism and Underdevelopment in Nigeria: The Dialectics of Mass Poverty*. London: Zed Books.

Organization of African Unity. 1981/1982. *Lagos Plan of Action for the Economic Development of Africa 1980–2000*. Geneva: International Institute for Labour Studies.

Prest, Alan Richmond and I.G. Stewart. 1953. *The National Income of Nigeria, 1950–1951*. London: Her Majesty's Stationery Office.

Rimmer, Douglas. 2000. 'African Development in Economic Thought.' In Rimmer, Douglas and Anthony Kirk-Greene (eds.) *The British Intellectual Engagement with Africa in the Twentieth Century*. London: Macmillan Press, 231–60.

Rodney, Walter. 1972. *How Europe Underdeveloped Africa*. London: Bogle-L'Overture.

Senghor, Leopold. 1964. *On African Socialism*. London: Pall Mall Press.

Sichone, Owen. 2003. 'The Social Sciences in Africa.' In Porter, Theodore M. and Dorothy Ross (eds.) *The Cambridge History of Science*, vol.VII. Cambridge: Cambridge University Press, 466–81.

Tete-Ansá, W. *Africa at Work*. 1930. New York: self-published.

Tignor, Robert H. 2006. *W. Arthur Lewis and the Birth of Development Economics*. Princeton: Princeton University Press.

Tilley, Helen. 2011. *Africa as a Living Laboratory*. Chicago: University of Chicago Press.

Tomori, Siyanbola. 1979. 'The Relevance of Economic Science to Nigeria's Economic Development.' *NJESS Special Issue*. 21:1–3, 33–56.

Toye, John. 1987. *Dilemmas of Development: Reflections on the Counter-Revolution in Development Theory and Policy*. Oxford: Basil Blackwell.

Wilks, Ivor. 1989. *Asante in the Nineteenth Century*. Cambridge: Cambridge University Press.

Wilks, Ivor. 1993. *Forests of Gold*. Athens, OH: Ohio University Press.

World Bank. 1981. *Accelerated Development in Sub-Saharan Africa: An Agenda for Action*. Washington: World Bank.

23

Southern Africa

Tidings P. Ndhlovu and Nene Ernest Khalema

The mercantile and colonial periods, including the post-1885 'Scramble for Africa', witnessed raging debates about whether European colonialists were agents of change who had a mission to civilise and modernise the 'Dark Continent'. Was colonial conquest and its economic intentions a means of showing superiority and humiliating Africans and their traditions (Falola, 2003)? Real or imagined, did the means for material ends, particularly in post-colonial southern Africa, lead to modifications of how people conceive their lived experiences, environments and lands? Did the 'exploitative' relationship between southern African countries and the colonizing powers alter the way the whole world saw Africa? Indeed, is dependency and 'underdevelopment' a legacy of imperialism?

To the extent that economic thought in southern Africa, particularly in Botswana, Zambia and South Africa, was shaped and re-shaped by the pre- and post-colonial system that was premised on class, race and gender divisions, we will trace how these developments were also influenced by changing political and social circumstances. Indeed, economic crises brought about upheaval in economic thinking at different historical periods. We outline contending views of indigenous economic thinking in the region. Post-colonial reaction and resistance to colonialism, which is anchored by what we frame as pre-colonial indigenous economic knowledge systems (IEKS) and practices, also gives us an insight into the development of economic thought in southern Africa.

Our argument is centred on the dynamics of development during what was in 1900 an overwhelmingly land-abundant region characterised by shortages of labour and capital, and by perhaps surprisingly extensive indigenous market activities. We argue that in reimagining economic thought in southern Africa, one must explain the muddle of social, political and economic nationalism, particularly as residuals of 'settler' and 'indigenous' economies persisted even after independence.

An overview of the long-term

The mercantilist period in the sixteenth to late eighteenth centuries was characterised by an insatiable thirst for acquiring territory to use as sources of cheap primary products and markets for manufactured goods. Arguably, the overriding belief was that restrictions in international trade, export subsidies and 'ring-fencing' (i.e. high tariffs and preventing acquired colonies from trading with colonies of rival imperialist countries) would enable merchants to accumulate wealth rapidly. The imposition of levies would help to sustain the mother country, ensuring that (high value) products such as sugar were then 're-exported' to 'client' colonies at a profit.

This is the context in which the Dutch people (latterly known as 'Afrikaners' or 'Boers'), for example, settled in South Africa in 1647 and 1652. To this end, the Dutch East India Company was involved in violent skirmishes with indigenous people for land, cattle and natural resources. The British colonialists did not arrive on the scene until the 1800s. After initial set-backs (such as the Battle of *Isandlwana* in 1879 in which the British were defeated by King Cetshwayo's Zulu army, and the protracted Boer Wars of 1880–1 and 1899–1902), the British, with their superior armoury, were finally able to subjugate both the indigenous people and the rival Dutch colonialists.

In pre-colonial Africa, farmers and peasants were producing for either their own use or to trade for other goods, though the concept of production for the others (i.e. foreign colonial masters) did not exist for them. Some authors (Gennaioli and Rainer, 2007; Heldring and Robinson, 2012, 2013) also contend that, before colonial expansion, politically centralised states such as the Tswana states in Botswana were shining examples of accountability of local chiefs to 'higher-level traditional authority'. Greater accountability in this hierarchical system is explicable from either pre-colonial states having been 'sociologically more advanced' to facilitate effective adoption of western technologies, or being able 'to organize politically and thus restrain abusive national leaders, fostering democracy' (Kittrell, 1973). Furthermore:

> In colonies of white settlement [such as the self-governing dominion of South Africa] the most important factor was that the highly extractive nature of colonial rule and land grabs manifested themselves . . . in quite serious immiseration of Africans during the colonial period. The evolution of the international dissemination and diffusion of technology plus the relative absence of slavery in this part of Africa makes it likely that, absent colonialism [*sic*], African living standards would have slowly improved.
>
> *(Heldring and Robinson, 2013, 2)*

However, similarly to Ferguson (2003) – who contends that, if there had been no British Empire (an essentially 'good' empire despite the racism, cruelty, snobbery and authoritarianism), then the situation would have been markedly worse under less scrupulous Spanish or German empires – counterfactuals are not easy to prove. How did classical economists conceptualise these earlier colonial 'invasions'? The ending of slavery, which was followed by the adoption of a free trade policy (1846), and the abolition of Navigation Acts (1849) and preferential customs, weakened mercantilist arguments. Protectionist ideas were denounced by classical economists and Evangelicals on economic (taxing trade and licensing monopolies) and moral grounds (a sense of 'unfairness').

Adam Smith's *laissez-faire* ideas were intended to address this so-called 'distorted and inefficient allocation of national resources' (Lorrain, 1991, 226) and perceived 'sense of unfairness'. Kittrell (1973, 88) notes that, for Smith, 'emigrants carry with them to the colonies superior knowledge of agriculture and of the useful arts, and the cultural attributes favourable to stable government. When this is combined with the colonial land that is cheap and plentiful, where there is no rents and taxes are nil, accumulation will progress rapidly'. However, it must be noted that, unlike other classical political economists (Malthus, Say, James Mill, J.S. Mill), Smith did not subscribe to the thesis of the 'civilising role/mission' of colonialism (Lorrain, 1991, 227–9; Backhouse, 1985).

The former argued that 'enlightened nations' with their 'superior civilisations' were duty bound to change 'savage nations' whose 'inferior civilisations' were characterised by cultures of superstition, preference for leisure, laziness and lack of motivation associated with hot climates, and the inability to save for a rainy day (Ferguson, 2003). Granted: 'Smith did not oppose colonialism in general . . . For Smith, colonial trade could be most advantageous for both the colonies and the colonial powers so long as there was no monopolistic control of it' (ibid., 227). Indeed, for both Smith and Ricardo, the struggle was against:

> a possible 'stationary state' of society . . . they assumed that those ['backward'] nations could not carry out their own transition [from various forms of feudalism] to capitalism without European colonial tutelage . . . Hence colonialism could even be justified as a way of establishing, enforcing and maintaining free trade in other parts of the world, thus securing development for both advanced and backward nations.
>
> *(ibid., 229; also see Ndhlovu and Cameron, 2013)*

Given readily available cheap land in the colonies, wages would be bid up, enticing more people to emigrate, and thus higher productivity would follow (Smith, 1937, 533; Ndhlovu, 2012; Ndhlovu and Cameron, 2013). There was therefore every reason to believe that more would be produced since, in these 'savage and barbarous nations', the relatively small size of the market limited the division of labour. It was against this background that McCulloch (1826, 64–5) argued that the pressures for labour as the market expanded would eventually lead to (white) settlement and the need for government to maintain growing emigration to the colonies.

In respect of settlement colonies such as Australia, South Africa and Zambia, this raised questions about the cost and methods of financing colonisation. E.G. Wakefield's (1829) theory of systematic colonisation and self-regulation seemed to provide the answer. If it was accepted that historical circumstances in the colonies differed from those of the imperialist country, then it stood to reason that plentiful land had to be sold to the colonists at such a restrictive price (the 'sufficient price') that it forced white settlers to work as labourers for a reasonably long time before they could become landowners. The government would be responsible for granting title of ownership, ensuring that only fertile land was cultivated, concurrently denying title on crown waste lands, and thus ensuring that no colonist's land was too large. The sale of land would thus constitute an 'emigration fund' that would give population relief in Britain and ensure that the colonial system was self-supporting (Kittrell, 1973, 89–90).

Wakefield

> did believe that his proposal for colonial self-government and selective emigration from all strata and both sexes, and especially young married couples, would make colonization easier, given a colonial lands sales policy based on his doctrines. The quantity and quality of the emigrating forces would be enhanced; and he felt these policies would certainly be instrumental in developing an old world society in the new world – a cherished dream – in the shortest period of time. Likewise the provision for using the proceeds of land sales to defray the costs of immigration was advocated by Wakefield. In the first place this would permit a lower price on the lands than otherwise; and secondly, he was keenly aware of the political appeal of a plan that transferred the cost of emigration to the colony.
>
> *(ibid., 99–100)*

Despite criticisms from James Mill, McCulloch, Malthus, Cairnes, Senior and James Spedding (of the Colonial Office), who questioned the computation of the 'sufficient price' and wondered whether government regulations from a distance would be effective, that is, imputed equilibrating forces of the free market (ibid., 91–103):

In practice, Wakefield felt that the best approach was for the government to fix a relatively low price, and as experience dictated, gradually raise the price until the rates of wages and profits indicated that the price was sufficient. He also felt that since the length of service a worker would give in the colony was dependent upon the wages rate, cost of living, fertility of soils, and the type of climate existing in the particular colony, these data could be used to establish the sufficient price.

(ibid., 91)

It is noteworthy that 'Wakefield . . . was asking that the abundant factor (land) be made relatively scarce through the instrument of the restrictive sufficient price. And as his critics noted, Wakefield conceived of some optimum combination of the factors in the colonies that rested on technological instead of economic considerations' (ibid., 93). Although Wakefield's writings were persuasive enough to convert Jeremy Bentham and Robert Torrens, the inertia at the Colonial Office, hostility from friends and foe and the Free Trade movement had begun to steal a march on his arguments.

In the meantime, from a very different perspective, Karl Marx was also grappling with issues surrounding the development of capitalism and colonisation. It is important to note the evolution in Marx and Engels' thought before and after 1860. Lorrain (1991, 229–32) argues that before 1860, Marx concentrated on national struggles whose success was inextricably linked with the class struggle in England. While acknowledging the 'immiseration' effects of capitalism, Marx nevertheless viewed the system as 'progressive' insofar as it 'advanced' the productive forces (Ndhlovu, 2012; Ndhlovu and Cameron, 2013). Sourcing cheap raw materials and extending the market as widely as possible helped to counter the tendency of the rate of profit to fall. In the circumstances, Marx believed that the English proletariat would play a leading role in the (world) liberation movement. However, for Marx after 1860, particularly in 1869 and 1875, the English working was no longer absolutely crucial to the liberation of colonies.

Furthermore, Lorrain (ibid., 232) notes that the 'early' Marx (in 1853) regarded the impact of colonisation (through infrastructural development i.e. railways) as crucial in industrialising 'backward' nations. However, by 1879 Marx was more cautious in his analysis; indeed, he was concerned about the widening disparities where 'the landed proprietor, the usurer, the merchant, the railways, the banker and so forth' were all repeating enormous benefits from the system, while 'the real producer', 'the masses' (Marx, as cited in Lorrain, 1991, 232) were suffering untold misery. On communal land rights, the 'early' (1853) Marx contended that British-imposed systems, despite their 'cruel features', were 'progressive' since they introduced private property, a necessary step on the linear and universal road to socialism. However, by 1881 Marx considered the substitution of communal land ownership as 'an act of English vandalism which pushed the indigenous people not forward but backward' (Marx, cited in Lorrain, 1991, 233), indicating that he was now open to multi-linear schemes of historical development. Finally, the 'early' Marx (in 1853) had been opposed to protectionism, but by 1867 he was in favour of self-government, agrarian reform and protective tariffs. While Marx did not believe that 'backward' nations would be permanently 'underdeveloped', he observed that 'every time Ireland was about to develop industrially, she was crushed and reconverted into a purely agricultural land' (Marx, cited in Lorrain, 1991, 233). Clearly, Marx's 'mature' historical materialism adopted a more cautious, nuanced approach that was less deterministic and more sensitive to complex circumstances.

Nevertheless, in Victorian Britain, colonial expansion was still being rationalised, not as a way of benefiting the mother country, but instead the Darwinian theory of evolution was used to invoke a racist ideology where European colonisation in the nineteenth century was presented as a civilising mission of primitive peoples under the guidance of a 'benign' imperialist state. Despite racial hierarchies, a sense of superiority and efforts to supplant indigenous cultures, features that had been noticeable in some of the classical economists' analyses, Ferguson (2003) argues that the enlightened British population were always at hand to curb the empire's worst effects. The lack of progress in curbing racism is put squarely on the shoulders of white settlers in the colonies. Moreover, the empire facilitated the spread of liberal capitalism and bequeathed Protestant Christianity and the English language on the colonies (ibid.). This ambiguity between capitalist principles of self-interest (individual freedom) and social justice is captured by Nelson Mandela (1995) in his autobiography, *Long Walk to Freedom*. Mandela recalls the arrogance of missionaries, whom he describes as benign dictators, during their 'civilising mission' of students like him at the University of Fort Hare. He contrasts this with their pious ideals of forgiveness, humility and equality in the eyes of God.

Notwithstanding Ferguson's (counterfactual) argument, it appears that 'there was a broad [Darwinian] acceptance of the idea that human societies progressed and that therefore the different "races" could be ranked within a hierarchy of primitive to civilised' (Hewitson, 2013, 92). In so far as concepts such as the nuclear family (with its patriarchal and hierarchical structures) distinguished the 'civilised' race from the 'savages' in the colonies, a body of thought could be built to rationalise the violent usurping of land in southern Africa by colonialists and subordinate its peoples in the name of progress. For those of a Smithian persuasion, once these peoples were 'liberated' from their 'uncivilised' ways or cultural chains, they could, imbued with self-interest, participate in free trade, while the 'invisible' hand was credited with bringing about the smooth workings of the market (Offer, 2012).

The twentieth century

The 1930s Great Depression, with its unprecedented falls in output and persistent and high levels of unemployment, ushered in new ways of thinking (such as Keynesianism) that were predicated on uncertainty (Cameron and Ndhlovu, 1999). In the southern African context, particularly in South Africa (during the apartheid period of 1948–94), Zambia (then Northern Rhodesia) and Botswana (then Bechuanaland), there was increasingly an emphasis on economic growth as a panacea for perceived 'backwardness'. For example, in South Africa, the Afrikaner nationalists not only extended and institutionalised the racist ideology, but they also justified it on the basis of religious beliefs within the Dutch Reformed Church (also see Freedman, 2013). Significant investment could justifiably be made to white sections of the population within the industrial and agricultural sectors, while the private sector could be given incentives to invest, thus ensuring increased productivity. Overarching national (indicative) sectorial and project planning became the key to rapid capital accumulation.

While the Second World War was characterised by Keynesian interventionist policies ('dirigiste dogma', to use Lal's term) and the introduction of technocratic skills ('getting technology right'), it also triggered a (re)evaluation amongst the newly educated 'natives' of economic growth; that it was not necessarily the same as development (which incorporates literacy, health, education, basic needs, etc.). Emphasis in analysis thus switched to 'redistribution with growth' ('getting income distribution right'). Ironically, the brutality of colonisation, combined with religious ideals of equality before God, had inspired African nationalists to oppose colonisation and policies of racial segregation. Recognition of this political dimension turned attention to the iniquities surrounding the racial and hierarchical system. The 1960s and 1970s were periods in which nationalist theories coalesced. The political struggles for independence from the (largely British) colonial yoke emphasised either rural/regional planning or under-development/dependency theories, which criticised ethnocentric models, and the role played by indigenous elites and intellectuals. These latter non-ethnocentric indigenous models rejected

'Western' models for their inapplicability to southern African historical and cultural experiences ('getting political relations right').

In so far as nationalist theories involved the ability of citizens to support and exercise their national identity, as well as national economic projects, there was increased resistance against the colonialists' divide-and-rule tactics ('One Zambia, One Nation', to use Kenneth Kaunda's rallying call in Zambia). Despite the difficulties in defining a 'nation', anti-colonial nationalism was a reaction to the subjugation of indigenous people by foreign, imperial powers. In the southern African context, African nationalists sought to resolve racial and ethnic divisions by either peaceful means (as in Botswana) or via militarism (as in South Africa). The establishment of African nationalism or civic nationalism also involved the active participation of trade unions (as in South Africa and Zambia); and it was also accompanied by advocacy of Christian socialism which emphasised social justice and human rights as a way of bringing together different strands of society for common economic and societal goals.

It is against this background that nationalists in southern Africa began to advocate Tanzanian President Julius Nyerere's populist version of socialism, that is, African communalism or *ujamaa* (familyhood or extended family in Swahili) philosophy. This was latterly known in South Africa as *umuntu ngumuntu ngabantu* (becoming a person through one's relations with others or through community) and in Zambia as 'Zambian humanism' (as advocated by Kenneth Kaunda). Not only was education and collectivised forms of production ('villagisation') to be emphasised, but social, economic and political equality was also seen as the key to progress (Nyerere, 1967; Ibhawoh and Dibua, 2003; Pauw, 1996; Saul, 1972). Although this was subsequently toned down in South Africa, Nelson Mandela and the African National Congress (ANC), for example, advocated a version of African nationalism or 'democratic socialism' ('a step towards bourgeois democracy', as enunciated in the 1956 Freedom Charter). This not only had similarities with the American civil rights movement of defiance against unjust laws (social justice), but was also influenced by the ANC's association with the trade union movement and the South African Communist Party (SACP) with respect to nationalisation of the commanding heights of the economy.

For his part, Goran Hyden (1980, 1983) took issue with the *ujamaa* philosophy and presented an alternative explanation that had echoes of neoclassical economic thinking. In his 'economy of affection', he depicted the post-colonial state in Africa as having 'no structural roots in society, which, as a balloon suspended in mid-air, is being punctuated by excessive demands and is unable to function without an indiscriminate and wasteful consumption of scarce societal resources' (Hyden, 1983, 19). He contended that, while the colonial government (allegedly) brought positive organisation to African states and aid for the poor, the modern African 'socialist structures' placed greater emphasis on social welfare rather than economic growth that was so important to colonial administrators. Inexperienced bureaucrats succumbed to 'excessive demands' on the state. When these demands were subsequently not met, the heroes' status of these leaders at independence quickly dissipated and was replaced by disillusionment where political leaders were seen in the same light as their colonial predecessors, the so-called cynical manipulators.

In the meantime, African states were unable to incorporate the independent peasantry that did not feel obliged to be part of the national economy. In so far as the peasant mode of production has its own informal system of reciprocal support that links together various social and economic units that are otherwise autonomous, the 'economy of affection' is thus central to the ability of peasant producers to survive without state assistance. And yet this system also enables peasant producers to take advantage of market incentives within the national economy, while redistributing any gains (derived from money invested in the welfare state) within the 'economy of affection'. Hyden (1983) describes peasant producers as having 'one foot in and one foot out of the state's sphere of influence'. Clearly, appropriation of the surplus from the peasant producers to boost national revenue is not possible, meaning that the state has to rely on alternative sources of income, such as in trade. Moreover, resources are likely to be diverted from the public in general (i.e. wasteful consumption) via white elephants such as unused 'conference hotels', high-technology weaponry and failed dam constructions. It was thus not surprising that some African leaders adopted authoritarian controls over society. In the circumstances, Hyden (1983) advocates full-scale capitalism in African countries and de-linking from the 'economy of affection'.

While Hyden (1983) has been criticised for over-generalisation and paying scant attention to historical specificity, the International Monetary Fund (IMF) and World Bank (joint conditionality) went along with this neo-liberal analysis in the 1980s and 1990s. In addition to Stabilisation Policies (1950–80) (devaluation of exchange rates; increasing import duties; raising interest rates), they introduced Structural Adjustment Policies (fiscal reform; removal or elimination of subsidies and price and wage controls; targeting of poverty programmes via user charges/fees and means tests; privatisation of public sector activities) for especially less developed countries (LDCs). At a time when many LDCs were using interventionist policies, across-the-board liberalisation involved the increased role of the market, increased openness, and 'getting prices right' (Lal, 1985, 2006). This medicine was to be taken until private and foreign investment, and economic growth, had risen substantially. These policies were implemented in, for example, Zambia with disastrous social consequences.

In South Africa, this neo-liberal economic thinking appeared in 1996 in the guise of the government's five-year macroeconomic strategy entitled Growth, Employment and Redistribution (GEAR). It was contended that privatisation, competition (liberalisation), with the state creating an investment-enabling environment, and elimination of exchange controls would not only address the legacy of apartheid, but also increase economic growth by six per cent per annum by 2000 and consequently increase employment (Ndhlovu, 2011). Unlike the earlier (1994) Reconstruction and Development Programme (RDP) that sought to address redistributive justice, GEAR did not mention inequality (Ramutsindela, 2006; Weeks, 1999). It must also be noted that analysis of women's work in southern Africa has been concentrated on social reproduction, services and so-called 'traditional work'. Although African States are arguably not neutral social arbiters, they are often presented as central to economic redistribution and therefore gender justice. Relatively few analyses examine the division of labour as central to the process of accumulation, and how power relations can be couched through the complex relationship between class, race and gender (Collins, 2000; Ndhlovu, 2014; Ndhlovu and Spring, 2009).

Notwithstanding this, the worsening global economic situation forced the South African government in particular to subsequently abandon GEAR in favour of the National Development Plan (NDP). Thinking switched to government being central to economic activity. In other words, it was the intention of the NDP to operationalise a version of the developmental state similarly to the 'Asian Four Tigers' (South Korea, Taiwan, Hong Kong and Singapore) and China. Investment in infrastructure would be prioritised, together with support for regional development plans. In addition, social grants and national health insurance would be put in place, while some market incentives were also part-and-parcel of this plan. This mixture of Keynesian interventionist policies and free market policies can be described as the New Institutional Economics (Cameron and Ndhlovu, 2000). Besides, meritocracy would arguably be intertwined with informal networks to facilitate the achievement of common economic and social goals. The government would also continue to redress racial and gender divisions via Broad-Based Black Economic Empowerment (2003) and other legislature (Buhlungu and Tshoaedi, 2012, 113).

The BRICS (Brazil, Russia, India, China and South Africa) countries reflect the challenge of balancing economic growth and accompanying social, political and cultural transitions; as well as constructing national identities and new geographical imaginaries. Indeed, the establishment of a Development Bank by the BRICS nations in 2013 to rival the IMF has given rise to various interpretations of this grouping; is it a neo-colonial relationship or the beginning of unshackling of the chains of dependency/underdevelopment?

Indigenous economic systems: thought and practice

South Africa, Botswana and, to some extent, Zambia have been hailed as economic miracles within a continent doomed with economic turmoil, upheaval and instability. However, recently more critical voices have started to emerge. What are the sources of that praise and what is the basis of the more recent critique? What makes Botswana, Zambia and South Africa so special, it seems, is that here, in southern Africa, they are examples of uninterrupted liberal democratic rule going back to independence. For example, those who praise the quality of Botswana's economy tend to base their arguments on a liberal democratic tradition (Beaulier, 2003; Nyamnjoh, 2007; Picard, 1987; Solway, 2009, 333). Here neo-liberal economic theories involving free trade, specialisation and the division of labour are dominant, while the marginalisation of women and other groups is a throw-back to the debates by classical economists. Moreover, the focus on a glowing review of the impressive economic performance of Botswana and South Africa also glosses over accompanying poverty and inequality.

Understandably, and given challenging and potentially unstable circumstances in neighbouring countries such as Zimbabwe, and now Mozambique, the two former countries' stability can be regarded as promising (du Toit, 1995; Solway, 2003). With South Africa and its cycles of political anxieties on her northern border and Zimbabwe gushing refugees to the West, it is certainly refreshing to note that Botswana and South Africa have held regular elections at five-year intervals since their respective independence (Buhlungu and Malehoko, 2012; Danevad, 1995).

These strains cannot be understated. Add to their liberal democratic qualifications, Botswana and South Africa and, to some extent, Zambia have had enormous economic good fortune, avoiding the descent into the kind of politics that characterise many primary commodity exporters. Undoubtedly, the role of sound leadership both for Botswana and South Africa is an important determinant of the remarkable economic growth experienced in the past decade. It is not surprising, given this level of praise, to find Paul Nugent (2010) remarking that, when writing of Africa, it is possible to posit a pattern common to pretty much all African countries, with the possible exception of Botswana and South Africa. To understand how economic thought has been couched in southern Africa, a grasp of indigenous economic thought and how these have developed over time, is necessary, particularly the historical impositions incubated during the pre- to post-colonial eras.

In southern Africa, particularly due to the length of colonialism, indigenous people sought ways to develop their products despite efforts to suppress their endeavours to commercialise their knowledge. For example, only in the 1990s and under the post-apartheid government in South Africa was government seen to support indigenous approaches to trade, commerce and business cultures based on indigenous knowledge systems, such as curios and muti (indigenous medicinal plants). Despite the policy pronouncements regarding the development of IEKS-based products and services, indigenous peoples often do not get the full benefit of their knowledge. Countries such as Zambia, Botswana and South Africa have developed indigenous ways of thinking that are based on *Ubuntu* principles of philanthropy that survived decades of colonial oppression and post-colonial neo-liberal interventions. *Ubuntu* is an African philosophy that states that one's standing in society is inextricably linked with one's relations with others. If respect (*inhlonipho*) is reciprocated, then this will ensure a harmonious society (see Ndhlovu, 2011, 85).

During the pre-colonial era, economic thought in these countries was characterised by international trade and economic exchange of goods based on traditional market systems centuries before the arrival of the European colonialists. According to Pouwels (2005), the bantu-language speaking people of southern Africa developed extensive trade links with lands as far away as China and India, from which they received porcelain, beads, and Persian and Arab pots. They traded domesticated beef, iron, ivory and gold (Pouwels, 2005). In Zambia and South Africa, economic exchange was based on the currency of cattle and livestock. In many instances, land was lineage-controlled, and cattle ownership dominated trading circles. Thus, through owning cattle, chiefdoms could gain power over a large number of groups and thus control trade goods and trading arrangements. The basic economic and social unit was the extended family, the lineage or the clan. The means of production was owned by the lineage that acted as a corporate unit and made decisions about family sustenance.

The economic understanding began to change under colonialism whereby indigenous peoples were actively encouraged to abandon their indigenous knowledge systems of commerce and market exchange. During this period, southern Africa was drawn increasingly into a world economic system that was dominated by the industrialising nations that colonised them and, in particular, there was growing trading contact with the south eastern coast of Africa, going to the far south. IEKS were denigrated and labelled 'primitive' and in extreme cases 'illogical'. Recent post-colonial critiques point to failures of neo-liberal market-driven economic approaches in addressing the fundamental socio-economic issues facing southern Africans. They specifically cite under-investing or under-allocation of resources in successful programmes as having a negative impact on intended beneficiaries (Cameron and Ndhlovu, 2000; Chamlee, 1993; Nandy, 2002; Tadasu, 2006; Yarrow, 2008). On his part Nandy (2002) decried the failure of a series of structural adjustment developmental projects to decisively deal with poverty, dubbing it a myth from which many have not woken up. Nandy's concerns call for a significant change in the manner in which economic understanding is defined, understood and treated. According to Ayittey (2011), cognisance must be taken of kingdoms that had to compete with many rulers in order to take advantage of new trading opportunities and possibilities for expansion.

Despite the onslaught on indigenous systems, they remained resilient. Thus trade in goods deriving from indigenous economic knowledge systems has for a long time thrived because there is a demand for the products based on culture. Such a market is not only limited to the indigenous people but is also found among tourists who seek products unique to this region (Ndhlovu and Lessassy, 2011). The informal trade in curios at the Durban Beachfront, the Johannesburg street vendors, the Muti trade along the Warwick triangle or the Gaborone Central Market or Lilongwe traders' corner are examples of industries based on IEKS (Ndinda, 1999). While trade in products based on IEKS provides economic opportunities for the small, medium and micro-enterprises, the vast majority of IEKS holders continue to languish in poverty in South Africa, Botswana, and Zambia.

Conclusion

This chapter sought to explain economic thought and knowledge in southern Africa, with special attention on South Africa, Botswana and Zambia. We argued that even though pre-colonial southern Africa was overwhelmingly a land-abundant region, characterised by simultaneous trade routes, indigenous capital and extensive indigenous market exchanges, colonial authorities developed African economies as primary-product exporters, consolidating power and exploiting Africans through large-scale land grabs to promote migrant labour flows in 'settler' economies.

Thus, colonial extraction in Africa could be seen most decisively in the appropriation of land for European settlers, a strategy used not only to provide settlers with cheap and secure control of land, but also to oblige Africans to sell their labour (power) to European owners (Palmer and Parsons, 1977).

In summary, colonial economic impositions and interventions need to be critiqued as a phenomenon that has imprisoned the African ways of understanding commerce, utilising indigenous economic ideas, traditions, beliefs and ideologies. Caution must be exercised whenever there are suggestions of combining neo-liberal theories with indigenous knowledge systems; more so since sustainability and development potentials of these cultural systems are often overlooked and perceived as primitive, uneconomic, environmentally destructive and incompatible with 'modernisation'. It is increasingly recognised in economic discourses that respect for indigenous economic knowledge stemming from African ways of relating to one another is an important aspect of addressing economic pressures. Thus, whilst IEKS are seen mainly as reactions to colonial economic impositions, they are also a solution to redress past economic injustices.

References

Ayittey, G.B.N. (2011). "Indigenous African Market Liberalism", *The Freeman*, http://www.fee.org/the_ freeman/detail/indigenous-african-free-market-liberalism, 1–4.

Backhouse, R.E. (1985). *A History of Modern Economic Analysis*. Oxford: Basil Blackwell.

Beaulier, Scott A. (2003). "Explaining Botswana's Success: The Critical Role of Post-Colonial Policy", *The Cato Journal*, vol.23, no.2, 227–40.

Buhlungu, S. and Tshoaedi, M. (2012). *COSATU's Contested Legacy: South African Trade Unions in the Second Decade of Democracy*, Cape Town: HSRC Press.

Cameron, J. and Ndhlovu, T.P. (1999). "Keynes and the Distribution of Uncertainty: Lessons from the Lancashire Cotton Spinning Industry and the General Theory", *Review of Social Economy*, vol.57, no.1, 99–123 (March).

Cameron, J. and Ndhlovu, T.P. (2000). "Development Economics: an Institutional Bastion", *Journal of Interdisciplinary Economics*, vol.11, nos.3/4, 237–53.

Cameron, J. and Ndhlovu, T.P. (2001). "The Comparative Economics of EU 'Subsidiarity': Lessons from Development/Regional Economic Debates", *Journal of Urban and Regional Research*, vol.25, 327–45.

Chamlee, E. (1993). "Indigenous African Institutions and Economic Development", *Cato Journal*, vol.13, no.1, 79–99 (Spring/Summer).

Collins, P.H. (2000). *Black Feminist Thought: Knowledge, Consciousness, and the Politics of Empowerment*, London and New York: Routledge.

Danevad, A. (1995). "Responsiveness in Botswana Politics: Do elections matter?" *Journal of Southern African Studies*, vol.33, no.3, September, 381–402, [www] http://www.jstor.org/stable/161482 [opens new window] (accessed April 24, 2014).

du Toit, P. (1995). *State Building and Democracy in Southern Africa: Botswana, Zimbabwe, and South Africa*, Washington, DC: United States Institute of Peace Press.

Falola, T. (2003). *The Power of African Cultures*, Rochester: The University of Rochester Press.

Ferguson, N. (2003). *Empire: The Rise and Demise of the British World Order and the Lessons for Global Power*, New York: Basic Books.

Freedman, S.G. (2013). "Mission Schools Opened World to Africans, but left an Ambiguous Legacy", *The New York Times*, 27 December, www.nytimes.com/2013/12/28us/mission-schools-ambiguous-legacy-in-south-africa.html?_r=0.

Gennaioli, N. and Rainer, I. (2007). "The Modern Impact of Precolonial Centralization in Africa", *Journal of Economic Growth*, vol.12, no.3, 185–234.

Heldring, L. and Robinson, J.A. (2012). "Colonialism and Economic Development in Africa", *NBER Working Paper No.18566* (November).

Heldring, L. and Robinson, J.A. (2013). "Colonialism and Development in Africa", http:www.voxeu.org/ article/colonialism-and-development-africa (January).

Hewitson, G. (2013). "Economics and the Family: A Postcolonial Perspective", *Cambridge Journal of Economics*, vol.37, 91–111.

Hyden, G. (1980). *Beyond Ujamaa in Tanzania: Underdevelopment and an Uncaptured Peasantry*, Berkeley: University of California Press.

Hyden, G. (1983). *No Shortcut to Progress: African Development in Perspective*, Berkeley: University of California Press.

Ibhawoh, B. and Dibua, J.I. (2003). "Deconstructing Ujamaa: The Legacy of Julius Nyerere in the Quest for Social and Economic Development in Africa", *African Association of Political Science*, vol.8, no.1, 60–83.

Kittrell, E.R. (1973). "Wakefield's Scheme of Systematic Colonization and Classical Economists", *American Journal of Economics and Sociology*, vol.32, no.1, 87–111 (January).

Lal, D. (1985). *The Poverty of "Development Economics"*, Harvard University Press.

Lal, D. (2006). *Reviving the Invisible Hand: The Case for Classical Liberalism in the Twenty-first Century*, Princeton University Press.

Lorrain, J. (1991). "Classical Political Economists and Marx on Colonialism and 'Backward' Nations", *World Development*, vol.19, no.2/3, 225–43.

Mandela, N. (1995). *Long Walk to Freedom: The Autobiography of Nelson Mandela*, Little Brown & Co.

McCulloch, J.R. (1826). "Emigration", *Edinburgh Review*, December.

Nandy, A. (2002). "The Beautiful, Expanding Future of Poverty: Popular Economics as a Psychological Defence", *International Studies Review*, vol.4, no.2, 107–21.

Ndhlovu, T.P. (2011). "Corporate Social Responsibility and Corporate Social Investment: The South African Case", *Journal of African Business*, vol.12, no.1, 72–92.

Ndhlovu, T.P. (2012). "Globalisation: A Theoretical Reflection", *World Journal of Entrepreneurship, Management & Sustainable Development (WJEMSD)*, vol.8, no.2, 95–112.

Ndhlovu, T.P. (forthcoming, 2014). "Economic Empowerment of Women in South Africa", *South African Journal of Development & Transformation*.

Ndhlovu, T.P. and Cameron, J. (2013). "Economics and 'Excess': Implications for Understanding and Combating Climate Change", *International Journal of Sustainable Economy*, vol.5, no.1, 15–35.

Ndhlovu, T.P. and Lessassy, L. (2011). "Prospects of African Ethnic Products in the EU", *Asia Pacific, Journal of Business and Management*, vol.2, no.1, 51–64.

Ndhlovu, T.P. and Spring, A. (2009). "South African Women in Business and Management: Transformation in Progress", *Journal of African Business*, vol.10, no.1, 31–49.

Ndinda, C. (1999). "Coping strategies of Women Micro-Enterprisers: The Case of Women Curio Sellers at the Durban Beachfront", *Business Management Review*, vol.6, no.1.

Nugent, P. (2010). "States and Social Contracts in Africa", *New Left Review*, vol.63, 35–68.

Nyamnjoh, F. B. (2007). "Ever Diminishing Circles: The Paradoxes of Belonging in Botswana", in Marisol de la Cadena and Orin Starn (eds), *Indigenous Experience Today*, Oxford, Wenner-Gren International Symposium Series, Berg Publishers.

Nyerere, J. (1967). *Freedom and Unity*, London and Nairobi: Oxford University Press.

Offer, A. (2012). "Self-interest, Sympathy and the Invisible Hand: From Adam Smith to Market Liberalism", *Economic Thought*, vol.1, no.2, 1–14.

Palmer, R. and Parsons, N. (1977). *The Roots of Rural Poverty in Central and Southern Africa*. London: Heinemann.

Pauw, C.M. (1996). "Traditional African Economies in Conflict with Western Capitalism", *SKRIF EN KERK Jrg*, vol.17, no.2, 373–85.

Picard, L.A. (1987). *The Politics of Development in Botswana: A Model for Success?* Boulder: L. Rienner Publishers.

Pouwels, R.L. (2005). *The African and Middle Eastern World, 600–1500*, Oxford University Press, 139–41.

Ramutsindela, M. (2006). "State Restructuring and Rural Development in South Africa", in Behera, M.C. (ed.) *Globalising Rural Development: Competing Paradigms and Emerging Realities*, New Delhi: Sage Publications.

Saul, J. (1972). "Planning for Socialism in Tanzania: The Socio-Political Context", *Development and Change*, vol.3, no.3, 3–25, September.

Smith, A. (1937). *An Inquiry into the Nature and Causes of the Wealth of Nations*, Edwin Cannan (ed.), New York: The Modern Library.

Solway, J. (2003). "In the Eye of the Storm: The State and Non-Violence in Southern Africa (Botswana)" *Anthropological Quarterly*, vol.76, no.3, 485–95.

Solway, J.S. (2009). "Human Rights and NGO 'Wrongs': Conflict Diamonds, Culture Wars and the 'Bushman Question'", *Africa: The Journal of the International African Institute*, vol.79, no.3, 321–46.

Tadasu, T. (2006). "African Imaginations of Moral Economy: Notes on Indigenous Economic Concepts and Practices in Tanzania", *African Studies Quarterly*, vol.9, nos.1/2: 105–21.

Wakefield, E.G. (1829). *A Letter from Sydney: The Principal Town of Australia*, J. Cross.

Weeks, J. (1999). "Stuck in Low GEAR: Macroeconomic Policy in South Africa, 1996–1998", *Cambridge Journal of Economics,* vol.23, no.6, 795–811.

Yarrow, T. (2008). "Negotiating Difference: Discourses of Indigenous Knowledge and Development in Ghana", *Political and Legal Anthropology Review*, vol.31, no.2, 224–42.

24

Angola and Mozambique

Marxist or market?

Steven Kyle

Many of the most important differences and similarities between Angola and Mozambique predate the arrival of the Portuguese in the fifteenth century. When we put the question of Marxist economic orientation in this context, the two decades of so-called Marxist development seems rather a small issue when compared to half a millennium of colonial history. The pre-existing conditions in each country had much more influence on their development prospects than did their years of Marxist economic policy. In fact, in many ways it is difficult to pinpoint actual "Marxist" policies distinct from those followed by other similar countries at the same level of development.

In terms of broad similarities, both countries contain within their borders a variety of African ethnic groups, many of which had no sense of common identity prior to the arrival of the Europeans. Both countries also contained substantial kingdoms, with well-defined borders and centralized political control: most notably the Kongo kingdom on the west coast of Africa, which had its capital in what is now Angola (though it extended northward into what is now Zaire and the Congo), and the kingdoms of Sofala and Muenemutapa in Mozambique.

The goals of the Portuguese were not primarily ones of conquest and settlement. Rather, the principal aim of the early explorers was to open routes for extraction of commodities, among which were spices, gold, ivory, and slaves. This had important implications for the local populations, as it meant that there was no overriding need for the Portuguese to control territory or to rule directly. Rather, it was more convenient for them to reach accommodations with local political leaders in order to develop trading relationships which would allow them to extract the desired export commodities. For the most part, there was no concerted effort to promote economic development, or to settle Portuguese colonists on these lands, and this remained the case until the twentieth century (Issacman and Isaacman, 1983; Newitt, 1995).

Until the partition of Africa by European powers in the late 1800s there was little effort by the Portuguese to settle or directly control the interior of either country. However, at that time it became clear that the main criterion for colonial borders was to follow the dictum "possession is 9/10 of the law" – or 100 percent in this case. Accordingly, the Portuguese began to push into the interior of both Mozambique and Angola, an effort that picked up speed in the 1930s when Portugal sought among other things to alleviate its own unemployment problems by exporting large numbers of settlers and peasant farmers abroad.

This massive influx of Europeans resulted in a situation in which virtually every formal sector job in the economies of both countries was dominated by whites. Every salaried job, including taxi drivers, waiters, ticket takers, etc. was held by the Portuguese, leaving no role whatsoever for Africans in the formal sector. Agriculture, too, became heavily Europeanized, with a large smallholder African peasant sector coexisting with a commercialized sector of medium-sized European farms and large plantations. Equally important was a virtual monopoly by the Portuguese on the network of rural traders who linked all agricultural producers to the market. These bush traders and shopkeepers provided an outlet for peasant production and in return served as providers of agricultural inputs, consumer goods and informal credit.

This chapter will argue that "Marxist" economic ideology as practiced in the Lusophone African context is virtually indistinguishable from general justifications for authoritarian extractive regimes of any political stripe, and that the extractive regimes of post-independence Angola and Mozambique are in many ways simply extensions of the old colonial regimes under new management. Though the newly independent governments in Angola and Mozambique were openly and avowedly "Marxist" in their economic convictions, this was more of a label of convenience than a real indicator of ideological conviction. The true conviction in each case was a determination to replace colonial hegemony and control with that of the ruling party, a goal which is shared by many political persuasions in Africa and around the world.

Marxist economics in Africa

What did it mean economically to be a Marxist state in the immediate post-colonial era of the 1970s in the former Portuguese colonies of Angola and Mozambique? If Marxist economics necessitates state ownership of the means of production, then we are in something of a definitional quandary because there simply *wasn't* very much in the way of "means of production" in either of these countries at independence in 1975. Nevertheless, to be avowedly Marxist certainly meant something to the governments in question so it is worth looking at exactly what it meant and how it evolved as time went on. By 2013 it is safe to say that Mozambique has taken a decided turn toward a market economy not just in rhetoric but in fact. Angola has taken a similar turn in rhetoric and to some extent in reality but lags behind Mozambique in its market reforms.

The stories of how these countries became "Marxist" economies in the first place was strongly influenced by the fact that their colonial occupiers were Portuguese, and were therefore members of NATO. When the predictable and necessary independence movements began to coalesce in the 1960s, there was no way they were going to get any assistance or encouragement from other NATO allies – their only viable sources of support were the communist bloc countries, particularly the USSR, East Germany and to some extent Cuba. Getting assistance and advice from these sources carried with it the Marxist economic mindset and developmental prejudices – a bias toward state control of the economy and a deep conviction that the political primacy of the party was more important than anything else. Accordingly, FRELIMO in Mozambique and the MPLA in Angola took control over all aspects of the polity and economy from top to bottom (Messiant, 1998).

To a very great extent this was forced on them. It is estimated that 95 percent of Portuguese settlers evacuated from both countries in the year during which Portugal relinquished power (Kyle, 1990, 2005). Some of them were reluctant to lose their Portuguese citizenship while many were frightened by the Marxist rhetoric of the incoming government and were unwilling to stay if all of their assets (farms, factories, etc) were to be nationalized. Given the extreme socio-economic segregation along racial lines enforced by the colonial rulers, this meant that managers and owners of virtually every economic entity, from large plantation down to rural convenience store, departed and in many cases destroyed their assets, rather than leave them to whoever was to come next. While both FRELIMO and the MPLA tried to continue established companies and plantations as going concerns, they quickly ran into a bottleneck. The racial laws preventing education or assimilation of most Africans meant that there was an extreme dearth of experienced managers after independence. Indeed, one observer in Mozambique stated that there were only 33 college graduates in the entire country after 1975 (Personal communication, Minister of Finance, 1988).

Another colonial legacy that is equally important is the fact that the Fascist Salazar regime exercised state control over the economy scarcely less comprehensively than what existed in many communist countries. Though large corporations did indeed control the "commanding heights" of the economy, the extent to which these were intertwined with government regulation and personnel should not be underestimated. Colonies were run with an eye toward extraction of surplus value and to the extent that corporations could assist in this they were encouraged and licensed by the government. Ownership of land and other productive assets was reserved for white settlers with the indigenous population relegated to less favorable zones where they were readily able to be called on for forced labor. Immigration was tightly controlled and the labor market explicitly segmented between occupations that were considered to be "white" (all formal sector jobs) or "black" (menial jobs).

Accordingly, it was no great leap to go from authoritarian "Fascist" control of the economy to authoritarian "Marxist" control. Neither regime countenanced political rivals and both employed police tactics to suppress opposition, and neither countenanced free-market economies. Both vested ownership of major productive assets in the ruling class (or state if we choose the Marxist nomenclature). All that was required in the first instance was a political "decapitation" of the old colonial regime and its replacement with new leaders. But it would be difficult to distinguish major differences between an exploitative centralizing regime run by Portuguese colonialists, and an exploitative centralizing regime run by a small indigenous ruling clique (Government of Angola, 1997, 2000 and 2006).

The degree of control and the institutional apparatus to enforce it were in some cases a holdover from the colonial era but also showed the influence of Eastern bloc economic advisors as in the formation of the "Economic Police," whose job was (putatively) to enforce pricing and distribution of goods, but whose actual function was to serve as merely one more point at which surplus value could be extracted from productive activities via bribes or other forms of corruption.

A vacuum of ideas – economic thinking in the early post-colonial era

When thinking about economic ideas and ideological biases in the early post-colonial era it is imperative to realize that there really were few or no trained economists (in the academic sense) who were part of the ruling parties or who were resident in Mozambique, apart from a very few foreigners. Of the "33 university graduates in the whole country" at independence, none were PhD economists. Angola's ruling MPLA was similarly bereft of internal debate of economic ideas at this level. This means that economic thought as typically conceived in Western universities simply did not exist, at least not in written form.

What did exist was a small cadre of revolutionary intellectuals who were schooled in Marxist economic ideology but who really did not participate in wider philosophical discussions of economic theory. Eduardo Mondlane, the father of Mozambican independence, was a sociology professor in the USA before joining the independence struggle in Africa and, before his assassination in 1969, could reasonably claim to be the most educated social scientist of the revolutionary era. Agostinho Neto, the father of Angolan independence was trained in medicine.

Insofar as these leaders and their successors followed standard Marxist economic doctrine from their Eastern Bloc supporters, they equated Portuguese colonialists with capitalists and oppressed African masses with the working class. Certainly, this was a reasonable interpretation of the facts on the ground but did not generate any question as to an appropriate course of action beyond defeating the Portuguese militarily. Sudden victory and independence in 1975 led to a situation where the victorious independence movements were thrust into *de facto* control of the economy and its consequent day to day emergencies, leaving theoretical debates over economics on the sidelines.

The economic vacuum created by the departure of the Portuguese settlers and the ensuing chaos left the newly minted states little option but to take over major production units such as plantations and factories. Managing such enterprises proved more difficult given the near total collapse of economic value chains, the inexperience of new managers, and the disappearance of the old forced labor arrangements that supported the profit margins of many of these concerns. Externally funded insurrections – RENAMO in Mozambique, funded by the white Rhodesian secret police and South Africa/the USA; and UNITA in Angola, funded by South Africa and the USA as well as their own diamond mines – reduced the actual governable space to a mere fraction of the national territory in both cases with a consequent crash in economic activity (Kyle, 1990; Andersson, 1992).

It could certainly be argued that the crash was a direct result not just of the civil conflict, though that would have been quite sufficient for the result, but also from the misguided attempt to exercise total economic control down to the micro level, as taken from traditional Marxist economic doctrine. Evidence for this could be seen in the virtual emptying of government-controlled marketing and distribution channels in favor of large informal markets which carried on outside of the regulatory regime. However, it was obvious in Mozambique by the early 1980s that not only was the government attempt at control failing to produce positive results, but external aid from the World Bank, the International Monetary Fund (IMF) and other agencies was conditional on a turn toward a market economy. In Angola the economic results of state control were no less obvious but impinged on the lives of the ruling elite far less due to their access to huge flows of oil revenue derived from newly exploited offshore oil fields.

The subsequent turn to the market in the 1980s/90s in Mozambique and to a lesser extent in Angola post-2002, definitely did have an intellectual basis in economic theory but this was more imposed from the outside than arising as the result of an economic debate in the countries themselves. FRELIMO in Mozambique saw clearly that their economy was suffering and that their control apparatus was not up to the task of promoting development or growth. The World Bank and the IMF had a clear alternative: they strongly promoted the "Washington Consensus" as laid out in John Williamson (1989). In many cases the turn to the market was simply an official recognition of ongoing commercial activity – simply allowing the "shadow economy" to be sanctioned by the government. But overall Mozambique clearly accepted the economic doctrines espoused by the donor community because there was little choice – if they wanted the aid, they needed to accept the policy changes and the ideology that underlay them. In short, they needed the money.

This meant in effect a massive retreat from government control of the economy. Reduction of government barriers to international trade were very much in line with research such as that by Anne Krueger (Krueger, 1997) and others at the World Bank extolling the virtues of neo-liberal market solutions to development issues. Subsequent high rates of growth in the

Mozambican economy served to justify and cement the "new thinking" in both the donor community and within Mozambique itself, at least for a time. Recently, some questions along the lines of those elaborated by Dani Rodrik (Rodrik, 2003) and others have arisen due to the very unequal distribution of growth across both space and class in Mozambique. In essence, some have benefited massively while others remain mired in poverty just as they were prior to the turn to the market in the 1990s. This remains as yet unresolved.

In Angola very similar (indeed indistinguishable) policy prescriptions were promoted with identical neo-liberal economics underpinnings. However, one major difference prevented their wholesale adoption in Angola – the government had massive flows of oil revenue and didn't need money nearly as much as their Mozambican counterparts. Certainly some degree of market opening did indeed take place at the micro level, but overall government policy has remained fundamentally unchanged – Angola is a resource-extraction-based regime and focuses its efforts on maintaining and increasing its mineral revenue.

Indeed, these oil fields contributed to Angolan elite cynicism about the motives of "development assistance," since the lip-service given to market reforms and good governance was coupled with a willingness to countenance a bloody civil war on the continent so long as oil continued to flow. Not only that, but the ruling elite had little or no direct economic need to reform since their own lifestyle could be amply supported by oil revenues. This promoted a mindset which, unlike almost all other countries in the region, did not see the need to cater to donor wishes. In terms of outside observers, the various explanations of the Resource Curse and Dutch Disease that are associated with W.M. Corden (1984) and Richard Auty (2002), who anchored their writings very much on empirical problems and low growth encountered by oil exporting countries. Angola is often cited as a prime example of how oil money can result in "rent seeking" behavior by favored elites. This strand of the economic literature remains directly relevant in Angola and has gained a new prominence in Mozambique given the discoveries of large deposits of natural gas in the past few years.

Portuguese land law and reform

Perhaps the most contentious economic issue debated in either country over the post-independence era is that of the ownership of land and the laws/regulations through which it is formalized (Bruce and Migot-Adholla, 1994). Both Angola and Mozambique have multiple sets of overlapping claims to land which can be mostly categorized as follows:

- Indigenous claims based on traditional occupancy, usually not formalized but widely recognized in the locality where they are located (Goody, 1969; Gluckman, 1969);
- Colonial-era ownership claims, mostly vacated for those settlers who left in 1975 but which survive in cases where settlers remained;
- Post-independence grants of land, which can be the result of claims or grants made at various levels of government up to and including the Presidency itself (Kloeck-Jenson, 1997, 1998; McGregor, 1995; Myers, 1993).

Of course, "Marxist" economic doctrine states that all land belongs to the "people" and is managed on their behalf by the state. This idea fits well with two important needs of any extractive regime, whether it be European or indigenous. The first is the need to be able to dispose of land as desired in order to reward supporters in a political sense. The second is the need to be able to monopolize extractive rents for mineral or other natural resource based wealth. This was particularly relevant early on in Angola where oil revenues formed the majority of the income of the government. Diamond mines were of secondary importance but are still large in absolute terms in Angola. In Mozambique such extractive goals were manifest in land grants to large farmers but also to foreign extractive companies interested in such things as logging or other extractive activities. It should be noted that many of these land grants simply ignored the fact that there were people already living on the lands involved.

Reform of the inherited Portuguese land law has proceeded in both Angola and Mozambique, and has been the subject of contentious debate both within the country and between the government and donors. Mozambicans and Angolans have taken it as a matter of fixed policy that land belongs to the nation as a whole and cannot be owned by individuals in perpetuity as is the case in most Western industrial countries. Many donors, in contrast, have argued for a land law that would support an active market in land.

While in theory the new land laws (allowing for varying periods of tenure for the purpose of using the land for farming, mining, habitation, etc) are quite specific in how tenancy is granted and held, in fact the resources to actually conduct a cadastral survey with the associated bureaucratic costs has been lacking in either country. Added to this is the problem that in some areas traditional farmers use shifting cultivation methods and so are not always farming the same plot. The result is a hodgepodge in which competing interests in any particular area vie for actual control over land. Peasants are routinely dispossessed in the interest of extractive interests promoted by the central or provincial governments, while large farmers also try to gain direct control over favored parcels.

None of this really resembles a "Marxist" system of land tenure either in economic theory or in terms of its application in existing Marxist countries anywhere in the world. Rather, we are witnessing an ongoing "land grab," in which moneyed or connected players have an advantage over the less well-off.

Mineral wealth and Marx – is there any detectable difference?

The short answer to the question posed above is "no." Both the Angolan and now the Mozambican governments have asserted unambiguously that the right to subsurface mineral wealth belongs to the government. In fact, the Angolan government has demonstrated quite clearly that they are willing to wage war in whatever manner and for however long it is necessary for them to exert control over the entirety of the national area and its offshore economic zones. This includes not only oil production areas but also diamond mines in the northeast part of the country. Extraction of the oil has been done almost exclusively by foreign contractors, including US, European, and other firms experienced in oil exploration and extraction. This might seem "un-Marxist" but was in reality part of a situation so confused that at one point Cuban soldiers were protecting US oil companies from South African mercenaries funded by the US and its allies.

But the question remains – is this Marxist economics in practice? In support of a negative answer we have to recognize that using foreign contractors for extraction is no more a hallmark of a particular ideology than is assertion of control over subsurface mineral rights: in short, everyone does it. The centralizing tendencies that go along with the economics of the Resource Curse may appear at first glance to have some resemblance to Marxist economic philosophy, but in reality they are simply a manifestation of the fact that power follows money – and in a resource rich country that money is located in the capital city (Kyle, 2006a, 2006b).

Marketing, distribution, and agricultural extension

It is in the area of marketing and distribution that Marxist economic thought has had the most pervasive, and arguably the most damaging effects on the economies of Angola and Mozambique. The Marxist glorification of the production worker and the vilification of commercial traders and marketers as "parasites" who produce nothing of value, has had a clear deleterious effect on the rural economy of both Angola and Mozambique (see FRELIMO, 1968 and Frelimo Party documents from 1977/78 for policies in these areas).

First, it is important to bear in mind that as discussed above, the pre-independence marketing system almost completely disappeared with the departure of the Portuguese settlers who had virtually monopolized these activities (Azzam and Faucher, 1988; Hilmarsson, 1995; Strachan, 1997; Arndt et al., 2000). This was particularly important in rural areas where small stores provided a broad spectrum of services including informal rural credit. Lack of capital together with the widespread destruction and chaos of civil war prevented reactivation of these rural markets and many remain not served by marketers to this day.

The problem is that wholesalers and traders were regarded as profiting from the "honest" work of peasants by selling their produce for a far higher price than they paid. The real services they provided – liquidity to peasants, willingness to bear market risk if prices changed, storage and most important, transportation services – were ignored or discounted in this view of the world. All that mattered was that these traders were earning what appeared to be a healthy profit, though even huge margins could be illusory in a highly inflationary economy (Pitcher, 2002).

Some districts in Angola, for example, went five years or more without once seeing a trader willing to purchase output from farmers. Any attempt to service these markets had first to overcome physical constraints of poor roads, land mines, destroyed bridges, etc. Even if these were surmounted, government regulations limited the profits that could legally be earned to a mere 25 percent, far below inflation rates during much of the 30 years following independence.

Indeed, this antipathy to traders extended to urban areas as well, leading to a situation where officially sanctioned retail outlets in the old city centers were virtually deserted, with no stock on their shelves, while bustling, open-air markets thrived on the outskirts of town. The well known "Roque Santeiro" market outside Luanda was one of the largest and most diverse markets on the continent, and though it has now been shut down with the reactivation of retail activity in more permanent facilities it was for many years the go-to place for a wide variety of products from food to consumer durables and even weapons.

This repression of the marketing system helped produce a disconnection between the producers in the countryside and the urban demand centers on the coast. Here, however, there were two big differences between Angola and Mozambique. In Angola, the pre-existing market links between city and hinterland were ruptured by the independence-associated evacuation of Portuguese and further stifled by war and banditry. Official repression prevented any real economic incentive from arising, and this was exacerbated by exchange rate overvaluation which made competing food imports cheap on the coast. Indeed, this situation persists to the present day, with command economy adherents in the government reactivating entities such as MECANAGRO, a state-run agricultural machinery service provider which is very similar to machinery brigades in the old USSR, but which in the Angolan context serves mainly large and well-connected plantations rather than small farmers.

In Mozambique there is domestic capacity to meet urban demand on the coast, principally in Maputo. However, these market links, unlike the Angolan case, were NOT pre-existing.

Rather, the southern part of the country imported food from abroad and paid for it by exporting labor to South African mines. Building market links for grain between the North and the South is therefore a question of development rather than rehabilitation.

Finally, we must address whether the repression of marketing is truly a "marker" for Marxist economic thought and management. Clearly, it is a characteristic common to many (virtually all) Marxist economies. However, it is not exclusive to these countries – distrust of middlemen runs deep in rural areas and is a routine feature of the rural worldview in many different countries – not just those with Marxist governments. Indeed, the antipathy to profiteering middlemen owes as much to the fact that they were Portuguese colonists in the pre-independence era as it does to any governing economic philosophy.

Agricultural extension services played an important role in promoting the state view of marketing and were also a mechanism for controlling information and political participation in rural areas. Clearly inspired by political goals, rural extension meetings were in some cases run by political appointees with little agricultural knowledge. Suspicion of the motives and/or expertise of such personnel grew to be a problem in some areas, though general under-funding of extension limited the role it could actually play in many areas (Gemo and Rivera, 2001; Eicher, 2002).

Conclusion

What are we to make of all of this? It appears that even in areas where "Marxist" economic thought appears to provide explanatory power there are equally good alternatives to explain what happened in Angolan and Mozambican economic policy. To declare one's party to be "Marxist" may well have been more of an artifact of shifting alliances and supporters than it was of any real ideological convictions. Another indicator that this might well be the case is the fact that both the MPLA in Angola and FRELIMO in Mozambique have now stated that they no longer consider themselves bound by the tenets of Marxist economic thought and are pursuing market-based approaches to economic development (see World Bank, 1996 or Republic of Mozambique, 1997/98). In Angola this development was somewhat later (see MINPLAN, 2006). This is no doubt at least partly due to the fact that major potential donors wanted them to make such a change – but this is yet another indicator that claims of adherence to particular economic doctrines are, in parts of Africa at least, more situational than ideological in origin.

References

Andersson, Hilary, *Mozambique, A War Against the People*, St. Martin's Press, 1992.

Arndt, C., H.T. Jensen, S. Robinson, and F. Tarp, "Marketing margins and agricultural technology in Mozambique", *Journal of Development Studies*, 37 (1): 121–37, 2000.

Austen, Ralph, *African Economic History*, London: James Curry, 1987.

Auty, Richard M., *Sustaining Development in Mineral Economies: The Resource Curse Thesis*, London: Routledge, 1993.

Auty, Richard M., "How Natural Resources Affect Economic Development", *Development Policy Review*, 18 (4): 347–64, 2000.

Azzam, J. and J. Faucher, "The Supply of Manufactured Goods and Agricultural Development – The Case of Mozambique", OECD, 1988.

Bruce, John and Shem E. Migot-Adholla (eds), *Searching for Land Tenure Security in Africa*, Kendall/Hunt Publishing Co., World Bank, 1994.

Corden, W.M., "Boom Sector and Dutch Disease Economics: Survey and Consolidation", *Oxford Economic Papers*, 36: 362, 1984.

Eicher, Carl, "Mozambique: Review of the Implementation of the Extension Master Plan and Proposals for Improvement", July 2002.

FRELIMO, "Documents of the Second Congress", Niassa, July 1968.

Frelimo Party, "Economic and Social Directives", Third Congress of Frelimo, 1977.

Gemo, H. and W. Rivera, "Mozambique's Move Towards a Pluralistic National System of Rural Extension", ODI Agren Network Paper No.110, January 2001.

Gluckman, M., *Custom and Conflict in Africa*, Barnes and Noble Books, 1969.

Gluckman, M., "Land Tenure: Group and Individual Rights" in Konczacki ed. *An Economic History of Tropical Africa*, Frank Cass, 1977.

Goody, J., "Land Tenure and Feudalism in Africa", *The Economic History Review*, vol.XXII no.3, December 1969.

Government of Angola – Council of Ministers (1997) Decree No. 17/99 of 29 of October, Decree on the organic structure of the Provincial governments and municipal and communal administrations, Luanda.

Government of Angola – Council of Ministers (2000) Decree No. 2/00 of 14 of January, Estatuto Orgânico DU Ministério da Saúde, Luanda.

Government of Angola – Council of Ministers (2006) Decree No. 27/00 of 19 of May, Paradigma de regulamento DUs Governos das Províncias, das administrações DUs municípios e das comunas, Luanda.

Governo de Angola IBAM. "Avaliação das Necessidades de Formação da Administração Local", UNDP/IBAM, 2006.

Hilmarsson, Hilmar, "Cashew Pricing and Marketing in Mozambique", World Bank, 1995.

Isaacman, A., *Cotton is the Mother of Poverty – Peasants, Work, and Rural Struggle in Colonial Mozambique, 1938–1961*, David Philip Publishers, 1996.

Isaacman, A. and B. Isaacman, *Mozambique: From Colonialism to Revolution: 1900–1982*, Westview Press, 1983.

Kloeck-Jenson, Scott, "Analysis of the Parliamentary Debate and New National Land Law for Mozambique", Land Tenure Center-Mozambique, September 1997.

Kloeck-Jenson, Scott, "Locating the Community: Local Communities and the Administration of Land and Other Natural Resources in Mozambique", Land Tenure Center, Mozambique, 1998.

Krueger, Anne, "Trade Policy and Economic Development: How We Learn", *American Economic Review*, vol.87 no.1, 1–22, 1997.

Kyle, S., "Economic Reform and Armed Conflict in Mozambique", *World Development*, 1990.

Kyle, S., "Mozambique: Political Choices and Rural Development", Paper presented to the World Bank Seminar on Rural and Agricultural Growth and Poverty Reduction in Mozambique, January 2004.

Kyle, S., "Resettlement and Development – Moving from Rehabilitation to Growth in Mozambique and Angola", Working Paper No.2004, 05 April, 2004.

Kyle, S., "The Transition from Stabilization to Growth: How and Why to Move Beyond Exchange Based Stabilization in Angola", Working Paper No.2004, 14 October, 2004.

Kyle, S., "Oil Revenue, the Real Exchange Rate and Sectoral Distortion in Angola", Working Paper No.2005, 19 August, 2005.

Kyle, S., "Macroeconomic Impact of Mineral Revenues on General Market Equilibrium and Poverty Alleviation in Sub-Saharan Africa" (with Ahmad Slaibi), Working Paper No.2006, 20 August, 2006a.

Kyle, S., "Oil Revenue, Non-Oil Trade, and Poverty Alleviation in Angola", Working Paper No.2006, 13 June 2006b.

MAP/MSU Research Team, "Smallholder Cash-Cropping, Food-Cropping and Food Security in Northern Mozambique: Summary, Conclusions, and Policy Recommendations", Working Paper No.25, June, 1997.

MINPLAN – Direcção de Estudos e Planeamento 2004 Estratégia de Combate à Pobreza – Reinserção social, reabilitação e reconstrução e estabilização económica, Versão revista em 2006, Luanda.

McGregor, J., "Staking Their Claims: Land Disputes in Southern Mozambique", St. Antony's College, Oxford, 1995, mimeo.

Messiant, Christine, "Angola, the Challenge of Statehood", in Birmingham and Martin (eds), *History of Central Africa*, Longman, 1998.

Myers, Gregory, "Land Tenure Issues in Post-War Mozambique: Constraints and Conflicts", Land Tenure Center, University of Wisconsin, April 1993.

Newitt, Malyn, *A History of Mozambique*, Indiana University Press, 1995.

Pitcher, M. Anne, *Transforming Mozambique – The Politics of Privatization, 1975–2000*, Cambridge University Press, 2002.

Republic of Mozambique, *Mozambique: Policy framework paper 1997–99*. Maputo: Republic of Mozambique, 1997.

Republic of Mozambique Ministry of Agriculture and Fisheries, "PROAGRI 1998–2003 Executive Summary", February 1998.

Rodrik, Dani (ed.), *In Search of Prosperity: Analytic Narratives on Economic Growth*, Princeton University Press, 2003.

Strachan, Lloyd, "Diagnostic Survey of Rural Trade Network and Proposal for Agricultural Marketing Support", INDER, April 1997.

Williamson, John, "What Washington Means by Policy Reform", in *Latin American Readjustment: How Much has Happened*, Washington: Institute for International Economics, 1989.

World Bank/Republic of Mozambique, *Mozambique: Policy framework paper 1996–98*, Maputo, 1996.

Part V

The Asia-Pacific region

25

Australia and New Zealand

A young tree dead?*

William Coleman

The history of the economics of Australia and New Zealand will be, at bottom, an account of that economics' confrontation of its marginality. For any story of economic thought in Australia and New Zealand will necessarily tell of the attempt to plant and cultivate in uncleared ground the long developed vine of older societies. It will relate how the cultivators pondered whether adapting the growth to local conditions would be more or less rewarding than simply perfecting their cultivation of the imported stem, and introducing its ever purer varieties. It will reveal that the adaptation of imported varieties to idiosyncratic conditions was in the event limited, though not wholly without significance; and even leaving some trace of cross-fertilisation of the wider world. For all that, the story, I contend, will conclude today with the local strains being submerged by the benefits and snares of globalisation.

The history of economics in Australia and New Zealand has been written before, both in detail and synoptically, with considerable scholarship and some panache (Goodwin, 1966; Groenewegen and McFarlane, 1990; La Nauze, 1949; King, 2007; Cornish, 2008; Blyth, 2008; Hight, 1939). The present history seeks to add through its focus on the predicament of any economics that rationally and usefully bears the adjective 'Australian'.

The cultural and economic context

Australia can claim several singularities, but for the present analysis its key feature will be taken to be the recurrent contention over the past two centuries between the aspirations of the state and those of society at large. The pre-eminent motive of the populace of this society has been economic advantage, to the near exclusion of any other. But the state – looming so large in Australian society since its genesis – has displayed a range of postures towards the economic. For a long period it was in profound conflict with the economic criterion. In inaugurating European settlement in 1788 by dispatching to 'Botany Bay' an expedition under military command, devoid of a medium of exchange, burdened by the full force of the Navigation Acts and the East India Company's monopoly on trade and restricted to the labour of criminals almost bereft of agricultural skill, the British state might be seen as designing its new extension to fail.

The colony's salvation lay in a clique of venal and rebellious army officers – the 'Rum Corps' – who saw in the penal settlement their road to personal enrichment. The broadest path they found was in wool. But the glisten of a golden fleece was descried guardedly by the imperial government: it scanned doubtful charts of the Australian continent and forbad the massing flocks to pass beyond certain rivers. (It was ignored.) It ordered the nascent banks to decline livestock as collateral, and not to assume unlimited liability. (It was ignored.) It insisted a sovereign right of ownership of every fleck of gold that might be gleaned from the dust; and in doing so provoked the one anti-constitutional convulsion in Australia's history, the 'Eureka Stockade' of 1854.

By underwriting the establishment of democratic governance throughout Australasia during the late 1850s, the Eureka stockade promoted a key re-coordination of the spacious presumptions of the older military state with the economic hunger of the now almost wholly free population. In facing their isolation, underdevelopedness and underpopulation, the infant Australasian democracies concluded that an active state could complement the potential for individual wealth making; a conclusion that was reinforced by the calamitous end of the wool, land and banking boom of the 1880s. A use of a constructivist means to serve individualist ends also supplied a tacit detente between the two ideological currents that the immigrant society brought with it; Benthamite constructivism and an individualist liberalism.

The epitome of this apparent realignment of the state with economic aspirations might be called 'Deakinism', after Alfred Deakin, the brilliant three-time Prime Minister of Australia between 1903 and 1910. Rejecting both socialism and '*laissez-faire*', he keenly propagated a system of extensive state manipulation of the economic game played by the manifold factors of production, on the presumption that, deftly done, it could benefit all interests and dispel conflict. If there is an 'Australian Ideology' it is Deakinism. Not even the emergence in Australia by 1914 of a powerful (and formally socialist) labour party – and the concomitant extinction of classical liberalism – would displace Deakinism from its position of sway. In New Zealand a variant of Deakinism was equally triumphant under the governance of the New Zealand Liberal Party from 1891–1912 (see Reeves, 1902 for an ardent statement of the creed, Metin, 1977 for a semi-incredulous nineteenth-century Marxist appraisal, and Hancock, 1930 for a liberal critique).

How does the cultivation of economics fit the Deakinite mindset? A particular kind – Utilitarian Economics – co-exists with it very well. A 'utilitarian' character coheres with Australia's bluntly 'pragmatic' attitudes. Through its imperative to instrumentalise everything, utilitarian economics neuters both the market and the state to harness them in the service of the maximum utility. Unencumbered by ideological or moral commitments, this sort of economics was free both to moot state remedies for various ills, and to shed them without qualms when they proved disappointing. In the same vein, in the eyes of utilitarian economics a free market was no more or less than an implement in the designing Benthamite tool box; and free trade – rather than being the economic ensign of political liberalism – could be either discarded as 'not applicable' or assimilated as one of the prudent moves of an all solving, all versatile state.

The development of economic ideas over the long-term

As Utilitarian economics had been brilliantly cultivated by British thinkers, it would seem inevitable for it to be reproduced in Australia. But the advent of any economics would not be a simple matter of the transportation of a doctrine from Britain to Australia, and the story of Australian economics opens with something of a false start: the passage across the Australian scene of three political economists of at least some world renown, W.S. Jevons (1835–82), W.E. Hearn (1826–88) and David Syme (1827–1908). In this episode of the pre-history of Australian economics, Australia, still more a frontier than a community, was effectively giving space for some of the wayward energy of the metropolis to express itself. But that very frontier character meant that there was little local institutional netting for their ideas to fasten to, and the promise of their fortuitous arrival was not obviously realised.

Syme, Jevons and Hearn – a Scotsman, an Englishman and an Irishman – were born within eight years of one another; all arrived in the wave of Gold rush emigration (Syme – 1852, Jevons – 1854, Hearn – 1855); and all were attracted to dissent in 'political economy'. All three, indeed, proposed new names for the discipline. Syme favoured 'Industrial Science', and it is on account of his *Outline of Industrial Science* (1877) that David Syme 'was known to many who would have been unable to name the capital of Victoria' (La Nauze, 1949). A brilliantly successful Melbourne newspaper proprietor, and friend of T.E. Cliffe Leslie, his fluent and glib prose does not attempt to theorise, but discharges a methodological critique of classical economics. But Syme's greater significance of the story of Australian economics lies in 'rare friendship' that he nurtured with Alfred Deakin. Rescuing him from legal failure, Syme employed Deakin in his mouthpiece, *The Age*, and converted him to protectionism, and in some way made Deakin the political embodiment of 'the Australian ideology'.

A far fainter impress on Deakin's mind was evidently made by W.E. Hearn, who taught the future prime minister free trade doctrines as the professor of 'modern history and literature, political economy and logic' from 1855 to 1873 at the newly established University of Melbourne. Hearn is, indeed, not remembered as a dispenser of standard classical policy prescriptions, but as the author of *Plutology or the Theory of the Efforts to Satisfy Human Wants* of 1863. An exercise in subjectivism without marginalism, *Plutology*'s 'curiously Jevonian' echoes (Schumpeter, 1954, 826) received the praise of Marshall, Edgeworth and Jevons (Moore, 2002). Yet it has no 'analysis'. Neither need we marvel at what Hearn did achieve, since as former student in the Trinity College, Dublin, Hearn was 'almost bound to be exposed to the infection of utility theory' (La Nauze, 1941, 257).

It is a teasing possibility that one of Hearn's students could well have included W.S. Jevons. For it was only after some indecision that Jevons in 1859 declined an offer of a generous position at the Melbourne mint, and instead returned to England, certainly without any contact with Hearn. The problem therefore that arises from Jevons' five-year sojourn in Sydney (1854–59) is, what significance – if any – might it hold for the genesis of his 'true theory' of political economy that he struck upon within 12 months of departing Australia? (see White, 1982, 2006). The most Jevons allowed for Australia is that it rendered 'peculiar service' by giving time to 'mature' his powers. We are really in matters of psycho-biography than intellectual history, and it is for others to divine the meaning of Jevons' remark on his arrival in England that he felt as if he had 'dreamt a great deal in a very short time' (5 October 1859, in Jevons, 1972).

What if Jevons had stayed? 'I could not have done much in Sydney', judged Jevons. 'I thought what I did very clever then, but it seems foolishness to me now'. A more objective indicator of the counter-factual may lie in the career of Alfred De Lissa (1838–1913). Both De Lissa and Jevons were religiously unorthodox; both attended University College at the same time; both had bankrupt fathers; and both arrived in Sydney, within a year of each other, in the wake of the gold rushes. But unlike Jevons, De Lissa stayed in Sydney, and nevertheless achieved something 'clever'. In 1890 De Lissa proclaimed in the *Australian Economist* a 'Law of Incomes', in which the impact on national income of any shock to primary production was a multiple of that shock (Goodwin, 1966). De Lissa's algebra not only sharply reminds the modern reader of the Keynesian multiplier, it was a sensible modelling of Australian national income. But it sank without trace, as did the prematurely launched Australian Economic Society (1888–98) and its organ, the *Australian Economist* (N.G. Butlin, 1988; S.J. Butlin, 1988).

William Coleman

The inter-war period

L.F. Giblin once declared, in hindsight, that 1924 'might perhaps be called A.E.1 – the first year of economists in Australia' (1947). Certainly, it was in the inter-war period that Australian economics progressed from the cogitations of solitaries to being a complex of intellectual and social capital that would assume a role as counsel to the nation in the economic tribulations of the period.

The occasion of this transformation was world war, and its twin offspring of economic turbulence and an effectively sovereign Australian state. At the same time the war's social dislocation, by revitalising the universities, fostered the brains to manage the state's problems. And so it was that the most prominent manifestation of the advent of economics was the rapid creation of specific Chairs and Departments and degrees in Economics and Commerce throughout Australia and New Zealand, where there had been almost nothing before (Anderson and O'Neil, 2009; Groenewegen, 2009; Kenwood and Lougheed, 1997; Williams, 2009). There followed, with a lag of 10 years, the first appointment of economists by the Treasury and the Commonwealth Bank.

But perhaps the key sign of the arrival of the economist was the foundation in 1924 in 'almost evangelical fervour' of the Economic Society of Australia and New Zealand (see Scott, 1988), with D.B. Copland assuming a vigorous leadership role. The Society quickly established the *Economic Record* (Giblin, 1947), with its first issue selling a very respectable 1,150 copies (compared to the 3,000 of the *Economic Journal* at the time).

The new profession was very small, perhaps 20 in all; of which the most senior twelve were Horace Belshaw (b. 1898), J.B. Brigden (b. 1887), Colin Clark (b. 1905), John Bell Condliffe (b. 1891), D.B. Copland (b. 1894), L.F. Giblin (b. 1871), K. Isles (b. 1902), R.C. Mills (b. 1886), Leslie Melville (b. 1901), E.O.G. Shann (b. 1884), Ronald Walker (b. 1907) and Roland Wilson (b. 1904). This 'intimate' circle was almost entirely native born; of these twelve there are only two partial exceptions (Belshaw arrived in New Zealand aged eight; Clark was British born, but his father had made his fortune in Queensland). All but one had formal education in economics, and most had post-graduate study, including three doctoral degrees (Belshaw, Walker, Wilson). Its intellectual orientation (with the solitary exception of Wilson) was strongly towards England rather than the United States.

Underlining this is that ten of the dozen had significant personal, professional or pedagogical association with J.M. Keynes. Keynes was, in fact, examiner for the University of New Zealand in economics 1919 (Blyth, 2007). Like Keynes, none of these were unalloyed academics; all had significant careers as public servants or advisors. Like Keynes, all of them pursued a method of 'realistic theory'. And, like Keynes, all of them – with the gaping exception of Shann and Melville – were sympathetic to the 'end of *laissez-faire*' New Liberalism that Deakinism was so clearly correlated with.

That doctrinal technicalities fell lightly upon them, but policy heavily, made them sensitive to the palpable facts of the Australian situation: it was a 'small open economy', whose exports were overwhelming produced by sector-specific natural resources with a price inelastic supply, and whose income (in consequence) included a large rent component, driven by fluctuating world demand. Having a high standard of living, the bulk of its income was spent on services. The now familiar classification of economic activity into the primary, secondary and tertiary sectors appears to be an antipodean neologism (Fisher, 1939). Australia was also a capital-hungry economy, with investment regularly exceeding saving, the size excess being determined by volatile net capital inflow driven by overseas sentiments, with the concomitant implication that any deficiency in aggregate demand would be a matter of its trade account.

These circumstances produced a novel economics of the open economy that can be summarised in three themes. First, the dependence of factor incomes on relative prices. In the opening issue of the *Economic Record* Brigden (1925) advanced the heterodoxical thesis that a tariff may enhance real wages. In Brigden's argument, labour is assumed to operate with diminishing marginal productivity in food (the exportable), but with constant marginal returns in manufactures (the importable). Given this, increasing tariffs will leave the marginal productivity of labour in manufactures unchanged (by assumption), but will induce a reallocation of labour from food towards manufactures, that thereby increased the marginal product of labour in food. The upshot is that the manufactures wage is unchanged, and the food wage is increased, and so the 'living standard' is raised.

This argument of Brigden became the key idea in the moderately protectionist semi-official *The Australian Tariff: an Economic Enquiry* of 1929. In Paul Samuelson's judgment the *Enquiry* helped 'set off an analytical controversy that has helped shape' the 1941 proof of Samuelson-Stolper that higher tariffs would unambiguously increase real wages if the country's import-competing sector is relatively labour intensive. In Samuelson's own words: 'I at least had very much in mind at the time of the Stolper-Samuelson investigations . . . the correctness of the "Australian case for the tariff"' (quoted in Coleman, Cornish and Hagger, 2006, 71).

Second, the dependence of the price of non-tradeables on net capital inflow. Wilson (1931) argued that, contrary to the contention of Mill and the presumption of the 'transfer problem' debate, net capital inflow need not be favourable to the recipient country's terms of trade. This was because there could be no presumption that mere reallocation of purchasing power from the donor to the recipient country (which capital inflow amounted to) would increase the world demand of the recipient country's exportable. However, argued Wilson, the reallocation of purchasing to the recipient country would certainly increase the demand for those outputs of the recipient country that only the recipient country could demand: it is non-tradeable.

Thus Wilson's contention was that the size of capital inflows governed 'the second terms of trade' – the price of non-tradeables in terms of tradeables, and this was to become a recurrent theme in Australian theorising throughout the twentieth century. The first fruit of Swan's digestion of Wilson's thesis was the 'Swan Diagram' (Swan, 1968), which demonstrated how, in a neo-Keynesian context, capital inflows would necessitate an increase in home costs (that is, non-tradeables). Wilfred Salter recast the same ideas in neoclassical form in the 'Salter Diagram' (Salter, 1959). The key equilibrating role of the relative price of non-tradeables was assimilated into international economics: James Meade was 'converted' during a 'DC flight from Canberra to Sydney' in 1956 (Arndt, 1985). But the most resonant application of the notions awaited the 'Gregory Thesis' of the 1970s that pressed a simple but socially significant implication of Wilson's thesis: that an increase in the value of non-tradeables would cause a depression in the production and incomes in the import-competing manufacturing sector.

Third, the export multiplier. In an economy composed mostly of services, a fall in the value of services amounts to a fall in national income, and so in pressing the link between the trade account and the value of services we are led to a vision of macroeconomy in which exports are significantly out of all apparent proportion to their size. This vision was captured by Giblin in 1930 through his articulation of a multiplier concept, in which (to use his example) a reduction of 700 pounds in export incomes would ultimately reduce national income by a total of 2,100 pounds, assuming a propensity to import of 1/3.

In *Australia, 1930* Giblin applied his multiplier logic to the onset of the Great Depression, 15 months before the Cambridge multiplier was in print. The logic of Giblin's multiplier differed from that of Cambridge; his was purely an export multiplier, and its roots appear to be correspondingly different and local (e.g. De Lissa). For all its distinctive logic and provenance, it is legitimate to be tantalised by the fact that King's College library does contain a copy of *Australia, 1930*. Giblin – a former student of King's College and friend of Keynes – had sent it, and it had arrived in June 1930. But there is no evidence that either Keynes or any 'Circus' members were aware of Giblin's multiplier. Neither was Giblin any more successful in April 1932 in securing Keynes' assent to his proposition that 'any increase of purchasing power directly by government expenditure or otherwise would result in a total purchasing power of three to four times the original amount' (Coleman, Cornish and Hagger, 2006, 97). Keynes' interest was caught, not by the work of Australia's professionals, but by a certain Australian partisan of Social Credit who, Keynes told Copland, had authored 'a most brilliant little book . . . with a touch of genius', and about whom Keynes asked Copland to dig about for details (see Millmow, 1997).

Nevertheless, Giblin did succeed in leaving one footprint on the *General Theory*. In 1935 he pressed on Keynes one peculiar condition of Australia; that industrial tribunals undertook to peg the aggregate *real* wage level. Presumably, this prompted Keynes to ask in the *General Theory*, what would be the implications for his model 'if, as in Australia, an attempt was made to fix by law the real wage'? (Keynes, 1936, 298).

The post-war period

The achievement of Australian economics in the inter-war period was to have created something where there had been (almost) nothing. The Second World War put this new creation to intensive use, without itself being transforming. But the economic context of the post-war was transforming; an 'age of opulence' had begun, and Australian economics was not excluded from its benefits.

Enrolments leapt; between 1940 and 1980 the annual output in Bachelor degrees in economics rose in Australia from 128 to 3,195 (Butlin, 1987). And a degree that had largely consisted of night classes given by part-time lecturers had by the 1960s become one taught by full-time staff to day students. Perhaps the most telling distinguishing mark from the inter-war era was the belated introduction of the PhD in economics (Melbourne – 1954; ANU – 1956; Sydney – 1964; Adelaide – 1971). This accelerated domestic production of human capital was complemented by the arrival of overseas talent escaping a fallen European continent: Fred Argy, Heinz Arndt, Harro Bernadelli, Max Corden, Peter Groenewegen, Fred Gruen, Helen Hughes, Jan Kmenta and Kurt Singer.

For all the transformation of its material situation, post-war Australian economics mostly followed tracks marked out by the previous generation. In economic history the massive narratives of Sydney and Noel Butlin of Australian growth and development were plainly stirred by the four volume chronology of Australian development authored 50 years before by T.A. Coghlan (1855–1926). Coghlan's example had a dual significance for the rapidly emerging sub-discipline of Australian economic history; he was the most eminent representative of a vigorous statistical movement in nineteenth-century Australia (Groenewegen and McFarlane, 1990, 92–117; Haig, 2006), a legacy of Australia being the costly possession of a mother country concerned for its expensive charge account for itself. And Coghlan, as Australia's most senior civil servant of his time, also implicitly heeded the Deakinite outlook by casting active governors and politicians as the most creative individuals in his history. Noel Butlin shared both Coghlan's vision of the partnership of the market and state, along with his statistical method; a specifically statistical (rather than econometric) quantitative method contributed to Australian economic history remaining distinct in style from its American counterpart (Coleman, 2014).

In international economics, the Brigden Report of 1929 was the starting point of Corden's investigations of the trade-policy small open economy, which yielded the earliest diagrammatic analysis of partial equilibrium of a tariff of an industry facing a given world-price, now found in all the text books (Corden, 1957). Still more novel was Corden's exploration of the notion of 'effective protection' that confronted tariffs in vertical production relations, 'an aspect until recently completely neglected in the literature of international trade theory' (Corden, 1968, 2004).

The post-war period did see the sudden germination of one new branch of Australian economics that was to have an impact out of proportion to its size: the marginal limb of agricultural economics. In New Zealand, Horace Belshaw had established firmly agricultural economics during the 1920s. But in Australia the genesis of this field came later, in reaction to the failure of government attempts to assist struggling agriculture. The Commonwealth Bank of Australia, whose finances had been marshalled into supplying cheap loans to the rural sector, began to generously fund the establishment of chairs in agricultural economics in Sydney, Melbourne, Adelaide, Monash, Western Australia and above all the University of New England (Bearman, 1985).

This sudden burgeoning of agricultural economics had two reverberations. First, the value of quantitative precision in designing agricultural policy, along with a good supply of data, made the field an excellent terrain for post-war econometric revolution; thus A.R. Bergstrom's first paper – also the first paper by a New Zealand author in *Econometrica* – concerned the British demand for New Zealand pastoral products. The extension of these techniques to general equilibrium models became a field in which Australia achieved a global prominence (see Challen and Hagger, 1979). Second, agricultural economics introduced a new strain of thought into the doctrinally inbred Australian scene: it introduced an American accent.

As one agricultural economist later explained 'it was quite obvious' that adequate training in agricultural economics was not to be had in the United Kingdom, and therefore, violating almost all precedent, post-graduate training was sought in the United States (Gruen, 1988). In 1950–1 Fred Gruen initiated what was to become a small chain migration to the University of Chicago; he was followed by Ross Parish, Alan Powell and K.O. Campbell. This Chicago training favoured 'price theory' over the mix of effective demand and monopolistic competition that was then the pith of local economics pedagogy, and Australian agricultural economists formed a novel constituency for deregulation of agriculture. More generally, the 'price theory' critique of the hapless state of Australian agricultural policy (e.g. Sieper, 1982) became one of the more powerful gusts in the gathering wind of 'economic rationalism' pressing against Deakinite presumptions.

One part of 'Chicago' that had almost no resonance in Australia was 'monetarism'. Australian macroeconomists of the post-war were satisfied with a hydraulic Keynesianism; the multiplier macroeconomics of Giblin – which had never disputed Say's Law – was ignored. It is true that in 1947, Murray Kemp (rightly) dismissed the *General Theory*'s assumption of exogenous money supply as redundant to Keynes' project of establishing the existence of 'unemployment equilibrium', by demonstrating that an infinite elasticity of the supply of money at some critical interest rate was sufficient to destroy the equilibrating effect of money wage adjustments (Kemp, 1948). But Kemp's point was totally ignored by macroeconomists, and it resurfaced quite independently as a 'post-Keynesian' tenet in the 1970s.

Neither did earlier Australian attempts at quantitative articulation of Keynesianism receive any development in the post-war period. Colin Clark's 1938 *The National Income of Australia* provided the first empirical assessment ('test') anywhere of Keynes' multiplier doctrine of national income, but his method was entirely neglected. Swan in 1945 (Swan, 1989) developed an elaborate econometric model that closely followed the *General Theory* (e.g. distinguishing aggregate supply and aggregate demand functions), but the first published Keynesian modellings of the Australian economy followed Klein. A student of Swan, John Pitchford, explored what became known as the 'AK' model of economic growth a generation before Barro *et al.* (Pitchford, 1960), but had had no impact. All this bespeaks the difficulty in a small intellectual community of keeping afloat and moving the stray bright ideas that it launches.

The antipodean contribution to macroeconomics that did launch a thousand papers was by someone not working in Australia or New Zealand, or working on Australasian data: A.W. Phillips. Phillips' performance is acutely singular, and is surely largely traceable to inborn brilliance and a lack of formal economics education, with little left over for his native land to claim. And yet it remains true that several decades before Isles (1932) had already drawn attention to the negative correlation between the unemployment rate and the rate of change in wholesale prices in Australia between 1913 and 1930.

If the inter-war Australian economics might be commended for making a good start from a low base, how might post-war economics be judged? Professional standards were established, certainly. Yet a critic can add some negatives to the balance. Australia managed to make only a very limited impact on the wider world of economics. Thus in a careful review of *Economic Record* in the mid-1960s, Butlin notes of it 'one finds depressingly few citations in overseas journals' (1966, 611).

Beyond international attention, Australian economics as an analytical entity did not seem to keenly serve its idiosyncrasies of the Australian context. The only real attention to minerals came from an economic historian (Geoffrey Blainey), until the early 1970s when, amidst an international focus on exhaustible exhaustion, analytical contributions were made by Ngo van Long, Murray Kemp and Neil Vousden. Despite her empty spaces there was little interest in spatial economics (save Blainey, 1966), although transport economics was pursued. In the matter of population, Australian economists largely ceded the area in the post-war period to demography. Australia's industrial tribunals – which Keynes at least noticed – received a considerable 'institutional' attention, but barely any theoretical analysis. Despite the precedent interest of Australian economists in capital inflows, it was a visiting Scotsman who first tackled the subject with analytical heft (MacDougal, 1960); and it took the arrival of a footloose Scot (Alex Hunter) to make the acutely monopolised state of Australian business an issue amongst Australian economists. In sympathy, one economist declared the existence of a vacuum in industrial organisation in Australia (Round, 1974).

Why this weakness?

Doubtless a degree of culpability lies in the post-war period being 'the age of macroeconomics'. Of course, macroeconomics meant Keynesian economics, and that in turn suggests another clue; Australian economics had drawn its intellectual capital too narrowly from Cambridge. It is remarkable how many of the personalities of the still compact world of post-war Australian economics had studied there: Austin Holmes, Maxwell Newton, Richard Downing, David Butt, Gerard Firth, Ronald Frank Henderson, Wilfred Salter, Eric Alfred Russel, Geoff Harcourt, John McCarty, Duncan Ironmonger, James Perkins, Allan Barton, Sydney Butlin, Michael Schneider, Burgess Cameron, Donald Cochrane, Peter Karmel, G.L.S. Tucker, not to mention Trevor Swan, who had distinct Cambridge ties if not formal qualifications (Harcourt, 2006).

Indeed, it may be argued that Cambridge in its 1950s formation actually constituted a burden to Swan. He had, of course, advanced in 1956 the 'neoclassical growth model', at essentially the same moment as Solow. It is uncertain if Swan's model was conceived independently of Solow's: the relevant issue of the *Quarterly Journal of Economics* had arrived in the library of the Australian National University by the time of Swan's first public outing of his ideas; on the other hand his contemporaries deemed Swan's paper original (see Pitchford, 2002). But despite Solow's (1997) generous salute to Swan, Swan's 1956 paper takes on a slight dimension when placed next to Solow's in the same year. Swan's paper is barely more than a note; 10 pages in length. It is dwarfed by an 18-page appendix of Swan's defending his use of a Clarkian capital aggregate against 'Joan Robinson's Puzzle'. How much more useful would have been 18 pages investigating the growth model?

In its broader Marshall-Pigou incarnation the 'Cambridge complex' was enervating. Marshall and Pigou loomed massive in the intellectual capital of post-war economists. Thus the *Principles of Economics* and the *Economics of Industry* were textbooks at Sydney University until the late 1950s (Groenewegen, 2010). A similar enduring prominence was found in New Zealand (Endres, 2010). Regrettably, economics is *not* 'all in Marshall'. And the presumption that 'economics' and 'Marshall' were synonymous encouraged the neglect, among other things, of Fisherian analysis of inter-temporal wealth and utility maximisation, which in the post-war period so palpably stimulated even enthusiastic American Marshallians such as Friedman.

A second ground for the deficiencies in post-war Australian economics might be sought in its utilitarian style. Such an economics is 'pragmatic'. It is not uncritical, but it is moderate, even unimaginative. It will not propose anything 'not in the political vocabulary'. (What would be the use of that?) And it is conservative in a literal sense; it tends to wait for an acrid smell to arise before concluding the mechanism needs repair. In the absence of any reek, its tendency was to appreciate, or perhaps recommend rationalising, the various peculiar institutions of Australian economy – the Commonwealth Grants Commission, Australian Conciliation and Arbitration Commission, the Loan Council, the Commonwealth Tariff Board – but not to judge them. The suggestion of something a bit mould-breaking was rare; it could only be, for example, a British economist who would propose in the 1960s the introduction of a consumption tax (Bensusan-Butt) or another (James Meade) who might suggest the Australian currency would be better off floating.

For all that, three volumes of *Surveys of Australian Economics* published from 1978 constitute a worthy testimony to the intellectual merit and strength of post-war Australian economics. Indeed, it was shortly thereafter that post-war economics enjoyed its day in the sun as the traditional formulation of the Deakinite project faltered, and the Hawke government (1983–91) sought to re-calibrate it with major assistance from economists. It was a hey-day, but the moment was brief.

Recent trends in economics

The post-war boom in Australian economics came to a crashing end in the late 1980s amidst a furious recoil at the retreat from the traditional Deakinite formulae of protection, labour regulation and state finance. This outraged reaction to the negation of old verities had parallels in other economies at the time, but in Australia it had a particular vehemence (see Coleman and Hagger, 2001). It was doubtless in sympathy with the scapegoating of economists that enrolments in economics began to shrink sharply. This was reinforced by a switch of students in the late 1980s to new more crudely vocational courses in 'business'. Thus the utilitarianism that had fed Australian economics was now withering it. Inevitably, this decline in student numbers was followed by the abolition of several economics departments and the total elimination of distinct departments of economic history.

At the same time as the casting of economists as a bugaboo by the rallied defence of the Deakinite project there arrived 'globalisation'. This produced a surge in enrolments that was vast at the graduate level. Whereas PhDs in the post-war period were a sprinkle, now departments established PhD assembly lines powered by foreign aid scholarships. Globalisation also revolutionised appointments. In the post-war years 'appointments from overseas were made cautiously' (Schedvin, 1978, 145) and sometimes grudgingly: in the 1950s John Harsanyi was denied promotion to Senior Lecturer by the University of Queensland, despite two papers in the *Journal of Political Economy*, one in *Econometrica* and one in the *Review of Economic Studies*. From the 1990s hiring directly from the United States became almost *de rigeur* for more highly ranked universities. This provoked complaints of 'Americanisation' (Gronewegen and McFarlane, 1990). But this term misrepresents the phenomenon; for the fields that are most resonant of American ideals – Law and Economics and Public Choice – have had little success in Australia. What Australia has absorbed in full measure is an 'international style'; a kind of economics that has no nationality, and looks the same wherever it is found across the world.

Both the anathemas of anti-economics and the enticements of globalisation operate in the same direction; to weaken Australian economics. One symptom is the struggles of the Economic Society of Australia to retain the engagement of academics, and its displacement by the Econometric Society. Another is the decline of text books with a significant Australian orientation. In the 1970s a genuine and careful adaptation was made of Samuelson, giving full recognition to Australian economics (Millmow, 2011). In the 1980s this text was not re-issued, but instead supplanted by adaptations of other US texts that were sometimes crude 'find and replace' operations. A third symptom would be the vanishing of Australian presence in international economics, once a stronghold of Australians. A co-editor of the *Journal of International Economics* was once quoted as saying 'All Aussies are good at trade theory' (Kenyon, 1992). Who would say that today? Perhaps the final 'proof' would be the seeming impossibility today of producing a 'Survey of Australian Economics' as was done a generation ago. In Australia today there is economics aplenty. But there is no Australia in economics any longer. Australian economics is at an end.

Does it matter?

It can be argued that an Australian economics is a misallocation of intellect. Is not the idiosyncratic the anomalous? And as a society gets smaller do not its idiosyncrasies become puny? Would not the most quintessentially Australian Economics be the economics of bushfires (Healey *et al.*, 1985)? Or perhaps the economics of brown snakes? Perhaps when economic journals took two months to arrive by sea-mail it was rational for some to pay attention to an 'Australian Model'. But distance has been abolished by various technological miracles, and the only rational choice for any talent is to participate in some global research project addressing 'big', universal and enduring questions.

In reply a sceptic might wonder whether distance has entirely lost its sting. Johnson's claim of 1969 on the inevitability of Canada and Australia being 'behind' remains true (1971). A sceptic might additionally declare that what globalisation has spelt for Australian economics is not so much integration but provincialisation. The aspiration of the post-war generation of cultural critics to reject a provincial self-relegation (e.g. A.A. Phillips, Robin Boyd) – an aspiration fully shared by economists like Butlin – now has little resonance, and Australian economists are content to borrow standards of judgement from the metropolis: the essential proof of the provincial mind. And when has provincialism added anything? Australia is now another Kansas. And what is the good of a second Kansas?

But if one was to commit to the pursuit of an Australian economics, we need to ask and decide wherein lies the value of any economics that rationally bears the adjective 'Australian'? Will it be that economics that successfully brings to the world's attention certain conditions peculiar to Australia, and thereby promotes their assimilation into a universal theory? Or will it be an economics which deems universal theories as empty of content, and therefore sees no choice but to deal with the Australian situation by means of a suite of special models?

The two positions have been well aired by Kenyon (1992, 1994) and Goodwin (2002). In reflecting upon his massive *Economic Enquiry in Australia* at the distance of four decades, Goodwin judged:

> So long as economic thought is defined as what has come out of Cambridge England and Cambridge Mass, with perhaps New York, Lausanne, Stockholm and Vienna thrown in, Australian economic thought ... will remain a non-subject – or at most a footnote ... But if Australian economic thought is taken to include ... how (for example) to build a racially and ethnically diverse nation with European roots but Asian location, then the subject takes on a new life and excitement.
>
> *(2002, 3)*

With that in mind Goodwin devoted a large part of *Enquiry* to 'oddballs' writing 'disreputable periodical literature ... beyond the pale of real economics'. Kenyon disputed the apparent identification of Australian economics with 'ratbags, heretics, cranks and *amateurs*', and the attendant suggestion that 'had the First fleet never sailed ... there would be very little in modern economics different from what there is today'. It is beyond the remit of this chapter to try to decide this dispute, but any choice over the orientation of Australian economics will need to weight the rival risks the two authors draw attention to.

Note

* I am indebted to the comments of Henry Ergas, Graeme Wells, Geoffrey Brennan, Mervyn Lewis, Alex Millmow, David Vines, Selwyn Cornish, Keith Rankin and George Fane.

References

Anderson, Kym and Bernard O'Neil 2009, *The Building of Economics at Adelaide, 1901–2001*, Adelaide: Barr Smith Press.

Arndt, H.W. 1985, *A Course Through Life: Memoirs of an Australian Economist*, Canberra: National Centre for Development Studies, Australian National University.

Bearman, Sally 1985, *Agricultural Economics in Australia*, Armidale: Dept. of Agricultural Economics & Business Management, University of New England.

Bergstrom, A.R. 1988, 'The History of Continuous-Time Econometric Models', *Econometric Theory*, 4(3) 365–83.

Blainey, Geoffrey 1966, *The Tyranny of Distance: How Distance Shaped Australia's History*, Melbourne: Sun Books.

Blyth, Conrad 2007, 'John Maynard Keynes: External Examiner for the University of New Zealand, 1919', *History of Economics Review*, 46, 151–62.

Blyth, Conrad 2008, 'Early Academic Economics in New Zealand: Notes on Its History from the 1870s to the 1950s', Wortung Paper Series, Dept. of Economics, University of Auckland, no.266.

Brigden, J.B. 1925, 'The Australian Tariff and the Standard of Living', *Economic Record* 1(1), 29–46.

Butlin, Noel 1987, 'Human or Inhuman Capital, The Economics Profession 1916–87', *Occasional Paper University of Newcastle Department of Economics*, no.146.

Butlin, N.G. 1988, 'The Life and Times of the Australian Economist 1888–1898', in *The Australian Economist 1888–1898*, Australian National University Press.

Butlin, S.J. 1966, 'The Hundredth Record', *Economic Record*, 42(1–4), 508–19.

Butlin, S.J. 1988, 'The Australian Economic Association', in *The Australian Economist 1888–1898*, Australian National University Press.

Challen, D.W. and A.J. Hagger 1979, *Modelling the Australian Economy*, Melbourne: Longman Cheshire.

Clark, Colin and J.G. Crawford 1938, *The National Income of Australia*, Sydney: Angus and Robertson.

Coleman, William 2006, 'A Conversation with Max Corden', *Economic Record*, 82(259), 379–395.

Coleman, William 2014, 'The Historiography of Australian Economic History' in *Cambridge Economic History of Australia*, Simon Ville and Glenn Withers eds, Cambridge University Press.

Coleman, William and Alf Hagger 2001, *Exasperating Calculators: the Rage Against Economic Rationalism and the Campaign against Australian Economists*, Sydney: Macleay Press.

Coleman, William, Selwyn Cornish and Alf Hagger 2006, *Giblin's Platoon: the Trials and Triumph of the Economist in Australian Public Life*, Canberra: ANU E Press.

Corden, W.M. 1957, 'The Calculation of the Cost of Protection', *Economic Record*, 33, 29–51.

Corden, W.M. 1968, 'Australian Economic Policy Discussion in the Post-War Period: A Survey', *American Economic Review*, 58(3), Part 2, Supplement, 88–138.

Corden, W.M. 2005, 'Effective Protection and I', *History of Economics Review*, 42 (Summer), 1–11.

Cornish, Selwyn 2008, 'Economics in Australasia', *The New Palgrave Dictionary of Economics*, Second Edition, Palgrave Macmillan.

Endres, Tony 2010, 'Marshallian Economics in New Zealand, c. 1890–1940' in *The Impact of Alfred Marshall's Ideas: the Global Diffusion of his Work*, Tiziano Raffaelli, ed., Cheltenham, UK: Edward Elgar.

Fisher, Allan G.B. 1939, 'Production, Primary, Secondary and Tertiary', *Economic Record*, 15(1), 24–38.

Giblin, L.F. 1930, *Australia, 1930*, Melbourne: Melbourne University Press.

Giblin, L.F. 1947, 'The Record and Its Editors', *Economic Record*, 23(1), 1–4.

Goodwin, Craufurd D. 1966, *Economic Enquiry in Australia*, Durham, NC: Duke University Press.

Goodwin, Craufurd D. 2002, 'Economic Enquiry in Australia: Reflections after 41 Years', *History of Economics Review*, 35, 1–3.

Groenewegen, Peter and Bruce McFarlane 1990, *A History of Australian Economic Thought*, London: Routledge.

Groenewegen, Peter 2009, *Educating for Business, Public Service and the Social Sciences: A History of the Faculty of Economics at the University of Sydney 1920–1999*, Sydney: Sydney University Press.

Groenewegen, Peter 2010, 'Marshall and Australia' in *The Impact of Alfred Marshall's Ideas: The Global Diffusion of his Work*, Tiziano Raffaelli, ed., Cheltenham, UK: Edward Elgar.

Gruen, Fred 1988, 'Of Economics and Other Things' in *Strauss to Matilda: Viennese in Australia, 1938–1988*, edited by Karl Bittman, Melbourne: Wenkart Foundation.

Haig, Bryan 2006, 'Sir Timothy Coghlan and the Development of National Accounts', *History of Political Economy*, 38(2), 339–75.

Hancock, W.K. 1930, *Australia*, London: E. Benn.

Harcourt, G. 2006, 'Australians in Cambridge in the 1950s: a Comment on William Coleman's Conversation with Murray Kemp', *History of Economics Review*, 43.

Healey, D.T., F.G. Jarrett and J.M. McKay 1985, *The Economics of Bushfires: the South Australian Experience*, Melbourne: The Centre for South Australian Economic Studies.

Hearn, William Edward 1863, *Plutology, or, The Theory of the Efforts to Satisfy Human Wants*, Melbourne: G. Robertson.

Hight, J. 1939, 'Preface', *Economic Record*, 15 (supplement), 3–6.

Isles, K.S. 1932, 'Australian Monetary Policy Reconsidered', *Economic Record*, 8(15), 191–203.

Jevons, William Stanley 1972, *Papers and Correspondence of William Stanley Jevons*, R.D. Colinson Black ed., vol.1, London: Macmillan.

Johnson, Harry 1971, 'Reflections on the Current State of Economics', *Australian Economic Papers*, 10(16), 1–11.

Kemp, M.C. 1948, 'Interest and the Money Supply in Keynes' Economics', *Economic Record*, 25(2), 64–73.

Kenwood, A.G. and A.L. Lougheed 1997, *Economics at the University of Queensland 1912–1997: Written on the Occasion of the Fiftieth Anniversary of the Department of Economics 1947–1997*, Brisbane: University of Queensland.

Kenyon, Peter 1992, 'Does Australia's Past have a Useful Economics?', *Murdoch University Economics Program*, Working paper No.61.

Kenyon, Peter 1994, Review of 'A History of Australian Economic Thought' by Peter D. Groenewegen and Bruce J. McFarlane, in *History of Political Economy*, 26(2), 341–45.

Keynes, J.M. 1936, *The General Theory of Employment Interest and Money*, London: Macmillan.

King, J.E. 2007, *A Biographical Dictionary of Australian and New Zealand Economists*, Cheltenham, UK: Edward Elgar.

La Nauze, J.A. 1941, 'Two Notes on Hearn', *Economic Record*, 17(33).

La Nauze, J.A. 1949, *Political Economy in Australia: Historical Studies*, Melbourne: Melbourne University Press.

MacDougal, G.D.A. 1960, 'The Benefits and Costs of Private Investment from Abroad; a Theoretical Approach', *Economic Record*, 36(73).

Metin, Albert 1977 [1899], *Socialism without Doctrine*, translator: Russel Ward, Chippendale, NSW: Alternative Publishing Co-operative.

Millmow, Alex 1997, 'Uncovering a "Touch of Genius": Keynes's Dealings with the Australian Underworld', *History of Economics Review*, 26, 131–5.

Millmow, Alex 2011, 'The Green and Gold Revolution: The Story behind the Australian Adaption of Paul Samuelson's Classic Textbook', *Economic Papers: A Journal of Applied Economics and Policy*, 30(4), 546–56.

Moore, Gregory C.G. 2002, 'Selling Plutology: Correspondence Relating to the Failure of Australia's First Economics Text', *History of Economics Review*, 35, 63–77.

Pitchford, J.D. 1960, 'Growth and the Elasticity of Factor Substitution', *Economic Record*, 36(76), 491–504.

Pitchford, J.D. 2002, 'Trevor Swan's 1956 Economic Growth "Seminar" and Notes on Growth', *Economic Record*, 78(243), 381–7.

Reeves, William Pember 1902, *State Experiments in Australia and New Zealand*, London: George Allen & Unwin.

Round, D.K. 1974, 'The Industrial Organization Vacuum in Australia', *Economic Record*, 50(2), 169–98.

Salter, W. 1959, 'Internal and External Balance: the Role of Price and Expenditure Effects', *Economic Record*, 35(71), 226–38.

Schedvin, C.B. 1978, 'Sydney James Butlin', *Economic Record*, 54(1), 143–6.

Schumpeter, Joseph A. 1954, *History of Economic Analysis*, New York: Oxford University Press.

Scott, R.H. 1988, *The Economic Society of Australia: its History 1925–1985*, East Ivanhoe: The Economic Society of Australia.

Sieper, E. 1982, *Rationalising Rustic Regulation*, St. Leonards, NSW: Centre for Independent Studies.

Solow, Robert 1997, 'Trevor W. Swan' in *An Encyclopedia Of Keynesian Economics*, Thomas Cate, ed., Cheltenham, UK: Edward Elgar.

Swan, T.W. 1956, 'Economic Growth and Capital Accumulation', *Economic Record*, 32(63), 334–61.

Swan, T.W. 1963, 'Longer Run Problems of the Balance of Payments' in H.W. Arndt and W.M. Corden, eds, *The Australian Economy*, Melbourne: Cheshire.

Swan, Trevor 1968, *Readings in international economics:* Richard E. Caves and Harry G. Johnson, eds, London: Allen & Unwin.

Swan, T.W. 1989, 'The Principle of Effective Demand – A "Real Life" Model', *Economic Record*, 65(4), 378–398.

Syme, David 1877, *Outline of Industrial Science*, London: Henry S. King.

White, Michael V. 1982, 'Jevons in Australia: a Reassessment', *Economic Record*, 58(160).

White, Michael V. 2006, 'Cultivated Circles of The Empire: Bibliographical Notes on W.S. Jevons's Antipodean Interlude (1854–1859)', *History of Economics Review*, 43.

Williams, Ross ed. 2009, *Balanced Growth: A History of the Department of Economics, University of Melbourne*, North Melbourne, Victoria: Australian Scholarly Publishing.

Wilson, Roland 1931, *Capital Imports and the Terms of Trade: Examined in the Light of Sixty Years of Australian Borrowings*, Melbourne: Melbourne University Press.

26

China

2,500 years of economic thought

Zagros Madjd-Sadjadi

There is a strong Eurocentric belief that Western civilisation represents the pinnacle of success that all other cultures ought to emulate. Even a cursory glance at most texts in the history of economic thought would erroneously suggest that China had little to contribute. An anti-Eastern bias is found in Weber's (1951) argument that Confucianism and Taoism, while not antithetical to wealth accumulation, lacked the work ethic and the drive to innovate of Protestantism. This is all the more curious when one considers that China had the most advanced economy on the planet prior to the Industrial Revolution, and thus must have had something positive to contribute.

In Beijing today, we find evidence of Western 'cultural imperialism' with children eating McDonald's for lunch, going to watch the latest Disney film, and listening to Chinese popular music with new lyrics superimposed on American melodies. Yet if we reversed our cultural lens, we would see Western culture has long been influenced by China: moveable type, paper money, gunpowder, the crossbow, the decimal system, vaccination and the suspension bridge all trace their origins to China (Temple, 1998). Chinese martial arts through the Hong Kong studios are seen widely around the world and their stars (Jackie Chan, Jet Li, and Michelle Yeoh) have entered the global mainstream. Chinese cuisine is found in every middle-American town and the extent of Chinese cultural influence ranks with only Japanese, French and Indian culture as being able to compete on the world stage with the American variety.

Yet culture has a profound influence on economies and many problems we see in imposing supposedly superior Western solutions onto other regions lie in a failure to understand this basic principle. Capitalism in the United States has been shaped by culture just as capitalism in Europe and Asia are different because of cultural differences, and it is to the Chinese business culture we now turn.

Cultural and business traditions

Harrison (2013, 83–5) uses a neo-Weberian analysis to argue Confucian-based Chinese and East Asian cultures score well on those dimensions of what he terms 'cultural capital', and that this leads to economic growth. An emphasis on merit and education, as exemplified by the Mandarin system of examinations of old and current *gaokao*, are seen in a positive light. Ancestor reverence implies not only a duty to the past but also one to the future, leading to a work ethic, future focus, pragmatism, innovation and entrepreneurship, since one will become the ancestor in whose memory others gather. This makes for a curious blend of collectivist and individualist culture quite unlike that of the West.

The West, especially the United States, is typified by an individualistic culture, and neoclassical economics takes the precept that society is composed of atomistic individuals who, in seeking only their own rational self-interests, end up serving those of society. Yet it is rather strange that neoclassical economics has evolved in this manner, given that Adam Smith in his *Theory of Moral Sentiments* never envisioned an atomistic individual abstracted from society.

If we think of rational self-interest as purposefully driven by cultural constraints, we can see why the Chinese version of capitalism is different. There are four fundamental strands of thought that make the Chinese who they are: the legalist, Confucian, Taoist and, in mainland China, Maoist traditions. Achievement is seen in the context of societal need as opposed to individual desire. Nowhere is this more evident than in attitudes towards parenting. Westerners believe that Chinese 'authoritarian parenting' stifles the independence of the child, while Chinese parents are disapproving towards Western 'permissive parenting' with its negative effect on the harmonious relationship between parent and child (Chao, 1996).

The European passion for individual liberty derives from the Enlightenment. American exceptionalism is a product of the Protestant work ethic, the American Revolution and the drive to conquer the 'wild west'. Chinese exceptionalism begins with the Yellow River. Confucius (founder of Confucianism) and Lao Tzu (the founder of Taoism) grew up on the river as near contemporaries, but their geographic distance brought about different solutions to the problem of flooding. Confucians seek to 'control the dragon' of the Yellow River through a levee and dam system, while Taoists prefer a more *laissez-faire* approach of simply not building on flood plains (Guo, 2010).

Coupled with these traditions are legalism and Maoism. The legalist philosophy is a rule of equality under a stable (though often harsh) legal system. Individuals have no rights under legalist doctrine for the law exists as a mechanism for ensuring social control (He, 2011). Emperors were obliged only to uphold equitable treatment under the law so as to ensure compliance with it.

Maoism, the political philosophy of Mao Zedong, holds the agrarian peasant class as the standard-bearers for a new China. The Agrarian Reform Law of 1950 reformed China's semi-feudalistic land tenancy regime by nationalising agricultural land and collectivising it into communes comprised of a few hundred households. Private industry was nationalized and progressive five-year plans were introduced to create a 'Great Leap Forward'. However, China was not ready for everyone to live in a communal fashion. The process destroyed the work ethic, thus ensuring no needs were met in what ordinary Chinese labelled the 'Great Leap Backward' (He, 2001, 57–9). Shortly after admitting the programme had been a failure, market liberalisation began under Deng Xiaoping and Liu Shaoqi, but increased social inequality scuttled this project. The resulting about-face led to Deng and Liu's removal as part of the Great Proletariat Cultural Revolution, a rebellion against traditional Confucian values as part of a rejection of 'the Four Olds: old thought, old culture, old tradition, and old custom' (Zhang and Schwartz, 1997, 197). The Cultural Revolution was a disaster but it was only the death of First Vice Premier Lin Biao, in what some believe was a staged plane crash in 1971, that allowed Mao to save face. Lin had been part of a failed coup that had shaken the Chinese leadership and led to the resignation of several high-ranking officials, and Premier Zhou Enlai was able to personally intervene with Mao to bring back Deng Xiaoping to the government as First Vice Minister.

As the health of Mao and Zhou deteriorated, the battle for China's soul emerged between the Gang of Four (Mao's widow Jiang Qing, Wang Hongwen, Yao Wenyuan and Zhang Chunqiao), who favoured a return to mass revolutionary movements, Hua Guofeng, who wanted a Soviet-style planning system, and Deng Xiaoping, who embraced market reforms. When Zhou died in January 1976, Deng lost his principal backer and the Gang of Four sought to discredit him. Mao's death, a mere eight months later, stopped Deng's persecution. He was again brought back into the leadership by the newly installed premier, Hua Guofang. Deng worked behind the scenes to consolidate power but did so with finesse. Even after engineering the removal of Premier Hua, Deng did not purge him from the party apparatus.

China turned towards economic reform once again and Confucianism and Taoism were again allowed to blossom. Maoism remains an important strand of thought within the Communist party and the public at large, especially in the minds of those who see corruption as endemic to the economic reform process.

Confucianism teaches of a reciprocal duty between subject and ruler, between friends, and between family members, as well as conveying the desire for stability. This reciprocity is epitomized by *guanxi* or, to the Western mind, 'connections'. *Guanxi* is more properly thought of as a network of individuals with whom each has an affinity to whom reciprocal duties are owed (*renqíng*, literally meaning 'a favour') and for whom failure to exercise these duties leads to a loss of social status, known as *mianzi* or 'face' (de Mente, 2009).

Chinese are reticent to voice displeasure openly with authority so as to avoid trouble, a lesson they learned during the Cultural Revolution, when those who openly criticised the regime were attacked. Still, foreigners who think Chinese are pushovers are forgetting the use of *mei yu ban fa*, which means 'there is no way' as a tactical strategy to prevent things by arguing that others will not allow it, *bu zhidao*, literally, 'I don't know' and *kaolǔ kaolǔ*, which means 'I'll look into it'. These phrases mean the same thing: it isn't going to happen, and are often used to dismiss those who lack good *guanxi*. Essentially, Chinese value relationships more than the rule of reason (Macleod, 1988, 162–5). They embrace a dualism that baffles the Western mind, as exemplified in the *yin yang*. Night cannot exist without day, male without female or, taking an economic example, maximisation of profit for business cannot exist without maximisation of utility for the consumer. These dualities are interrelated principles rather than contradictions, leading to an emphasis on situational ethics, whereby one always keeps one's options open.

The ceremonial-instrumental tension of the Veblenian dichotomy is found throughout China, which relies more on cash than credit, the Chinese viewing debt as something inherently negative in keeping with Confucian tradition to eliminate debts with each new year. This self-reliance on internal financing and desire for familial control was noted by Chen, Kiani and Madjd-Sadjadi (2007, 79–80) in a study of 300 publicly traded Taiwanese companies: 'Firms in Taiwan mostly . . . avoided usage of borrowed funds for firm growth. This is crucial in understanding why Taiwan did not suffer much when compared to the other economies in the region in the 1997 Asian Financial crises.' Following up on that study, Kiani, Chen and Madjd-Sadjadi (2012, 1299) noted 'long-run solvency was negatively related to firm growth', suggesting long-term strategies emphasising sustainability and balance, key Taoist and Confucian elements.

China is no monolith. There are critical regional differences. There is greater emphasis on legalism and Confucian values in the north than in the south, which incorporates Taoism: the Cantonese are fond of saying, 'The mountains are high and the emperor is far away'. Similarly, Singapore's regime is more legalist than Hong Kong's or Taiwan's. These tendencies mean that policies that work in one region may not work in another. Indeed, differences within a culture outweigh differences between cultures. However, if one is to speak meaningfully of culture, one must examine it through a long lens and generalise, even while warning against turning generalisations into stereotypes (Sun, 2010).

As we turn to the history of Chinese economic thought, we should look at how Chinese culture interfaces with the main challenges of achieving an equitable society as well as a sustainable one. All East Asian countries have very high levels of savings, which have translated into low interest rates. Yet Taiwan, Japan and South Korea all have a more equitable distribution of wealth using the Gini Coefficient than China, which is nominally still Communist, and all of the above referenced countries, along with Hong Kong and Singapore, have a lower ratio of wealth held by the top 20 per cent of society as measured against the wealth held by the bottom 20 per cent of society (World Bank, 2013).

Economic ideas over the long-term

Taoism reflects a basic belief in non-interventionism and Taoists have been called 'the world's first libertarians' (Rothbard, 1995, 23). In Chapter 3 of the *Tao Te Ching*, written by Lao Tzu (604–531 BC), governments are counselled to 'do that which consists in taking no action, and order will prevail' (as translated by Lau, 1963, 7). In Chapter 9, the ruler is advised 'To be overbearing when one has wealth and position is to bring calamity upon oneself' (as translated by Lau, 1963, 13), and in Chapter 17, to be 'but a shadowy presence to his subjects' (as translated by Lau, 1963, 21). Later, in Chapter 57, Lao Tzu provides this warning against what would become legalism: 'The more taboos there are in the empire the poorer the people . . . The better known the laws and edicts the more the thieves and robbers there are. Hence the sage says, I take no actions and the people are transformed of themselves . . . I am not meddlesome and the people prosper of themselves' (as translated by Lau, 1963, 64).

These sentiments are echoed by Chuang Tzu (369–286 BC): 'Let things be what they are. Have no personal views. This is how everything under Heaven is ruled' (as translated by Palmer and Breuilly, 1996, 61). Yet little economics appears beyond these simple aphorisms. There is simply nothing there (which might be the best concise summary of Taoism). This does not mean Taoism had no influence. Instead, its influence was more to temper the importance of the state in the minds of the populace rather than having any real impact on policy.

In contrast, the Confucians had a definitive system of economic thought. Confucius (551–479 BC), writing only a few decades after Lao Tzu, founded Confucianism and took a low-regulatory but mixed-state approach, as opposed to the pro-state legalism and asceticism of Taoism. Confucianism is concerned with the place of an individual *within* society rather than the atomistic conception of self found in modern economics. Everyone within society has reciprocal obligations, including the emperor, which puts it at odds with legalism. Yet, this reciprocity is practical, as well as moral, as indicated when the Duke of Ai asks how to raise revenues for the state, to which the reply given is to set the tax rate at 10 per cent. The duke is indignant. His tax is currently set at 20 per cent, so wouldn't lowering it reduce revenues? The reply, from the *Analects of Confucius* 12:9 (Legge, 1893, 255) is pure supply-side economics: 'If the people have plenty, their prince will not be left to want alone. If the people are in want, their prince cannot enjoy plenty alone.'

It took a challenge, known as Mohism, to Confucian thought by Mo Tzu (490–403 BC) to get Chinese philosophy to go beyond axioms and platitudes and towards systematic analytical reasoning. Mohism was a utilitarian-based ethical system that dispensed with what was seen as wasteful expenses, such as the largesse that Chinese spent on the dead. It has now been largely incorporated into Taoism, but Mo Tzu is noteworthy as being the first to distinguish between use value and exchange value, using the same commodity/example used by Aristotle a century later, leading one to wonder if the Greek philosopher knew of Mo Tzu's argument: 'A straw sandal used as a medium to buy something else is a straw sandal no more' (Hu, 1984, 10).

The Confucian scholar, Mencius (371–289 BC), discusses at great length the division of labour and why the exchange of goods is the only way society can get all that it needs: 'Why does [the farmer] exchange things in such confusion with the various artisans [rather than] avoid all this trouble [by doing it himself]? ... The activities of the various artisans inherently cannot be done along with farming' (as translated by van Norden, 2008, 70). He also counselled that a 'benevolent government' was one that 'lessens punishments [and] reduces taxes', while traditional commentator Zhu Xi stated 'the people will be able to fully apply their strength in farming the fields' (as translated by van Norden, 2008, 6). The rationale was two-fold: first, it increased prosperity and second, it ensured a loyal populace.

Confucianism was not always amenable to the free market. Indeed, with one exception, it soon took a more centrist position. Scholars such as Xun Kuang (312–230 BC) pushed against limited government. In contrast to Mencius, who viewed man as inherently good, Xun Kuang believed 'Human nature is evil [and] he is born with a love of profit' (as translated by Knoblock, 1994, 150–1), leading him to argue that government must create laws that will lead individuals to become good. His students, Han Fei and Li Si are considered two of the founders of legalism, which heavily influenced Confucian thought as it jockeyed for favour with the ruling elites. These two philosophies, though derived initially from the same principles, ended up being at odds with one another in a battle over China's soul. Nowhere was this more in contrast than on the advice to governments. Whereas Confucianism would stress having few laws and keeping the punishments light, legalism taught punishment should be heavy but equally applied to the powerful and the weak.

During these battles, legalism tempered Confucianism and it was left to the great historian, Ssa-Ma Chi'en, to reassert the original Confucian conception of a *laissez-faire* attitude towards the economy, even if it was only short-lived (Spengler, 1964). China would show a Confucian face over its legalist character for most of its history, a policy known as *rubaio fali* (Wang, 2011, 110).

Coupled with the philosophical traditions, there was a lot of practical economic advice. According to Hu (1988, 17–18) 'The Tribute System of Yu', a fifth century BC document, details the first exposition of the doctrine of equal sacrifice in public finance. Land quality was the dominant rationale for assessment of taxes, although it was modified by factors such as the distance from the central authority and the locality's relative level of wealth.

The Art of War by Sun Tzu (544–496 BC) is a military classic still studied around the world. Yet buried within its text is a clear understanding of key economic concepts. For example, the idea of diminishing marginal returns is found in this passage: 'When you do battle, even if you are winning, if you continue for a long time it will dull your forces and blunt your edge' (Cleary, 1988, 57). This point was refined by Jia Lin, a Tang Dynasty (AD 618–906) commentator: 'Even if you prevail over others in battle, if you go on too long there will be no profit' (Cleary, 1988, 57). A ninth-century commentator to the text Du Mu states 'When provisions go for three hundred miles, the country is out a year's supplies; when provisions go for four hundred miles, the country is out two years' supplies' (Cleary, 1988, 61). Sun Tzu notes the military drives up prices in its vicinity, demonstrating an understanding of how demand affects prices. Karagiannis and Madjd-Sadjadi (2007, 183) argue passages such as these show '[a]lthough actually dealing with warfare, the book is really about maximising gain in all arenas'.

Huan Kuan in the *Discourses on Salt and Iron* documents the debates in the imperial court in 81 BC on whether to keep government monopolies on salt, iron and liquor. The debate on iron centred on the efficiency of government enterprises, with Confucian scholars (who were arguing for a return to *laissez-faire*) stating that the quality of state production was inferior since it was 'produced to meet quotas rather than to provide for real needs' (Wagner, 2008, 187). Government officials pointed out that having the iron and salt monopolies in the hands of the government had greatly expanded production due to economies of scale, giving a case of natural monopoly some two millennia before Smith and Mill formalised the concept (Hu, 1988, 266–7). The court was convinced of the correctness of this line of reasoning for both iron and salt, but returned the liquor industry to private hands, though it imposed heavy taxes on its production to offset lost revenue.

Sophisticated price supports were proposed by Fan Li in the fifth century BC and implemented by Sang Hongyang in 110 BC (Hu, 1988, 270–1). By having grain trade within bands, so it was bought when it was 'too low' and sold when it was 'too high', the government could help assure domestic order. These bands were set so they would only be triggered in extraordinary cases, and normal trading did not cause government intervention nor lead to a sustainable black market.

The *Book of Guan Zi*, a legalist policy primer dating from the fourth century BC, provides one of the earliest formulations of the quantity theory of money in the 'Shan Guo Gui'. After beginning with an example of how to increase prices tenfold by removing coinage from circulation, it advises 'While cash is in short supply and valued and goods are plentiful and cheap, buy up goods, paying for them with cash. Money will then be in the hands of the people below, but goods will be in the hands of the government and increase in value tenfold' (Rickett, 1998, 392). There is no indication of rational expectations kicking in where the public realises that they are being duped by the government, which controls the monetary supply. To increase demand, the government is advised to engage in deficit spending during contractionary times and in saving during expansionary times, since an individual's income provides the basis for his consumption and if there is no income, there can be no consumption. It also states that individuals will find it difficult to do these things even as the state can.

By the ninth century, it was generally acknowledged that hoarding of money had reduced the level of transactions, but Shen Kuo (1031–95) was the first to detail the effect that foreign trade could have. He noted (Hu, 1988, 394) 'the barbarian lands in every direction all rely on the copper coins of China', and he believed government monopolies on necessities would exacerbate the situation, since the higher monopoly prices would encourage imports and thus an exodus of Chinese coins. The solution was to ban imports to decrease the outflow of foreign exchange rather than banning export of coins directly, as others advocated.

We conclude this section with a discussion of the Chinese Malthus, Hung Liang-Chi (1746–1809). Writing five years before Malthus, in the *Zhi Ping Pian* (On Peaceful Governance), Hung noted China's population, which had reached 400 million people and was doubling every two generations, increased at a faster rate through geometric expansion than the land that could come under cultivation (which grew in a linear fashion). He believed unless arable land could be increased by land reclamation, or by altering the tax burden so as to discourage agriculture, the government would either have to intervene with policies designed to curb population growth in the country, or 'natural checks' to population growth (disease, drought, murder, war) would occur as resources per person dwindled. The more pressing concern for Hung was not demand outstripping the food supply but rather rising joblessness (Silberman, 1960).

Recent advances and trends in economics

Western economic thought was first introduced to China by Karl Gutzlaff (1803–51), a German missionary, who wrote two Chinese texts on economics, *Outlines of Political Economy* in 1839 and *Treatise on Commerce* in 1840. By the 1880s the first Western economics texts were being translated and studied in China. However, these texts were modified to reduce what was seen as a bias towards low tariffs, regarded as an imposition of Western thought onto Chinese autonomy. Intellectuals such as Ma Jianzhong, one of the first Chinese educated in the West, viewed Western thought in more mercantilist terms, stressing increased exports to achieve wealth (Trescott, 2007).

The first attempt to directly translate the *Wealth of Nations* in Chinese was made by Yan Fu in 1902. Although not an economist by training, it was the first attempt to translate the classic and is even more important because of the translator's inclination to interpret, rather than merely translate, in a manner that could accommodate, rather than supplant, Chinese intellectual traditions (Lai, 1989). This was part of a trend towards rehabilitation of Chinese thought and only nine years later Chen Huan-Chang (1911) introduced the Western world to Confucian economic principles in his masterwork *The Economic Principles of Confucius and His School*, which contains a brilliant exposition of Confucian economic theory and its relationship to Western economic theory.

From 1920 to 1939, the works of many Western economists were translated into Chinese, including J.M. Keynes, F. List, K. Marx, I. Fisher, H. George, A. Marshall, T. Veblen and D. Ricardo. However, there was a strong anti-imperialist current coupled with the socialist philosophy of Sun Yat-Sen, who was heavily influenced by George rather than Marx. This laid the groundwork, not for mainstream economics, but for the introduction of institutional economics in the Veblen-Ayers-Commons tradition, since institutionalism was not antagonistic to socialism. For example, at Yenching University most of the economics faculty had studied under institutional economists from the United States (Trescott, 2007).

Until Mao took power in 1949, Marxist economists were removed from their posts due to strong anti-communist Kuomintang policies. After 1949, Marxist thought became ascendant but with a Maoist flavour. Most Western economists were suppressed, but ironically Smith and Ricardo were taught since both were referenced favourably by Marx (Trescott, 2007, 320). Still, while Marx believed the rising organic composition of capital led to a declining rate of profit and to economic crises, Mao did not focus on this aspect since China was predominantly an agrarian society without large-scale industrialisation. Instead, Maoist theory concentrated on the development of the peasantry, and most economics of the time dealt not with theory but rather with practical questions of how to engage in industrialisation without losing China's rural character. However, with China's industrialisation more traditional Marxian analysis has come from the Chinese New Left, including Minqin Li and Cui Zhiyuan.

Minqi Li (b. 1969) attended the University of Massachusetts, Amherst and is one of the foremost Chinese Marxists. He believes the insertion of China into the world economy will hasten the decline of the worldwide rate of profit, bringing about the end of the capitalist world system. His argument rests not on traditional Marxian analysis but on the squeeze between competitive prices and the rising cost of energy due to climate change. He views the coming collapse as necessitating a transition to communism so as to ensure a fair distribution of resources in its wake (Li, 2008).

Cui Zhiyuan (b. 1963) was heavily influenced by John Mill and James Meade, explicitly calling for the creation of a 'shareholder-cooperative system' that would pay a 'social dividend' in a similar fashion as Meade's 'labour-capital partnership' (Cui, 2005). He regards social inequality and uneven regional development as critical issues for China.

The Chinese New Left was a reaction against the reform movement, which was developed by Gu Zhan (1915–74). During the 1950s, he dared, along with Sun Yefeng (1908–83) to argue that the market, not the state, was the proper vehicle for socialist planning. These two economists heavily influenced Liu Shaoqi and Deng Xiaoping and are the intellectual fathers of Chinese economic reforms (Song, 2013). They, in turn, influenced Wu Jinglian.

Wu Jinglian (b. 1930) is known as 'Market Wu' for his unbridled championing of markets. A protégé of Gu Zhan, Wu also cites James Buchanan and Douglas North as his main influences. As someone involved in the decision-making process, he has written the definitive study of the evolution of China's economic reforms from the 1950s to 2002 (Wu, 2005). He believes China has become a crony capitalist society with high levels of rent-seeking behaviour, and has publicly condemned the Chinese New Left for advocating 'restarting the Cultural Revolution and establishing a total dictatorship over the bourgeoisie' (Wu, 2012).

Zhang Weiying (b. 1959) worked with Wu Jinglian and introduced the 'dual-track price system' to China. This system provides a centrally planned price for a predetermined quota amount of production, and then allows all production above that quota to be set by the market. By reducing the quota over time, one can successfully transition to a market economy. In recent years, Zhang has become an Austrian economist, declaring that it is time to 'bury Keynesianism' in a speech to the China Entrepreneurs Forum (Bhattacharya, 2012).

Since 1976, a dialogue has opened between China and the West, mostly in the form of orthodox economic thought as well as two strands of heterodoxy: institutionalism and Post Keynesian. However, there are gaps in the knowledge base with J.K. Galbraith and G. Myrdal seen as prime proponents of neo-institutional thought and little attention paid to such important luminaries as Clarence Ayers, Marc Tool or Paul Bush (Zhang and Xu, 2013, 320).

Gregory Chow (b. 1929) is one of the world's top econometricians and developer of the Chow (1960) test that checks the stability of a regression either over time or across groups. He also demonstrated the superiority of the Lagrangian technique over other more complex dynamic programming methods (Chow, 1997).

Stephen Ng-Sheong Cheung (b. 1935), former Professor of Economics at the University of Hong Kong and a former colleague of Ronald Coase at the University of Chicago, is probably the most important of all contemporary Chinese economists from the standpoint of economic theory. A leading member of the New Institutional School of economics, in his 'simplistic general equilibrium theory of corruption' (Cheung, 1996), he argues international competition in private markets limits the ability of officials to obtain bribes. Corruption tends to increase in areas where competition is inherently limited, such as antiquities and state-owned enterprises that have been granted a monopoly. Moving from a hierarchical-based property rights system, where claiming resources depends on your position in the party, to a private-property-based approach opens opportunities for corruption and this can cause institutional sclerosis, preventing a full transition to a market-based economy. This worsens under democratically formed governments since individuals vote themselves opportunities to be corrupt.

In 'Irving Fisher and the Red Guards' (Cheung, 1969), he asserts that Mao's interpretation of a 'social contradiction' between individuals who desire limited resources is inherently superior to Marx, but still fundamentally flawed. Whereas Marx believed a communist state would end competition since man was inherently good, Mao believed it would endure, but in an unstable form, unless something could be done about human nature itself. This presented a rationale for government action: if human nature does not change naturally, it must be forced. The Red Guards, acting on Mao's instructions to abolish private property, took it to the logical extreme of eliminating all differential rents, even those due to superior intellect or ability, leading to the disaster of the Cultural Revolution.

Two other articles are considered seminal reading in transaction cost economics. Cheung (1983) discussed the problem of defining a firm as a set of contractual arrangements existing to reduce market transaction costs, and notes that piece-rate payment and other endeavours that treat workers as independent contractors threaten to destroy the notion of what a firm actually is. In 'The Fable of the Bees' (Cheung, 1973), he demonstrates the traditional view on reciprocal externalities was inaccurate. So long as both parties could exchange services and benefit from that interaction, a market can develop. Similarly, he has shown that the use of bride prices (payments from the groom's family to the bride's) and foot binding served to enforce property rights at a time when children were viewed as an economic good, and this consequently reduced female infanticide (Cheung, 1972).

In 1957, Ma Yinchu (1882–1982) proposed his 'New Population Theory', advocating China begin state-enforced family planning (Ma, 1997). Ma had been one of the first Chinese graduates from Columbia University and was influenced by Malthus. Initially decried as a reactionary who did not uphold socialist values, by 1979, his viewpoint had become government dogma with the introduction of the 'One Child Policy'. Solving one problem may lead to others, as suggestions arise for the Chinese government to re-examine this policy in light of a demographic crisis of too many males and a rapidly aging workforce. After all, Taiwan, Hong Kong and Singapore, none of which have had a population control policy, all have birth rates lower than mainland China. Still, pointing to these counterexamples as a rationale for abandoning the one child policy is problematic, since levels of development differ.

Zhou Xiaochuan (b. 1948), governor of the People's Bank of China, has argued that using SDRs (special drawing rights) rather than the US dollar as the world's reserve currency will resolve the Triffin paradox whereby the reserve currency country (in this case the United States) ends up with a permanent trade deficit as it attempts to provide liquidity for the rest of the world (Zhou, 2009), a policy the International Monetary Fund has cautiously endorsed.

Yu Yongding (b. 1948) has been influenced by Nobel Laureates Robert Shiller and Paul Krugman. He argued that China needs to reduce its capital and current account surpluses. The ongoing US budget deficit, the dysfunctional US political system and the aforementioned Triffin Paradox make a rapid devaluation of the US dollar more likely, which will negatively impact China's investments. He believes diversification, including into gold and away from US treasuries, is beneficial for this reason and will act as a steriliser for the vast amounts of foreign currency coming into the country, so that it does not lead to mal-investment. China suffers from severe overinvestment in the property market (both commercial and residential) and this is causing a major bubble. Indeed, this overinvestment might be masking actual *underinvestment* in productive capital and infrastructure (Yu, 2006, 2013).

Yang Xiaolai (1948–2004), then called Yang Xiguang, spent 10 years (1968–78) in prison after writing a notoriously scathing critique of the Chinese Communist Party from a leftist perspective entitled 'Whither China?' It set the stage for the 'bourgeois democracy' and the desire for a 'privatized economy' (Unger, 1991, 34). In deriding 'the red capitalist class', it is cited as a precursor for the backlash against corruption that is now manifested throughout the country (Unger, 1991, 3). While in prison, he taught himself calculus and later undertook a PhD in economics. He contributed to our understanding of infra-marginal economics. Infra-marginal decisions are those that cause discrete future path-dependency that closes off some alternatives while opening others. Infra-marginal analysis also leads to endogenous specialisation, reduced transaction costs, and network effects that contribute to increasing returns in society (Yang, 2001).

Dissemination of national traditions overseas

As the Qing Dynasty crumbled under the weight of misguided policies and European colonial expansion, many Chinese emigrated. They sought better opportunities and reacted to greater despotism among ruling elites who had abandoned Confucian values. The Chinese used familial connections to create an insular network that gave them an advantage in business dealings. They were hated for their successes and were stereotyped as being greedy and having little allegiance to their new countries. Later, overseas Chinese lost their connection to their homeland when, in the 1960s, China revoked their ability to hold two passports, and in 1980 the right to immigrate back to China for overseas Chinese descendants was removed.

Despite this, the Chinese continue to be determined not to assimilate on anything other than their own terms. There are three main reasons why the Chinese remain Chinese and succeed regardless of where they go: education, cultural acceptance and the *huis*.

There is a Confucian saying on a banner in our family's Chinese ancestral home: 'All other occupations are ordinary; only scholarly pursuits are held in high regard'. The Confucian philosophical belief that education is of primary importance has led to success around the world and the Chinese tend to concentrate their endeavours in subjects leading to well-paying jobs (business, economics, engineering, sciences). This is less evident in mainland China due to the Cultural Revolution (1966–77) where *all schools* closed from June 1966 to February 1967 (and in the case of urban schools and universities even longer), and educational attainment was interrupted for millions, sometimes as long as five years. There is still a pronounced reduction in educational attainment for those who came of age during that time (Guo, 2010).

Cultural acceptance is high among the Chinese, who incorporate 'Chinese characteristics' into foreign ways. It is not merely for public consumption that the Chinese describe their economy as 'socialism with Chinese characteristics', or perhaps more appropriately 'capitalism with Chinese characteristics'. The Chinese may dress in Western clothes and use English in business dealings but they do so without abandoning traditional culture or their use of their native tongue at home and with other Chinese.

The *huis*, small credit associations organised under the term 'family association' and found in almost all overseas Chinese enclaves, are, in theory, merely social clubs where those with the same family name can congregate and receive assistance. In reality, they serve as a back-channel banking system that provides credit to Chinese who are often discriminated against (at least the Chinese perceive themselves to be discriminated against) by local banks. Monetary obligation serves to bind the community together and reinforce their identification with other Chinese.

The Chinese have always given their host countries a blend of Chinese and local culture. Fortune cookies (authentic Chinese restaurants would serve oranges as an after-dinner treat instead) and chop suey are unheard of in China, but have made an indelible mark in Western countries. Confucianism and Taoism are studied, as are ancient Chinese classics such as the *Art of War*, in universities around the globe. Still, the biggest influence of Chinese culture on other lands (other than through the emigration of Chinese citizens) is the Chinese written language and the Chinese philosophies sent to other Asian countries, specifically Korea, Vietnam and Japan.

Chinese characters, called Hanja in Korean, Han tu in Vietnamese and Kanji in Japanese, served as the basis for literate society in those three countries for millennia. They came by way of trade and conquest. Buddhism, with its various Chinese literary texts, was incorporated into the cultures of these countries. Legalism and Confucianism in its more state-oriented configuration bridged the gap to Korea and Japan. Taoism influenced ordinary ethnic Chinese rather than elites and there was a great deal of intermarriage between Vietnamese and Chinese due to a long history of rule by China of Vietnam. Taoism, though present in both Japan and Korea for 1,400 years, never became a major philosophical influence and was relegated to folk religion status in Korea and Japan.

Korean and Japanese society ended up with a corporatist form of governance giving rise to Japanese *zaibatsu* and *keritsu* and Korean *chaebols*, the large interlocking industrial conglomerates that control much of the Korean and Japanese economies. Taiwan, Singapore and Hong Kong tend to have smaller companies more focused on single industries, greater emphasis on equity financing due to negative Confucian attitudes towards debt and more economic freedom. It is nonetheless a mistake to regard the Chinese experience as a model for the world stage. Even within Chinese society, the blend of legalist, Confucian, Taoist and Maoist elements causes friction and disagreement. To the extent it works, it relies upon human nature transformed by centuries of philosophy, and it cannot be wholly lifted into another context without considering the cultural foundations upon which it lies.

Bibliography

Bhattacharya, A. 2012. Zhang Weijing: China's anti-Keynesian insurgent, *Wall Street Journal*, October 13: A11.

Chao, R. K. 1996. Chinese and European American mothers beliefs about the role of parenting in children's school success, *Journal of Cross-Cultural Psychology* 27, 403–23.

Chen, H.-R., K. Kiani, and Z. Madjd-Sadjadi. 2007. Impact of control type on firm growth in Taiwan, *International journal of applied economics* 4(1), March, 76–84.

Cheung, S. N. S. 1996. A simplistic general equilibrium theory of corruption, *Contemporary Economic Policy* 14(3): 1–5.

Cheung, S. N. S. 1983. The contractual nature of the firm, *Journal of Law and Economics* 26(1): 1–26.

Cheung, S. N. S. 1973. The fable of the bees: an economic investigation, *Journal of Law and Economics* 16(1): 11–33.

Cheung, S. N. S. 1972. The enforcement of Property Rights in Children, and the Marriage Contract, *Economic Journal* 82(326): 641–657.

Cheung, S. N. S. 1969. Irving Fisher and the Red Guards, *Journal of Political Economy* 77(3): 430–3.

Chow, G. C. 1960. Tests of equality between sets of coefficients in two linear regressions, *Econometrica* 28(3): 591–605.

Chow, G. C. 1997. *Dynamic economics: Optimization by the Lagrange method*. Oxford: Oxford University Press.

Cleary, T. trans. 1988. *The art of war*. London: Shambhala Publications.

Cui, Z. 2005. Liberal socialism and the future of China: a petty bourgeoisie manifesto, in T. Y. Cao, ed., *The Chinese model of modern development*. London: Routledge.

Guo, R. 2010. *An introduction to the Chinese economy: The driving forces behind modern day China*. Singapore: John Wiley & Sons (Asia).

Harrison, L. E. 2013. *Jews, Confucians, and protestants: Cultural capital and the end of multiculturalism*. Lanham, MD: Rowman & Littlefield.

He, H. Y. 2001. *Dictionary of political thought of the People's Republic of China*. Armonk, NY: M. E. Sharpe.

He, P. 2011. The difference of Chinese legalism and Western legalism. *Frontiers of Law in China* 6(4): 645–69.

Heritage Foundation. 2013. *2013 Index of economic freedom*. Retrieved on October 13, 2013 from http://www.heritage.org/index/

Hu, J. 1984. *Chinese economic thought before the seventeenth century*. Beijing: Foreign Language Press.

Hu, J. 1988. *A concise history of Chinese economic thought*. Beijing: Foreign Language Press.

Huang, M. K.-W. 2008. *The meaning of freedom: Yan Fu and the origins of Chinese liberalism*. Hong Kong: Chinese University Press.

Karagiannis, N. and Z. Madjd-Sadjadi. 2007. *Modern state intervention in the era of globalisation*. Cheltenham, England: Edward Elgar Publishing.

Kiani, K., E. H. Chen, and Z. Madjd-Sadjadi. 2012. Financial factors and firm growth: evidence from financial data on Taiwanese firms, *Quantitative Finance* 12(8): 1299–1314.

Knoblock, J. 1994. *Xunzi: A translation and study of the complete works, books 1–6*, Stanford, CA: Stanford University Press.

Lai, C.-C. 1989. Adam Smith and Yen Fu: Western economics in Chinese perspective, *Journal of European Economic History* 18(2): 371–81.

Lau, D. C., trans. 1963. *Lao Tzu: Tao Te Ching*. Baltimore: Penguin Books.

Legge, J., trans. 1893. *Confucian analects, the great learning and the doctrine of the mean*. Oxford: Clarendon Press.

Ma, Y. 1997. New population theory, in *Ma Yinchu's collected papers on population*. Hangzhou: People's Press, 67–107.

Macleod, R. 1988. *China inc.: How to do business with the Chinese*. New York: Bantam Books.

de Mente, B. L. 2009. *The Chinese mind: Understanding traditional Chinese beliefs and their influence on contemporary culture*. North Clarendon, VT: Tuttle Publishing.

van Norden, B.W. 2008. *Mengzi: With selections from traditional commentaries*. Indianapolis, IN: Hackett Publishing.

Palmer, M. and E. Breuilly. trans. 1996. *The book of Chuang Tzu*. London: Penguin Books.

Rickett, W. A., trans. 1998. *Guanzi: Political, economy and philosophical essays from early China, volume II*. Princeton, NJ: Princeton University Press.

Rothbard, M. N. 1995. *Economic theory before Adam Smith*. Aldershot, England: Edward Elgar.

Silberman, L. 1960. Huang Liang-Chi: a Chinese Malthus, *Population Studies* 13: 257–265.

Song, Y. 2013. *Biographical dictionary of the People's Republic of China*. Jefferson, NC: McFarland & Company Publishers.

Spengler, J. 1964. Ssu-Ma Ch'ien: unsuccessful exponent of *laissez-faire*, *Southern Economic Journal* 30(3): 223–43.

Sun, T. 2010. *Inside the Chinese business mind: a tactical guide for managers*. Santa Barbara, CA: ABC-CLIO.

Temple, R. 1998. *The genius of China: 3,000 years of science, discovery and invention*. London: Prion Books.

Trescott, P. B. 2007. *Jingji Xue: The history of the introduction of Western economic ideas into China, 1850–1950*. Hong Kong: Chinese University Press.

Unger, J. 1991. Whither China? Yang Xiguang, red capitalists, and the social turmoil of the Cultural Revolution, *Modern China* 17(1): 3–37.

Wagner, D. B. 2008. *Science and civilization in China, vol. 5, part 11: ferrous metallurgy*. Cambridge: Cambridge University Press.

Wang, F.-L. 2011. China's evolving institutional exclusion: the *hukou* system and its transformation, in X. Huang, ed., *The institutional dynamics of China's Great Transformation*. New York: Routledge.

Weber, M. 1951. *The religion of China: Confucianism and Taoism*, trans. H. Gerth. Glencoe, IL: The Free Press.

World Bank, 2013. Calculated by author from data retrieved on October 13, 2013 at http://data.worldbank.org/topic/poverty.

Wu, J. 2005. *Understanding and interpreting Chinese economic reform*. New York: Thomason Texere.

Wu, J. 2012. The challenges in China's economic policy and system reforms in a changing global economy, public lecture given at Oxford University, December 5.

Yang, X. 2001. *Economics: New classical versus neoclassical frameworks*. New York: Blackwell Publishers.

Yu, Y. 2013. China's investment addiction, Project Syndicate, October 7. Retrieved on October 14, 2013 at http://www.project-syndicate.org/commentary/the-roots-of-chinese-overinvestment-by-yu-yongding.

Yu, Y. 2006. IMF reform: a Chinese view in E. M. Truman, ed., *Reforming the IMF for the 21st century*. Washington, DC: Institute for International Economics: 519–25.

Zhang, L. and Y. Xu. 2013. The transmission of heterodox economics in China, 1949–2009, in M. Ying and H.-M. Trautwein, *Thoughts on economic development in China*. New York: Routledge.

Zhang, T. and B. Schwartz. 1997. Confucius and the Cultural Revolution: a study in collective memory, *International Journal of Politics, Culture and Society* 11(2): 189–212.

Zhou, X. 2009. Zhou Xiaochuan: Reform the International Monetary System. 23 March. *BIS Review* 41/2009.

27

Southeast Asia

Indonesia and Malaysia

Cassey Lee and Thee Kian Wie

The early history of "classical" development economics is closely intertwined with the experiences of developing countries during the period from the 1940s to the 1960s. This was a period which witnessed the decolonization of many Southeast Asian countries. Much of the economic thought that emerged in these countries during this period was very much related to the economic challenges faced by these countries after gaining independence. These challenges include rebuilding of infrastructure and the productive apparatus, poverty eradication, expansion of education and health facilities, and economic diversification away from its agricultural sector towards manufacturing. Economic ideas about development also evolved as these countries underwent political and structural changes in subsequent years.

In the case of Southeast Asia, there have been relatively few studies that have attempted to review how economic thought has evolved. The main purpose of this chapter is to address this gap by providing a concise narrative of what can be termed as a brief history of economic thought in Indonesia and Malaysia. The reader might ask: why Indonesia and Malaysia? In a sense, there is an element of arbitrariness in this choice – the two contributors specialize in Indonesia and Malaysia. However, the two countries provide a useful opportunity for a comparative study of economic thought in two geographically proximate states. Whilst the national languages of the two countries are very similar ("Bahasa" in Indonesia and Malaysia), the economic and political trajectories have been very different since the countries' independence, and were also rather distinct before this time. The structure of the chapter is as follows. The first section will provide a brief historical background that will serve as a context for the history of economic thought in the two countries. The second section dwells briefly on economic thought in the pre-independence period. The core of the chapter then focuses on post-independence economic thought, while a final section concludes.

Brief background

Indonesia and Malaysia are two neighboring countries that have sometimes been collectively grouped together into what is known as the Malay Archipelago. The basis for the term "Malay Archipelago" could have been language and/or ethnicity (Pribumi/Bumiputra). Of the two, Indonesia is by far the larger country, both in terms of land size (1.9 million sq. km compared to 0.3 million sq. km) and total population (243.8 million against 28.8 million in 2013). However, Malaysia's current income per capita is about twice that of Indonesia. The political and historical trajectories of both countries were also very different.

The total territory of Indonesia was a Dutch colony (when it was referred to as the Netherlands Indies) since 1815. On March 8, 1942, the Commander of the Royal Netherlands Indies Army, General ter Poorten, signed the act of surrender to the Japanese Commander in Subang, a small town in the province of West Java. Subsequently, Indonesia was occupied by Japan until August 15, 1945, when Japan surrendered unconditionally to the Allied Forces. Indonesia's two foremost nationalist leaders, Sukarno and Mohammad Hatta, seized the opportunity to proclaim Indonesia's independence on August 17, 1945 after Japan's surrender, whilst the British resumed their rule of Malaya (Peninsular Malaysia prior to the formation of Malaysia in 1965) until August 31, 1957, when Britain granted it its independence. The Malayan peninsula and Northeast Borneo were occupied by Britain for 117 years.

There were some similarities in the economic challenges encountered by Indonesia and Malaysia in the countries' early post-independence years. Infrastructure development and achieving a more balanced structure of the economy (away from an overdependence on the export-oriented agricultural and mining sectors) were priority areas for both countries. Both countries shared similar concerns over the dominance of foreign-owned firms as well as Chinese-owned firms in these economies.

Another major area of focus was the development of the manufacturing sector – especially the need to enhance the sector's production to meet domestic needs. Whilst both countries began with import substitution industrialization, the duration of these policies differed – Indonesia from the early 1950s until the early 1980s (after the first oil boom ended) and Malaysia from the 1950s to the 1960s.

For Indonesia, macroeconomic stabilization was of greater importance following economic instability during the period from the mid-1950s to the mid-1960s, involving the twin deficits (balance of payments and budget) and hyperinflation, which had reached a staggering 600 percent in 1965 (Thee, 2012). Greater economic stability and more sustained growth was only achieved in Indonesia in the first decade of Suharto's New Order Era (1966–98). The two oil booms in the 1970s enabled the Indonesian government to undertake significant investments in physical infrastructure and in health and education facilities, particularly in primary education, as well as support for the agricultural and manufacturing sectors.

However, the first oil boom, which ended in 1982, had the unfortunate effect of the resource curse, which adversely affected exporting activities as Indonesia's real exchange rate appreciated. However, after the price of oil dropped steeply in early 1986, the Indonesian government finally embarked on a more determined path of export-oriented industrialization. This scheme turned out to be very successful, as from 1987 manufactured exports rose very rapidly, thus following in the footsteps of the East Asian newly industrialized economies.

Malaysia's oil boom came much later in the mid-1990s with important discoveries in the East Coast of Peninsular Malaysia and in East Malaysia. As in the case of Indonesia, Malaysia also used its windfall earnings from oil to undertake a second round of import-substitution by focusing on heavy industries (automotive, steel and cement). Despite this new emphasis, export manufacturing activities continue to be important in Indonesia and Malaysia. The Asian financial crisis in 1997/98 had a significant adverse impact, especially on Indonesia. The sharp economic contraction in 1998 was followed by the downfall of Suharto on May 21, 1998. In Malaysia, the Mahathir administration survived the crisis by shielding domestic capital via exchange controls and bailouts in the banking sector.

Pre-independence economic thought

It is useful to briefly examine the cultural/business traditions and economic thought that existed prior to the Second World War. Documentation relating to these topics is relatively scarce, especially before the colonial period. Much of what exists is the work of historians/economic historians. Then there is the problem of how far back should we look. A useful starting point or benchmark is the publication of Adam Smith's *Wealth of Nations* in 1776 or circa the late eighteenth century. This was a period which saw the early history of colonial rule in the region. Two points of view are of relevance here – those of the Colonial office/officers (British and Dutch) and the indigenous population.

In the case of Indonesia, Arndt (1981) has opined that the Dutch were purely interested in trade and profit-seeking. It is less clear whether the views of the Dutch were driven by mercantilist theories. Whilst the extraction of resources (such as spices) for trade did benefit the Dutch, Indonesia (Java, primarily) was not yet targeted as a market for manufactured goods (ibid.). This was rather different from Malaya (Peninsular Malaysia), where mercantilist-type thinking may have informed colonial policy and where raw materials (tin, rubber) were exported from Malaya and manufactured goods were imported from Britain (Li, 1982).

Perhaps a more important idea related to development that has received some attention relates to the nature of the indigenous population within Southeast Asia. For example, Arndt (1981) discussed the "theory of dualism" propounded by J.H. Boeke, who argued that Indonesian people lacked the desire to improve their material (economic) welfare. Boeke's "theory of dualism" argued that there were major differences between Western and non-Western economic cultures and objectives at a fundamental level. This theory, which was subsequently rejected by many later development economists, had parallels in the sociology literature in the form of the "myth of the lazy native" (Alatas, 1977). Related to such studies are the historical examinations of the material culture of indigenous societies in the Southeast Asian region (Reid, 1988).

There are likely to be much fewer records pertaining to economic ideas and reactions of the indigenous population (compared to colonial records and views). Also, the "indigenous population" in these countries was not an entirely homogenous group. One important indigenous group was the local rulers (sultans/kings). Another was the nationalists. In the much-cited work by Gullick (1988), indigenous political leaders within the feudal system extracted an economic surplus (via taxation) to maintain their political power. There is no evidence on how "Western economic theories" influenced such practices, if they did at all. As for the nationalists, their main concern was for overcoming relative economic backwardness (Roff, 1967). Some of these concerns were manifested as part of a more general concern for inequality, sometimes under the influence of early socialist ideas (Boestaman, 2004). Overall, pre-independence economic thought amongst the indigenous population in Indonesia and Malaya is a relatively unexplored topic, and therefore more research needs to be carried out on the pre-independence and pre-colonial periods.

Early post-independence contributions: 1950s/1960s

The economic debates and policy orientation in Indonesia and Malaysia during the early post-independence were strongly influenced by their decolonization experiences, economic performance, and economic structure. In 1949, the Dutch had attempted, successfully, to protect its commercial interests in Indonesia as part of the negotiations to recognize Indonesia's independence during the Round Table Conference in The Hague in the autumn of 1949. This was achieved when the Dutch delegation insisted on including a Financial-Economic Agreement

(Finec) in the Round Table Conference (RTC) Agreement, which guaranteed that all the Dutch firms could continue their business operations as usual, including the remittance of profits (Meier, 1994, 157).

Nationalization of the Dutch enterprises required mutual agreement, with compensation to be determined by a judge on the basis of their actual worth (Meier, 1994, 46). On December 15, 1951, the Indonesian government nationalized the Java Bank, which was the bank of circulation during the Netherlands Indies, by purchasing all the shares of the Java Bank held by Dutchmen and other foreigners. The sale of the shares of the Java Bank proceeded smoothly (Saubari, 2003, 27). Thereafter the Java Bank was renamed Bank Indonesia, which became Indonesia's central bank. It is unclear whether any economic theories were articulated to support these actions.

In the case of Malaya, the process of gaining independence and transfer of power was peaceful and more gradual. Whilst the studies of foreign ownership were important – by scholars such as James Puthucheary – no nationalization policies were implemented in Malaya during the 1950s. Large-scale takeover (via equity purchase) of British-owned enterprises operating in Malaysia were only undertaken by government-linked corporations (GLCs) in the early 1980s. There is more documentation on the theories that have influenced the work on ownership in Malaysia. Puthucheary (1960) argues that foreign capital was primarily focused on primary industries and thus had limited impact on industrialization in developing countries. This idea was influenced by the works of Hans Singer and Gunnar Myrdal from the 1950s.

Debates about ownership in the modern sector (distributive trade and manufacturing) also took on an ethnic dimension. In Indonesia, this took the form of the *Benteng (Fortress) Program* which was introduced in 1950 to develop indigenous entrepreneurs (Thee, 2012). This was achieved by giving preferential treatment to indigenous Indonesia importers. There were other programs aimed at constraining ethnic Chinese businesses which were implemented in 1954, such as ownership restrictions in weaving mills, rice mills, and port services. Such policies were supported by some economists (Sumitro Djojohadikusumo, who from 1950 to 1957 was the Dean of the Faculty of Economics, University of Indonesia), whilst they were rejected by others (Sjafruddin Prawiranegara, the first Indonesian Governor of Bank Indonesia).

Ownership debates were also intense in Malaysia but took place after the late 1960s. The race riots on May 13, 1969 were the key event that triggered the implementation of the *New Economic Policy* (NEP) which was to become the most important affirmative-action based policy in Malaysia. The Policy was formulated during the period 1969–70. There was a major disagreement on economic thought within the circle of policy makers on NEP (Faaland et al., 1990). The "EPU School," representing key planning and policy-making agencies such as the Economic Planning Unit (EPU), the Treasury and Bank Negara (central bank), emphasized economic growth: most likely, the Keynesian-inspired growth theories of Harrod, Domar, and Solow. The "DNU School" (Department of National Unity) favored a more radical approach involving more direct government intervention to correct the ethnic imbalance in income, employment and ownership of assets and capital (ibid., 32). The approach of this school was underpinned more by political economy considerations (equality and political stability) than by any identifiable economic theories. The subsequent implementation of NEP, which signified the "victory" of the DNU School, was very much reminiscent of the dominance of the history-minded leaders (or solidarity makers) over the economics-minded (administrators) in the 1950s in Indonesia (Thee, 2012, 44–5).

In hindsight, the EPU school's emphasis is understandable, based on the economics literature in the 1950s and 1960s, which focused much more on economic growth and structural change. This was a period that witnessed the development of various growth theories by Harrod (1939),

Domar (1946), Lewis (1955), Robinson (1956), and Solow (1956). This literature did influence the economic studies in both Indonesia and Malaya, albeit gradually and indirectly. In the case of Malaya, there was much emphasis on factor accumulation in terms of population growth and investment – both of which were seen as key factors driving the growth of the economy (Silcock, 1961). During this period, economists emphasized the open economy nature of economies of Indonesia and Malaya and how this impacted on economic growth. More specifically, economic growth was seen as being driven primarily by demand for primary commodities, such as rubber and tin.

Industry studies on rubber and tin also became important during this period. In the case of the Malaysian rubber industry, the focus of these studies has mainly been on the production structure (cost, smallholding versus plantation, replanting), government regulation, ownership (foreign versus local, ethnic groups), and the competition between natural and synthetic rubber. Important contributors in the 1950s and 1960s include P.T. Bauer and T.H. Silcock. Due to the nature of tin production – the most important topics studied in the tin industry were the nature and role of capital accumulation (tin being a capital-intensive industry) and commodity control agreements. Major contributors in this literature include K.E. Knorr, Siew Nim-Chee, Yip Yat-Hoong, and Ooi Jin-Bee. The heavy dependence on exports of primary commodities also led to discussions on the need for export diversification. This coincided with the theories of export pessimism associated with Raúl Prebisch and Hans Singer, who argued that development strategies based on exporting of primary commodities suffered from declining terms of trade. As a consequence, developing countries should undertake the development of their manufacturing sector via import-substitution strategies.

Finally, starting after March 11, 1966 (when President Sukarno authorized General Suharto to take control of the government), General Suharto turned to a group of US and Canadian-trained economists at the Faculty of Economics, University of Indonesia (FEUI), referred to as the "Berkeley Mafia" (although not all had studied at the Department of Economics, University of California, Berkeley) for policy advice. The group include Widjojo Nitisastro (PhD, Berkeley, 1961), Ali Wardhana (PhD, Berkeley, 1962), Emil Salim (Berkeley, 1964), Moh, Sadli (M.Sc. MIT, Doctor in Economic Science, FEUI, 1957), and Subroto (M.A. McGill and Doctor of Economic Science, FEUI, 1957).

This group of economic advisers, even though it was not associated with any strong singular ideological orientation, was regarded by some as instrumental in the implementation of market-oriented policies, such as the removal of price controls and trade liberalization (Yasui, 2002). It is plausible that the thinking of the "Berkeley Mafia" evolved over time from one focused on Keynesian thinking (the Harrod-Domar model) and development planning (Mahalanobis), to a more market-oriented approach (Sadli, 1993).

Oil boom years and economic reforms: 1970s/1980s

The two oil shocks in the 1970s and the stagflation that followed had significant impact on mainstream debates on Western macroeconomics (e.g. the Phillips curve), but the impact of the oil shocks was a bit different for oil-producing countries such as Indonesia and Malaysia. The rise in oil prices marked the beginning of the oil-boom years in these countries which provided more resources for development programs.

In Indonesia, the impacts of the oil booms were more destabilizing. Economists such as Arndt and Sadli were quick to point out that the gains from the first oil boom (1973/74) were quickly dissipated with the bankruptcy and bailout of the country's national oil company, Pertamina, due to poor governance structures. The Indonesian rupiah was also devalued by 50 percent in 1978 just prior to the onset of the second oil boom (1979) to deal with the "Dutch Disease" problem from the first oil boom. During the second oil boom period (1978/79), policy-making was likely dominated by economic nationalists (rather than the economic technocrats belonging to the "Berkeley Mafia"). A manifestation of this is the implementation of a new industrial strategy based on a second round of import-substitution, which focused on state-owned enterprise, up-stream, basic, and resource-processing industries (Thee, 2012, 100). The economic arguments that were put forward by A.R. Soehoed (from 1978 to 1983 Minister of Industry) to support the strategy were premised upon market failures in the presence of the required high capital intensity, gestation period, and physical infrastructure. These arguments aside, the strategy was prematurely terminated with the end of the oil boom in the early 1980s.

In Malaysia, economic discussions and policy focused on the formulation of integrated regional development programs that would serve to achieve the objectives of the New Economic Policy. Interests in this approach to development were partly in response to the failure of aggregative Harrod-type growth models in bringing about more equitable growth (Higgins, 1982). By the early 1980s to mid-1980s, economists began writing extensively on the implications and impact of NEP. These studies emphasized the importance of achieving high-growth rates in order to achieve the NEP targets without zero-sum effects on other ethnic communities (Young et al., 1980; Snodgrass, 1980). The implementation of NEP also motivated a number of major economic studies on income distribution in Malaysia in the late 1970s and early 1980s (Meerman, 1979; Tan, 1982). In addition to these studies, there were also class-based approaches to interpreting economic development and the NEP (Hua, 1983; Jomo, 1986).

The end of the oil boom in 1982 (due to a weakening of the world oil market) and the economic slowdown in the mid-1980s shifted economic debates and policy focus to trade and policy reforms in both countries. Whilst these developments coincided with the advent of neo-liberal economic ideas and policy reforms in the US and UK, the economic performance in Indonesia and Malaysia as well as external pressures were the main drivers of trade and policy reforms since the mid-1980s. In Indonesia, the rapidly deteriorating economy finally convinced the government to implement policy reforms that were advocated by efficiency-minded economists in the country (Pangetsu, 1996). Later works such as Feridhanusetyawan and Pangetsu (2003) highlighted the role of external events such as the Uruguay Round Agreement and the World Trade Organization in providing an impetus to trade liberalization during this period.

Malaysia also underwent significant change shifts in economic policy orientation beginning in the early 1980s. A second phase of import-substitution focusing on the development of heavy industries was pursued under the leadership of Mahathir Mohamad. This approach was heavily influenced by the industrialization strategies adopted in Japan and South Korea, although a minority of economists was openly critical of this approach (Chee, 1985). Other economists during this period were more concerned about technological development and transfer in the manufacturing sector (Fong, 1986; Ali, 1992). The Mahathir administration also embarked on an extensive privatization and liberalization program, and it took another ten years before comprehensive and often critical reviews of privatization programs emerged.

The Asian financial crisis and regional integration: 1990s/2000s

The literature on privatization in Malaysia emerged beginning in the mid-1990s – more than ten years after the privatization was implemented. The early study by the World Bank

(Galal et al., 1994) had a positive review of the privatization outcomes (MAS, KCT and Sports Toto). Later studies by Malaysian academics were more critical of privatization programs (Jomo, 1995; Tan, 2008). These studies were part of the larger emerging literature on political economy in Malaysia, emphasizing the rent-seeking nature of the ruling coalition party in Malaysia (Gomez and Jomo, 1997). The literature on privatization in Indonesia is sparse as little progress was made in this area despite the announcement of ambitious plans in the late 1980s (McLeod, 2002).

The key economic event in the 1990s was, without doubt, the Asian financial crisis in 1997. Analyses of the financial crisis have attributed the crisis to both economic factors (exchange rate system, private debt levels, and a weak financial system) which were compounded by political factors (Hill, 1999; MacIntyre, 1999). In the case of Malaysia, short-term capital flows, high leverage, and an equity bubble have been identified as factors contributing to the economy's vulnerability during this period (Athukorala, 2001). Factually, the impact of the crisis was more severe for Indonesia than on Malaysia. The different policy responses in Indonesia and Malaysia brought to light economic debates on the pro-market ideas dubbed the "Washington Consensus" (advocated by International Monetary Fund (IMF)/World Bank) as well as the role of political economy in development. Indonesia was forced to implement the IMF/World Bank's structural adjustment policies, which later brought about severe political crisis and the end of the Suharto regime. In Malaysia, a different policy response was adopted involving greater state intervention via capital controls, which was regarded as going against IMF-type policy prescriptions (Mahani, 2002; Dornbusch, 2002).

Political economists have also entered the debate by highlighting the role of politics (e.g. governing coalitions) in explaining the different policy response and subsequent developments (Pepinsky, 2009). The slower pace of growth in the period after the 1997 financial crisis has also prompted further analyses, especially on the role of institutions and politics. For example, the rent-seeking critique of government policies continues to have significant traction in the political economy literature in Malaysia (Hill et al., 2012). This trend is perhaps consistent with increasing interest amongst mainstream economists in the role of institutions and politics in long-term economic growth (Acemoglu et al., 2005).

Conclusion

Economic thought in Indonesia and Malaysia has, in the past, evolved in response to the countries' colonization experiences and subsequent post-independent developmental challenges. What emerges from this broad and short survey is a sense that there is no singular or identifiable school of thought in these countries. Much of the writings that have emerged in the past fifty to sixty years were primarily driven by challenges posed by prevailing economic and political problems. By undertaking a survey of economic thought/problems side-by-side, this comparative study argues that there are both similarities and differences in emphases over time.

Early economic writings were pre-occupied by similar problems associated with the inheritance of colonial economies – post-war reconstruction and ownership. The ethnic dimension in development – involving an inequality in wealth between the indigenous and ethnic Chinese communities – has featured prominently in both countries. The resulting debates and others in the 1950s/1960s have often pitched professional economists (adhering to conventional economic thinking) against other non-economist groups (nationalists, politicians). After the Asian financial crisis in 1997, there was perhaps greater convergence as economists have begun looking more deeply into the role of institutions and politics in generating and sustaining long-term growth.

Bibliography

Acemoglu, Daron, Johnson, Simon and Robinson, James. (2005). "Institutions as a Fundamental Cause of Long-Run Growth", in *Handbook of Economic Growth*, Volume 1, edited by Philippe Aghion and Steven Durlauf. Amsterdam: Elsevier.

Alatas, Syed Hussein. (1977). *The Myth of the Lazy Native*. London: Frank Cass.

Alavi, Rokiah. (1996). *Industrialisation in Malaysia*. London: Routledge.

Ali, Anuar. (1992). *Malaysia's Industrialization: The Quest for Technology*. Singapore: Oxford University Press.

Arndt, H.W. (1981). "Development and Equality: Themes in Economic Thought about Indonesia", *Journal of Southeast Asian Studies*, 12:2, 464–75.

Aswicahyono, Haryo, Hill, Hal and Narjoko, Dionisius Narjoko. (2010). "Industrialisation after a Deep Economic Crisis: Indonesia", *The Journal of Development Studies*, 46:6, 1084–1108.

Athukorala, Prema-Chandra. (2001). *Crisis and Recovery in Malaysia: The Role of Capital Controls*. Cheltenham: Edward Elgar.

Boestaman, Ahmad. (2004). *Memoir Ahmad Boestaman*. Bangi: UKM Press.

Bruton, Henry. (1992). *The Political Economy of Poverty, Equity and Growth: Sri Lanka and Malaysia*. New York: Oxford University Press.

Bulletin of Indonesian Economic Studies. "Survey of recent developments", various issues.

Chee, Peng Lim. (1985). "The Proton Saga – No Reverse Gear!: The Economic Burden of Malaysia's Car Project", in *The Sun Also Sets*, edited by Jomo K.S. Kuala Lumpur: INSAN.

Dick, Howard, Houben, Vincent, Lindblad, J. Thomas and Thee Kian Wie. (2002). *The Emergence of a National Economy: An Economic History of Indonesia, 1800–2000*. Crows Nest, NSW: Allen & Unwin.

Dornbusch, Rudi. (2002). "Malaysia's Crisis: Was It Different?", in *Preventing Currency Crises in Emerging Markets*, edited by Sebastian Edwards and Jeffrey A. Frankel. Chicago: University of Chicago Press.

Drabble, John. (2000). *An Economic History of Malaya, c.1800–1990*. London: Macmillan.

Faaland, Just, Parkinson, J.R. and Saniman, Rais. (1990). *Growth and Ethnic Inequality: Malaysia's New Economic Policy*. Kuala Lumpur: Dewan Bahasa dan Pustaka.

Feridhanusetyawan, Tubagus and Pangetsu, Mari. (2003). "Indonesian Trade Liberalisation: Estimating the Gains", *Bulletin of Indonesian Economic Studies*, 39:1, 51–74.

Fisk, E.K. and Osman-Rani, H. (eds) (1982). *The Political Economy of Malaysia*. Kuala Lumpur: Oxford University Press.

Fong, Chan Onn. (1986). *Technological Leap: Malaysian Industry in Transition*. Singapore: Oxford University Press.

Galal, A., Jones, L., Tandon, P. and Vogelsang, I. (1994). *Welfare Consequences of Selling Public Enterprises: An Empirical Analysis*. New York: Oxford University Press for the World Bank.

Gomez, T. and Jomo, K.S. (1997). *Malaysia's Political Economy: Politics, Patronage and Profits*. Cambridge: Cambridge University Press.

Gullick, J.M. (1988). *Indigenous Political Systems of Western Malaya*, Revised Edition. London: Athlone Press.

Henderson, Jeffrey, Hulme, David, Phillips, Richard and Noorul Ainur, M. Nur. (2002). "Economic Governance and Poverty Reduction in Malaysia", Working paper No.44, Manchester Business School.

Higgins, Benjamin. (1982). "Development Planning", in *The Political Economy of Malaysia*, edited by E.K. Fisk and H. Osman-Rani, Kuala Lumpur: Oxford University Press.

Hill, Hal. (1999). "An Overview of the Issues", in *Southeast Asia's Economic Crisis*, edited by H.W. Arndt and H. Hill. Singapore: ISEAS.

Hill, Hal, Tham, Siew Yean and Ragayah Mat Zin. (eds) (2012). *Malaysia's Development Challenges: Graduating from the Middle*. London: Routledge.

Hua, Wu-Yin. (1983). *Class & Communalism in Malaysia: Politics in a Dependent Capitalist State*. London: Zed Books.

Jomo. K.S. (1986). *A Question of Class: Capital, the State and Uneven Development in Malaya*. Singapore: Oxford University Press.

Jomo K.S. (ed.). (1995). *Privatizing Malaysia: Rents, Rhetoric, Realities*. Boulder, CO: Westview Press.

Jomo, K.S. (ed.) (2007). *Malaysian Industrial Policy*. Singapore: NUS Press.

Jones, Gavin. (2012). "Demographic and Labour Force Dynamics", in *Malaysia's Development Challenges: Graduating from the Middle*, edited by Hal Hill, Tham Siew Yean and Ragayah Mat Zin. London: Routledge.

Li, Dun Jen. (1982). *British Malaya: An Economic Analysis*. INSAN: Petaling Jaya.

Lim, Chong Yah. (1967). *Economic Development of Modern Malaya*. Kuala Lumpur: Oxford University Press.

Lim, MahHui. (1981). *Ownership and Control of the One Hundred Largest Corporations in Malaysia*. Kuala Lumpur: Oxford University Press.

Lim, Teck Ghee. (1977). *Peasants and Their Agricultural Economy in Colonial Malaya 1874–1941*. Kuala Lumpur: Oxford University Press.

MacIntyre, Andrew. (1999). "Political Institutions and the Economic Crisis in Thailand and Indonesia", in *Southeast Asia's Economic Crisis*, edited by H.W. Arndt and H. Hill. Singapore: ISEAS.

Mahani, ZainalAbidin. (2002). *Rewriting the Rules: The Malaysian Crisis Management Model*. London: Prentice Hall.

Manning, Chris and Roesad, Kurnya. (2007). "The Manpower Law of 2003 and its Implementing Regulations: Genesis, Key Articles and Potential Impact", *Bulletin of Indonesian Economic Studies*, 43:1, 59–86.

McLeod, Ross. (2002). "Privatisation Failures in Indonesia", mimeo.

Meerman, Jacob. (1979). *Public Expenditure in Malaysia: Who Benefits and Why*. Washington DC: World Bank.

Meier, H. (1994). *Den Haag – Jakarta: De Nederlands-Indonesische Betrekkingen, 1950–1962 (The Hague – Jakarta: Dutch Indonesian Relations, 1950–1962)*. Utrecht: Aula.

Pangetsu, Mari. (1996). *Economic Reform, Deregulation and Privatization: The Indonesian Experience*. Jakarta: Centre for Strategic and International Studies.

Pepinsky, Thomas. (2009). *Economic Crises and the Breakdown of Authoritarian Regimes: Indonesia and Malaysia in Comparative Perspective*. New York: Cambridge University Press.

Puthucheary, James. (1960). *Ownership and Control in the Malayan Economy*. Singapore: Eastern Universities Press.

Rao, V.V. Bhanoji. (1980). *Malaysia: Development Pattern and Policy*. Singapore: Singapore University Press.

Reid, Anthony. (1988). *Southeast Asia in the Age of Commerce 1450–1680*. New Haven: Yale University Press.

Reid, Anthony. (1992). "Economic and Social Change", in *The Cambridge History of Southeast Asia*, vol.1, part 2, Cambridge: Cambridge University Press.

Roff, William. (1967). *The Origins of Malay Nationalism*. New Haven: Yale University Press.

Sadli, Mohammas. (1993). "Recollections of My Career", *Bulletin of Indonesian Economic Studies*, vol.29, no.1, 35–51.

Saubari, Mohammad. (1987). "Reflections on Economic Policy-Making", *Bulletin of Indonesian Economic Studies*, vol.23, no.2, August, 118–121.

Saubari, Moh. (2003). "Reflections on Economic Policymaking, 1945–51". In *Recollections: The Indonesian Economy, 1950s–1990s*, edited by Thee Kian-Wie.

Seers, Dudley. (1968). "From Colonial Economics to Development Studies", *IDE Bulletin*, 1:1, 4–6.

Silcock, T.H. (ed.) (1961). *Readings in Malayan Economics*. Singapore: Eastern Universities Press.

Snodgrass, Donald. (1980). *Inequality and Economic Development in Malaysia*. Kuala Lumpur: Oxford University Press.

Tan, J. (2008). *Privatization in Malaysia*. London: Routledge.

Tan, Tat Wai. (1982). *Income Distribution and Determination in West Malaysia*. Kuala Lumpur: Oxford University Press.

Thee, Kian Wie (ed.). (2003). *Recollections: The Indonesian Economy, 1950s–1990s*. Singapore: ISEAS.

Thee, Kian Wie. (2012). *Indonesia's Economy Since Independence*. Singapore: ISEAS.

World Bank. (1955). *The Economic Development of Malaya*. Richmond: Johns Hopkins Press for the World Bank.

World Bank. (2006). *World Development Report 2007*. Washington, DC: World Bank.

Yasui, Shin. (2002). "How was the Market Economy Implanted in Developing Countries? The Cases of Chile and Indonesia", mimeo.

Young, Kevin, Bussink, Willem, and Parvez, Hasan (eds). (1980). *Malaysia: Growth and Equity in a Multiracial Society*. Baltimore and London: Johns Hopkins University Press for the World Bank.

Yusuf, Shahid and Nabeshima, Kaoru. (2009). *Tiger Economies Under Threat: A Comparative Analysis of Malaysia's Industrial Prospects and Policy Options*. Washington, DC: World Bank.

28

The Asian Tigers

Takashi Kanatsu

The Asian Tigers refer to the following four economies: Hong Kong, Singapore, South Korea and Taiwan, which showed remarkable economic development from the 1960s to the 1990s. There are some similarities among these four economies: however, each economy is significantly distinct. The naming of the Asian Tigers focuses more on the outcome represented in GDP growth rates, rather than the causes of such economic growth.

The following are the major similarities of the Asian Tigers. First, all four economies are located in the east of the Eurasian continent. This is not a trivial issue in relation to the post-World War Two world order. During the Cold War, which coincided with the time of the Tiger's rapid economic growth, this location was often the frontline between communist and capitalist countries. The relations between these economies and the United States (or Great Britain in the case of Hong Kong) are therefore not a negligible factor. Second, all four economies invested significantly in human capital. They rank very high – almost always top contenders – in various international educational achievement tests such as the Programme for International Student Attainment and Trends in International Mathematics and Science Study. Third, there are similarities of ethnicity – all but South Korea are of Chinese ethnicity, with the main religion and philosophy being Confucianism and Buddhism, and the language of three is Chinese, with a strong influence even in South Korea.

Fourth, these economies received significant Japanese influence as a coloniser before World War Two. Japan was also a predecessor in rapid economic development after World War Two, although its influence varied economy by economy. Fifth, all economies have focused on export-oriented industrialisation. Historically, all the Asian Tigers have had marked trade surpluses since the 1960s. Finally, all economies had political regimes of so-called 'developmental dictatorship'. Although Hong Kong and Singapore were more of a soft authoritarianism, no Tiger was under full-fledged democracy during the height of its economic growth.

The differences among these economies, however, are more significant in terms of the causes of their economic growth. The economic ideas employed in these economies in order to facilitate development can be gauged in terms of the level of similarities/differences between the United States as the most liberal market-oriented economy, at least conceptually if not in reality, and Japan, where government intervention in the economy has played a key role since the Meiji Restoration of 1868. They can be situated in this US–Japanese axis in the following order: Hong

Kong, Singapore, Taiwan and South Korea. Hong Kong's economic development is the most similar to the *laissez-faire* free-market model, while the heaviest government intervention took place in South Korea, reminiscent of Japan. As such, this chapter will eventually discuss the four economies one by one. However, it is helpful to first map out the basic uniqueness of the economic thought that applies in the Asian Tigers, although the level of application varies among the four economies.

Developmental state theory

The most important economic idea that has guided the growth of these economies over the last few decades can be categorised as the developmental state theory. This idea was born out of the study of Japan, which showed significant economic growth after World War Two, although the origin of the story would go back to Friedrich List, who guided Japanese government officials in the nineteenth century. Chalmers Johnson wrote the seminal work articulating the current theory in 1982. This idea, with variations, spread in the 1980s and early 1990s. During this process, the theory has been used to explain the development of other successful East Asian economies dubbed as 'Asian Miracles'. In 1989, Alice Amsden published a book explaining how the South Korean government 'took prices wrong' intentionally, and in 1990, Robert Wade introduced the concept of *Governing the Market*, which discussed the Taiwanese case in detail.

The developmental state theory of generating economic development claims that there is a critical role that the government can play in the development of a country's economy in a way that is very different from the traditional idea of socialist-style government intervention. Developmental state theory does not deny the role played by the market as, fundamentally, this theory is based on a capitalistic market economy. Yet, the role played by the government is much bigger than in a neoclassical model of a market economy, whose role there is defined mainly as regulatory and with minimal intervention in the economy.

The role of the government in developmental state theory can be summarised as an industrial policy. This prototypically consists of five stages. First, the government identifies industries that are expected to grow in the next one/two decades; second, the government identifies private companies that can achieve development in the identified industries; third, in order to make the companies competitive in the world market, the government encourages and supervises merger and acquisitions or suggests a specialisation of each company's products; fourth, the government provides support to the companies selected by setting up a consortium to develop critical technology, government research institutes and preferential loans or tax breaks; finally, the government judges the performance of each selected company, particularly in its export performance to the US market. Based on a final evaluation, some companies continue to receive the government support while others lose such privileges. To enable this industrial policy and upgrade the industrial level of the country, the government establishes higher education institutions that specifically target technological aspects of industry.

The economic rationale of this developmental state theory was drawn from several ideas. First, there is a role that the government can play in a developing country where financial industries are underdeveloped. For example, Japan's MITI (Ministry of International Trade and Industry) used its leverage of the allocation of foreign currency, which was still restricted in the 1950s, to manoeuvre private firms to join its efforts to participate in industrial policy schemes. Second, the developmental state theorists argue that 'pure' comparative advantage based on trade theory in neoclassical economics is unrealistic, as investing in certain fields can actively create 'competitive' advantage. This view reflects the idea that economic growth is fundamentally dynamic and not static like the equilibrium theory of neoclassical economics. This is an idea taken from Joseph Schumpeter's notion of 'creative destruction'.

What makes capitalism such a powerful mechanism for economic growth is not the narrow idea of allocative efficiency as explained by neoclassical economics, but the entrepreneurial ability to introduce very innovative products and technologies, and thus to destroy the existing equilibrium and engender dramatic change. Therefore, the developmental state theorists claim that so-called market 'distortions' created by government initiatives do not create a problem but are actually part of the solution to kick-starting development. Indeed, with many of the products that Japan or the Asian Tigers dominate, it cannot be considered that they would have a comparative advantage without government intervention. Various other economic ideas complement the validity of state intervention in developmental state theory. For example, the idea of transaction costs, originally developed by Ronald Coase, suggests the important contribution of signalling effects, or credible commitments, by the government to industry.

There was a major international debate on developmental state theory in the 1990s. The World Bank published a book called *The East Asian Miracle* in 1993, responding to various claims made, particularly by the Japanese government, that state intervention can promote economic growth. The majority of neo-liberal economists in the World Bank opposed this theory, and the 1993 book emphasized the importance of stable macroeconomic management based on neoclassical economics as a root of success, rather than government intervention. The 1997 *World Development Report* by the World Bank, however, conceded that there was a significant role that the state can play in economic development.

The 1997 Asian financial crisis that affected one of the Asian Tigers, South Korea, seriously but not others encouraged neoclassical economists to claim that developmental state theory was mistaken. However, various studies of the crisis suggested that it was not necessarily the fault of the developmental state. Indeed, the South Korean economy went back to its growth path within two years. The reason that the South Korean economy was more affected by this crisis was related to the nature of South Korean industrial organisation, which relies so much on a few giant *chaebols* (family-owned conglomerates) that focused on market share predominantly rather than profits. There are, however, significant failures of industrial policies even in Japan, in industries like petrochemicals and aluminium. Therefore, theoretical debates over developmental state theory have not yet ended.

Another issue is: how/why the government can identify industries for promotion and assess various technological needs, while it is not engaged in business itself. Although developmental state theory is different from socialist intervention, where governments create national/state corporations, there is still doubt about how bureaucrats can predict at the forefront of future industries. To answer this, Peter Evans articulated the notion of 'embedded autonomy'. The government bureaucrats face a dilemma. On the one hand, they need industrial information from a private sector that is making or losing money every day. On the other hand, they do not want to be 'captured' by these business interests, as these interests have incentives to lie in order to extract resources from the government: traditional industrial lobbying. Evans argues that there must be a mechanism for government bureaucrats to extract unbiased information from industries, yet not be affected by sectoral interests.

To do so, the governments of a developmental state set up frequent meetings with corporations and let the corporations compete with each other, in order to avoid being captured by their provincial interests, and thereby remain autonomous. Evans argues that because the balance between 'embeddedness' and autonomy is extremely delicate, there have been few successful developmental states. Even among the Asian Tigers, only South Korea and Taiwan can be listed as successful cases, while Singapore is less a typical developmental state. Hong

Kong is clearly not an example. Evans' argument can be supported by various theories of collective action. Repeated communications among actors and the logic of the prisoner's dilemma made coordinated actions by industry to deceive the government difficult in the cases of South Korea and Taiwan, leading to developmental success.

Industrialisation strategy

All the Asian Tigers had significant trade and current account surpluses regardless of industrialisation strategy. Except for Hong Kong, the industrialisation strategies of the Asian Tigers fit the model of export-oriented industrialisation (EOI). The importance of exports for economic development was discussed widely by, for example, Béla Balassa. However, there has been an argument about industrialisation and the deteriorating terms of trade for exports, which was most notably discussed by Raúl Prebisch, who recommended import-substituting industrialisation (ISI). However, ISI-only policies would result in huge trade deficits, as the Latin American countries experienced in the 1980s. According to Gary Gereffi, industrialisation strategies take five steps in their relation to trade strategies. First, any developing economy that lacks capital, foreign currency reserves and technology must start with a commodity phase by exporting items such as agricultural goods and minerals to earn enough foreign currency to purchase machines and technologies from developed countries. The economy cannot stay in this stage for very long, however, because the terms of trade of agricultural goods deteriorate over the long-term, as mentioned above, as productivity increases in primary commodities are limited. Furthermore, the economy in this stage is vulnerable because of the weather and other uncontrollable factors that can affect the economy tremendously.

Once currency reserves are accumulated, the economy moves into the next stage called primary import-substituting industrialisation. In this process, the government needs to protect domestic companies in order to nurture infant industries by raising tariffs and instituting other subsidies to combat foreign imports that have quality advantages. At this point, the economy focuses on labour-intensive products such as clothes, processed foods and shoes. Once they obtain a certain level of technology and capability of manufacturing these products, the economy can then compete in the international market due to its lower labour cost. This is the third stage called the primary export-orientated industrialisation. This will provide the country with enough capital and foreign currency reserves to step up to the next phase. The economy has no luxury to stay in this stage, as other developing countries will catch up while the economy will face rising wages as development succeeds. Besides, at this level, the economy still needs to import expensive machinery to make these labour-intensive products. Therefore, the trade surplus at this level can be very small.

Therefore, the economy then needs to 'deepen' its industrialisation by focusing on more highly value-added products such as consumer durables, intermediate goods such as steel, petrochemicals and machinery, and high technology goods. Again, the government needs to protect domestic companies from foreign competition as developed countries have higher levels of technology. The developing economy at this point must face a steep learning curve in science and technology, and cheap labour does not provide significant advantage any more. This fourth stage is called the secondary import-substitution industrialisation. Once the economy masters the top-level technologies of the international standard, it can then move into the final, fifth stage called the secondary export-orientated industrialisation. At this final stage the structure of industry becomes one of developed economies.

South Korea and Taiwan reached this final stage in a wide variety of their products while Singapore achieved this in limited industries. All three economies had to go through two ISI stages quickly as the protection cannot last long, due to potential damage to the economies during ISI. During the ISI stages, the government faces major dilemmas. On the one hand, it needs to purchase technologies or machines from developed countries. In order to make these imports cheaper, the government maintains the local currency at an appreciated level. However, this will make their exports more expensive, which makes their products, whether commodities or labour-intensive products, less competitive internationally. Therefore, the trade surplus will shrink during the ISI stage, or it may result in trade deficits. In order to shorten the ISI periods, the economies need to accelerate the learning process, which requires a focus on science/technology education that is very close to commercial technologies. Let's now examine each Asian Tiger historically and individually.

Hong Kong and Singapore

Hong Kong's case is unique among Asian Tigers because of its rather strict following of neoliberal economic thought. This has been consistent even when Great Britain was cajoling Keynesian ideas. According to Leo Goodstadt, this is the policy preference of Hong Kong's Chinese business elite and has been supported by the governors of Hong Kong since 1947, when the governor was Sir Alexander Grantham. Hong Kong became a separate economic entity from China in 1842 after the Opium War, but its return to China in 1997 did not make this economy completely merge with the Chinese economy, although relations between the two have been closer since 1997. Hong Kong never developed a significant manufacturing sector like the other three Asian Tigers. Its manufacturing sector remained less sophisticated, such as cheap garments and other industries, while the three other Tigers made a significant progress in high-technology and heavy industries.

Nevertheless, Hong Kong shares similar traits with the other Asian Tigers such as investing heavily in human capital and in exporting products. Hong Kong's main strength was in its financial industry and it became a financial hub of Asia. Hong Kong has also retained one of the most competitive education systems in the world. The University of Hong Kong and Hong Kong University of Science and Technology are in the top twenty science and engineering universities in the world. As discussed above, Hong Kong did not have a significant industrial policy, which makes it rather different from the other Tigers.

Singapore is located between Hong Kong and Taiwan/South Korea in terms of the level of government intervention. It is one of the freest economies in the world, yet, it was not satisfied with an entirely *laissez-faire* economy like Hong Kong. The government put significant efforts into industrialising the economy in some limited areas. The major architect of Singapore's economic development was Lee Kuan Yew. Singapore features some high-tech industries, particularly in semiconductors and media storage. The National University of Singapore is listed as the highest in Asia and is the sixteenth in the world in the engineering and technology field.

Taiwan

Taiwan, along with South Korea, took a unique approach known as the developmental state approach. The similarity between Taiwan and South Korea is that they both are prototypical examples of developmental state theory: utilising industrial policies to promote targeted industries. Taiwan, however, differs from South Korea in that its more complex industrial organisation resulted from the unique political history of Taiwan.

Taiwan has one of the most competitive education systems in the world. In addition, Taiwan's uniqueness is that it tried to emulate Stanford University/Silicon Valley by connecting science and technology oriented universities, National Chiao Tung University and National Tsing Hua University, to the industry in the Hsinchu Science and Industry Park (HSP).

Taiwan's industrial policies have been as extensive and intensive as South Korea's. A pilot agency, the Committee for Economic Planning and Development (CEPD), developed these policies. The government established a technology research institute, the Industrial Technology Research Institute (ITRI), which played a key role in Taiwan's high-tech industrial development, particularly in the field of information technology. Unique aspects of the government involvement in industry are the establishment of the HSP mentioned above. Considering that the chronic trade deficit with Japan was problematic due to heavy imports of semiconductors, in spite of the development of consumer electronics, the Taiwanese government decided to launch a programme to start semiconductor production. However, due to a rift between the Taiwanese and the mainlanders, local Taiwanese corporations were reluctant to join this plan. Facing a lack of interest among Taiwanese companies, the government decided to use government laboratories to develop a semiconductor, having established the Electronic Research and Service Organisation, or ERSO, under the ITRI. Once a product is developed, the Taiwanese government allows the laboratory to be 'spun off' from the ITRI to become a private company. Government engineers quit their government jobs and became private entrepreneurs. This 'spin-off' business worked well. For example, the largest semiconductor company in Taiwan, TSMC, and the second largest, UMC, are both the products of this 'spin-off' scheme in the HSP.

Taiwan is connected to Japan in two ways. First, Taiwan was the first colony of Japan before World War Two. From 1895 to 1945, Taiwan was under Japanese control. During this time, Taiwan experienced a predecessor of industrialisation particularly in the 1930s when Japan invested in heavy and chemical industries in colonised Taiwan. Even prior to this, Japan tried to make Taiwan a model of successful colonial management to impress Western powers under the governorship of Shinpei Goto. After World War Two, Taiwan became a major destination for Japan's foreign direct investment.

Taiwan's connections with the United States are the highest among the Asian Tigers. After World War Two, the United States became a key protector of Taiwan as well as the source of investment, and many Taiwanese migrated to the United States. The expatriates who moved to the United States, particularly in California, never severed connections to Taiwanese businesses. As Taiwan's economy moved to more sophisticated manufacturing, particularly in the IT industry, the demand for the engineers who were trained in US higher education rose dramatically. Organisations such as the Monte Jade Science and Technology Association helped nurture continuous ties between the Taiwanese expatriates, particularly in Silicon Valley, and the companies in Taiwan.

What makes Taiwan's case unique in its relation to the United States is the government effort to connect to US expatriates upon initiating the semiconductor industry. As discussed above, the Taiwanese were reluctant to accept the government invitation to develop a semiconductor industry. The government decided to communicate with expatriates in the United States and ask for their return to Taiwan, providing them with favourable monetary and patriotic incentives. Morris Chang, who headed the TSMC, was a typical example. Chang was an engineer at Texas Instruments for years but had faced a glass ceiling for promotion as being non-Caucasian. He accepted the government invitation and worked in the ITRI and eventually spun-off to establish the largest Taiwanese semiconductor company TSMC. Thus, the relation between the United States and Taiwan is strong through multiple channels. Without this connection, Taiwan's IT development would have been much harder to achieve.

South Korea

South Korea is the most typical example of developmental theory among the Asian Tigers, only next to the originator of the theory, Japan. Like Japan, it took various steps through industrial policies: identifying promising industries and corporations; providing support for the development of technology through government research institutes; providing various subsidies and tax incentives; judging the corporate successes/failures and rewarding the successful corporations by renewing subsidies and tax incentives.

South Korea is also one of the leading countries in the K-12 aptitude test, and its focus on technological education is very similar to Japan's. The government created a graduate school focusing on technology and science totally separate from the traditional school system: the Korea Advanced Institute of Science and Technology (KAIST). Later, they added undergraduate schools. Many of their graduates found jobs in *chaebols* such as Samsung and LG. The KAIST is ranked one of the top science and technology institutions in the world.

South Korea's industrial policies are prototypical industrial policies as discussed above. Yet, there are several differences between Japan and South Korea. First, the pilot agency of South Korea's industrial policies, the Economic Planning Board (EPB), was filled with US-trained economists, while Japanese MITI was filled with locally trained economists. Therefore, South Korea's industrial policies were slightly more market-oriented than the Japanese counterpart. Second, the South Korean industrial policies gave up coordinating among corporations in the process of acquiring advanced technologies, as rivalries among *chaebols* were too strong to allow collaboration. Although South Korea established the government-owned industrial research institute, the Korean Institute of Science and Technology (KIST) in 1966, it realised that the individual *chaebols'* laboratories could produce products much more efficiently. Third, the South Korean industrial policies focused on nurturing *chaebols* rather than supporting small and medium enterprises (SMEs). Later, the South Korean government realised the danger of excessive focus on the large enterprises and established Daedeok Science Town, currently called Daedeok Innopolis, in 1973 in order to facilitate the synergy between government research laboratories and private corporations, having as models Silicon Valley and Tsukuba of Japan. In contrast to South Korea, Japanese SMEs compose two-thirds of the total number of corporations as well as the number of employees.

The relations between Japan and South Korea are long-standing and complex. Japan colonised Korea from 1910 to 1945. The president of South Korea, Park Chung-Hee, was a member of the Japanese army and studied in the Imperial Japanese Army Academy. When Japan lost World War Two, he was a lieutenant in the Japanese Imperial Army. Also, many of the post-Korean War South Korean bureaucrats were from the Japanese colonial government. Furthermore, upon the conclusion of the Treaty on Basic Relations between Japan and the Republic of Korea in 1965, there has been economic cooperation between the two, including about 1.1 billion US dollars of aid. The similarities between South Korea and Japan are influenced by these historical relations.

The personal relations between the United States and South Korea are not as strong as the relations between Taiwan and the United States. Although Korean immigrants live in the United States, the connection between the expatriates and the indigenous Koreans is not as strong as in the case of Taiwan. Yet, due to the fact that the United States was the protector of South Korea after World War Two and the Korean War, the security relation is strong. Nonetheless, South Korea's economic development focusing on nurturing *chaebols* is much closer to the path of Japan than that of the US free-market economy. The fact that the US protected South Korea's security interests, while at the same time allowing it significant freedom to diverge from the Western free-market economic model, is an interesting combination to end with.

Bibliography

Amsden, Alice. H. 1989. *Asia's Next Giant: South Korea and Late Industrialization*. New York, NY: Oxford University Press.

Aoki, Masahiko, Kevin Murdock and Masahiro Okuno-Fujiwara (eds). 1996. *The Role of Government in East Asian Economic Development*. New York, NY: Oxford University Press.

Chang, Ha-Joon. 1994. *The Political Economy of Industrial Policy*. Basingstoke, UK: Macmillan Press.

Evans, Peter B. 1995. *Embedded Autonomy: States and Industrial Transformation*. Princeton, NJ: Princeton University Press.

Gereffi, Gary and Donald L. Wyman (eds). 1990. *Manufacturing Miracles: Paths of Industrialization in Latin America and East Asia*. Princeton, NJ: Princeton University Press.

Goodstadt, Leo F. 2010. 'Fiscal Freedom and the Making of Hong Kong's Capitalist Society'. *China Information*. 24 (3): 273–94.

Johnson, Chalmers. 1982. *MITI and the Japanese Miracle: The Growth of Industrial Policy, 1925–1975*. Stanford, CA: Stanford University Press.

Kim, EunMee (ed.). 1998. *The Four Asian Tigers: Economic Development and the Global Political Economy*. San Diego, CA: Academic Press.

Mathews, John A. and Dong-sung Cho. 2000. *Tiger Technology: The Creation of a Semiconductor Industry in East Asia*. Cambridge, UK: Cambridge University Press.

Nelson, Richard R. (ed.). 1993. *National Innovation System: A Comparative Analysis*. New York, NY: Oxford University Press.

Wade, Robert. 1990. *Governing the Market: Economic Theory and the Role of Government in East Asian Industrialization*. Princeton, NJ: Princeton University Press.

Woo-Cumings, Meredith (ed.). 1999. *The Developmental State*. Ithaca, NY: Cornell University Press.

World Bank, The. 1997. *World Development Report 1997: The State in a Changing World*. New York, NY: Oxford University Press.

World Bank, The. 1993. *The East Asian Miracle: Economic Growth and Public Policy*. New York, NY: Oxford University Press.

29

India

Balakrishnan Chandrasekaran

As human civilization evolved and developed a workable theory of the nation-state, economic thought gradually became more distinct from other subjects. By virtue of being an old civilization, India has a long tradition of progressive 'economic thinking' understood in a broad sense. Of course historically, Indian political economy is rooted in the social, cultural and political conditions of India (Parthasarathi, 2012). Though India is very diverse culturally, certain basic value systems and a traditional understanding of life have made its 'thought' compatible across different regions of the country.

Economic thinking in India is based fundamentally on the liberty and freedom of individuals within the ambit of the family system, which is also placed within wider society. But unlike Western 'standalone' individualistic culture, 'family-based' individualistic culture is the bedrock of Indian socio-economic values (Mukherjee, 1916). Therefore the family household is usually the basic unit considered in Indian economic thought, rather than the solitary individual.

The secular development of Indian economic thought can be classified into four phases:

(1) The ancient Indian phase that produced very diverse traditions of 'economic thought' which are completely different to what is considered as economics today.
(2) The pre-independent phase from around 1850, when the nationalist school attempted to unite the different provincial forces and provided various platforms for discussions about then-prevailing Western economics and also indigenous Indian thought. This phase helped Indian thinkers to look again at their own traditions and to work on a new framework for a future India. This continued until the beginning of the twentieth century and was usually critical of classical economics, because the British government in India invariably used classical economics for policy-making and often underestimated the relevance of Indian economic thought.
(3) The independent India phase after 1947, when the scenario became completely different as far as economic thought was concerned, partly because of the influence of Marxism. At the same time, the emergence of powerful analytical currents like neoclassical and Keynesian economics had sidelined the indigenous ideas of Indian economists in the first half of the twentieth century. This third phase continued until 1991, when an economic crisis was

triggered by excessive government/state control, which had believed for decades in the theories of Marxism and Keynesianism.

(4) A liberal economic phase that was thrust upon the country as a way out of the crisis after 1991. This helped the country to move out of crisis quickly and sustained India on a completely different path, and created a new passion for free market economics amongst some. Now the debate amongst Indian economists is between three basic schools of thoughts: free market, Keynesian and Marxist.

Ancient economic thought

Schumpeter said that 'the history of economic thought starts from the records of the national theocracies of antiquity whose economies presented phenomena that were not entirely dissimilar to our own' (1954, 49). As Ajit Dasgupta (1993) explained:

> the third argument advanced by Schumpeter in favour of studying the history of economics is that it throws light on the workings of the human mind. For a history of economic thought in India this is, I believe, especially important . . . In ancient cultures the workings of the human mind tended to be closely linked to religion. A history of economic thought must therefore take the religious factor into account. If one is writing a history of economic thought for a country outside the mainstream of Western culture, this could give rise to special difficulties. These were particularly emphasised by Max Weber in his highly influential work on the sociology of religion.

However, Dasgupta included a caveat that 'studying the history of Indian economic thought can indeed help illuminate the workings of the Indian mind. The illumination would be the more effective if we discarded the distorting mirror of Weberian sociology'. Hardly anyone has followed these warnings, without which the crux of his interpretation would be misleading.

Many unique features of Indian economic thinking were depicted in ancient texts from the very early period of civilization, and they invariably contain an ocean of economic ideas conceived very broadly (Thanawala, 1997; Ambirajan, 1997). According to Ambirajan (1936–2001) 'many of the classical Indian writings on ethics, economics, law or philosophy are somewhat like mathematical theorems whose proofs have not been written out. Hence we have to work out how and why these terse statements came about' (1997, 32).

The classical literature relevant for understanding ancient economic thought in India includes *Vedas, Arthasasthra, Ramayana, Mahabharata, Manusmriti, Sukraniti, Nithisasthra* and *Thirukkural* (Basu and Sen, 2008). Kautilya, the foremost economic thinker of ancient India, treated economic topics along with political and military matters in his *Arthasasthra*. Indeed, *Arthasasthra* is one of the earliest tracts of economic science, written at least twenty centuries before Adam Smith. Another source of ideas on economics was the *Santi Parva* of the *Mahabharata*, an epic wherein advice concerning the accumulation and distribution of wealth was interspersed with advice on how to run a country (Ambirajan, 1997).

But the two outstanding works among the ancient literature are *Thirukkural* and *Arthasasthra*. These texts have many original economic ideas premised within social and political contexts. *Thirukkural* (couplets or aphorisms), which is believed to be written 2,400 years ago by Thiruvalluvar, a Tamil Poet, has 1,330 couplets in 133 chapters covering all aspects of human life in relation to the state, economy and society. Moreover, *Thirukkural* is a universal work as it deals with a wide range of issues from ploughing a piece of land and the method of ruling a country, to the code of purposeful life in society (Kalam, 2010). The book is divided into three broad sections that discuss virtue, wealth and human emotions (love).

Arthasasthra discusses various elements of economics, the title being translated as the science of political economy or science of material gain. It is now accepted that its author Kautilya was a contemporary of Aristotle. At the centre of Kautilyan economics is an obligation of the state to provide for the welfare of the people. *Arthasasthra* also deals extensively with international trade, taxation and the labour theory of value. According to Charles Waldauer (Waldauer et al., 1996), Kautilya

> explicitly recognizes that international trade (trade among kingdoms) in goods and services is a major vehicle for increasing the sovereign's wealth as well as that of his subjects. Kautilya also counsels his monarch that the wealth and well being of the realm can be most advanced by a fair and efficient system of taxation, one which will supply the king with tax revenue while not stifling economic growth. Finally Kautilya advocates a wage system which rewards workers for the value they have created and encourages them to work harder and more efficiently.

The most common features in both *Thirukkural* and *Arthasasthra* are the wisdom of wealth creation and prosperity within society engendered by individual economic agents, as well as the importance of family culture with or without the help of a modern notion of the state. Both elements are intertwined and equally necessary.

The nineteenth century

Since the middle of the nineteenth century, when the movement for independence gained momentum, the debate between different currents of thought in India was usually expressed in relation to the functioning of the British government in the undivided Indian sub-continent. On the one hand, there were mass movements against the British Raj for reforming the social, economic and political systems. On the other hand, there were disturbing trends within Indian society, including the domination by one community of others on the basis of social norms such as caste, which were often accentuated by British colonial rulers for political gain.

Against these movements, many thinkers studied the systemic issues at hand, the method of economic analysis and its uses, including varieties of historical economics. Most of the prominent leaders highlighted India's rich tradition of knowledge in the ancient and later periods. According to Shib Chandra Dutt (1934, 5), during this early period, 'a considerable portion of economic thinking in India is of an economic-political character. To socio-economic questions a part of the thinking has addressed itself, while economic history has arrested the attention of a large number of scholars'. Thus, the first new wave of Indian economic thought was born against the backdrop of the emergence of systemic social reforms as well as the independence movement.

A basic impetus for social reforms in India was given by Rammohan Roy (1772–1833), who 'stressed the importance of private property' in general, and particularly for women as early as 1822 (Spengler, 1971). In his 1822 work, *Brief Remarks Regarding Modern Encroachments on the Ancient Right of Females according to the Hindu Law of Inheritance*, (3–4), Roy argued that in ancient India women had property rights in an absolute form, and he referred to key legal authorities as support. According to Roy, in ancient India, property rights for women were not restricted. Roy was one of the early proponents of liberalism in India, expounding the values of individual freedom and liberty, constitutional methods for achieving independence, and a free press. He strongly believed that without liberty, human development could not be achieved. According to S.P. Aiyar (1985), Roy was quick to perceive the significance of the great changes on which India was poised during the first quarter of the nineteenth century.

Following in the footsteps of Roy, there were other pioneers of Indian economic thinking. A promising new line of ideas began with the works of Dadabhai Naoroji (1825–1917), Mahadeo

Govind Ranade (1842–1901), Romesh Chunder Dutt (1848–1909) and Gopal Krishna Gokhale (1866–1915). There were also several social reformers, philosophers and radicals like Swami Vivekananda (1863–1902), Sri Aurobindo and Bankim Chandra Chatterjee (1838–94), who contributed significantly to economic thought.

Dadabhai Naoroji is often given the title 'Grand Old Man of India' for his contributions to Indian economics during British rule. He was a Professor of Mathematics and Natural Philosophy at the Elphinstone Institution in Bombay in 1855. He published a book in 1876 entitled *Poverty of India* based on papers read before the Bombay Branch of the East India Association. He outlined reasons for the drain of India's wealth to Britain, which he argued was taking place at a time when the country was in dire need of industrialization and other reforms. Naoroji, a proponent of free trade, was one of the first to calculate the economic costs of the drain of resources from India. He estimated a £200–300 million loss of revenue to Britain that was not returned. This book brought his ideas to the public at large and become a stepping stone for the emergence of movements to end British rule.

According to R.P. Masani (1939, 192–3):

> Dadabhai's paper was the most illuminating document ever published on that most contentious problem of Indian economics. His method of approach was rough and ready . . . Nevertheless, his estimate of the national income was roughly as accurate as it could then have been, and the best corroboration of his calculations was the estimate given by Evelyn Baring (Lord Cromer) and Sir David Barbour in the year 1882.

However, later Indian economists like Benoy Kumar Sarkar (1887–1949) disagreed with Naoroji's argument about the draining of resources from India to Britain. In fact, Sarkar 'rejects the theory of exploitation and holds that just as India is drained of her raw materials or her foodstuffs through her connection with Great Britain, similarly India has been draining Great Britain of her capital, her organizing ability and her expert training for her own development' (Dutt, 1934, 179). Thus, Naoroji's calculation had ignored the intangible elements of the relationship, such as knowledge transfers. John Maynard Keynes was Sarkar's mentor, and Sarkar began studying at King's College, Cambridge, in 1911 and stayed in England until 1920: Keynes's own analysis of India was similar to Sarkar's on the drain issue. Keynes remarked about Sarkar that 'He is a strange and charming creature' (Moggridge, 1992). Indeed, the relationship between Keynes and Sarkar was quite intimate. However, the broader debate moved on to what is usually known as the negative policies of the British government in India.

M.G. Ranade was among the first generation of thinkers who made important contributions to Indian political economics, as it was famously called. From 1893 until his death in 1901, he served as Judge of the High Court of Bombay. He published a book entitled *Revenue Manual of the British Empire in India* in 1877, which documented the provincial systems of land revenue sources. Ranade also published *A Note on the Decentralization of Provincial Finance* in 1894. His lectures, delivered during 1880–93, were published as *Essays on Indian Economics* in 1898. They provided a critical view of established economic theories, including the cultural aspects of Western and Indian traditions. This book has been called one of the greatest works of Indian economics.

Ranade not only debated all the prevailing issues of the British Raj, but also gave consideration to the usefulness of classical economics in India, particularly methodology. He studied the economic systems of European countries and arrived at the conclusion that the inductive or historical method of analysis was the best. He railed against what he called 'the Deductive School' of Adam Smith, David Ricardo and Thomas Malthus and instead argued, 'The Method to be followed is . . . the Historical Method, which takes account of the past in its forecast of the future; and Relativity, and not Absoluteness, characterizes the conclusions of Economical Science'.

Thus he called for a specifically 'Indian Political Economy' (Gallagher, 1988, 14). Ranade argued that 'The same Teachers and Statesmen, who warn us against certain tendencies in our Political aspirations, forget this salutary caution when the question at issue is one of Indian Economics. They seem to hold that the Truths of Economic Science . . . are absolutely and demonstrably true, and must be accepted as guides of conduct for all time and place . . . Social, Juristic, Ethical, or Economical differences in the environments are not regarded as having any influence in modifying the practical application of these Truths'. Ranade thus believed that the principles of classical economics may not be applicable to countries other than Britain.

John Adams (1971) has argued that Ranade was an Institutionalist and took much from the German historical school, especially Sismondi, Hamilton, Carey, Ludovico, Muller and List. However, Ranade was arguing in the context of Britain's imported economic policies, and had imbibed India's long-standing value systems: Indian nationalism was emerging. Ranade was conscious of the cultural element involved with economic prosperity, although some feel that 'Ranade's complete rejection of the Western classics was somewhat extreme' (Pani, 2011). Still, he was to some extent influenced by Institutionalists like J.R. Commons, Thorstein Veblen and the historian Henry Maine. In fact, all of these thinkers were influential in India.

Romesh Chunder Dutt was a civil servant, political economist and writer. His publications dealt with British economic policies in India: *England and India* (1897), *Famines in India* (1900) and an *Economic History of India*. According to D.R. Gadgil, Dutt's work 'contains, in essence, a preview of what came later to be called the economics of colonialism' (Dutt, 1968). One of Dutt's telling analyses was that 'while British Political Economists professed the principles of free trade from the latter end of the eighteenth century, the British Nation declined to adopt them till they had crushed the Manufacturing Power of India, and reared their own Manufacturing Power . . . in India the Manufacturing Power of the people was stamped out by protection against her industries, and then free trade was forced on her so as to prevent a revival'. Thus, Dutt concluded that as a consequence of deindustrialization, there was increased dependence upon agriculture, which also came under severe pressure with British rule, chiefly because of high taxation (Parthasarathi, 2001). These conclusions were later corroborated by David Clingingsmith and Jeffrey Williamson (2005).

Gopal Krishna Gokhale pioneered a new radical economic thought in India. Initially he taught mathematics and for a time lectured on English, but then turned his attention to history and economics. He was also a Fellow at Bombay University. He was largely responsible for the drafting of new courses in history and economics. Gokhale was a strong advocate of the decentralization of power, particularly in matters related to finance. In 1896, he gave evidence before the Royal Commission under Lord Welby, which made his reputation as one of the foremost Indian economists. In a speech delivered at the Annual Financial Statement discussions in the Supreme Legislative Council of British Rule, Gokhale argued for a free banking system and against the government monopoly of currency and legal tender. He favoured the gold standard and specifically stated that 'an automatic self-adjusting currency' would be a better way to manage the demand for currency, which would automatically adjust with trade in the market (Ambedkar, 1947, 240).

The early twentieth century

The growth of neoclassical economics in the twentieth century has had significant impact on Indian economists. As argued controversially by Parthasarathi (2012): 'the growing influence of neoclassical economics and its universalization has eliminated the need for a historical approach in contemporary Indian economics'. Many leading twentieth-century Indian economists, either directly or indirectly, were trained in Western ideas, especially at the London

School of Economics (LSE), Cambridge and Oxford. Individuals like Harold Laski, Lionel Robbins, Joan Robinson, Hicks, Kaldor, Allen, Lerner, Kalecki, Shackle, Karl Popper and Friedrich Hayek were all major influences. Early Indian economists and others who studied at the LSE included B.R. Ambedkar, B.R. Shenoy, Sardar Tarlok Singh, V.K. Krishna Menon, K.R. Narayanan, Minoo Masani, C.R. Pattabhiraman, R.K. Amin, Mahesh P. Bhatt, and C.D. Rajesvaran. Many were influenced by Laski's school of politics and economics. Ramachandra Guha (2003) explained that 'LSE did indeed have a deep impact on the policies and politics of independent India. I forget who it was who said . . . that "in every meeting of the Indian Cabinet there is a chair reserved for the ghost of Professor Harold Laski'". P.G. Mavalankar, who studied under Laski in England, founded the Harold Laski Institute of Political Science in Ahmedabad in 1954 with funds from the Indian government.

The Department of Economics at the University of Madras was one of the earliest established in India in 1912. Subsequently, the Department of Economics at the University of Allahabad and the University of Calcutta were both created in 1914 (the university was inaugurated by H. Stanley Jevons in 1915). The Department of Economics of the University of Mumbai was established in 1921. At College level, the Sydenham College of Commerce and Economics was created in 1913 and is also one of the earliest colleges created in Asia. Similarly, the Department of Economics at St. Agnes College in Mangalore in south India was one of the oldest departments established in 1921.

Alongside this growth of economics departments, in the first half of the twentieth century, colonial India produced several economists of repute who anticipated debates in development economics well before it became part of the mainstream. J. Krishnamurty (2009) has studied 'the lives and careers of the first generation of Indian professional economists', who did cutting-edge work on what was later to become development economics. He traced contributions made during the period 1900–45 by B.R. Ambedkar, Brij Narain (1889–1947), L.C. Jain, C.N. Vakil (1895–1979), Radhakamal Mukherjee (1889–1968), Rajani Kanta Das, Jehangir C. Coyajee (1875–1943), V.G. Kale (1876–1946), Gyanchand (1893–1983), P.J. Thomas (1895–1965), P.S. Lokanathan (1894–1972), V.K.R.V. Rao (1908–91) and B.P. Adarkar (1903–88). For example, in a 1929 paper on indigenous banking, L.C. Jain lamented the slow but sure disappearance of many indigenous banking systems which were centuries old, and the loss of ancient banking methods and practices which, if retained and judicially mixed with modern developments, could be a source of strength to the Indian banking system as a whole.

Brij Narain contributed something distinct on universalization. He said in 1934 that 'the study of economics, coupled with careful observation of facts, shows that economic life and development are governed by laws of universal validity. This realisation has not yet come to India'. Narain was influenced by economists like W.E. Weld and Othmar Spann, who rejected the idea of economics tailored for each country. A year before India attained independence, Narain published a book on *The Economic Structure of Free India* (1946), where he argued for the appropriate type of economic system that India should adopt, after rejecting Gandhi's village Swaraj system. Narain considered two basic systems, *laissez-faire* and the planned economy.

B.R. Ambedkar (1891–1956) was an authority on Indian currency and banking in the early decades of the twentieth century. He was familiar with the works of Carl Menger, but he remained independent, favouring empiricism and logic, rather than any particular system or ideology (Chandrasekaran, 2011a). Ambedkar pursued Gokhale's idea of free banking when he was studying at the LSE for his PhD, completed under Edwin Cannan.

One of Ambedkar's most illuminating works was the Statement of Evidence given before the Royal Commission under Hilton-Young on Indian Currency and Finance 1924–5. Ambedkar said:

one of the evils of the Exchange Standard is that it is subject to management . . . by adopting the convertible system we do not get rid of the evil of management which is really the bane of the present system . . . When the management is by a bank there is less chance of mismanagement. For the penalty for imprudent issue . . . is visited by disaster directly upon the property of the issuer. But the chance of mismanagement is greater when it is issued by Government because the issue of government money is authorised and conducted by men who are never under any present responsibility for private loss in case of bad judgment.

His recommendations for free banking were ignored not only by the Commission but also the Indian government. The Commission submitted its Report in 1926 and its recommendations were instrumental in the establishment of the Reserve Bank of India.

Ambedkar was trained in the West, receiving a Masters' degree in economics from Columbia University in 1915. His major works included: *Administration and Finance of the East India Company* (1915), *The Problem of the Rupee* (1923), *The Evolution of Provincial Finance in British India* (1917) and *Provincial Decentralisation of Imperial Finance in British India* (1921). Many of his ideas reflected a path-breaking interest in the Austrian school of economics (Chandrasekaran, 2011b). There is a close similarity between Ambedkar's ideas and those of Carl Menger, Ludwig von Mises, F.A. Hayek and William Graham Sumner. Ambedkar was one of the earliest Indian economists to understand the central issue of the use of knowledge in society. His theory of free banking was built on Menger's works as well as Gokhale's treatise on finance and money. Ambedkar's (1947, 279) view of the distinguishing differential quality of money (its almost unlimited saleable-ness) was influenced by Menger's idea of the sale-ability of money, as expressed in his 1892 article 'On the Origin of Money'.

Further, Ambedkar understood the impossibility of a successful centralized administration or planning for British rule in India in a society so extensive and diverse. Taking into account the Hayekian knowledge problem, Ambedkar advocated an absolute form of decentralized planning. In his thesis 'The Evolution of Provincial Finance in British India', Ambedkar (1925, 179) said 'a Central Government for the whole of India could not be said to possess knowledge and experience of all various conditions prevailing in the different Provinces under it. It, therefore, necessarily becomes an authority less competent to deal with matters of provincial administration than the Provisional Governments'. Ambedkar also made important contributions to development economics; a paper published in 1918 'on the problem of small holdings in Indian agriculture is almost prophetic in its anticipation of several themes in later development economics, including the existence of disguised unemployment in farming. He showed why India needs to industrialize to absorb this surplus labour' (Rajadhyaksha, 2013).

B.K. Sarkar was one of the most prominent Indian social scientists of the period before independence (Sen, 2013). In 1925, he started as a lecturer at the Department of Economics, University of Calcutta, and in 1947 he became a professor and head of the department. Sarkar published works on a variety of topics, and edited two leading journals, *Economic Progress* and *Journal of the Bengal National Chamber of Commerce*. Further, he was one of the early founders of the Indian school of sociology. His major writings included: *Economic Development* (1926), *Studies in Applied Economics and World Economy* (1932), *Indian Currency and Reserve Bank Problems* (1933) and *Imperial Preference vis-à-vis World-Economy in Relation to International Trade and National Economy of India* (1934).

Radhakamal Mukherjee was Professor of Economics and Sociology of the University of Lucknow. He wrote 50 books ranging from rural studies to class analysis, personality theory to regional ecology, population problems to mysticism and Indian arts (Celarent, 2013), and he was one of the leading economists of modern India. His early work dealt with issues of 'Indian' economics and its relation to universal economics. Mukherjee published various books including: *The Foundations of Indian Economics* (1916), *Principles of Comparative Economics* (1921), *Borderlands of Economics* (1925), *The Institutional Theory of Economics* (1939), *Economic Problems of Modern India* (1939), *The Economic History of India, 1600–1800* (1940) and *The Culture and Art of India* (1959). In *The Foundations of Indian Economics*, he said that 'in India we have heard and seen enough of theories as well as practices attempting to force economic systems and methods which have not been wholly successful in the West, but which are unsuited to the socioeconomic traditions of the country . . . the time has come for a clear analysis of the social and ethical ideals of India to which all economic institutions must be adapted'.

Mukherjee was an early proponent of the Indian family thesis: 'Founded on the virtues of affection and self-control, this system tends to develop a spirit of self-sacrifice, and mutual control and dependence, which are quite opposed to the competitive individualistic spirit . . . while in the West it is the individual's own scale of wants, his standard of comforts . . . which regulates the growth of the population, in India the family mode of enjoyment or standard of life is the main factor'. Mukherjee was also a proponent of Institutional economics in India (Sinha, 1992), and he was strongly influenced by Veblen, Mitchell, Commons and Hobson. In his book *The Institutional Theory of Economics* (1939, 89), Mukherjee wrote that 'Institutional economics deals not only with the abstract laws governing the relations between restricted or scarce goods and satisfactions or services, but also with the entire social and institutional structure and standards which blend and interpenetrate with and over-reach economic values'. He was an Intuitionalist but in a less-developed context.

Keynes and Indian currency

The legendary figure Vedagiri Shanumugasundaram (b. 1926), who taught Indian economic thought while serving as Head of the Department of Economics at the University of Madras, expressed a blind adoration so characteristic of recent Indian scholarship: J.M. Keynes had become the synonym of economics (1979).

Keynes published his first book *Indian Currency and Finance* in 1913, analysing the workings of India's monetary system. In the same year, he was appointed as member of the Royal Commission on Indian Currency and Finance chaired by J.A. Chamberlain. Many of the chapters were already drafted before Keynes was appointed, while Sir Shapurji Burjorji Broacha was the only Indian member. Both Keynes's book and the Commission's report created a heated debate. J. Shield Nicholson criticized the Commission's report and believed that 'a large part of the report is substantially in accord with the treatment (sic) by Mr J.M. Keynes in his recent book' (Doraiswami, 1914). One of the key aspects was that Keynes believed that the gold-exchange standard was suitable for India, rather than the traditional gold standard. This was strongly contested by many within India and abroad as well.

S.V. Doraiswami was a well-known economist from Madras (now Chennai) who criticized Keynes's arguments. In December 1914, Doraiswami published his own book entitled *Indian Finance, Currency and Banking*. He had already published his views in outlets like London's *Statist*, and his book was reviewed internationally. According to Doraiswami, Keynes 'seems to have dominated the Commission, and he holds the view that the gold exchange standard marks an advanced stage in monetary evolution. I am not aware of any economist of repute who holds that view. Be that as it may, the Indian currency system should not be tampered with to suit the whims of an armchair doctrinaire' (1914, 109). Doraiswami believed that a central bank 'should be an instrument for allowing and encouraging the free and unfettered inflow of gold to India' (168). Further, he went on to argue that 'a gold standard without a gold currency is an absurdity' (7).

Moreover, in the early 1920s, B.R. Ambedkar also criticized Keynes's arguments on the gold-exchange standard. Ambedkar (1923, 256) declared that 'if stability of purchasing power in terms of commodities in general is the criterion for judging a system of currency, then few students of economics will be found to agree with Prof. Keynes'. Ambedkar argued that the gold-exchange standard did not have the institutional stability of the gold standard, as in the former system additions to the supply of currency depended on the actions of the issuer, and in the Indian context at least, he demonstrated that prices varied significantly more under the former system than the latter. He (1923, 257) continued, 'Keynes scoffs at the view that there cannot be a gold standard without a gold currency as pure nonsense. He seems to hold that a currency and a standard of value are two different things. Surely there he is wrong. Because a society needs a medium of exchange, a standard of value, and a store of value to sustain its economic life, it is positively erroneous to argue that these three functions can be performed by different instrumentalities'.

Bhalchandra P. Adarkar (d. 1988) was unique among Keynes's many Indian students both personally and intellectually. Adarkar was Professor of Economics in Allahabad University. He produced works such as *Theory of Monetary Policy* (1935), *The Indian Constitution* (1938) and *Indian Fiscal Policy* (1941). His contributions on monetary theory, federal finance and fiscal policy are classics (Khatkhate, 1988). The high esteem in which Adarkar was held by Keynes, who was not only his supervisor for the Economics Tripos at King's but also a mentor (Chandavarkar, 1988), was shown by the fact that in 1932 Keynes wrote: 'I consider him to be the most promising Indian student of economics, as far as original work is concerned'.

After independence

After India attained independence in 1947, the country took the path of a socialist and centralized regime, largely influenced by the rise of Marxist-Leninist philosophy, ignoring the millennia-old indigenous traditions of Indian philosophy and cultural values. Indian economic planning was initially modelled by P.C. Mahalanobis using the existing Soviet literature on planning techniques, with little opposition from most Indian economists. But as Milton Friedman said 'there is only one prominent professional economist, Professor B.R. Shenoy of Gujarat University, who is openly and publicly and at all effectively opposed to present policies and in favour of greater reliance on a free market. He is a remarkable and courageous man'.

Shenoy was a student of Austrian economist F.A. Hayek in the early 1930s at the LSE. In his book *Post-War Depression and the Way-Out* (1944) he pointed out the dangers of financing the Bombay Plan of government intervention through newly created money and bank credit, i.e. through massive deficit spending. Other important works by Shenoy include *Ceylon Currency and Banking* (1941), *The Sterling Assets of the Reserve Bank of India* (1953), *Problems of Indian Economic Development* (1958), *Fifteen Years of Indian Planning* (1966), *Indian Economic Crisis: A Program for Reform* (1968), *Food Crisis in India: Causes and Cure* (1974) and *Economic Growth and Social Justice* (1977).

For decades before the 1991 economic crisis, Shenoy advocated sound finance based on free market ideas, but his voice was ignored. His contemporaries had a blind faith in centralized planning, and these policies were responsible for creating a crisis in India's foreign exchange in the early 1990s. Shenoy died in 1978, after which the thrust of economic policy moved away from the worship of planning, and most economists now agree that India's long tryst with Nehruvian socialism was an economic disaster.

Initially, some Indian economists had argued in favour and some against neoclassical economics. The critics based their arguments on its suitability for the Indian economy. However, neoclassical economics eventually became the most popular of all economics in independent India. Indeed, Nachane (2008, 85) stated 'belief that neoclassical economics is universal (widely prevalent among large sections of the Indian intelligentsia) is attributable the fact that the subject of Indian Economics . . . now survives only as an exotic species . . . the spirit of independent thinking that characterised the writings of 19th-century nationalists such as Dadabhai Naoroji and Mahadev Govind Rande, and of their intellectual heirs . . . has virtually disappeared from the current generation'.

D.M. Nachane (2008) pointed out the 'virtually unshakeable position that neoclassical economics occupies currently in mainstream economic thinking'. But his view on 'what exactly constitutes neoclassical economics and when it originated' is interesting. As pointed out by Nachane, 'Dasgupta refrains from the appellation neoclassical while referring to the works of Jevons, Walras, Menger, J.B. Clark, Wicksteed and others, preferring to use the term marginalist instead'. Dasgupta believed the term neoclassical was suited only for Marshall, whose 'analysis of equilibrium points to a dynamic element'. Further, in Nachane's words 'Dasgupta's position is thus close to Veblen (1900) and contrasts strongly with the more inclusive use of the term neoclassical introduced by Hicks (1932) and Stigler (1941)'.

Nachane's basis for neoclassical economics was that 'modern orthodox economics incorporating the important contributions to information theory, transaction costs and externalities by Arrow, Stigler, Stiglitz, Townsend, Coase, etc., does not constitute a departure from neoclassical economics, only its continuation and reaffirmation under more general boundary conditions' (2008, 82). Dissatisfied with the role of neoclassical economics in India, Nachane concluded that 'the economics profession in India will overcome its traditional intellectual dependency on Western mainstream economics, and imbibe a little bit of the spirit of free inquiry and critical appraisal of dogmas, that characterised A.K. Dasgupta's life and work'. Noted Keynesian economist A.K. Bagchi (1976, 81) also criticized neoclassical economics, arguing that it 'has no tools for dealing with essentially non-capitalist social formations or their interaction with capitalist formations'.

Amartya Sen (b. 1933) is undoubtedly the greatest economist of independent India and has contributed to both economic theory and policy. Sen is a product of the long tradition of West Bengal achievements, being the second Nobel Laureate from West Bengal after Rabindranath Tagore, who won for Literature in 1913. Bengal was the early powerhouse of colonial India before the British administration was shifted to Delhi. Sen's corpus of works since 1970 has fulfilled his basic objective to expand the scope and flexibility of three central tools of economics: the concept of preference, rational choice theory, and social choice theory (Anderson, 2005). He has also contributed to welfare economics on topics such as poverty, famine and inequality, this work re-energizing the field of development economics. In 1998, he was awarded the Nobel Prize for Economics for 'his contributions to welfare economics'. In his Nobel lecture, Sen discussed the challenges faced by social choice theory, by sketching a perceptive view of the origin of that theory. His basic argument for expanding the scope, objectives and boundary of social choice theory were drawn from Kenneth Arrow's *Social Choice and Individual Values* (1951).

In 1953, Sen was only in his late teens when he went to study in Cambridge at Trinity College for a BA in Economics, although he already had a BA in Economics from Calcutta University. After finishing the BA he enrolled for a PhD. But he later returned to Calcutta on a two-year period of leave from Cambridge and was appointed as Professor of Economics and founding Head of the Department of Economics at Jadavpur University, Calcutta. At that time, Sen was 'not yet even 23' years old, and this created a storm at the university. After two years at the department he returned to Cambridge to complete his PhD. Sen wrote his thesis on 'The Choice of Techniques' under the supervision of Joan Robinson.

When Sen was at Cambridge, a heated debate between the Keynesians (Richard Kahn, Nicholas Kaldor and Joan Robinson) and the neoclassicals (Dennis Robertson, Harry Johnson, Peter Bauer and Michael Farrell) was occurring. But Sen had 'close relations with economists on both sides of the divide', and he maintained this position throughout his career. However, he did make greater criticism of the neoclassical school, and it seems that Sen underwent a significant ideological migration (Briggeman, 2013). Both the left and right have claimed Sen, but he said that he had read the writings of both and agreed with neither (Goyal, 1999).

Sen's first major book was *The Choice of Techniques* published in 1960, based on his PhD thesis. It explored choices over the optimal combination of techniques for industrial production, whether to use more labour-intensive methods of production or capital-intensive methods, assuming there was abundant labour and scarcity of capital (Atkinson, 1999). Sen criticized purely market-based criteria for choice of technique and criteria that sought to modify the market solution only by taking account of market failures in the static allocation of resources. But he recognized that market prices and costs should shape planners' choices, when such prices could not be altered without imposing too high a fiscal burden or social cost (Bagchi, 1998).

In 1970 Sen published a book on *Collective Choice and Social Welfare*, which was concerned with investigating the dependence of judgements about social choice and public policy on the individual preferences of members of a society. He argued that, just as social choice was based on individual preferences, the latter in turn depended on the nature of the society in which they occurred. Thus, rules of collective choice were linked to specific social structures.

Another contribution of Sen was on the behavioural theory of self-seeking egoistic agents which he called rational fools (1977). His theory of rational fools combined two different philosophical schools, the rationalistic school and the phenomenological school. Sen argued that adopting too narrow a definition of 'rational' behaviour neglected important factors such as commitment, but in a way that neglected the distinction between reason as such, and knowledge as the basic problem of human activity. Thus his criticisms were mainly targeted at the neoclassical rather than the Austrian approach.

Sen's work on the 'capabilities approach' to development created a new methodological debate among economists. Capabilities are the alternative combinations of functionings that a person is feasibly able to achieve. Sen argued for five components in assessing capability: the importance of freedoms in the assessment of a person's position; individual differences in the ability to transform resources into valuable activities; the multivariate nature of activities producing happiness; a balance of materialistic and non-materialistic factors in evaluating welfare; and concern for the distribution of opportunities within society. This work helped to make the capabilities approach a paradigm for policy debates in human development. Sen refined Adam Smith's principle of sympathy and added a modernised concept of the impartial spectator in the form of commitment (Eiffe, 2008). Sen drew not only on Smith's *Wealth of Nations*, but also on *The Theory of Moral Sentiments*. These two books were the main instruments for redefining a different approach to human progress.

Unlike liberal economists like Ambirajan (1976, 1978), Sen argued in his book *Poverty and Famines* (1981) that it was not the decline of food availability, but the 'failure of exchange entitlements', which caused famine. Thus, such failures can arise when the rate at which products or labour power can be exchanged against food turns sharply against the producers and labourers (Patnaik, 1997). Sen remains India's most well-known economist.

Conclusion

The commitment to indigenous Indian economic thought continued into the early decades of the twentieth century, but was mainly lost after independence. Despite pioneering work on Indian ideas, now there is hardly any school or centre in any university/institute which recognizes the importance of Indian economic thought from a contemporary perspective.

After India became a republic in 1950, many universities and colleges were created across the country, some with teaching and research programmes in Indian economic history, although not so much for Indian economic thought. The teaching of Indian economic thought as a core subject was continued until 2004 at the University of Madras, but was then discontinued. There are some colleges and universities created recently that teach the history of Indian economic thought, but only as optional subjects for undergraduate students.

However, after the emergence of Western free market economics, India has not attempted to look back at its own indigenous tradition of market economics once practised decades or even centuries before. This is a point which few are willing to take from Indian economists like S.V. Doraiswami, C. Rajagopalachari, Mohandas Karamchand Gandhi, Gopal Krishna Gokhale, B.R. Ambedkar, B.R. Shenoy and Radhakamal Mukherjee. Looking forward the future of India is promising and, if nurtured properly, it could reengage with the 'lost' path of the pioneering contributions of Indian economists who envisioned distinctive ideas for India's own needs.

It is clear that there was a large amount of literature in ancient India providing moral, social and economic codification for ways of pursuing prosperity. It is also clear that the independence movement in India shifted radically the way in which economic thinking prevailed in India after British colonial rule. In the process, the insightful ideas of ancient India vanished, partly because of the social divisiveness of aspects of the Hindu religion. Western thinking also played a role in highlighting social ills within the broad structure of Indian society. While it is true that many useful ideas depicted in ancient literature were sidelined, at the beginning of the twentieth century there were some pioneering Indian economists who re-employed elements of ancient economics. But this tradition was only briefly rediscovered and quickly vanished. Since then it has been a long journey of forgotten traditions, while the academic community engaged on the paths of Marxist and neoclassical economics up to very recently. Nevertheless, there is hope that the past antiquities of Indian economic thought could be re-introduced to young minds, who may pursue them rigorously and with great interest.

References

Abdul Kalam, A.P.J. (2010) Address during the Presentation of the Chinese Edition of Thirukkural, Taipei.

Adams, John (1971) The Institutional Economics of Mahadev Govind Ranade, *Journal of Economic Issues*, vol.5, no.2, 80–92.

Aiyar, S.P. (1985) *The Concept of Liberalism and its Relevance for India, Freedom and Dissent*, Democratic Research Service, Bombay.

Ambedkar, B.R. (1918) Small-Holdings in India and their Remedies, *Journal of Indian Economic Society*, vol.1.

Ambedkar, B.R. (1923) *The Problem of the Rupee: Its Origin and Its Solutions*, P.S. King & Son, Ltd, London.

Ambedkar, B.R. (1925) *The Evolution of Provincial Finance In British India*, P.S. King & Son, Ltd, London.

Ambedkar, B.R. (1947) *History of Indian Currency & Banking*, Thacker and Company Ltd, Bombay.

Ambirajan, S. (1976) Malthusian Population Theory and Indian Famine Policy in the Nineteenth Century, *Population Studies*, vol.30, no.1 (March).

Ambirajan, S. (1978) Classical Political Economy and British Policy in India, *Cambridge South Asian Studies*, no.21. Cambridge University Press.

Ambirajan, S. (1997) The Concepts of Happiness, Ethics, And Economic Values in Ancient Economic Thought, in B.B. Price (ed.) *Ancient Economic Thought*, vol.1, Routledge, London.

Anderson, Elizabeth (2005) Critical Notice of Amartya Sen, *The Philosophical Review*, vol.114, no.2 (April).

Annadurai, C. (1933) Moscow Mob Parade, published in the *College Magazine*.

Atkinson, A.B. (1999) The Contributions of Amartya Sen to Welfare Economics, *The Scandinavian Journal of Economics*, 101(2).

Bagchi, A.K. (1976) Cropsharing Tenancy and Neoclassical Economics, *Economic & Political Weekly*, January 17.

Bagchi, A.K. (1998) Amartya Kumar Sen and the Human Science of Development, *Economic & Political Weekly*, vol.33, no.49 (December 5–11).

Basu, Ratan Lal and Sen, Raj Kumar (2008) *Ancient Indian Economic Thought – Relevance for Today*, Rawat Publications, New Delhi.

Berg, Maxine (1979) Classical Political Economy and British Policy in India: Review, *Journal of Economic Literature*, vol.17, no.2.

Briggeman, Jason (2013) Amartya Sen – Ideological Profiles of the Economics Laureates, *Econ Journal Watch* 10(3), September.

Celarent, Barbara (2013) The Dynamics of Morals by Radhakamal Mukerjee – Book Review, *American Journal of Sociology*, vol.118, no.6, 1736–44.

Chakraverti, Sauvik (2003) Review of Amartya Sen's Rationality & Freedom, *The New York Sun*, 26 February.

Chandavarkar, Anand (1988) B.P. Adarkar and Keynes: The Ganges and the Cam, *Economic & Political Weekly*, October 22.

Chandrasekaran, B. (2011a) India's Great Free-Market Economist, *Mises Daily*, Tuesday July 5.

Chandrasekaran, B. (2011b) The forgotten liberal ideas of M.K. Gandhi, *The Cobden Centre*, 22 July.

Chaudhuri, K.N. (1979–80) Classical Political Economy and British Policy in India – Book Review, *Pacific Affairs*, vol.52, no.4.

Clingingsmith, David and Williamson, Jeffrey G. (2005) India's Deindustrialization in the 18th and 19th Centuries, Department of Economics, Harvard University.

Dasgupta, Ajit (1993) *Indian Economic Thought*, Routledge, London.

Doraiswami, S.V. (1914) *Indian Finance Currency and Banking*, The Commercial Press, Madras.

Dutt, R.C. (1968) *Romesh Chandra Dutt: Builders of Modern India*, Publication Division, Ministry of Information and Broadcasting, Government of India.

Dutt, Shib Chandra (1934) *Conflicting Tendencies in Indian Economic Thought*, N.M. Ray-Chowdhury & Co., Calcutta.

Eiffe, Franz F. (2008) The Smithian Account in Amartya Sen's Economic Theory, Vienna University of Economics and Business Administration.

Friedman, Milton (1963) Indian Economic Planning in *Friedman on India*, edited by Parth. J. Shah, The Centre for Civil Society, New Delhi, 2000.

Gallagher, Robert (1988) M.G. Ranade and the Indian system of political economy, *Executive Intelligence Review*, vol.15, no.22, May 27.

Ghosh, Arun (1991) Trade Reform for Restructuring the Economy, *Economic & Political Weekly*, vol.26, no.24, June 15.

Goyal, Ashima (1999) Interpreting Amartya Sen's Work, *Economic & Political Weekly*, April 10.

Guha, Ramachandra (2003) The LSE and India, *The Hindu*, November 23.

Gundappa, D.V. (1987) Liberal Position Paper – 7, Liberalism in India, *Freedom First*, July.

Harnetty, Peter (1979) Classical Political Economy and British Policy in India, Review, *The Journal of Asian Studies*, vol.38, no.3, May.

Khatkhate, Deena (1988) An Economist Whose Present Was in the Past, *Economic & Political Weekly*, October 8.

Krishnamurty, J. (2009) *Towards Development Economics: Indian Contributions 1900–1945*, Oxford University Press, New Delhi.

Masani, R.P. (1939) *Dadabhai Naoroji: The Grand Old Man of India*, George Allen & Unwin Ltd, London.

Menger, Carl (1892) On the origin of money, *Economic Journal*, 2 (6).

Moggridge, Donald (1992) *Maynard Keynes: An Economist's Biography*, Routledge, London.

Mukherjee, Radhakamal (1916) *The Foundations Of Indian Economics*, Longmans, Green and Co, London.

Mukherjee, Radhakamal (1939) *The Institutional Theory of Economics*, Macmillan & Co. Ltd, London.

Mukherjee, Sumita (2010) *Nationalism, Education and Migrant Identities*, Routledge, London and New York.

Nachane, D.M. (2008) The Unity of Science Principle and the 'Unreasonable Effectiveness' of Neoclassical Economics, *Economic & Political Weekly*, vol.43, nos.12/13.

Narain, Brij (1934) *Tendencies in Recent Economic Thought*, Lectures delivered as Sir Kikabhai Premchand Reader, University of Delhi.

Pani, Narendar (2011) Gadgil on Indian economics, *The Hindu*, May 9, 2011.

Parthasarathi, Prasannan (2001) *The Transition to a Colonial Economy: Weavers, Merchants and Kings in South India 1720–1800*, Cambridge University Press.

Parthasarathi, Prasannan (2012) The History of Indian Economic History, LSE, May.

Patnaik, Utsa (1997) The Fourth Indian Nobel: Amartya Sen and His 'Ethical' Economics, *Social Scientist*, vol.25, nos.11/12.

Rajadhyaksha, Niranjan (2013) Ambedkar, rupee and our current troubles, *Livemint*, 20 August.

Ranade, M.G. (1898) *Essays on Indian Economics: A Collection of Essays and Speeches*, Thacker & Company Ltd, Bombay.

Roy, Rammohan (1822) *Brief Remarks Regarding Modern Encroachments on the Ancient Right of Females According to the Hindu Law of Inheritance*, The Unitarian Press, Calcutta.

Schumpeter, Joseph (1954) *History of Economic Analysis*, Allen & Unwin Ltd.

Sen, Amartya (1977) Rational Fools: A Critique of the Behavioral Foundations of Economic Theory, *Philosophy and Public Affairs*, vol.6, no.4.

Sen, Satadru (2013) Benoy Kumar Sarkar and Japan, *Economic & Political Weekly*, 16 November, 2013, vol.XLVIII nos.45/46.

Shanumugasundaram, Vedagiri (1979) A General Theory of Change from Poverty to Plenty, Presidential Address at the 63rd Annual Conference of the Indian Economic Association held at Surat on 27th December.

Sinha, Dipendra (1992) Institutional Economics of Radhakamal Mukherjee, *Journal of Economic Issues*, vol.26, no.2.

Spengler, Joseph J. (1971) *Indian Economic Thought: A Preface to Its History*, Duke University Press, Durham, NC.

Stokes, Eric (1979) Classical Political Economy and British Policy in India – Book Review, *Modern Asian Studies*, vol.13, no.4.

Thanawala, Kishor (1997) Kautilya's Arthashastra: A neglected work in the history of economic thought, in *Ancient Economic Thought* edited by B.B. Price, vol.1, Routledge, London.

The Thirukkural, (2008), *Tamil Guardian*, Culture Editor, January 23.

Waldauer, Charles J., Zahka, William and Pal, Surendra (1996) Kautilya's Arthashastra: A Neglected Precursor to Classical Economics, *Indian Economic Review*, vol.XXXI, no.1.

30

Conclusion

Vincent Barnett

What can be concluded from the rich tapestry of economics within nation–state boundaries that has been documented above? The most obvious conclusion must be that 'economics' is still not an entirely homogenous subject, either in its contemporary manifestation, and even more so throughout its long history. Although it will now be evident to readers, having reached this conclusion at the end of the volume, that authors with a wide range of perspectives were deliberately chosen to write the individual chapters, this on its own does not wholly explain the degree of variance that has been presented.

Two basic and opposed positions have been articulated. Those that see (mainstream) economics as a universal and increasingly international phenomenon (e.g. William Coleman on Australia and New Zealand and Roger Middleton on England), and those that see national particularities as being very important as limiting or determining factors in setting what 'correct' and/or 'useful' economics is/should be seen to be (e.g. Veronica Montecinos on Spanish-speaking South America and Zagros Madjd-Sadjadi on China), at least for the specific countries in question. These are not necessarily the only/absolute positions that are possible, there are intermediate/ median stances between the two opposite poles that have been well articulated (e.g. Renee Prendergast on Ireland and Patrice Franko on Brazil). But does this lead to anything more than: you pay your money and you take your choice (anything goes, regionally speaking)? As merely the editor of this volume, I cannot provide a definitive answer.

However, in addition to the international diversity of economic understandings, what has also been documented is the growing influence of mainstream economics over the last century or so in many different parts of the world, and the increased institutionalization of economics in university departments, think tanks, government bodies and other institutions. Much of this has been mainstream Western economics, but certainly not exclusively so. An ability to creatively adapt mainstream economics to local/national conditions has also been demonstrated in some instances. But the precise nature of this 'influence' should be clearly specified: it is of course mainly influence within ruling elites, and less so amongst the general population. And as Middleton rightly implied, the globalization of economics that has occurred after World War Two should more accurately be described as its 'Americanisation/internationalisation'.

Roger Backhouse has convincingly argued that after World War Two, economics became much more international, with the result that 'the nationality of economic ideas has become harder than ever to pin down – there is a real sense in which it has become a meaningless concept. Economic ideas have become essentially international' (Backhouse, 2002, 307). If by 'economic ideas' Backhouse means 'mainstream textbook-style economics' then there is certainly a large element of truth in his assertion. But such a view has some difficulty in explaining the contemporary Chinese paradox: how has a Communist-controlled economic ideology assisted in creating one of the fastest-growing export booms in world history? What about the success of the Asian Tiger economies, where conventional neoclassical economics has exerted little influence on state development policy? How is 'internationalized economics' relevant to a country/region that has no or few formally-trained economists, as was seen in the case of Mozambique and Angola under 'Marxist' control? And how is it possible to explain the acceptance of large levels of quantitative easing (QE) in the US economy after 2008, an idea which was not really part of 'American/international' economic discourse before this time?

One answer is found in Backhouse's own idea of 'subtle differences between different types of socialist and capitalist systems' (310). But if there are different types of capitalism, might there then be a need for different variants of economics which are adapted to the different geographical regions where the distinct types of capitalism are situated? If so, then economics might not quite be as universal as some would have us believe. The case of QE is instructive. QE was a policy first pioneered in Japan in 2001 in response to its own unique economic circumstances, which was then adapted after the onset of the Great Recession for use in other Western countries. This was brought out in the chapter on Brazil, where the effect of US QE on other countries was considered. The national/international paradox is also highlighted by the dual role of the US currency. The American dollar is a national currency, but it plays an international role as a global reserve currency. The US economy has been dealing (or not dealing) with the conse-quences of this dual role for some considerable time.

Another question raised in the introduction was Joseph Schumpeter's idea that national differences were more apparent in economists' general social philosophy rather than in their technical analysis. In one sense this has been confirmed across this volume, with significant differences in underlying world-views sometimes remaining in specific countries over long periods of time, alongside a greater homogenization in what is taught as 'economics 101' in universities across much of the (Western) world. But in another sense the range of chapters that have been presented demonstrate that the reality is more complex than this simply dichotomy. For example, 'technical economics' has been employed by those promoting development in the Asian Tigers but to foster a state-assisted industrial policy that is very different from the type of approach usually advocated by mainstream economists in the West, where a more *laissez faire* attitude to development is widespread. Thus, technical economics can be used for a variety of ends depending on the underlying social philosophy that is prevalent in any given country/region.

An apt way to express this duality might be to say that economics is sometimes international in its methods and techniques, but simultaneously national in its uses and applications. As J.M. Keynes concluded, economic theory is not a body of settled conclusions applicable to policy: instead it is 'a method rather than a doctrine, an apparatus of the mind, a technique of thinking, which helps its possessor to draw correct conclusions' (Keynes, 1922, 856). How such 'techniques of economic thinking' are applied in specific national/regional contexts often depends at least in part on factors outside what is conventionally defined as economics, and the 'correct conclu-sions' that are drawn are sometimes conceived by those making the deductions (or experiencing the consequences of them) as correct national/regional conclusions.

Instead of offering further general conclusions, it is illuminating to finish with a very specific example of the international dissemination of economic ideas that is especially intriguing: the

1935 Russian (Soviet) edition of Adam Smith's *Wealth of Nations*, which was published in two volumes in 'Moscow-Leningrad' by the Soviet State Social-Economic Press with a print-run of 20,000 copies (Barnett, 2002, 40). Is this the most bizarre and incongruous translation of Smith's classic ever to have been published? Whilst arranging for the murder of hundreds of thousands of Soviet citizens for their alleged 'bourgeois' attitudes in the mid-1930s, Joseph Stalin allowed a new Russian translation of the founding text of free market economics to be published. If an obvious instance of an economics text having multiple political and cultural overtones is sought by historians, then this is a classic example.

The meanings gained in this translation must have been immense, but the actual influence of this text in the USSR on its publication was probably tiny. Despite suggesting a universal mechanism for market activity (the 'invisible hand'), Smith's analysis must surely have been overwhelmed by the oppressive Soviet context. In this negative sense at least, no one can deny the importance of national/regional circumstances in influencing the impact of economic ideas.

References

Backhouse, Roger. 2002. *The Penguin History of Economics*. London: Penguin.

Barnett, Vincent. 2002. 'Mr Smith Goes to Moscow: Russian Editions of *The Wealth of Nations*', *Research in the History of Economic Thought and Methodology*, vol.20-A, 35–42.

Keynes, J.M. 1922. Introduction to the Series. In *Collected Writings*. Cambridge: CUP, vol.XII. 1983.

Author index

Place index

For Product Safety Concerns and Information please contact our EU
representative GPSR@taylorandfrancis.com Taylor & Francis Verlag GmbH,
Kaufingerstraße 24, 80331 München, Germany

Printed and bound by CPI Group (UK) Ltd, Croydon, CR0 4YY
08/05/2025
01864327-0013